THE BOUNTY

THE

The True Story of the Mutiny

on the Bounty

BOUNTY

CAROLINE ALEXANDER

VIKING

VIKING

Published by the Penguin Group

Penguin Group (USA) Inc., 375 Hudson Street, New York, New York 10014, U.S.A.

Penguin Books Ltd, 80 Strand, London WC2R 0RL, England

Penguin Books Australia Ltd, 250 Camberwell Road, Camberwell, Victoria 3124, Australia

Penguin Books Canada Ltd, 10 Alcorn Avenue, Toronto, Ontario, Canada M4V 3B2

Penguin Books India (P) Ltd, 11 Community Centre, Panchsheel Park,
    New Delhi – 110 017, India

Penguin Books (N.Z.) Ltd, Cnr Rosedale and Airborne Roads, Albany, Auckland, New Zealand

Penguin Books (South Africa) (Pty) Ltd, 24 Sturdee Avenue,
    Rosebank, Johannesburg 2196, South Africa

Penguin Books Ltd, Registered Offices:
80 Strand, London WC2R 0RL, England

First published in 2003 by Viking Penguin,
a member of Penguin Group (USA) Inc.

10 9 8 7 6 5 4 3 2 1

LIBRARY OF CONGRESS CATALOGING-IN-PUBLICATION DATA
Alexander, Caroline
    The Bounty : the true story of the mutiny on the Bounty / Caroline Alexander.
        p. cm.
    Includes bibliographical references (p.) and index.
    ISBN 0-670-03133-X
        1. Bounty Mutiny, 1789.   2. Oceania—Description and travel.   3. Bligh, William,
    1754–1817—Journeys—Oceania.   4. Christian, Fletcher, 1764–1793—Journeys—Oceania.
    5. Bounty (Ship).   I. Title.
    DU20.A53 2003
    996.1'8—dc21   2003050158

This book is printed on acid-free paper. ∞

Printed in the United States of America
Designed by Carla Bolte
Set in Scala, with Michelangelo display
Breadfruit leaf motif derived from a watercolor by George Tobin, 1702, courtesy of Mitchell Library, State
Library of New South Wales

TO SMOKEY

CONTENTS

SHIP'S COMPANY

COMMANDER	Lieutenant William Bligh
MASTER	John Fryer
BOATSWAIN	William Cole
GUNNER	William Peckover
CARPENTER	William Purcell
SURGEON	Thomas Huggan
MASTER'S MATES	Fletcher Christian†
	William Elphinstone
MIDSHIPMEN	John Hallett
	Thomas Hayward
	Peter Heywood*†
	George Stewart*†
	Robert Tinkler*
	Edward Young*†
QUARTERMASTERS	Peter Linkletter
	John Norton
QUARTERMASTER'S MATE	George Simpson
BOATSWAIN'S MATE	James Morrison†
GUNNER'S MATE	John Mills†
CARPENTER'S MATES	Charles Norman D
	Thomas McIntosh D
SAILMAKER	Lawrence Lebogue
MASTER-AT-ARMS	Charles Churchill
ARMORER	Joseph Coleman D
SURGEON'S ASSISTANT	Thomas Denman Ledward

CAPTAIN'S CLERK	John Samuel
CAPTAIN'S SERVANT	John Smith
COOPER	Henry Hilbrant *†
SHIP'S COOK	Thomas Hall*
BUTCHER	Robert Lamb*
COOK'S ASSISTANT	William Muspratt *†
ABLE SEAMEN	Thomas Burkett †
	Michael Byrn D
	Thomas Ellison †
	William McCoy †
	Isaac Martin †
	John Millward †
	Matthew Quintal †
	Richard Skinner †
	Alexander Smith †
	John Sumner †
	Mathew Thompson †
	James Valentine
	John Williams †
GARDENER	David Nelson
ASSISTANT GARDENER	William Brown †

* Mustered as able seaman for wages
† Mutineer
D Loyalist detained with mutineers

AUTHOR'S NOTE

Every attempt has been made to use and quote from firsthand source material wherever available. In such quotations, the original and often erratic spelling, punctuation, grammar and typographical conventions (e.g., liberal use of uppercase initial letters) have been retained. In the case of John Fryer's "Narrative" alone, punctuation has on occasion been added for more straightforward reading. Similarly, a few abbreviations common in the era ("wr." for "weather," "larbd." for "larboard") but now unfamiliar have been spelled out so as not to cause unnecessary stumbling over sense.

Personal names are particularly variable, and I have attempted to use the form the individual in question used where this can be ascertained, rather than to rely on *Bounty* story conventions. In the case of the ten mutineers brought to court-martial, this is not difficult to establish, as each of the ten defendants left a deposition signed with his signature: thus "Burkett," not "Burkitt"; "Byrn," not "Byrne"; although the alternate forms occur frequently in the language of second parties. In other cases, problematic names were established by correspondence, wills or similar personal documentation. Midshipman John Hallett's father signed his correspondence "Hallett"—not, as Bligh and others wrote, "Hallet"—and so forth. There is strong evidence to suggest that Matthew Quintal, one of the mutineers, regarded himself as Matthew "Quintrell," but here deference is made to the spelling adopted by his present-day descendants. Geographical places are referred to by their names at the time, with the modern equivalent in parentheses on first mention: Coupang (Kupang), Endeavor Strait (Torres Strait).

A nautical day began and ended at noon, with the noon sighting, not at midnight as in civil time. Thus the mutiny on the *Bounty* occurred on the morning of April 28, 1789, in both sea and civil time; some four hours later, however, it was April 29 by nautical reckoning. There is occasional awkwardness when the two systems collide, as when a returning ship comes into port, and a running commentary begun at sea resumes on land. No attempt has been made to convert sea to civil time; dates of events recorded at sea are given as stated in the ship's log.

All mileage figures for distances at sea are given in nautical miles. A nautical mile consisted at the time of 6,116 feet, or one degree of latitude; a statute mile consists of 5,280 feet. All temperatures cited in the ship's log are in degrees Fahrenheit.

One pound sterling (£1) comprised twenty shillings (20s.); a guinea equaled £1 plus 1s. The valuation of currency of this time can be gauged by certain standard-of-living indicators. Fletcher Christian's mother expected to live comfortably on 40 guineas a year. A post-captain of a first-rate ship received £28 0s. 0d. (28 pounds, 0 shillings, 0 pence) a month in pay; a lieutenant, £7 0s. 0d. (7 pounds, 0 shillings, 0 pence); an able seaman, £1 4s. 0d. (1 pound, 4 shillings, 0 pence)—less deductions!

THE BOUNTY

PRELUDE

Spithead, winter 1787

His small vessel pitching in the squally winter sea, a young British naval lieutenant waited restlessly to embark upon the most important and daunting voyage of his still young but highly promising career. William Bligh, aged thirty-three, had been selected by His Majesty's government to collect breadfruit plants from the South Pacific island of Tahiti and to transport them to the plantations of the West Indies. Like most of the Pacific, Tahiti—Otaheite—was little known; in all the centuries of maritime travel, fewer than a dozen European ships had anchored in her waters. Bligh himself had been on one of these early voyages, ten years previously, when he had sailed under the command of the great Captain Cook. Now he was to lead his own expedition in a single small vessel called *Bounty*.

With his ship mustered and provisioned for eighteen months, Bligh had anxiously been awaiting the Admiralty's final orders, which would allow him to sail, since his arrival at Spithead in early November. A journey of some sixteen thousand miles lay ahead, including a passage around Cape Horn, some of the most tempestuous sailing in the world. Any further delay, Bligh knew, would ensure that he approached the Horn at the height of its worst weather. By the time the orders arrived in late November, the weather at Spithead itself had also deteriorated to the extent that Bligh had been able to advance no farther than the Isle of

Wight, from where he wrote a frustrated letter to his uncle-in-law and mentor, Duncan Campbell.

"If there is any punishment that ought to be inflicted on a set of Men for neglect I am sure it ought on the Admiralty," he wrote irascibly on December 10, 1787, "for my three weeks detention at this place during a fine fair wind which carried all outward bound ships clear of the channel but me, who wanted it most."

Nearly two weeks later, he had retreated back to Spithead, still riding out bad weather.

"It is impossible to say what may be the result," Bligh wrote to Campbell, his anxiety mounting. "I shall endeavor to get round [the Horn]; but with heavy Gales, should it be accompanied with sleet & snow my people will not be able to stand it. . . . Indeed I feel my voyage a very arduous one, and have only to hope in return that whatever the event may be my poor little Family may be provided for. I have this comfort," he continued with some complacency, "that my health is good and I know of nothing that can scarce happen but I have some resource for— My little Ship is in the best of order and my Men & officers all good & feel happy under my directions."

At last, on December 23, 1787, the *Bounty* departed England and after a rough passage arrived at Santa Cruz, in Tenerife. Here, fresh provisions were acquired and repairs made, for the ship had been mauled by severe storms.

"The first sea that struck us carryed away all my spare yards and some spars," Bligh reported, writing again to Campbell; "—the second broke the Boats chocks & stove them & I was buryed in the Sea with my poor little crew. . . ."

Despite the exasperating delay of his departure, the tumultuous passage and the untold miles that still lay ahead, Bligh's spirits were now high—manifestly higher than when he had first set out. On February 17, 1788, off Tenerife, he took advantage of a passing British whaler, the *Queen of London,* to drop a line to Sir Joseph Banks, his patron and the man most responsible for the breadfruit venture.

"I am happy and satisfyed in my little Ship and we are now fit to go round half a score of worlds," Bligh wrote, "both Men & Officers tractable and well disposed & cheerfulness & content in the countenance of every one. I am sure nothing is even more conducive to health. —I have no cause to inflict punishments for I have no offenders and every thing turns out to my most sanguine expectations."

"My Officers and Young Gentlemen are all tractable and well disposed," he continued in the same vein to Campbell, "and we now understand each other so well that we shall remain so the whole voyage. . . ."

Bligh fully expected these to be his last communications on the outward voyage. But monstrous weather off Cape Horn surpassed even his worst expectations. After battling contrary storms and gales for a full month, he conceded defeat and reversed his course for the Cape of Good Hope. He would approach Tahiti by way of the Indian Ocean and Van Diemen's Land (now Tasmania), a detour that would add well over ten thousand miles to his original voyage.

"I arrived here yesterday," he wrote to Campbell on May 25 from the southernmost tip of Africa, "after experiencing the worst of weather off Cape Horn for 30 Days. . . . I thought I had seen the worst of every thing that could be met with at Sea, yet I have never seen such violent winds or such mountainous Seas." A Dutch ship, he could not resist adding, had also arrived at the Cape with thirty men having died on board and many more gravely ill; Bligh had brought his entire company through, safe and sound.

The *Bounty* passed a month at the Cape recovering, and was ready to sail at the end of June. A still arduous journey lay ahead but Bligh's confidence was now much greater than when he had embarked; indeed, in this respect he had shown himself to be the ideal commander, one whose courage, spirits and enthusiasm were rallied, not daunted, by difficulties and delays. Along with his ship and men, he had weathered the worst travails he could reasonably expect to face.

The long-anticipated silence followed; but when over a year later it was suddenly broken, Bligh's correspondence came not from the Cape, nor any other port of call on the expected route home, but from Coupang (Kupang) in the Dutch East Indies. The news he reported in letters to Duncan Campbell, to Joseph Banks and above all to his wife, Elizabeth, was so wholly unexpected, so unconnected to the stream of determined and complacent letters of the year before as to be almost incomprehensible.

"My Dear Dear Betsy," Bligh wrote with palpable exhaustion to his wife on August 19, 1789, "I am now in a part of the world that I never expected, it is however a place that has afforded me relief and saved my life. . . .

"Know then my own Dear Betsy, I have lost the *Bounty*. . . . "

PANDORA

At daylight on a fine, fair, breezy day in March, a young man in his late teens said good-bye to his wife and stepped out of his neat cottage picturesquely set amid citrus trees at the foot of a hill for an excursion to the mountains. Darkly tanned and heavily tattooed with the traditional patterns of manhood across his backside, the youth could have passed for one of the Tahitians who met him outside. Peter Heywood, however, was an Englishman, not an "Indian," and close observation would have revealed that one of the tattoos inked on his leg was not native, but the symbol of the Isle of Man. Young Heywood had been living here, in his idyllic garden home just beyond Matavai Bay, since September 1789, when the *Bounty*, under the command of Master's Mate Fletcher Christian, had deposited him and fifteen other shipmates at Tahiti—and then vanished in the night, never to be seen again.

Peter Heywood, former midshipman on the *Bounty*, had been only a few weeks shy of seventeen on the morning the mutiny had broken out and his close friend and distant relative Fletcher Christian had taken the ship. At Christian's command, Lieutenant Bligh and eighteen loyalists had been compelled to go overboard into one of the *Bounty*'s small boats, where they had been left, bobbing in the wide Pacific, to certain death.

Fletcher Christian's control of the mutineers was to last no more than five months. When he eventually directed the *Bounty* back to Tahiti for what would be her final visit, he had done so because his company had disintegrated into factions. The majority of his people wished to bail out and take their chances at Tahiti even though, as they knew, a British naval ship would eventually come looking for them; some of these men had been loyal to Bligh, but had been held against their will on board the *Bounty*.

Peter Heywood had been one of the last men to take his farewell of Christian, whom he still regarded with affectionate sympathy. Then, when the *Bounty* had departed for good, he had turned back from the beach to set about the business of building a new life. Now, on this fresh March day, a year and a half after Christian's departure, Peter was setting out for the mountains with friends. He had gone no more than a hundred yards from his home when a man came hurrying after him to announce that there was a ship in sight.

Running to the hill behind his house, with its convenient lookout over the sea, he spotted the ship lying to only a few miles distant. Peter would later claim that he had seen this sight "with the utmost Joy," but it is probable that his emotions were somewhat more complicated. Racing down the hill, he went to the nearby home of his close friend midshipman George Stewart with the news. By the time he and Stewart had splashed their way out to the ship, another man, Joseph Coleman, the *Bounty*'s armorer, was already on board. On introducing themselves as formerly of the *Bounty*, Heywood and Stewart had been placed under arrest and led away for confinement. The ship, *Pandora*, had been specifically commissioned to apprehend the mutineers and bring them to justice in England. These morning hours of March 23, 1791, were the last Peter Heywood would spend on Tahiti.

The news of the mutiny on board His Majesty's Armed Vessel *Bounty* had reached England almost exactly a year before. How the news arrived was even more extraordinary than the mutiny—for the messenger had been none other than Lieutenant William Bligh himself. After Fletcher Christian had put him and the loyalists into the *Bounty*'s launch off the island of Tofua, Bligh, against all imaginable odds, had navigated the little 23-foot-long craft 3,618 miles over a period of forty-eight days to Timor, in the Dutch East Indies. Here, his starving and distressed company had been humanely received by the incredulous Dutch authorities. Eventually, passages had been found home for him and his men, and Bligh had arrived in England in a blaze of triumph and white-hot anger on March 13, 1790.

Notice of the mutiny and a description of the mutineers were swiftly dispatched to British and Dutch ports. In Botany Bay the news inspired seventeen convicts to escape in an attempt to join the "pirates" in Tahiti. Although it was at first supposed that two Spanish men-of-war already in the Pacific might have apprehended the *Bounty,* the Admiralty took no chances and began to mobilize an expedition to hunt down the mutineers. The expense and responsibility of sending yet another ship to the Pacific was not appealing: England seemed poised on the verge of a new war with Spain, and all available men and ships were being pressed into service. However, putting a British naval officer overboard in the middle of the Pacific and running away with His Majesty's property were outrages that could not go unpunished. Eventually, a 24-gun frigate named *Pandora* was dispatched under the command of Captain Edward Edwards to hunt the mutineers.

Departing in early November 1790, the *Pandora* made a swift and uneventful passage to Tahiti, avoiding the horrendous storms that had afflicted the *Bounty* three years before. Whereas the *Bounty* had carried a complement of 46 men, the *Pandora* bore 140. The *Pandora*'s commander, Captain Edwards, had suffered a near mutiny of his own nine years earlier, when in command of the *Narcissus* off the northeast coast of America. Eventually, five of the would-be mutineers in this thwarted plot had been hanged, and two more sentenced to floggings of two hundred and five hundred lashes, respectively, while the leader of the mutiny had been hanged in chains. As events would show, Captain Edwards never forgot that he, the near victim of a mutiny, was now in pursuit of actual mutineers.

Also on the *Pandora,* newly promoted to third lieutenant, was Thomas Hayward, a *Bounty* midshipman who had accompanied Bligh on his epic open-boat journey. With memories of the thirst, near starvation, exposure and sheer horror of that voyage still fresh in his mind, Hayward was eager to assist in running to ground those responsible for his ordeal. His familiarity with Tahitian waters and people would assist navigation and island diplomacy; his familiarity with his old shipmates would identify the mutineers.

So it was that in March 1791, under cloudless skies and mild breezes, the *Pandora* sighted the lush, dramatic peaks of Tahiti. Closer in, and the mountain cascades, the graceful palms, and the sparkling volcanic black beaches could be seen beyond thundering breakers and surf. The few ships that had anchored here had all attempted to describe the vision-like beauty of the first sight of this island rising into view from the blue Pacific. Bligh had called Tahiti "the Paradise of the World."

Now, as the *Pandora* cruised serenely through the clear blue waters, bearing justice and vengeance, she was greeted by men canoeing or swimming toward her.

"Before we Anchored," wrote Edwards in his official report to the Admiralty, "Joseph Coleman Armourer of the Bounty and several of the Natives came on board." Coleman was one of four men whom Bligh had specifically identified as being innocent of the mutiny and detained against his will. Once on board, Coleman immediately volunteered what had become of the different factions. Of the sixteen men left by Christian on Tahiti, two had already been responsible for each other's deaths. Charles Churchill, the master-at-arms and the man described as "the most murderous" of the mutineers, had in fact been murdered by his messmate Mathew Thompson, an able seaman from the Isle of Wight. Churchill's death had in turn been avenged by his Tahitian friends, who had murdered Thompson and then offered him "as a Sacrifice to their Gods," as Edwards dispassionately reported.

Meanwhile, on his way to the anchored ship, Peter Heywood had learned from another Tahitian friend that his former shipmate Thomas Hayward was on board. The result of this friendly inquiry, as Peter reported in a long letter he wrote to his mother, was not what he had ingenuously expected.

"[W]e ask'd for him, supposing he might prove our Assertions," Peter wrote; "but he like all other Worldlings when raised a little in Life received us very coolly & pretended Ignorance of our Affairs. . . . So that Appearances being so much against us, we were order'd in Irons & look'd upon—infernal Words!—as piratical Villains."

As the *Pandora*'s company moved in, inexorably bent upon their mission, it became clear that no distinction would be made among the captured men. Coleman, noted as innocent by Bligh himself and the first man to surrender voluntarily, was clapped in irons along with the indignant midshipman. Edwards had determined that his job was simply to take hold of everyone he could, indiscriminately, and let the court-martial sort them out once back in England.

From the Tahitians who crowded curiously on board, Edwards quickly ascertained the likely whereabouts of the other eleven fugitives. Some were still around Matavai, others had by coincidence sailed only the day before, in a thirty-foot-long decked schooner they themselves had built, with much effort and ingenuity, for Papara, a region on the south coast where the remainder of the *Bounty* men had settled. With the zealous assistance of the local authorities, the roundup began and by three o'clock of the second day, Richard Skinner, able seaman of the *Bounty*, was on board *Pandora*.

A party under the command of Lieutenants Robert Corner and Hayward was now dispatched to intercept the remaining men. Aiding them in their search was one John Brown, an Englishman deposited on Tahiti the year before by another ship, the *Mercury*, on account of his troublesome ways, which had included carving up the face of a shipmate with a knife. The *Mercury* had departed Tahiti only weeks before Christian's final return with the boat—she had even seen fires burning on the island of Tubuai, where the mutineers had first settled, but decided not to investigate. Brown, it became clear, had not been on terms of friendship with his compatriots.

At Papara, Edwards's men discovered that the mutineers, hearing of their approach, had abandoned their schooner and fled to the mountain forest.

"[U]nder cover of night they had taken shelter in a hut in the woods," wrote the *Pandora*'s surgeon, George Hamilton, in his account of this adventure, "but were discovered by Brown, who creeping up to the place where they were asleep, distinguished them from the natives by feeling their toes." British toes apparently lacked the telltale spread of unshod Tahitians'.

"Tuesday, March 29th," Edwards recorded in the *Pandora*'s log. "At 9 the Launch returned with James Morrison, Charles Norman and Thomas Ellison belonging to His Majesty's Ship *Bounty*—prisoners." Also taken in tow was the mutineers' schooner, the *Resolution,* an object for them of great pride and now requisitioned by the *Pandora* as a tender, or service vessel.

The three newcomers were at first housed under the half deck, and kept under around-the-clock sentry. Meanwhile, the ship's carpenters were busy constructing a proper prison, a kind of low hut to the rear of the quarterdeck, where the prisoners would be placed, as Edwards reported to the Admiralty, "for their more effectual security airy & healthy situation." The prisoners in their turn assessed their circumstances somewhat differently, referring sardonically to the shallow, cramped structure, with its narrow scuttle, as "Pandora's Box."

At some point during the pursuit of James Morrison and the men on the *Resolution,* Michael Byrn, the almost blind fiddler of the *Bounty,* either was captured or came on board of his own accord. Insignificant at every juncture of the *Bounty* saga, Byrn, alone of the fugitives, arrived on the *Pandora* unrecorded. Eight men had now been apprehended and were firmly held in irons; six men remained at large, reported to have taken flight in the hill country around Papara.

Over the next week and a half, while searches were made for the fugitives under the guidance of the ever helpful Brown, Captain Edwards and his officers got a taste of life in Tahiti. Their immediate host was Tynah, the stately king, whose girth was proportionate to his outstanding nearly six-foot-four-inch height. Around forty years of age, he could remember William Bligh from his visit to the island in 1777, with Captain Cook, as well as his return eleven years later with the *Bounty.* Upon the *Pandora*'s arrival, Edwards and his men had been greeted by the islanders with their characteristic generosity, with streams of gifts, food, feasts, dances and offers of their women.

"The English are allowed by the rest of the world . . . to be a generous, charitable people," observed Dr. Hamilton. "[B]ut the Otaheiteans could not help bestowing the most contemptuous word in their language upon us, which is, Peery, Peery, or Stingy."

Generous, loyal, sensual, uninhibited—the handsome people of Tahiti had won over most who visited them. By now the *Bounty* men were no longer strangers, but had lived among them, taken wives, had children. . . .

"Sure Friendship's there, & Gratitude, & Love," young Peter Heywood would later write, exhibiting a poetic bent:

Sure Friendship's there, & Gratitude, & Love,
Such as ne'er reigns in European Blood
In these degen'rate Days; tho' from above
We Precepts have, & know what's right and good . . .

Now, sitting shackled in the sweltering heat of Pandora's Box, Heywood and his shipmates had more than usual cause, and time, to contemplate this disparity of cultures.

On Saturday, the last fugitives began to trickle in. Henry Hilbrant, an able seaman from Hanover, Germany, and Thomas McIntosh, a young carpenter's mate from the north of England, were delivered on board; as predicted, they had been captured in the hill country above Papara. By the following evening, the roundup was complete. Able seamen Thomas Burkett, John Millward and John Sumner, and William Muspratt, the cook's assistant, were brought in, also from Papara.

As the "pirates" were led into Pandora's Box, ship activities bustled around them. Carpenters and sailmakers were busy making repairs for the next stage of their long voyage and routine disciplinary activities continued. On Sunday, the ship's company was assembled for the weekly reading of the Articles of War: "Article XIX: If any Person in or belonging to the Fleet shall make or endeavour to make any mutinous Assembly upon any Pretence whatsoever, every Person offending herein, and being convicted thereof by the Sentence of the Court-martial, shall suffer Death." After the reading, three seamen were punished with a dozen lashes each "for theft and drunkenness." It was a cloudy evening and had rained the day before. This was the last the *Bounty* men would see of Pacific skies for several months.

Fourteen men were now crowded into the eleven-by-eighteen-foot space that was their prison. Onshore, they had kept themselves in different factions and were by no means all on good terms with one another. Strikingly, both Thomas McIntosh and Charles Norman, who had been among those who fled from the *Pandora*'s men, had been exonerated by Bligh. Perhaps family attachments on the island had made them think twice about leaving; or it may be, less trusting than Coleman who had so quickly surrendered, they did not believe that innocence would count for much in the Admiralty's eyes.

Within the box, the prisoners wallowed in their own sweat and vermin.

"What I have suffer'd I have not power to describe," wrote Heywood to his mother; he had characterized himself to her as one "long inured to the Frowns of Fortune" and now waxed philosophical about his situation.

"I am young in years, but old in what the World calls Adversity," he wrote; Peter Heywood was not quite nineteen. "It has made me acquainted with three Things, which are little known," he continued, doggedly. "[F]irst, the Villainy & Censoriousness of Mankind—second, the Futility of all human Hopes,—& third, the Enjoyment of being content in whatever station it pleases Providence to place me in."

Among the possessions confiscated from the mutineers were journals kept by Stewart and Heywood in their sea chests, and from these Edwards was able to piece together the history of the *Bounty* following the mutiny, up to her final return to Tahiti. Two days after Bligh and his loyalists had been left in the Pacific, Fletcher Christian and his men had cut up the ship's topsails to make jackets for the entire company—they were well aware of the impression made by a uniformed crew.

Soon all the breadfruit—1,015 little pots and tubs of carefully nurtured seedlings, all, as Bligh had wistfully reported, "in the most flourishing state"—were thrown overboard. More sails were cut up for uniform jackets, and the possessions of those who had been forced into the boat with Bligh were divided by lot among the ship company. But in a telling report made by James Morrison, the *Bounty* boatswain's mate and the mastermind behind the ambitious *Resolution,* "it always happend that Mr. Christians party were always better served than these who were thought to be disaffected."

Tensions among the men already threatened to undermine Christian's tenuous control. In this state of affairs, the *Bounty* made for Tubuai, an island lying some 350 miles south of Tahiti, and anchored there on May 24, nearly a month after the mutiny.

"Notwithstanding they met with some opposition from the Natives they intended to settle on this Island," Edwards wrote in his official report, gleaning the diaries of Heywood and Stewart. "[B]ut after some time they perceived they were in want of several things Necessary for a settlement & which was the cause of disagreements & quarrels amongst themselves." One of the things they most quarreled about was women.

Consequently, only a week after landing at Tubuai, the *Bounty* sailed back to Tahiti, where they had lived and loved for five memorable months while gathering Bligh's breadfruit. Here, as the men knew, their loyal friends would give them all they required. The story they prepared was that they had fallen in with the great Captain Cook (in reality long dead), who was planning to make settlement on the island of Whytootackee (Aitutaki), and that Bligh had remained with his old commander and delegated Christian to sail with the *Bounty* for supplies. The Tahitians, ever generous and overjoyed at the news that Cook, whom they regarded with worshipful esteem, would be so close to them, gave freely of hogs, goats, chickens, a variety of plants, cats and dogs. More important, nine women, eight men, seven boys and one young girl left with the *Bounty* when she returned to Tubuai.

For three months the mutineers struggled to make a settlement on the tiny island. Construction was begun on a defensive fort that measured some fifty yards square, surrounded by a kind of dry moat or ditch. A drawbridge was planned for the entrance facing the beach, while the walls were surmounted by the *Bounty*'s four-pounder cannons and swivel guns. Patriotically, the mutineers had christened their fortress Fort George, after their king.

Again, there were early signs that this would not be a successful experiment.

"On 5th July Some of the people began to be mutinous," according to an extract made by Edwards from Peter Heywood's journal. "& on 6th 2 of the Men were put in Irons by a Majority of Votes—& drunkenness, fighting & threatening each other's life was so common that those abaft were obliged to arm themselves with Pistols." The following day, an attempt was made to heal the growing breach and "Articles were drawn up by Christian and Churchill specifying a mutual forgiveness of all past grievances which every Man was obliged to swear to & sign," according to an extract from Stewart's journal. "Mathew Thompson excepted who refused to comply." Despite this gesture, an inner circle evolved around Christian. When John Sumner and Matthew Quintal spent the night onshore without leave, declaring that they were now their own masters and would do as they pleased, Christian clapped the pistol he now always carried to the head of one, and had both placed in leg irons.

Violence also escalated without as well as within this fractious company, erupting as the *Bounty* men fought with the Tubuaians over property and women. In one particularly bloody encounter, Thomas Burkett was stabbed in the side by a spear and Christian wounded himself on his own bayonet. When the dust settled, sixty-six Tubuaians were dead, including six women, and the *Bounty* men were masters of the field. One of the gentle Tahitian youths who had journeyed to Tubuai with his English friends, according to James Morrison, "desired leave to cut out the jaw bones of the kill'd to hang round the quarters of the Ship as Trophies," and was much displeased when this request was denied.

In September, in recognition that the different factions could not coexist, a collective decision was made to return once more to Tahiti. Here, the ship's company would divide. Those who chose to remain on the island could do so; the rest would depart with Christian, taking to sea once again in the *Bounty*. Each man remaining onshore was given a musket, a pistol, a cutlass, a bayonet, a box of cartridges and seventeen pounds of powder from the ship's arms and lead for ball—everyone save Michael Byrn, that is, who, as Morrison stated, "being blind and of a very troublesome disposition it was thought that arms put into his hands would be only helping him to do some mischief."

On anchoring for the third and final time in Matavai Bay, Christian and many of the eight men who had cast their lots with him did not even bother to go ashore. Arriving on September 21, 1789, they departed secretly the same night, quietly cutting the *Bounty*'s anchor cable. Joseph Coleman, the most relentless loyalist, had been once again held against his will for his skills as an armorer; but as the ship slipped away, he dived overboard and swam to land. At dawn, the sixteen men deposited onshore saw their ship hovering off Point Venus; by midmorning she was gone.

When here with Bligh, each man had acquired a *taio*, or special protector and friend, and to these each now turned. Soon, the fugitives had settled down, either with their *taios'* families or, like Heywood and Stewart, in cottages of their own. They took wives and some had children, and so a year and a half had passed, until the day the *Pandora* loomed out of the early morning to drag them back to England.

Now captured and pinned inside Pandora's Box, the *Bounty* prisoners listened in anguish as their wives and friends wailed and grieved under the *Pandora*'s stern. Standing in canoes around the ship, the women enacted their terrible rites of mourning, hammering at their heads with sharp shells until the blood ran. As the day of departure approached, more canoes came from across the island, filling the harbor around the ship. Men and women stripped their clothes and cut their heads in grief, and as the blood fell, cut again and cried aloud. Tynah came on board and, with tears streaming down his cheeks, begged to be remembered to his friend, the King of England.

"This I believe was the first time that an Englishman got up his anchor, at the remotest part of the globe, with a heavy heart, to go home to his own country," wrote Dr. Hamilton—an astonishing admission from a naval official who had come in search of deserting mutineers.

On May 8, 1791, under pleasant breezes, the *Pandora*, recaulked and overhauled, left Tahiti with the mutineers' schooner, *Resolution*, in tow.

Edwards's commission was far from fulfilled. Still missing was His Majesty's stolen ship as well as the ringleader of the mutiny and his most hard-core followers.

"Christian had been frequently heard to declare that he would search for an unknown or an uninhabited Island in which there was no harbour for Shipping, would run the Ship ashore, and get from her such things as would be useful to him and settle there," Edwards recorded in his official report to the Admiralty, continuing with admirable understatement, "but this information was too vague to be follow'd in an immense Ocean strew'd with an almost innumerable number of known and unknown Islands." Specifically, the Pacific contains more than twenty thousand islands scattered over some 64 million square miles. Christian and the *Bounty* had departed Tahiti in September 1789—a twenty-month head start, long enough to have taken the *Bounty* not only as far as North or South America, but, in theory, around the globe.

Edwards's instructions from the Admiralty offered some guidance: If no knowledge of the mutineers had been gained at Tahiti, he was to venture west to Whytootackee (Aitutaki), "calling, in your way, at Huaheine and Uliatea." If nothing was found here, he was to make a circuit of the neighboring islands. If nothing here, he was to continue west to the Friendly Islands (Tonga), "and, having succeeded, or failed," to return to England, through the Endeavour Strait (Torres Strait) separating New Guinea from New Holland (Australia). Be mindful of prevailing winds, the Admiralty admonished, "there being no dependence (of which we have any certain knowledge) of passing the Strait after the month of September. . . ."

For roughly the next three months Edwards doggedly followed the Admiralty's prescribed itinerary in a desultory chase from island to island. At each landfall, a uniformed officer was disembarked and in the cloying heat tramped along the beach, offering presents and seeking information. Anchored offshore, the *Pandora* received the now customary canoe loads of eager visitors. Spears, clubs and other curios were collected, differences among the islanders, who appeared "ruder" and less civilized as the *Pandora* progressed, were duly noted, but no hint of the *Bounty*'s whereabouts emerged.

A week out from Tahiti, Hilbrant, one of the mutineers, volunteered that Christian had spoken to him on the day before his departure of his intention to make for an uninhabited island that he knew from earlier accounts to be "situated to the Westward of the Islands of Danger." This description seemed to refer to Duke of York Island (Atafu) but was to prove to be another dead end. En route, however, Edwards stopped off at Palmerston Island (Avarau) and sent his boats ashore to search that isle's bays and inlets. Two of these returned in the late afternoon full of coconuts, and nothing more. But that night the tender arrived with hopeful news: it had discovered some spars and a yard marked "Bounty's Driver Yard" embossed with the Admiralty's broad arrow mark.

Over the next two days, all the ship's craft—a cutter, two yawls and the mutineers' schooner—were dispatched to examine the island as well as islets and even reefs in the vicinity. The belief that the mutineers might be at large nearby caused everyone to move with great circumspection. One party camping overnight on the island were woken abruptly when a coconut they had placed on their campfire exploded. "[E]xpecting muskets to be fired at them from every bush," Dr. Hamilton explained, "they all jumped up, seized their arms, and were some time before they could undeceive themselves, that they were really not attacked."

As the various small craft tacked to and fro around the island, Edwards remained with *Pandora*, cruising offshore and making the occasional coconut run. On the afternoon of May 24, one of the midshipmen, John Sival, returned in the yawl with several striking painted canoes; but after these were examined and admired, he was sent back to complete his orders. Shortly after he left, thick weather closed in, obscuring the little craft as she bobbed dutifully back to shore, and was followed by an ugly squall that did not lift for four days. When the weather cleared on the twenty-eighth, the yawl had disappeared. Neither she nor her company of five men was ever seen again.

"It may be difficult to surmise what has been the fate of these unfortunate men," Dr. Hamilton wrote, adding hopefully that they "had a piece of salt-beef thrown into the boat to them on leaving the ship; and it rained a good deal that night and the following day, which might satiate their thirst."

By now, too, it was realized that the tantalizing clues of the *Bounty*'s presence were only flotsam.

"[T]he yard and these things lay upon the beach at high water Mark & were all eaten by the Sea Worm which is a strong presumption they were drifted there by the Waves," Edwards reported. It was concluded that they had drifted from Tubuai, where the mutineers had reported that the *Bounty* had lost most of her spars. These few odds and ends of worm-eaten wood were all that were ever found by *Pandora* of His Majesty's Armed Vessel *Bounty*.

The fruitless search apart, morale on board had been further lowered by the discovery, as Dr. Hamilton put it, "that the ladies of Otaheite had left us many warm tokens of their affection." The men confined within Pandora's Box were also far from well. Their irons chafed them badly, so much so that while they were still at Matavai Bay, Joseph Coleman's legs had swollen alarmingly and the arms of McIntosh and Ellison had become badly "galled." To the complaint that the irons were causing their wrists to swell, Lieutenant John Larkan had replied that "they were not intended to fit like Gloves!" Edwards had an obsessive fear that the mutineers might "taint" his crew and, under threat of severe punishment, had forbidden any communication between the parties whatsoever; but from rough memos he made, it seems he was unsuccessful. "Great difficulty created in keeping the Mutineers from conversing with the crew," Edwards had jotted down, elsewhere noting that one of his lieutenants suspected that the prisoners had "carried on a correspondence with some of our people by Letter."

From Duke of York Island down to the rest of the Union Islands (Tokelau), thence to the Samoas, the *Pandora* continued her futile search. To aid them in making rough landfalls, Lieutenants Corner and Hayward donned cork jackets and plunged boldly into the surf ahead of the landing boats. Parakeets were purchased on one island, splendid birds resembling peacocks on another, and on others still the use of the islands' women. Striking sights were enjoyed—the large skeleton of a whale, for example, and a deserted shrine with an altar piled with white shells. They had even discovered whole islands, whose newly bestowed names would form a satisfying addition to the report Edwards would eventually turn over to the Admiralty. In short, the *Pandora* had discovered a great deal—but nothing at all that pertained to the missing mutineers and the *Bounty*.

Thousands of miles from England, adrift in one of the most unknown regions of the earth, Hamilton, who seems to have enjoyed this meandering sojourn, mused tellingly on the strange peoples he had seen and their distance from civilized life: "[A]nd although that unfortunate man Christian has, in a rash unguarded moment, been tempted to swerve from his duty to his king and country, as he is in other respects of an amiable character, and respectable abilities, should he elude the hand of justice, it may be hoped he will employ his talents in humanizing the rude savages," he wrote, in an astonishing wave of sympathy for that elusive mutineer who had, after all, consigned his captain and eighteen shipmates to what he had thought was certain death.

"[S]o that, at some future period, a British Ilion may blaze forth in the south," Hamilton continued, working to a crescendo of sentiment, "with all the characteristic virtues of the English nation, and complete the great prophecy, by propagating the Christian knowledge amongst the infidels." Even here, at the early stage of the *Bounty* saga, the figure of Christian himself represented a powerful, charismatic force; already there is the striking simplistic tendency to blur the mutineer's name— Christian—with a christian cause.

In the third week of June, while in the Samoas, Edwards was forced to report yet another misfortune: "[B]etween 5 & 6 o'clock of the Evening of the 22nd of June lost sight of our Tender in a thick Shower of Rain," he noted tersely. Edwards had now lost two vessels, this one with nine men. Food and water that were meant to have been loaded onto the tender were still piled on the *Pandora*'s deck. Anamooka (Nomuka), in the Friendly Islands, was the last designated point of rendezvous in the event of a separation, and here the *Pandora* now hastened.

"The people of Anamooka are the most daring set of robbers in the South Seas," Hamilton noted matter-of-factly. Onshore, parties who disembarked to wood and water the ship were harassed as they had not been elsewhere. Edwards's servant was stripped naked by an acquisitive crowd and forced to cover himself with his one remaining shoe. "[W]e

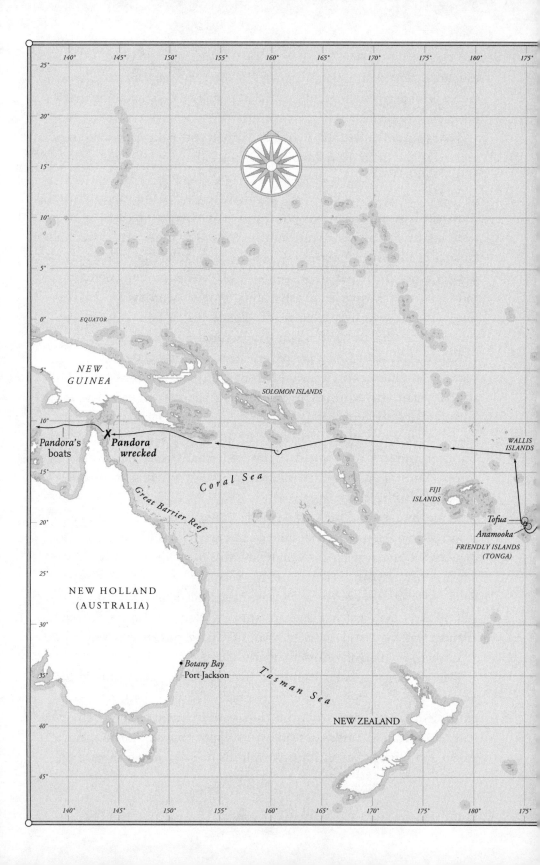

SANDWICH ISLANDS

VOYAGE
of
THE *PANDORA*

0 Miles   500   1000

0 Kilometers   1000

Scale at Equator

Pacific Ocean

Atafu (Duke of York Island)

UNION ISLANDS
(TOKELAU)

Savaii

SAMOA
ISLANDS

Huahine

SOCIETY
ISLANDS   Papeete

COOK ISLANDS

Avarau
(Palmerston)

Tahiti (Otaheite)

Aitutaki
(Whytootackee)

Route of *Pandora*

Rarotonga

Tubuai

Pitcairn

© 2003 Jeffrey L. Ward

soon discovered the great Irishman," Hamilton reported, "with his shoe full in one hand, and a bayonet in the other, naked and foaming mad." While overseeing parties foraging for wood and water, Lieutenant Corner was momentarily stunned on the back of his neck by a club-wielding islander, whom the officer, recovering, shot dead in the back.

There was no sign of the tender.

Leaving a letter for the missing boat in the event that it turned up, Edwards pressed on to Tofua, the one island on which Bligh, Thomas Hayward and the loyalists in the open launch had briefly landed. One of Bligh's party had been stoned to death here, and some of the men responsible for this were disconcerted to recognize Hayward.

From Tofua, the *Pandora* continued her cruising before returning to Anamooka, where there was still no word of the missing tender.

It was now early August. Edwards's laconic report reveals nothing of his state of mind, but with two boats and fourteen men lost, uncowed mutineers on board and a recent physical attack on the most able of his crew, it is safe to hazard that he was anxious to return home. His own cabin had been broken into and books and other possessions taken as improbable prizes (James Morrison, with discernible satisfaction, had earlier reported that "a new Uniform Jacket belonging to Mr. Hayward" had been taken and, as a parting insult, donned by the thief in his canoe while in sight of the ship). Now, "thinking it time to return to England," Edwards struck north to Wallis Island, then west for the long run to the Endeavour Strait, the route laid down by the Admiralty out of the Pacific—homeward bound.

The *Pandora* reached the Great Barrier Reef toward the end of August, and from this point on Edwards's report is closely concerned with putting on record his persistent and conscientious depth soundings and vigilant lookout for reefs, bars and shoals. The *Pandora* was now outside the straits, the uncharted, shoal-strewn divide between Papua New Guinea and the northeastern tip of Australia. From the masthead of the *Pandora*, no route through the Barrier Reef could be seen, and Edwards turned aside to patrol its southern fringe, seeking an entrance.

After two days had been spent in this survey, a promising channel was at last spotted, and Lieutenant Corner was dispatched in the yawl to

investigate. It was approaching dusk when he signaled that his reconnaissance was successful and started to return to the ship. Despite the
reports of a number of eyewitnesses, it is difficult to determine exactly
how subsequent events unfolded; a remark made by Dr. Hamilton suggests that Edwards may have been incautiously sailing in the dark. Previous depth soundings had failed to find bottom at 110 fathoms but now,
as the ship prepared to lay to, the soundings abruptly showed 50 fathoms; and then, even before sails could be trimmed, 3 fathoms on the
starboard side.

"On the evening of the 29th August the Pandora went on a Reef,"
Morrison wrote bluntly, adding meaningfully, "I might say how, but it
would be to no purpose"; Morrison had prefaced his report with a classical flourish, *"Vidi et Scio"*—I saw and I know. In short, despite soundings, despite advance reconnaissance, despite both his fear and his
precautions, Edwards had run his ship aground.

"[T]he ship struck so violently on the Reef that the carpenters reported
that she made 18 Inches of water in 5 Minutes," the captain was compelled to write in his Admiralty report. "[I]n 5 minutes after there was 4
feet of water in the hold." Still chained fast in the darkness of Pandora's
Box, the fourteen prisoners could only listen as sounds of imminent disaster broke around them—cries, running feet, the heavy, confused
splash of a sail warped under the broken hull in an attempt to hold the
leak, the ineffectual working of the pumps and more cries that spread
the news that there was now nine feet of water in the hold. Coleman,
McIntosh and Norman—three of the men Bligh had singled out as being innocent—were summarily released from the prison to help work
the pumps, while at the same time the ship boats were readied.

In the darkness of their box, the remaining prisoners followed the
sounds with growing horror; seasoned sailors, they knew the implication
of each command and each failed outcome. The release of the exonerated
men added to their sense that ultimate disaster was imminent, and in the
strength of their terror they managed to break free of their irons. Crying
through the scuttle to be released, the prisoners only drew attention to their
broken bonds; and when Edwards was informed, he ordered the irons to be
replaced. As the armorer left, the mutineers watched in incredulity as the

scuttle was bolted shut behind him. Sentinels were placed over the box, with the instructions to shoot if there were any stirring within.

"In this miserable situation, with an expected Death before our Eyes, without the least Hope of relief & in the most trying state of suspense, we spent the Night," Peter Heywood wrote to his mother. The water had now risen to the coamings, or hatch borders, while feet tramped overhead across the prison roof.

"I'll be damned if they shall go without us," someone on deck was heard to say, speaking, as it seemed to the prisoners, of the officers who were heading to the boats. The ship booms were being cut loose to make a raft, and a topmast thundered onto the deck, killing a man. High broken surf around the ship hampered all movement, and compelled the lifeboats in the black water to stay well clear.

The confusion continued until dawn, when the prisoners were able to observe through the scuttle armed officers making their way across the top of their prison to the stern ladders, where the boats now awaited. Perhaps drawn at last by the prisoners' cries, the armorer's mate, Joseph Hodges, suddenly appeared at the prison entrance to remove their fetters. Once down in the box, Hodges freed Muspratt and Skinner, who immediately scrambled out through the scuttle, along with Byrn who had not been in irons; in his haste to break out, Skinner left with his handcuffs still on.

From above, some unseen hand suddenly closed and barred the scuttle again. Trapped with the prisoners, Hodges continued to work, striking off the irons in rapid succession, while the confined men renewed their pleas for mercy.

"I beg'd of the Master at Arms to leave the Scuttle open," Morrison wrote; "he answered 'Never fear my boys we'll all go to Hell together.'"

As he spoke, the *Pandora* made a fatal sally, rolling to port and spilling the master-at-arms and the sentinels into the water. The boats had already left, and Morrison claims he could see Edwards swimming toward his pinnace. Nowhere in his long report of the wreck and abandonment of his ship does Edwards make any mention of the prisoners.

With the ship under water as far as the mainmast, Pandora's Box began to fill. Hen coops, spars, booms—anything that would float had been cut loose and flung overboard as a possible lifesaver. Passing over the top of the prison roof on his way into the water, William Moulter, the boatswain's mate, heard the trapped men's cries, and his last action before he went overboard was to draw the bolt and hurl the scuttle away.

Scrambling inside the box, the men fought their way toward the light and air. Peter Heywood was one of the last to get out, and when he emerged in the sea he could see nothing above the water but the *Pandora*'s crosstrees. All around him, men floundered and called for help, lurching to take hold of anything afloat. A gangway floated up with Muspratt riding on one end. Coleman, Burkett and Lieutenant Corner were perched on top of the old prison. Heywood, stripped stark naked, had grasped a floating plank.

"The cries of the men drowning in the water was at first awful in the extreme," Hamilton wrote, "but as they sunk, and became faint, it died away by degrees."

Slowly the lifeboats circled the wreckage, gathering up distressed men as they found them. After an hour and a half in the water, Morrison was picked up by the master's mate, and found Peter Heywood already on board. One by one, the boats made their way to a sandy key, some three miles distant, and here when a muster was held it was discovered that eighty-nine of the ship's company and ten prisoners were accounted for; thirty-one of the company and four prisoners had drowned—but, as Morrison pointedly noted, "all the Officers were Saved." Of the prisoners, Richard Skinner had gone down while still in handcuffs, along with John Sumner and Peter's closest friend, George Stewart, both of whom had been struck and killed by a falling gangway; Henry Hilbrant, also still in irons, had never made it out of Pandora's Box.

On the day following the disaster, a boat was sent back to what remained of the *Pandora*, to see what could be salvaged. Nothing much was gained, and the boat returned with the head of the topgallant mast, some rigging, the chain of the lightning conductor—and the ship's cat, who had made his way to the crosstrees.

As the blazing Pacific sun rose over the sandy key, Edwards took a survey of his new situation. An assessment was made of the supplies that had been saved, which were now spread out along the sand to dry.

Somehow, with the whole of the night to prepare for certain disaster, no orders seem to have been given for the salvaging of provisions.

"Providentially a small barrel of water, a cag [keg] of wine, some biscuit, and a few muskets and cartouch boxes, had been thrown into the boat," Hamilton wrote, suggesting that what little supplies there were had been saved by chance. A daily ration was determined of three ounces of bread, two small glasses of water and one of wine, with the occasional addition of an ounce of portable soup, or cakes of dried soup, and half an ounce of essence of malt. Edwards's plan was to sail for the Dutch East Indies settlement of Coupang, in Timor, the same port that had received Bligh and his company at the end of their ordeal in the *Bounty*'s launch. The irony that the *Pandora*'s boats were to replicate part of Bligh's famous voyage is unlikely to have escaped anyone—least of all poor Thomas Hayward, who had been with Bligh and was thus about to embark on his second Pacific open-boat journey in a little more than two years. A voyage of some eleven hundred miles lay ahead.

On August 31, the third day after the *Pandora* had struck the reef, the little squadron set sail, with Captain Edwards leading the way in his pinnace, followed by the red and blue yawls and the launch. The prisoners had been carefully apportioned among the vessels. Peter Heywood, in the launch under the sympathetic Lieutenant Corner, had drawn what was probably the happiest boat, while James Morrison, as he reported, "had the good or evil fortune, call it which you please to go in the Pinnace with Capt. Edwards."

Proceeding northwest, the little squadron now at last passed through the reef by way of a channel that, as Edwards reported to the Admiralty, was "better than any hitherto known"—a discovery that had come rather late in the day. In the morning of the following day, they came to the desolate, treeless coast of New Holland. Here, the parched men had the rare good fortune to find a spring rushing onto the beach. The prisoners in particular were tortured by the sun; their skin, pale and tender after five months of confinement, had quickly burned and blistered. Peter wrote, "[W]e appeared as if dipped in large tubs of boiling water."

The company passed the night off a small island, where they were awakened by the howling of dingoes, which they mistook for wolves. On the afternoon of September 2, they passed a series of distinctive islands that were recognized from Bligh's account and a chart made during his boat voyage. By the evening, the boats were in sight of Cape York, the northernmost tip of New Holland, and the end of the strait. Ahead was the Indian Ocean and a one-thousand-mile run to Timor.

"It is unnecessary to relate our particular sufferings in the Boats during our run to Timor," wrote Edwards, with his usual literary sangfroid, "and is sufficient to observe that we suffered more from heat & thirst than from hunger." The weather, at least, was good and the overloaded boats made satisfying progress. At dawn on the sixteenth the Dutch fort at Coupang, Timor, was at last hailed. Edwards had lost no men on this leg of the journey, although they had been reduced to drinking the blood of captured birds and their own urine.

Backed by gentle, verdant, wooded hills, the small settlement of Coupang was built at the head of a deep natural harbor. It consisted of little more than a fort and a handful of houses, a church, a hospital and company stores serving a population of Dutch officials, Chinese merchants and Malay slaves. A European ship at anchor amid other small craft offered a comfortingly familiar sight. The *Pandora*'s four boats hailed the fort, and the men were welcomed ashore.

While the *Pandora*'s officers and men were dispersed in different houses around the settlement, the prisoners were taken to the fort itself and put in stocks. Again, Edwards's report makes no mention of the prisoners at all during this sojourn, but Morrison's account is graphic: "Immediately on our landing Provisions were procured which now began to move our bodys and we were forced to ease Nature where we lay." Most of the men had not moved their bowels for the duration of the journey, and some were now administered enemas through a syringe.

"[T]he Surgeon of the Place who visited us could not enter the place till it had been washed by Slaves," Morrison continued. "[W]e had laid 6 Days in this situation. . . ." A compassionate Dutch officer of the fort, clearly appalled at the prisoners' treatment, arranged to have the men released from the stocks and placed in leg irons, manacled two by two, but otherwise at liberty to walk about. The prisoners were still almost naked, but with "some of the leaves of the Brab Tree . . . set to work to make hats," a skill undoubtedly learned in those faraway days in Tahiti. These hats the enterprising prisoners then sold and with the little money earned bought tobacco.

As it turned out, the *Pandora*'s company were not the only distressed British sailors at Coupang. Some months earlier, seven men, a woman and two children had arrived at the fort in a small six-oared cutter with the story that they were part of the crew and passengers of a wrecked brig called *Neptune*. They too had been treated with great compassion by the Dutch authorities. And when Edwards and his men came ashore, the kind Dutchmen had hastened to their guests to bring them the good news that their captain had arrived.

"What Captain! dam'me, we have no Captain," Hamilton reports one of them had unwisely exclaimed. The small party, it turned out, had not been shipwrecked, but were convicts who had made a daring escape from Botany Bay ("they were discovered to be Cheats," as Morrison noted self-righteously).

On October 6, having recovered strength, Edwards led his entire company to sea again, this time as passengers on a Dutch East Indiaman, the *Rembang*. Their destination was the Dutch settlement of Batavia, on Java, from where Edwards expected to get passages to Cape Town. Here, there would be other company ships bound for Europe.

This short passage from Timor to Batavia proved to be as eventful as any in the men's now protracted travels. On the sixth day out, while they were off the coast of Flores, a tremendous storm erupted. According to Dr. Hamilton, within a few minutes "every sail of the ship was shivered to pieces. . . . This storm was attended with the most dreadful thunder and lightning we had ever experienced."

At the height of this crisis, when the ship was in imminent danger of being driven onto the lee shore, the Dutch seamen, Hamilton reported, "went below; and the ship was preserved from destruction by the manly exertion of our English tars, whose souls seemed to catch redoubled ardour from the tempest's rage." This appears to have been no exaggeration. Morrison himself, hardly one to volunteer praise for his captors,

stated matter-of-factly that the ship was "badly found and Worse Managed and if Captain Edwards had not taken the Command and set his
Men to work she would never have reached Batavia."

On October 30, the *Rembang* limped into Semarang, on the north coast
of Java. The prisoners had been let out of irons during the battle with the
storm to take turns at the pumps but had discovered they no longer had
strength for this routine duty. But the spirits of the whole company were
raised by an entirely unexpected and welcome surprise: the *Pandora*'s little
schooner, *Resolution*, awaited them, safely anchored in the harbor. After
having lost sight of *Pandora* in the gale four months earlier, the *Resolution*'s men set out from the Samoas to the Friendly Islands, skirted the
southernmost of the Fiji group, made northwest for the Endeavour Strait,
struck out for the Indonesian islands and came, through the Strait of Bali
to Surabaya, on the north coast of Java. Their navigational equipment had
consisted of two quadrants, a volume of Robertson's *Elements of Navigation*
and an edition of Guthrie's *Geographical Grammar,* but no charts.

At Surabaya, the vessel's young commander, Master's Mate William
Oliver, had presented himself to the Dutch authorities. All Dutch settlements, however, had been alerted to the fate of the *Bounty;* and as David
Renouard, one of the *Pandora*'s midshipmen, said, it was "a singular coincidence that the mutineers who quitted Otaheite in the *Bounty* corre-
sponded with ourselves both in rank and numbers." The *Resolution,* built
in fact by mutineers, was moreover hand-hewn from Otaheitan wood.
Distrustful of Oliver's story, the Dutch authorities politely detained the
small company for a month. At length, Oliver persuaded them to let him
make for Batavia, by way of Semarang, where by another uncanny coincidence the *Resolution* had arrived on October 29, the day before the
Rembang. Between *Bounty, Pandora, Resolution* and the boat from Botany
Bay, four epic voyages had been accomplished within a two-and-a-half-
year period; the Dutch authorities, ever picking up the wreckage, must
have wondered if the British had a penchant for this kind of business.

The *Rembang* and the *Resolution* proceeded together to Batavia, the principal port of the Dutch East Indies. Founded in 1618, it was now a spacious
town set at the head of a deep bay half a mile from the sea, its streets cut,
Dutch style, by tree-lined connecting canals. Picturesque from afar, it was

also reckoned to be one of the most fever-ridden and pestilential places on earth. Out of the surrounding swamp and stagnant canals, malarial mosquitoes spread like miasma. A "painted sepulchre, this golgotha of Europe," Dr. Hamilton described the city. Dead bodies floating into the sea from the canals had struck their ship on arrival, which, as Hamilton noted, "had a very disagreeable effect on the minds of our brave fellows." Two years earlier, four of Bligh's men had died of fever here, after successfully weathering their great boat journey, and Bligh himself had fallen gravely ill.

On arrival, Edwards arranged for his men to be housed on board a Dutch East India Company ship then in the road, or anchorage outside the harbor. Thirty of his sick were borne to a hospital—a number of these were men from the *Resolution* who had suffered badly in the course of their impromptu journey.

In the nearly seven weeks they were detained at Batavia, the majority of the prisoners were allowed on deck only twice, although once again Coleman, Norman and McIntosh enjoyed more freedom. But it may be that the confinement afforded the men some protection from the mosquitoes. "[H]ere we enjoyed our Health," Morrison stated, noting with satisfaction that "the *Pandora*'s people fell sick and died apace."

Edwards had negotiated an arrangement with the Dutch authorities to divide the *Pandora*'s complement among four ships bound for Holland by way of the Cape, "at no expense to Government further than for the Officers and Prisoners," as he somewhat nervously informed the Admiralty. A disaster such as the loss of a ship did not allow a captain of His Majesty's Navy carte blanche in extricating himself from the disaster. All accounts for the £724 8s. od. in expenses incurred between Coupang and Batavia would have to be meticulously itemized and justified on return.

Edwards also used the sojourn at Batavia to write up his report to the Admiralty relating all that had transpired subsequent to January 6, 1791, the date of his last dispatch from Rio. Edwards's report, in his own hand, filled thirty-two large, closely written pages and ranged over all his adventures—the capture of the mutineers, the fruitless search for Christian and the *Bounty*, the wreck of the *Pandora*, and the voyage to Timor. The events are narrated in strict chronological order, like a story, with discursive material about the customs and country of the islands visited and anecdotal asides ("I took this opportunity to show the Chief what Execution the Canon and Carronades would do by firing a six pound shot on shore . . ."), so that their lordships of the Admiralty would have had no clue until page twenty-six that the *Pandora* had in fact been lost. Boldly noting that he was enclosing "Latitudes & Longitudes of several Islands, & ca discovered during our Voyage," with his report, Edwards then offered a tentative conclusion:

"Although I have not had the good fortune fully to accomplish the Object of my Voyage," he ventured, ". . . I hope it will be thought . . . that of my Orders which I have been able to fulfil, with the discoveries that have been made will be some compensation for the disappointment & misfortunes that have attended us"; and, with a last rally of optimism:

> [S]hould their Lordships upon the whole think that the Voyage will
> be profitable to our Country it will be a great consolation to,
>> Sir,
>>> Your most obedient humble servant,
>>>> Edw. Edwards.

Also before leaving Batavia, Edwards presented the mutineers' schooner, *Resolution*, to the governor of Timor as a gift of gratitude for his kindness. Morrison watched this transaction closely. He had been the architect of the plan to build the schooner and although she was the handiwork of many, he had placed the greatest stake in her. Her timbers had been hewn from Tahitian hibiscus, and both her planking and the bark gum used as pitch had come from that versatile and fateful tree, the breadfruit.

On Christmas Day 1791, the Dutch Indiaman *Vreedenburg*, Captain Christiaan, weighed anchor and sailed out of the straits at the harbor's entrance carrying a cargo of coffee beans, rice and arrack, a liquor distilled from coconut milk. On board as passengers were Captain Edwards, twenty-seven officers and men of the *Pandora*, twenty-six Chinese and the ten mutineers. The remainder of the *Pandora*'s company, including the Botany Bay prisoners, were divided among two other ships. Lieutenant Larkan and a party of twenty had departed a month earlier on the *Zwan*. Edwards had also taken on board a distressed English seaman from the *Supply*. In turn, he had been forced to leave in the deadly hospital one of his own men, who was too ill to be moved. All in all, Edwards lost fifteen men to the Batavian fever, one being young William Oliver, the twenty-year-old master's mate who had commanded the *Resolution* with such leadership and skill on her unexpected voyage.

A few days from the Cape of Good Hope, nearly three months out on what had been a slow passage, the mutineers were released from their irons and allowed to walk the deck. Here, testing the wind, Morrison noted that the men "now found the weather Sharp and Cutting." The balmy Pacific lay far behind.

On March 18, the *Vreedenburg* anchored in Table Bay, at the Cape of Good Hope. Close by the harbor was the fortress that safeguarded the Dutch East India Company stores, and indeed the whole town had been established solely to serve the Company. Here ships could break the long journey between Europe and the East Indies, restock and refit and, if coming from Batavia, offload their sick at the Cape Hospital.

The *Vreedenburg* joined other sail at anchor, including to the universal joy of the *Pandora*'s company, a British man-of-war, the *Gorgon*, Captain John Parker. This 44-gun frigate had arrived from Port Jackson in New South Wales, where she had dropped off much anticipated and desperately needed supplies, including livestock and thirty new convicts. Seeing an opportunity to return directly to England, instead of by way of Holland where the Dutch Indiamen were bound, Edwards arranged passages for part of his mixed company on the *Gorgon*.

Thus, two days after arrival, Edwards added himself, the Botany Bay convicts and the *Bounty* mutineers to the *Gorgon*'s company, joining other passengers that included a detachment of marine privates and their families leaving Port Jackson, and fifteen distressed British seamen picked up at the Cape. Among the mixed cargo, boxes of dispatches for the colonial office were probably the most important. More burdensome were the sixty tubs and boxes of plants destined for the Royal Botanic Gardens at Kew, under the direction of the great naturalist and president of the Royal Society, Sir Joseph Banks. Specimens of New South Wales lumber cramming the main and quarter decks were for the Navy Board, while a dingo was a gift for the Prince of Wales. Similarly, two kangaroos and opossums were also gifts for Joseph Banks, whose tentacles of influence stretched to the remotest corner of all parts of the globe; it was Banks who had been the driving force behind the *Bounty*'s breadfruit venture.

The arrival of the mutineers was noted offhandedly in the *Gorgon*'s log, along with the more important additions: "Recd Wine fresh Meat; Bread for Ships Company; also Water. Caulkers Caulking within and without board. Carpenters as necessary. Armourer at his forge; Sent to Sick quarters 1 Supernumerary Marine. Came on board from the Dutch Ship Vreedenburgh 10 Pirates belonging to His Majesty's Ship Bounty. . . ."

At four in the afternoon of April 5, 1792, the *Gorgon* at last set sail for England, exchanging salutes with the fort as she passed. Blessed with fine weather and "a charming Breeze," as one of the marines, Lieutenant Ralph Clark, noted in his private journal, the *Gorgon* passed the island of St. Helena in under two weeks. Five days later they anchored at Ascension Island, primarily to refresh their food stock with local turtles. Although each passing mile brought the prisoners closer to their day of reckoning, they enjoyed the return to familiar British naval routine. Their confinement had been made less rigorous than under Edwards, and as Morrison noted, they had begun to regain their health and strength.

May 1 brought an extraordinary diversion: two sharks were caught and in the belly of one was found a prayer book, "[q]uite fresh," according to Lieutenant Clark, "not a leaf of it defaced." The book was inscribed "Francis Carthy, cast for death in the Year 1786 and Repreaved the Same day at four oClock in the afternoon." The book was subsequently confirmed as having belonged to a convict who had sailed to Botany Bay in 1788 with the first fleet of prisoners consigned to transportation.

In the early rainy hours of May 6 died Charlotte Bryant, the child of Mary Bryant, the escaped convict who had sailed so boldly into Coupang before the arrival of the *Pandora*. Amid the mixed humanity that the *Gorgon* carried, it was not the pirates of the *Bounty* who appear to have stood out, but the young widow from Cornwall, age twenty-seven, "height 5'4",

grey eyes, brown hair, sallow complexion," as the register of Newgate
Prison records, who had been sentenced to transportation for stealing a
cloak. By coincidence, Marine Captain Watkin Tench, returning from
Botany Bay, had gone out with Mary five years before, and recalled that
she and her husband-to-be "had both of them been always distinguished
for good behaviour." Now, he got from her the details of her extraordinary 3,254-mile voyage, coasting the shores of New Holland, harassed by
the "Indians" when attempting to land, foraging for food and water—
this story, which surely circulated around the ship, was one every sailing
man on board would appreciate.

On June 19, the *Gorgon* completed her long voyage and on an overcast
day anchored at Spithead off Portsmouth alongside three of His
Majesty's ships, the *Duke*, *Brunswick* and *Edgar*, three frigates and a
sloop of war. Captain Parker immediately notified Sir Andrew Snape Hamond, the port's commander on duty, of his ship's arrival and awaited
further instructions. Meanwhile, his crew busied themselves with the
numerous tedious and chaotic duties that awaited the end of a long voyage. The officers and men of the Portsmouth and Plymouth Divisions
were disembarked, and water and victuals were brought onboard. The
carpenter made his customary report, noting that the ship's "works in
general is very weak from carying large quantities of water and hay &
tubs of Plants."

Captain Edwards, a passenger, had nothing to do with these transactions. Most of his men were still behind him, on the other Dutch ships,
and the pirates and convicts would now be turned over to the proper
authorities. Disembarking early at the Isle of Wight, he was safe in
Portsmouth by the time the *Gorgon* came to anchor. At some point in
their wanderings, most probably during the sultry, sickly sojourn at
Batavia, an anonymous member of the *Pandora*'s crew had immortal-
ized their journey, and their captain, with a long doggerel poem:

> *Brave Edwards then with freindly Care*
> *for men and boat began to fear . . .*
> *by hard fatigue Our men were Spent,*
> *the Ship keel'd Over and Down She went*

An Equel Chance Our Captain Gave
to All Alike their Lives to Save . . .

Edwards's last semiofficial duty had been to accompany the captain's wife, Mary Ann Parker, to shore, a journey that, perhaps predictably, turned into a four-hour ordeal, as she noted, "rowing against the wind." Once onshore, nothing remained for Edwards but to await his own court-martial; like Bligh, he had returned without his ship.

On the day after the *Gorgon's* arrival, Captain Hamond informed Captain Parker that their lordships of the Admiralty had directed that "the ten Prisoners belonging to the *Bounty*" be sent to the security of one of the port guardships. The following day, a longboat, manned and armed, was sent from the *Hector*, Captain George Montagu, to collect the mutineers. Put over the side of the *Gorgon* in chains into the waiting boat, the prisoners were able to enjoy the sights of the busy, lively anchorage in the course of their short journey. The cloudy weather had briefly cleared and showed breezy and fair—an English summer day. Their arrival on board was mentioned briefly in the *Hector's* log: "Post-noon received the above Prisoners, Wm Muspratt, James Morrison, Jn Milward, Peter Heywood, Thomas Ellison, Michl Burn, Thos Burkett, Josh Coleman, Thos. McIntosh & Charles Norman . . . and secured them in the Gun Room." A sergeant's guard of marines was sent over to provide additional security. For Thomas Burkett, at least, the *Hector* was familiar territory: he had served as an able seaman on this same ship, six years previously.

Peter Heywood had brought away a single possession from his long ordeal, a *Book of Common Prayer*, which he had carried in his teeth as he swam from the wreck of the *Pandora*. On the flyleaves, he had made some notations of events and dates important to him: "*Sept. 22 1789, Mya TOOBOOAI mye; Mar. 25 1791, We ta Pahee Pandora . . . We tow te Vredenberg tea . . . Pahee HECTOR*"—the most striking thing about Peter's entries is that he had written them in Tahitian.

Back in Tahiti, the *Bounty* men who had cast their lot in with the islanders were remembered largely with affection. Less than eight months after the *Pandora* left Matavai Bay, Captain George Vancouver arrived with his two ships, *Discovery* and *Chatham*. Through conversations with the Tahitians, he and his men learned a great deal about the mutineers' lives on the island: they had built a schooner; they had each taken a wife and treated their women well; Stewart and Heywood had laid out gardens that were still in a flourishing state; these two had conformed to Tahitian manners to such an extent that they ceremonially uncovered their upper bodies when in the presence of King Tynah, as was local custom.

One day the *Chatham*'s men were "surpized at seeing alongside in a double Canoe, three women all dress'd in White Linen Shirts, and having each a fine young child in their arms, perfectly white," as Edward Bell, a young clerk on the *Chatham,* reported in his journal. These were the women who had lived with the *Bounty*'s mutineers, and their children.

"One call'd herself Peggy Stewart, after Mr. Stewart, one of the Bounty's midshipmen, and her child which was very beautiful was called Charlotte," wrote Bell. "[A]nother's name was Mary MacIntosh and the other's Mary Bocket [Burkett]."

Following this first meeting, Peggy Stewart frequently came to visit, often bringing small gifts and always inquiring after her husband. At length, it was time for the ships to depart, and she came to make her affectionate and tearful farewell.

"Just before she went away, she came into my Cabbin," wrote Bell, "and ask'd me the same question she had often done, whether I thought Stewart would be hung." Deeply moved, he replied that he didn't know—perhaps not.

"She then said 'If he is alive when you return, tell him that you saw his Peggy and his little Charlotte, and that they were both well, and tell him to come to Otaheite, and live with them, or they will be unhappy.' She then burst into Tears and with the deepest regret forced herself into her Canoe and as long as we could see her she kept waving her hand." The next ship that came from Tahiti brought word that Peggy had pined away and died of a broken heart.

BOUNTY

England, 1787

The passion for exploration and discovery, the hunger to learn all things about all aspects of the physical world, the great and preposterous optimism that held that such truths were in fact discoverable—these remarkable traits that so characterized the British eighteenth century were embodied by one remarkable eighteenth-century man, the admired, envied and uniquely influential Sir Joseph Banks. Banks was forty-four years old in 1787, and already a national treasure, as powerful in his way as any member of government. And it was the interest of Banks, more than any other consideration, that ensured that the government undertook the *Bounty*'s breadfruit mission to the South Seas.

Banks had been born in 1743, to a prosperous and well-connected landowning family. Somehow he had managed to be educated at both Eton and Harrow and at Oxford, although under a tutor he had privately hired from Cambridge. He was only eighteen when his father died and he had inherited the first of his estates, and from this time, for the remainder of his life, Banks was the master of his own destiny. From an early age he had shown a passion for natural history, above all botany, and this he now pursued. At the age of twenty-one, having established himself in London society, where he quickly became the friend of distinguished men some decades his senior, Banks set out for a summer of botanizing along the coasts of Labrador and Newfoundland. Returning with a professionally compiled collection of novel specimens never before seen in Europe, and the basis of what would become his world-famous herbarium, he was, at twenty-three, elected a fellow of the Royal Society. Still restless, still implausibly young, Banks then decided that his next venture in gentlemanly inquiry would be with Lieutenant James Cook in the Pacific.

The first of what would be Cook's three magnificent voyages left England in the *Endeavour* in August 1768. The primary objective was to enable British astronomers to observe the transit of Venus from Tahiti, but after accomplishing such observations, the expedition was to proceed in search of the fabled Southern continent, surveying New Zealand and other islands en route. Banks was footing the bill for his own passage as well as that of his considerable entourage—his colleague and employee Dr. Daniel Solander, a distinguished Swedish naturalist and disciple of Linnaeus, two artists to make records of what was seen, his secretary, four servants and his two greyhounds. It was popularly rumored that Banks's expenses for the trip had cost him some ten thousand pounds.

Cook's first voyage made discoveries in New Zealand, Australia (where Botany Bay was named for Banks's botanizing) and a multitude of new islands, but it was the visit to Tahiti that became most memorably etched in the English imagination. Tahiti had been "discovered" before Cook—Captain Samuel Wallis of the *Dolphin* had touched here, on what he called "King George III Island," in 1767—but it did not become a subject of popular and fashionable fascination until the return of the *Endeavour* in 1771.

And at least one reason for the fascination was Joseph Banks. He had not just returned to England with thousands of unknown and expertly preserved botanical specimens, professional botanical drawings and watercolors (as well as landscapes and ethnological studies) from his artists; Banks had also returned as the subject of romantic, even titillating stories. With his zeal for new experiences, he had thrown himself into Tahitian life, learning its language, attending burials and sacrifices and dances, endearing himself to its people, even having himself discreetly tattooed. The happy promiscuity of the Tahitian women was already well known from Wallis's reports and Banks's adventures on this front provided additional spice. Outstanding among the stories that made the rounds of London social circles was the tale of the theft of Mr. Banks's fine waistcoat with its splendid silver frogging, stolen, along with his shoes and pistol, while he lay sleeping with his "old Freind Oberea" in her canoe:

Didst thou not, crafty, subtle sunburnt strum
Steal the silk breeches from his tawny bum?
Calls't thouself a Queen? and thus couldst use
And rob thy Swain of breeches and his shoes?

The romance of Banks and Queen Oberea, broadcast in facetious verse and "letters," helped ensure that the most-talked-about phenomenon to emerge from Cook's long, exotic voyage was Joseph Banks. To paraphrase one historian, Banks had no need to return to London with a lion or tiger—he was the lion of London. A few years after his return, he would make one more far-flung journey of discovery, this time a self-financed expedition to Iceland. In the course of his three rather eccentrically determined voyages, he had pursued natural history from Iceland to Tierra del Fuego, from extreme northern to extreme southern latitudes—a range unmatched by any naturalist of his day.

With these travels behind him, Banks purchased a London town house in fashionable Soho Square and settled into the sedate but stimulating routine he was to maintain until the end of his life. In 1778, he was elected president of the Royal Society—and would be reelected annually for the next forty-two years—and he was raised to a baronetcy as "Sir Joseph" in 1779. On his return from the South Seas, he had been introduced to King George, who also shared Banks's enthusiasm for natural history; Banks had been appointed botanical adviser to the King, and the two men became enduring friends. From their conversational strolls together were laid the plans for what would become the Royal Botanic Gardens at Kew, an enterprise made successful by Banks's energetic enthusiasm and dazzling connections with botanists and collectors throughout the world. This dedication would continue from his appointment in 1775 until his death. Banks's nearby villa, Spring Grove, and its extensive land became a model of experimental farming, another interest he shared with the King. The stud stock of Spanish merino sheep, which had had acquired with much difficulty and bred at Spring Grove, was, with the royal stud, which he also managed, the foundation for the growth of the British export wool trade in the next century.

But mostly what occupied Banks, apart from his duties at the Royal Society, was his correspondence. In his town house, with his fine library and unique collection of specimens, beautifully mounted in cabinets of his own design, he was furnished with much of what he required for his further researches. The rest came to him from the eager outside world. Reports of the prodigious appetite of a cuckoo raised by hand, and of the tonal qualities of Tahitian wind instruments; descriptions of battles between spiders and flies; introductions to promising students of botany and natural history; queries about prospective African expeditions, proper methods of raising ships from riverbeds, the correct authorship of "*God Save the King*"; reports of unicorn sightings, of the later years of the famous German Wild Boy and his fondness for gingerbread; descriptions of destruction done to wall fruit by insects, the superiority of olives to other oil-producing trees; gifts of newly published treatises, specimens of seed, of insects, of fighting flies and remains of the spiders they had conquered—all streamed into 32 Soho Square. The kangaroos, opossums and plants that would so inconvenience the *Gorgon* in 1792 were all destined for Joseph Banks.

His correspondence, most of it now lost, is estimated to have comprised anywhere from 50,000 to 100,000 letters. His correspondents included great names such as William Pitt the Younger, Lord Nelson, Benjamin Franklin and distinguished scholars of many nations. But there were also captains who offered interesting specimens from their travels, farmers and a letter forwarded from a schoolmaster giving testimony that he had seen a mermaid.

Anywhere in the world, everywhere in the British Isles, people noted curious phenomena, came up with curious questions, observations or theories and thought, "I'll write to Joseph Banks." When Samuel Taylor Coleridge wanted "hashish," he contacted Banks. Without straying far from London and his well-managed Lincolnshire estates, Banks knew everyone, and everything. Studiously apolitical, he was respected and trusted by most parties. Few British expeditions of discovery of any kind, whether to Africa or Iceland, were mounted without consultation with Sir Joseph Banks. In Banks's correspondence is mirrored the British eighteenth century, with all its energetic, questing optimism, its dazzling sophistication and its occasional startling innocence; an age in which geographical and scientific discoveries surpassed anything previously dreamt of, and yet an age in which it was still, just barely, possible to believe in mermaids and unicorns.

Amid this flood of gloriously mixed correspondence came an insistent trickle from those with interest in the plantations of the West Indies, with the suggestion that the importation of exotic fruit-bearing trees would be useful to the islands. As early as 1772, Valentine Morris, a planter who would later be governor of St. Vincent, had approached Banks regarding the "possibility of procuring the bread tree, either in seed or plant so as to introduce that most valuable tree into our American Islands."

The virtues of the *Artocarpus incisa*—the handsome, broad-leafed tropical tree that bore fruit the size of a man's head—had been related by early explorers, who gave accounts of the fruit's tastiness and uncanny similarity to bread. Lord Anson's account of his circumnavigation of the world, published in 1748, told how on the Pacific island of Tinian, where his scurvy-stricken crew had fortuitously washed up, the breadfruit had been "constantly eaten by us instead of bread: and so universally preferred that no ship's bread was expended in that whole interval."

Such reports by Anson, Cook and others were taken very seriously by the West India Committee, which was composed of merchants and property owners with island interests. At a meeting in February 1775, a letter was read to the chairman "relative to the introduction into England of the Bread-fruit tree and Mangostan from the East Indies, in order for their being sent over and propagated in the West Indies." A month later, a resolution was passed offering a hundred pounds to "the captain of an East India ship, or any other person" who brought "the true Bread-fruit tree in a thriving vegetation" to England. The matter dragged on over the years, the subject of various letters, treatises and resolutions put forth by the committee. And thus things might have remained indefinitely, with a vague and rather lowly bounty offered to any willing taker, if the enterprise had not caught the interest of Joseph Banks.

Banks had privately discussed the possibility with several eager planters and botanists: needless to say, he had himself tasted the fruit on Tahiti, but had personally preferred plantains, finding that breadfruit "sometimes griped us." By 1785, Matthew Wallen, a botanist living in Jamaica to whom Banks had sent various exotic seeds for experimental planting, wrote to Banks with the bold observation that the "King ought to send a Man of War, a Botanist & Gardener for the Plants we want," adding he would not then "want the Example of the King of France who sends Duplicates & Triplicates of all valuable Plants to his Colonies." Banks was in agreement that a proper government-sponsored expedition was desirable; it was also the case that he lacked breadfruit specimens of his own for Kew. That the British had fallen behind the French on this front provided useful leverage, and in February 1787, a breadfruit expedition was formally announced to the West India Committee by Prime Minister Pitt.

Simultaneous with these proposals for the breadfruit expedition were the plans, now well under way, for the transportation of the first convicts from England to Botany Bay in New South Wales. Banks, who was instrumental to both ventures, had originally intended to combine the two, and had at first proposed an ambitious itinerary: a single vessel would carry the convicts to New South Wales, deposit them and then continue on to collect breadfruit in Tahiti. It did not take long, however, for Banks to awake to the fact that the two enterprises, although destined for roughly the same part of the globe, had wholly distinct requirements. An expedition devoted solely to the breadfruit was, he allowed in March 1787, "more likely to be successful."

Thus some months later, Lord Sydney, a principal secretary of state, informed Banks that the Admiralty had "purchased a Vessel for the purpose of conveying the Bread-Fruit Tree and other useful productions from the South Sea Islands to His Majesty's West India Possessions." The ship, formerly named *Bethia*, was one Banks had approved, and it had been purchased by the Admiralty for the sum of £1,950. She was to be commissioned within a few days, according to Sydney, and was "to be called The Bounty, and to be commanded by Lieutenant Bligh."

Exactly how, or through whose recommendation, William Bligh came to receive the command of the *Bounty* is not known. It does not appear to be the case that Banks knew Bligh personally, although he had undoubtedly heard of him, since Bligh had served as sailing master of the *Resolution* on Cook's last expedition, which had departed England eleven years before, in 1776. It is possible that Banks had made a recommendation that the breadfruit expedition was best entrusted to one of Cook's men. William Bligh, on the other hand, had certainly heard of Joseph Banks, and in his mind there was no question of to whom he was indebted.

"Sir, I arrived yesterday from Jamaica," Bligh wrote to Banks on August 6, with an outflowing of gratitude. ". . . I have heard the flattering news of your great goodness to me, intending to honor me with the command of the vessel which you propose to go to the South Seas, for which, after offering you my most grateful thanks, I can only assure you I shall endeavour, and I hope succeed, in deserving such a trust."

William Bligh had been christened on September 9, 1754, in the great naval town of Plymouth, where his father, Francis Bligh, was chief of customs. The Blighs were originally from Cornwall, and could claim such distinguished men as Admiral Sir Richard Rodney Bligh and the Earls of Darnley. Bligh's mother, Jane Pearce, had been a widow when she married Francis Bligh, and had died before her son was sixteen. William Bligh appears to have been the only child of this union. Francis Bligh married twice again after the death of his wife, and had himself passed away at the age of fifty-nine in December 1780—three months after his son's return to England from Cook's third Pacific voyage.

Bligh first appears in naval records in 1762, as a captain's servant on the *Monmouth*, when he would have been all of seven years old. This should not be taken to mean that young William had actually gone to sea; more likely, he had been entered on the books of an accommodating captain. This well-established, if strictly improper, tradition enabled a captain to draw extra rations and the child to enjoy some early friendly patronage and "sea time." Widespread as the practice was, it was only extended to families with some degree of "interest," or influential connections. In Bligh's case this appears to have come through a relative of his mother, although his father undoubtedly had connections through the customs office. Bligh's name does not appear again in naval records until 1770, shortly after his mother's death, when he was entered on the muster of the *Hunter* as an "able seaman," a common, temporary classification for "young gentlemen," or potential officers in training who found themselves on ships where the official quota of midshipmen was already filled. And indeed, six months after signing on, a midshipman position did open up and Bligh was duly promoted.

Bligh was to serve on his next ship, the *Crescent*, for three years as a midshipman, or from the age of seventeen to a few weeks shy of twenty. This period, which saw tours to Tenerife and the West Indies, was undoubtedly a formative period of his professional life. Paid off in 1774, Bligh next joined the *Ranger*—not as a midshipman, but once again, initially, as an able seaman; such was the expected fickleness of a naval career. The *Ranger*'s principal duty was hunting smugglers, and she had been based where smuggling was known to be particularly egregious, across the Irish Sea at Douglas, on the Isle of Man. Manx men and women were to figure heavily in Bligh's later life.

Then, at the age of twenty-one, Bligh received the news that would represent a turning point in his life: he had been chosen to join Captain Cook on his third expedition as master of the *Resolution*. Again, how or by whom he had been singled out for this prestigious commission is not known. Cook himself had stated that the young officers under his direction "could be usefully employed in constructing charts, in taking views of the coasts and headlands near which we should pass, and in drawing plans of the bays and harbours in which we should anchor." Given Bligh's later proven abilities, it may be that even at the age of twenty-one a reputation for these skills had preceded him and recommended him to Cook. To work side by side, in this capacity, with the greatest navigator of the age was for Bligh both a great honor and an unparalleled opportunity.

It was also, however, strictly speaking, if not a step backward in the command hierarchy of his profession, at least a step sideways. For a young man of Bligh's background and aspirations, the desired position following a successful midshipman apprenticeship was that of lieutenant, which would put him securely on the promotional ladder leading to the post of captain. A master, on the other hand, for all the rigor of his responsibilities, received his appointment not as a commission from the Admiralty, but by a warrant from the Naval Board. These were important distinctions, professionally and socially. And while it was not unusual for a young man to bide his time by serving as a master until a lieutenancy was offered, there was the danger of proving too useful in that rank and advancing no further. Most masters had not been young gentlemen and were not destined for the captain's list. In Bligh's case the risk seemed justified. If he did his job well, he could count on the "interest" and recommendation of Captain Cook, the most highly regarded royal naval officer of his day as a cartographer and explorer.

With Cook's expedition, Bligh sailed to Van Diemen's Land, New Zealand, Tahiti, and the Pacific islands. He patrolled the west coast of North America and searched for the Northwest Passage. Cook was justly famous for maintaining the health of his crew on his long, demanding voyages, and Bligh's own later practices would reveal that he had closely observed and learned from his mentor's innovations in diet and ship management.

From Cook's own log, one catches only glimpses of the earnest young sailing master, usually being sent ahead of the ship in a reconnaissance boat to make a careful survey of some ticklish coast or bay. After Cook himself, Bligh was responsible for most of the charts and surveys made in the course of this last expedition, and had thus honed his already exceptional abilities.

Most unforgettably, Bligh had been present at Kealakekua Bay, Hawaii, when on February 14, 1779, James Cook was murdered by the island natives. The events that led to this shocking tragedy would be long disputed; dispassionate reading of the numerous, often conflicting accounts suggests that Cook behaved with uncharacteristic rashness and provocation to the islanders—but that at the moment of crisis he had been betrayed by the disorder and panic of the armed marines whose duty had been to protect him. In the horrified and frightened aftermath of their loss, Cook's officers assembled an account of the events at Kealakekua Bay that vindicated most and made a scapegoat of only one man, a Lieutenant Rickinson. Some years later, William Bligh would record his disgust with this closing of the ranks in marginal annotations made in a copy of the official publication of the voyage: "A most infamous lie"; "The whole affair from the Opening to the end did not last 10 Minutes, nor was their a spark of courage or conduct shown in the whole busyness"; "a most Hypocritical expression"; "A pretty Old Woman Story."

In Bligh's opinion, the principal cause of the tragedy at Kealakekua Bay lay with the marines: they had failed to do their duty. After firing a first panicked volley, they had fallen back from the menacing crowd of islanders in fear, splashing and flailing to their waiting boat. "The Marines fir'd & ran which occasioned all that followed for had they fixed their bayonets & not have run, so frightened as they were, they might have drove all before them." The person most responsible for the marines' disorder was their commander, Lieutenant Molesworth Phillips, characterized by Bligh as a "person, who never was of any real service the whole Voyage, or did anything but eat and Sleep."

Bligh was at least in some position to pass judgment, for the day following Cook's murder he had been sent onshore to oversee a party of men repairing the *Resolution*'s damaged mast. Shortly after landing, Bligh had found himself faced with a menacing crowd and had ordered his men to stand and fire; and he had held this position until joined by reinforcements from the ship.

The shock and tragedy apart, Cook's death deprived Bligh of the valuable interest he had counted on at the expedition's end, and which it would appear by this time he otherwise lacked; his own modest connections had been sufficient to secure him a young gentleman's entry to naval service, but do not appear to have been extensive enough to have advanced him further. In both the subsequent flurry of promotions and the published account of the voyage, Bligh found himself somewhat marginalized; whether this was because he had made known his highly impolitic views of the expedition cannot be determined. But to his intense annoyance and mortification, the carefully drawn charts he had made throughout the voyage were published under another's name.

Following his return to England, Bligh had indulged in a rare holiday and returned to the Isle of Man, with, as subsequent events would suggest, a determined objective; only months after his return, in February 1781, William Bligh was married to Elizabeth Betham, the pretty, twenty-seven-year-old daughter of well-to-do and exceptionally well-educated parents. Richard Betham, Elizabeth's father, was the receiver general, or collector of customs, in Douglas, and the friend of such distinguished men as philosopher David Hume and economist Adam Smith, with whom he had been a student at university. William Bligh, prudent, diligent and ambitious, would have had much to recommend him as a husband. For Elizabeth Betham, intelligent and brought up in a family of enlightened thinkers, Bligh's participation in a high-profile expedition of discovery and exploration was also an attraction, evidence that the young officer was a cut above the usual naval man. By now Bligh had not only served with, and been deeply affected by, the most progressive sea captain of his age, but also, as his ship logs would reveal, he shared Cook's unflagging interest in recording not only the coasts and harbors but also the people and places he encountered. As Elizabeth Bligh had undoubtedly appreciated, William Bligh not only was ambitious in the naval line, but also possessed the diligent, inquiring curiosity that might destine him for association with the "scientifically" minded men of the Royal Society.

Following his marriage, Bligh had served as a fifth or sixth lieutenant in a series of short commissions during the winding down of the American War of Independence. By 1782, the navy had begun to scale back and reverted to offering the meager fare of peacetime—two shillings a day and no opportunity for prize money from enemy ships. William Bligh, newly married and now with a young daughter to support, had at first lain low in the Isle of Man, where life was famously cheap, and where, as he told a relative, he could at least get plenty of books and "improve" himself by reading. But these circumstances were tolerable for only so long, and by the middle of 1783, Bligh had received permission from the Admiralty to take mercantile employment abroad; so for four years, until his appointment to the *Bounty*, Bligh had plied the rum and sugar trade from England to the West Indies for his wife's wealthy merchant uncle, Duncan Campbell.

Bligh was of average to below-average height. His hair was black, his skin "of an ivory or marble whiteness"; in later years, it would be remarked of him that "[h]is face, though it had been exposed to all climates, and to the roughest weather, was, even as years began to tell upon him, far from appearing weather-beaten, or coarse." He did not, then, have the look of a rough "salt." Nonetheless, he was widely experienced, having served in time of war, in voyages of discovery and in the merchant trade, from the Pacific to the West Indies. Other considerations are likely to have recommended him in Admiralty eyes. While it was the often expressed opinion of Joseph Banks that the *Bounty* voyage was now exclusively about breadfruit transportation, the Admiralty had one other, highly regarded objective, as was clear from the sailing orders Bligh eventually received: after leaving Tahiti, his orders instructed him, "you are to proceed from thence through Endeavour Streights (which separate New Holland from New Guinea)." The navigation and survey of this important, little-known and dangerous passage—where Cook himself had run aground—was of great interest to the Admiralty, and there were few naval men better qualified, or available, to undertake this than Captain Cook's able sailing master.

For William Bligh, now not quite thirty-three years old and a lieutenant in His Majesty's Navy, the command of Sir Joseph Banks's prestigious breadfruit journey implied more than a return to naval service from the obscurity of the sugar trade—it put Bligh squarely in Cook's footsteps.

"The object of all the former voyages to the South Seas," Bligh himself wrote, "has been the advancement of science, and the increase of knowledge. This voyage may be reckoned the first, the intention of which has been to derive benefit from those distant discoveries."

———

The vessel that Bligh would refer to with habitual affection as "my little ship" awaited him at Deptford Dockyard, on the Thames. The *Bounty* was a beautiful craft, lying solid and low in the water like the full-bodied merchant ship she was, blunt nosed and square sterned, surmounted by her three spirelike masts. Riding under her bowsprit was the painted figurehead of a lady dressed in a riding habit. But for all the neatness of her lines, Bligh could have been forgiven for a momentary loss of heart at his first sight. *Resolution* and *Discovery,* the two ships carefully chosen by Captain Cook for his last expedition, had been 462 and 295 tons, respectively—and *Discovery,* as a consort, was markedly smaller than any of Cook's previous ships, which averaged around 350 tons burthen. The *Bounty* was of 220 tons. At 85 feet 1⅓ inches long, and with a beam of 24 feet 4 inches, she was rated as only a cutter. Of more consequence to Bligh, a cutter did not rate a captain as her commanding officer, or even a commander (the rank Cook had held on his second voyage). William Bligh would therefore not be promoted as he had optimistically hoped, but would sail as a lieutenant; if he were addressed as "Captain Bligh," it would be only out of courtesy. Given that he was to be gone for at least two years, this was an acute disappointment; at the very least, it meant two years more on a lieutenant's pay.

It was Banks who, in consultation with David Nelson, the gardener chosen for the voyage, had made the final selection of the vessel from the few candidates the Admiralty had deemed suitable. A merchantman had been chosen, since carrying capacity was the main object. Banks had very definite ideas about how exploration vessels should be fitted out—so definite that they had cost him a place on Cook's second expedition of 1772. At that time, it had been assumed by everyone, including Banks, that he would participate in this next grand adventure. But after the ship selected by Cook had been completely reconfigured under Banks's supervision to accommodate his entourage—heightened, re-decked, fitted with a new raised poop to compensate for the scientists' quarters—the ship had proven too top-heavy to sail. She was restored to her original state, and Banks withdrew from the enterprise in pique.

Fifteen years later, Banks's ideas on how botanical expeditions were to be conducted were still adamantly precise. "As the sole object of Government in Chartering this Vessel in our Service at a very considerable expense is to furnish the West Indian Islands with the Bread-Fruit & other valuable productions of the East," Banks wrote in a draft of his instructions in early 1787, "the Master & Crew of her must not think it a grievance to give up the best part of her accommodations for that purpose."

There were to be no dogs, cats, monkeys, parrots, goats or any of the other animals traditionally found on ships, excepting those kept in coops for food. Arsenic must be kept out for cockroaches and rats and "the Crew must not complain if some of them who may die in the ceiling make an unpleasant smell." Banks had estimated that "a Brig of less than 200 Tons Burthen would be fully sufficient." He also wanted a small crew—"no more than 30 Souls," including the gardener—so as not to take up space that could be used by plants. An astronomer had also sought to go along "to observe the expected comet," but Banks refused; in his eyes, the *Bounty*'s voyage had one object only—breadfruit.

This was made clear to Bligh personally from the moment he first looked over his new ship. Descending the companionway from the upper deck, Bligh entered the great cabin, the captain's private quarters that encompassed the breadth of the vessel and extended from the transom almost to the mainmast. Paned windows at the stern and quarter windows flooded the spacious area with light. This was where the captain could retire for privacy and rest, where he could invite his officers and young gentlemen. For a navigator and draftsman like Bligh, it was also his library, where he could spread out his charts and drawings, and store his collection of books.

But the *Bounty*'s great cabin was not destined for the personal use of Lieutenant Bligh—it was to be converted into a nursery for the plants. Fitted with skylights and air scuttles, it would contain staging cut with holes for 629 pots; it also had a stove to ensure that the plants would be warm in cold weather. An ingenious drainage system provided a catchment for surplus water, which could be recycled. Bligh's quarters would be improvised immediately forward of the nursery, to the starboard side of the companionway. A windowless cabin measuring eight by seven feet would form his sleeping area. Adjoining it was a small pantry where he would take his meals; if he wished to invite others to his table, they would meet him here, in this cramped, undignified space. Cook, too, on his first voyage, had shared his day cabin with Banks and his scientist and draftsman, but on that occasion the usurpation of the captain's space into a kind of gentleman's working library had not resulted in any symbolic loss of dignity. Unlike Cook, Bligh was not to enjoy an active and collegial engagement with his partner in this enterprise. Shunted into his cramped, dark solitude by the pots of Joseph Banks, he was effectively relegated to the role of botanical courier.

With the interior refinements out of his hands, Bligh spent the months of August and September making his ship as seaworthy as possible for her long, dangerous voyage. Her masts were shortened so as to make her more stable, and her wooden hull was sheathed with copper against the ravages of ship worm. Nineteen tons of iron ballast were stowed instead of the customary forty-five; Bligh reckoned that the eighteen months of stores he was carrying would make up the balance.

The *Bounty*'s rating as a cutter also determined the establishment she would carry. There would be no commissioned officers apart from Bligh; the warrant officers would include a master, boatswain, carpenter, gunner and surgeon. In the interest of economy, and as was not uncommon, the role of purser had been dispensed with. A purser, the purveyor of all official stores, in effect purchased provisions from the Navy Board at the outset of a voyage, and sold back what had not been used on his return. Because he was expected to supplement his lowly salary by profits received, he had strong self-interest to stint on provisions, for which reason he was generally regarded by the sailors with suspicion and contempt. On the *Bounty*, the duties of this office were to be fulfilled by the commanding officer—Lieutenant Bligh.

Bligh's commission had commenced on August 16, and was followed only days later by the appointment of the first warrant officers. John Fryer, the *Bounty*'s new master, was slightly older than Bligh; with his rather refined features and pensive air, he called to mind a dignified school headmaster. Fryer had been assigned the small cabin opposite Bligh's, on the other side of the aft hatchway.

Only weeks before he joined the *Bounty*, Fryer, a widower, had married a "Spinster" named Mary Tinkler, from Wells-next-the-Sea, in Norfolk, where he too had been born. This marriage held some consequence for the voyage. Fryer, using his modest interest, had secured a position for his brother-in-law, Robert Tinkler, nominally as an AB, or able seaman, with the understanding that he was to be considered a young gentleman. Although Tinkler was entered on the ship's muster as being seventeen years of age, he was in fact only twelve.

Fryer had entered the navy only seven years earlier. As was common for a master, he had transferred from the merchant service, where he had seen some excitement; around 1776, he had been mate on a vessel captured by French privateers and had spent over a year and a half in prison. John Fryer's role as master on the *Bounty* was the same as that played by Bligh on Cook's *Resolution*. However, Bligh had been a precocious twenty-one-year-old lieutenant-in-waiting, while John Fryer was a thirty-five-year-old man who was unlikely to advance higher in nominal rank.

Bligh's failure to gain promotion for this breadfruit voyage bore implications well beyond the fact that he would continue to be paid as a lieutenant, and nowhere were the consequences to become more overtly apparent than in his relationship with Master Fryer. While Bligh considered himself to be only a formality away from the coveted promotions that would secure him his captaincy, in the eyes of John Fryer, Mr. Bligh was still merely a lieutenant. In theory, the master bore responsibility for the navigation of a ship; however, William Bligh was by now an expert navigator, trained under Captain Cook, and one of the few men in the British navy with experience in the South Seas. It was not then to be expected that he would surrender his own expertise on so critical a subject to the middle-of-the-road know-how of Master Fryer. Under William Bligh, the master was in fact redundant.

Thomas Huggan, an alcoholic surgeon, was the second warrant officer appointed. "My surgeon, I believe, may be a very capable man, but his indolence and corpulency render him rather unfit for the voyage," Bligh wrote as tactfully as he could to Sir Joseph Banks, whom he was careful to keep apprised of all developments. "I wish I may get him to change."

Although this proved impossible, Banks did succeed in getting the Admiralty to agree to an assistant surgeon. Eventually this position was taken by Thomas Denman Ledward, a man in his late twenties from a distinguished family of apothecaries and physicians and the first cousin of Thomas Denman, destined to become Lord Chief Justice.

"I am to enter as A.B.!" Ledward wrote to his uncle shortly before sailing—the ever handy "able seaman" designation being invoked to comply with the ship's official numerical establishment. "[B]ut the Captain is almost certain that I shall get a first Mate's pay, & shall stand a great chance of immediate promotion," and—a further agreeable incentive—"if the Surgeon dies (& he has the character of a drunkard) I shall have a Surgeon's acting order." An additional inducement to take on what surely promised to be a thankless job was that Sir Joseph Banks had offered his "interest to any surgeon's mate who would go out as able seaman."

On the same day that Fryer and Huggan were appointed, Thomas Hayward also joined the *Bounty*, nominally as another AB but shortly to be promoted to one of the two coveted midshipman allotments. This nineteen-year-old officer had been recommended by one of Banks's old and admired colleagues, William Wales, who had been the astronomer on Cook's second voyage, and who was now mathematical master at Christ's Hospital, that extraordinary charity school that educated, among other luminaries, Charles Lamb and Samuel Taylor Coleridge; indeed, some of the haunting ice imagery of Coleridge's "Rime of the Ancient Mariner" comes from William Wales's description of crossing into Antarctic waters on Cook's voyage. Wales taught mathematics, astronomy, navigational skills and surveying at Christ's Hospital, the object of his particular attention being that circle of boys destined for sea careers. Lamb, describing his old teacher, claimed that "[a]ll his systems were adapted to fit them for the rough element which they were destined to encounter. Frequent and severe punishments, which were expected to be born with more than Spartan fortitude, came to be considered less as inflictions of disgrace than as trials of obstinate endurance. To make his boys hardy, and to give them early sailor-habits, seemed to be his only aim."

Wales was also secretary to the Board of Longitude and had been responsible for publishing the scientific observations of Cook's voyage—he was, then, a man for whom Banks had high regard.

"I beg leave to trouble you with the Name of the Young Gentleman who is desirous of going with Capt. Bligh and whom I mentioned to you sometime since," Wales wrote to Banks on August 8. "It is Mr. Thomas Hayward, Son of Mr. Hayward, a surgeon at Hackney." The young man who was the object of Wales's interest was the eldest son of nine surviving children. Thomas Hayward had entered the navy's books as a captain's servant aboard the *Halifax* at the tender age of seven, where he served, on the books at least, for the next four years. From age eleven to fourteen, however, Hayward was not at sea, but was presumably being schooled. In 1782, he was back on the navy's books and for the next five years served as able seaman or midshipman aboard a number of ships. He came to the *Bounty* from the 24-gun frigate *Porcupine,* which had been patrolling off the Irish coast. Possibly no other promising young gentleman in His Majesty's Royal Navy was to endure such a spectacular run of bad professional fortune as Thomas Hayward.

Over the next weeks, the rest of the crew continued to trickle in, acquired from other ships, from former service with Bligh or from those with interest to get them their positions. A number of these deserted: the names John Cooper, George Armstrong, William Hudson, Samuel Sutton, marked "R" for "Run," are among those that appear on the *Bounty* muster only briefly before vanishing from this story. These desertions included the company's only two pressed men, seamen forced against their will into the King's service. Bligh claimed that it was only after leaving Tenerife that he "now made the ship's company acquainted with the intent of the voyage," but it is unlikely that the men had remained in ignorance until this time; the preparations themselves would have given much away. Thomas Ledward, the young assistant surgeon, reported excitedly to his uncle before the *Bounty* sailed that he had agreed to go "to Otaheite to transplant Bread fruit trees to Jamaica," which would indicate there were no secrets here. It is a striking fact that, with the desertion of the pressed men, the *Bounty* carried an all-volunteer crew; surely her destination—Tahiti, the Pacific islands—was one reason.

Little is known of William Cole, the boatswain and another of the warrant officers, apart from the fact that this was the third naval ship on which he had served. A great deal is known, however, about the boatswain's mate, James Morrison—fortunately, for he was to play an important role in the story of the *Bounty*. Morrison was a native of Stornoway, on the isle of Lewis off the western coast of Scotland. His family was descended from several generations of educated Lewismen and even local hereditary judges, while his father was a merchant and land entrepreneur of education and some means. As events would show, the twenty-seven-year-old Morrison was exceptionally—dangerously—well educated, and although almost certainly Gaelic speaking, fluent and literate in English, and with at least a passing knowledge of Latin. One of the ways in which Morrison was to exercise his superior intellect was by writing a narrative of the *Bounty* voyage, which included a lengthy and well-observed description of life on Tahiti, as well as the voyage and aftermath of the *Pandora*. It was written several years after the events described, while he was a prisoner on the *Hector* awaiting trial for his life, circumstances that very directly colored some of his "recollections."

At five foot eight, Morrison was of above-average height and of slender build, with sallow skin and long black hair; a musket wound on his arm was a memento of action seen in service. He had joined the navy at the age of eighteen, and had since served on several ships in an intriguing variety of capacities: as a clerk on the *Suffolk*, a midshipman on the *Termagant*, acting gunner on the *Hind*. In 1783, at twenty-three, Morrison passed his master gunner's examination, having shown proficiency, according to the examiners, in "Vulgar and Decimal Arithmetic, the extraction of the Square and Cube Roots, and in practical Problems of Geometry and Plain Trigonometry." This success, however, did not provide any material advantage. Like many during those "weak, piping times of peace," Morrison seems to have been without a ship. At any rate, he does not surface in any known naval records until he appears as a boatswain's mate on the muster of the *Bounty*.

In this capacity, his duties were to assist William Cole in his continual inspection of sails, rigging and boats. It was also Morrison who would administer all floggings; on a ship of the line, the boatswain's mate was said to be "the most vocal, and the most feared, of the petty officers." Still, boatswain's mate was a step down from master gunner and one must suspect either an urgent need for employment or a passion to see something of the world in his willingness to sign on to the *Bounty* in this lower position.

William Peckover, the *Bounty*'s actual gunner, had sailed with Cook on every one of his voyages. He therefore knew Tahiti and was also known to Bligh from the third expedition. William Purcell, the carpenter, made up the complement of warrant officers; the *Bounty* was his first ship of naval service. All of these men were at least minimally educated, as the Admiralty regulations stated that no person could be placed in charge of stores "unless he can read and write, and is sufficiently skilled in arithmetic to keep an account of them correctly"; all warrant officers had responsibilities for stores of some kind. Importantly, too, no warrant officer could be flogged.

Joseph Coleman, the thirty-six-year-old armorer, had also sailed with Cook and Bligh, having been mustered as an AB on the *Discovery* in 1776. Another man from Cook's third voyage was David Nelson, the gardener, who had originally been recommended to Banks by a Hammersmith nurseryman. Banks had personally selected him for the breadfruit voyage on respectable terms of £50 a year. According to a shipmate from the *Discovery*, Nelson was "one of the quietest fellows in nature." His assistant, William Brown, aged twenty-three and from Leicester, had also been selected by Banks. Although now a gardener, Brown had formerly served as a midshipman, when he had seen fierce action against the French—how or why he had gone from the one profession to the other is not known. Both Nelson and Brown were practical, hands-on gardeners, not botanists; Banks was adamant that there be no competing interests to the sole object of caring for the shipment of plants.

The three men joining the *Bounty* who had sailed on Cook's last voyage were old acquaintances of Bligh's—they had all been paid off together in 1780, seven years before. A more substantial number of the crew, however, had sailed with Bligh more recently, and were joining the *Bounty* from the West Indian ships Bligh had commanded for Duncan Campbell. These men knew Bligh as a commanding officer: Lawrence Lebogue, age forty, the sailmaker from Nova Scotia; John Norton, a quartermaster, age thirty-four, from Liverpool; Thomas Ellison, able seaman, age fifteen, from Deptford, where the *Bounty* now lay; and Fletcher Christian, the master's mate, aged twenty-three, cited on the muster as being from Whitehaven, in Cumberland.

According to Bligh, Fletcher Christian was "Dark & very swarthy," with "Blackish or very dark brown" hair. Standing about five foot nine, he was strongly built, although his "knees stands a little out and may be called a little bow legged." Others would later describe his "bright, pleasing countenance, and tall, commanding figure." While born in Cumberland, in the north of England, Christian had more recently been based on the Isle of Man, where his family had old, strong connections, and where Bligh had been living after his marriage.

Fletcher, it was said by his family, had "staid at school longer than young men generally do who enter into the navy." His first sea experience had been as a midshipman on the *Eurydice* in 1783, when he was eighteen and a half years of age—remarkably late in the day for a young man with his sights set on a naval career. After six months spent at anchorage in Spithead, the *Eurydice* had sailed for India, and for the next twenty-one months, Christian had been exposed to some of the most exotic parts of the world: Madeira, Cape Town, Madras and the Malabar Coast. Christian's biographer would conjure the steaming coastal settlements the new midshipman encountered on this first voyage: most notably, the British Fort Saint George at Madras, defiantly set to survey the sea and surrounded by the residences of the English traders and officials, the busy traffic of lumbering oxen and sweating palanquin bearers, the rowdy trade of fine cotton, spices and green doves. The *Eurydice* was a ship of war, with a complement of 140 men, including a unit of marines, and Christian had also experienced for the first time British naval life in all its coarseness—bad food, complete lack of privacy, irregular sleep and rough discipline. Yet he must have prospered, or at least shown promise, for the ship muster indicates that some seven months out from England, he had been promoted from midshipman to master's mate.

Christian had returned from India in high spirits, telling a relative that "it was very easy to make one's self beloved and respected on board a ship; one had only to be always ready to obey one's superior officers,

and to be kind to the common men." This promising start was somewhat derailed by the inconvenient peace, which had put so many ships
out of commission and, like Bligh, Christian had turned his sights from
naval service to the merchant trade. The decision to approach Bligh,
then working for Duncan Campbell, had been prompted, as a relative
advised, because "it would be very desirable for him to serve under so experienced a navigator as Captain Bligh, who had been Sailing-master to
Captain Cook."

To Christian's request for a position, however, Bligh had returned the
polite response that he already had all the officers he could carry. This
was undoubtedly true, but the fact that Bligh did not stretch himself to
accommodate the eager young man, as he was to do for so many young
gentlemen on the *Bounty,* suggests that he was not in any way beholden
to the Christian family; Fletcher had approached Bligh, it would appear,
without benefit of interest.

Upon receiving this rebuff, Christian was undeterred; indeed, he rose
to the occasion, volunteering to work before the mast until a vacancy
arose among the officers.

"Wages were no object, he only wished to learn his profession," he
had told Bligh, adding, "we Mid-shipmen are gentlemen, we never pull
at a rope; I should even be glad to go one voyage in that situation, for
there may be occasions, when officers may be called upon to do the duties of a common man."

To this honorable request Bligh had responded favorably. Christian
was taken on board the *Britannia* as a seaman, and on his return from
the West Indies, according to his brother, "spoke of Captain Bligh with
great respect." He had worked hard alongside the common sailors, but
"the Captain had been kind to him," instructing him in the art of navigation. At the same time Christian had observed "that Captain Bligh was
very passionate; yet he seemed to pride himself in knowing how to hu-
mour him." On their second voyage Christian was entered as nominal
"gunner" but, as Bligh made clear, was to be treated as an officer. Christian, it would seem, had become Bligh's protégé. Bligh had taken pains
not only to instruct the ambitious young man, but to elevate him, regularly inviting him to join him and his officers at his table for dinner.

Christian for his part must have passed muster with his captain, for Bligh was not one to suffer fools, and it was Bligh who recommended Christian to the Admiralty as midshipman on the *Bounty*. "[A]s it was understood that great interest had been made to get Midshipmen sent out in this ship," Fletcher's brother would write, "Christian's friends thought this recommendation . . . a very great obligation." On the return from the South Seas, Fletcher could expect to be promoted to lieutenant.

This promising naval career had not been in the Christian family's original plans for its second-youngest son; and as the family itself was to play a significant part in the shaping of the events ahead, it is well to introduce its members here. Fletcher Christian was born on September 25, 1764, in his parents' home in Cumberland, and had been baptized that same day, in Brigham Church, some two miles distant. Baptism on the day of birth was unusual, and implies that the newborn child was not expected to live. His parents, Charles and Ann, had already lost two infants.

Charles Christian came from an old Manx family that had been settled on the English mainland since the seventeenth century. At the age of twenty-two he had married Ann Dixon, the daughter of a dyer and a member of the local gentry well connected with other important north-country families. Ann's mother was a Fletcher, another old and established Cumberland family. It was for his grandmother's family that Fletcher Christian was named.

Charles had grown up in the Christians' ancestral home, Ewanrigg, a forty-two-bedroomed mansion with crenellated battlements overlooking the sea. Reputedly, the property had been won by the Christians from the Bishop of Sodor and Man in a card game. Charles's mother, Bridget Senhouse, could trace her ancestry back fourteen generations to King Edward I. Such distinctions bore little practical weight, however, and as a younger son (and one of eleven children), Charles inherited only his name and some shares in various family interests. Like all but the eldest son, he was expected to make his own way, which he did as an attorney-at-law, and later as coroner for Cumberland. The main boost to his fortune was his marriage—Ann brought with her a small but respectable property called Moorland Close, just outside Cockermouth, described locally as "a quadrangular pile of buildings, in the style of the mediæval manor house, half castle and half farmstead." The surrounding wall, originally built to rebuff Scottish border raiders, during Fletcher's boyhood benignly enclosed an orchard and gardens, while the former guard stand had been converted into a little summer house.

Ten children were born to the young couple, six of whom survived infancy. Fletcher was the fifth surviving child, born twelve years after his eldest brother, John. Although Fletcher was raised in a large family, with cousins and relatives nearby in every direction, his childhood was made precarious by the early death of his father, who passed away in 1768. A month before he died, Charles Christian had written his will declaring himself "weak of body," which suggests a protracted illness.

Ann Christian was now left to raise six children on her own. Fletcher was not yet four; his elder brothers, John, Edward and Charles, were sixteen, ten and six, respectively; his sister, Mary, was eight, while little Humphrey was just three months old. Money was, and evidently had long been, a problem. As early as the year of his first son's birth, Charles Christian senior had borrowed from his eldest brother, and family records indicate a series of other large "loans" made in later years. Still, under Ann's management, care was given to Fletcher's education, and he was sent first to Brigham's one-room parish school and then to the Cockermouth Free School, which he attended for seven years—and where a younger contemporary was William Wordsworth, the future Poet Laureate.

Cockermouth and Moorland Close stood on the edge of the Lake District, "the wildest, most barren and frightful" landscape in England. Years later, Wordsworth would romanticize and memorialize the savage grandeur of fractured crags and sweeping valleys, scored with streams and dark tarns. Cockermouth, situated against the backdrop of Mt. Skiddaw on the Derwent and Cocker Rivers, was by all accounts a pleasant market town, its two main streets lined with stout stone houses roofed with thatch and blue slate.

Little is known of Fletcher Christian's Cumberland upbringing, but his schoolmate William Wordsworth never forgot the wild freedom this countryside gave his childhood:

> *Oh, many a time have I, a five years' child,*
> *In a small mill-race severed from his stream,*
> *Made one long bathing of a summer's day;*
> *Basked in the sun, and plunged and basked again*
> *Alternate, all a summer's day, or scoured*
> *The sandy fields, leaping through flowery groves*
> *Of yellow ragwort; or when rock and hill,*
> *The woods, and distant Skiddaw's lofty height,*
> *Were bronzed with deepest radiance, stood alone*
> *Beneath the sky, as if I had been born*
> *On Indian plains, and from my mother's hut*
> *Had run abroad in wantonness, to sport,*
> *A naked savage, in the thunder shower.*

While Fletcher Christian rode back and forth between the orchards and gardens of Moorland Close to Cockermouth, his two oldest brothers, John and Edward, went off to Cambridge and to professions in law. It was Edward who, as a new fellow of his college, handled his mother's affairs when her finances finally and fatally bottomed out. The crisis occurred in 1779, although to judge from the size of her debts it had been building for years. Somehow, together with her eldest son, John, she had managed to accumulate debts to the tune of £6,490 0s. 11d. The family, it appears, had been living for years with no regard for reality, and now Ann Christian was faced with the humiliating prospect of debtor's prison. John Christian, her husband's wealthy brother and head of the family, once again bailed them out, but seems to have made it clear that he could not be counted upon to do so again. In partial compensation, John Christian assumed ownership of Moorland Close and all effects attached to it.

Through Edward's special pleading and contributions from his own modest fellowship, he succeeded in scraping together an annuity of forty guineas per annum for his mother, with which, as he observed, she would "be able to live comfortably any where, so that if she is not secure from arrests at Moorland Close, I should have now no objections to the family's removing to the Isle of Man." In the course of these negotiations with his wealthy uncle, Edward indicated the hope that "in time perhaps some of us may be in such circumstances as to think it a desirable object to redeem the place of our nativity." This touching aspiration was never to be realized. In October 1779, an advertisement was run on the front page of the *Cumberland Pacquet* for "that large commodious House situated in the Market Place of Cockermouth" formerly belonging to John Christian, Fletcher and Edward's oldest brother. Edward briefly became headmaster of Hawkshead Grammar School in Cumberland, where one of his pupils was Wordsworth. After seeking a position as a naval surgeon, Charles junior, the third son, entered the West Yorkshire Militia Regiment, commanded by Sir George Savile, who wrote glancingly of him, noting that "Mr. Christian [is] well satisfied & happy I believe in his situation. Indeed he is very deserving," which suggests the special attention of an aristocratic patron with "interest" in his new recruit. When the regiment disbanded, Charles Christian went to Edinburgh to study medicine, and then qualified as a surgeon aboard an East India vessel called the *Middlesex*.

The fact that Ann Christian, with her daughter, Mary, and young Humphrey, immigrated to the Isle of Man suggests that she was not, after all, "secure from arrest": debts acquired on the mainland could not be pursued here, and the island had become a haven for financially distressed gentry. Fletcher, now about fifteen, attended St. Bees School, close to Whitehaven in Cumberland, but would have been a summer visitor to the island between school terms, where he encountered another part of his heritage. Here, on the Isle of Man, the Christians were an ancient and distinguished family who could trace their lineage back in an unbroken line of male successors to 1408, the year in which John Mac-Crysten, deemster or judge of the island, had put his signature on a deed.

It was not, however, in the magnificent, castlelike Christian family home of Milntown, with its sixteenth-century gardens and doors reputedly made from the wreckage of the Spanish Armada, that Ann and her family had settled. Bound to live within the means of her modest annuity, Ann Christian had taken her family to Douglas, where she rented property. Facing the Irish Sea and backed by miles of rolling, sparsely inhabited countryside, Douglas was more isolated and more remote than Cockermouth. It was home to just under three thousand souls. Herring sheds, a small shipyard and a brewery represented local industry. Douglas society, according to a contemporary English diarist, was "not of the best kind, much like that in our common Country Towns." But life here was cheap: no taxes, a "good living House at £8 a year," and port wine for ten pence a bottle.

Between Cumberland and the Isle of Man, then, young Fletcher Christian had lived within the shadow of family greatness, even if the shadow was not cast by his own immediate kin. No evidence survives of how he passed the years between St. Bees School and his sudden resurfacing in the muster roll of the *Eurydice* in 1783. The younger sons of Charles and Ann Christian would have been brought up to look forward to university and careers in law, following the paths of John and Edward; but the money had run out. Fletcher's late coming to his profession, his staying "at school longer than young men generally do who enter into the navy," may have been the result of family stalling, a hope that something "would come up" to change their fortunes. Nevertheless, Fletcher's proposal to Bligh—that "he would readily enter his ship as a Foremast-man"—indicates that the young man had accepted with great grace and optimistic courage this abrupt change of destinies.

Another of the *Bounty*'s newly recruited young gentlemen had a family background remarkably similar to that of Fletcher Christian. In fact, Peter Heywood was distantly related to the Christians: his great-aunt Elizabeth had married another John Christian of Douglas, and both the Christians and his mother's family, the Speddings, had married into the ancient Cumberland family of Curwen. On his father's side, Peter Heywood could trace his ancestry back to Piers E'Wood in 1164, who had settled after the Norman invasion near Heywood, Lancashire. A branch of the family eventually immigrated to the Isle of Man, of whom the most famous member had been Peter "Powderplot" Heywood, who had apprehended Guy Fawkes and so forestalled the plot to blow up Parliament in 1605.

Peter was born on June 5, 1772, on the Isle of Man, in his father's house, the Nunnery, a romantic former abbey set in extensive gardens about half a mile up the hill from Douglas, and the most imposing property in the area. Peter's father, Peter John Heywood, like many of the Manx Christians before him, was a deemster of the island, and took a scholar's interest in the Manx language, unusual for his time.

But while Heywood may have been a learned man, he appears not to have been highly practical. The next year, he was forced by debts to sell the Nunnery, surrender his position as deemster, and move to White-haven, close to where Fletcher Christian was to go to school.

Exactly how the Heywoods survived over the next few years remains unclear, but in 1781, Mr. Heywood was offered the appointment as seneschal, or agent, of the Duke of Atholl's estate and holdings on the Isle of Man. Young Peter had moved back to the island with his large family of ten brothers and sisters, and settled in Douglas, where Fletcher's mother was now also residing, and where the presence of the Nunnery must have been a constant, bitter reminder of more prosperous days.

In July 1787, only a month before Bligh received his orders for the *Bounty*, Peter's father was unceremoniously fired by the Duke of Atholl when it was discovered that he not only had been wildly mishandling the Duke's estate, but had also pocketed several thousand pounds of his employer's income. Confronted with his wrongdoing, Mr. Heywood had responded with self-righteous hauteur; among other tactics, he pointed out that his family could be traced as far back as the Atholls. This inability to assume any responsibility, let alone culpability, for his actions so incensed his employer that the Duke felt compelled to offer a personal rebuke. For years, he observed to Mr. Heywood, "you have been living in a Stile of profusion far beyond your fortune, and to the detriment of your own Children spending money belonging to another."

Mr. Heywood's sudden loss of employment had brought disaster to his family, who were forced to move out of their house, which was the Duke's property. On the other hand, the disgrace of Mr. Heywood's offense was studiously concealed and there is no whisper of any misdeed in all the Heywood papers down through the decades after this. Apparently unashamed, the children seemed to have passed through life with all their illusions of superior gentility intact.

Peter had been sent away to school at the age of eleven, first to Nantwich school in Cheshire and then, briefly, also to St. Bees, at which establishments he would have received a gentleman's usual diet of religious instruction and Latin. His teacher at Nantwich had published books on Livy and Tacitus, and so one may hazard that young Peter had his fill of these. Unlike Fletcher, however, a seagoing career of some kind had probably been in the cards for Peter, regardless of changed family circumstances; the number of naval and military careers in the Heywood pedigree suggests this was an honored tradition. Peter's first naval service had been aboard the *Powerful*, in 1786. The *Powerful*, however, had never left Plymouth Harbour. As this represented his only naval experience prior to joining the *Bounty*, he had not yet served at sea.

Peter's position as a young gentleman and an AB on the *Bounty* came through the sympathetic and pitying offices of William Bligh's father-in-law, Richard Betham, a friend of the Heywoods. "He is an ingenious young Lad & has always been a favorite of mine & indeed every body here," Betham wrote to Bligh from Douglas, thanking him for taking Peter under his wing. "And indeed the Reason of my insisting so strenuously upon his going the Voyage with you is that after I had mentioned the matter to Mrs Bligh, his Family have fallen into a great deal of Distress on account of their Father's losing the Duke of Atholl's Business, and I thought it would not appear well in me to drop this matter if it cou'd be possibly be done without any prejudice to you, as this wou'd seem deserting them in their adversity, and I found they wou'd regard it as a great Disappointment." Betham did not apparently envisage young Peter's duties as being particularly nautical. "I hope he will be of some Service to you, so far as he is able, in writing or looking after any necessary matters under your charge," Betham had added, vaguely.

In the summer of 1787, Mr. Heywood accompanied his son from the Isle of Man to Liverpool. Here he bade Peter good-bye, entrusting him to the care of friends who were traveling to London by chaise along the long, rough road, each carrying a pair of loaded pistols as a guard against highwaymen. Once at Deptford, as another token of Bligh's efforts for the young man, Peter stayed with Bligh and his wife at their lodgings while the *Bounty* was being equipped. Christian had relatives in London of his own to visit, including an uncle and his brother John, who had moved here after his bankruptcy. Given Christian's already close association with Bligh, it would be incredible that he too did not visit the Bligh household at this time. "You have danced my children upon your knee," Bligh would remind the master's mate at a later date.

Also joining the *Bounty*, rated as a nominal AB, was another fallen aristocrat of sorts, twenty-one-year-old Edward Young. Edward was the nephew of Sir George Young, a distinguished naval captain and future admiral who had served in both the Royal Navy and the East India Company. "As I do not know all his exploits," one memorialist offered breezily, "I can only state that he was employed . . . in several services requiring nautical skill and British courage." Since 1784, George Young had been an advocate, with Sir Joseph Banks, of establishing the New South Wales colony, which he envisaged would serve as a port of call for ships on the China trade and more unexpectedly a center for the cultivation of flax. A paper outlining his proposal became a cornerstone of the government's eventual establishment of a penal colony near Botany Bay. It is probable that it was through his connection with Banks that Young had approached Bligh about a position for Edward.

However, there is no family record of a nephew called Edward. On the *Bounty* muster, Edward is entered as coming from "St. Kitt's," and a near contemporary reference mentions him as "half-caste." He was described by Bligh as roughly five foot eight in height, with a dark complexion "and rather a bad look." Young had dark brown hair, was "Strong Made" and had "lost several of his Fore teeth, and those that remain are all Rotten; a Small Mole on the left Side of the throat." If Edward was indeed a nephew of Sir George, it is most likely that his father had been Robert Young, a younger brother who had died in 1781 on St. Helena while captain of the East India Company's *Vansittart*. Whereas other distinguished families associated with the *Bounty* would be loud in their opinions, news of the mutiny was met with a thundering silence by the

Youngs. If Edward had been born on the wrong side of the blanket, there may have been relief when he vanished from the picture altogether.

Yet another young gentleman, George Stewart from the Orkney Islands, joined the *Bounty* as a midshipman, but was rerated AB before the ship sailed (the ship's fixed allotment of two midshipman positions required judicious management on Bligh's part). Bligh had met Stewart seven years earlier, when the *Resolution* had called at Stromness at the end of her long and harrowing voyage. In their home, the Whitehouse, overlooking the harbor and the bustling town with its inns and taverns, Alexander and Margaret Stewart, George's parents, had entertained Bligh.

Like so many of the *Bounty*'s young gentlemen, George Stewart could trace an old and distinguished lineage. His father's family could be traced back to King Robert II, in the thirteenth century; his mother could trace her descent back to Danes who had settled the Orkneys in the ninth century. Alexander Stewart had been born and lived on Ronaldsay in the Orkneys, but had moved to Stromness for his children's schooling; he and his wife had eight children, of whom George was the eldest. Apparently, when word of the *Bounty*'s voyage reached them, the Stewarts had reminded Bligh of their former acquaintance; surely the stories the young master had told the Stewart family seven years earlier, upon his return from the Pacific had made George's interest in this particular voyage especially keen.

When he came down to Deptford to join the *Bounty*, George Stewart was twenty-one years old and "five feet seven inches high," according to Bligh, who continued with an unprepossessing description: "High, good Complexion, Dark Hair, Slender Made, Narrow chested, and long Neck, Small Face and Black Eyes."

The last of the *Bounty*'s young gentlemen was fifteen-year-old John Hallett from London, the son of John Hallett, an architect, and his wife, Hannah. He had four younger brothers, all of whom would later be employed by the East India Company, and one half sister, the "natural child" of Mr. Hallett. Midshipman Hallett's father was a wealthy man, with a residence in Manchester Buildings, a gentlemen's row of private houses situated just off the Thames, almost opposite Westminster Bridge and in strolling distance of St. James's Park. The Halletts, like the Haywards, belonged to the energetic, gentlemanly professional class possessed of actual skills—doctors and architects as opposed to seneschals or bankrupt country lawyers.

Hallett Senior moved in a distinguished circle of artists, including members of the Royal Academy. His niece had married into a prosperous family of merchants and shipbuilders, with a home in fashionable Tunbridge, where Mr. Hallett was often found. From diarist Joseph Farington, who recorded a number of dinners and other social occasions at which Mr. Hallett was present, we are given a glimpse of the *Bounty* midshipman's circle: "Mr. Hallett spoke of several persons who from a low beginning had made great fortunes," Farington noted after a London dinner, going on to describe a leather breeches maker now established on Bond Street and said to be worth £150,000. War with Russia would only ruin Russia's trade, as England could do without her goods. A neighbor recently died having "expended £50,000 it was not well known how"—all good solid, middle-class, mercantile discussion.

Young John Hallett was already well on the road to a naval career when he joined the *Bounty*. He had been entered on the books as a lieutenant's servant in 1777, at the age of five, and on the books of four subsequent ships as a captain's servant. Prior to joining the *Bounty*, he had been on the *Alarm*, which had paid off in Port Royal, Jamaica, when the ship was taken out of commission. This had occurred four years previously, and one assumes young Hallett, at age eleven, was getting his schooling during the interim. John Hallett Sr. appears to have been acquainted with Banks, and wrote to him thanking him for getting his son's position. While the *Bounty* was swarming with young gentlemen—officers in training, midshipmen in waiting—the only two to hold the coveted midshipmen's slots were Thomas Hayward and John Hallett, both protégés of Banks.

In early October, Bligh prepared the *Bounty* to leave the Thames for Spithead, Portsmouth, where he was to await official orders to sail. The ship, now copper sheathed, had been completely refitted and was stuffed with supplies—not just the food stores, clothing or "slops," fuel, water, rum and bulk necessities, but all the miscellaneous minutiae of the gardener's trade, as inventoried on a list supplied by Banks: paper, pens, ink, India ink, "Colours of all kinds," spade, pins, wire, fly traps, an insect box, bottles, knives, "Journal Books & other usefull Books," guns and gunpowder, shot and flints, and "Trinkets for the Natives," which included mirrors and eighty pounds of white, blue and red glass beads. Bligh had also been given sixty-one ducats and forty-five Spanish dollars for the purchase of plants. Eight hundred variously sized pots for the breadfruit plants had been stowed, but as David Nelson reported to Banks plaintively, "as I have only room for 600, the remainder may possibly be broken." The pots had been made extra deep for drainage by "Mr. Dalton, potter," near Deptford Creek.

Every British naval seaman brought certain expectations to each ship he joined. He expected to endure hard labor in raw conditions, and was ever mindful that he was vulnerable to harsh and often arbitrary punishment at the hands of his officers. He expected to eat very specifically measured amounts of rank food, and to drink much liquor. Above all, he expected to exist for the duration of his service in stifling, unhygienic squalor. There would be no privacy. As the official naval allotment of fourteen inches sleeping space for each man suggests, space was always at a premium—but nowhere more so than on the little *Bounty*, now crammed with supplies for eighteen months' voyaging and trade. Her fo'c'sle, an unventilated, windowless area of 22 by 36 feet, was shared by thirty-three men, while the maximum height between decks amidships was 5 feet 7 inches—the average height of the men she carried. The master's mates, midshipmen, and young gentlemen—Fletcher Christian and a William Elphinstone, Hayward and Hallett, Peter Heywood, George Stewart, Edward Young and Robert Tinkler—were all quartered directly behind Bligh's little pantry, separated, it is suggested, merely by canvas walls.

On deck, amid the piles of stores, were the *Bounty*'s three boats. The Navy Board had placed an order for these as early as June, but the usual supplier, swamped with other work, had been forced to beg off. The Board then turned to a private contractor to build a launch of 20 feet in length with copper fastenings, and to the Deal boatyard for a cutter and a jolly boat of 18 and 16 feet, respectively. For reasons known only to himself, Bligh requested of the Navy Board that the launch and cutter, which had already been supplied, be replaced with larger models. The Board complied, and thus was acquired one of the most historic craft in maritime history, the *Bounty*'s 23-foot-long, 2-foot-9-inch-deep launch.

On October 9, 1787, a drear, dull day, the pilot arrived to take the *Bounty* out of the Thames on the first leg of her voyage. In the Long Reach she received her gunner's stores. Officially designated as an "Armed Vessel," she was equipped with "four short four-pounder carriage guns and ten half-pounder swivel guns," to quote the Admiralty's directive—a laughably meager firepower. Additionally, there were small arms, muskets, powder and bayonets, all locked in the arms chest, supposedly at all times under the key of the ship's master, John Fryer.

The *Bounty* herself was in her glory—newly fitted out to the tune of thousands of pounds, sails set, piled with stores, guns gleaming and swarming with her men, the midshipmen in their smart blue coats, Bligh in his blue-and-white-piped lieutenant's uniform with its bright gilt buttons, and the seamen in their long, baggy trousers and boxy jackets: Charles Churchill, with his disfigured hand showing "the Marks of a Severe Scald"; German-speaking Henry Hilbrant, strong and sandy-haired, but with "His Left Arm Shorter than the other having been broke; Alexander Smith, "Very much pitted" with smallpox, and bearing an axe scar on his right foot; John Sumner, slender, fair and with a "Scar upon the left Cheek"; William McCoy, scarred by a stab wound in the belly; William Brown, the gardener, also fair and slender, but bearing a "remarkable Scar on one of his Cheeks Which contracts the Eye Lid and runs down to his throat." With the knowledge of hindsight, they are a piratical-looking crew.

The *Bounty* lingered at Long Reach for nearly a week before receiving orders to proceed to Spithead, the naval anchorage outside Portsmouth Harbour. But "the winds and weather were so unfavorable," in Bligh's words, that the short journey down the Thames and around the coast took nearly three weeks to complete.

"I have been very anxious to acquaint you of my arrival here, which I have now accomplished with some risk," Bligh wrote Banks on November 5 from Spithead. "I anchored here last night, after being drove on the coast of France in a very heavy gale." His plan, as he now related, was to make as swiftly as possible for Cape Horn in order to squeak through a diminishing window of opportunity for rounding the tempestuous Cape so late in the season; as he observed to Banks, "if I get the least slant round the Cape I must make the most of it." Bligh was awaiting not only a break in the weather, but also his sailing orders, without which he could not sail. He did not, however, anticipate any difficulties, noting that "the Commissioner promises me every assistance, and I have no doubt but the trifles I have to do here will be soon accomplished."

The days passed and the weather broke, and still Bligh's sailing orders did not arrive. As the delay lengthened, his wife, Betsy, broke off nursing their youngest daughter, who was stricken with smallpox, and came down from their home in Wapping to take lodgings in Portsmouth. With impotent exasperation, Bligh watched other ships weigh anchor and slip serenely down the Channel, in the fair, fine weather. Each day that passed, as he knew, reduced the odds of a good passage around the Horn.

There had already been warning signs that the *Bounty*'s voyage, so beloved to Joseph Banks, did not stand quite so high in Admiralty eyes. Back in September, Bligh had received a distinguished visitor at the Deptford docks. Lord Selkirk, a Scottish earl, ostensibly came down to use his interest to find a position for his son's tutor, William Lockhead, who was "an enthusiast in regard to Natural History" and "most anxious to go round the World with Mr. Bligh"; Selkirk's son, the Honorable Dunbar Douglas, was already set to join the *Bounty* as yet another gentleman "able seaman." With his own son destined to sail with her, Selkirk took a closer look than most at the *Bounty;* alarmed at what he had seen, he wrote a frank and urgent report to Banks, drawing attention to ominous deficiencies.

The rating of Bligh's vessel as a cutter, and not a sloop of war, was "highly improper for so long a voyage," Selkirk wrote on September 14, pointing out that the ship's establishment did not include "a Lieutenant, or any Marines." Marines essentially served the role of the commander's security force, and Cook had never sailed on his Pacific voyages with fewer than twelve.

But perhaps most troubling to Lord Selkirk was the issue of Bligh's own status: "I was sorry to find . . . Mr. Bligh himself is but very indifferently used, or rather I think realy ill used," Selkirk had written with some force. "It would have been scrimply Justice to him to have made him Master & Commander before sailing: nay considering that he was, I believe, the only person that was not in some way or other prefer'd at their return of all who went last out with Capt. Cook, it would be no unreasonable thing to make him Post Captain now." Cook, on his very first Pacific voyage, had also sailed as a lieutenant—but the prestige of that voyage had never been in question.

Although Selkirk did not disclose the fact, he was an old friend of Bligh's father-in-law, Richard Betham, and it is probable that he had been leaned upon to communicate family concerns to Banks. These concerns were openly expressed in the farewell letter Betham himself wrote to Bligh a week later, offering his good wishes for the long voyage ahead: "I own I have a different Idea of [the voyage] from what I had conceived before I was acquainted with the Circumstances of the Vessel, & the manner in which it is fitted out," he told his son-in-law. "Government I think have gone too frugally to work: Both the Ship and the Complement of Men are too small in my opinion for such a voyage. Lord Howe may understand Navy matters very well, but I suppose mercantile Projects are treated by him with Contempt."

"Contempt" is perhaps too strong a word; but the accumulation of troubling details—the miserably small ship, the determinedly lower rating, Bligh's own status and the apparent lack of urgency in getting sailing orders—tend to suggest that collecting breadfruit in Tahiti was not at the top of the Admiralty's list. Among other things, England seemed poised for yet another war, this time with Holland.

"Every thing here wears the appearance of War being at hand," Duncan Campbell had written to a Jamaican colleague on September 29. "Seaman's Wages & every naval Store have of course risen to War prices." To an Admiralty intent on mobilizing ships and men, the Bounty's breadfruit run to the Pacific was only a distraction. Three weeks would pass before Bligh received his sailing orders, by which time the fair conditions had changed.

On November 28, 1787, Bligh headed the *Bounty* out to sea, and got as far as St. Helens on the Isle of Wight, an inconsequential distance, where he was forced to anchor. For the next twenty-four days, the *Bounty* bounced between Spithead and St. Helens as each successive attempt to get down Channel failed in the teeth of contrary winds. Master Fryer and William Peckover, the gunner, were laid up by the bad weather with "rheumatic complaints" and a number of his men had severe colds. Resentment and anxiety that had been mounting in Bligh for months rose to the fore.

"If there is any punishment that ought to be inflicted on a set of Men for neglect I am sure it ought on the Admiralty for my three weeks detention at this place during a fine fair wind which carried all outward bound ships clear of the channel but me, who wanted it most," Bligh fumed in a letter to Duncan Campbell. It was December 10, and he was back at St. Helens, pinned in the cabin. "This has made my task a very arduous one indeed for to get round Cape Horn at the time I shall be there. I know not how to promise myself any success and yet I must do it if the ship will stand it at all or I suppose my character will be at stake. Had Lord Howe sweetened this difficult task by giving me promotion I should have been satisfied."

The question of promotion worried Bligh grievously. At the very least, as he had written to Banks, "that one step would make a material difference to Mrs. Bligh and her children in case of any accident to me." Moved by Bligh's entreaties, Banks personally approached Lord Howe, the revered First Lord of the Admiralty, but without success, being told such advancement "was designed intirely as a reward to those who had engaged in the War equipment"; in other words, breadfruit expeditions did not count.

"The hardship I make known I lay under, is that they took me from a state of affluence from your employ," Bligh continued, unburdening himself to Duncan Campbell, "with an income five hundred a Year to that of Lieut's pay 4/- per day to perform a Voyage which few were acquainted with sufficiently to ensure it any degree of success."

But interest had gone as far as it could. Meanwhile, if war was indeed at hand, this would be the occasion for promotions, although not for Lieutenant Bligh, off in the Pacific.

"Poor fellow," Campbell would say of Bligh, somewhat later. Ignobly batted back and forth across the Channel entrance, Bligh, while not quite getting cold feet, was clearly assessing the risks of the voyage to which he was committed. Low pay was to have been compensated by promotion and the prestige of the undertaking; but there was no promotion and the prestige had already evaporated. Frustrated, demoralized, already tested by the weather, Bligh had not yet even left England.

"[I]t is wished to impress it strongly on your mind that the whole success of the undertaking depends ultimately upon your diligence and care," Banks wrote in an oppressively stern letter to the poor gardener David Nelson—but the warning applied equally to Bligh. "[A]nd that your future prospects in life will greatly depend upon your conduct on this occasion."

One person on board, at least, benefited from the delay in the *Bounty*'s departure. Thanks to the rough weather, Fletcher Christian was able to meet his brother Charles, who had recently returned to England on the *Middlesex,* the East Indiaman on which he had been ship's surgeon.

"When the *Middlesex* returned from India, the *Bounty* lay near to where she was moored," Charles Christian recounted in an unpublished memoir many years later. "Fletcher came on Board coming up the River, and he and I and one of our Officers who had been in the Navy went on Shore, and spent the Evening and remained till next Day." There were family matters to discuss; their sister Mary had died in her twenty-sixth year, more than eighteen months before; their youngest brother, Humphrey, was soon to go to Africa. Doubtless, too, the brothers conferred over family finances. Things were looking up for Fletcher who, returned from the West Indies, could report that he was now off to Tahiti, with Cook's sailing master.

But all of this was overshadowed by the news Charles Christian had to tell his younger brother. Certain events had transpired on the *Middlesex* that had shaken him to his core—indeed, they were eventually to lead to his mental breakdown. Two weeks before the arrival of the *Middlesex* in England, Charles Christian had been involved in a mutiny.

Trouble had begun as early as Fort Saint George, in Madras. David Fell, the second officer, claimed that he had been unlawfully confined on the ship, and that the governor of the fort had interceded and ordered him re-leased. The Company's surviving records tend to bear this out, showing that in July 1787 the Directors praised the governor for the "manner in which you interfered in the Disputes on board the Middlesex."

The real trouble came to a head two months later, however, as the ship approached English shores. On September 5, according to the log of Captain John Rogers, Mr. Grece, seaman, was placed in irons "for Pre-senting a Loaded Pistol to my Breast with a threat that he would put the first Man to death who would offer to touch him." The first and second of-ficers attempted to aid John William Grece and were dismissed "for aiding & assisting in the above Mutinous Conspiracy" as well as "for Drunkeness, Insolent Language & striking at me on the Quarter Deck. . . . The Surgeon also in the Conspiracy."

Two days later, George Aitken, the dismissed first officer, came on deck when Captain Rogers was present, an action the captain interpreted as hostile. Calling on his other officers, Rogers had Aitken and David Fell confined below, "battened them both in their Cabbins," with a scut-tle cut in the door for air. Twelve days later, the *Middlesex* reached the Downs, the sheltered anchorage between Dover and the Thames estuary.

The captain's log, however, did not give the entire story. Upon return to England, the *Middlesex* officers and men sent a stream of furious and aggrieved letters into the East India Company's Court of Directors, charging Captain John Rogers with brutal conduct.

"I see myself bearing with Silence, insults, excessive severe to my Feelings, considering the Character I held," wrote seaman William Grece. Shortly before the fateful day of the mutiny, he claimed to have been "wantonly insulted" by one of the passengers in the presence of the commander, who later "sent for me, Bent me, Ordered me to be Flogged to Death, and I believe, there was not much Hyperbole in this Order," Grece wrote, his rage still palpable in the fraught diction of his letter. "I am sure if He had dared, He would have done it, and ordered me in Irons, in which Situation, he treated me with inhumanity unparrelled, this every man in the Ship knows—all commanders of the Royal Navy al-low Prisoners to do the necessary calls of Nature in another place than the small space, that they are confined in. . . .

"I think much Stress was laid with regard to the Pistol," poor Grece now ventured, knowing he was on thin ice: such an act in the navy would have meant his death. "I for a moment thought, to prevent myself being Seized, to be Flogged, but my conduct shews I had no intention of using it."

The first and second officers leaped to Grece's assistance, implicating themselves in the mutiny. They were joined by Charles Christian, whose own intervention resulted "from a sudden ebullition of passion springing from humane sympathy at seeing cruel usage exercised towards one who deserved far different treatment—on putting an ingenious, unoffending, insulted, oppressed, worthy young man into irons, by the capricious orders of tyranny influenced by a hollow sycophant," to quote Charles's own, impassioned and inimitable account. Grece, Aitken and Fell were all roughly imprisoned, a punishment Charles escaped.

The Court of Directors deliberated, and handed out penalties all around. Captain Rogers was rebuked for not informing the Company of his actions toward his officers, and fined £500 and a year's suspension for the unrelated offense of refusing passage to a Company seaman at Madras. Grece, Aitken, Fell and Christian were all handed suspensions—Grece for his lifetime, Charles Christian for two years.

But the incident did not end here. Although the final accounting would not be given until long after the *Bounty* had sailed, it has much bearing on Charles Christian's credibility. The aggrieved parties brought civil suits against the captain.

"I had to appear as the principal, the sole witness in their favour," Charles reported. "Lord Loughborough complimented me in court for the impartial and steady manner in which I gave my testimony." By juries' verdicts, the plaintiffs were awarded £3,000 in damages—an enormous sum, which must be taken as a reflection of the strength of their suit.

No doubt Charles Christian told the same story that had so impressed Lord Loughborough to his brother Fletcher, as they talked through the stormy night at the riverside inn. Charles's friend First Officer George Aitken would have had his own heated version to relate of having been battened inside his cabin for his principled stand. But it seems that it was Charles who had been most affected by the events.

"I went on board of this ship in hopes," he wrote, "as a tree in a state of pleasing promising blossom—full of life and active vigour. I returned as one withered with blight, palsy-struck, disappointed, dispirited, and full of heart-damping trouble." He was also broke. Before setting out he had borrowed £500 on credit for trade goods, but the "markets were glutted at Madras and at Canton in China, by the unusual number of ships sent out that season," and the money was lost.

For Fletcher Christian, these were unsettling stories to hear on the eve of departure, and he left his brother a broken man, with the judgment of the mutiny still hanging over him. In his turn, Charles's last memory of Fletcher was more cheerful: "[H]e was then full of professional Ambition and of Hope. He bared his Arm, and I was amazed at its Brawniness. 'This,' says he, 'has been acquired by hard labour.' He said 'I delight to set the Men an Example. I not only can do every part of a common Sailor's Duty, but am upon a par with a principal part of the Officers.'"

When the weather at last permitted the *Bounty* to sail on December 23, both Bligh and Christian had much upon their minds—Bligh, demoralized and resentful; Christian, ambitious, but burdened with family matters, and shaken with the revelation of how a man could be broken by an oppressor's tyranny. Both had everything to gain or lose on the *Bounty* voyage.

After many exertions on their behalf, neither Lord Selkirk's son, the Honorable Dunbar Douglas, nor his eager tutor sailed with the *Bounty*. The tutor never obtained a position, and the young gentleman departed the ship just before she left Long Reach for the open sea. Perhaps his father had continued to mull over the ship's troubling deficiencies—her improper size, Bligh's lack of a single commissioned officer, the absence of marines to back his authority—and concluded that this was not, after all, an enterprise on which he cared for his own son to stake his life.

VOYAGE OUT

On December 23, the *Bounty* sailed at break of a boisterous, cloudy day. By night she was already battling heavy squalls. Near disaster occurred within the first twenty-four hours, when one of the sailors fell from the main topgallant sail, and narrowly saved himself by grabbing a stay. As rain and sleet drove down, Bligh ordered the sails close-reefed, the dead-lights in and hatches battened. Heavy seas struck the ship, carrying away extra sails and a yard. By the evening of the twenty-fifth the weather had abated, which, as Bligh noted in his log, "allowed us to spend our Christmas pleasantly." Beef and plum pudding were served for dinner, washed down with an allowance of rum.

The well-timed respite was brief, and in the following days the heavy gales increased to a storm that piled up alarming, huge seas. Sleet and rain stung the men as they lurched and fumbled at their duties, and the *Bounty* herself was slammed with great waves that stove all the boats, almost washing them overboard.

"[W]e were an entire Sea on Deck," Bligh recorded. The sham windows of the great cabin were also stove in, and water flooded inside. So severe was the wind that Bligh dared not attempt to turn his ship to lie to but, dangerously, was forced to scud ahead of the great following sea.

"[B]ut the Ship scuds very well," he allowed—Bligh's pride in the *Bounty* never flagged. When conditions allowed, he ordered fires lit to dry his men's sodden gear. "Thick Rainy Weather" continued, and belowdecks he found that casks of rum and stores of fish and bread had been damaged or destroyed by the thundering, incoming seas.

On December 29, the weather diminished to a moderate gale. "Out all Reefs, Up Top G[allan]t Yards & set the sails," Bligh's log sang out. Slowly the ship regrouped. Bligh ordered the men to wash all their dirty linen, and by noon shirts and breeches were hung all around the ship, fluttering in a fresh, drying breeze. Additional clothing and tobacco were given to the men, always a good move for restoring morale.

On January 5, following a good run through the night, Tenerife was sighted, its landmark peak hidden in clouds. By break of the following day, the *Bounty* was safely moored off Santa Cruz. It was drizzling, but the winds were calm and the temperature pleasant, hovering just below 70 degrees.

Once anchored, Bligh detailed an officer to go ashore to pay respects to the governor. The officer in question is not named in Bligh's log, but in a subsequent published narrative he pointedly reported that this was "Mr. Christian." The delegation of the master's mate for this vaguely prestigious function would suggest that at this early date Bligh regarded Christian as his de facto lieutenant. Christian had been instructed to request the governor's permission to restock supplies and to repair the damaged ship. He was also to inform His Excellency that Lieutenant Bligh was willing to salute him provided that the salute was returned with the same number of guns; "but as his Excellency never returned the same Number but to persons equal in Rank to himself, this ceremony was laid aside." Still, Bligh was able to meet with the governor personally, thanking him "for his politeness and Civility," and was later to dine with him.

While his ship was being prepared and stocked, Bligh toured Santa Cruz and made an informal survey of the harbor. He had been here before with Captain Cook, and this first port of call must have impressed upon him again the flattering thought that he was indeed following in his distinguished mentor's footsteps. Although Santa Cruz was by now well-trodden ground, Bligh's description of the town in his log is characteristically detailed and fulsome. In its barest form, a ship's log was a record of daily weather, winds, mileage, position, and "Remarks," which

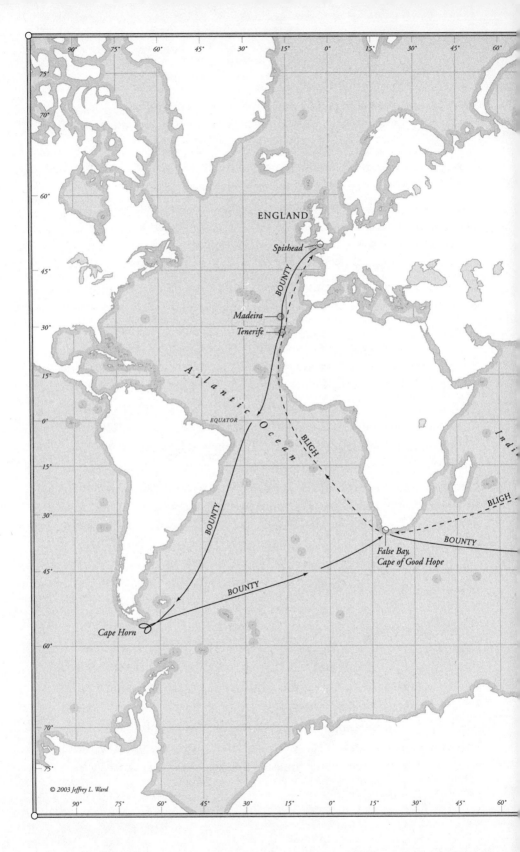

ENGLAND

Spithead

BOUNTY

Madeira

Tenerife

Atlantic Ocean

EQUATOR

BLIGH

BOUNTY

Indi

BLIGH

False Bay,
Cape of Good Hope

BOUNTY

BOUNTY

BOUNTY

Cape Horn

© 2003 Jeffrey L. Ward

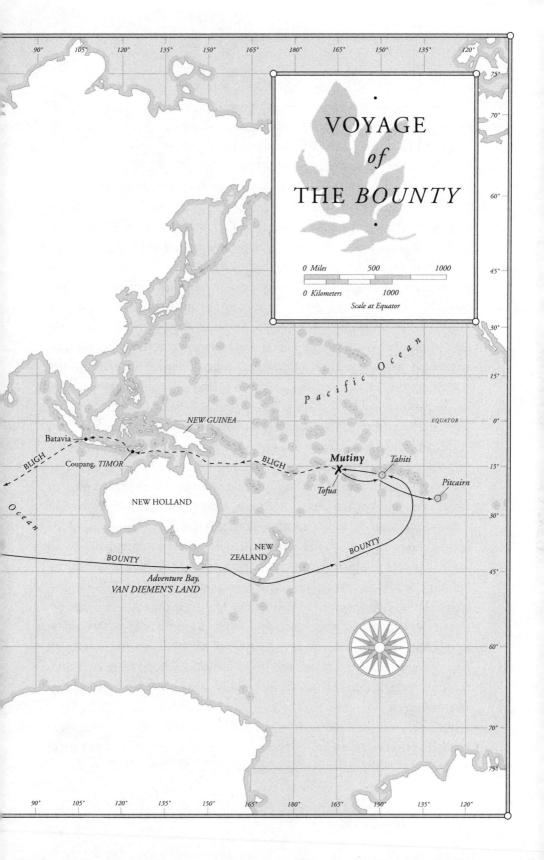

VOYAGE
of
THE *BOUNTY*

0 Miles   500   1000

0 Kilometers   1000

Scale at Equator

Pacific Ocean

NEW GUINEA

BLIGH

Batavia

Coupang, *TIMOR*

BLIGH

Mutiny

Tahiti

Pitcairn

Tofua

Ocean

NEW HOLLAND

EQUATOR

NEW
ZEALAND

BOUNTY

BOUNTY

Adventure Bay,
VAN DIEMEN'S LAND

could be as spare as a simple notation of sails set and duties performed, or as descriptive as a proper journal, depending upon the nature of both the captain and his mission. Fortunately, Bligh was as meticulous in keeping his log as he was in performing all other aspects of nautical duty; by "Cloudy Weather," he observed in his preface, "is to be understood the Sun is not to be seen or but very seldom. Fair Weather or Open Cloudy Weather is when the Sun can be frequently seen . . ."—nothing was left to chance. A log was also a legal document, a true and accurate account of daily proceedings, to be deposited with the Admiralty at voyage's end. Bligh was to leave two logs of the *Bounty* voyage, one private and one official. Parts of each have been lost, but most of each survive, and when laid side by side they are identical in most respects. Where they do differ is enlightening; in general, Bligh was much freer with criticism of individuals, often named, in his private account, while such passages have been tactfully omitted in his official copy. Bligh's logs of the *Bounty* are the only contemporary, running accounts of her voyage, written as events unfolded.

In the best expeditionary tradition, while at Santa Cruz Bligh had been careful to receive from the governor permission for David Nelson to do some botanizing in the surrounding hills. For his part, this time was mostly spent in overhauling his ship. His plan to replace damaged stores with fresh provisions, however, was disappointed, and in the end Santa Cruz supplied only 230 pounds of inferior beef, some pumpkins and potatoes. The *Bounty* had been victualed before departure with all the usual stores—biscuit, salt beef, pork, cheese, butter, malt, sauerkraut, peas, raisins, rum, spirits and beer, as well as the fairly innovative "portable soup," slabs of dried bouillon intended as a defense against scurvy—calculated for approximately eighteen months of what would be at minimum a two-year voyage. Additional supplies, particularly fresh meat, greens and fruit, water and wood for fuel, were to be obtained en route at strategic ports of call, either by purchase or, where there were no settlements, by foraging.

Judging from the letters he wrote before leaving Tenerife, Bligh was in high spirits as he set out, despite his knowledge that the most problematic part of his journey—the rounding of Cape Horn—still lay ahead.

"I have the happyness to tell you my little ship does wonderfully well," he wrote to Campbell. "I have her now the completest ship I believe that ever swam & she really looks like one fit to encounter difficulties. . . ." Before signing off, Bligh was pleased to inform him that a protégé of Campbell's, young Tom Ellison, was "improving [and] will make a very good seaman." To Banks, Bligh reported that he and his men were "all in excellent spirits and I have still the greatest confidence of success in every part of the Voyage."

On January 11, 1788, the *Bounty* fired a farewell salute and got under way. Only hours out to sea the ship was taken aback by rainy squalls. To ensure that his small crew would be as rested as possible for the almost certainly arduous passage ahead, Bligh ordered them into three watches, instead of the traditional two. In this manner, each watch was ensured a period of eight unbroken hours of sleep, instead of the traditional watch-and-watch—four hours on duty, four hours of sleep.

"I have ever considered this among Seamen as Conducive to health," Bligh recorded in his log. "[A]nd not being Jaded by keeping on Deck every other four hours, it adds much to their Content and Cheerfulness." This was one of Cook's innovations, and it undoubtedly was appreciated by Bligh's men. In a decision that was to have unimagined consequences, Bligh designated Fletcher Christian, "one of the Mates," as officer of the third watch.

As another measure against the uncertainties of the immediate passage ahead, Bligh mustered his company and announced that he was putting them on a ration of two-thirds allowance of bread or ship's biscuit to ensure that it would last as long as possible. The sailors, respectful of what they knew the Horn could offer, understood this precaution, and according to James Morrison, it "was cheerfully received."

The cloudy weather was soon cleared by fresh, light breezes. Four days out and the ship was actually becalmed, making only five miles in twenty-four hours. The men were kept busy airing bedding, drying bread, rechecking stores and sails. The light breezes returned and by January 17 the *Bounty* was ambling under clear skies through smooth seas.

"Very pleasant Weather," Bligh logged. "All Sails set before the Wind."

In these easygoing conditions he ordered the entire ship washed and then rinsed down with vinegar, which served as a disinfectant. This was to be a regular routine, as were his Sunday inspections of his mustered men, whose clothing and even fingernails he personally checked for cleanliness. Bligh's model in this almost fetishistic concern for hygiene was Captain Cook. When Cook had found a man with dirty hands, he had stopped his grog. In an age in which more seamen were lost to disease than to naval wars, Cook had managed to return from voyages of several years' duration with minimal fatalities. A diet of sauerkraut and sweet wort, or malt extract, the procuring of fresh produce wherever possible, the endless rigorous washings and inspections, the three watches—all these practices had been conscientiously noted by the young Bligh during his service to his formidable mentor and were now earnestly applied on his own little ship. Mandatory, and soon despised, dancing sessions were implemented under this same improving philosophy.

"Sometime for relaxation and Mirth is absolutely necessary," Bligh had opined in his log, "and I have considered it so much so that after 4 O'Clock, the Evening is laid aside for their Amusement and dancing. I had great difficulty before I left England to get a Man to play the Violin and I prefered at last to take One two thirds Blind than come without one." This much-sought-after musician was the disagreeable Michael Byrn.

As the fair weather continued, the *Bounty* passed flying fish and porpoises, and occasionally spotted a shark. Toward the end of January, a fine moon shone on her as she sailed the dark night sea. Boobies, shearwaters and a man-of-war bird were seen, although far from land.

The pleasant and orderly passage was spoiled for Bligh by the discovery that his surgeon, the corpulent, lazy Thomas Huggan, was "a Drunken Sot." Bligh was forced to record, "[H]e is constantly in liquor, having a private Stock by him which I assured him shall be taken away if he does not desist from Making himself such a Beast." After all the effort and energy required to keep his ship clean scrubbed, his men in clean linen and clean habits, this was a bitter blow to Bligh. His worthy goal was to return his men as soundly as Cook would have done, and now the very individual he most required as an ally—his surgeon—had proven unfit. This meant increased vigilance of his men's health and habits on Bligh's part.

As the *Bounty* headed south, the weather thickened, becoming warmer—into the eighties—cloudier and wet. "Sultry & Hot," Bligh recorded on January 26. "Got everything up from below & gave all the Air possible between Decks." The rainfall was never intense, but thunder and lightning often spread across the unbroken sky. Airing of the ship continued and on the last day of January, the *Bounty* was washed, yet again, with vinegar, so that "by the Evening the Ship was perfectly Sweet & refreshing." That same night, lightning played all around the heavens, while "a prodigious number of Porpoises" swam with the ship through a sea aglow with luminous fish. The following evening as Bligh stood enjoying the spectacle of the *Bounty*'s long wake at the close of a fine, clear day, he was horrified to see "a dreadfull breaking shoal" rising directly in their tracks. How had he and his sharp lookouts missed this? Staring again, Bligh saw the "shoal" resolve itself into a school of porpoises, their backs breaking the waves as would a sandbar.

The close, occasionally thunderous weather continued and on February 8, the *Bounty* crossed the equator. A somewhat modified version of the traditional ceremony for crossing the line was enacted, with the old hands presiding as King Neptune and his court. The twenty-seven officers and men, or over half the ship's company, who had never crossed before now underwent the rough initiation—covered with tar, "shaved" with the edge of an iron hoop, and compelled to give Neptune gifts of rum. The rum was in lieu of the most fearful part of the usual ceremony—ducking from the yardarm—which Bligh forbade, on the grounds that "of all the Customs it is the most brutal and inhuman."

The day after the ceremony, a Sunday, Bligh "[m]ustered the People and saw every thing Clean." Divine service was performed, by Bligh, and "every person attended with decorum & much decency." A few days later, a sail was seen in the early morning; next day they fell in with the *British Queen,* a whaler bound to the Cape of Good Hope. This fortuitous meeting allowed the *Bounty* to send letters via the Cape to England. To the Heywoods, Bligh wrote a "flattering" account of young Peter's progress. To Duncan Campbell, Bligh reported that the passage had been pleasant and that he had acquired some fine wine for Campbell, which he would present on his return.

"My Men all active good fellows," Bligh wrote, "& what has given me much pleasure is that I have not yet been obliged to punish any one." Food and wine were good: "with fine Sour Krout, Pumpkins and dryed Greens and a fresh Meal five times a week I think is no bad living. My Men are not badly off either as they share in all but the Poultry, and with much content & chearfullness, dancing always from 4 untill eight at Night I am happy to hope I shall bring them all home well." Once again, Bligh ended with a note about Campbell's protégé: "Tom Ellison is a very good Boy and will do very well."

To Joseph Banks, Bligh reported nothing but contentment. "I am happy and satisfyed in my little ship and we are now fit to go round half a score of worlds," he wrote—how different from the fretful, worried letters penned before departure! "[B]oth Men & Officers tractable and well disposed & chearfulness & content in the countenance of every one. I am sure nothing is even more conducive to health. I have no cause to inflict punishments for I have no offenders and every thing turns out to my most sanguine expectations." This repeated reference to the fact that there had been no need for punishment—flogging—is revealing. It would seem that to Bligh, infliction of punishment was like sickness, and scurvy, something that had no place on a well-run ship. William Bligh had set out to make the perfect voyage.

To Banks, as to Campbell, Bligh concluded with an update on the progress of a protégé. "Young Hallet is very well and is a very fine young man," he informed Banks, "and I shall always attend to every thing that can be of service to him."

Parting company with the British Queen, the Bounty continued south and days later "passed the limits of the Southern Tropic." Incrementally, the temperature began to drop. Vast numbers of seabirds were noted—shearwaters, albatross—as well as turtles and numerous whales; one afternoon a cloud of butterflies was blown past the ship. Then, on Sunday, March 2, after divine service and the usual inspection of his men, Bligh made an announcement. "I now thought it for the Good of the Service to give Mr. Fletcher Christian an Acting Order as Lieut. I therefore Ordered it to be read to all hands." This was another clear indication of Bligh's patronage, if not favoritism, of Christian; a long stint as acting lieutenant would in the normal course of things ensure the master's mate of promotion on his return.

A week later, out of the blur of notations about butterflies and shearwaters, porpoises and whales, Bligh's log records an event that returned him squarely to the world of his men: "Untill this Afternoon I had hopes I could have performed the Voyage without punishment to any One," Bligh wrote, with evident regret, "but I found it necessary to punish Mathew Quintal with 2 dozen lashes for Insolence and Contempt."

In a subsequent published narrative, Bligh expanded on the event. "Upon a complaint made to me by the master, I found it necessary to punish Matthew Quintal, one of the seamen, with two dozen lashes, for insolence and mutinous behaviour. Before this, I had not had occasion to punish any person on board."

Now began the whole grim ritual; the crew mustered to watch Quintal, age twenty-two, from Cornwall, stripped to the waist and strapped, spread-eagled, by the wrists and ankles to an upright deck grating. With no marines to drum or pipe, this would have been a lackluster ceremony, itself stripped down to its most pertinent and brutal elements. By all later reports, Quintal, of middle height and "strong made," was a dangerously disaffected troublemaker. It does not appear from the manner in which the incident was logged, however, that Bligh himself had been witness to Quintal's insubordination; no matter. Once his master logged the event and brought it to Bligh's attention, Bligh was compelled to administer punishment, and his perfect record was now spoiled.

While the small crew stood formally mustered to witness the punishment in the damp, hazy weather, Boatswain's Mate James Morrison—the literate diarist, with his smattering of classical education—administered the flogging. For Bligh, whose humane principles had forbidden men's being ducked when crossing the line, the familiar ritual must have been a singularly unpleasant landmark on his voyage. The natural coarseness of men's habits—their dirty clothes and fingernails, his surgeon's "beastly" drunkenness, their cruel and brutal pranks—all offended him. He had chosen a profession infamous for poor conditions and dirty habits, in which men counted on taking brutal poundings from their fellow men and from the sea. Yet Bligh expected his ship to be "perfectly sweet" and scented with vinegar, hardened seamen to wear clean clothes and scrub their hands, cheerfulness to be seen on every countenance and merry dancing in the evening. There was no dirt or disease in Bligh's vision of the perfect voyage, and no punishment. Busily intent on his many burdensome responsibilities, Bligh was unlikely to have taken note of his men's practiced and scrutinizing gazes. Did they perceive that it was their fastidious, bustling captain who avoided the lash?

The damp, hazy weather closed in and by the following day had become dense fog. The temperature continued to drop, and when the fog cleared the air was felt to be cold. In the afternoon, one of the men shot an albatross that fell dying into the ocean, and a boat was sent out to collect it. On board its wingspan was gravely measured. The superstition that the killing of an albatross brought bad luck was not yet prevalent; Coleridge had not yet written "The Rime of the Ancient Mariner"—this would follow later.

The *Bounty* was now as far south as the fortieth latitude, the "roaring forties," and was drawing parallel with the coast of Patagonia. A wet, dense fog forbade sight of land, although south of Puerto Deseado the men "saw what was supposed to be the looming of it." Whales appeared in great numbers and seemed to enjoy lying in groups of two and three windward of ship, expelling great blasts of spray over the men.

A strong gale arose on March 20 as the *Bounty* approached the Jasons, the northwesternmost of the Falkland Islands. Albatross, petrels and snowbirds flocked and hovered around the rigging, as if wishing to perch. The wind and sea became violent and Bligh was anxious to get south of the islands; he had by now given up his earlier plan of stopping here for wood and water. The weather was fast deteriorating and he could afford no delays.

Before dawn on March 23, the goats and single dog on board began to agitate, and the men declared that the animals could smell land. Soon, in the moonlight, hills could be made out to the west, and when daylight broke the mountains of Tierra del Fuego could be seen, mostly free of snow.

"I realy look upon the bad or Winter Weather not yet to be set in," Bligh wrote. "[B]ut as I must expect it hourly I have no right to loose a Moment. . . ."

Skirting Le Maire Strait, they passed the desolate, mountainous country of Staten Island to the east. Now, at nearly the 55° latitude south, the *Bounty* was fast approaching the Horn. A hint of the weather they were in for hit the ship on March 27, with the arrival of a strong gale and an "exceedingly High" sea.

"It would not be possible for a laboursome Ship to keep her Masts," Bligh observed. His ship, as he had often proudly noted, was not "laboursome," but well behaved. Her hatches were all battened down, and although towering seas broke over her, so far the men kept "tolerably dry." The temperature was now in the upper thirties, and the weather wet and raw.

"I Ordered the People to have Wheat [porridge] served every day with Sugar & Butter to enable them to have a comfortable hot breakfast," Bligh logged. Hour after hour, his men were required to reef and hand the sails; then reset them; then reef again, up and down the perilous, pitching rigging in the menacing cold. The sea, Bligh wrote wonderingly, "exceeds any I have seen."

When the gale moderated, Bligh ordered the belowdecks cleaned and dried. The sea was still so huge that he had difficulty taking sightings, as the mountainous waves swamped his horizon. Over the next few days the gales moderated, then increased, moderated, then "blew a Storm of Wind and the Snow fell so heavy that it was scarce possible to haul the sails up and furl them from the Weight and Stiffness." With the great sea running confused and contrary, sleet and hail began to fall.

"At 6 In the Morning the Storm exceeded anything I had met with and a Sea higher than I had ever seen before," Bligh entered in his log. The ship was carrying only her staysails, all the canvas that could be risked.

"My next business was to see after my People who had undergone some fatigue," Bligh wrote, his ship safe for the time being. A fire blazed continuously in the galley and someone was set to dry clothes around the clock. Bligh ordered large quantities of the "Portable Soup" of which he was very proud, added to the men's "Pease," or pea pudding, "which made a Valuable and good dinner for them."

Incredibly, the gales increased, carrying blasts of snow and sleet, the sharp winds piling the sea to windward "like a Wall." Still, Bligh could note that blue petrels and pintados, "two beautiful kinds of birds," followed their wake. The *Bounty* was losing ground, being driven back the hard-won miles. At the close of April 3, she was farther north than she had been six days before.

"All I have to do now is to Nurse my people with care and attention," wrote Bligh, "and like Seamen look forward to a New Moon for a Change of Wind and Weather." The gale moderated in the early hours of the following morning, and although a cold rain fell, the men were able to check and service rigging as well as clean up and dry below. With fresh gales and mere squalls, the *Bounty* made headway, and over the next few days, under close-reefed sails, clawed her way to 60° 14' south; this was to be the extreme limit of her southing. For ten days, Bligh pushed the *Bounty* and her men through squalls of sleet and hail, "dark wet nights" and strong gales, through fog and high confused seas. At midnight on the thirteenth, the ship was hit by so severe a gale that the decks were "twice filled with the Sea." Now all pumps were worked every hour. Although the hatches were closed—and had been for close to three months—the belowdecks was awash and Bligh turned over his great cabin "to the Use of those poor fellows who had Wet Births." It is not noted if Bligh himself slept at all.

Despite all exertions—the constant fires, dry clothes, dry berths and hot food at every meal—the weeks since passing Staten Island had begun to take their toll. Huggan had his shoulder thrown out when the ship lurched, and in the midst of a "Very Severe" gale and "a high breaking sea," Thomas Hall, the cook, fell and broke a rib. William Peckover, the gunner, and Charles Norman, carpenter's mate, were laid up with rheumatic complaints. Every man out of commission increased the burden of the remaining small crew.

"I have now every reason to find Men and Ship Complaining, which Will the soonest determine this point," Bligh confided to his log.

That point soon came, and on April 17, Bligh determined to abandon the Horn. Only shortly before his departure from England, almost as an afterthought, he had received (through the intercession of Joseph Banks) discretionary orders from the Admiralty to make for the Cape of Good Hope if the Horn proved impossible. This Bligh now determined to do. From here, he would approach the South Seas from the opposite side of the globe. The detour would add some ten thousand miles to the voyage, but there was nothing to be done. After twenty-five days of battle with the sea, the *Bounty* was, at 59° 05' south, more or less where she had begun.

At eleven in the morning of the seventeenth, Bligh summoned all hands aft and publicly thanked them for attending to their duties throughout the trials of the last month. He then announced that he had decided to bear away for southern Africa. "The General Joy in the Ship was very great on this Account," Bligh noted. His announcement was received with three hearty cheers.

It was, for Bligh, a bitter, difficult decision—so difficult that only days later when the weather took a moderate turn he was induced to make one last attempt, but this was quickly abandoned. Eight men were now on the sick list, mostly with "Rheumatick complaints." This, as Bligh ruefully noted, was "much felt in the Watches, the Ropes being now Worked with much difficulty, from the Wet and Snow." The men aloft on whom fell the monstrous task of handling the sails were at times incapable of getting below in the face of the storm blasts, and when they did return they "sometimes for a While lost their Speech." Reconciling himself to defeat, Bligh "ordered the Helm to be put a Weather," and the *Bounty* headed for the Cape of Good Hope.

She arrived in False Bay, the preferred anchorage across the spit from Cape Town, on May 24, after an uneventful passage. The sick men had recovered during the intervening four weeks, and refurbishment of the ship began almost at once. The day after mooring, Bligh administered a second punishment: six lashes for John Williams, a seaman from

Guernsey, for neglect of duty "in heaving the lead." In this case there was no expression of regret from Bligh.

The *Bounty* remained in False Bay for thirty-eight days, during which time she was overhauled from top to bottom, from her rigging to new ballast in her hold, as well as resupplied. Fresh meat, celery, leeks, onions, cabbages and—as a luxury—soft bread were brought on board for storage, while Bligh's log daily notes "Fresh Meat & Greens" served at dinner. This sojourn also allowed some pleasant diversions. In Colonel Robert Gordon, the half-Dutch, half-Scottish commander of the now considerable Dutch forces at this Dutch settlement, Bligh found an entertaining companion who shared a fondness for natural history and amateur exploration. Needless to say, Sir Joseph Banks had an associate out this way, botanizing at his behest. Francis Masson, once an undergardener at Kew, had been at the Cape for a number of years, sending back specimens and seeds to Banks. From Masson's collections would come plants familiar to generations of British gardeners—gladioli, geraniums and freesias.

A few days after mooring, Bligh set out for Cape Town proper to pay his respects to the governor. The twenty-five-mile journey was made by carriage along a partly treated, mostly sandy road that led across a central tableland skirted by mountains. Bligh was greeted warmly by Governor van der Graaff, who most gratifyingly expressed his wonderment that "any ship would have ventured to persist in a passage" around Cape Horn.

Bligh's record of his visit to Cape Town speaks only of his own impressions and it is not clear whether he made this short trip alone; but it is very possible that Acting Lieutenant Fletcher Christian accompanied him, for it was here at the Cape that Bligh advanced Christian money. Bligh's attitude toward his personal finances was, and would be throughout most of his life, one of incessant anxiety and concern. Although securely a "gentleman," William Bligh had from an early age been forced to make his own way in the world and, like many an officer on half pay, he had become accustomed to count and turn every penny. The road ahead offered no immediate source of improvement, and

Bligh, as fastidious in his personal economy as in the running of his ship, was reconciled to a life of calculation, self-discipline and sacrifice; to the slow accumulation of security and comfort that would come only through a steady career. Unlike the Christians and Heywoods, whose anciently established sense of entitlement allowed them unblushingly to pile up debts amounting to thousands of pounds beyond any possibility of repayment, Bligh expected to balance his books. Worries about money had beset him as he departed Spithead, since, as he had noted to everyone, taking the commission had resulted in a calamitous drop in pay. Bligh's loan to Christian, then, amounted to a significant act of friendship—one wonders whether Christian fully appreciated the compromise and anxiety this must have entailed. For his part, although freely given, this was not a gift that Bligh allowed himself or Christian to forget.

Some three weeks after the *Bounty* came to anchor, the *Dublin*, an East Indiaman, arrived in False Bay carrying part of the Seventy-seventh Regiment, under Colonel Balfour; saluting *Bounty* with eleven guns, she was returned with nine. A few days later, Bligh, Colonel Gordon, botanist Masson and a Mr. Van Carman were invited on board for dinner.

"We had a very merry Day of it and a great deal of dancing with the Ladies in the Evening to fine Moon light," one officer who was present recorded in his diary; it is gratifying to imagine Lieutenant Bligh indulging in a little social levity. Colonel Gordon entertained the company with stories of his remarkable travels into the interior and, to the astonishment of his fellow diners, even managed a Gaelic song.

In these agreeable circumstances, amidst the sympathetic company of fellow seamen from around the world who well knew the dangers of the southern ocean, Bligh reflected on what he had accomplished. "A Dutch Ship came in to day having buried 30 Men & many are sent to the Hospital," he wrote to Campbell, "altho they have only been out since the last of January." He, Bligh, had been out since the end of December. "This is a credit I hope will be given to me," Bligh continued, confessional as always to Campbell. "Indeed had I not been very conversant in these matters I believe poor Fellows they would scarce ever have got here"; Bligh was referring to his own men, for whose lives he took full credit.

"Upon the whole no People could live better," he exclaimed to Campbell, embarking on a description of his nutritious hot breakfasts and portable soups. "I assure you I have not acted the Purser with them," he let Campbell know, "for profits was trifling to me while I had so much at Stake."

It was not only in his private correspondence that Bligh enlarged upon this flattering theme of his own successful man-management. His official log offered a short dissertation on the subject: "Perhaps a Voyage of five Months which I have now performed without touching at any one place but at Tenarif, has never been accomplished with so few accidents, and such health among Seamen in a like continuance of bad Weather," he began, not mincing words. "[A]nd as such a fortunate event may be supposed to have been derived from some peculiar Mode of Management it is proper I should point out what I think has been the cause of it."

The mode of management was, needless to say, hot breakfasts, clean dry clothes, clean hammocks and a clean ship ("in cleaning Ship all dark holes and Corners the common receptacles of all filth were the first places attended to"), dancing, infusions of malt, portable soup and sauerkraut. Once again, it is evident that in Bligh's eyes, his small ship and forty-six-member company were embarked upon a historic enterprise.

"Seamen will seldom attend to themselves in any particular and simply to give directions . . . is of little avail," Bligh added, echoing the sentiments of many a captain. "[T]hey must be watched like Children."

Bligh was not the only man to take advantage of the layover to send reports to England. Thomas Ledward, the assistant surgeon who had joined the *Bounty* at the eleventh hour, wrote to his uncle describing "a continual series of the most violent and distressing weather that ever was experienced." The ship was in danger of becoming unfit from her exertions, he reported, continuing that he had no doubt the captain "will gain much credit by his resolution & perseverance & by the extreme care he took of the Ship's company."

Ledward had been in the habit of keeping a diary, but had just learned that all such private documents would have to be turned over to the Admiralty at journey's end. While Ledward might not have known it, this had become standard practice since Cook's first voyage, the purpose being to ensure that any officially sanctioned publication was not undercut by a private, competing work. Once the official account was out—in this case, to be written by Lieutenant Bligh—other accounts were usually permitted.

In the face of this new knowledge, Ledward determined, as he informed his uncle, to drop his diary. Other of his shipmates, however, were less circumspect. Someone, probably Charles Churchill, the master-at-arms, wrote an elegant memoir to the Reverend John Hampson, with the hint that he was "very desirous to have [it] publish'd and beg you will cause it to be inserted in the Public Papers as soon as possible." The report commenced with a brief essay on the breadfruit and references to Cook's voyages and then briefly sketched the tempestuous voyage to Tenerife, the crossing of the "Equinoctial Line," which he stated was celebrated with "the usual Ceremonies of Shaving and Ablution"—no self-respecting seaman would confess that ducking, or "ablution," had been prohibited.

Meanwhile, in the north of England, there appeared in the *Cumberland Pacquet* an "[e]xtract of a letter from a midshipman (aged sixteen) on board his Majesty's ship 'Bounty'"; this could only be from Peter Heywood. Either he too had requested publication, or his proud family felt the letter relating his adventures must be shared; they had already sent copies to various relations. Heywood's report was mostly concerned with the attempted passage around Cape Horn, which had been "one continued gale as it seldom ceased for four hours together." But, echoing his captain's sentiments, Heywood allowed that "the *Bounty* is as fine a sea boat as ever swam."

All known firsthand contemporary accounts of the first five months of the *Bounty*'s outward voyage, then, indicate that after a passage of unprecedented severity, the *Bounty*'s crew were in good health, good spirits, forward looking and, if anything, proud of what had so far been accomplished. There were not, judging from these letters, complaints worth writing home about.

The *Bounty* dropped anchor in Adventure Bay off the southern coast of Van Diemen's Land, now Tasmania, seven weeks after departing the Cape. The passage had seen ferocious weather and much severe lightning; once the *Bounty* had been pitched almost on her beam ends, but as Bligh logged, "no damage was done but the overturning [of] some Tubs with Plants I had brought from the Cape." The plants were intended as useful gifts for the Tahitians.

With his ship safely anchored, Bligh set out by boat to scout the surroundings. The largely mountainous land appeared unchanged from when he, along with Nelson, Peckover and Coleman, had been here with Cook. Among the stands of massive trees that overlooked the island-studded bay, Bligh examined stumps that had been cut for the *Resolution*, eleven years previously. Later, Thomas Hayward pointed out to Bligh a tree trunk carved with a date from Cook's second expedition, "as distinct as if it had not been cut a Month, even the very slips of the Knife were as discernable as at the first Moment." There was much Bligh encountered at Adventure Bay to put him in mind of his own voyage with Cook; "I cannot therefore help paying this humble tribute to Captn. Cook's memory," he reflected in his log, "as his remarkable circumspection in many other things has shown how little he has been wrong."

The following morning, Bligh divided his men into different parties, and sent them out on various duties. He had determined to work from Cook's old base, where a gully disgorged water conveniently close to the chosen landing. One man was detailed to wash all dirty linen, while Nelson and his assistant, William Brown, set out to explore the country. Acting Lieutenant Fletcher Christian and William Peckover, the experienced and reliable gunner, were put in charge of the parties detailed to cask water and fell wood.

The weather blew squally, then fair, then squally with rain and rapid, racing clouds throughout the following days. The watering party rolled casks of water along the beach, loading them with difficulty into the waiting boats. The surf was troublesome enough to require the wood party, under Christian, to raft the timber out in bundles. In off-hours, some of the men went shooting and fishing with mostly disappointing results, although two black oystercatchers, largish black-and-white birds with long red bills, were shot by Mr. Christian. All the men kept an inquisitive lookout for local people, but it was some days before any turned up. Dressed in little but kangaroo skins and with painted faces, they appeared to the *Bounty* men as "the most miserable creatures on the face of the Earth," as James Morrison bluntly put it.

On August 23, there was the first unequivocal sign of trouble. Going onshore to inspect the various work parties, Bligh found William Purcell, the carpenter, cutting crude, unwieldy billets of wood. When Bligh complained that the billets were too long, Purcell accused his captain of coming onshore "on purpose to find fault." Words were exchanged, Purcell became insolent and Bligh lost his temper and sent the carpenter back to the ship.

Now Bligh was made to feel the consequences of his inconveniently small company. He had no commissioned officer to turn to for authority and moral support—and no marines to back him up. Under the Articles of War, Purcell's refusal to obey Bligh's commands—let alone insolently talk back to him—was an offense punishable by court-martial. Yet, the prospect of holding a court-martial was well over a year away.

"I could not bear the loss of an able Working and healthy Man," Bligh logged; "otherwise I should have committed him to close confinement untill I could have tryed him." As a warrant officer, the carpenter could not be flogged, and Bligh could find no recourse but to order him back to the ship to assist Fryer in other duties. Purcell seems to have had a keen appreciation of Bligh's dilemma, for three days later Bligh was forced to log a second, lengthy complaint against him for disobeying Fryer's orders to help load water.

Fryer informed Bligh of Purcell's disobedience when Bligh returned to the ship with other members of the shore parties, who would have watched the encounter closely. Facing the broad Pacific and backed by a mountainous land so remote that only four ships from the outside world had ever previously touched it, Bligh had only his own authority with which to confront the carpenter.

"[M]y directions and presence had as little effect," Bligh recorded ominously. Purcell had refused to back down. Confinement of Purcell until such time as he could be brought to court-martial would rob Bligh of the carpenter's skills and, in theory, other able-bodied work. Or so Bligh himself reasoned as he matter-of-factly devised a novel form of punishment: "I therefore Ordered the different Persons evidence to be drawn out and attested, and then gave Orders that untill he Worked he should have no provisions, and promised faithfully a severe Punishment to any Man that dared to Assist him."

Bligh was satisfied with the result of this action, "which immediatly brought [him] to his senses. . . . It was for the good of the Voyage that I should not make him or any Man a prisoner," Bligh concluded his account of the event. "The few I have even in the good State of health I keep them, are but barely sufficient to carry on the duty of the Ship."

James Morrison gives an oblique, deliberately evasive reference to the confrontation, from which it is impossible to cull hard facts. But a single statement is unambiguous: here, says Morrison, in Adventure Bay "were sown seeds of eternal discord between Lieut. Bligh & the Carpenter, and it will be no more than true to say, with all the Officers in general." Fryer was probably one of these other officers; Bligh's observation that he had to repeat his orders to the master ("I repeated my injunctions to the Comm'g Officer Mr. Fryer") is subtly troubling. Christian was in charge of the wood party, whose task of rafting timber through heavy surf seems to have been particularly difficult; now under personal obligation to Bligh, had he too been found lacking?

Bligh's log ticked on, with descriptions of native encounters, lists of shrubs and herbaceous plants, and careful surveys of adjacent land. For him, the crisis with the carpenter had been satisfactorily addressed and the incident was closed.

The *Bounty* left the wooded shores of Adventure Bay on September 5 and headed into more wet, misty weather. A few days out, the southern lights, "as Red as blood," inflamed the clouded sky. At night, phosphorescent medusae, long tentacled jellyfish, glowed from beneath the sea. South of New Zealand, the ship unexpectedly came upon "a parcell of Rocky Islands," devoid of all greenery, but patched with late snow—a discovery. Their position was duly laid down by Bligh and logged. "I have called them the Bountys Isles," he recorded solemnly.

The *Bounty* plowed onward through often dark, cloudy weather and thick fogs, punctuated with gales of rain. Bligh's log checked off each day's consumed miles: 177, 175, 141. From England to Tahiti, the *Bounty* would eventually log 28,086 miles. Between his duties on deck, Bligh retired amid the pots to his cabin, and there, while his ship thrummed through the Pacific swells, carefully wrote up his log, made his natural history observations, and refined his charts and sketches. The odds and ends of plants he had collected at the Cape for Tahiti held majestic sway over the great cabin, where he checked them approvingly from time to time. There are few more touching images in his ship's saga than this, the industrious lieutenant conscientiously acting the role of Captain Cook in his own miniature ship.

Crowded in their own quarters, the *Bounty*'s men stoked the galley stove that both dried their wet clothing and filled the air with choking smoke. The entire company was again on two-thirds rations of bread, or unpalatable hardtack, sensibly so, as the remainder of the voyage was unpredictable. In accordance with naval regulations, the men would receive monetary compensation for such reductions on return to England.

Now nine months out, friendships and factions had been formed. Among the young gentlemen, Peter Heywood and George Stewart had become firm friends. Fletcher Christian and young Heywood also had so much in common it was natural they too sought each other out, and Christian appears to have taken Heywood under his wing, helping him, Heywood claimed, with his mathematical and classical studies. Heywood was greatly admiring of his older friend, who had impressed the entire company with his athletic feats: Christian could balance a musket on the palm of his outstretched arm and could make a standing jump from inside one barrel to another. Of the first ship on which he had served, the *Eurydice*, it had been reported to Christian's family that the young man had ruled over his inferiors "in a superior pleasant Manner," that he had made "Toil a pleasure"; Christian's stint before the mast under Bligh in the West Indies may have enhanced his instinctive, easy dealings with the lower deck, and all evidence suggests he was well liked on the *Bounty*.

In accordance with naval custom, and as Cook had done in turn for him, Bligh had his young gentlemen and other officers join him in rotation at his table. The habit was to be somewhat revised on this last leg.

"During this passage Mr. Bligh and His Mess mates the Master & Surgeon fell out, and seperated," wrote Morrison, with his infallible eye for trouble, "each taking his part of the stock, & retiring to live in their own Cabbins, after which they had several disputes & seldom spoke but on duty; and even *then* with much apperant reserve." When Bligh invited his young gentlemen to dine, they joined his solitude.

The causes of the disputes with Fryer and the disagreeable Huggan are described at length by Bligh in his private and official logs. On the morning of October 9, as the *Bounty* cut through a rare smooth sea, Bligh sent the ship's several expense books to Fryer for the master's usual bimonthly inspection and signature. The books were shortly returned to Bligh accompanied by a certificate drafted by Fryer, "the Purport of which," Bligh recorded, "was that he had done nothing amiss during his time on board." Unless Bligh signed the certificate, Fryer would not sign the books.

Summoning the master, Bligh informed him that he "did not approve of his doing his duty conditionally," at which Fryer abruptly left. This time, Bligh's instincts were sure and his reaction swift. Ordering all hands on deck, he read the Articles of War, "with particular parts of the Instructions relative to the Matter." Fryer was instructed to sign the books or "express his reasons [for not complying] at full length at the bottom of the Page."

"I sign in obedience to your Orders, but this may be Cancelled hereafter," Morrison reported that Fryer intoned as he signed. Morrison's sly suggestion was that Bligh had been caught fiddling the books, which if true would have cost him his career. But his very public actions defy this interpretation: Bligh was not about to countenance a furtive quid pro quo with his Master. "[T]his troublesome Man saw his error & before the whole Ships Company signed the Books" was Bligh's report.

There are indications that Fryer might have had reason for concern about his performance as master—Bligh's glancing reference to his need to repeat orders about Purcell at Adventure Bay being one. More immediately, Fryer may have had in mind the events of just three days earlier—events Bligh described with shock and anger in his private log but omitted in the official log he presented to the Admiralty.

On this day, William Elphinstone, one of the master's mates, came to Bligh with wholly unexpected news: James Valentine, a twenty-eight-year-old able seaman, had incurred a bad infection after being bled by surgeon Huggan for an ailment contracted at Adventure Bay. Bligh was informed that Valentine was delirious "and had every appearance of being in a dying state."

"This shock was scarce equal to my astonishment," Bligh almost gasped, "as the Surgeon had told me he was getting better, and had never expressed the least uneasyness about him." When summoned, Huggan explained that, oh yes—he had meant to tell Bligh the night before at dinner, only Bligh had a guest (the officer of the watch) and he had not thought it proper to say anything at the time, but, yes, it was true: James Valentine had only hours to live.

Where was the ship's master? Where was the acting lieutenant? Above all, where was the assistant surgeon? How had it transpired that Bligh had only learned, belatedly and almost by happenstance, of so serious a development? Bligh immediately visited the stricken man, who was "seized with a violent hollow Cough and spit much." He had been treated by Huggan with blisters, applied to his breast, for what the surgeon had diagnosed as an asthmatic complaint.

On October 10, the day after the altercation with Master Fryer, Bligh recorded the death of Seaman Valentine in his official log.

"This poor man was one of the most robust People on board," he reflected, "and therefore the Surprize and shock was the greater to me." Forgoing the customary auction of the deceased man's effects, Bligh directed that his meager possessions be given to the two men who had cared for him on his deathbed "with great care and Affection." On the following day, as the ship progressed under light breezes and fine rain, Valentine's remains were committed to the deep.

Bligh's perfect record of health was now irrevocably spoiled, and it had been spoiled by his beastly sot of a surgeon, aided by the apparent indifference of his officers. Four days after Valentine's death, three of the older seamen who had formerly complained of "the Rheumatism" were diagnosed with symptoms of scurvy. Bligh was beside himself with frustration and disbelief; had he himself not written in his dissertation on the healthful "Mode of Management" that "the Scurvy is realy a disgrace to a ship"?

Bligh embarked upon a frantic application of his most trusted defenses—portable soup and essence of malt, the latter served at a ratio of three tablespoons to a quart of water, "[t]his being the Surgeons opinion was sufficient"; despite his misgivings and distaste for Huggan, Bligh was still dependent on his professional opinion, such as it was.

Was it scurvy, or was it something else? Throughout the rest of the voyage, all the way to Tahiti, the question hounded Bligh, who returned to it again and again in his log. On October 17, he dosed up the three men who had complained of rheumatism with malt, sauerkraut, and less usefully, vinegar and mustard—everything, it would seem, that he could think of. The next day he examined other men "who the Doctor supposed had a taint of the Scurvy" but found only the symptoms of prickly heat. The *Bounty* was now back up to the twenty-fifth parallel, after all, and temperatures had risen well into the seventies.

On the afternoon of the nineteenth, as the ship ambled along in fair but windless weather, John Mills, the forty-year-old gunner's mate from Aberdeen, and William Brown, the assistant gardener, refused to participate in the mandatory evening dancing. Perhaps the higher temperature was taking a toll, or perhaps the men were just fed up with what they regarded as tedious nonsense. On being informed, Bligh's response was to stop the offenders' grog, "with a promise of further punishment on a Second Refusal"; the stopping of grog had been one of Cook's stratagems.

"I have always directed the Evenings from 5 to 8' O'Clock to be spent in dancing," Bligh registered with a tone of aggrieved self-righteousness in his log, "& that every Man should be Obliged to dance as I considered it conducive to their Health."

Only hours later, Bligh had to log a second entry about the incident: "Wm Brown complaining of some Rheumatic Complaints which he has had these three Weeks past, the Doctor insists upon it that it is Scurvey."

So Brown, it seems, had turned to the doctor for moral support. Bligh himself, however, could discover no such symptoms. Determinedly, he pushed forward with his "decoctions" of essence of malt, noting, "I have Ordered the Doctor to issue it himself."

"If able," he had added in the original entry of his private log, which also noted that Huggan had been "constantly drunk these last four days." Toward the end of this frustrating Sunday, all hands were mustered for the usual inspection.

"I think I never saw a more healthy set of Men and so decent looking in my life," Bligh exclaimed in exasperation to his log. Bligh knew what scurvy looked like and could find no symptoms—no "eruptions or swellings," no bleeding gums or loose teeth. Yet the real interest in this protracted incident, of course, has less to do with whether or not there was scurvy on the *Bounty* than whether or not Bligh was being toyed with. Was Huggan getting back at Bligh for his anger over Valentine's death with a vindictive but unassailable diagnosis of the disease Bligh most feared—a gambit instantly appreciated and exploited by the appreciative and all-knowing seamen?

On October 23, Huggan sent Bligh an updated sick list, with his own name on it under the complaint "Rheumatism." Twenty-four hours later, he issued a revised list that gave his complaint as "Paralytic Affection." Later in the same day, however, as Bligh noted, Huggan was "discovered to be able to get out of bed and look for liquor," his paralysis notwithstanding. With this, Bligh's patience snapped and he gave orders for the surgeon's filthy cabin to be searched and all liquor removed, an "operation that was not only troublesome but offensive in the highest degree." Successfully deprived of alcohol, Huggan made a shaky appearance on deck the next day, tenuously sober. The timing of his recovery was excellent, as the *Bounty* was less than a day away from Matavai Bay and only hours away from sighting land. Bligh urgently wished his surgeon to perform one important medical office before landfall. Ever since the first European ship had arrived at Tahiti, sailors had infected the islanders with "the venereals"; the French claimed the English were responsible for the devastation the disease had wrought, while the English pointed out that the Tahitians themselves had implicated the French. Bligh wanted Huggan "to examine very particularly every Man and Officer" for any sign of the disease before arriving at the island. Huggan did so and, to the universal joy of the company, declared "every person totally free from the Venereal complaint."

The next day brought the *Bounty* to Tahiti.

TAHITI

Beneath the island's volcanic pinnacles, the *Bounty* passed around the surf-pounded reef beyond Point Venus. Already she was hailed by throngs of canoes; and when Bligh called out that he had come from Britain, or "Pretanee," the delighted islanders swarmed onto the ship, "and in ten Minutes," wrote Bligh, "I could scarce find my own people."

The old-timers—Nelson, the gardener, William Peckover, the gunner, Armorer Joseph Coleman and Bligh himself—greeted and were greeted with warm recognition. The remainder of the crew now learned that the stories that had filled their ears throughout the long, hard outward voyage—about the island's beauty, its sexually uninhibited women, its welcoming people—were not tall tales, or sailors' fantasy. Beyond the ship, its undulating slopes and valleys, gullies and dramatic peaks casting shifting green-blue shadows in the morning sun, rose the vision of Tahiti. Below, the blue sea around them was clogged with cheerful canoes that had come laden with gifts of plantains, coconuts and hogs. And filling the deck, milling and laughing around them, were the tall, clean-limbed, smooth-skinned Tahitians. The *Bounty* men—bowlegged, pockmarked, scarred and misshapen, toothless and, despite Bligh's best efforts, very dirty—regarded the improbably handsome, dark-haired islanders with both appetite and awe. Their brown skin gleaming with perfumed oil, garlanded with flowers, and flashing smiles with strong white teeth such as few Englishmen had ever seen, these superior men and women were also friendly and accessible. Significantly, all cases of scurvy were quickly cured; even Morrison allowed "that in a few days of arrival there was no appearance of sickness or disorder in the ship."

The following day, October 27, maneuvering around canoes and people, Bligh successfully worked the *Bounty* into Matavai Bay, and dropped anchor. Under the escort of a chief named Poeno, Bligh was taken to Point Venus, the peninsula that formed the northeast point of Matavai Bay, from where in 1769, Cook had observed the transit of Venus. Standing under the graceful and now familiar coconut palms, the surf breaking against the lava-black beach, Bligh seems to have drawn a deep breath of happiness.

It had been Bligh's original plan to conceal Captain Cook's death from the Tahitians; Cook was held in such high esteem that a portrait of him, left as a gift eleven years earlier, was still in good repair. But some three months before the *Bounty*'s arrival, another foreign ship—apparently the first since Cook's departure—had brought news of his terrible death at the hands of the Sandwich Islanders. Nonetheless, David Nelson— with or without Bligh's prompting is unclear—introduced Bligh as "Cook's son" to the local dignitaries; they are reported to have received this news with much satisfaction, although subsequent interactions suggest this was not perhaps taken by them as a literal truth.

On November 1, Bligh set out on a scouting trip to Oparre, a district to the west of Matavai. In order to uproot and carry off the large number of breadfruit he sought, he needed the permission of all the various chiefs with jurisdiction over the areas in which he would be working. A visit to pay his respects to the Ari'i Rahi, the six-year-old king of Oparre, took him inland toward the hills, "through the delightful breadfruit flats of Oparre," which were cut by a serpentine river. In the course of the day, the two parties entertained each other, the Tahitians offering an impromptu *heiva*, or dancing festival, Bligh a demonstration of his pocket pistol.

Before returning to his ship, Bligh contemplated the scenes of the day—the sparkling streams and green glades of the interior, and the dramatic sweep of the palm-rimmed lava beach of Matavai Bay. "These two places," he reflected, "are certainly the Paradise of the World, and if happiness could result from situation and convenience, here it is to be found in the highest perfection. I have seen many parts of the World," he continued in this remarkably personal entry, "but Otaheite is capable of being preferable to them all."

Tynah, the paramount chief of Matavai and the adjoining region, soon became the local dignitary with whom Bligh and his men had the most communion. He and his outgoing wife, Iddeeah, were both large, impressive persons, Tynah standing over six foot three and weighing some three hundred pounds. Now around thirty-seven years old, Tynah had been known to Cook and Bligh previously as "Otoo." Adroitly, Bligh conveyed to Tynah and the other lesser chiefs that the gift his sovereign, King George of Pretanee, would most welcome in exchange for the gifts his ship carried was the breadfruit tree. Delighted that King George could be so easily satisfied, the chiefs readily gave their assent, and Bligh, much relieved, began to organize his land base.

The Admiralty's delay in getting Bligh his orders had ensured that the *Bounty* arrived in Tahiti near the outset of the western monsoon season, which ran from November to April, a period of rain and gales avoided by sailors. Additionally, as he had been directed to return by the Endeavour Straits, Bligh knew he had to await the eastern monsoon, which would begin at the end of April or early May; in short, the *Bounty* would not be departing Tahiti until April, five months away, and several months longer than had originally been planned.

On November 2, Bligh sent a party to Point Venus that included William Peckover, Peter Heywood, four of the able seamen, as well as Nelson the gardener and his assistant William Brown, all under the command of Fletcher Christian. It was their job to establish and maintain the camp for the gardeners' work. Eventually, two tents and a shed, built of bamboo poles and thatched with palm branches, were erected on Cook's old site and a boundary line drawn, "within which none of the Natives were to enter without permission and all were cautioned against it." The compound was to serve as a nursery where the transplanted breadfruit could be closely supervised before being transported to the *Bounty*. Here, in the shade of the coconuts and breadfruit that rolled down to the dark shore, as palm fronds clattered and rustled in the sea breezes far above their heads, Christian and the rest of his small land party were to live and work for the next few months. Their less fortunate companions were expected to spend the night on board their ship.

Bligh himself divided his time between an anxious monitoring of his plants, and careful, if enjoyable, diplomacy. The success of his breadfruit operation depended upon the continued goodwill of such powerful friends as Poeno and Tynah (the father of the boy king), both of whom he knew from his former visit. Based upon his earlier experience, there was little reason to imagine this goodwill would in fact waver, but there was reason to fear the curiosity and acquisitiveness of the common man. So far, as Bligh had noted, the thefts the *Bounty* had suffered had been insignificant, but he was keenly aware that this situation could quickly change. He had already had to administer the third flogging of the voyage, in this case twelve lashes to Alexander Smith, able seaman, "for suffering the Gudgeon of the large Cutter to be drawn out without knowing it." The flogging had horrified the watching Tahitians—especially the women, who, according to Bligh, "showed every degree of Sympathy which marked them to be the most humane and affectionate creatures in the World."

The temptation for Bligh to take personal advantage of his circumstances, to strike out on short expeditions, making discoveries and taking the surveys in which he was so expert, all to his own greater glory, must have been very great. But Bligh had virtually promised Banks a successful outcome to the voyage, and Banks had made it patently clear that he cared about nothing but breadfruit. The nursery, therefore, and everything that concerned the nursery, were to be the sole objects of his attention. Bligh could not risk some fatal lapse of discipline; nor, as it appears, could he trust his officers or men.

This was most apparent in Bligh's attempt to regulate the ongoing torrent of trade between his ship and his island hosts. The establishment of a fixed market, as opposed to a free-for-all run by the sailors' whim, was of immediate advantage to his own ship, as well as to future British vessels. As Cook had done—and based closely on Cook's own rules—Bligh drafted a set of injunctions intended to govern his men's conduct among the Tahitians:

1st. At the Society or Friendly Islands, no person whatever is to intimate that Captain Cook was killed by Indians or that he is dead.

2nd. No person is ever to speak, or give the least hint, that we have come on purpose to get the breadfruit plant, until I have made my plan known to the chiefs.

3rd. Every person is to study to gain the good will and esteem of the natives; to treat them with all kindness; and not to take from them, by violent means, any thing that they may have stolen; and no one is ever to fire, but in defence of his life.

4th. Every person employed on service, is to take care that no arms or implements of any kind under their charge, are stolen; the value of such thing, being lost, shall be charged against their wages.

5th. No man is to embezzle, or offer to sale, directly, or indirectly, any part of the King's stores, of what nature soever.

6th. A proper person or persons will be appointed to regulate trade, and barter with the natives; and no officer or seaman, or other person belonging to the ship, is to trade for any kind of provisions, or curiosities; but if such officer or seaman wishes to purchase any particular thing, he is to apply to the provider to do it for him. By this means a regular market will be carried on, and all disputes, which otherwise may happen with the natives will be avoided. All boats are to have every thing handed out of them at sun-set.

These orders were nailed to the mizzenmast immediately upon anchoring—so Morrison reports, citing a garbled version of only item number six on Bligh's list. Bligh's orders, Morrison recalled, prohibited "the Purchase of Curiosities or *any* thing except Provisions," adding that "there were few or no instances of the order being disobeyd, as no curiosity struck the seamen so forcibly as a roasted pig. . . ."

Nonetheless, it was this last order that appears to have been responsible for the only complaints worth recording during the twenty-three weeks spent on Tahiti. Bligh's directive aimed to avoid the disputes that would inevitably arise if trade were conducted by forty-five individuals following no particular rules, and to ensure that, as commanding officer and purser, he could reliably provision his ship.

Captain Cook himself, who in the course of his long career had seen many a promising market ruined, had been very clear on this point: "Thus, was the fine prospect we had of geting a plentifull supply of refreshments of these people frustrated," Cook had lamented, after one of his men had volunteered a quantity of rare red feathers for a pig, inadvertently establishing red feathers as the currency for all future pigs. "[A]nd which will ever be the case so long as every one is allowed to make exchanges for what he pleaseth and in what manner he please's."

Morrison undoubtedly understood Bligh's motivation for the directive, and John Fryer, as master, most certainly did. Yet Morrison complained that when the trade in hogs began to slacken, "Mr. Bligh seized on all that came to the ship big & small Dead or alive, taking them as his property, and serving them as the ship's allowance at one pound per Man per Day." According to Morrison, Fryer also complained to Bligh, apparently publicly, that his property was being taken. The site designated for trade was one of the tents at the nursery compound, where the boundary marker kept crowds at bay. William Peckover had been placed in charge, a sensible choice given his knowledge of Tahitian language and customs picked up in the course of several visits he had made to the island with Cook. Nonetheless, the sailors continued to encourage their Tahitian friends to come to the ship surreptitiously.

"The Natives observing that the Hogs were seized as soon as they Came on board . . . became very shy of bringing a hog in sight of Lieut. Bligh," Morrison reported, and he went on to describe with relish the ways in which the sailors and islanders conspired to trick their commanding officer. The Tahitians "watched all opportunity when he was on shore to bring provisions to their friends." Not for the first time—and certainly not for the last—Bligh must have wished for the support of even a small party of marines, armed sentinels who would have stood apart from the fraternity of seamen, and whose loyalty to his commands he could have counted on when his back was turned.

Despite Morrison's lengthy complaint, time passed pleasantly enough for the seamen who were entrusted with minimal duties and allowed onshore regularly "for refreshment." Joseph Coleman set up a forge to make and repair goods for the ship and islanders alike. The usual wood-

Joseph Banks, 1771, by Benjamin West *(Courtesy of Lincolnshire County Council, Usher Gallery)*

William Bligh, c. 1775, portrait attributed to John Webber *(Courtesy of Stephen Walters)*

Sheer draft and deck plans of the *Bounty*, showing the fittings for transporting breadfruit plants
(Courtesy of National Maritime Museum, London)

Master John Fryer, c. 1807, by Gaetano Calleyo
(Courtesy of Mitchell Library, State Library of New South Wales)

Wood Hall, near Cockermouth, Cumberland, c. 1834 *(Courtesy of Richard Nicholson)*

Peter Heywood as a young man
(Courtesy of Manx National Heritage Library)

The Nunnery, Isle of Man, c. 1795 *(Courtesy of Manx National Heritage Library)*

Douglas Harbour, Isle of Man, 1804 *(Courtesy of Manx National Heritage Library)*

The Cape of Good Hope, South Africa, by Jacques Arago
(Courtesy of National Library of Australia)

Adventure Bay, Van Diemen's Land, 1792, by George Tobin
(Courtesy of Mitchell Library, State Library of New South Wales)

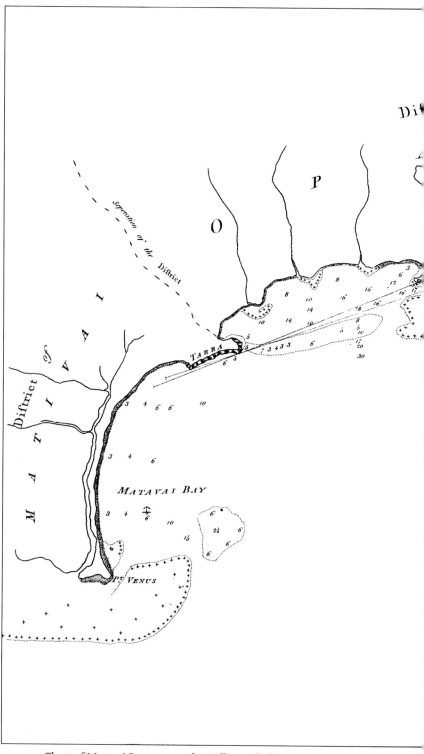

Chart of Matavai Bay, c. 1790, by William Bligh

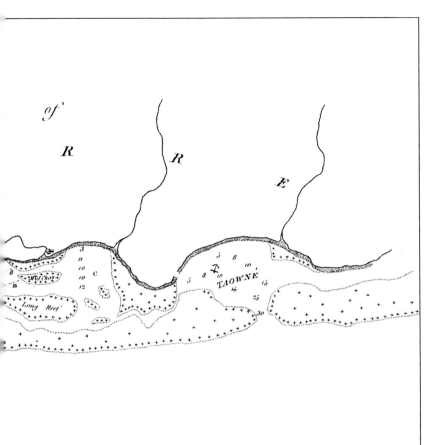

of

R

R

E

Mid Chan

Long Reef

TAOWNE

SKETCH

From recollection *and* anchor-bearings
of the
NORTH PART of OTAHEITE

From Point Venus *to* Taowne Harbour

References .

A Bounty-Rock, *where the Ship struck,* 9 feet water.
B Toahroah Harbour *where the Ship lay.*
C Tettyoorah Harbour .

by

Wm Bligh

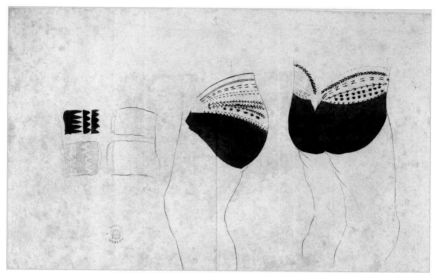

Tahitian tattoos, from *The Endeavour Journal of Joseph Banks, 1768–1771*, J. C. Beaglehole, ed. *(Courtesy of the British Library)*

"Voyage of the *Bounty*'s Launch," by Lieutenant Colonel Batty, from *The Eventful History of the Mutiny and Piratical Seizure of H.M.S. Bounty*, by Sir John Barrow, 1831

Entry from Bligh's notebook, kept in the *Bounty*'s launch

(Courtesy of National Library of Australia)

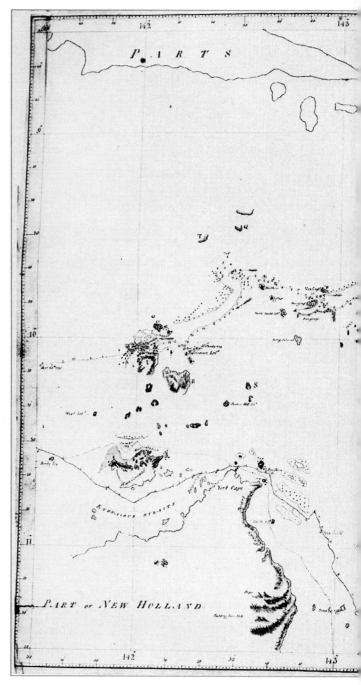

Bligh's survey of
the straits between
New Holland and
New Guinea

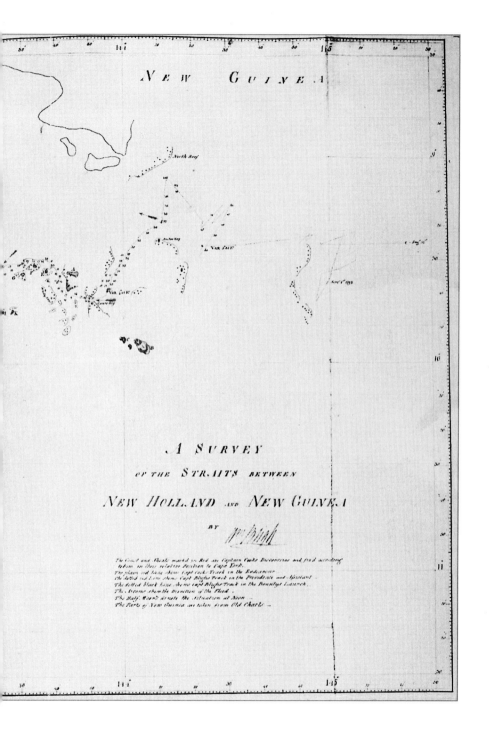

NEW GUINEA

North Reef

L. VAR FALL

A SURVEY

OF THE STRAITS BETWEEN

NEW HOLLAND AND NEW GUINEA

BY

Coupang, Timor, 1801, by François Peron and Charles LeSeur
(Courtesy of Mitchell Library, State Library of New South Wales)

Arrival of Bligh and his men at Timor, 1791, by Charles Benazech
(Courtesy of National Library of Australia)

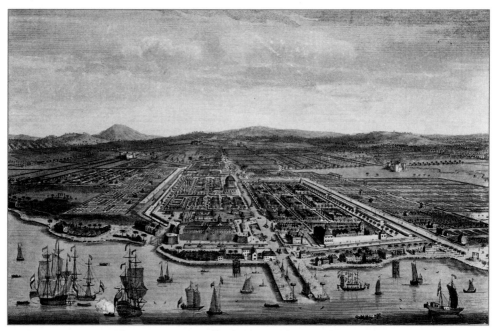

City of Batavia, Java, c. 1780, by Ivan Rynne *(Courtesy of Art Archive)*

ing parties were sent off to cut timber, while others prepared puncheons of salted pork for the return journey. The great cabin was refitted for the pots waiting in the land nursery, only, as Bligh logged, "the Carpenter running a Nail through his Knee very little was done." Charles Norman, a carpenter's mate, had been ill for several days with a complaint diagnosed by Huggan variously as rheumatism and "Peripneumonianotha," and the quartermaster's mate, George Simpson, also according to Huggan, had "Cholera Morbus." Bligh bought a milch goat for Norman, believing its milk would help the patient's chronic diarrhea. The men recovered and Bligh was able to report a clean sick list, save that the "Venereal list is increased to four"; sadly, the European disease was now endemic.

Bligh met almost every day with Tynah and his family and retinue, and each day he logged some new discovery about his hosts' culture. Along with the ship's officers, he was entertained by lascivious *heivas,* in which the women, "according to the horrid custom," distorted their faces into obscene expressions. He discussed the tradition of infanticide among the flamboyant *arioi,* and he recorded the recipe for a delicious pudding made from a turniplike root. One day, Bligh engaged in long theological inquiry, in which he was questioned closely about his own beliefs: Who was the son and who was the wife of his God? Who was his father and mother? Who was before your God and where is he? Is he in the winds or in the sun?

When asked about childbirth in his country, Bligh answered as well as he was able, and inquired in turn how this was done in Tahiti. Queen Iddeeah replied by mimicking a woman in labor, squatting comfortably on her heels between the protective arms of a male attendant who stroked her belly. Iddeeah was vastly amused on learning of the difficulties of Pretanee's women.

"[L]et them do this & not fear," she told Bligh, who appears to have been persuaded by this tender pantomime.

In the evenings, Bligh entertained his hosts on board the *Bounty,* which none seemed to tire of visiting. As Tynah's royal status forbade him to put food or drink into his own mouth, Bligh himself sometimes served as cupbearer if attendants were unavailable; Iddeeah, according to custom, ate apart from the men. After the meals, the company lounged lazily around the small deck area, enjoying the offshore breezes, and the muffled pounding of the surf on shore and reef, and the lap of the waves below. Not infrequently, Bligh's guests stayed the night on board the *Bounty*, loath to depart.

How Bligh passed his time at Tahiti can be followed, day by day, event by event, as recorded in his fulsome log. What is not known with any clarity is how time was passed onshore. All midshipmen were required to keep up their own logs, to be produced at such time as they applied to pass for lieutenant, and one would give much to have Fletcher Christian's. As it is, life at Point Venus can be sketched only in broad outline. Every evening, when the work of the shore party was winding down, the Tahitians gathered at "the Post" before sunset. Almost all of the *Bounty* men had found *taios,* or protective friends, who took them into their homes and families. At least two of the men, George Stewart from the Orkneys and, perhaps less predictably, the critical James Morrison, had women friends to whom they were particularly attached, while all the men seemed to have enjoyed regular sexual partners; whether or not Fletcher Christian had formed an attachment to any one woman was to become a hotly contested question—at the very least, he, like young Peter Heywood, had to be treated for "venereals." The women of Tahiti, as Bligh would later famously write, were "handsome, mild and cheerful in their manners and conversation, possessed of great sensibility, and have sufficient delicacy to make them admired and beloved." They were also by European standards not only very beautiful, but sexually uninhibited and experienced in ways that amazed and delighted their English visitors.

"Even the mouths of Women are not exempt from the polution, and many other as uncommon ways have they of gratifying their beastly inclinations," as Bligh had observed, aghast. Famously, favors of the Tahitian women could be purchased for mere nails. Both on ship and at the camp, Bligh allowed female guests to stay the night, at the same time trying, through Ledward, his assistant surgeon, to keep track of the venereal diseases. When dusk came, the shore party were left more or less to their own devices. The sundown gatherings brought entertainments—

wrestling matches, dances and games, feasts, martial competitions—but also a sexual privacy, even a domesticity, not allowed to the men still on board ship. From the curving arm of Point Venus, Christian and his companions could look back toward Matavai Bay, past the *Bounty* riding gently at anchor, to the darkening abundance of trees that seemed to cascade from the grave, unassailable heights of the island.

As the weeks passed, the potted plants began to fill the nursery tent, and by the end of November, some six hundred were "in a very fine way." Meanwhile, other ship duties were intermittently carried out. Bligh ordered the sails brought onshore, where they were aired and dried under Christian's supervision. The large cutter was found to have a wormy bottom and had to be cleaned and repainted, under the shade of a large awning that Bligh had made to protect the workmen from the sun.

These duties were accompanied by the usual problems. Mathew Thompson was flogged with a dozen lashes "for insolence and disobedience of Orders." Also, Bligh logged, "by the remissness of my Officers & People at the Tent," a rudder was stolen, the only theft, as Bligh observed, so far, of any consequence; the officer in charge of the tent was of course Fletcher Christian. There is no record of punishment.

Most seriously, Purcell once again had begun to balk at his orders. When asked to make a whetstone for one of the Tahitian men, he refused point-blank, claiming that to do so would spoil his tools. On this occasion, at last, Bligh punished the carpenter with confinement to his cabin—although, as he recorded, he did "not intend to lose the use of him but to remitt him to his duty to Morrow."

Toward the end of November, strong winds began to accompany what had become daily showers of rain, and by early December the dark weather brought an unfamiliar, heavy swell. The *Bounty* rolled uncomfortably at her anchorage, while the surf breaking on Dolphin Bank, the outlying reef, had become violent. On December 6, Bligh described a scene "of Wind and Weather which I never supposed could have been met with in this place." From midnight until well into the morning, amid torrents of rain, a foaming sea roiled the ship "in a most tremendous manner." Onshore, Christian's party was cut off by the swelling of the nearby river and an alarming influx of the sea. In the morning,

Tynah and Iddeeah fought their way to the *Bounty* in canoes through a sea so high that, as Bligh wrote, "I could not have supposed any Boat could have existed a moment." On board, the couple offered their tearful greetings, saying they had believed the ship lost in the night. The rainy season, which Europeans had never experienced before, had commenced, and it was at once clear that Matavai Bay was no longer a feasible anchorage. The plants had been threatened by salt spray as the winds and high sea raged, and Bligh was determined to move them to safer ground as soon as he was able. On Nelson's advice, he delayed an immediate departure until plants in an apparently dormant state showed signs of being alive and healthy.

Some days after the storm, Huggan, the quondam surgeon, at last succumbed to his "drunkenness and indolence."

"Exercise was a thing he could not bear an Idea of," Bligh wrote by way of an epitaph. Since his death had been projected even before the *Bounty* departed Deptford Dockyard, Huggan had a good run for his money. He was buried the following day to the east of Point Venus, across the river that cut the point and not far from the sea.

"There the Sun rises," Tynah said as the grave was being dug, "and there it sets, and here you may bury Terronnoo, for so he was called." Joining Huggan's shipmates for the funeral were all the chiefs of the region and a great many other people, respectful and solemn for the surgeon's perhaps undeservedly dignified rites. Huggan was only the second European to be buried on the island.

It was Christmas by the time the dormant plants had put forth the desired shoots, and the men began the cumbersome task of moving camp. A reef harbor at Oparre, to the west of Matavai, had been chosen as the *Bounty*'s new anchorage. With a watchful eye on the weather, which had continued to be troubled, Bligh ordered the *Bounty* readied for her short journey, and had his 774 potted breadfruit plants carefully carried on board. At half past ten in the morning, the ship weighed anchor and cautiously set out to follow the launch, which was carrying the tents and which Bligh had sent ahead as a pilot.

The second camp, according to Bligh, was "a delightful situation in every respect." The ship lay in sheltered, smooth water, where the tide lapped at the beach and no surf broke. Dense stands of trees shaded the new nursery, which was established along the same lines as the Matavai camp with the addition of a hut supplied by Tynah. Tynah, who had lobbied hard not to lose the *Bounty* and all the amusements and lucrative trade she brought, was delighted with the relocation, as he also had jurisdiction of Oparre. *Taios* left behind were still close enough to visit, and the easy social routine that had been enjoyed at Matavai was soon resumed, with people promenading along the beach opposite the ship "every fair Evening." Bligh directed the ship "to be laid up and everything put below" in part so as to avoid more thefts, but this was also a sign that the men on board could look forward to only perfunctory duties.

Nonetheless, the very day the plants and ship were safely reestablished, Bligh had William Muspratt, the cook's assistant, flogged with a dozen lashes for "neglect of duty." Two days later Robert Lamb, the butcher, was also flogged with a dozen "for suffering his Cleaver to be Stolen." This now brought the total number of men punished up to six.

Although the temperature remained warm, this new season brought torrential rain and squalls, and skies so dense with sodden clouds that for an entire month Bligh was unable to take a single celestial observation. It was on one of these dark, impenetrable nights that three of the *Bounty*'s men deserted. When the watch was relieved at four in the morning of January 5, 1789, Charles Churchill, the master-at-arms, John Millward, able seaman, and William Muspratt, who had only recently been flogged, were found missing. Gone with them were the small cutter along with eight stand of arms and cartouches of ammunition.

Bligh responded to the news with an icy resolve that he had hitherto not displayed. To his Tahitian friends, he stated in very clear, straightforward and polite language that he expected the men returned. Laughing nervously, they asked Bligh if he would hold them hostage on board his ship, as Cook had done. This was an unexpected and revealing question. In 1769, during his first visit to Tahiti, Cook had lost two marines to desertion and had retaliated by holding the chiefs hostage, his rationale being that his men could not survive on the island without the complicity

of the islanders. That Bligh's friends raised this concern twenty years after the event suggests that Cook's actions had left a deep impression.

Bligh reassured his friends that he would not resort to such a strata-
gem, adding, in his log, that he had "never shown any Violence or
Anger" at any of the petty thefts that had occurred and had enjoyed such
mutual goodwill that he knew his friends had confidence in him, and
that he had "therefore no doubt but they will bring the Deserters back"—
but, if they should not, he would "make the whole Country Suffer for it."
Having issued his warnings, there was little Bligh could do but wait, relying on local intelligence to flush out the fugitives.

That some of his men would try to desert probably did not take Bligh
completely by surprise; again, he had his experience with Cook to draw
upon. Cook had suffered desertions on Tahiti during all three of his expeditions. Recognizing that the inducements to leave ship were many,
Cook had summoned his crew and lectured them at length on the "spirit
of Desertion," informing them that "they Might run off if they pleased,"
as one of the company later recorded, "[b]ut they might Depend upon it
he would Recover them again." Stern as it was, the speech did not deter
other, also futile attempts. Some years later, on learning of the *Bounty*'s
fate, James Matra, a midshipman on Cook's first journey, would report
to Banks the astonishing news that a mass desertion had been planned
by "most of the People" and some of the gentlemen of the *Endeavour*.
Mr. Midshipman Matra had been instrumental in dissuading them, so
he would claim, his principal line of argument being that the men could
be certain of "dying rotten" of the pox if they were to live out their lives
on the island.

Within his own company, Bligh must have seen evidence that his officers and people were settling down into Tahitian life and adopting local
customs, most visibly in their passion for being tattooed. The first tattoos had arrived in England with sailors returning from the Americas or
the Pacific, and especially from the *Endeavour* (with Joseph Banks) at the
end of Cook's first voyage, when they had become tokens of great prestige. The Bountys' tastes were varied, some sticking conservatively to English iconography. James Morrison, of all people, for reasons only to be

guessed at, had had himself tattooed with the Order of the Garter around his leg and the Knights of the Garter's motto: *"Honi soit qui mal y pense"*—"Shame on him who evil thinks." Thomas Ellison wore simply his name and "October 25th 1788" on his right arm—the date he had first sighted Otaheite.

But several of the men had undergone traditional Tahitian tattooing over large parts of their body, particularly on their buttocks. In Tahitian tradition, a man was not eligible to marry unless he had undergone the lengthy and painful operation of having his entire backside blacked over. Bligh left descriptions only of the mutineers, and with one exception (John Mills, the Scottish gunner's mate) every one of them was tattooed, and usually "very much tatowed" or "tatowed in several places." Peter Heywood was in this company, being "[v]ery much tattowed," among other things with the three-legged emblem of the Isle of Man. Those who had received the elaborate tattoos of Tahitian manhood included George Stewart, Matthew Quintal and Fletcher Christian.

Still, Bligh himself had encouraged friendly relations with the Tahitians, and his men's enthusiasm for the more eye-catching aspects of their culture was not something to be readily, or fruitfully, legislated. But now, as he conducted his own grim investigation of the events, he made other discoveries. On examination of the men's personal effects for clues, a piece of paper was found inside Charles Churchill's chest on which he had written his own name and the names of three of the shore party. The deserters would later say darkly that "many others intended to remain among the islands," and making a list of men committed to an illegal act such as desertion—or mutiny—was an old trick. When Captain Edward Edwards, back in his happier days before he captained the *Pandora,* had thwarted the mutinous plot on board his ship *Narcissus,* a list of names of the men involved in the plot had been discovered on one of the would-be mutineers; perhaps the rash act of committing a name to paper was perceived as a kind of security that bound the man in question to one's cause.

Some years later, in personal correspondence, Bligh reported that "[t]his List had Christian, Heywood and several other Names in it," and that he had approached his protégé "not conceiving Christian could be guilty of such a thing, and who, when I showed it to him, laughed as well as myself." To a man, the shore party professed their innocence to Bligh, and "denyd it so firmly, that He was inclined from Circumstances to believe them and said no more to them about it," according to Morrison. In the official log no mention is made of this mysterious list; Bligh's personal log, in which he would have been most expected to have made some remarks about the event, ends on October 23, and does not resume until April 5, 1789; a comprehensive index, in Bligh's own handwriting, is all that can be found of the missing portion. The official log, submitted to the Admiralty, makes no mention of his suspicions whatsoever and shows Bligh's professionalism at its best. If the men had convinced him of their innocence, then he was bound to "say no more about it." Or, was the incident omitted for more self-serving reasons—because later events proved he had been duped? At least "three of the Party on shore" would remain among the mutineers: Peter Heywood, William Brown and Fletcher Christian.

One curious and generally unremarked incident occurred four days after Churchill and his companions deserted. As Bligh reported, "one of my officers on shore" cut a branch of an oil-nut tree growing at a *marae*, or sacred site, and, "accidently bringing it into the dwelling where my people are at, all the Natives both Men and Women suddenly left." The branch had tabooed the shore hut; no Tahitian would set foot here until the appropriate ceremony lifted the taboo. Curiously, however, as Bligh noted, "[w]hen I came on shore I found a branch of this Tree tyed to one of the Posts, altho they saw the effect it had of keeping the Natives from the House." Is it significant that in the immediate aftermath of the desertion one of the officers—Christian or Heywood—tabooed the house in which three men implicated on Churchill's list happened to live? Was this a sign to Tahitian *taios* and allies to stay away, perhaps in the wake of an aborted plot? A whimsical amulet to ward off further trouble? Or, as Bligh clearly believed, mere happenstance?

Bligh seems to have accepted that the outcome to this adventure did not lie in his hands, and he returned his company to their former routine while awaiting whatever news his Tahitian friends brought him of the deserters. His own time was once again divided between the nursery and inquiry into local customs, and he observed with delight "the swarms of little Children which are in every part of the Country," flying kites, playing cat's cradle, and skipping rope, the latter game, as he noted being "common with the Boys in England." While onshore on January 16, he received a message from Fryer that a man known to have given conveyance to the deserters was on board the *Bounty*: did Bligh want Fryer to detain him? Incredulous, Bligh returned to the ship to find the informant had escaped by diving overboard and that no attempt had been made to follow him.

"As he knew perfectly my determination in punishing this Man if ever he could be caught, it was an unnecessary delay in confining him," Bligh wrote of Fryer. The following day, he had even greater cause for anger. Spare sails that Bligh had ordered to be taken out of storage and aired were found to be mildewed and rotting.

"If I had any Officers to supercede the Master and Boatswain, or was capable of doing without them, considering them as common Seamen, they should no longer occupy their respective Stations," Bligh fumed. "Scarce any neglect of duty can equal the criminality of this, for it appears that altho the Sails have been taken out twice since I have been in the Island, which I thought fully sufficient and I had trusted to their reports, Yet these New Sails never were brought out." Bligh had the sails washed in the sea, then hung to dry "to be ready for repairing," a laborious task. The *Bounty*'s voyage was only half over; an estimated ten months of sailing lay ahead.

Almost three weeks passed before word was brought that the deserters had been located in Tettahah, some five miles distant. Bligh at once set out to apprehend them, although darkness was coming and it was a rainy, windy night. Surprised by Bligh where they had taken shelter, the three men resignedly surrendered without resistance. Once back at the ship, Bligh read the Articles of War and administered punishment: twelve lashes for Charles Churchill, two dozen each for William Muspratt and John Millward—to be repeated at a later date. In between the floggings, the men were confined in irons and found time to write Bligh an extraordinary letter:

> Sir,
>
> We should think ourselves wholly inexcusable if we omitted taking this earliest opportunity of returning our thanks for your goodness in delivering us from a trial by Court-Martial, the fatal consequences of which are obvious; and although we cannot possibly lay any claim to so great a favour, yet we humbly beg you will be pleased to remit any farther punishment; and we trust our future conduct will fully demonstrate our deep sense of your clemency, and our stedfast resolution to behave better hereafter.
>
> We are,
>
> Sir,
>
> Your most obedient, most humble servants,
>
> C. Churchill, Wm. Muspratt, John Millward.

If the men believed that a submissive, honey-toned letter would charm their captain into dropping the second part of the punishment, they were proven mistaken when, eleven days later, the second round was indeed administered. Why Charles Churchill should have received a lesser punishment than his fellows is unclear. The punishment as a whole was, in any case, lenient; convicted deserters—with good service and character taken into consideration—could expect to receive 100 to 150 lashes. Bligh's leniency had been carefully considered. As he wrote in his log, "this affair was solely caused by the neglect of the Officers who had the Watch." The officer in question, identified by Morrison as Midshipman Thomas Hayward, had been asleep at his station, a crime under the Articles of War no less serious than desertion. ("No Person in or belonging to the Fleet shall sleep upon his Watch, or negligently perform the Duty imposed on him, or forsake his Station, upon Pain of Death. . . .") Bligh disrated the officer, turning him before the mast. According to an approving Morrison, he had also been clapped in irons until the runaways were returned.

"I was induced to give them all a lecture on this occasion," Bligh continued, referring to his other officers, "and endeavored to show them that however exempt they were at present from the like punishment, yet they were equally subject by the Articles of War to a condign one." In other words, although his officers were exempt "at present" from being flogged, they were liable to "a severe and well-deserved" punishment. It is within this remarkable lecture that the tensions so fatal to the voyage can be discerned most transparently.

"An Officer with Men under his care is at all times in some degree responsible for their conduct," Bligh wrote in his log, paraphrasing his lecture, "but when from his neglect Men are brought to punishment while he only meets with a reprimand, because a publick conviction by Tryal will bring both into a more severe and dangerous situation, an alternative often laid aside through lenity, and sometimes necessity, as it now is in both cases; it is an unpleasant thing to remark that no feelings of honor, or sense of shame is to be Observed in such an Offender."

The list of his officers' transgressions while in Tahiti, quite apart from incidents in the earlier part of the voyage, is impressive: when moving from Matavai to Oparre, Fryer had allowed the ship to run aground; a midshipman had slept on his watch and allowed three men to desert; the sails had been allowed to rot; on returning from capturing the deserters, Bligh had discovered that the ship's timekeeper, critical to accurate navigation, had been allowed to run down; the ship's rudder had been stolen from the camp; and in early March, an azimuth compass had been taken from under the noses of the men onshore, for which, according to Morrison, "Mr. Bligh . . . went on shore and rebuked the Officers at the tent for neglecting their duty." In addition, there are two enigmatic entries in the index Bligh composed to his missing personal log that refer to "Mr. Hallet's contumacy" and "Mr. Hallet's behaviour."

No wonder, then, that Bligh had raged after learning of the desertion that "[s]uch neglectfull and worthless petty Officers I believe never was in a Ship as are in this. No Orders for a few hours together are Obeyed by them, and their conduct in general is so bad, that no confidence or trust can be reposed in them, in short," he concluded ominously, "they have drove me to every thing but Corporal punishment and that must follow if they do not improve." The tenor of these occasional outbursts suggests that many more aggravations had passed unrecorded. It is a striking fact that, with one exception, Fryer and Purcell are the only offi-cers named by Bligh in his official log. The names of Hallett, Hayward, Christian—other known offenders—have all been edited out, perhaps along with other of his young gentlemen. Bligh was later, privately, to re-fer to Edward Young, for example, as "a worthless wretch," which at the very least suggests dereliction of some duties; and yet Young's name is never mentioned in the Admiralty's log. All of these young gentlemen were friends of the friends and patrons Bligh would have to rub shoul-ders with once back in England.

On February 4, two nights after the second part of the deserters' pun-ishment was meted out under cover of heavy rain, the cable of the *Bounty*'s bower anchor was cut, an act that could have brought the ship to disaster by allowing it to drift upon the reef. No explanation for what Bligh termed "this Malicious act" could be made; indeed, the mystery would be cleared up only much later, when the mutineers returned to Tahiti and learned that the agent had been the *taio* of Midshipman Hayward. His mo-tive had been to wreck the ship so as to ensure that his friend never left Tahiti. More alarming, he declared that he had watched as the deserters were flogged and vowed that if a lash were laid on Hayward, he would kill Bligh for it. But now, perplexed and affronted, Bligh threatened "instant revenge" unless the perpetrator was produced. To underscore his displea-sure, Bligh held aloof from Tynah and Iddeeah for two days, approaching them only to reiterate his anger. But for all his efforts, the unhappy chief was unable to produce the villain, and at length burst into tears.

"I could no longer keep these people under an Idea that I mistrusted them," Bligh wrote, already repentant. "Our reconciliation therefore took place, and they came on board with me at Noon to dine."

February and March, the last two months the *Bounty* was to be in Tahiti, were spent readying the ship for departure. Under the great low-ering cloud banks that filled the sky with violent color and claimed the island heights, the *Bounty* men worked through the daily fits of rain that ranged from light to torrential. Their very visible activities—caulking, re-pairing sails, mending iron fittings, stowing provisions and all the bustle preparatory to a long voyage—caused consternation among the Tahi-tians, now faced with the imminent certainty of losing their friends.

Tynah began an unsuccessful bid to persuade Bligh to carry himself and Iddeeah to England. This period also saw an increase in the number of thefts, as many Tahitians saw their last chance for a little profit fading. As Bligh wrote, "it is to be expected when a ship is near the time of Sailing," adding that he attached no blame to the Tahitians, because he was "perfectly certain that had the Ship been lying in the River Thames, a hundred times as much would have been Stolen." Nonetheless, when, thanks to Tynah's efforts, the thief of the azimuth compass was found, Bligh felt the time had come to deter all such future acts with a demonstration of Pretanee's might.

"Kill him," said Tynah, committed to demonstrating his unwavering good faith. Bligh was not inclined to do so, but instead administered the most severe punishment of his voyage: one hundred lashes to the thief, who was then confined in irons until the departure of the ship.

"His back became very much swelled," Bligh recorded with a kind of wonderment, "but only the last stroke broke the Skin." The incident is also recorded by Morrison, who administered the flogging and makes no adverse comments on it, only remarking that Bligh had gone "in a passion" to Tynah when the theft was first discovered.

Still the rains continued, and on the dawn watch of a day and night that had seen "much Rain," the mate of the watch heard a splash over the side of the ship, which on investigation turned out to be the sound of the confined thief diving overboard to his freedom. The thief's escape—according to Morrison, he had picked his lock—elicited a last strenuous outburst from Bligh.

"I have such a neglectfull set about me," he wrote, after castigating the mate of the watch, whom, exceptionally, he named as George Stewart (it is worth noting he had not come to Bligh through a patron), "that I beleive nothing but condign punishment can alter their conduct"—this was the second occasion Bligh had adverted to the possibility of "condign" punishment of his officers. "Verbal orders in the course of a Month were so forgot that they would impudently assert no such thing or directions were given, and I have been at last under the necessity to trouble myself with writing what by decent Young Officers would be complied with as the common Rules of Service."

As preparations for departure continued, it is likely that at least some of the *Bounty*'s men looked up from their work on the ship, through the rain and its steaming aftermath, across the water to the rustling skirt of palms and the dense canopies of fragrant trees they now knew so well . . . and dreaded the day of departure. Not just a life of ease, but friends, lovers, common-law wives, in some cases their future children would be left behind. William Bligh, on the other hand, for all the praise he showered on the island and for all his ease and professed friendships with his hosts, had always had his eye on the homeward run. His outbursts at his officers significantly increased in the final months of the Tahitian sojourn. Whether this was simply because Bligh had reached the limit of tolerance for their irresponsible behavior, or because he responded to the increased pressures of the approaching departure by lashing out at those next in pecking order, is impossible to know. Certainly Bligh had much to think about even without the worry over unreliable officers. His ship and everything in her had to be overhauled and provisioned for the long voyage still ahead; he had to take final surveys of the coast and harbor, which would be submitted to the Admiralty for the use of future navigators; he had to rerate the ship timekeeper, and keep a clear head for the Endeavour Straits. Relationships with Tynah and all local dignitaries had to be massaged until the last moment, so that future British vessels would receive as much goodwill as had the *Bounty*. And he had to nurse the 1,015 breadfruit and other miscellaneous plants through the vicissitudes of a twelve-thousand-mile voyage home.

"One day, or even one hours negligence may at any period be the means of destroying all the Trees and Plants which may have been collected," Banks had written in his final orders to Nelson with characteristic directness, noting earlier, "You will take care to remind Lieutenant Bligh of that circumstance."

On March 27, Bligh ordered all cats and the two dogs disembarked in preparation for bringing the plants on board, an operation that he characterized as "tedious." Now firmly rooted in boxes, tubs and pots, they had all to be sorted by size and arranged in their appropriate holdings.

"Thus far I have accomplished the Object of my Voyage," Bligh wrote, days later, when the operation was finished. Complacently surveying his flourishing plants neatly arrayed in the great cabin, he noted he had managed to stow 309 additional breadfruit to what had originally been planned; he was, then, safely covered for any losses.

With the ship crammed—"lumbered," to borrow Morrison's term—with gifts of cocoa nuts, yams and plantains, the men made their good-byes. Tynah and Iddeeah wept bitterly, begging Bligh to spend one last night in Matavai, but this he gently declined. He had grave misgivings about leaving his friends, knowing, as did they, that once the protection of the *Bounty* was removed they would be vulnerable to attacks from other chiefs from other parts of the island, jealous of the many gifts that the English visitors had showered upon them.

"I hope," Bligh had logged earlier, "that they will never be forgot by us." He had complied with Tynah's wish to be left two muskets and two pistols for protection. Purcell, unexpectedly, had thrown in an American musket that was much appreciated; Iddeeah in particular had impressed the *Bounty*'s men with her proficiency in firearms (as she had done with her surfing and wrestling).

"If therefore these good and friendly people are to be destroyed from our intercourse with them, unless they have timely assistance," Bligh logged by way of a pointed note to the Admiralty, "I think it is the business of any of his Majestys Ships that may come here to punish any such attempt." As he noted, he and his men had for twenty-three weeks been "treated with the greatest kindness: fed with the best of Meat and finest Fruits in the World."

In the early afternoon of April 5, Bligh, with his officers, took affectionate leave of Tynah and Iddeeah on board the *Bounty,* and then ordered the cutter to carry them ashore near Point Venus. As the ship rode at anchor in the lee of the outlying reef, all on board could watch the small, bobbing boat make its way to the black shore one last time. The weather was squally, the palms clattering unheard across the water as Tynah and Iddeeah bade good-bye to the boatmen, and then turned to face the *Bounty* and the sea.

MUTINY

Everybody, according to Morrison, "seemd In high spirits and began already to talk of Home"; but one must wonder how true this was, and if he was not merely at pains, writing with hindsight, to show that no man had left his heart on the island. The returned cutter, full of coconuts as a final gift from Tynah, was hoisted aboard, and the *Bounty* made sail. Tynah's request to have the ship's guns fired as a salute had to be denied, as Bligh was concerned that this might hurt the plants; instead all hands gathered and shouted three cheers across the darkening water. Some hours later, Tahiti lay behind them, and when dusk descended, the green, cloud-tipped peaks were gone.

A week after departing Tahiti, traveling west and following heavy rain, an unknown island was spotted through the persistent cloud. Outlying reefs and the unsettled weather made it too difficult to go ashore, but from visitors who paddled out to the ship Bligh learned that his discovery was called "Whytootackee." The island, some ten miles in circumference, had beaches of dazzling white sand and appeared to be covered with trees. While Bligh compiled a short working vocabulary of their language, some of his men contracted with the island men to bring women with them the next morning.

In the years to come, Lawrence Lebogue, the *Bounty*'s Nova Scotian sailmaker, claimed that he clearly remembered that Bligh "came on deck one night and found fault with Christian, because in a squall he had not taken care of the sails. It was after we left Whytootackee." Bligh himself, denying the charge that he had "frequent" quarrels with Christian, maintained, "I had never one untill after I left Otaheite." At this point, yet another account comes to bear; in a highly uneven narrative, commencing with the events immediately before the mutiny, Master John Fryer substantiated Lebogue's memory: While working the ship "to exercise the People" on April 21, Fryer recalled, close to midnight of a dark, brooding day that had seen much rain, "Mr. Bligh and Mr. Christain had some words—When Mr. Christain told Mr. Bligh—Sir your abuse is so bad that I cannot do my Duty with any Pleasure. I have been in hell for weeks with you."

With these, the first recorded words of Fletcher Christian in the entire course of the voyage, the tensions between Bligh and his chief officer leap into focus. Fryer's account is not to be taken entirely at face value—Christian's claim that he had been in hell would become a famous set piece in the telling of the *Bounty*'s story, placed by different people at different places. Nonetheless, something of Christian's state of mind had been reliably evoked.

Perhaps the most telling fact about the various narrations of the *Bounty*'s voyage up until this point is how little overlap there is between them. Bligh's rages against his officers while at Tahiti are generally only hinted at by Morrison, or ignored. Fryer's narration commences after the departure from Tahiti, and rarely looks back at past events. Complaints made by Morrison of the outward voyage have no counterparts in the other accounts. But now, as the *Bounty* continued westward, approaching Anamooka, in the Friendly Islands (Tonga), there is a dramatic and unequivocal convergence of narratives. To everyone looking back, this—not on the outward voyage, not on Tahiti—was where the trouble really began.

Bligh had nostalgic reasons for wishing to visit Anamooka, where he had come with Cook in 1777, and on arrival he made inquiries "after our old Friends." The *Resolution* had stayed here for two weeks and in the Friendly Islands for nearly two months, where Bligh joined Cook in making observations and surveys. Cook, by the time of this third and, as it would turn out, final voyage, had acquired the reputation of being an immaculate navigator and seaman, and a brilliant manager of men. His far-ranging accounts of his voyages, moreover, revealed a remarkable respect for the foreign peoples he met, and a striking reluctance to condemn outright even those alien practices that his own culture held to be immoral.

And yet, by consensus, Cook was not entirely "himself" on this third voyage. It had been here in the Friendly Islands that his new disposition had first become most disturbingly apparent. On Anamooka itself Cook had flogged a minor chief for some small theft, and then had the offender bound and taken unceremoniously onshore, where he was ransomed for the price of a hog. In Tongatapu, Cook had punished theft and stone throwing by administering floggings by the dozen and then, in a fury of impotent exasperation, slashed crosses on the thieves' naked arms. After he journeyed onward to Tahiti, Cook's punishments had become more severe. The theft of a goat prompted him to order the destruction and plunder of an entire village; the loss of a sextant led him to outright cruelty, ordering the thief's head shaved and both his ears cut off. Aghast, Cook's officers expressed their disapprobation, but for the most part were powerless to do more than mutter discontentedly in their journals. When a Tahitian prisoner escaped, Cook had his own men turned before the mast and disrated, and the errant sentinel flogged over three successive days. It is interesting to speculate what might have happened had Cook lived to return to England. Would his officers' journals have been read and searched for evidence of their captain's unworthiness to command? Would the great man have suffered the humiliation of a reprimand? Or, would he have been knighted for the accomplishment of a third magnificent voyage?

This was the man with whom William Bligh had worked side by side for almost two and a half years, and from whom he had learned some of his most valuable lessons of command. But in one respect, at least, Bligh proved himself the better man. Even in his most towering rages, Bligh was incapable of the vengeful brutality that characterized Cook at his worst on his final voyage. Bligh's threat to Tynah on Tahiti, that if the deserters were not returned he "should make the whole Country Suffer for it," had been modeled on Cook's punitive campaign through the villages; but one must doubt whether Bligh could have found it in him to destroy the pretty houses and plantations he had so enjoyed, any more than he could have cut and maimed any offender. And because of his fundamental humanity, Bligh had fewer defenses than Cook to counter the exasperating and increasingly sinister thievery and provocation that he now encountered on Anamooka Island.

From the moment Bligh arrived onshore he was unfavorably struck by the appearance of the island's people. "We met frequently both Men and Women with dreadfull Sores on their Legs, Arms and Breasts," he wrote. A woman who had recently given birth and her child were stained a macabre yellow. Many people, even children, bore the dreadful self-inflicted wounds of ritual mourning, their heads bloodied, their hair torn out by the roots and whole fingers amputated.

"Several fine Boys about 6 Years Old had lost both their little fingers," Bligh observed with horror.

On landing, Bligh dispatched two work parties: four men to go for wood under the command of the mate of the ship, William Elphinstone, who had already disgraced himself on arrival at the island by allowing the bower anchor buoy to sink "for want of a little exertion"; and eleven men for water under the command of Fletcher Christian.

"To the Waterers I ordered Arms," Bligh logged, "but to be Kept in the Boat & there only to be Used, considering them much Safer on Shore without them, unless I could have encreased the Party." He also strenuously enjoined the parties "to keep themselves unconnected with the Natives. . . . I not only gave my Orders but my advice," Bligh noted. Needless to say, both were ignored; the Indians were allowed to crowd around and distract the men, and an axe and an adze were shortly stolen.

As so often, Bligh made a distinction between the culpability of his men and of his officers. The men, he allowed, could not simultaneously do their duty—fell trees and keg water—and keep all their tools in hand. But "[a]s to the Officers I have no resource," Bligh wrote, with a kind of deadly resignation. "[O]r do I ever feel myself safe in the few instances I trust them."

Christian and his men had been harassed by a crowd at the watering place; it is not clear if they had actually been prevented from accomplish-

ing their job. Bligh's response, on being informed of these circum-
stances, is vividly recorded by both Morrison and Fryer. Bligh damned
Christian "for a Cowardly rascal, asking him if he was afraid of a set of
Naked Savages while He had arms," according to Morrison, "to which
Mr. Christian answerd 'the Arms are no use while your orders prevent
them from being used.'"

The following day, Christian was sent back with his party to finish the
work. Somewhat later, Fryer was sent ashore to "Hurry Mr Christian off
with the Launch." On landing, Fryer had to ask the way to the watering
place of a man and woman who stood nearby. Pointing to meandering
lanes that led between plantations, the couple encouraged him to follow
them. A short distance along the path, Fryer, feeling, one senses, very
much alone, encountered Matthew Quintal rolling a barrel of water
toward the boat. After delivering the cask, both men turned back for the
watering place.

"Quintal call'd out Mr Fryer there a man going to knock you down
with his club," Fryer recalled. "I turn myself round rather surprised,
when I saw the Man Brandishing his club over my head." The man escaped into the plantations, and Fryer, "not arm'd even with a stik," arrived at the watering place, about a quarter of a mile from shore. Here
Fryer found "Mr Christain was getting the water fill'd as fast as he
could—but there was a number of Natives about him some heaving
stones frequently and one cheif with a Very long spare [spear] frequently
point'd at Mr Christain." (It would be at Anamooka that Lieutenant Corner of the *Pandora* was also to run into trouble, also while getting water;
when clubbed on the back of his head, Corner turned and shot his assailant.) With some panic, Fryer told Christian to get the casks to the
waiting cutter, "empty or full," while he fobbed off the milling crowd
with gifts of nails. On reaching the cutter, it was discovered that her
crew, according to Fryer, "in stead of complying with my orders in keeping the Boat off with their oars—had let the grapnail go—and got playing tricks with the Boys & Girls that came into the water." While the
diverting children gamboled in the water, the grapnel, or small anchor,
was slipped off its line by an enterprising diver and stolen.

"[H]e was very warm about the lost of the Grapnail," was how Fryer described Bligh's reaction to this piece of news. Immediately, Bligh proposed a plan for its recovery; he would "detain" some of the chiefs who were on board until the theft was made good. This ploy, of course, had been used with mixed success by Captain Cook. Badly rattled by events onshore, Fryer weakly informed his commanding officer that, as there were several more grapnels on board, the "loss was not very great."

"[N]ot very great Sir," Bligh replied furiously. "[B]y God Sir if it is not great to you it is great to me."

"I told him," said Fryer, flailing in the hole he had dug, "that I was very sorry that we had lost the Grapnail—but being sorry I thought was of no use."

Bligh's own account is brief. Noting that he had sent Fryer with the watering party, along with Nelson who wanted plants, his log reports that "[o]ne lost the Grapnel and the other a Spade and met with some insults." Bligh thought highly of Nelson, and this fact may have mitigated his anger, for he appears to have been focused only on regaining the grapnel; no report is given of his anger toward the men involved.

In the midst of this confusion, two hours' leave was granted to the men still on the ship for trade, since, as Morrison noted, "this was likely to be the last Island where Iron currency was the most valuable." Curiosities such as spears, clubs and mats, as well as large quantities of yams and coconuts, were purchased by all hands in exchange for their all-valuable nails. When everything was stowed on board—piled even into the cutter and jolly boat for lack of deck space—Bligh, in his own words, "gave directions to unmoor" and "secretly determined to confine" the chiefs; this, after all, was what Cook had done.

"[W]e had hoistd the fore topmast Staysail and the Ship was easting, two hands up loosing the Foretopsail," Fryer wrote, "when I heard Mr. Bligh call out, hand the arms up."

"Why dont you come to assist me Sir," Bligh greeted Fryer. The master now discovered that the call for arms was in order to guard the detained chiefs. Local rumor, however, already reported the grapnel had been carried away to another island.

"[M]ean while we were under arms some of the People was rather awkward, when Mr. Bligh made a speech to them told them that they were all a parcel of good for nothing Rascals." This was the first time, on record at least, that Bligh had complained about his "People," as opposed to his officers. Morrison recalled the incident somewhat differently. After taking the detained chiefs below, Bligh returned on deck.

"He then came up and dismissd all the Men but two, that were under arms, but not till he had passd the Compliment on officers & Men to tell them that they were a parcel of lubberly rascals and that he would be one of five who would with good sticks would disarm the whole of them." The day had clearly seen an unpleasant dressing-down of the entire company, either rightly, or quite possibly wrongly. The detained and frightened chiefs—"those poor miserable fellows," as Fryer described them—were, according to Bligh, "Vastly Surprized" at their predicament and assured Bligh that a canoe would be sent after the thieves and the grapnel.

As the hours passed, great long canoes followed the ship, "full of People making sad lamentations for their chiefs," as Fryer wrote. By late afternoon, all but one impressive double canoe had left them, full of weeping women and the oldest chief, all lamenting and inflicting on themselves the wounds of ritual mourning.

Still, no grapnel had appeared.

"I however detained them untill Sun Down," wrote Bligh of the chiefs, "when they began to be very uneasy, beat themselves about their Eyes with their fists and at last cried bitterly." As before, when he had tried to stay aloof from Tynah, Bligh appears not to have had the stomach to carry out his charade.

"I now told them I should not detain them any longer and called their Cannoes alongside to take them in, at which they were exceedingly rejoiced," was Bligh's account of the abrupt termination to the standoff. Each of the captives was given a hatchet, saw, nails and other desirable ironware, at which they "showed such gratitude and thanks for my goodness that it affected all of us," is how Bligh concludes this bewildering chapter. Two of the chiefs, according to Morrison, "[s]eemd as if they only smotherd their resentment, seeing that they could not revenge the insult."

At the end of this fraught day, Bligh had gained absolutely nothing by his heavy-handed mismanagement of almost everything recorded of this harried and unsettling visit to Anamooka. His losses, on the other hand, were disastrous. To his men, only three weeks out of Tahiti, with the memories of *taios* and lovers and many kindnesses received still vivid, the treatment of the chiefs was probably genuinely shocking. Nothing like it had been enacted onshore, and Bligh must have lost much moral stature in their eyes. He had also, as it were, lost the game. When the chiefs and *Bounty* parted company, the chiefs left with their many presents, the *Bounty* without her grapnel.

But it is the milling confusion at the watering place that stands at the tantalizing center of the Anamooka sojourn, for it is here that Fletcher Christian was most specifically and directly embroiled. No report makes clear what Christian had in fact done to warrant Bligh's damning him for a "cowardly rascal."

Bligh's very specific instructions regarding the use of arms, which surely struck his men as being almost incomprehensibly unreasonable, were firmly based, once again, upon experience with Cook. Bligh had seen how useful arms had been in February 1779, at Hawaii's Kealakekua Bay. Here, the *Resolution* and the *Discovery* had come for repairs, and here Cook and his men suffered the usual petty thieving. But when the ship's cutter was stolen, Cook had loaded his double-barreled musket, one barrel with shot and one with ball, and accompanied by Lieutenant Molesworth Phillips at the head of nine armed marines, had strode ashore. The crowd he met with on arrival was suspicious and hostile; it was also armed with spears and stones, and the people gathered protectively around their chief, whom, indeed, Cook had intended to take hostage. A man made a menacing movement at Cook, something was thrown and Cook fired his shot—to no effect, for his assailant was protected by stout matting. The crowd grew more threatening, throwing stones, and Cook fired ball. This time he killed a man; his lieutenant of marines fired, the marines fired and the crowd overwhelmed them all. Minutes later, the men in the waiting boats watched with stunned horror as Cook was clubbed from behind and fell facedown into the water as he attempted to reach one of the boats. He was then clubbed to death in the shallows.

"I not only gave my Orders but my advice," Bligh had told Christian and his men, as they set out on the wood and watering parties; his advice was a personal admonition, concerned, perhaps even friendly. It was based upon what he, Bligh, knew: that no word or gesture should be made to engage a suspect crowd, that loaded arms endowed their bearers with fatal confidence, that the wrong shot fired at the wrong time could precipitate trouble, not quell it. Morrison's account vindicates Bligh's concerns.

The crowd, Morrison wrote, was "very rude & attempted to take the Casks from the Waterers and the axes from the Wooding party; and if a Musquet was pointed at any of them produced no other effect than a return of the Compliment, by poising their Club or Spear with a menacing look." Morrison's account also confirms that Bligh's orders had been ignored: Bligh had stipulated that the arms be kept in the boats, knowing that if events took an ugly turn, the boats providing the getaway were the objects that must at all cost be safeguarded.

Like most of the crew, Christian had not sailed with Cook. He did not perhaps know that the taking of hostages had, as it were, naval precedent and was not merely some underhanded act of tyranny devised by Bligh; nor was the ship's company likely to have appreciated Bligh's insights into the finer points of crowd management.

It was now April 27, 1789. For the past several days the weather had been unremarkable, with light easterly winds, and cloudy. On leaving Anamooka, the *Bounty* headed north toward Tofua, the northwesternmost of the Friendly Islands. By night, the air had become so light and still that the ship made little progress. Away to the west, a volcano on Tofua erupted, shooting flame and columns of smoke into the night sky, a spectacle enjoyed by the men on ship. The same still, calm weather held into the morning when Bligh came up for a turn about the quarterdeck and, taking a hard look at the coconuts piled between the guns, sent for Fryer.

"Mr. Fryer," said Bligh, according to Fryer, "don't you think that those Cocoanuts are shrunk since last Night?"

"I told him," said Fryer, "that they were not so high as they were last night, as I had them stowd up to the Rail but," as he added diplomatically, "that the people might have pull them Down—in walking over them in the Night."

Bligh thought not. "[H]e said No that they had been taken away and that he would find out who had taken them." Churchill, the master-at-arms (Morrison says it was Elphinstone, the master's mate), was then ordered to bring up all the nuts from belowdecks, along with their owners.

"'Every Body,' he repeated several times."

One by one, Bligh addressed his officers. "'Mr. Young—how many Nuts did you bye?' 'So many Sir.' '& How many did you eat?'" Young did not know, but there was the remainder to be counted. Morrison implied that the interrogation was only of the officers, while Fryer specifically noted "then all the other Gentlemen was calld and likewise the People." Fryer made no mention at all of Fletcher Christian; indeed, Edward Young is the only person singled out in his version. But in Morrison's narration, Christian is placed front and center.

Bligh, according to Morrison, "questioned every Officer in turn concerning the Number they had bought, & coming to Mr. Christian askd Him, Mr. Christian answerd 'I do not know Sir, but I hope you dont think me so mean as to be Guilty of Stealing Yours.' Mr. Bligh replied 'Yes you dam'd Hound I do—You must have stolen them from me or you could give a better account of them—God dam you you Scoundrels you are all thieves alike, and combine with the men to rob me—I suppose you'll Steal my Yams next, but I'll sweat you for it you rascals I'll make half of you jump overboard before you get through Endeavour Streights.'"

"'I take care of you now for my own good—but when I get you thro the Straits you may all go to hell,' and if they did not look out sharp that he would do for one half of them" was how Fryer condensed this same speech.

In Fryer's account, Bligh concluded this showdown by telling "Every Body that he allowd them a pound and a half of yams, which was more than there Allowance—but if he did not find out who took the Nuts that he would put them on ¾ of a pound of Yams." Fryer's almost parenthetical aside—"which was more than there Allowance"—is such an oddly reasonable qualification of Bligh's threat that it must, one senses, be true; Fryer's narrative was not intended to be complimentary to Bligh, and this detail was unlikely to have been invented. This same concluding threat, however, Morrison reported somewhat differently.

"Stop these Villains Grog, and Give them but half a Pound of Yams to-morrow," Bligh is said to have commanded his clerk, Mr. Samuel. "[A]nd if they steal then, I'll reduce them to a quarter." Bligh went below, according to Morrison, at which "the officers then got together and were heard to murmur much at such treatment, and it was talkd among the Men that the Yams would be next seized."

Later reports would depict Christian as having been not only wounded but shattered by this confrontation. William Purcell would state that Christian came from Bligh with tears "running fast from his eyes in big drops."

"What is the matter Mr. Christian?" Purcell had asked—which is itself intriguing; if all had happened as reported, surely he knew?

"Can you ask me, and hear the treatment I receive?" Christian had asked; to which Purcell had replied, "Do I not receive as bad as you do?"

"[Y]ou have something to protect you," Christian said to Purcell. He was referring to the carpenter's warrant, which forbade that he be flogged; although designated "acting lieutenant" of the voyage by Bligh, Christian was still officially a master's mate, which amounted more or less to a senior midshipman.

"[Y]ou have something to protect you, and can speak again; but if I should speak to him as you do"—apparently the carpenter's verbal defiance was well recognized—"he would probably break me, turn me before the mast, and perhaps flog me; and if he did, it would be the death of us both, for I am sure I should take him in my arms, and jump overboard with him."

"Never mind it, it is but for a short time longer," was Purcell's parting, buck-up-it's-not-as-bad-as-you-think advice. To this Christian is said to have replied, "In going through Endeavour Straits, I am sure the ship will be a hell." Hell was to come up a good deal in Christian's later speeches.

All reports agree that after this blowup, Bligh went contentedly about his business; the coconut incident receives no mention whatsoever in either his private or official log. Afterward, he resumed his custom of inviting Christian to dine with him, as Christian had done every third evening of the voyage. Christian declined, sending word he was indisposed, upon which Thomas Hayward accepted Bligh's offer, and, according to Fryer, was hissed by the other young gentlemen when he left.

Writing to Bligh some years after the events, Edward Lamb, who had sailed with Bligh and Christian on the *Britannia*'s last voyage as chief mate, back when they were working in the West Indies, made some skeptical observations about Fletcher Christian. "When we got to sea, and I saw your partiality for the young man," the former mate told Bligh, "I gave him every advice and information in my power, though he went about every point of duty with a degree of indifference, that to me was truly unpleasant; but you were blind to his faults, and had him to dine and sup every other day in the cabin, and treated him like a brother, in giving him every information."

All available evidence indicates that this favoritism had continued on the *Bounty*. Of Christian—and of Peter Heywood—Bligh was shortly to write, "These two were objects of my regard and attention . . . for they realy promised as professional Men to be an honor to their Country." This was high praise from Bligh and suggests that in spite of whatever specific causes of complaint he may have had against the master's mate, he was not, all in all, dissatisfied with his protégé's progress. It was then not Bligh who broke with Christian, but Christian who broke with Bligh.

Exactly why or precisely when Christian had began to succumb to the pressure of serving under his irascible commander is impossible to ascertain. In reports that would later emerge he was quoted as saying he had been in hell "for weeks past," "for two weeks," or in other words, since the *Bounty* left Tahiti. Central to Christian's state of mind appears to have been the extraordinary idea that Bligh might either break or flog him. Bligh's log hints darkly at "condign" and "corporal punishment" being in order, so it is not impossible that he made such a threat in one of his passions. But if so, one would expect an event of such blazing significance to be referred to by Morrison or Fryer; or Heywood in his letters; or in testimony in the court-martial; or in later rumored accounts. No such allegation was ever made.

Sixteen months earlier, at the riverside inn with his brother Charles before the *Bounty* sailed, Fletcher Christian had gained a breathtaking insight into how powerless a man could be made, officer or seaman, in

the hands of a tyrannical captain, as his brother related all that had happened on the *Middlesex*.

"His passions were raised against me, to a more violent degree than
formerly. Let him speak the truth, and he cannot assign a reasonable
cause . . . sent for me, bent me, ordered me to be flogged to death"; so
had Fletcher learned one of the men in the *Middlesex* mutiny had
protested his treatment. From his impassioned brother, who had leaped
into the fray, Fletcher had also learned there was honor in resistance.

The fact that Bligh invited Christian to join him on the usual terms of
friendship at his table suggests that Bligh himself, for all his passionate
language, did not seriously entertain any such thoughts of violence
against his master's mate. "Passionate" was a term that would be used of
Bligh throughout his life, even by his supportive relatives. Cook had
been passionate too; behind his back his men had referred to his impressive foot-stamping, fist-shaking rages as "*heivas*," after the exuberant
Tahitian dances. The impotence of young officers in the face of their captains' intemperate rule was, moreover, simply an established fact of
naval tradition. "The state of inferior officers in his majesty's service is a
state of vassalage," an officer of this era had reflected. "[T]hat power of
reducing them to sweep the decks, being lodged in the breast of a captain, is often abused through passion or caprice."

Bligh's passions were verbal, not physical, and it is unlikely that he
was aware of half of what he said. Nonetheless, something had shaken
Christian to the core.

"He is subject to violent perspirations, and particularly in his hands,
so that he soils any thing he touches," Bligh would write of Christian, in
his description of this apparently well-made, well-looking young man.
One may be sure that Christian was sweating now.

By late afternoon of this unpleasant day, Bligh headed the *Bounty* due
west, so as to pass to the south of Tofua, and be on course for her jog to
the Endeavour Strait; this represented a decisive stage on the homeward
voyage, since to turn back, for any reason, would be to sail against the
now prevailing easterly wind. The evening passed without incident, and
if Bligh was oblivious that some dark and critical line had been crossed

in Christian's mind, it appears everyone else was too. Only in relentless painstaking retrospect would anything be detected amiss.

John Fryer had the first watch of the night, eight P.M. to midnight, and noted with pleasure that at about ten o'clock the weather cleared. About an hour later Bligh came on deck, as was customary, to give Fryer his orders for the night.

"We at that time was upon speaking terms," Fryer noted.

A welcome breeze had arisen, promising better sailing than had been seen for some days. Both men stood looking out over the ruffled night water and observed the new moon, which Fryer noted would be "lucky for us to come on the coast of New Holland."

"Yes, Mr. Fryer," replied Bligh, "it will be very lucky for us." Shortly afterward, Bligh took his leave and went below.

At midnight, Fryer was relieved by William Peckover, who, according to Fryer, "had a very pleasant watch."

"[E]very thing very quiet on board," as Fryer wrote. Four hours later, at four A.M., Peckover in turn was relieved by Fletcher Christian. The *Bounty* was by now some ten leagues south of Tofua.

After taking leave of Fryer, Bligh had retired to his small and windowless cabin; perhaps he had looked in on the nursery to admire the well-ordered ranks of flourishing plants and the pleasing wake of his ship through the great cabin window. As was his habit, Bligh left his door open and unlocked, so as to be immediately accessible if he were needed. Presumably, he would have fallen asleep by midnight.

He was awoken five hours later, at dawn, by the weight of hands being pressed upon him. In sheer astonishment, he came to his senses to find Fletcher Christian, Charles Churchill, John Mills, the gunner's mate, and Thomas Burkett, seaman, under arms. Bligh was roughly seized and his hands bound behind his back.

"Murder!" Bligh shouted at the top of his voice, as he was pushed up the stairway in his nightshirt, passing other men, also under arms, stationed outside his cabin door. Once on deck, there was a blur of confused activity, voices shouting, mocking, giving orders, whispering encouragement. Christian was calling for a boat to be lowered; first one was chosen and then another. Some two and a half hours later, the ship's large launch was in the water, and Christian was giving orders for men to enter it.

Different people made different pleas to Christian. Bligh, tied in his nightshirt and naked from the waist down, was hoarse from shouting. One by one, with small bundles of belongings, the men Christian ordered passed over the side of their ship into the boat below.

John Samuel, the clerk, at considerable personal risk had secured Bligh's log, commission and the all-important "pursery" books. "All this he did with great resolution, being guarded and Strictly Watched," wrote Bligh. Nevertheless, fifteen years of charts, surveys and drawings had to be left behind.

Christian, so distracted and in such disarray as to frighten those who looked on him, continued to hold the rope that bound Bligh, and to point a bayonet at his chest.

"[H]e seemed to be plotting instant destruction on himself and everyone," Bligh would write, "for of all diabolical looking Men he exceeded every possible description." Hayward and Hallett had been ordered into the boat, while Fryer begged to remain but was sent over the side. But, contrary to all the mutineers' expectations, other men, with Purcell in the lead, voluntarily filed over the side to join their captain.

The launch measured 23 feet in length; at its widest, it had a breadth of 6 feet 9 inches; its depth was 2 feet 9 inches. Eighteen men were now stowed in her, along with the possessions and supplies they had been able to garner: 150 pounds of bread, 32 pounds of pork, 6 quarts of rum, 6 bottles of wine and 28 gallons of water—enough, under normal circumstances, for some five days.

"Come, Captain Bligh, your Officers and Men are now in the Boat and you must go with them," Christian said, addressing Bligh with haunting formality.

"When they were forcing me out of the ship, I asked him, if this treatment was a proper return for the many instances he had received of my friendship," Bligh recorded. He also implored Christian more directly: "Consider Mr. Christian, I have a wife and four children in England, and you have danced my children upon your knee.

"[H]e appeared disturbed at my question, and answered with much emotion, 'That!—captain Bligh,—that is the thing—I am in hell—I am in hell.'"

Christian would later confess to being taken aback by the number of men who of their own volition left the *Bounty*. The launch was by now a fearful sight, so overcrowded that she showed no more than seven inches of freeboard above the calm morning water. Later, a defense made by those who remained on the ship would be that it was evident to all that to join the boat would have been tantamount to suicide. "Something more than fear had possessed them to suffer themselves to be sent away in such a manner without offering to make resistance," was Christian's own wondering assessment.

Men loyal to Bligh, who had sought to join the launch and been turned away, now called out to Bligh to remember them. In the confusion of those few terrible and incomprehensible hours, many would forget who said what, who stood where, even who stood under arms. Words would be remembered and misremembered, facial expressions recalled with ambiguity. But one incident was graven into the memory of everyone who saw it. With his ashen men crowded into the launch, surrounded by the boundless Pacific, with no charts and little food, their captain addressed the loyalists detained on board. In a voice that carried across what seems to have been a sudden silence, Bligh called out, "Never fear, my lads; I'll do you justice if ever I reach England!"

RETURN

On the evening of March 13, 1790, moving cautiously through dangerous, foggy weather, a Dutch East Indiaman approached the Isle of Wight. Impatiently peering through the fog, and taking pointed note that the Dutch captain was "very much frightened" by the thick conditions, was Lieutenant William Bligh, a passenger. Catching an Isle of Wight boat, Bligh was in Portsmouth by midnight. The following morning he left by post chaise for London, and by Monday morning the fifteenth, he was at the Admiralty's door. It was ten and a half months—321 days—since the mutiny on the *Bounty*, and William Bligh had returned to England.

The story of the extraordinary events in the Pacific, and of Lieutenant Bligh's 3,618-mile voyage in an overloaded open boat, was immediately the talk of London. In all the centuries of the kingdom's remarkable naval history, no feat of seamanship was deemed to surpass Bligh's navigation and command of the *Bounty*'s 23-foot-long launch, and few feats of survival compared with his men's forty-eight-day ordeal on starvation rations. For months afterward, national and local press carried stories about the *Bounty* and Bligh's "wonderful escape at sea."

"This officer only holds the rank of Lieutenant in our navy," the *English Chronicle* stated, "and the distresses he has undergone, entitle him to every reward—In navigating his little skiff through so dangerous a sea, his seamanship appears as matchless, as the undertaking seems beyond the verge of probability."

Those with keen interest in the story were soon able to look forward to reading Bligh's remarkable adventure in his own words. Less than two months after his return to England, the imminent publication of Lieutenant Bligh's "Narrative," illustrated and with charts, was announced in the London press. In June the book appeared: a slender work of only eighty-eight quarto pages, entitled *A Narrative of the Mutiny, on Board His Majesty's Ship Bounty; and the Subsequent Voyage of Part of the Crew, in the Ship's Boat, From Tofoa, one of the Friendly Islands, to Timor, a Dutch Settlement in the East Indies.* Taken directly and with little embellishment from Bligh's log and the notebook he had kept in the launch, this essentially modest work was the first public account of both his ordeal in the boat and the mutiny of the *Bounty.* From the outset, the *Narrative* had been conceived as only part of what would eventually be a more expansive and complete work, but even in its abbreviated form it received enormously favorable reviews.

Bligh's *Narrative* began with the mutiny, with the taunts and rough laughter, the threats to blow out his brains and the oaths of the pirates—"Damn your eyes, you are well off to get what you have." As the *Bounty* slipped behind the launch, cries of "Huzza for Otaheite" had been raised by the mutineers.

"As soon as I had time to reflect, I felt an inward satisfaction, which prevented any depression of my spirits," Bligh reported in his published book. This was not after-the-fact bravado, but taken directly from his running log, which he continued to maintain, along with a rough notebook, until his return to England. Indeed, his personal log had expressed his immediate state of mind even more optimistically.

"I had scarce got a furlong on our way when I began to reflect on the vicisitude of human affairs"—Bligh had written these words either as the launch made slow progress toward Tofua, or, under yet more trying circumstances, on the beach of Tofua itself—"but in the midst of all I felt an inward happyness which prevented any depression of my spirits; conscious of my own integrity and anxious solicitude for the good of the service I was on—I found my mind most wonderfully supported, and began to conceive hopes notwithstanding so heavy a calamity, to be able to account to my King & Country for my misfortune."

The boat's immediate course lay for Tofua, at only ten leagues distant the nearest landfall, where it was hoped that supplies of fruit and water could be acquired. The provisions in the launch amounted to five days of rations for the nineteen men under normal ship usage. The sea remained calm and unthreatening and by nightfall of the following day the launch was riding off the island's rocky shore; the *Bounty*, with her cheering crew, had long since vanished into the haze of the horizon. At daybreak, Bligh began a patrol of the shoreline, searching for a landing and scavenging for water, plantains and coconuts. After three days of this routine, some of the island's inhabitants had appeared, friendly at first, bringing coconut shells full of water to Bligh's parched men, and trading food for buttons and beads. In response to the islanders' inquiries, Bligh replied that their ship had been wrecked.

"[T]hey seemed readily satisfyed with our Account," Bligh logged, "but there did not appear the least mark of Joy or Sorrow in their Faces, altho I fancied I discovered some signs of surprize." All of the *Bounty* men were on edge, knowing from their experience at Anamooka that even a large company of British sailors, armed with muskets and with a ship at their backs, did not necessarily inspire awe.

Stormy weather as well as the hope of obtaining further provisions held the men at Tofua, and over the next few days the size of the crowd of curious islanders increased. Several professed to having heard of the *Bounty*'s visit to Anamooka—a statement of ambiguous significance, given the events at that place; a young man appeared whom Bligh had seen at Anamooka, and who expressed "much pleasure" at seeing him. Eventually, Bligh logged, "I observed some symptoms of a design against us." Some of the crowd had attempted to draw the launch up onshore. Quietly, Bligh ordered his men to gather their possessions while he continued to make purchases of breadfruit and the occasional spear; four cutlasses, tossed over the side of the *Bounty* at the last minute, were held in readiness in the boat.

The ensuing events would prove to be as harrowing as any the company encountered in their long ordeal. Nothing met with at sea terrified the men so much as the sudden, palpable hostility of the crowd that now lined the beach. No words were spoken; there was only an ominous clacking of stones knocked against one another.

"I knew very well," wrote Bligh, "this was the sign of an attack." The same *clack-clack* had presaged an attack on Cook's voyage and was drilled into his memory. As his men drifted with studied casualness down to the launch, Bligh sat at the entrance of the cave where they had set their camp and, while the increasingly raucous crowd pressed close round him, made a great show of writing up his log.

"Stay the night onshore," said two of the chiefs, who now approached him.

"No, I never sleep out of my boat," Bligh replied.

"You will not sleep onshore?" was the response. "Then *Mattie*," which, as Bligh observed, "directly signifies we will kill you." The knocking of stones continued and the mounting tension on both sides betrayed that decisive action was imminent. Taking one of the men, Nageete, firmly by the hand, Bligh made his way with Purcell to the boat through the jostling, pressing mob, "every one in a silent kind of horror." By the boat, Nageete broke free of Bligh's grasp; all the men piled into the launch save one, big John Norton, a quartermaster from Liverpool, who, impelled by long years of dutiful training, splashed out into the water to cast off the stern line. While Fryer and others frantically called Norton back, Bligh clambered on board. A shower of stones fell on Norton like heavy hail, knocking him to the beach, where he was set upon by five of the Tofuans. Others began hauling on the stern line, dragging the launch toward the shore. Struggling with his knife, Bligh cut the line and the launch was free. As the boat pulled away, twelve of the Tofuans leaped into their canoes and began chase. Onshore, the men around Norton could be seen beating the fallen man's head with stones, while others pulled off his trousers. As the canoes closed in, Bligh and Peckover hurled out clothes and other valuable provisions. The ruse worked, and as the canoes stopped to collect the plunder, the launch pulled away.

"The poor man I lost was John Norton," Bligh recorded. "[T]his was his second voyage with me as a quarter-master"—Norton, then, had also

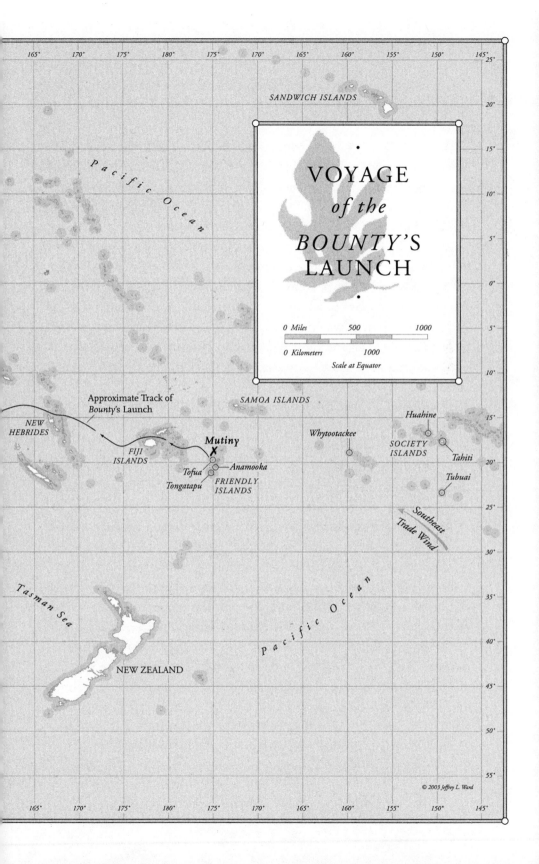

165°   170°   175°   180°   175°   170°   165°   160°   155°   150°   145°
25°

SANDWICH ISLANDS

20°

15°

VOYAGE
of the
BOUNTY'S
LAUNCH

10°

5°

0°

P a c i f i c   O c e a n

0 Miles   500   1000

0 Kilometers   1000

Scale at Equator

5°

10°

Approximate Track of
Bounty's Launch

SAMOA ISLANDS

Huahine

15°

*NEW
HEBRIDES*

Whytootackee

*SOCIETY
ISLANDS*

Mutiny
✗

*FIJI
ISLANDS*

Tahiti

20°

Tofua   *Anamooka*

Tongatapu   *FRIENDLY
ISLANDS*

Tubuai

*Southeast
Trade Wind*

25°

30°

T a s m a n   S e a

P a c i f i c   O c e a n

35°

40°

NEW ZEALAND

45°

50°

55°

165°   170°   175°   180°   175°   170°   165°   160°   155°   150°   145°

sailed with Christian—"and his worthy character made me lament his loss very much. He has left an aged parent, I am told, whom he supported."

Wounded by the rain of stones, and horribly shaken, the men in the launch now made a fateful and historic decision. There would be no more island visits. Tahiti was out of the question on account of the risk of running into the mutineers. There remained, as Bligh told his men, "no hope of relief . . . until I came to Timor," some 3,600 miles away. There was a Dutch settlement, civilization and ships that could carry them to Europe—although "in what part of the island I knew not." Coldly assessing the boat's "stock," Bligh extracted the "sacred promise" from each man to live upon the rations he would set: one ounce of bread and a quarter pint of water per day. A set of scales was later improvised from coconut shells and on this the ration of bread and occasional salt pork was balanced against a musket bullet weighing a twenty-fifth of a pound.

The plan of action having been determined, the men set about making the boat shipshape. The company was divided into three watches, not only for the usual ship functions, but to enable the men to find physical space in the impossibly overcrowded boat. While others lay prone on the boards, attempting to sleep, the watch on duty gained the space necessary to sit up, bail and work the sails.

Before retiring on this first night of the great voyage, the men offered prayers of thanks for their "miraculous preservation." The wind had arisen sufficient to warrant reefing the foresail; the launch carried two sails, both lug-rigged, fore and midships. Despite her service to the men, she never acquired a name, being known throughout all the years her story would be told as simply "the Bounty's launch."

On the morning of May 3, the sun "rose very firey and Red, a sure indication of a Severe Gale." By eight in the morning, the launch was in a violent sea, with waves running so high that she floundered becalmed when in the troughs of their valleys. Despite the men's nonstop bailing, a following sea threatened to swamp them. "A situation more distressing has, perhaps, seldom been experienced," Bligh wrote. The precious bread was stowed in the carpenter's chest and all superfluous items—

clothes, sails, lines—were thrown overboard. The fearsomely slender freeboard—the length of a man's hand as one man described it, in calm seas—was of the greatest concern, and no excess weight of any kind could be accommodated.

The terrors and discomforts that the men experienced during the first twenty-four hours at sea would be endured for the next twenty-four days: Downpours of rain and nights of numbing cold, and the small boat continually awash with the onslaught of unremitting waves. At times, great storms of prodigious lightning crackled and forked around them, the sky booming and thundering as the launch dipped and skittered across the face of the Pacific. The bailing, bailing without respite took a severe toll on the increasingly exhausted and starving men. A frightening lassitude claimed them, so that some could barely stir their limbs; all the men were unbearably cramped, from the cold, from the impossibility of ever stretching. As the voyage progressed, the men were wracked by a dreadful tenesmus, the ineffectual straining of their unvoided bowels.

Three times a day—at breakfast, at dinner and at supper—Bligh weighed and distributed the pitiful rations. On days and nights when the wet cold took more than its usual toll, he administered carefully measured teaspoonfuls of rum. As the sea was at all times warmer than the air, the men repeatedly soaked their clothes in the ocean.

"I would recommend to every one in a similar situation the method we practiced," Bligh advised, straight-faced, in his published *Narrative*, "which is to dip their cloaths in the salt-water, and wring them out. . . . We had occasion to do this so often, that at length all our cloaths were wrung to pieces."

Bligh had set course first to the west northwest, by way of the Fiji Islands, which had been rumored by islanders' reports to lie this way, and then west toward the Endeavour Strait and New Holland. Although the launch carried no charts, Bligh had a quadrant, a compass and the necessary tables required for basic navigation, along with a broken and unreliable sextant. Bligh had a knotted log line made from extra rope and taught lubbers like David Nelson to count off the seconds between knots.

"I have hitherto been only able to keep an imperfect account of our

Run," Bligh recorded on May 5, "but have now got ourselves a little better equipped and a line Marked, & having practiced at counting Seconds,
every one can do it with some exactness." The instruction in itself provided valuable diversion. Bligh also "amused all hands, with describing
the situation of New Guinea and New Holland," taking care to convey to
them all he knew "in case any Accident happened to me." Although
William Peckover, the gunner, had been to Timor on Cook's first voyage,
that had been nearly twenty years ago, when he had been barely nineteen,
and the charts they were steering by resided mostly in Bligh's memory.

The launch met with the Fiji Islands as supposed, an event Bligh
logged with a careful description of the high and low land, the isles and
reefs and rocky places for future navigators. This passage in the *Bounty*
launch, in fact, represented the first European navigation through this
important group.

The long days and nights of rain at least enabled the parched men to
gather water and slake their thirst, although as Bligh noted, "being extremely wet, and no dry things to shift or cover us, we experienced cold
and shiverings scarce to be conceived."

By May 17, some of the men had begun to implore Bligh to increase
their rations, "but," Bligh recorded, "I positively refused it." The night
had been wracking, "truly horrible," dark, thick, and starless, but rent by
great outbursts of lightning and thunder. When the long run of rain at
last abated, "[e]very person now complained of violent pain in their
Bones."

After a fleeting day of respite, the rain began again, a deluge in a
night "so dark we could scarce see each other." At daybreak, Bligh began
to fear for his men; "some of my People half dead," he logged. "Our appearances were horrible, and I could look no way but I caught the Eye of
some one in distress. Extreme hunger is now evident." As an almost
sublime record of extreme suffering and undaunted resolution, few documents can compare with the log William Bligh kept in the *Bounty*'s
launch. In its stark phrases, dutifully penned at each day's end, are conjured both the horror of the men's ordeal and Bligh's own firm and unwavering attention to all the responsibilities of his command: "Our
situation to day highly perilous. . . . I however got propped up and made

an Observation. . . . Not a Star to be seen to Steer by and the Sea break-ing constantly over us . . . We are covered with Rain and Sea that we can scarce see or make use of our Eyes . . . every person complaining, and some of them solliciting extra allowance, but I positively refused it. . . . At Noon after writing up my Account I divided the two Birds. . . . For my own part a great share of spirits and no doubt of being able to accomplish the Voyage seems to be my principal Support. . . ."

In the following days, new, strong gales brought not just more days and nights of heavy, unassailable rain, but very high seas.

"Our situation to day was highly perilous," Bligh wrote, "the least Error in the Helm would in a Moment be our destruction." The people bailed "with horror and anxiety"; the bone-deep cold, the dreadful constriction of every muscle in their bodies and the frightening numbness had debilitated many. But at noon on May 23, the weather broke, somewhat, the gales and high seas continuing but now under fair, clear skies. The capture of several boobies on the twenty-sixth had an immediate effect on morale. The birds were divided according to sailors' tradition, with one man turning his back on his fellows, and answering the question "Who shall have this?" as each unseen portion was prepared. The blood was given to "three of the most distressed."

By now, Bligh knew that he was off the coast of New Holland, and began to strategize his approach to the Great Barrier Reef. "From my recollection of Captn. Cooks Survey of this Coast I considered the situation of it to be N.W. . . . the Wind mostly to the Southward of East, I could range such a barrier of Reefs until I found a passage," he logged, demonstrating how keenly he had retained his wits and navigational acumen, when others were already sunk by hunger and exposure into deadening lethargy.

On the morning of May 28, the men caught sight of the reef, over which the sea broke in warning foam. Beyond lay quiet water and beyond this, land. With the wind rising, Bligh did not dare more than range along the reef, with all eyes straining for sight of a safe passage to the peaceful water beyond. Eventually, such a break was spotted a mile distant, and the exhausted men sailed and rowed through; Providential Channel, Bligh called the passage.

"Soon after I had got within the Reefs the Coast began to show itself very distinctly," Bligh wrote. Toward dark, a small, sandy-beached island loomed up, and when closer inspection proved it to be deserted, Bligh gave the order for the launch to land. In his *Narrative* Bligh described this event characteristically, with little fanfare, but Fryer's recollection was vivid.

"[W]e were like so many drunken men," he wrote, "in setting so long in the Boat and being so weak that when I first landed my head was so light that I fell down." Half the company sprawled out in the boat, half stumbled out to sleep on land. They remained for two full days, sleeping, eating oysters and, despite Bligh's warning, gorging on berries, which so disastrously shocked their attenuated systems that the men feared they had been poisoned. Bligh busied himself with his journal, entering long descriptions of the types of berries, birds, insects and flora, as well as taking observations. A full month had passed since he had been roughly awoken in his snug cabin; the *Bounty*, Tahiti, breadfruit, even Fletcher Christian, must have all seemed very far away.

Over the next four days, the men island-hopped along the coastline of New Holland, which Bligh roughly charted as he passed along, steadily working northwest toward Endeavour Strait, that passage whose navigation the Admiralty had so ardently desired. Methodically, Bligh conned the launch around and through the false islands, shoals and reefs that made a treacherous maze of these waters. On the afternoon of June 4, the launch arrived at the northernmost tip of New Holland. The Barrier Reef and the strait were now safely behind and all that remained was the 1,100-mile stretch of open water to Timor.

"At eight o'clock in the evening, we once more launched into the open ocean," Bligh wrote. He was surprised to see his men looking almost cheerfully restored; they fancied they could see the end of their ordeal.

"So much confidence gave me great pleasure," Bligh continued, and added a flash of insight that suggests he may have been more psychologically attuned to his men than he was accustomed to let on: "[A]nd I may assert that to this cause their preservation is chiefly to be attributed; for if any one of them had despaired, he would most probably have died before we reached New Holland."

On June 14, the launch approached the outer waters of Coupang's harbor and was greeted by the sound of two cannons firing. The preceding ten days had tested the men's strength perhaps more than any other part of their long voyage. Once again, they had been awash in the incoming sea, once again forced to bail, without rest and with ever failing strength, for their very lives. The resumption of this relentless regime had been especially brutal following the brief taste of near ease and security offered by their island landfall; the men were also now approaching the bitter end of their physical abilities to endure. Most had wanted only to sleep, which as Bligh recognized, "seemed to indicate that nature was almost exhausted." Lassitude, swollen legs and, most ominously of all, "an apparent debility of Understanding" characterized the mortally exhausted crew. Still, Bligh took his observations, made soundings, kept his expansive log, drew sketches, measured out the rations and, as Timor hove in view, kept a lookout for any sign of a European settlement.

The report of the cannon firings "gave new life to every One." Now Bligh unfurled the ultimate banner of his naval professionalism. From a bundle of signal flags that had been in the launch, he had had made, in the course of the long passage, the British Jack; this he now raised, for, wrote Bligh, "I did not choose to land without leave." Eventually, the eighteen men walked shakily ashore, "their limbs full of Sores and their Bodies nothing but Skin and Bones habitated in rags," as Bligh described. Due to his management, eleven days of rations remained.

Forty-eight days had passed since the launch left the *Bounty,* and more than 3,600 miles at sea. With the exception of poor John Norton, none of the men Christian had sent to their deaths had been lost. Sadly, the greatest toll was taken of the crew after they were safe on land. David Nelson, Banks's loyal and resourceful gardener; Thomas Hall, cook; Peter Linkletter, quartermaster; William Elphinstone, who at thirty-eight had served as a somewhat aged master's mate with Fletcher Christian; Robert Lamb, the butcher who had been flogged in Tahiti for allowing his cleaver to be stolen—all would die in the Dutch East Indies or on the homeward voyage.

Bligh and his men remained in Coupang for nearly two months, recuperating and, in Bligh's case, searching for a means to make the next stage of the journey back to England. It was in Coupang that David Nelson died and was buried, and although he was given a fitting funeral, Bligh mourned his inability to provide the loyal gardener with a proper tombstone. A week after the burial, while in the midst of preparations to find passage to Batavia, Bligh had observed the mango and jambula trees in blossom, all signs of "the advance of Spring."

He reflected, "All these circumstances recalls to me the loss of Mr. Nelson and the object of my Voyage, which at times almost bear me down, but for the impropriety to let so much Weakness get the better of me."

It was also in Coupang that Bligh had written a long and loving letter to his wife, Betsy, his children and the new child—the "little stranger"— he knew would have been born in his absence. Apart from his rough notebook and log, this was the earliest report made of the mutiny—written when his greatest concern was only the accounting he would have to give to the Admiralty for the loss of his ship:

> My Dear Dear Betsy
>
> I am now in a part of the world that I never expected, it is however a place that has afforded me relief and saved my life, and I have the happyness to assure you I am now in perfect health. . . . What an emotion does my heart & soul feel that I have once more an opportunity of writing to you and my little Angels, and particularly as you have all been so near losing the best of Friends—when you would have had no person to have regarded you as I do, and must have spent the remainder of your days without knowing what was become of me, or what would have been still worse, to have known I had been starved to Death at Sea or destroyed by Indians. All these dreadful circumstances I have combated with success and in the most extraordinary manner that ever happened, never dispairing from the first moment of my disaster but that I should overcome all my difficulties.
>
> Know then my own Dear Betsy, I have lost the *Bounty*. . . . On the 28th. April at day light in the morning Christian having the morning watch, He with several others came into my Cabbin while I was a Sleep, and seizing me, holding naked Bayonets at my Breast, tied my Hands behind my back, and threatned instant distruction if I uttered a

word. I however call'd loudly for assistance, but the conspiracy was so well laid that the Officers Cabbin Doors were guarded by Centinels, so that Nelson, Peckover, Samuels or the Master could not come to me. I was now dragged on Deck in my Shirt & closely guarded—I demanded of Christian the cause of such a violent act, & severely degraded him for his Villainy but he could only answer—"not a word Sir or you are Dead." I dared him to the act & endeavored to rally some one to a sense of their duty but to no effect. Besides this Villain see young Heywood one of the ringleaders, & besides him see Stewart joined with him. Christian I had assured of promotion when he came home, & with the other two I was every day rendering them some service—It is incredible! these very young Men I placed every confidence in, yet these great Villains joined with the most able Men in the Ship got possession of the Arms and took the *Bounty* from me, with huzza's for Otaheite. I have now reason to curse the day I ever knew a Christian or a Heywood or indeed a Manks man. . . .

The Secrisy of this Mutiny is beyond all conception so that I cannot discover that any who are with me had the least knowledge of it. Even Mr. Tom Ellison took such a liking to Otaheite that he also turned Pirate, so that I have been run down by my own Dogs. . . .

My misfortune I trust will be properly considered by all the World—It was a circumstance I could not foresee—I had not sufficient Officers & had they granted me Marines most likely the affair would never have happened—I had not a Spirited & brave fellow about me & the Mutineers treated them as such. My conduct has been free of blame, & I showed every one, that tied as I was, I defied every Villain to hurt me. Hayward & Hallet were Mate & Midshipman of Christian's Watch, but they alarmed no one, & I found them on Deck seemingly [unconcerned] untill they were ordered into the Boat—The latter has turned out a worthless impudent scoundrel, but I beg of you to relate nothing of them untill I come home.

I know how shocked you will be at this affair but I request of you My Dear Betsy to think nothing of it all is now past & we will again looked forward to future happyness. Nothing but true consciousness as an Officer that I have done well could support me. I cannot write to Your Uncle or any one, but my publick letters, therefore tell them all that they will find my character respectable & honor untarnished. I have saved my pursing Books so that all my profits hitherto will take place and all will be well. Give my blessing to my Dear Harriet, my Dear Mary, my Dear Betsy & to my Dear little stranger & tell them I shall soon be home. . . . To You my Love I give all that an affectionate Husband can give—

> Love, Respect & all that is or ever will be in the power of your ever affectionate Friend and Husband Wm Bligh.

Once Bligh's party were sufficiently recovered, Bligh's next object was to get them from Coupang to Batavia, in Java, by October, when the ships of trade departed for Europe. With no means of ready passage at hand, he was eventually forced to purchase and provision a small schooner that he himself would command for the voyage. This in turn meant having to draw upon credit with His Majesty's government, a common enough transaction in the international seafaring world; and for this reason, Bligh was greatly taken aback on being informed that the governor desired him to "suffer the Names of my Officers to be joined with my own as an additional security." This Bligh refused to do, replying that he "could give him no other or could he have any better security than my bills of Exchange on the Government of Great Britain." This was a potentially serious development. If Bligh was not advanced the cost of the hired schooner, he and his men would lose valuable time and risk losing a passage with the fleet when it sailed from Batavia; this in turn would mean waiting additional months until the monsoon passed and sailing resumed. Most disconcerting, however, was the governor's slighting implication that Bligh's security was insufficient.

A week after this awkward impasse, Bligh had learned more from the sympathetic Mr. Wanjon, the governor's son-in-law and the settlement's second-in-command.

"My Master who I am under the necessity to keep strictly to his Duty, and is a vicious person, it is hinted to me has been the cause of the Governor's demur," Bligh wrote in his private log. It transpired that Mr. Fryer had struck up a friendship with a Captain Spikerman, whose wife was the governor's sister. Fryer had made dark suggestions that all would not go well with Bligh on his return to England, thus destabilizing the Dutch authorities' confidence that Bligh's notes of credit would be honored. That Fryer's activities had hurt Fryer himself, who was as anxious to return to England as was Bligh, is not the kind of realization that came easily to the master. The tensions between Bligh and his disaffected officers were to leave a lasting and unpleasant impression upon the Dutch authorities. Bligh's contempt for Fryer, Purcell and, to a lesser extent, Hallett and William Cole (the boatswain responsible for the mildewed sails) appears by this stage to have been undisguised. Barely recovered from his extraordinary sufferings, Bligh had now to shoulder the burdensome responsibility of overseeing all the logistical and bureaucratic difficulties of burying the men who had died, and leading the survivors on yet another vessel and yet another voyage.

The journey from Coupang to Batavia in the newly purchased Dutch schooner, renamed by Bligh the *Resource,* took exactly six weeks, from August 20 until October 1. With the launch in tow, the *Resource* hopped along the Java coast, landing at Surabaya and Semarang, replacing rotten parts and begging for basic supplies and water. Throughout this tedious voyage, Fryer, with relentless tenacity, continued to dog and counter Bligh's every word and deed. To Bligh's command that Fryer keep an eye on Purcell while the carpenter worked on the new schooner, Fryer had responded that "he was no Carpenter." When Hallett and Elphinstone were found "beastly drunk," Bligh reacted with the partly rhetorical question "Are they drunk or Ill?," to which Fryer replied, "Am I a Doctor?"

This last altercation took place at Surabaya, on the coast of Java, and was the cause of a near mutinous showdown.

"What do you mean by this insolence?" Bligh had asked the master, referring to his coy response.

"It is no insolence," Fryer replied, buoyed for this confrontation by his drunken and disgruntled audience, of whom the most significant member was William Purcell. "You not only use me Ill but every Man in the Vessel and every Man will say the same."

"Yes by God we are used damned Ill," began the muttering chorus. This entire episode is logged by Bligh himself, along with all the complaints the disgruntled party chose to lodge against him—that he would be hanged or shot from the mouth of a cannon on his return to England; that he had overbilled His Majesty's government for stores purchased in Coupang (this from Fryer); that "the cause of the Ship being taken was owing to my stoping provisions" (this from Purcell). Bligh's unsqueamish report of the range of complaints against him would tend to indicate that these were not issues in which he feared public scrutiny. The one heartening development was a sudden, emotional outburst from Thomas Hayward in support of his captain. Hayward, Bligh now learned, had earlier been taunted by his fellow officers for being Bligh's "lackey." Now, throwing himself into Bligh's arms, amid a torrent of tears he begged Bligh to believe that he had never been guilty of disloyalty.

"The Honor and integrity of this young Man made the Wretches about him tremble" was Bligh's approving summation.

Bligh had learned much since his first tentative and ineffectual punishment of Purcell, all those months ago, in Van Diemen's Land; this, or his patience had by now been worn so paper-thin that he had thrown his previous caution to the winds. In either event, his reaction to the new crisis had been to call instantly for the arrest of Purcell and Fryer by the Dutch authorities. Next, addressing his "tumultuous" men, Bligh publicly asked that those who had complaints to make against him step forward. Three men did so, John Hallett, William Cole and, surprisingly, Thomas Ledward, the assistant surgeon. Bligh requested the Dutch authorities to hold all men separately until questioning on the morrow, to ensure that they did not prepare complicit statements.

The next day, an examination was held onshore, presided over by the commandant of the considerable Dutch troops, a captain of the marines and a third high-ranking Dutch official.

"Have you anything to say against your Captain?" asked the commandant of John Hallett.

Yes, replied Hallett: "He beat me once at Otaheite."

"For what reason?"

"Because I was not got into the boat."

"Why did not you go into the Boat?"

"The Water was too deep." This is in all probability the event enigmatically referred to in Bligh's index to the missing portion of his private log as "Mr. Hallet's contumacy."

"Have you no other complaint against your Captain?"

"None."

And so it went.

To Mr. Ledward: "Have you anything to say against your Captain?"

"I have nothing to say against my Captain only the first time the Boat went on Shore I ask'd leave to go with him & was refused until he came on board again."

To Mr. Cole: "Have you anything to say against your Captain?"

To which Cole, suddenly addressing himself directly to Bligh, had replied, "I alledge no particular complaint against you, God forbid." Thus had Fryer's intent to rally resistance to Bligh ended with a whimper.

Fryer himself, now confined, sent Bligh a series of contrite letters, begging forgiveness and declaring that all parties could unite as friends. This vacillating tendency in Fryer Bligh had long despised, having noted in his log, a month earlier, that the "vicious & troublesome disposition of this Man can be only equalled by his ignorance & meanness, always ready to make concession & supplicate my forgiveness in the most abject manner." Fryer's misdeeds were substantial. It was he who had set a bush fire on one of the landfalls by his stubborn insistence on having his own fire; it was he who had intervened in a squabble between William Cole and Robert Tinkler, by advising Tinkler "to stick his knife into the Boatswain." When Bligh had stopped to make camp, Fryer loudly advocated moving on; when under way, he had advocated making landfall.

Somewhere in Fryer's brain there appears to have been lodged the fancy that he was Bligh's equal with respect to all things nautical; that a mere quirk of command had placed one man on a higher footing than the other; that he, Master Fryer, was entitled not only to his own opinion on every observation and duty of ship life, but to the right to air and advocate that opinion. In Bligh's handling of his cockleshell of a ship around the Horn; in his zealous and unremitting application of Cook's most enlightened sea practices; in his successful transplanting of the breadfruit; in his excellent relations with the Tahitians, conducted over a demanding five-month period; in his abilities, widely acknowledged, to survey and chart and navigate; in the fact that at the age of twenty-one he had performed, with distinction, as Cook's sailing master; above all, in his extraordinary leadership during a voyage by open boat so attenuating it had robbed men under him of their wits—in none of these accomplishments had Fryer perceived a man above his own modest and unremarkable stature. He, John Fryer, was not William Bligh, and against this adamantine fact the imperceptive master battered himself like a moth against a lighted windowpane.

Ten days after arriving in Batavia, the *Resource* and launch were sold to a visiting English captain named Hogendor, at public auction and at a great loss. "The services she had rendered us, made me feel great reluctance at parting with her," Bligh allowed in a later account, "which it would not have done, if I could have found a convenient opportunity of getting her conveyed to Europe." The *Bounty*'s company dispersed throughout the town, the officers to the dirty and ill-ventilated hotel in which all visitors ended up, the men to the convalescent hospital, some four miles distant; William Purcell, who had arrived separately on a spice boat from Surabaya, was transferred at Bligh's request to another ship, still under arrest. John Fryer had been released on Bligh's receipt from him of a written apology for his behavior. Bligh himself, as Joseph Banks and other gentlemen had done before him, after spending six nights in the hotel, fled as soon as was feasible to "the country" outside the pestilential town. His offer to take his officers with him to the country hospital was declined—according to Bligh—with them professing that "they could not bear the Idea of being there." Alone at the home of the surgeon general, close by his men in the convalescent hospital, Bligh nursed an intermittent fever and at times a crippling headache, and became convinced that he would not survive unless he took the first available passage to Europe; his complaint was probably malaria. But illness quite apart, it is transparently clear from his log that with no ship to claim his responsibility Bligh had become uncharacteristically disengaged from his surroundings and quite simply wanted to go home.

About a week after arrival, while Bligh was convalescing in the country, John Fryer wrote to his wife, Mary, in Wells-next-the-Sea, with the news of his own adventures. The letter is remarkable not only for what it says but, given Fryer's record of complaints against Bligh, for what it does not say. Written without outside interference, it is the master's most sincere, private and unadulterated representation of all that had passed and contains no hint of dissatisfaction with his commander.

"I have the pleasure to inform you that I [am] well & likewise Robert," he began (Robert Tinkler was his wife's young brother),

> but am sorry to tell you that we have lost our ship, by a stratagem that never happened before, in the memory of man. On the twenty eight of April at Day break the captain & me were surprised by Misters Christian, Stewart, Young & Haywood & the Master at Arms, with twenty one of the people. Christian & the Master at arms, went into Mr. Bligh Cabin, & tyed his hand behind him two men came into my cabin, with musquitts & Bayonets, told me if I spoke, that I was a dead man, that Mr. Christian had taken the ship and that they was intended to put us on shore upon one of the friendly Isles. I expostulated with them but all to no purpose, they hoisted the Long boat out, and all them that would not join with them in the mutiny they obliged to go into the boat. I was the last that received that order, when I was obliged to beg hard of Christian to let Robert come with me—he at last consented that he should go with me . . . they gave us about two Hundred pound of bread & sixteen small pieces of Pork, a compass and an old Quadrant with some few cloaths. . . .
>
> [At Timor] Mr. Bligh purchased a small Vessel to bring us to Batavia at which Place we are waiting to embark in a Dutch ship, which will sail in three weeks so that My Dearest Girl I hope to be with you in May . . . or the beginning of June. We have been at this place a week— our living here is very Dear it cost me Every Day for Robert and myself three Dollars, which in this country is fifteen shillings—and Cloaths likewise are very Dear. . . . I shall be very happy if one Hundred pounds besides my pay will clear me—but hope that Government will take our Misfortunes in consideration and make some allowance for

our losses—I was obliged to draw on Mr. Wilson at Timor for 228 Rix
Dollar—which is about forty five pounds I likewise gave Mr. Bligh a
bill of sixteen pounds, which I was indebted to him for the Expense of
the Mess as he wished all matters settled fearing that one of us might
Die . . . this letter come in a packit to Holland, which we suppose will
be home some time before us—so that the People in England will hear
of our misfortunes & forget them before we get home—I will not trouble you with any more of our Adventures. Robert join with me in Duty
love & best wishes to all friends & conclude with prayers to the
Almighty that my Dearest Mary may be well.

from your Affectionate
Husband.

Back in the civilized world, where Dutch rix dollars and shillings had
to be paid for all bodily needs, the men were soon smarting at the long
lists of expenses they incurred just in the act of staying alive. The Dutch
authorities had offered food, shelter and passages home—but, canny
merchants all, had charged breathtaking sums for these services. His officers had borrowed from Bligh, or, like Fryer, drawn money on their own
accounts, to be reimbursed on return; if any of the men who had borrowed from Bligh were to die before getting home—Bligh might be out
of pocket. With the prospect of imminent departure, therefore, Bligh's
self-interest became highly practical, and he began methodically collecting "securities" from all those to whom he had advanced money. The extent to which these financial considerations worried Bligh is made
brutally and unhappily clear in a letter Ledward the surgeon wrote to his
uncle. "You will be surprised when you hear I am deprived of my own
Ship with every individual thing I took out with me, besides effects to a
considerable amount which I purchased at the Surgeon, Mr Huggan's,
Death," he began.

The sad affair happened early in the Morning Watch; as soon as I was
informed fully how the matter stood, I instantly declared I would go
with the Captain, let the consequence be what it would, & not stay
among Mutineers. . . .

There is one thing I must mention which is of consequence: the Captain denied me, as well as the rest of the Gentlemen who had not Agents, any Money unless I would give him my power of Attorney & also my Will, in which I was to bequeath to him all my property; this he called by the name of *proper security*. This unless I did, I should have got no money, though I shewed him a letter of Credit from my Uncle & offered to give him a Bill of Exchange upon him. In case of my Death I hope this matter will be clearly pointed out to my Relations.

A ship due to leave in early October was found to have space for three passengers aboard. With no compunction, Bligh quickly claimed these for himself, John Smith, his servant and John Samuel, his clerk. His explanation, pleaded often in the log, was continued grave ill health, but it is also clear that for William Bligh, his duties to his troublesome, turbulent crew were over.

"... I expected after all my distresses that I was finally to close my Carreer of life in this sad place Batavia," he wrote on the very day after arrival. In all the long and debilitating days at sea he had never confessed to fear for his own life. Now, on dry land, with nothing much more to concern him, the prospect of early death by pestilence or fever seemed to haunt him like a specter. Having arranged with the Dutch authorities for his men to be sent out with the first ships on which space could be found, Bligh delegated John Fryer to take responsibility for them.

"You want a taste of being commanding officer?" one can imagine Bligh thinking. "Here! You manage everything from now on!"

In his last days in Batavia, Bligh busied himself with settling all accounts and arranging for his men's care and passage, and in writing letters to Banks, Duncan Campbell and the Admiralty. He had by now also written a list and description of all the mutineers, which was translated into Dutch and disseminated to all ports, including Port Jackson and the Dutch East India Company posts, at which the *Bounty* might conceivably make call.

"Thus happily ended through the assistance of Divine Providence without accident a Voyage of the most extraordinary Nature that ever happened in the World," Bligh summed up in his log and letters, both private and official, regaining the tone of indomitable complacency that had characterized his early log, back when he had had a ship; "let it be taken in its extent, duration and so much want of the Necessaries of Life." This extravagant claim would, in fact, be unchallenged for the next 127 years.

On October 16, 1789, Bligh gathered up what few effects remained to him and with his small and threadbare entourage embarked on the Dutch East Indiaman *Vlijt*, bound for the Cape and then on to Holland. The men with whom he had endured the defining ordeal of his career he left behind him, so it seems, without a backward glance.

The captain of the *Vlijt* had received special dispensation from the Batavian authorities to drop Bligh off in British waters, en route to Holland, and on Saturday afternoon, March 13, Bligh was landed at the Isle of Wight. Days later, he was presented to King George, and "laid his journal of the voyage to the South Seas before his Majesty."

In London, the news of Bligh's ordeal, followed by the success of his *Narrative*, quickly inspired an anonymous and titillating sequel advertised as an account of the mutiny "To which are added, Secret Anecdotes of the Otaheitean Women, whose charms, it is thought, influenced the Pirates in the commission of the daring conspiracy." The ingredients of beautiful, uninhibited island women, English sailors, mutiny and valor at sea, all set against the "paradise of the world," made the story of the loss of the *Bounty* a great hit from the very outset. Even before Bligh's publication, popular fascination with the romantic tale had been quickly exploited. By early May, London newspapers had begun advertising a new production at the Royalty Theatre entitled *The Pirates; Or, The Calamities of Capt. Bligh*. The elaborate catalogue of the new play's offerings illustrated what would be the *Bounty* story's enduring highlights: Otaheitean dances, and "the Attachment of the Otaheitan Women to, and their Distress at parting from, the British Sailors"; an "exact Representation" of Bligh's capture in his cabin. There would be songs by the Dutch captain ("To relieve a fellow-creature") while Miss Daniel would sing "Loose ev'ry sail"; the "whole to conclude with a correct view of that superb monument of British benevolence Greenwich Hospital," the royal naval hospital for seamen. Ralph Wewitzer, a veteran of the London stage, would play Captain Bligh. Moreover, the production, so it was claimed, had been "rehearsed under the immediate Instruction of a Person who was on board the Bounty. . . ." It is impossible to know if this last claim held any truth.

The fate of the *Bounty* was also discussed in more sober circles. In early May, Fanny Burney, the novelist and diarist and, at this period, a lady-in-waiting to Queen Charlotte, was on her way to the House of Lords to attend the greatest entertainment in London at the time, the impeachment trial of Warren Hastings, governor general of India, for alleged mismanagement of the East India Company's affairs. Accompanied by her brother, James Burney, an erudite and well-connected captain who had sailed with both Cook and Bligh, she was accosted by William Windham, a member of Parliament active in Hastings's impeachment.

"But what officers you are!" Windham cried to Captain Burney. "*[Y]ou men of Captain Cook;* you rise upon us in every trial! This Captain Bligh,—what feats, what wonders he has performed! What difficulties got through! What dangers defied! And with such cool, manly skill!"

James Burney had just come from breakfast with Sir Joseph Banks at his Soho Square residence. Banks, of course, had been one of the first to learn of the *Bounty*'s fate. There was no person or entity—not the lords of the Admiralty, not the West India merchants, not His Majesty's government—to whom Bligh felt so accountable and apologetic as to Banks; especially grievous was the death of David Nelson, Banks's handpicked emissary. Many others, too, felt for Banks (and, to a lesser extent, for Nelson) and a flurry of commiserative letters arrived at Soho Square from far-flung colleagues—from naturalists who hinted, discreetly, that it was hoped Banks would try a second breadfruit venture; from a German colleague who had been promised a Tahitian skull for his cranial studies; and of course from the West Indies: "[T]o have all these pleasing Prospects blasted by a set of Miscreants raises such Resentment in my Mind, that the only consolation I can receive on the occasion, is to hear that those Villains have been all taken, and made to expiate their crime on the Gallows," one planter raged in a letter from Jamaica.

"The escape of poor Bligh by his companions is a miracle that has not been equalled these 1700 years," wrote James Matra, the former midshipman who had been with Banks on the *Endeavour*. "Inglefield may now burn his old Blanket," he added facetiously; Captain John Inglefield had been widely admired for an open-boat journey in the North Atlantic, following the loss of his ship in 1782, in which he had improvised a sail from an old blanket. There was no question but that Bligh was the hero of the *Bounty* saga. Fletcher Christian received scant public attention, being singled out only by one syndicated story, which had reported that the leader of the mutineers was "a man of respectable family and connections, and a good seaman."

A formal court-martial on the loss of the ship could not be held until all the *Bounty*'s men arrived from Batavia. In all, of the nineteen men who had left the *Bounty*, as Bligh later recorded, "[i]t has pleased God that twelve should surmount the difficulties and dangers of the voyage, and live to re-visit their native country." Besides Bligh himself, those who survived to return were John Samuel, his quietly courageous clerk; John Smith, his loyal servant; Thomas Hayward and John Hallett, the two somewhat lacking midshipmen; William Peckover, the gunner and veteran, now, of four Pacific voyages; Lawrence Lebogue, the Nova Scotian sailmaker; George Simpson, quartermaster's mate; William Cole, the boatswain; William Purcell, the cantankerous carpenter; John Fryer, Bligh's querulous master, and his young brother-in-law, Robert Tinkler. The whereabouts of Thomas Denman Ledward, the surgeon, remained unknown. The ship he had embarked on in Batavia had been lost at sea and it was presumed he had gone down with her.

In the meantime, while recovering with his now large family, Bligh was also in contact with the shocked and horror-stricken families of the men still with the *Bounty*. Privately, Bligh met with Captain Hugh Cloberry Christian (a relation of the Cumberland Christians); with Fletcher's brother Edward; with Captain John Taubman, who had married one of Fletcher's cousins and first recommended that Fletcher apply to Bligh for a position; and with Fletcher's first cousin John Christian

Curwen, now married to one of the wealthiest heiresses in northern England and a well-connected and reform-minded member of Parliament—Curwen was a future patron of Samuel Taylor Coleridge. To some of these men, Bligh had unfolded his theory that Christian's mishandling of the *Bounty* in the storm off Whytootackee had been deliberate; that Christian had intended "to cripple the ship, that they might be obliged to return to Otaheite to repair." Evidently, Bligh had mulled over all the events leading to the mutiny in the course of the long boat voyage; he would never believe that the mutiny had not been planned well in advance. Whether Bligh's theory was correct or not, it is illuminating, as it indicates that Christian's actions at the time had been so wildly uncharacteristic as to have, in retrospect, raised suspicion—this was the period, of course, when he had been "in hell."

Still, despite many long months of speculation, no rational explanation for the mutiny could be given. Fletcher's brother Charles had written an agonized letter to Bligh's father-in-law, Richard Betham, prophesying that "it would be found that there had been some Cause not then known that had driven Fletcher to this desperate Step." The Christians and Bethams, along with the Heywoods, could expect to bump into one another on the Isle of Man.

"Fletcher when a Boy was slow to be moved," Charles recalled agonizing over the events, but drawing on his memories of the *Middlesex,* acknowledged that "when Men are cooped up for a long Time in the Interior of a Ship, there oft prevails such jarring Discordancy of Tempers and Conduct that it is enough on many Occasions by repeated Acts of Irritation and Offence to change the Disposition of a Lamb into that of an Animal fierce and resentful."

To Captain Taubman, who had asked straight out "what could possibly have been the Cause" of Christian's actions, Bligh had replied simply, "Insanity."

Although the newspapers had not made great play of the Christian family's involvement, the mutiny could only be perceived as a blight upon the family reputation; nor does it appear that the Christians put up any public resistance to Bligh's report, bowing their heads as it were, and quietly submitting to the unwelcome notoriety. Charles Christian's feelings "were so harrowed up with this unlooked for and unhappy Intelligence," he had written to Richard Betham, that he would have him believe that "instead of Ink, it was my Heart's Blood I wrote with."

No family, however, responded with more visible anguish than the Heywoods. When the news of the mutiny had reached Peter's recently widowed mother on the Isle of Man, she "in a State of Mind little short of Distraction," according to a Heywood family report, had written an imploring letter of inquiry to Bligh, who responded with characteristic, unmitigated directness:

> Madam,
>
> I received your Letter this Day & feel for you very much, being perfectly sensible of the extreme Distress you must suffer from the Conduct of your Son Peter. His Baseness is beyond all Description but I hope you will endeavour to prevent the Loss of him, heavy as the Misfortune is, from afflicting you too severely. I imagine he is with the rest of the Mutineers returned to Otaheite.

To a similarly anxious letter from Colonel James Holwell, one of Peter's several concerned uncles, Bligh replied in much the same tone:

> SIR,
>
> I have just this Instant received your Letter; with much Concern I inform you that your Nephew, Peter Heywood is among the Mutineers: his Ingratitude to me is of the blackest Dye for I was a Father to him in every Respect & he never once had an angry Word from me thro' the whole Course of the Voyage, as his conduct always gave me much Pleasure & Satisfaction. I very much regret that so much Baseness formed the Character of a Young Man I had a real regard for & it will give me much Pleasure to hear his Friends can bear the Loss of him without much concern.
>
> I am Sir, your Obt. servant . . .

Such reports threw the Heywoods into a state of bewildered despair. They were under an enormous obligation to Bligh who, as they were keenly aware, had taken on young Peter out of compassion for his family's fallen circumstances. Bligh and his wife had cared for Peter in their own home while the *Bounty* was being readied. And if Bligh himself had been taken aback by Peter's actions in the fraught and fateful hours of mutiny, having previously, by his own admission, had only pleasure in the young man's conduct—how much greater was the wounded incredulity of Peter's doting family. Uncles, family friends, naval colleagues were all approached with anguished entreaties to find out something, anything, that would ameliorate the charges, that would, in short, allow them to continue to believe in Peter's character and "honour."

Around this time, Bligh met personally with James Modyford Heywood, a fourth cousin of Peter's father, who had earlier interested himself in young Peter. Mr. Heywood's written report of the meeting was not made to Peter's mother, who was by now too despairing to absorb anything more to do with the lamentable affair, but to Peter's older sister, Hester, or "Nessy" as she was known to the family; Nessy had also approached Thomas Hayward for news, but the young midshipman, questioning the propriety of answering any question before the court-martial on the loss of the *Bounty* had taken place, had his father return a private letter in his stead.

At their meeting, Bligh "expressed his Astonishment" at Peter's involvement, Mr. Heywood told Nessy, adding, along with expressions of sympathy, his hope that Peter's mother would remain "ignorant of the true cause of your Brother's not returning." The true cause had to be conveyed with some delicacy to a young maiden of only twenty-two, such as was Nessy, for it seemed that "Mr. Bligh, & the whole of the Ship's Crew who came away with him are unanimous in ascribing the cause of this horrid Transaction to the Attachments unfortunately formed to the Women of Otaheite." Bligh would almost certainly have informed Heywood that young Peter, like Christian, had been treated for "venereals" in Tahiti. At any rate, Mr. Heywood continued, as tactfully as he could, Peter's "strange conduct" would probably make it rather difficult for him to return to England any time soon.

"[T]he only consolation I can hold out to you is that when he does return, his general good conduct & Character previous to this unhappy Business, may with some Allowance for the unbridled Passion of youth plead for his Pardon; You must have the Philosophy for the present to consider him as lost forever," Mr. Heywood concluded, echoing in gentler terms Bligh's more bluntly expressed opinion that young Peter was best forgotten. "[B]ut I trust that Providence will restore him to you & enable him to make Atonement." With such philosophical reflections, Nessy and the rest of Peter's immediate family had to console themselves for the next two years.

On October 22, 1790, the court-martial was finally held on the loss of the *Bounty*, the last of the loyalist company having arrived from Batavia. The purpose of the court-martial was "to enquire into the Cause and Circumstances of the seizure of His Majesty's armed Vessel the *Bounty* . . . and to try the said Lieutenant Bligh and such of the Officers and Ship's Company as are returned to England for their conduct on that occasion." Essentially, what the court required was official reassurance that Bligh and his men had done all that was possible to prevent the loss of the ship. This was the specific point over which Bligh agonized with an almost morbid intensity. Every one of the depositions he had made to the various Dutch authorities had stressed the fact that he personally had done all he could, and he came back to the same point again and again in his log and in all letters.

"My conduct has been free of blame," he had told his wife, in his long letter from Timor. "I showed every one, that tied as I was, I defied every Villain to hurt me."

"My Character & honor is spotless when examined," Bligh wrote to Duncan Campbell, shortly before his departure from Batavia. "I shall stand to be tried disspising mercy or forgiveness if it can be found I have been guilty of even an error in Judgement."

But while close inquiry made among the men in the course of the boat journey had satisfied everyone that there had been no discernible hint of approaching disaster prior to the mutiny, Bligh appears not to have been as easy in his mind that the loss of the ship was inevitable. Once captured, he had shouted himself hoarse, had given ignored commands, had implored, had incited bystanders to knock Christian down, all this while securely bound and guarded at the mizzenmast. But had Fryer, who had kept a pistol in his cabin, really done all he could? What if all the young officers had behaved with determined resistance? Four loyal men were known to have been forced to remain with the mutineers on the *Bounty*—might there have been more potential loyalists among the seamen who could have been swayed by a show of determination on the part of the officers? The image of the compliant men filing meekly into the waiting launch was difficult to exorcise. The fact that "out of forty-five men eighteen should suffer themselves to be pinioned and put on board a boat, at the almost certainty of death, without the least resistance" was one of the striking circumstances, as a disquieting article in the *Times* had put it, that were perhaps "unparalleled in the annals of mutiny."

"I had not a Spirited & brave fellow about me & the Mutineers treated them as such" was Bligh's private assessment to his wife. The loss of the ship, then, could have been prevented, in Bligh's opinion, although not by William Bligh. But it would do him personally no good if any hint of fecklessness should be discovered in his men at the court-martial; the Admiralty would not be investigating the cause of the mutiny—an act that was by definition indefensible—but only seeking reassurance that once the mutiny broke nothing had been left undone to quell it. All participants would have to put aside their most secret doubts, as well as animosities, to present for this solemn occasion a united front.

The court-martial was held at Spithead, on board the *Royal William*, presided over by Admiral Samuel Barrington. The first to be examined was Bligh, who when put the traditional question of whether he had "objection or complaint" against any man or officer, had replied that, William Purcell excepted, he had not (the carpenter had remained a prisoner since Surabaya). All the other officers played their parts; no one had anything to say against anyone else. Hallett and Hayward, who had been on watch when the mutiny broke, were not quizzed or reprimanded for failing to sound the alarm. John Fryer corroborated Bligh's account that he had been bound and held under armed guard by Christian himself.

"I asked Mr. Christian, who had then hold of Mr. Bligh with a bayonet in his hand, what he could think of himself or what he was after, or words to that effect," Fryer told the court. "[H]e told me to hold my tongue for he had been in hell for a week." The court appears to have expressed no interest in this insight into Mr. Christian's state of mind; the cause of the mutiny was, after all, not the point under examination. In any case, there was for every mutiny a presupposition that some mutineer had found his breaking point for one reason or another.

The court deliberated and concluded that "the *Bounty* was violently and forceably taken from the said Lieutenant William Bligh by the said Fletcher Christian and certain other Mutineers" and that Lieutenant Bligh and his officers and men were thereby honorably acquitted.

William Purcell alone was made to face the music. On the same day that Bligh and the other loyalists were acquitted, Purcell was brought onto the *Royal William* to face six charges that ranged from his insolence at Adventure Bay to an astonishing mutinous episode that had occurred toward the end of the boat voyage. Unusually, Bligh had not edited this last event out of his published narration, which in itself indicates its seriousness—and how ably Bligh believed he had handled it. The incident had occurred at a small island on which Bligh had sent his men out to scavenge for oysters.

"On this occasion their fatigue and weakness so far got the better of their sense of duty, that some of them began to mutter who had done most, and declared they would rather be without their dinner than go in search of it," Bligh had written in his *Narrative*. "One person, in particular, went so far as to tell me, with a mutinous look, he was as good a man as myself." This person had been William Purcell. Swiftly determining that he would "preserve my command, or die in the attempt," Bligh took up his cutlass. "I ordered him to take hold of another and defend himself; on which he called out I was going to kill him, and began to make concessions."

"I could not help laughing to see Capt. Bligh swagering with a cutless over the carpenter," was how Fryer described his reaction to this fraught moment; his sniggering tone apart, his record factually accords with Bligh's. "I said—no fighting here—I put you both under an arrest," Fryer had unwisely intervened. To which Bligh had responded, as might have been expected, "By God Sir if you offerd to tuch me I would cut you Down."

George Simpson, John Samuel, Thomas Hayward and John Fryer were called upon to give evidence of Purcell's insolence. No one contradicted Bligh's charges and most were in strong agreement that, as Samuel put it, the "general Tenor of [Purcell's] Conduct has not been such as is usual in the Service from an inferior to a superior Officer." Even Fryer reported that Purcell would "sometimes drop improper words."

The court placed most emphasis upon the first incident at Adventure Bay, Van Diemen's Land, and the witnesses seem to have been chosen because of their presence at this event. The court was clearly interested to know whether Purcell had been called upon to perform tasks beyond the duties of his warrant.

"Was it absolutely necessary for every Man to assist in the Duty of the Ship?" the court asked John Samuel at one point.

"It was," the clerk replied. How difficult to conjure now, snug in home port, the sweaty multitude of tasks—gathering and billeting wood, foraging for greens, washing laundry in the bay, filling keg upon keg with water from the grudging stream, all the while on guard for a surprise appearance from the island's natives.

"I could not bear the loss of an able Working and healthy Man," Bligh had logged at the time of his showdown, "otherwise I should have committed him to close confinement."

The surprise witness was William Peckover, the gunner, who both substantiated the charges against Purcell, and added some background color of his own. At Adventure Bay, he reported, Mr. Purcell said to Bligh that he had come "on shore for nothing but to find fault"; when the carpenter had been ordered back to the ship, Bligh called after him, "I'll put a Rope about your Neck."

At the end of the inquiry, the court found that "the Charges had been in Part proved against the said William Purcell and did adjudge him to be Reprimanded." There are several possible reasons for this relative leniency, one being that survival of the boat journey was in itself deemed a mitigating circumstance. Bligh himself was awarded a rapid and unorthodox promotion to the coveted position of post-captain after his court-martial; now officially "Captain Bligh," his professional future was more or less secure, since he had only to stay alive and his further advancement would proceed as senior captains died above him. This swift promotion, aided by the "interest" of Joseph Banks, was clearly a reward for his achievement. On the same principle, it may have been thought most just to allow Purcell to get on with his career. Bligh hints as much in a letter to Banks, in which he noted that a "great part of my evidence was kept back as it affected his life," adding, however, that this magnanimous gesture was "all thrown away on the Wretch, for he began to abuse & threaten some of the evidences as soon as he got on shore." In later years, it would be said of Purcell that he too had obtained his position on the *Bounty* through Banks, a claim that is impossible to prove or disprove—but if true, it would explain a great deal.

The exact terms upon which Bligh and Master Fryer eventually parted remain unclear. Subsequent events would show that their mutual antipathy was never overcome. Yet Bligh did not bring Fryer to court-martial as he had done Purcell. This may have been simply because two courts-martial ordered on two of his officers could only have raised eyebrows. Additionally, despite his continued ill will, Fryer had made a formal apology to Bligh, even signing a letter of contrition that had been drafted by Bligh.

Still, all was not over between the two men; and it was sometime after these trials that Fryer set down to write his own narrative of events, the straightforward intent of which appears to have been the denigration of Bligh—perhaps as a guard against future charges Bligh might make against him. Strikingly, however, for all its ill will, apart from its citation of mismanaged events at Anamooka Island, the document recorded nothing more damaging than Bligh's passionate outbursts of temper against his inept officers. Fryer made no mention at all of the books he had so conspicuously refused to sign on the outward voyage, for example, or of the allegations he had spread in Coupang that Bligh's receipt books would not be honored in England. Rather, his memoir is characterized by a litany of petty personal slights and oversights: Mr. Bligh took the only paper and ink in the launch, so he, John Fryer, had been unable to keep a log; a bedstead intended for him in Coupang had been given by Bligh to someone else (the soon-to-die David Nelson!); Bligh had not solicited his opinion about the location of a reef—one pictures Fryer, tight-lipped and self-righteous, sitting in pious, wounded silence less than twenty feet distant from his captain with the sea rising around them, steadfastly refusing to offer an opinion because he had not been formally asked to do so. In a typical entry, concerning an order Bligh had given Fryer to keep the carpenter at his duties, Fryer's tedious and roundabout defense mostly serves to illustrate just how wearisome Bligh's responsibilities had become by the end of the voyage. No, Fryer had responded to Bligh's query, he had not been down to check on Purcell's work, contrary to his orders, because he was unwell.

"What is your complaint?" said Bligh.

"I told him the prickly heat was much out on me & that the Doctor told me to take care, and not catch cold."

"Is that all your complaint?" was Bligh's incredulous response—medical excuses were usually reserved for scurvy, the flux, fever, injuries, wounds.

"I told him the Doctor was the only man to prescribe on that matter. He said 'Sir it's my order that you see the Carpenter at work every morning by Day break & keep him at work.' I said, Sir I am not a judge of Carpenter work neither do I think it my Duty to attend the Carpenter. He said 'it is your Duty Sir & you shall do it,'" and so on.

Whether Fryer wrote his narrative to keep on hand "just in case" or hoped it would have a more public airing is difficult to tell. Probably, bearing in mind Fryer's characteristic tendency to back down under close scrutiny, he had sort of half hoped someone might see it—without his being perceived as actively advocating this. This is borne out by a telling exchange that he reports between himself and David Nelson midway through his boat journey.

"O Mr. Fryer Sir, Captain's Oeconomy have upset our Voyage," Nelson is alleged to have said.

"I use to say never mind Mr. Nelson, have a good heart we shall see old England and tell them all our grievances by & by."

"—aye Mr. Fryer, Sir Joseph Banks will ask me a number Questions—and be assured that I will speak the truth—if ever I live to see him."

Nelson, of course, was long dead and not around to verify or refute the conversation. Elsewhere Fryer consistently refers to Nelson, in grudging, resentful tones, as one of Bligh's few confidants, in light of which the reported exchange does not ring quite true. Nonetheless, the coy reference to Banks suggests that Fryer may have hoped it would end up in his hands. And in fact, Fryer had occasion to meet with Banks, or at least to catch his ear: Francis Masson, Banks's intrepid botanist at the Cape, had met Fryer when his ship called in at Table Bay en route to Europe; Masson had requested Fryer to deliver some "curious Euphorbia" seeds to his patron, along with boxes of other seeds and bulbs. One can imagine the pensive master arrived in England, making his way through the broad, spacious streets that flanked the handsome houses of Soho Square, seeds in hand, on his way to Sir Joseph Banks; or perhaps, if he had been lucky, waiting on the great man in his high-windowed study with its calm view over the square's gardens. From Banks himself there is no record of any meeting, and if Fryer made it past the butler, it seems likely that, his courage failing, he simply delivered his seeds and departed.

But Fryer did use his return to London to pay a visit to Joseph Christian, a linen draper who owned a fashionable shop in the Strand—Jane Austen shopped here in later years. Although a somewhat distant cousin of Fletcher, Joseph Christian was closely connected with the powerful Christian Curwens, and thus at the heart of the Christian family power base—when John Christian, the future member of Parliament, had eloped with his own cousin, the heiress Isabella Curwen, the couple had lain low in Joseph's small apartment over his shop. To Joseph Christian, less intimidating, perhaps, to a man of Fryer's standing than Sir Joseph Banks, John Fryer made a report that at least in some part unburdened him of his resentment toward Bligh. What he said about Fletcher can only be guessed. There is no evidence that Joseph Christian did anything at all with this information at this point, but his influence would prove more discernible at a later date.

As it happened, Bligh was also in touch with Joseph Christian, although, as it would seem, for professional reasons. Sometime after his return, Mr. Christian sent him a package containing "3 Handsome printed callicoe Dresses," yards of cotton chintz, two dozen ribbons and a walloping order of twelve dozen shirts. Bligh may simply have been shopping for his family through a well-known merchant; or perhaps the order, which amounted to £82 8s. 0d., represented a creative means of repaying the loan Bligh had made to Christian at the Cape. Given Bligh's extraordinary sensitivity to being out of pocket on anyone's account, it is hard to believe that he would not have recouped this irksome debt in some fashion or another. One can only hope he received a liberal discount.

In attempting to recoup his losses from the Admiralty, on the other hand, Bligh appears to have been less successful. In the first instance, he had submitted accounts for the not insignificant expense of getting his men home, as well as for the sixty-one ducats and forty-five Spanish dollars that the Navy Board had given him for supplies when he set out and which had remained with the *Bounty*. But in addition to these well-documented losses, Bligh also felt compelled to submit a painfully itemized account of the personal effects he had lost with his ship. There were his shoes and boots and silver buckles, his woolen stockings and hats, his china and wineglasses and three dozen shirts, his pillowcases and waistcoats, every one of the forty-eight books in his small library, his sword and pistols, and his "Box of Pencils" valued at two shillings and sixpence.

"Take that this account cannot be allowed," was the Admiralty's scribbled—and perhaps incredulous—notation. There was something almost unmanly in this untoward fussiness. As events turned out, Bligh was not to be out of pocket. Although the breadfruit expedition had failed, the Jamaican House of Assembly voted to award Bligh five hundred guineas for his efforts. This gesture was unlikely to have been made without some consultation with Sir Joseph Banks. While Banks himself does not appear to have known Bligh personally, or at least well, before the departure of the *Bounty*, on Bligh's return he became his committed patron.

In mid-April 1791, Bligh was informed by the Admiralty of his new commission. With the encouragement of Banks, the government had determined to mount a second breadfruit expedition to Tahiti—and Captain William Bligh would command it. As Bligh knew, this represented the most public expression of the government's—and Banks's—trust. Doggedly, the newly appointed captain began preparing for a second two-year, thirty-thousand-mile round-trip voyage to the island that had been his undoing. His health was not recovered from the boat journey and he was still oppressed by the headaches and intermittent fevers that he believed had nearly killed him in Batavia.

In early August, Bligh sailed with the *Providence,* a three-decked frigate, and the *Assistant,* a sixty-three-foot, 4-gun brig acting as tender, for Tahiti, by way of the Cape; there would be no attempt to sail the Horn on this second voyage. Bligh had drafted a memorandum for Banks of those particulars that he believed, this time, had to be observed: his ship should be at least of 350 tons, with three decks; there should be lieutenants, officers and twenty marines—the "Establishment as Capt. Cook." They would not proceed by way of the Horn. Ideally, there should be a second, smaller vessel that could "render the Navigation of Endeavor Streights less hazardous," for the Admiralty had reiterated its desire to accomplish this dangerous task.

Banks, also drawing on hard lessons learned, affixed a new preface to his orders for the expedition's gardeners: "The first duty to be inculcated into the mind of a man who undertakes to serve his Majesty is obedience to the orders of those His Majesty is Pleasd to put in command over him." Although poor David Nelson had died loyal to his commander, Banks's assistant gardener, William Brown, was one of the inner circle of mutineers, leaving Tahiti with Christian and the *Bounty.* Lawrence Lebogue, who had served with Bligh in the West Indies, and John Smith, Bligh's servant, now accompanied their captain once again, back to the Pacific. Peckover, the gunner, also sought a position on this second expedition, but Bligh turned him down.

"Should Peckover my late Gunner ever trouble you to render him further services," Bligh wrote to Banks, "I shall esteem it a favor if you will tell him I informed you he was a viscious and worthless fellow." One would like to imagine that Banks had come to enjoy Bligh's blasts of candor. Apparently, it had not occurred to the gunner that his impromptu comments at Purcell's court-martial had not been calculated to gain his captain's favor. In any event, as Bligh confided to Banks, he had determined he would never sail again with an officer of the *Bounty.*

Before he departed, Bligh had made preparations for the publication of an expanded narrative of the *Bounty* voyage, entrusting his private log to his old friend Captain James Burney. Burney's job was mostly editorial, and he made few embellishments to Bligh's original text. Burney had also assisted in the publication of Bligh's first, abbreviated account of the boat voyage, and the degree of personal interest he had taken in the project is made clear by an amusingly double-edged entry in his sister's famous journal.

"We read a good deal of Captain Bligh's interesting narrative," Fanny Burney had written in March 1790, "every word of which James has taken as much to heart as if it were his own production." In later years Bligh would be accused of deliberately omitting certain events from his published work; but, on the contrary, the fact that he had so casually turned this project over to a colleague can only indicate that for William Bligh the events on the *Bounty* had been, quite literally, an open book.

PORTSMOUTH

1792

Nestled between two sturdy peninsulas on England's southern coast, facing the Isle of Wight, Portsmouth Harbour seemed to have been designed by nature for the security of His Majesty's Royal Navy. It was said that its capacious basin could contain the entire naval fleet and its waters were so deep that a first-rate man-of-war could ride in the harbor at the tide's lowest ebb. It was guarded by the batteries, forts and towers strung along the Solent, the long channel lying between the mainland and the Isle of Wight, and in time of crisis, a chain could be strung across the harbor mouth.

Outside the harbor, Spithead was Portsmouth's principal anchorage; at twenty miles long and as much as three miles in breadth, it could accommodate a thousand ships at one time, so it was said, "without the least difficulty or danger." In time of mobilization, this was where the Royal Navy's ships, manned and provisioned, were mustered before heading out on the campaigns that would carry them across whole oceans as coherent majestic fleets.

A clutter of busy traffic of vessels and crafts of all rigs and sizes constantly plied back and forth between the great ships at anchor and the mainland, where lay Portsmouth town and, on the harbor's eastern arm, Portsmouth Dockyard. Britain's Royal Dockyards were the largest industrial enterprise on the planet, and Portsmouth Dockyard was the greatest in the kingdom or, in the words of one local guidebook, "the completest Dockyard in the universe."

A self-contained walled town, the great yard encompassed every activity required to send a ship to sea. Even in time of peace some two thousand men were employed here, working ten- to twelve-hour days. There were offices and storehouses, and neat brick homes for the principal officers as well as the massive infrastructure required to produce a ship. In the Rope-house all cordage was spun, from light line to massive anchor cable, in lengths of more than a thousand feet, some so thick that eighty men were required to handle them in maximum shifts of four hours—longer than this being beyond any man's ability. Timber balks and spires of wood lay submerged in the Mast Pond, seasoning until called to use. In the blacksmith's shop were wrought ninety hundred-weight anchors in furnaces that put visitors in mind of "the forge of Vulcan." And on the slips, or docked along the waterfront, were the 180-foot-long hulls of men-of-war, the great battle-wounded ships brought for recovery, or the skeletons of new craft, their hulking, cavernous frames suggesting monstrous sea animals from a vanished, fearsome age.

On the western side of the harbor, south of Gosport and only a quarter of a mile from the sea, stood the imposing brick complex of Haslar Hospital, the refuge of the naval "sick and hurt," enclosed by a twelve-foot-high sentry-guarded wall. Intricate pedimental sculpture depicted Navigation as a female goddess pouring balm on a wounded sailor, with the North Star over her head. Opposite her, sitting amid full chests and bales, was Commerce, in the words of the contemporary guide, "distributing money, fruit, and flowers."

One of the finest views in all of England was that from the ramparts of Portsmouth town, north of the dockyard. Forming a circuit a mile and a quarter around, the broad ramparts were edged with well-tended elms, where visitors and townspeople could promenade. From here, one could look behind to the rolling prospect of farmlands and meadows, and in the other direction out toward the sea. Below, in Spithead anchorage flocked the great vessels of the kingdom, their creamy sails and occasional flashes of brass shining out from the shimmering and, just here, decep-tively unruffled water. It was to Portsmouth that Bligh had arrived after disembarking the *Vlijt*, his hired boat splish-splashing past the great ships at anchor, looming out of the night fog. Few places in the kingdom were more symbolic of "home" for a returning sailor. For the prisoners arriving in the *Gorgon* in June 1792, caught by the long arm of the law, few were also more symbolic of His Majesty's naval might.

Those men who had remained with the *Bounty* had not been forgot-ten by their families during the intervening years since the news of the mutiny reached England. Away on the Isle of Man, Peter Heywood's family anxiously awaited word of the *Pandora*'s arrival, an event both ex-citedly anticipated and, as Peter's sister Nessy admitted, feared. From the very outset it was known to all families that any man captured would be on trial for his life, and that the most probable outcome of the trial would be the sentence of death. A story in the London press as early as April—two months before the captured mutineers' actual arrival in England—had borne ambivalent news, reporting that Midshipman Peter Heywood and Armorer Joseph Coleman, two "of Christian's crew," had swum to the *Pandora* when she anchored at Tahiti—and the two men "were so tattoed, and exhibited so many other characteristic stains," that they had been mistaken for Tahitians. This last was the kind of de-tail guaranteed to rivet popular interest, if also to worry the Heywoods.

With the advance notice of the fugitives' capture and imminent ar-rival, a flurry of correspondence began to whirl from Nessy Heywood's prolific pen. Once again, James Modyford Heywood, visiting London from his Devon estate outside Plymouth, responded to his niece's ap-peals for advice and assistance by extending his sincere sympathies to the family and pledging that as soon as he was informed of Peter's ar-rival, he would "pay every Attention to his situation." Referring to the news story, he stated his belief that the "Circumstances of his having swam to the *Pandora* will, I trust, be strong in his Favor." Mr. Heywood was not indelicate enough to mention Peter's new tattoos.

By early June, Nessy had contacted everyone associated with the *Bounty* that she could flush out. John Hallett, now Lieutenant Hallett and back in service on the sloop *Savage* off the coast of Scotland, replied with an icy letter stating that in the event he were called as a witness, "notwithstanding the Friendship I had for your Brother, I shall be strictly bound by Oath to adhere to Truth." Peter's youth "at the Time he committed the rash Act" might mitigate the case against him, Hallett allowed. Peter's other messmate, Thomas Hayward, who had accompanied the *Pandora* on her hunt for the pirates, had not yet returned to England, but his father took it upon himself to respond on his son's behalf, offering Nessy bracing and pragmatic advice: "I will take the Liberty my dear young lady of requesting you to make all possible Interest with all your Friends that Application may be made to his Majesty, so as to be prepared against and to avert the most painful consequences of the impending Trial," Francis Hayward wrote in early June, when the prisoners were some two weeks away from Spithead. "I well know that Mr. Bligh's Representations to the Admiralty are by no means favorable."

A surviving, highly stylized portrait shows Nessy as the ideal young woman of her time, with large, limpid eyes and a small "rosebud" mouth, her slim, pale face framed by a mane of soft curls—a portrait that does not accord entirely with Peter's own fond and forgiving description. His sister's features, he allowed, "were by no means regular," although her long-lashed eyes "redeemed the whole face." Nessy was also "below the middle height but well-formed, and graceful in her movements." Nessy was now twenty-four, four years older than Peter.

The Heywood family had suffered another blow since the shameful dismissal of Peter and Nessy's father by the Duke of Atholl just before the departure of the *Bounty*. In February 1790, only a month before Bligh arrived in England with news of the mutiny, Mr. Heywood had suddenly and mysteriously died. Every circumstance—his hopeless bankruptcy, the striking fact that this amateur lawyer had left no will, the family's determined silence about the nature of this death—suggests suicide; to a family friend, Nessy ingenuously declared that her father had died of a severe attack "of gout," although in a passage in a letter to Peter that was later edited out of copies of his correspondence, she allowed that gout, "and distress of mind from the repeated disappointments he met with, put an end to his existence." Elizabeth Heywood,

Nessy's mother, was now raising eight children on her own and had been hauled in before various increasingly exasperated creditors to account for her husband's debts; the defiant behavior of the Heywood women had added to the creditors' displeasure. Rescue must have come from some undiscoverable source, for by the time the *Gorgon* arrived with Peter at Spithead, the Heywoods were living in Douglas on the Parade, a new and fashionable street directly facing the sea. Just around the corner was Fort Street, where Fletcher Christian's mother also lived in modest but genteel circumstances.

The Isle of Man received all its news of the outside world from the mail, gazettes or random passengers arriving by the regular Liverpool packet, which was itself entirely at the whim of prevailing weather. As events unfolded across the Irish Sea, the Heywoods, frantic for information, knew themselves to be oppressively, maddeningly isolated. Mrs. Heywood, overwhelmed by all that had overtaken the family and with the responsibility of her many children (the youngest, Edwin, was nine), increasingly followed events at second hand, relying on Nessy's reports from her widening circle of correspondents.

Chief of these was Nessy's uncle by marriage, Captain Thomas Pasley, now in command of the 74-gun *Vengeance*. Pasley knew Bligh personally, and had in fact sent a favorite midshipman, Matthew Flinders, to join Bligh's second breadfruit expedition. Nearly sixty years old, this bluff, straight-talking Scotsman was respectfully regarded as "old school," a characterization born out by his inimitable personal diary: "A very dull stupid Cruize this, not one Yankie on the Seas I believe—already out 17 Days and have not seen one—hard, very hard. . . ."

" . . . At ½ past 4 our Stupid Rascal of a Pilot run the Ship's stern upon the Crow Rock. . . . The Shock was so great that it broke several Bottles in one of my Cases of Rum. . . . I hope we shall be able without further disaster to bundle the Old Bitch into one King's Port or other."

Pasley had gone to sea at sixteen and seen much action against the French and in the West Indies. While stationed off the Isle of Man, he met Maria Heywood, sister of Peter John Heywood (and Nessy's aunt), and the two married in 1774. Pasley had helped discreetly in other Heywood family troubles, as his diary makes clear. In 1778, while on patrol at the Leeward Islands, he met a new sister-in-law, a fourteen-year-old "Child," now pregnant by one of the Heywood men, a "D———d Rascal," who had absconded. Although finding the girl a "large, course [*sic*], clumsy piece, with a flat broad face and small peeping Eyes," Captain Pasley was moved by her plight and did what he could to aid her.

Corpulent and with a stern-featured face, Captain Pasley was an imposing figure, but the kind of rough man who melted before a woman in distress. He was also the commander in chief in the Medway, based at Sheerness, a fact not lost on Nessy Heywood. And if this gallant officer had been moved by his pudding of a sister-in-law, how much more was he affected by the grief and anxiety of his charming niece! Pasley was genuinely fond of Nessy, who had on occasion stayed with him and his wife at their Bedfordshire estate. He had even been induced to enter into one of Nessy's interminable poetic exchanges:

> *Lines by Capt. Pasley to his niece, Miss Hester Heywood, with a present to her of some pairs of gloves, on her having stolen a kiss from him when he was asleep in his chair:*

> *Accept, my dear Nessy, the tribute that's due*
> *Poor the kiss that so sweetly was given by you.*
> *But be cautious, my fair one; for had I been single*
> *One kiss such as that would have made my heart jingle . . .*

At the beginning of June, Nessy sat down to write a letter to Peter. It was not yet known when he and the *Gorgon* would arrive, and Pasley had forewarned her that in any case she would have "no chance of seeing him, for no bail can be offered." A letter, then, would be her only means of communication. Sitting in the windswept house in Douglas, Nessy had written as if speaking to the young, well-educated man of budding honor who had left the family nest five years before. Peter's adventures on the far side of the globe would have been beyond the boundaries of her maiden imagination, experiences she would not have known to guess at—the adventures in love and lust, mutiny and power, the wars and bloodletting on Tubuai, the tattoos and settled domestic life on Tahiti, the wreck of the *Pandora* in the night sea and the long journey home in chains.

"I will not ask you my beloved Brother whether you are innocent of the dreadful crime of Mutiny," Nessy began. Curiously, she addressed the letter to the care of Francis Hayward, the father of Thomas Hayward, who had accompanied the *Pandora;* Hayward Sr. at least appears to have remained kindly disposed toward the Heywood family.

"[I]f the Transactions of that Day were as Mr. Bligh represented them, such is my Conviction of your worth & Honor, that I will without hesitation stake my Life on your Innocence," Nessy had continued loyally, but illogically. "—If on the Contrary you were concerned in such a Conspiracy against your commander I shall be as firmly persuaded his Conduct was the Occasion of it—But," she hastily added, "alas Could any Occasion justify so atrocious an Attempt to destroy a Number of our fellow Creatures?"

When the *Gorgon* was still at least a week away, more news was brought by a batch of the *Pandora*'s crew just arrived from Holland and, as luck would have it, delivered specifically to Pasley's care at Sheerness. This was the advance party that had sailed from Batavia on the Dutch East Indiaman, *Zwan,* under the charge of the despised Lieutenant Larkan. On arrival, the men had been whisked to Pasley's ship, the *Vengeance,* for a thorough debriefing. From these men, who had lived on top of Peter and the other prisoners for a full nine months, eavesdropping on their every word and—if one is to believe Captain Edwards—inclined to regard their captives with a troubling sympathy, Pasley learned disheartening news.

"I cannot conceal it from you my dearest Nessy, neither is it proper I should," Pasley reported in his blunt way, "—your Brother appears by all Account to be the greatest Culprit of all, Christian alone excepted. Every Exertion you may rest assured I shall use to save his Life—but on Trial I have no hope of his not being condemned." Pasley was compelled to disclose one more piece of bad news to Nessy: the report that Peter had been the first to swim to the *Pandora*—a circumstance very much in his favor—was, he had learned, untrue. There was little to do now except await the arrival of the prisoners themselves and hope subsequent accounts would offer more encouragement.

The summer of 1792 promised to be one of the worst and wettest in memory. Toward the middle of June, the weather turned blustery with lightning storms seen to the south, before settling back to a calmer pattern of dull skies and showers of rain. Two days after the *Gorgon* dropped anchor, a longboat was sent out from the 74-gun guardship *Hector* to collect the prisoners. As the boat made its way across the broad, busy anchorage to Portsmouth Harbour, the weather broke and it was under the light, fair skies of an English summer day that the prisoners beheld their native land. Once on the *Hector,* the prisoners were taken down to the gun room for confinement.

A week later, Captain Montagu warped the *Hector* farther down harbor to moorings off Gosport, where she would lie until the court-martial was assembled. Several conditions had to be met, which might take many months. All of the men from the *Pandora* had to have returned, especially Lieutenant Hayward, who would certainly be called on as an "evidence," or witness, and twelve captains of sufficiently senior rank had to be assembled in port. Finally, much depended upon the movements of Vice Admiral Lord Hood, commander in chief at Portsmouth and a First Lord of the Admiralty, who would preside over the proceedings.

With the *Gorgon's* safe arrival, relatives and well-wishers felt it their duty to prepare Nessy and her family for the heartbreak that inevitably lay ahead. James Modyford Heywood, the helpful relation who lived close to Plymouth and had previously offered only words of consolation and support, now felt it proper to disabuse Nessy of any illusions: Peter's character "will I fear avail him little when he is convicted of a Crime, which, viewed in a political Light, is of the blackest Dye," he wrote darkly, in language that ominously echoed Bligh's.

Similarly, from his private island in Lake Windermere, Cumberland, John Curwen (Fletcher Christian's well-connected first cousin) wrote to Nessy that "however painful, I think it just to say that unless some favourable Circumstance should appear any Interest which can be made will have little Weight." Only Peter's "extreme youth" was in his favor. However, as Curwen undoubtedly knew, Peter's youth was neither extreme nor, in a profession in which young boys were sent to sea as children, even remarkable. Peter was now twenty; on the day of the mutiny, he had been five weeks shy of his seventeenth birthday. In a postscript to his letter, Curwen added that it was "not unlikely" that he might be on the Isle of Man for a few days on unspecified business with his friend and relation Captain Hugh Cloberry Christian, "who has more the Power of serving you than any Person I know."

This seems to have been a broad hint of support, for it was not long afterward that Captain Christian took the liberty of approaching the lost *Pandora*'s captain, Edward Edwards, with queries on Peter's behalf. Regarding "the unfortunate Young Man Peter Heywood," Edwards duly responded that he well understood the young man had not taken an active part *against* his commander; the question, however, was "how far he may be reprehensible for not taking an active & decided part in his favour in the early part of the business." As for possible allowance being made for Peter's youth, "I have only to observe," wrote the unaccommodating Edwards, "that he appeared to me to be much older and I understand that he passed for and was considered to be so on board the *Bounty*." Edwards had also witnessed, all those months ago on Tahiti, the evidence of Peter's manhood—the little houses where he and Stewart had lived with their Tahitian wives, for example. Despite a certain guardedness that suggested that Edwards might not be the ideal witness in Peter's favor when he took the stand, Edwards offered a glimmer of good news. Peter "certainly came on board the Pandora of his own accord almost immediately after she came to an Anchor." Also, Peter was a young man of abilities; for instance, "he made himself Master of the Otaheitian Language." This last point, however, like the incriminating tattoos, was not the kind of information the family felt needed to be bandied about.

At last, toward the end of June, Peter's own long-awaited voice reached his family. The letter that arrived from him to the frantic Douglas household had not been written on arrival at Spithead, but was addressed and dated "Batavia, November 20th 1791," written while he and the other captured men had been confined off Java's pestilential shore. Now came the flood of words, the description of the fateful and confused day, the capture by Edwards, the loss of the *Pandora*, the brutal captivity. But above all else the letter carried the voice of Peter's misunderstood innocence, and the first declaration of his version of that day's events.

"[W]hat has since happen'd to me," Peter wrote, had "been grossly misrepresented to you by Lieut. Bligh, who by not knowing the real Cause of my remaining on board, naturally suspected me, unhappily for me, to be a Coadjutor in the Mutiny." On that dreadful morning, Peter said, he had awoken at daylight and, leaning out of his hammock, seen a shipmate sitting with drawn cutlass on the arms chest. He was told that Christian had taken the ship and was going to take Bligh home as prisoner, "to have him tried by a Court Martial for his long tyrannical & oppressive Behaviour to his People!—I was quite thunderstruck. . . ."

Once on deck, Peter discovered a different story. Bligh was being threatened with cutlass and pistol by Christian, and the launch was being lowered. All who did not wish to remain with Christian were given a choice: they could get into the launch "or be taken in Irons as Prisoners to 'Taheite & be left there." The launch meant certain death, whereas at Tahiti he could wait for the arrival of another ship. As he assisted in clearing the launch of the yams stored in her, Thomas Hayward had asked him what he intended to do, and Peter had replied that he would remain in the ship.

"[N]ow this Answer I imagine he has told Mr. Bligh I made to him, from which together with my not speaking to him that Morning his Suspicions of me have arose, construing my Conduct into what is foreign to my Nature—Thus my dearest Mother 'twas all owing *to my Youth & unadvised Inexperience*."

Peter urged his mother to convey his innocence to Richard Betham, Bligh's father-in-law, who had been responsible for getting him on the *Bounty;* "perhaps his Assistance in interceding with his son in Law Mr. Bligh in my Behalf might undeceive him in his groundless ill Opinion of me, & prevent his proceeding to great Lengths against me at my approaching Trial." Although he could not know it, Betham had died in 1789. Peter, his mind already racing ahead, had other practical requests: "If you should likewise apply to my Uncle Pasley & Mr. Heywood of Plymouth, their timely Aid & friendly Advice might be the Means of rescuing me from an ignominious Lot!"

The effect of this letter on the Heywood household was electrifying. Two other letters were next received in rapid succession, along with, in

the best family tradition, a poem from Peter, which sent Nessy into raptures:

> Oh! Hope—thou firm Support against Despair,
> Assist me now stern adverse Fate to bear . . .

On June 29, Nessy and her mother replied warmly to Peter in separate letters. Nessy, predictably, was effusive: "My dearest & most beloved
Brother . . . Your fond, anxious, & till now, miserable Nessy is at last permitted to address the Object of her tenderest Affection in England!—
Oh! my admirable, my heroic Boy—what have we felt on your
Account. . . . Surely my beloved Boy, you could not for a Moment imagine we ever supposed you guilty of the Crime of Mutiny. . . ."

Nessy was by now intent on going to the mainland, as she told Peter,
"to fly into your Arms"; Uncle Pasley's solemn reckoning that "you have
no chance of seeing him" had already been forgotten.

Peter, as he had told his mother, had been forced to write his long
Batavian letter "by stealth," but on the *Hector* he suffered no such restric-
tion. By a happy quirk of fate, as Pasley reassured his niece, "Captain
Montague of the *Hector* is my particular Friend."

George Montagu was from a distinguished naval family. He had entered the Royal Naval Academy, gone to sea at thirteen and as a young
lieutenant accompanied his father to the North American station in the
early 1770s. During the American Revolutionary War, he had been active
in the reduction of New York. Now forty-two years old, Montagu had
been in command of the *Hector* since 1790, following an eight-year
stretch of unemployment—the usual naval casualty of peace.

Under Montagu's care, the *Bounty* prisoners were being kept in the
gun room at the stern of the lower deck. Lit only by its gun ports, it was
a dark and airless cavern, although in a rated ship of the line this
traditionally served as living quarters and schoolroom for the captain's
servants and midshipmen, or junior young gentlemen in training.
Canvas-walled cubicles along each side provided sleeping berths, while
small arms, such as cutlasses and pistols, were stored aft.

Although kept shackled in leg irons, the prisoners were otherwise

treated well and made no complaints about the conditions on board the
Hector. As Pasley told Nessy, "every attention & Indulgence possible is
granted to him." Friendly interest from another quarter made Peter's circumstances yet more comfortable. As luck would have it, Captain Albemarle Bertie of the *Edgar,* already at moorings when the *Gorgon* arrived,
was also a relative, his wife, Emma, being the daughter of the helpful
James Modyford Heywood. In fact, after moving down the harbor, the
Hector was now moored beside the *Edgar,* making it extremely convenient for the Berties to keep an eye on young Peter. Soon Mrs. Bertie
was writing to Mrs. Heywood the kind of letters calculated to calm a
mother's fears: "I think it will be a great satisfaction to you to know, that
he has a Friend and Relation on the spot," Mrs. Bertie reassured her.
Many emissaries were soon crowding the *Hector*'s deck on Peter's behalf; officers from the *Edgar* (Lieutenant Bayne was a friend of Uncle
Holwell), messengers from Mrs. Bertie daily delivering baskets of fresh
vegetables and other tokens of kindness, other friends of her father's.
Days after arrival, Peter wrote to his mother for money so "that I may be
enabled to cloath myself with that decency which is a requisite," and
shortly afterward a package of new linen was duly delivered. Less tactfully, Peter also wrote to Mrs. Bligh asking for the return of certain attire
he had left to be laundered before departing with her husband on the
Bounty.

Peter was keenly aware that as the only officer among the prisoners
he was sure to draw the most interest and also might be held to a higher
standard of behavior. How his shipmates regarded the shower of special
attention the young midshipman received is not known. Most probably
they were encouraged and gratified, as it could only be useful to their
common cause to have one of their number viewed with such evident favoritism.

On the other hand, as was swiftly becoming evident, the interest
shown in Peter's case amounted to more than just better living conditions. Captain Pasley's pronouncements on the bleakness of Peter's case
notwithstanding, his efforts on his nephew's behalf had been tireless; he
already acquired a legal adviser, John Delafons, who was a senior purser

with the reputation for being an authority on naval courts-martial. Under Delafons's friendly direction, Peter had promptly sent a petition to the Lords Commissioners of the Admiralty requesting the favor of a speedy trial. As Peter told Nessy, this had been done so as to "have the desired effect of speedily making my guilt or Innocence known to the world"; all parties had been strictly advised, as they repeatedly reminded one another, that Peter's correspondence, ingoing and outgoing, would be closely read by outside parties. Nonetheless, even without matters spelled out, Nessy was quick to perceive that a speedy trial had advantages to Peter other than allowing him to clear his name. As she herself discreetly wrote, "Mr. Bligh is gone to the South Sea—but we must hope for the best." The best was obviously that the trial would take place before Bligh returned.

On July 10, amid a haze of early morning rain, Captain Sir Andrew Snape Hamond and Captain John Colpoys hoisted their pennants on their respective ships, the *Bedford* and the *Hannibal*. Colpoys was one of the hardest-serving captains around, having been at sea in active service for an unbroken period of thirty-seven years, even though he had just turned fifty. Before being appointed to the *Hannibal* in 1790, he had served in the East and West Indies, the North American station, the Channel and the Mediterranean.

Sir Andrew Snape Hamond was a protégé of the great Lord Howe—Richard "Black Dick" Howe, the former First Lord of the Admiralty, commander of the Channel fleet, and the recently appointed Vice Admiral of England. Hamond, a fearless and brilliant tactician, had proved himself worthy of such a mentor, as he pulled off a number of audacious feats during the American war. Handsome and aristocratic, Hamond exuded an air of dashing impetuosity. Now in his midfifties, he had been captain of the third-rate *Bedford* for just under a year; he too, as Pasley reassured Peter, was another "particular friend."

The *Hannibal* and *Bedford* got under way to join the rest of Lord Hood's fleet on patrol. Since Hood's presence was absolutely required to convene the court-martial, the movements of the fleet were followed with close attention. Although the interested parties were still in dreadful suspense, it was possible to forecast a trial sometime within the next few months.

Nessy Heywood's desire to fly to her brother had been thwarted by the concerned advice of all her male relatives, Peter included, who were concerned that the sight of her brother in leg irons would send her into shock. In any case, "no female relations would be permitted," as Peter told her; and Nessy at length was forced to concede, as Mr. Heywood had advised her, that it was best for Peter to remain "cool & composed," a state of mind that seems to have been tacitly and universally acknowledged as impossible to maintain with Nessy present. A vague plan to send out Peter's brother James was also scotched, on the grounds of his well-known "Warmth of Temper"; as Nessy told Peter, even the appearance of "the least Imprudence or want of Caution" was to be dreaded while he was in his present precarious situation.

Instead, Peter and Nessy attempted to catch up with each other's lives through their now faithful correspondence. While his first, lengthy letter had given the outline of his many tumultuous adventures, even on the quiet home front there was news to report. Peter would find his family in a new house, Nessy told her brother, one with a fine view of the sea. As for the family parlor, it was now chiefly decorated with Nessy's organ, "upon which I practice with unceasing assiduity that I may entertain my loved Peter; & which while sorrowing for his mournful & tedious absence was my chief amusement & consolation. . . ." Grandfather Spedding had died but not left an expected bequest; Henry, Peter's thirteen-year-old brother, was in Jamaica, after a fearful, tempestuous passage; old Birket, the family servant, was still alive, God bless her; an uncle had had the good fortune to win £15,000 in the lottery; Peter's drawing of Nader Shah was now hung over the mantelpiece—just why this young teenager should have chosen to immortalize the sacker of Delhi and plunderer of the Peacock Throne is not addressed.

It was probably around this time that Peter received the last letter his father had written to him, at the end of 1788. While recounting local and national news, such as the death and health of various Manx neighbors and the crisis caused by the insanity that had recently gripped the King, the letter was mostly a painful exercise in desperate pride as Peter John Heywood attempted to provide his son with a believable if wholly false explanation of why the Duke of Atholl had fired him. Enclosed with the letter were twelve tiny woodcock wing feathers to be used as delicate brushes for Peter's miniaturist paintings. These appear to have been the only legacy his father left Peter. The letter closed with a request to give his "respectful Compliments to Captain Bligh."

For his part, Peter sent to his family skillful sketches of the wreck of the *Pandora* and the camp established on the white-hot key, all those months and miles ago in the Pacific. In answer to Nessy's request, he also attempted a portrait of himself wearing one of the straw hats he had woven to pass the time in Batavia.

"I had no Looking Glass, therefore drew it from Recollection; & 'tis now one year at least since I saw my own Face," he told her. Nessy did not recognize the thin, pale face of this miniature and was shocked at the news that her brother stood only five foot seven and one half inches in his stocking feet.

"I am surpized you are not taller," exclaimed Nessy, who was perhaps handicapped by a conventional sense of what a young hero should look like. "I fully expected you wou'd have been 5 Feet 10 at least." The brother who had left with the *Bounty* was a well-proportioned young man, with a fair complexion and light brown hair.

"[L]et me ask you this," Peter rejoined with some energy, recalling the horror of Pandora's Box. "[S]uppose the last two years of *your* growth had been retarded by close Confinement nearly deprived of all kinds of necessary Aliment—shut up from the all-chearing Light of the sun for the space of five months—& never suffered to breathe the fresh Air . . . without any kind of Exercise to stretch & supple my Limbs— . . . how tall shou'd you have been my dear sister?"

As the dismal, overcast summer wore on, naval life at Portsmouth continued with serene indifference to the fate of the captives. The lords of the Admiralty paid a visit to the *Hector* on business unrelated to the

Bounty's men. Down in the gun room, the ten prisoners would have been unlikely to have missed the sounds of pomp and ceremony overhead, the thirteen-gun salute and tramp of smart boots. In fact there were many salutes given this summer, twenty-four guns for the Duke and Duchess of York as they left Portsmouth Dockyard, nineteen guns as the lords of the Admiralty passed the *Hector* on their way to Spithead, salutes on the arrival of various captains and foreign dignitaries. Above and below deck, the mundane routine of a working ship carried on, deliveries and stowage of provisions, washing of decks, and administration of punishment. A court-martial of the boatswain of the *Edgar* "for charges of embezzlement of stores" was held on August 1.

Shackled as they were, the prisoners spent most of their time sitting and waiting for news, reports, visitors and any diversion. Peter at least whiled away the days drawing sketches and reading the books that were delivered to him by his many well-wishers. But all this was difficult in the bare, dim room whose only light fell in long, low horizontal bars through the gun ports. And Montagu's special care notwithstanding, the weeks of impotent waiting had begun to take a toll.

"I fear owing to Perturbation of Mind I felt I may have inserted some weak & foolish Nonsense unworthy of a Man," Peter apologized to Nessy for words written in a previous letter. Nessy for her part was also becoming increasingly wrought and inclined to be less sympathetic than before to Mr. Bligh for branding her "amiable Brother with the vile appellation of Mutineer. . . .

"His cruelty and Barbarity in loading you with so approbrious an Epithet is therefore the more unpardonable or will so far from injuring you my dearest Peter recoil upon himself," wrote Nessy in loyal but incoherent passion. She derived much satisfaction from the report of a family friend that "every lady" believed in Peter's innocence. From time to time, the voices of Peter's other brothers and sisters intruded, expressing deference to Nessy as much as support of Peter; there was little question who was running the family show.

"My Dearest Brother," wrote Isabella Heywood, in a brief epistle, "[m]y sister Nessy has permitted me to express my joy in your arrival."

"[W]e envy Nessy the pleasure she will have in being with you," wrote Eliza. This was long after the official family determination had been made *not* to allow Nessy to travel to the mainland, but evidently Nessy kept hope alive in the Douglas parlor.

In early August, the *Hector*'s lieutenant of marines informed the prisoners that the Dutch East Indiaman carrying their old shipmate Thomas Hayward had been spoken off the Isle of Wight. The ship was bound up channel to Holland, but Hayward was expected in England shortly via a packet. His arrival would mean that all the "evidences" for the court-martial were returned.

The sobering news was shortly followed by a letter from Nessy containing a trumpet blast of her poetry (*"Come gentle Muse, I woo thee once again . . ."*). And it may be that her poetic effort, combined with the arrival of his former shipmate, stirred memories in Peter, for only days later he sent his sister a long and remarkable poem that he, in his turn, had written in Tahiti. Weaving together regret for events past and submission to his eventual fate, the poem is above all a passionate hymn to Tahiti. The poem, Peter explained to Nessy, had been composed following a dream whose powerful effect he would never forget. Remarkably, the dream had occurred on February 6, 1790, which, as Peter had only recently learned, had been the very day of his father's death.

"I *hammer'd* at it while at 'Taheite," Peter wrote of his poem, "& after writing it I learnt it by Heart." The poem described his soulful and solitary walks along Matavai's black beach at night, under the stately fronded palms when the only companions to his thoughts had been the "wakeful crickets" and moon-reflecting sea. Here in the paradise of the world Peter had nursed his "secret Melancholy," the painful knowledge that he was an exile.

> *Of all the flatt'ring Hopes which reign'd within*
> *His Breast, when first his native Home he left,*
> *Now baffled all! by one Man's fatal Sin,*
> *Hopeless alas!*

In Peter's dream, a divine presence had answered his lamentations with the reminder that whatever might befall him was God's will:

Nor can there ever happen an Event,
But Providence hath wisely it thought fit;
And 'tis by his Omnisciency, meant
Some greatly good, and useful End to hit.

To this dream, Peter now wrote to Nessy, "I owe . . . all my present serenity, & it was this alone which enabled me to support the many Troubles I
have had to encounter." This state of religious submission was what Peter strove to maintain throughout the harrowing weeks ahead. He would
be bombarded with advice, encouragement, solace and the prattle of
Nessy's bright optimism; but through it all Peter attempted to enter
some quiet, dark, interior place that he had long prepared for himself—
and to brace for the worst.

From early August, Portsmouth enjoyed a rare spell of fair, mild weather.
Captain Montagu had his people busy working up junk, or old cordage,
into swabs, sitting on deck to enjoy the fine clear days. The Prince of
Liechtenstein came on board for a brief visit, and was solemnly received
with thirteen guns. On Sundays, divine service was performed by the
ship's chaplain, the Reverend Mr. Cole; the prisoners too were permitted
benefit of clergy.

Tuesday, August 14, had closed on the *Hector* with the usual firing of
the evening gun, and when dawn broke the next day it revealed the fleet
at anchor off the Isle of Wight: Lord Hood had returned. By Thursday
the entire fleet was anchored at Spithead, the very names of the great
men-of-war conjuring all that was destructive and powerful from the
realms of nature, man and god—the *Bedford, Orion, Brunswick, Hannibal, Alfred, Niger, Juno, Racehorse, Rattlesnake, Tisiphone, Spitfire* and *Ores-
tes,* and Lord Hood's flagship, the *Duke.*

At the arrival of the fleet salutes thundered from all the ships at anchorage, and the noise of human traffic bounced around the water—the
cries and splashing of boats come to service the ships, the halloos and
oaths and laughter. For the prisoners in the dark belly of the *Hector,* the
arrival of Lord Hood represented the turning point in the long, open-

ended ordeal of waiting. Their trial would take place within the following month.

Hood had received the Admiralty's notification to prepare for the court-martial only two days earlier, when a ship bearing the orders had intercepted the fleet off the Lizard. The orders had stipulated that Hood return to Spithead with certain ships under his command, but this notice had come too late, as three of the stated ships had already been dismissed to their home stations on entering the Channel. However, as Hood informed the Admiralty when he arrived at Spithead, he had taken the liberty to make up the deficiency and "to supply their places by the *Hannibal Orion* and *Alfred*." By such random chance were the participating judges assembled.

The *Hannibal* was, of course, still under the command of the able Captain Colpoys. The *Orion*'s captain, John Duckworth, although now forty-four, was still in the very early stages of what would eventually become a distinguished career. The son of a clergyman, Duckworth had gone to sea at the age of eleven. Short, stout and muscular, he was said to be "never happy but when actively employed." His career to date had been somewhat erratic. During the American war, Duckworth, then a first lieutenant, on arriving off Rhode Island, had fired a friendly and enthusiastic salute, unwittingly blasting a transport ship in so doing and causing five men to be killed. The ensuing court-martial was a messy affair, due to a number of irregularities of protocol. Nevertheless, Duckworth was acquitted. Promoted to post-captain at the age of thirty-two, he gained the reputation with his men of being a humane and compassionate commander, serving the food from his own table to the ship's invalids. He also was known for keeping pigs on board, and an anecdote told of his reaction when one was swept overboard in heavy weather.

"Back the yards, back the yards; lower a boat, there's a pig overboard; my pig—pig—pig will be drowned," Duckworth had stammered.

"It's *our* pig," a watching midshipman had interjected.

"What—what? *their* pig—their pig: Keep on your course . . . we must not risk—risk—risk men's lives for a pig. . . ."

The captain of the *Alfred*, by contrast, was nearing the end of a not particularly remarkable career at fifty-two. Captain John Bazely's most distinguished service to date appears to have been as lieutenant of the *Alert* during the American war, when, after a dogged chase and much damage sustained, he once overpowered a rebel ship of superior force. His appointment to the *Alfred* was very recent—indeed, this would be the last but one ship on which he would serve.

The other captains of the fleet who would sit on the court-martial were Sir Roger Curtis, of the *Brunswick,* and Richard Goodwin Keats, of the *Niger.* Curtis was one of the most versatile and able officers in the service. While he was only a commander, and the youngest in his squadron at that, his abilities and "spirit" had caught the eye of Admiral Lord Howe and he had served as captain of the admiral's flagship. Subsequently promoted to post-captain, Curtis had distinguished himself at the siege of Gibraltar in 1781. Later appointed ambassador to the Emperor of Morocco and the Barbary States, he proved a clever and adroit diplomat. Back in Gibraltar, Curtis subdued a mutiny on one of the ships of the fleet "with great bravery and presence of mind."

A popular anecdote was told of a coach journey Curtis made to Portsmouth in civilian attire. Sharing the carriage was a young mate who delighted in regaling his fellow passengers with nautical jargon. Playing the lubber, Curtis had asked him leading questions: How could sailors see at night? Did they tie their ships up to posts in the darkness? Rolling his eyes, and with many a contemptuous "damn me," the young mate had put his companion straight. Soon after arriving in Portsmouth, the mate bumped into Sir Roger, now dressed in full naval splendor, with gold laced hat and an attentive retinue. Enjoying the mate's discomfiture, Curtis invited him to "splice the main brace" with him that evening. While Hamond remained a protégé of the great Lord Howe, Curtis—witty, worldly and entertaining—became one of the admiral's closest and most confidential friends. Curtis was familiar with the *Bounty* case, having been one of the judges at Bligh's court-martial on the loss of the ship.

Keats, the *Niger*'s captain, now thirty-five, was another clergyman's son. His swift rise through the ranks had been greatly aided by the fact that while he was a lieutenant on the *Prince George,* Prince William Henry (later King William IV) had served as a midshipman under his watch. Keats had so far seen action in the siege of Gibraltar and North America.

Lord Hood's flagship, the Portsmouth guardship *Duke,* was captained by John Knight, the son of a rear admiral. Under his father's tutelage, Knight had gone to sea at about the age of ten and had served almost twenty years in or off North America, as both surveyor and belligerent. After taking part in the attack on Bunker Hill, he "had the misfortune to fall into the hands of the enemy" and was held prisoner in Massachusetts for several months. On being released he had joined Hood in the West Indies, where he had seen many "skirmishes," including a brilliant encounter with superior French forces off St. Kitts, which had concluded with Knight's receiving his defeated enemy's sword. Physically Knight had the features and bearing of a gentleman, but the fiery, covetous eye of a buccaneer. He had joined the *Duke* only in June, days before the arrival of the *Bounty* "pirates" in the *Gorgon.*

Just as the news of Hayward's return had coincided with Peter's decision to share his most soulful Tahitian poem with his sister, so the arrival of the fleet coincided with a revealing letter to his mother. That same day, Peter decided the time had come to respond to some earlier, searching questions from Mrs. Heywood.

"The Question my dear Mother in one of your Letters concerning my swimming off to the Pandora is one Falsity among the *too many* in which I have often thought of undeceiving you & as frequently forgot," Peter began, as it were clearing his throat. Shackled in his dark prison with the prospect of the trial for his life now imminent, Peter allowed his mind to return to the island he loved, and to those few hours in which the entire balance of his life had been upset. On that fair and breezy morning in March 1791, he had left his house just after first daylight, setting out for the mountains with two Tahitian friends. He had gone about one hundred yards when a man came hastening after them to say that a ship had been spotted. Running to a place of rising ground that made a lookout, Peter had seen "with the utmost Joy" the *Pandora* laying off Hapiano, "a District two or three Miles to Windward of Matavia where I lived." Thinking immediately to share "such pleasing News" with his friend Coleman, who lived a mile and a half away, Peter had sent off one of his servants to alert him. On hearing the word, Coleman had at once set out in a canoe for the *Pandora;* Coleman's reluctance to remain with the mutineers had never seriously been questioned by anyone. Coleman attempted to intercept the ship as she was tacking into Matavai Bay, but the wind tippled his canoe, he capsized and was picked up by the *Pandora.* Meanwhile, Peter was onshore with his messmate Stewart, ready to set out with a double canoe, eventually reaching the *Pandora* as she streamed her anchor buoy.

As for being taken for a native: "being dressed in the *country* Manner, tanned as brown as themselves & tattowed like them in the most curious Manner, I do not in the least wonder at their taking us for *Natives,*" wrote Peter, rather breezily and with a just detectable note of pride.

And as for those tattoos: "I was tattowed, not to gratify my own Desire, but their's," he wrote defensively. In Tahiti, tattoos brought esteem; the more tattoos a man had, the more he was respected. A man without tattoos was an outcast. Besides, as Peter concluded, "I always made it a Maxim 'When I was in Rome to act as Rome did.' . . . "

For Mrs. Heywood, whose life had been mostly lived within the bounds of Douglas and Cumberland, these images her son conjured so casually—"the Mountains," "my house," the lookout point over Matavai Bay, the shore, his tattoos—must have seemed both threateningly vivid and incomprehensibly mysterious. Although, like most Englishwomen from strong, naval traditions, she had personally heard firsthand accounts of the West Indies or the Leeward Islands, North America, India or China, the glimpses Peter offered of an entire, alternate life were confounding. "I was an universal Favorite amongst those Indians," he declared in this same letter, "& perfectly conversant in their Language. . . . I was the greatest favorite of any Englishman on Shore & treated with respect by every Person on the Island in whose Mouths *my* Name ever was, as an Object of their Love and Esteem." Again, that near boastful, almost defiant tone: "perhaps you may think I flatter myself, but I really do not. Adieu my dearest Mother believe me your truly dutiful & most obedient Son," and Peter had signed off.

If his mother had not yet taken in the fact that the sojourn in Tahiti, during which her son had lived tanned and tattooed like a native, had changed him forever, one must suspect that Peter himself knew. What it cost him to conjure those green, cloud-tinged mountains, the neat and friendly plantations, the rattle of palms over Matavai's black beach, his home and wife in the gun-room prison is impossible to imagine. As each day closed, and the long bars of light vanished from the gun ports, he was left to contemplate many weighty issues; his approaching trial would bring either death, or life and freedom. And if the latter—then what?

Several days later, Hood departed for the Admiralty in London to give a report of his cruise. Around this time, the Admiralty sent notices in turn to those who were to appear at the court-martial. This included John Fryer, currently superintendent master at Chatham Dockyard; William Cole, now boatswain of the *Irresistible* at Pasley's port, Sheerness; the cantankerous William Purcell, now carpenter of the *Inspector* at Deptford yard; and William Peckover, the gunner on the *Ocean* at Woolwich. John Hallett was to travel the farthest, from Loch Ryan in Scotland. Captain Edwards seems to have been in London, while other of the *Pandora's* men were still quartered on the *Vengeance,* Pasley's ship. Robert Tinkler, John Fryer's young brother-in-law, was not summoned; why he was not is unclear, but in the event this was fortunate for the Heywoods. The fact that young Tinkler had just turned fourteen at the time he joined Bligh and Fryer in the open boat would have been highly inconvenient to Peter's plea of "youth and inexperience."

Pasley had already met a number of these "evidences" and had made some encouraging progress; indeed, the commander in chief in the Medway seemed to have been spending a great deal of time away from his station at Sheerness. After meeting with Cole and Fryer, Pasley reported to Peter that he had found "both favourable witnesses"— although it is difficult to imagine how he could possibly have found his meeting with Fryer reassuring. It was Fryer who had, after all, stated to his wife in his letter from Batavia that "the captain & me were surprised by Misters Christian, Stewart, Young & Haywood & the Master at Arms." But perhaps the embittered master, under the urgent, imposing—and flattering—attention of Commander in Chief Pasley, had begun to recollect events somewhat differently.

"Keep up your spirits," Fryer now took it upon himself to write to Peter, in the wake of Pasley's visit. "[F]or I am of opinion no one can say you had an active part in the mutiny; and be assured of my doing you justice when called upon."

In addition to seeking out the witnesses one by one for close questioning, Pasley had also been to the Admiralty to read the various depositions submitted by Bligh and his officers on the loss of the *Bounty*, as well as the minutes of Bligh's own court-martial. Nothing in these, Pasley was reassured to see, had specifically implicated Peter. He also made a personal visit to Captain Edwards—"that *Fellow*," as he indignantly called him, whose "inhuman Rigour of Confinement" of the prisoners he would never forget; "even" Edwards had allowed that Peter had voluntarily identified himself as "late of the *Bounty*" when he had come aboard the *Pandora*.

But from a legal point of view, the nub of the issue—as Pasley was compelled to remind Nessy—was that "the Man who stands Neuter is equally guilty with him who lifts his arms against his Captain." It was not enough to prove that Peter had not actively abetted the mutineers; acquittal could be won only if it could be shown he had helped resist them.

Almost from the outset, Peter had been benefiting from the friendly advice of John Delafons. But what Pasley now had in mind was someone who could offer coaching and a proper legal strategy. When the matter was put to Peter's family, they had instantly declared that only Erskine and Mingay could be trusted to represent their Peter: Lord Erskine and James Mingay were two of the most eminent lawyers of the day, as well as the most fiery and intimidating. Mingay had lost his right hand in an accident and had replaced it with a hook, which he wielded to great effect in the courtroom. However, as Pasley pointed out, a gift for fiery oratory would be to no point since barristers could not "exhibit" at a naval court-martial, which was not run like a civil trial. A naval court would first summon the various evidences for the prosecution, who could in turn be cross-examined both by the court and directly by the individual defendants. In the second part of the proceedings, each prisoner would be allowed to give a statement and to call upon witnesses in his defense. His Majesty's Navy also had an aversion to lawyers, as it turned out, and so what was required was not a high-flying personality, but a sound adviser working discreetly behind the scenes.

"Any sensible sound Lawyer to point out the proper Questions . . . & capable of writing a good defense will answer the Purpose," Pasley advised Peter. But from subsequent correspondence it appears that Pasley did not quite succeed in making his point. Suddenly a notification came from John Beardsworth of Lincoln's Inn, the lawyer of Peter's father, that Francis Const had been hired, and not it appears with Pasley's blessing.

"I am glad Erskine & Mingay are not retained," he would later confide to Peter, "and am almost sorry Const is." The jittery Heywood family appears to have jumped the gun.

On the morning of August 23, Lord Hood raised his flag on the *Duke*, having returned from London the previous night. Pasley received orders to send the *Pandora*'s men by sea round to Portsmouth when they had all finally arrived from Holland, along with William Cole, the *Bounty* boatswain, who was to hitch a ride as a passenger. The other evidences were to make their way to Portsmouth by land. Lieutenant Hayward, also under Pasley's direction, was to make his way to London for a visit to the Admiralty before venturing on to Portsmouth. As Pasley wrote to Peter, "no Trial can take Place without my knowing it."

Meanwhile, Peter continued to receive a stream of helpful directives. Following Mrs. Bertie's advice, he ordered a suit for his court appearance and, abetted by her feminine eye for detail, a mourning band of black crepe for the memory of his father. More relatives and well-wishers entered the picture. Attorney John Beardsworth was now also advising. Uncle Colonel James Holwell, writing from his estate near Tunbridge Wells, in Kent, offered the kind of sentimental support that was welcome, but ultimately to no purpose.

"[Y]ou have given of filial duty . . . to the best of parents," wrote Colonel Holwell; he himself was the son of the heroic Governor Zephaniah Holwell, a director of the East India Company and one of the few survivors of the Black Hole of Calcutta. "[Y]our education has been the best; & from these considerations alone without the very least evidence of your own Testimony, I would as soon believe the Archbishop of Canterbury would set fire to the city of London, as suppose you could directly or indirectly join in such a d——d piece of Business."

With time running out, Pasley was keenly aware that although much useful background work had been done, Peter was still not prepared specifically to face his day in court. And it was with matters in this irresolute state that a man who was to become one of the most important figures in Peter's life entered the family picture.

"A Friend of Mine, Mr. Graham who has been Secretary to the different Admirals on the Newfoundland Station for these twelve years, consequently Judge Advocate at Court-Martials all that Time, has offered me to attend you," wrote Pasley to Peter, the dark clouds that had oppressed him visibly parting. "[H]e has a thorough Knowledge of the Service, uncommon Abilities, & is a very good Lawyer—he conducted Capt. P——'s Court Martial who wou'd have been broke unassisted by him."

Aaron Graham had first met Pasley in 1771, when at nineteen he had served as clerk on the *Sea Horse* under Pasley's command off the coast of Africa. He seems to have impressed Pasley even then, as he was to impress other superiors in his somewhat unorthodox naval career. For it was, as one memorial stated, in *civil* service—the business art of balancing accounts and numbers and adroit paperwork—not strictly in naval work, that Graham excelled: "At length, in consequence of his abilities, and conciliating manners, he was appointed secretary to a Flag Ship, and in this capacity, attained the friendship and confidence of all the Admirals with whom he sailed, no less by the amiableness of his disposition, than by a strict and scrupulous integrity, that invited investigation, and set suspicion at defiance"—so curious and suggestive is this last sentence that the memorial is worth quoting in full.

Aaron Graham had been born in Gosport, close by Portsmouth Harbour. He had, then, grown up within sight of the glorious comings and goings of His Majesty's fleets. Graham's naval service seems to have been clerical rather than nautical from the beginning. After impressing Pasley, he had moved on to other ships before landing on the Newfoundland station. In this bleak and remote outpost of British jurisdiction, Graham officially served as secretary to four successive governors, but his gift for bureaucratic duties ensured that he wore many unofficial hats and essentially ran the station. Quietly, unthreateningly, adroitly, he was the ingratiating subordinate who mastered any task or crisis, and on whom his grateful superiors came to rely. Graham superintended all things afloat; he cheerfully handled all paperwork and all legal issues; he organized theatrical events; he was also an agent for prizes, thereby obtaining a share of all that was captured by the station during the American war. On his return to England in late 1791, he was appointed a police magistrate.

Graham, we are told by his memorial, was "rather under the middle size." He was neat in dress and person, with unoffensive manners, "insinuating in his address." He was constantly employed, it would seem, in helping deserving superior officers, with money, with advice, just as he had now stepped forward to offer assistance to Peter Heywood.

But the full range of Graham's talents can be appreciated only by a glance at what he would go on to accomplish in the years immediately ahead. During the later part of the "great mutiny" of 1797—the politically radicalized sailors' strike at the Nore—Aaron Graham would serve the Admiralty as a spy. He would also for several seasons be a manager of the Theatre Royal, Drury Lane, serving the statesman and playwright Richard Brinsley Sheridan in the same able manner in which he had served the Newfoundland governors.

And it would be in this latter managerial capacity that he would form an important friendship with a young, exceptionally pretty actress of no particular professional standing named Harriet Mellon. When Miss Mellon, who was in her twenties, caught the eye of the banker Thomas Coutts, age seventy, married, and said to be the richest man in England, it was Aaron Graham who was entrusted with their clandestine correspondence.

Graham, then, was not only exceptionally clever; he was also a great student of human character. He was the person whom a certain kind of gentleman—a gentleman in a bit of a pickle—might seek out, and upon whose knowing, discreet, confidential advice and actions he could rely. He was exactly the kind of knowledgeable guide Pasley had been seeking. Francis Const might be a very good barrister, but Aaron Graham

Artocarpus incisa, or the breadfruit, c. 1769, by Sydney Parkinson
(Courtesy of National Maritime Museum)

View of part of Oaitepeha Bay, Tahiti, 1773, by William Hodges *(Courtesy of National Maritime Museum)*

Vaitephiha Bay, Tahiti, 1777, by John Webber *(Courtesy of Art Archive)*

Opposite: Poedua, daughter of a chieftain, c. 1782, by John Webber *(Courtesy of National Library of Australia)*

The mutineers turning Bligh and some of the officers and crew adrift from the *Bounty*, 1790, by Robert Dodd *(Courtesy of Stephen Walters)*

Bligh's attempt to land on Tofua, 1790, by Robert Cleveley *(Courtesy of National Library of Australia)*

A view of the Cape of Good Hope and Table Bay from the *Vlijt*, December 1789, by William Bligh
(Courtesy of Stephen Walters)

"The small blue Paroquet of Otaheite," 1792, by William Bligh
(Courtesy of Mitchell Library, State Library of New South Wales)

Transplanting breadfruit trees from Tahiti on the *Providence* voyage, 1796, by Thomas Gosse
(Courtesy of National Library of Australia)

Landing at Bounty Bay, Pitcairn Island, c. 1825, by Richard Beechey
(Courtesy of Mitchell Library, State Library of New South Wales)

knew not only law but what people—especially in naval circles—thought about the law. Const was an aspiring amateur writer, and can be credited with a number of "epilogues" and "prologues" to presumably lost or never published plays and he kept literary company—including that of Richard Sheridan. Aaron Graham managed men like Sheridan, read their weaknesses, knew their finances, and told them what they could and could not safely do.

Graham volunteered his services in late August, and immediately got to work. On the mild, fair evening of September 5, Pasley stumped over to Const's chambers in the Middle Temple, off Fleet Street, to meet with Const and Graham. Whatever was discussed between the three men at this night session apparently shed new, promising light upon the entire proceedings. "I shall say Nothing of what I expect the Result may be but at present Appearances are favorable," Pasley wrote to Nessy the following day, in a complete reversal of his earlier cautions against undue optimism. He had now seen Graham's fabled skills at work, and could not refrain from praising this "intimate & very particular Friend."

"I have every Reason to think you may look forward with pleasing Hopes," Pasley wrote to Peter with the same new exuberance. "I refer you to my Friend Mr. Graham for Information."

Of great significance was the fact that Graham had already met with most of the evidences prior to this important meeting. It is noteworthy that when Graham would do his undercover work during the Nore crisis, he was willing to pay for information. From his wide experience of human nature—with sailors, with the range of questionable types passing through his hands in his capacity as a police magistrate, with gentlemen in straitened circumstances—it is a safe bet that Graham knew how to work the witnesses better than had Commander in Chief Pasley.

Meanwhile, in Portsmouth, Lord Hood had his hands full. The day on which Pasley had held his meeting with Peter's new counsel had seen a lot of activity around the harbor. The *Scourge,* a sloop coming to Spithead with a small capture in tow, had sent a boat to shore that had foundered in rough water. Some of the boat's party were picked up after floating for nearly seven hours; but two midshipmen spotted earlier clinging to wreckage had slipped beneath the water and been lost.

On this same day, Lord Hood began to focus on the practical logistics of the trial. He conferred with the captains and all were in agreement with him that "it will be extremely inconvenient" to assemble anywhere other than Portsmouth Harbour. At the same time, anticipating a larger than average crowd, "as Counsel are to attend from London," he suggested to the Admiralty that they use one of the three-decked ships in ordinary, or out of commission, laid up near the dockyard. Finally a bar of some kind needed to be erected in the ship for the prisoners.

On the purely legal front, Hood also asked the Admiralty's counsel for a decision whether the mutineers were to be tried separately, as he understood they wished, or as a group. He personally was of the opinion that they should be tried together, "the whole being involved in one criminal act." This issue was still pending.

The Admiralty had already made other legal determinations concerning the *Bounty* affair, such as whether the prisoners' alleged offense amounted to an act of piracy under common law. The precedents for this offense—such as Captain Kidd's theft of a ship—had, however, been found to pertain to "ships belonging to private owners." Consequently the Admiralty's counsel concluded that "the proper way of proceeding in this Case will be by a Court Martial according to the Articles of War." The main changes were clear enough under Article XIX: "If any Person in or belonging to the Fleet shall make or endeavour to make any mutinous Assembly upon any Pretence whatsoever, every Person offending herein, and being convicted thereof by the Sentence of the Court-martial, shall suffer Death."

Hood himself, distracted by his many responsibilities as commander in chief of the port, was also for personal reasons not in a particularly happy mood. He had recently applied for and lost the prestigious position of Vice Admiral of England, for which he had been in competition with his younger brother. The Right Honorable Samuel, Lord Hood, had been born the son of a clergyman and a gentleman's daughter of humble means. Both he and his brother, Alexander, Lord Bridport, had gone to sea and achieved enormous distinction. Following a steady, solid career pursued since his first naval service at age sixteen, Hood had, in 1778, been appointed commissioner of Portsmouth Dockyard, "an honourable and lucrative position," as one biographer recorded, and one greatly aided by the fact that he had married the daughter of a mayor of Portsmouth. This and his simultaneous appointment as governor of the royal naval academy at the age of fifty-three were seen as the graceful winding down of his active service. Two years later, however, to the astonishment of many, Hood was promoted to rear admiral and sent out at the head of a squadron to reinforce Admiral Sir George Rodney in the West Indies. It was in this second wind of his career that he gained the most distinction, and in 1782, following a series of decisive actions against the French, he had been created Baron Hood of Catherington.

Despite this solid, satisfying advancement, despite the prizes, honors and titles achieved, Lord Hood was a bitter and disappointed man. As recently as June, he had written his distinguished brother Lord Bridport (whom he addressed as "Sir Alexander") a letter rehashing his grievances of years past as well as more recent, familial hurts. His surrender of a hard-won seat in Parliament to accommodate the Admiralty in 1788—all of four years before—had been particularly harmful; by this, he told his brother, "I am beggar'd and thereby broken hearted." This was something of a smoke screen for his real cause of grief—namely, that his brother, this same "Sir Alexander," had put his name forward for the position his own heart was set upon, Vice Admiral of England.

"Whether you will have it is more than I can tell but this I know, that I shall not or anything else," Samuel told his brother, bitterly, of the contested position. "I believe there never was a man, who had lent himself to an administration, with that zeal & attention I have done, that was ever so neglected."

Lord Hood was now sixty-seven years of age, on the cusp of the final tier of his career. Either some final flurry of advancements would catapult him into the legion of true naval immortals—or he would die as another vaguely important career officer. His long thin face, tight lips and introspective, disappointed eyes betrayed the fact that it was the latter he expected. Only days before the court-martial commenced, he would learn both that he had not received the appointment he had applied for and that his brother had been advanced, if not to Vice Admiral—that coveted position had gone to Lord Howe—to Rear Admiral of England.

Beyond the Portsmouth ramparts, out beyond the shelter of the harbor and the anchorage, there were other causes for grave concern. Across the Channel in France, the revolutionary politics of *Liberté, Égalité, Fraternité* had swung wildly out of control. The Bastille had fallen to the mob in 1789 and the King and Queen were currently imprisoned and under imminent threat of ignoble and brutal deaths. Only a month before, in August 1792, the Tuileries had been stormed and the King's Swiss Guard massacred. By September stories of the massacre of aristocrats were filling the London papers. The Countess of Chèvre and her five young children had been mutilated and then butchered; the Countess of Perignon and her two daughters had been stripped naked, covered with oil and roasted alive in the Place Dauphin while France's new *citoyens* danced and cheered. Like the aristocrats, churchmen were a favorite target and some three hundred terrified priests had recently escaped across the Channel, washing up in Portsmouth. Where this all might end was impossible to fathom; Prime Minister Pitt was struggling to maintain peace, but Englishmen were also advised to keep an eye "on certain coffeehouses in Jermyn-street and about the Haymarket," an area alleged to be the haunt of French sympathizers and spies. These circumstances were of first importance to those captains gathered in Portsmouth from their recent cruises. At the end of the day, their business was war. And at this unsettled time, they may have had difficulty extending keen interest to the faraway and famously peaceable South Seas, where two of His Majesty's ships under Captain William Bligh were now searching again for breadfruit.

"[O]ne useful lesson offers itself to mankind," the *Times* was to opine on the very day the court-martial commenced: "Revere your Laws."

On September 8, Peter at last met Aaron Graham. The following day, a Sunday, Graham returned to the *Hector* with Const and, with Captain Montagu's permission, conferred privately with his client. As had Pasley's, Peter's spirits soared as a result of his *tête-à-tête* with Graham: "I have something to say that will give you pleasure tho' my Trial is not yet over," Peter wrote to his mother two days later, informing her of his meeting with Mr. Graham. "[F]rom what Information I had the Happiness to receive I have every reason, as may you my Dear Mother, to look

forward with the most pleasing Hopes of——————I need not——————indeed
I should not say much to you. . . ." Like his sister, however, Peter could
never resist the chance for a piece of verse, and he now affixed to his letter as tactless a couplet as ever a mother received:

The awful Day of Trial now draws nigh
When I shall see another Day—or—Die!

"[T]ell my sisters to *set taught* the *Topping-lifts* of their Hearts from an
Assurance that with God's Assistance all will yet *end well!*" he concluded
on a more jocular note.

For her part Nessy, knowing that the usual delays in the mail packet
could mean that the family might hear nothing of Peter's fate until some
time after verdict had been rendered, had already sent her final good
wishes. As if binding her brother with protective spells and incantations,
Nessy offered Peter her blessing, her prayers, and consigned him to the
care of all the powers in heaven: "May that Almighty providence whose
tender Care has hitherto preserved you be still your powerful protector—
may he instill into the Hearts of your Judges every sentiment of justice,
Generosity, & Compassion—May Hope, Innocence, & Integrity, be your
firm Support—& Liberty, Glory, & Honor your just Reward—May all
good Angels guard you from even the Appearance of Danger, & may you
at length be restored to us. . . ."

While Peter and his family had prepared for the trial with all the considerable means at their disposal, the other prisoners also took what
measures they could. Confined together in the gun room, every man
would have been aware of Peter's resources, the emissaries, the letters
and words of advice from visiting officers and relatives, the visits from
Delafons, Const, Beardsworth and finally Aaron Graham. If they had not
known before this time, they had surely learned by now that when the
stakes were high one did not sit idle and trust to the impartial law of His
Majesty's appointed judges, nor look to Providence.

James Morrison, boatswain's mate, and Thomas Burkett, able seaman, had both received letters bearing testimony to their good character
from officers under whom they had formerly served. Captain Stirling
represented that he could "perfectly recollect" Morrison's "sobriety and

attention to his duty" while on the sloop *Termagant,* back in 1782; more to the point, he had always "paid due respect to his superiors." Commander John Doling recalled that Burkett had behaved with such "sobriety and attention to his duty" that he had been "confidentially considered" when, in 1786, they had both served on the *Hector,* that same ship on which Burkett was now confined; the *Hector,* then as now, had never left Portsmouth Harbour. It is probable that other prisoners made similar unsuccessful attempts to establish their "characters"; a lot would have depended on pure chance—a captain at sea, for example, could not be reached. Moreover, the most recent former service could only have been in 1787, just before the *Bounty* sailed: how many able seamen could count on being remembered five years after the fact from a crew of hundreds?

Only one other man had the wits, gumption and capability to hire outside legal counsel. William Muspratt, assistant to the *Bounty*'s cook, had retained the services of Stephen Barney, a lawyer of the Inner Temple and a former town clerk of Portsmouth. How Muspratt of all men had the means to take this step is a question that has long been debated, but it is possible to venture at least one explanation. His brother Joseph, with whom he was particularly close, was employed at this time as a groom at Cam's Hall, in nearby Fareham, the town where Stephen Barney lived. Cam's Hall, recently built and reputed to be one of the most elegant estates in the area, belonged to the wealthy Delmé family, and it may be that they had put up the funds for their groom's brother's defense. More conventional than Aaron Graham, and with no reputation for Graham's intellectual flair, Barney nonetheless would prove an able agent for his client.

As September 12, the date designated for the start of the trial, loomed closer, Lord Hood was further inconvenienced by the opinion of some of his captains that on reflection the court-martial should be assembled not on a spare three-decker, but on his own ship, the *Duke.* The propriety of holding a court-martial on a ship in ordinary had been questioned, and was believed to be without precedent. With their eyes on the suspect "Counsel from London" who would be in attendance, the concerned captains pointed out that such an irregularity might give later grounds for an appeal of the sentence. Consequently, even though the weather had turned unpleasantly squally, Hood weighed anchor and brought his ship from Spithead closer to the harbor.

Two captains who had arrived separately from the fleet completed the muster of court-martial judges. Sir Andrew Snape Douglas of the *Alcide*, age thirty-one, was the nephew of Sir Andrew Snape Hamond. Although he was an officer of enormous promise, the feats for which he would achieve lasting glory still lay ahead. Douglas was destined to live a short life, and to die a gallant, painful death.

Captain John Nicholson Inglefield had achieved renown on two occasions. In 1782, having seen hazardous action against the French in the West Indies, Inglefield was returning to England in command of the *Centaur* when a hurricane hit his convoy. In the howling turmoil, a number of ships went down with great loss of life. The *Centaur*, dismasted and thrown on her beam ends, was for a while kept afloat by the exertions of Inglefield and his crew, but on the eighth day she too suddenly went down. In wild high seas Inglefield and eleven other survivors had set out in the ship's pinnace, with little food and little equipment; at one point, they were forced to use blankets to improvise a sail. After sixteen days of great suffering and the loss of one life, they had arrived in Fayal, in the Azores. Like Bligh, Inglefield had published an account of this sensational adventure, which had attracted much attention—Byron's great shipwreck scene in *Don Juan* was lifted almost verbatim from Inglefield's narrative:

> *Nine souls more went in her: the long-boat still*
> *Kept above water, with an oar for mast,*
> *Two blankets stitch'd together, answering ill*
> *Instead of sail, were to the oar made fast . . .*

It was this great voyage that Sir Joseph Banks's correspondent James Matra had waggishly referred to on learning the news of Bligh's voyage in the *Bounty* launch. Until Bligh's journey, Inglefield's travails in the *Centaur*'s pinnace had been one of the most highly regarded feats of survival and seamanship.

Inglefield's other great claim to fame was as the cuckolded husband in a notorious divorce case. This too had been published from "an Authentic copy" of the shorthand notes of the trial. Interested readers were thus able to learn that Mrs. Ann Inglefield, after nearly thirteen years of marriage and four children, had "cast lustful eyes upon the negro lad" whom Inglefield had taken into his family, that the lad wore an apron and that Mrs. Inglefield "would not let that apron alone." Also disclosed was the fact that Inglefield was a jealous husband who had used spies to monitor his wife while he was away at sea, and that persons listening at her locked door had heard such noises "precisely as if . . . two persons, upon the floor, or a chair, or something of that kind, were doing what men and women are apt sometimes to do in the dark." Somehow, Byron resisted this material, and somehow poor Inglefield weathered this second storm.

Now forty-four, Inglefield had just returned from the coast of Africa in the 50-gun *Medusa*. Early in his career, Inglefield had served under both Lord Hood and his brother. He was especially close to the former, naming his son Samuel Hood Inglefield after his friend and mentor. Inglefield was a humane man. Only a year before, he had taken some pains to plead for the lives of seamen who were charged with piracy on his African station, pointing out to the Admiralty that the men had been ill treated and were only trying to obtain their liberty.

The sum experience of the twelve captains brought together for the court-martial represented England's great naval campaigns of the past few decades. Collectively, the men had seen wars and blockades, foul weather and shipwreck; they had been wounded and been prisoners of war. They had commanded 74-gun ships and been responsible for companies of hundreds of men. As sea warriors, they were mindful of the Articles of War, which bound them never to display fear in combat, never to hang back, never to retreat against orders. All were braced to embark upon new campaigns if the developments in France warranted. None had ever been involved in a venture such as the breadfruit voyages of Sir Joseph Banks.

Curiously, the least experienced of these men, by a long shot, was the amiable Albemarle Bertie, Peter's relative by marriage. Although Bertie was now thirty-seven, his naval résumé could be told in a few short lines.

Promoted to lieutenant in December 1777, after previous service so obscure it has not been recorded, Bertie was captured by the French eight months later. Released after four months' captivity, he saw no further service of any kind until 1782, when he was nonetheless made postcaptain, at the tender age of twenty-seven. Subsequently he had command of one other Channel ship before being appointed to the *Edgar,* now moored so cozily beside the *Hector.*

In a delightful crossing of paths, Bertie would later make the acquaintance of that most discerning judge of character, Jane Austen, who declared there was "nothing to like or dislike" about him. And it would have to be allowed that, with his somewhat pampered expression and vague unfocused gaze, he was not a man naturally to command attention. But Captain Bertie had one great asset: he was married to Emma Heywood, the daughter of James Modyford Heywood, the same "Mr. Heywood of Plymouth" spoken of with such deference by Peter's family. This same Mr. Heywood, in his turn, had the happy fortune to have married the sister of the great Lord Howe and was thus known in royal, government and Admiralty circles as "a relation of Lord Howe." Indeed, to this familial connection Mr. Heywood owed one of the only two offices he appears to have held in the course of his entire life, six months' service as a lord of the Admiralty. Only a few summers before, Mr. Heywood had played host to the royal family, who had come out to his beautiful Devon estate at Maristow to admire the grounds. Another of his daughters, Sophia Heywood Musters, had been the toast of London and was rumored to have had an affair with the Prince of Wales.

Lord Howe's relationship to the Heywoods does not appear to have been much known outside their immediate family circle, nor does he appear to have taken much interest in their affairs before the events leading to the court-martial. It was he, indeed, who had been partly responsible for Bligh's maddening delay in receiving sailing orders for the *Bounty,* when young Peter had been on board. However, his lordship had been kept abreast of Peter's activities through James Modyford Heywood, who read him letters Peter had written from the *Bounty*—Lord Howe had been pleased to comment on Peter's fine nautical description of the *Bounty*'s attempt to round the Horn. That he now came to take a personal interest in the court-martial is evident from a discreetly worded letter Howe wrote four days before the trial commenced to his close friend Sir Roger Curtis, one of Peter's judges, requesting that Curtis stay close to Portsmouth until his "court-Martial business" was over.

There is no sure knowing what Aaron Graham saw in Peter's apparently hopeless circumstances that had made him so confident of winning his client's freedom. But it may be, with his astute understanding of how life in the navy worked, that Graham had instantly grasped that the salient facts of the issue at hand were not Peter's guilt or innocence. The sudden "favourable" nature of the evidences; Peter Heywood's relationship to the most powerful naval figure in the land; his relative's presence as a judge on his court-martial; Pasley's two "particular friends" also sitting as judges; the presence of Captains Curtis and Hamond, who owed their careers to Lord Howe—these may have been the facts that most interested Graham.

On September 12, when the court-martial was at last convened, Captain Bligh was navigating the Endeavour Strait en route to the West Indies; once again, he had made a successful collection of Tahitian breadfruit. Thus Nessy's fondest, guilty hope was to be fulfilled: as unorthodox as it might be, the chief witness for the prosecution would not, after all, be present at the mutineers' court-martial.

COURT-MARTIAL

At eight A.M. on September 12, the *Duke* hoisted the signal for a court-martial, and then fired a single gun for it to assemble. At half past eight, the ten *Bounty* prisoners were led from their quarters in the *Hector*'s gun room and embarked into one of the her boats, where a guard of marines stood at stiff attention.

Conspicuous in their red coats, the marines remained at attention throughout the short journey, which still took the oarsmen over an hour in the choppy, ragged weather. Under a low, gray, dispiriting sky, the prisoners were carried among the great ships at anchor toward the outer harbor, where the *Duke* was moored. Here, they were solemnly taken on board with much formality, and finally led to the captain's great cabin at the stern of the ship, where their judges were assembled, along with the various counsel and the men to be called upon as evidences, or witnesses.

In theory, Lord Hood, as President, acted the role of counsel for the prisoners; once the trial was under way, it was he who was to intervene and caution them as to when they should or should not respond. But the actual running of the court was delegated to a Judge Advocate, Moses Greetham, who had also served the same role on the courts-martial of Bligh and William Purcell and so was more intimately familiar with the *Bounty* affair than most. Greetham opened the trial by reading the "Circumstantial letter," a preamble laying out the particulars of the case before the court—the history of the *Bounty*'s breadfruit commission, the large cargo of plants "in a very flourishing State," the seizure of the ship off Tofua by Fletcher Christian, officer of the watch, and the voyage of the *Pandora* to bring the mutineers to justice. It was particularly noted that the men captured on Tahiti were divided into two groups: persons who "came on board the Pandora," and those who "were taken a few Days afterwards on another Part of the Island." Listed as the former were "Peter Heywood, George Stewart, Joseph Coleman, and Richard Skinner." Stewart and Skinner had, of course, died in the *Pandora*.

The preamble concluded, Greetham swore in the judges. Standing with heads uncovered, left hand on the Act of Parliament that vested authority in the proceedings, right hand on the Bible, each captain solemnly responded to the pronouncement of his name: "I, Andrew Hamond," "I, George Montagu," "I, John Bazely" . . . The roll completed, the captains took their seats. Arrayed behind a long table, with the great cabin window at the backs, the twelve men formed an awe-inspiring wall of blue dress coats, gold lace and buttons. The prisoners before them, who had arrived from the East Indies in the nankeen clothing of their own make, were a ragged lot, Peter Heywood excepted. He was in the smart new suit and mourning crepe suggested by Mrs. Bertie. Some—perhaps most—of the men standing humbly before the court were undoubtedly destined to be found guilty, and all Heywood's associates understood the need for Peter to stand apart from his ill-fated fellows as conspicuously as possible.

Only two days earlier, Peter had given notice that he would submit at the court-martial itself a last formal petition to Lord Hood, "By the Advice of my Friends," that he be tried alone. This issue had been broached earlier, and Hood had deferred the decision to the Admiralty's legal advisers, who in their wisdom had replied that the matter was entirely up to the court. Hood himself had particularly strong feelings on the subject that did not bode well for any of the accused.

"The *Bounty*'s Mutineers being charged with and were guilty of the same atrocious Crime, committed at the same moment," he had stated on record, well before the court had even convened. It was true, as he acknowledged, that Lieutenant Bligh noted that three and possibly four men (if including Michael Byrn) had been held against their will; yet, as he now observed, "two of these three fled from the *Pandora*'s Officer, and did not surrender themselves until compelled from necessity." Additionally, as Hood pointed out, each individual prisoner would be able to put questions on his own behalf to each witness giving evidence for the prosecution, and would later be able to call on witnesses when presenting his defense, so that his case would be in no way compromised. After some discussion, Hood's view prevailed and it was announced to the court that "the whole of the Prisoners must be tried together."

Before any evidences were presented, Greetham read to the court Bligh's long and vivid report from Coupang. This and excerpts from his official log would be Bligh's only contribution to the trial. Now Bligh's angry and amazed words conjured the day of mutiny, his own humiliating bondage, the shouts and threats on the *Bounty*'s deck, and the horror of the overloaded launch.

Beyond the listening blue-coated captains, Portsmouth Harbour could be seen through the great paneled window that formed almost the entire stern wall of the cabin. Dirty weather, "squally with some rain," as it would be logged for this day, swept past the window. Outside on deck, the *Duke*'s master fussed with the small bower anchor whose cable was found to be worn. Back on the *Hector*, deeper in the harbor, carpenters on loan from the dockyard had come to dismantle bulkheads that had previously been installed in the captain's cabin for an earlier court-martial. Otherwise, the day's main event was the opening of a cask of pork.

Along one side of the great cabin, facing the captains, were crowded the witnesses and interested onlookers. Many of these were officers from the *Duke* and other nearby ships. Perhaps nothing could so poignantly underscore how small a venture, how desperately unimportant, the *Bounty* had been than this casual assemblage of captains and lieutenants who thronged the big men-of-war. The *Duke* alone carried five lieutenants; by contrast, Lieutenant Bligh had been the *Bounty*'s single commissioned officer. Gathered with the naval officers were also such well-known personages as Sir Archibald Macdonald, the Attorney-General; Lord McCartney, the new envoy to China; Sir Nash Grose and William Ashurst, both distinguished judges of the Court of the King's Bench; and Secretary of State George Rose. Lieutenant Hallett's father,

John Hallett, was also in attendance. Captain Pasley—perhaps to his relief—had been unable to attend.

Because Bligh's letter to the Admiralty from Coupang had been written to report the circumstances of the loss of his ship, it was not a detailed report of the mutiny itself; the actual criminal act with which the ten men before the court were charged amounted to very little of the entire document. In this very general overview, the only individuals specified by Bligh were "Fletcher Christian, who was Mate of the Ship and Officer of the Watch," and "the Ships Corporal [Charles Churchill]"; these designated perpetrators were "assisted by others," none of whom were named. Toward the end of his report, Bligh broke the company down into two lists, "[t]he people who came in the Boat" with him and "the people who remained in the Ship" with Christian. The latter list, of course, included the names of all the men now standing before the blue-coated judges: Peter Heywood, James Morrison, Charles Norman, Thomas McIntosh, Joseph Coleman, Thomas Burkett, Thomas Ellison, John Millward, Michael Byrn and William Muspratt. With the exception of Norman, McIntosh and Coleman, whom Bligh had specifically stated as having been held by the mutineers against their will, there was no further reference of any kind to any other individual's role or culpability.

Bligh's official log, on the other hand, was more explicit: "Just before Sun rise Mr. Christian, Mate, Chas. Churchill, Ships Corporal, John Mills, Gunners Mate, and Thomas Burkett, Seaman, came into my Cabbin while I was a Sleep and seizing me tyed my hands with a Cord behind my back," read the entry for Tuesday, April 28, 1789. Outside his cabin Alexander Smith, John Sumner and Matthew Quintal stood sentinel. All of the men named save for Burkett were dead or had departed with Christian. Here, as in his report, Bligh had affixed his lists of loyalists and mutineers, but with additional commentary—particularly expansive in his private log: "Christian the Capt. of the Mutineers is of a respectable family in the North of England, & from my connection with a part of them I had taken this Young Man to bring him forward in life"; Heywood was "also of a respectable family in the North of England and a Young Man of Abilities as well as Christian, and is connected with a most respected officer in our service captain Thos. Pasley. . . . These two became therefore objects of my attention, and with much unwearied zeal I instructed them, for I considered them very worthy of every good I could render to them, and they really promised as professional Men to be an honor to their Country."

Crowded together in the great cabin, witnesses and defendants alike must have been stirred by the vivid readings that had evoked their shared adventures. All had set out optimistically on the grand voyage to the South Pacific; all had lived to savor the unimagined beauty of Tahiti; all were survivors of their respective ordeals at sea. Now, with the conclusion of the preamble, the witnesses—Fryer, Cole, Purcell, Peckover, Hallett and Hayward, joined by Captain Edwards and Lieutenants Corner and Larkan from the *Pandora*—were asked to withdraw. Each witness was to be examined in isolation from his colleagues. This scrupulous precaution was somewhat redundant, given that both Captain Pasley and Aaron Graham had met with at least the first four men, in great part specifically to ensure that their defense would not be surprised by inconsistencies in their stories. This informal preliminary interview may have necessitated some gentle "memory jogging."

The first witness to be summoned was John Fryer. Since the court-martial on the loss of the *Bounty* in October 1790, Fryer had been the superintending master of the *Thunderer*, at Chatham Dockyard, upriver from Sheerness. A son, Harrison, had been born during his absence on the *Bounty*, and more recently his wife had borne him a daughter. John Fryer had recently turned forty.

The lengthy prepared statement that Fryer now read to the court commenced with the *Bounty* tacking off Tofua as he took the first watch on the fine, promising night of April 28, 1789. Beguiled by the new fair weather, with the slender moon showing in its first quarter, Bligh and Fryer had exchanged civil, almost friendly words. At the end of his watch, Fryer had gone to bed. His cabin was opposite Bligh's toward the ship's stern and, like Bligh's, opened onto the companionway leading to the upper deck. At dawn, Fryer was awoken by the noise of shouting and then, more clearly, by the voices of John Sumner and Matthew Quintal, able seamen, telling him that he was a prisoner, that if he did not hold his tongue he was a dead man. Raising himself up on his elbow, Fryer saw Bligh, clad only in his nightshirt, being led up the ladder that stood between their cabins with his hands tied behind him and Christian holding the cord.

Fryer's tenacious ear for dialogue retained a memory of the abusive language hurled at Bligh by the mutineers: "Damn his Eyes . . . put him into the Boat, and let the Bugger see if he can live upon three fourths of a Pound of Yams a day"; "recollect that Mr Bligh has brought all this upon himself"; "the Boat is too good for him." Still a prisoner in his cabin, Fryer made futile attempts to reason with the mutineers, and he next learned that Bligh was to be turned out into a boat.

"I hope they are not going to send Captain Bligh adrift by himself," Fryer reported he had exclaimed with horror. The mutineers had answered, "No—his Clerk Mr. Samuel, Messrs. Hayward and Hallett, are going with him."

According to Fryer, it was in part his own strenuous efforts that had won the bigger launch for Bligh, instead of the wormy-bottomed cutter first planned—subsequent witnesses would make the same claim for themselves. After much pleading, he was allowed on deck to speak with Christian, and found the mutineer standing guard over Bligh by the mizzenmast, the tail of the cord that bound his captain in one hand, a bayonet in the other.

"'Mr. Christian, consider what you are about—'

"'[H]old your tongue Sir,' he said, 'I have been in Hell for Weeks past—Captain Bligh has brought all this on himself.' I told him that Mr. Bligh and his not agreeing was no reason for taking the ship. 'Hold your tongue Sir,' he said. I said, 'Mr. Christian you and I have been on friendly terms during the Voyage, therefore give me leave to speak; let Mr. Bligh go down to his Cabin and I make no doubt but that we shall all be friends again in a very short time.' He then repeated, 'Hold your tongue, Sir, it is too late.'"

After further threats, Fryer was led back down to his cabin.

"At the Hatchway I saw James Morrison the Boatswain's Mate, he was at that time getting a tackle to hook upon the Launch's Stern, apparently so I said to him 'Morrison I hope you have no Hand in this Business?' He replied, 'No Sir I do not know a Word about it,' or Words to that effect. 'If that's the case,' I said in a low Voice, 'be on your Guard, there may be an opportunity of recovering ourselves.' His answer was 'go down to your Cabin, Sir' "; and, echoing Christian, " 'it is too late.' "

Seaman John Millward, like Morrison one of the prisoners, had been placed as armed guard over Fryer; but Fryer said he "seemed friendly. . . . I winked at him and made a motion for him to knock the Man down that was next to him, which was John Sumner. Millward immediately cocked his Piece and dropt it, pointed towards me, saying at the same time, 'Mr. Fryer be quiet, no one will hurt you.'"

"Millward, your Piece is cocked," Fryer replied, showing a rare glint of dry humor, "you had better uncock it as you may shoot some Person." By way of response, Millward lifted his gun and said, "There is no one who wishes to shoot you."

"No," Sumner had affirmed, "that was our Agreement not to commit Murder."

All the while, Bligh's clerk, the quietly redoubtable Mr. Samuel, had been busy getting things out of his master's cabin. After some discussion, Fryer had succeeded in being taken down to the cockpit, directly below, where Nelson, the botanist, and Peckover were confined.

" 'Mr. Fryer what have we brought on ourselves?' Mr. Peckover, the Gunner, said, 'What is to be done Mr. Fryer?' I told him that I had spoke to Captain Bligh desiring him to keep his Spirits up"—the same words Fryer had written to Peter in his captivity—"that if I staid on board the Ship I hoped soon to follow him." The conversation had been interrupted by Henry Hilbrant, the Hanoverian cooper who was next door in the breadroom, getting hardtack for the boat. Fryer was ordered back to his cabin, but on the way learned that Christian had decided to give Bligh the bigger, safer launch, "not for his sake but the safety of those who were going with him."

"I then asked if they knew who was going into the Boat with Captain Bligh, they said no, but believed a great many. I then heard Christian say, 'Give every Man a dram out of Captain Bligh's Case, that is under Arms.' " This, thought Fryer, was an optimistic turn, as the pirates would shortly become drunk and the ship could be retaken.

Later, Christian summoned Fryer and ordered him into the boat.

"I said 'I will stay with you if you will give me leave.' 'No Sir,' he replied, 'go directly into the Boat.'

" 'Mr. Fryer, stay in the Ship,' " Bligh now called from the gangway. His hands had been untied.

" 'No by God Sir,' Christian said, 'go into the Boat or I will run you through,' pointing his Bayonet at my breast." Seeing that there was no way out, Fryer pleaded that Robert Tinkler, his young brother-in-law, be allowed to come with him, and at great length, Christian reluctantly agreed. It transpired that Churchill had it in mind to make Tinkler his servant.

Once Fryer and Bligh joined the launch, the verbal abuse increased. "[T]he People at the same time making use of very approbrious Language—I heard several of them say, 'shoot the Bugger.' " In the launch, the men begged for firearms; pleas for better navigational equipment had already been denied. On board the *Bounty,* the captain's liquor was flowing freely, and the men in the launch agreed it would be safer to gain some distance. There was very little wind and so they took to the oars, seeking to get out of range of the guns.

"As soon as the Boat was cast off I heard Christian give Orders to loose the Top Gallant Sails, they steered the same course as Captain Bligh had ordered W.N.W.—and continued to do so for the time we saw them." This was the last Fryer had seen of the *Bounty.*

Fryer was able to give a list of all those he had seen under arms, which of the prisoners included only Thomas Burkett and John Millward. Joseph Coleman had "called out several times to recollect that he had no hand in the Business—Thomas M'Intosh, Carpenter's Mate, another of the Prisoners, and Charles Norman another of the Prisoners were leaning over the rail apparently to me to be crying—Michael Byrn another of the Prisoners, in one of the Boats crying—I heard him say that if he went into the Boat, that the People who were in her would leave him when they got on Shore as he could not see to follow them. . . . Mr Peter Heywood another of the Prisoners I did not perceive on Deck at the seizure of the Ship."

Under examination from the court, Fryer recalled that in the several times he had been up on deck, he had seen no more than eight to ten people, and that most activity at those times seemed to have centered on hoisting the boats.

"Do you think that the Boats could be hoisted out by eight or ten People?" Professional seamen all, the captains understood the import of such details. "No," was Fryer's response, which established that the list of men he had seen under arms was in no way a complete list of the mutineers; other compliant participants must have been involved. Further questioning established that Millward and Burkett seemed to be taking orders from the mutineers—whether reluctantly or not was another matter. Also, Fryer had seen Ellison, "who was a Boy at that time," up upon the yards in obedience to Christian's order to loose the topgallants.

Fryer did not recall any of the prisoners before the court abusing Bligh from the ship: "I saw Millward upon the Taffrel Rail with a Musquet in his Hand; there was so much Noise and Confusion in the Boat that I could not hear one man from the other."

"Was the remark you made of your not having seen Peter Heywood on Deck during that Day of the 29th of April [sic] made at Timor or since you knew that he had been apprehended by the Pandora?" In answer to this astute question, Fryer conceded that he had made the remark since "I knew he was apprehended, but," he added, "I had frequently told Captain Bligh in our Conversations that I had not seen the Youngsters on Deck" ("the captain & me were surprised by Misters Christian, Stewart, Young & Haywood & the Master at Arms," Fryer had earlier written to his wife).

"What did you suppose to be Mr. Christian's meaning when he said he had been in Hell for a fortnight?" came another question from the court.

"From the frequent Quarrels that they had had, and the Abuse which he had received from Mr. Bligh," Fryer responded with, one suspects, eager alacrity.

"Had there been any very recent Quarrel?"

"The Day before Mr. Bligh challenged all the young Gentlemen and People with stealing his Cocoa nuts." Within the context of the courtroom, this now seemed a very slight pretext for a mutineer and would-be murderer of nineteen souls to have been "in Hell."

Each defendant having the right to cross-examine each of the prosecution's witnesses, the first to step forward now was Peter Heywood. However, instead of directing questions at Fryer, he handed the judges a prepared statement informing them that he would defer his questions until the occasion of his own defense; he would prefer "an examination in Chief, than a cross examination of Witnesses in the usual Manner," and did not wish to delay the court at this time. The effect of the statement, which was read aloud by Greetham, was not remarked upon.

Of the few who did venture questions at this point, the most effective was James Morrison, the boatswain's mate and well-educated diarist.

"Do you recollect when you spoke to me, what particular Answer I made?" Morrison asked Fryer, seeking to neutralize the dangerously ambiguous exchange the master had reported having with him in the companionway. "[A]re you positive that it was me who said, 'Go down to your Cabin'?" Yes was Fryer's response; he was indeed positive.

Morrison tried another tactic. "Do you recollect that I said 'I will do my endeavour to raise a Party and rescue the Ship'?" Fryer had no memory of such words at all; but Morrison's ploy was a good one, and the court itself picked up this leading thread, asking Fryer directly whether "Morrison's speaking to you, and telling you to keep below, [might] be from a laudable Motive."

"Probably it might," was now Fryer's response, adding that had he remained with the ship Morrison "would have been one of the first that I should have opened my Mind to."

With the conclusion of the cross-examination, Fryer was retired and led outside and back onto the upper deck. The story of the great boat journey and bitter comments about Bligh would be handed down to his growing family over the years to come. He would be called upon in the days immediately ahead as a witness for one defendant or the other, and undoubtedly he had friends and associates to visit in the area, former shipmates from other less memorable voyages; but when such visits and the telling of yarns was over, John Fryer traveled back to Chatham Dockyard to resume his mundane duties. Here, on this gray September day, with the long view of the harbor stretching ahead and Spithead at his back, Fryer's role as master of the *Bounty* concluded.

Below, in the *Duke*'s great cabin, William Cole, the boatswain, was sworn in. On that morning of the mutiny, he told the court, in his cabin down in the fore hold, he was awoken by the voice of Matthew Quintal informing Purcell that Christian had taken the ship. Jumping out of his hammock, Cole had exclaimed to the carpenter, "For God's sake I hope you know nothing of this." As he was getting dressed, Cole discussed the situation with Lawrence Lebogue, who was apparently in the next-door storeroom with the spare sails, and then hastened on deck. On his way, in passing through the midshipmen's berths in the deck above, Cole saw Heywood "leaning over his own Hammock in the larboard Birth" and Edward Young doing the same in his starboard berth. Coming up the fore hatchway onto the upper deck, Cole noticed five men under arms, none of them any of the defendants. But looking aft, he saw Bligh, with hands tied behind him, under the guard of three armed sentinels, one of whom was Thomas Ellison; Burkett, another of the prisoners, was watching from the quarterdeck.

Greatly alarmed, Cole jumped back down the hatchway and ran to the seamen's quarters to awaken Morrison, Millward and McIntosh, all prisoners before the court.

"I asked them if they knew anything of it and they told me not, Millward the Prisoner, said he was very sorry for it, he said he had a hand in the foolish Piece of Busines before, and that he was afraid they would make him have a Hand in that also." The former foolish business had been his desertion at Tahiti with Charles Churchill and William Muspratt. Millward's fears were quickly confirmed when Churchill suddenly walked in on this furtive conference and "called out to Millward, desired him to come upon Deck immediately to take a Musquet." Dressing as he went, Millward complied; Churchill, of course, was armed.

Going back on deck, Cole went directly aft to ask Christian what he intended to do.

"[H]e then ordered me to hoist the Boat out and shook the Bayonet, threatening me and damning me if I did not take Care." Minutes later, Fryer came on deck and tried to plead with Christian, telling him that "if he did not approve of the Captain's behaviour to put him under an Arrest and proceed on the Voyage"; to which Christian had replied "that if that was all he had to say to go down to his Cabin again for he had been in Hell for Weeks and Weeks past." One of the men standing by sardonically excused Fryer, noting that he had a wife and family, "but that would be all forgot in a few Months." This comment could refer only to the amnesia-inducing seductiveness of Tahiti, and was evidence that at the earliest stage of the mutiny Tahiti—as much as the deposition of William Bligh—had been the mutineers' objective. Equally important, Cole's testimony next revealed that Hayward, Hallett and Bligh's clerk, Samuel, were to be sent in the boat, which accorded with Fryer's recollection.

The launch was at this time out of commission, only a shell with thwarts and hardware still to be assembled. While it was being made ready, Christian continued to issue his threats and ordered rum to be brought up and served to all who were under arms. Michael Byrn, the blind fiddler, was in the worm-eaten cutter lying beside the launch, "but how he came into her I do not know." Bligh's servant, John Smith, obediently brought rum while Christian continued to call out to the loyalists, "'Take care you carry nothing away'—threatening and shaking the bayonet."

Cole continued, "I saw Mr Peter Heywood one of the Prisoners, who was standing there lending a Hand to get the Fore Stay fall along, and when the Boat was hooked on he spoke something to me, but what it was I do not know, for Christian was threatening me at the time and Mr. Heywood then went below and I do not remember seeing him—afterwards, whilst we were in the Ship." As the sails, masts, oars "and other Necessaries" were lowered into the boat, Churchill and Quintal walked about saying, "Damn them, they have enough."

"At this time looking about I saw William Muspratt one of the Prisoners with a Musquet in his Hand, I don't recollect seeing him before I heard Churchill call out to keep somebody below, but who it was I do not know."

As people were forced into the boat, a stream of supplies and possessions was lowered into her. Coleman was in the act of joining the boat when Christian ordered him to be detained, along with McIntosh and Norman.

"[T]hen they were forcing the People out of the Ship who were going and who were not on their Side—and I went into the Boat," Cole told the listening court. Peckover, Nelson, Hayward and Hallett had followed, and finally Bligh.

"Coleman and Norman were standing at the Gangway crying all this Time, after they were ordered not to go into the Boat, and McIntosh was standing there also and would have wished to come into the Boat—and Byrn was in the Cutter all the time crying." Why he was in the cutter was never answered—it appears the fiddler had simply got into the wrong boat. From the ship, John Sumner yelled at Cole to hand up his boatswain's call, or whistle.

"I asked him at the same time in the Indian tongue if he would give me anything for it," Cole had replied, thus nonchalantly opening a window on yet another way the men had been changed by Tahiti. Why he had replied "in the Indian tongue" was not clear. Poor John Norton, who would shortly be stoned to death on Tofua, begged to be given a jacket, only to be told by one of the mutineers, "You Bugger if I had my Will I would blow your Brains out." Not all the bad language, then, had been directed at Bligh. With this threat, the men in the boat decided it was time to cast free of the *Bounty*. As they did so, Coleman called out from the ship, crying and begging notice "that he had no Hand at all in it; if ever any Body should live to get to England he beg'd them to remember him to a Mr. Green in Greenwich." Cole's last sight of the ship "was seeing Thomas Ellison loosing the Main top Gallant Sail."

"Did you see any attempt made by any one of the Prisoners to put an End to the Mutiny?" Cole was asked by the court when his own testimony was complete; to which he had replied, "None."

"You have said that Coleman, Norman and McIntosh were detained in the 'Bounty' against their Will—Have you reason to believe that any other of the Prisoners were detained against their Inclinations?" the court now asked.

"I believe Mr. Heywood was," replied Cole. "I thought all along he was intending to come away—I did not think anything else, he had no Arms and he assisted to get the Boat out and then went below."

"What was the Cause of Coleman, Norman and Michael Byrn's—crying as you have represented them to be?"

"They wanted to come away," Cole answered, then added with something approaching disdain, "as to Byrn I do not know why he was crying. I suppose for no other reason he was blind and could not see."

"You have said that Coleman, Norman and McIntosh assisted at the Tackle fall in getting the Launch out," the court now pressed. The tackle fall was the hoisting end of the block-and-pulley assembly, by which the launch was swung out and lowered from the ship. "[D]id you suppose they meant to be of use to Captain Bligh and to accompany him in the Boat or that they were well disposed to the Mutineers and wished to get rid of their Captain?"

"I believe they wished to go with him."

"Do you suppose that Peter Heywood acted from the same motive when he assisted at the Tackle fall?"

"I had no reason to think otherwise; he assisted at the Tackle fall."

"Where about was Muspratt when you saw him under Arms?"

"Just abaft the Fore Hatchway." Muspratt's berth had been down in the fo'c'sle with the other seamen; while others had been closely watched, he seemed to have enjoyed freedom of movement.

It was now approaching four o'clock. Inside the cabin, lamps had been lit as dusk fell. It had been a long, intense day and although the cross-examination of Cole still remained, the court was adjourned until the following morning. Onlookers stirred and murmured to one another; the captains sat back in their chairs. The scarlet-coated marine guard gathered the prisoners and led them up the companionway and out into what remained of the day. Lights were showing throughout the harbor and in the distance from Gosport and Portsmouth town. In the longboat the prisoners were conveyed into the harbor to where the *Hector* was moored, her stern windows glowing like a lantern in the dusk above the water.

———

At eight A.M. on the following day, a Thursday, the ten prisoners were once again ferried to the *Duke;* this conspicuous routine, announced by the firing of the court-martial gun, was to continue throughout the following week. Once again the weather was bleak and blustery, making heavy work for the oarsmen.

The prisoners had been able to mull over Cole's testimony, and when the court resumed Michael Byrn sprang into action, aggressively launching a series of questions at Cole intended to demonstrate that he, like Coleman, Norman and McIntosh, had shown goodwill to Bligh by helping to launch the boat. Cole, however, would have none of it.

"When you and Mr. Purcell came up did I not say the People are in Arms and the Captain's a Prisoner?" demanded Byrn, at the end of his exasperating and so far pointless interrogation.

"I do not remember seeing him," Cole sniffed, addressing himself as protocol demanded to the court and not to Byrn. "[H]e may be there, he is a Person whom I should take very little Notice of upon such an Occasion being nearly blind." Once again, Morrison was more successful. "Do you recollect, when you came upon Deck after you called me out of my Hammock, that I came to you abaft the Windlass, and said, 'Mr. Cole, what is to be done?' and that your Answer was, 'By God, James, I do not know, but go and help them with the Cutter'?" "Yes," said Cole, he did remember this.

Cole's testimony completed, he was asked to withdraw and William Peckover was sworn in. It was Peckover who had sought to accompany Bligh back to Tahiti in the *Providence* and been summarily rejected.

Peckover's testimony began with a bang, with the "confused Noise" that had yanked him out of sleep in his cabin in the hold, next to the breadroom. As he was pulling on his trousers, he met Nelson at the door, who told him that "the Ship was taken from us."

"We are a long way from land" was his amazed response; he was thinking they were victims of the Friendly Islanders.

"Mr. Nelson answered, 'It is by our own People and Mr. Christian at their head,'—or 'has got the command,' I don't know which—'but we know whose fault it is,' or, 'we know who is to blame'—I do not know which of those Expressions it was," Peckover reported coyly. Attempting to go on deck, the men were at first stopped by two of the mutineers holding fixed bayonets. Shortly afterward, the dogged Mr. Samuel came up and informed the two men that he, Hallett and Hayward were going in the small cutter with Bligh, and asked advice on what he should bring with him.

"I told him that if I was in his Place, I should take but very few things" was Peckover's somewhat insensitive response. While the fated Samuel was stuffing a pillowcase with shirts and socks, Fryer came down to the quarters in the cockpit and asked Peckover what he intended to do.

"[I replied] that I wished to get Home if I possibly could, for by staying behind we should be reckoned as Pirates." It was a while before Peckover, Nelson and Samuel were allowed to leave their quarters and go on deck. When he was finally summoned up, Peckover saw "Captain Bligh, and Mr. Christian standing alongside of him, with a naked Bayonet." He also saw Burkett "in Arms on the Quarter Deck" and Muspratt upon the fo'c'sle; the fact that Muspratt had been free to move about while others were detained was once again noteworthy. Now he appeared to Peckover to be busy with something in the woodpile.

Stepping onto the gangway, Peckover had gone over the ship's side and into the launch, which was already filled with about ten or twelve people. Some five minutes later, the rest of the boat's passengers appeared with Bligh. When the overfilled boat was veered astern of the *Bounty,* Burkett leaned over the side of the ship and called down to Peckover, asking if he wanted anything.

"I told him, I had only what I stood in, a Shirt, and a pair of Trowsers; he told me if I would send my Keys up, he would go and get me some Cloaths." Mistrustful, Peckover had replied that he had lost his keys. Nonetheless, Burkett duly returned some ten minutes later "with a Handkerchief and different Cloaths," which he tossed into the boat. Coleman called out that he wished to come, and begged Peckover to "call upon a friend in Greenwich and acquaint him of the matter." Cole now pressed Bligh to cast off, and so the boat had drifted away from the *Bounty.*

Questioned by the court, Peckover stated, and then was asked to repeat, the names of all those he had seen under arms—of those so named, only Thomas Burkett was a prisoner.

"What were your particular reasons for submitting, when you saw but four Men under Arms?" asked the court. The strangely passive, bloodless acquiescence to the handful of mutineers confounded these veterans of many battles as much as it had Christian.

"I came naked upon the Quarter Deck with only my Trowsers on," replied Peckover.

One by one, the court now went through the names of the defendants:

"Did you on that Day see Joseph Coleman?"

"Yes."

"What was he doing when you saw him?"

"Looking over the Stern."

"Did you see Peter Heywood, Midshipman on that Day?"

"No."

". . . In the former part of your Evidence in Conversation with Mr. Nelson, the Botanist he said to you that you knew whose fault it was, or Words to that effect—do you apprehend that Mr. Nelson alluded to any of the Prisoners?"

"No," Peckover replied. He himself had of course been alluding to Bligh; but now, having successfully directed the court's attention to this conversation Peckover backpedaled, adding, unconvincingly, "It is impossible to judge what he meant."

"Those Men who remained in the Ship did you believe them to be of Mr. Christian's Party, except Coleman Norman, McIntosh and Byrn?"

"We had every reason to suppose so," Peckover replied. The point-by-point examination of who had been seen where, who was under arms, was ultimately beside the point. No, Peckover had not seen anyone under arms apart from those he had named; but, yes—he believed that, with the noted exceptions, everyone who had remained with the ship was "of Mr. Christian's Party."

The final question put to Peckover revealed how far the court still stood from grasping the reality of conditions on board the *Bounty*.

"Were there any Centinels usually placed on board the 'Bounty' in any part of the Ship at Sea?" Commanders of 74-gun ships, these naval judges were accustomed to the services of divisions of marines and hundreds of seamen. Bligh, with his sparse company divided into three watches for their healthful repose, had scarce men enough to spare for sentinels, a role normally assumed by marines, so conspicuously absent from the *Bounty*. In any case, so confident had Bligh been of the security of his small ship that he had slept with his cabin door open.

"No," was Peckover's simple answer to this uncomprehending question.

The day was still young when William Purcell, the carpenter and one of Bligh's most stubborn adversaries, was summoned by the court. Pasley had complacently deemed his account "favorable" to Heywood, but now the Heywoods would discover what Bligh had long ago learned to his great cost—namely, just how independent this bloody-minded and fearless seaman could be. Until Purcell's performance, things had drifted along promisingly for Peter Heywood, with few mentions of his name to snag the attention of the listening judges. But Purcell's electrifying testimony would turn all this on its head.

His account began with the now familiar images: the sudden announcement that the ship was taken, Bligh with his hands lashed behind him and Christian brandishing his naked bayonet.

"Mr. Christian has the Command—the Captain is confined all resistance will be in vain, if you attempt it you are a Dead Man," as Matthew Quintal had informed him. Purcell had been in his quarters in the fore hold, with Cole and Lebogue, when he learned the news. On going up the companionway ladder, he passed the midshipmen's quarters and saw Heywood and Stewart "in their Birth abreast of the Main Hatchway on the Larboard Side." Sentinels posted at the hatchway entrances controlled who came and went by way of the ladders.

After arguing with Christian about which boat was to be given to Bligh, Purcell went straight to work on preparing the more seaworthy launch. Of all the people who claimed responsibility for obtaining the bigger, safer boat, Purcell was the most likely really to have done so. Without immediately saying as much, he had, it seems, determined to join Bligh from the outset.

"I asked Mr. Christian if he meant to turn us adrift in the Boat, to let us have the Launch and not make a Sacrifice of us," he now told the court. Purcell's facing down Christian caused the mutineer to flinch. He had done nothing, he told Christian, "to be either ashamed or afraid of," and he wished to see his native land.

In his workmanlike way, Purcell had gone about procuring "such Things as I thought would be useful"—a bucket of nails, saws, a looking glass and clothes. He then approached Christian and asked for his tool chest, "[w]hich after much Altercation he granted." By "Altercation," one gathers Purcell stood toe-to-toe with Christian and fearlessly argued with him, naked bayonet notwithstanding. Fryer now came on deck and, addressing the men under arms, begged them "in the Name of God to lay down their Arms," asking them what they were about and "if the Captain had done anything to confine him."

"No, Damn you," Churchill had growled in reply, "you ought to have done that Months ago."

During this exchange, Purcell went into the boat and was busy stowing the considerable supplies he had managed to gather. Suddenly, Isaac Martin—a thirty-year-old able seaman from Philadelphia, and one of the mutineers who had been under arms—appeared in the boat with a bag of possessions and told Purcell he was coming along.

"I replied if ever we get to England, I'll endeavour to hang you myself," Purcell responded. Hearing him, two of the mutineers "presented their Pieces" at Martin and ordered him out of the boat; the sailor reluctantly complied. More ominously, other mutineers began to harangue Christian to order Purcell out of the boat as well, claiming that if the carpenter was allowed to leave with his tool chest, Bligh's party would "have another Vessel in a month." Like Coleman, the armorer, Purcell was highly valued for his skills. Christian, however, may have reflected upon the undesirability of having the uncompromising carpenter along as a reluctant passenger, for when the boat finally cast off from the *Bounty*, Purcell was in her.

"When the Boat left the Ship," Purcell told the court, "she had about 7½ Inches amidships above water."

Of the prisoners before the court, Purcell had seen Ellison, Burkett and Millward under arms, but he repeated the incident described by Cole when Millward expressed his fear that he would be compelled to join the mutineers on account of the "former foolish Affair."

"When you came upon Deck did you see any one of the Prisoners?" the court asked Purcell.

"I did," he replied.

"Did you see Mr. Heywood?"

"No."

"Had you any Conversation with him?"

"Not at that time."

It was this vaguely qualified response that prompted a fatal query: "At any other time?"

"Yes."

"Did you see Mr. Heywood standing upon the Booms?" This was following up on Cole's recollection that Heywood had helped launch the boat.

"Yes," said Purcell.

"Had he a Cutlass in his Hand?" This startling question from the court came from nowhere—no hint of such a thing had been given in any of the other evidence.

"He was leaning the Flat part of his Hand on a Cutlass on the Booms," said Purcell, "when I exclaimed, 'In the Name of God Peter what do you do with that?' when he instantly dropped it. One or two of the People had previous to that laid down their Cutlasses, being Armed with Cutlasses and Pistols to assist in hoisting the Launch out."

Under the ensuing intense cross-examination from the court, Purcell attempted to undo some of the obvious damage wrought by his almost offhand statement: He had looked upon Mr. Heywood, he now explained, "as a person confused and that he did not know that he had the Weapon in his Hand, or his Hand being on it, for it was not in his Hand." Probably Heywood had gone below "to collect some of his Things to put into the Boat."

"How long was it after the Launch was hoisted out before she went from the Ship?"

"I think it must be near two Hours."

"Do you think then," came the skeptical query from one of the court, "that Mr. Heywood was so long employed in collecting his Things as you have before supposed?" And Purcell, whose characteristic blunt clarity was becoming ever more fuzzy, backtracked to say that Heywood had not after all left immediately, but had stayed to help other people with their things, and then only gone below "but a very short time, ten Minutes or a Quarter of an hour," before the launch pulled away from the ship.

For the next fifteen minutes, the court hammered away at the cutlass. Where was the arms chest in relation to Heywood's berth? Did he drop the cutlass accidentally or on purpose? Did others do the same? Were the mutineers aware of Heywood's having a cutlass? Would they have permitted him or any other "well disposed Person to the Captain" to have touched a weapon? Were they so careless of the arms as to leave them unattended for anyone to pick up? Had Heywood expressed "any Desire or Inclination to follow his Commander?"

Previous to Purcell's testimony, it had appeared that all of the defendants were more or less accounted for in terms of where they had physically stood during the approximately two and a half hours the events unfolded. But now, here was Peter Heywood wandering at will around the deck when the clear loyalists had been confined or guarded; here was a loose bayonet that had not been used in defense of the ship; here was Peter dawdling on the booms after the launch had been lowered into the water—dawdling for close to two hours, by Purcell's own reluctant arithmetic.

Others significantly affected by the carpenter's testimony were Morrison and Muspratt; Morrison had desired Purcell "to take Notice in the face of the whole of the Mutineers that he was prevented from coming into the Boat." This Purcell stated with some vigor. On the other hand, he had not seen Muspratt under arms but *had* seen him handing "some Liquor up to the Ship's Company."

Michael Byrn, as was his wont, used his right of cross-examination to pepper Purcell with questions that did nothing to advance his cause; he appeared not to comprehend that things were going well enough for him as they were. As always, his cross-examination seemed only to irritate the witness from whom he was beseeching support.

"Do you recollect my saying, 'Mr. Purcell, if you live to go home, I hope you will go to my Friends and let them know, I know nothing of this Transaction, nor had any hand in it?'" he now asked, in what appears to have been a shameless mimic of Coleman's parting plea to seek out his friend in Greenwich.

"No," said Purcell. All of Byrn's questions were similarly dismissed. Perhaps cowed by this example, if not stunned by the new turn the testimony had taken, none of the other defendants were inclined to raise their voices, and the court was adjourned until the morrow.

The testimony of the warrant officers completed, the *Bounty*'s midshipmen were now introduced. Of all the *Bounty*'s young gentlemen, only Thomas Hayward and John Hallett had officially been midshipmen. Captain Pasley had indicated to Peter Heywood that he intended to speak to these young men, but there is no evidence that he had actually done so. Although the socially inferior warrant officers had been found, in his view and presumably Aaron Graham's, to be "favorable," both Hayward and Hallett had sent very clear advance messages that they thought Peter culpable. It had been Thomas Hayward's father who advised Nessy to seek all "interest" she possibly could on her brother's behalf. Similarly, John Hallett had informed Nessy that notwithstanding his former friendship to Peter, he would if called upon "be strictly bound by Oath to adhere to Truth."

One of the most striking facts to emerge from the evidence given thus far was that from the very outset the mutineers had planned to put Hayward and Hallett in the boat with Bligh and his clerk, Samuel. Every witness testified that he had learned of Bligh's intended fate in the same breath he learned of that of the two midshipmen. Perhaps no other circumstance so clearly betrayed that the actions of Christian and his fellows had been purely personal, and had little to do with professional complaints against their commander.

Hayward and Hallett had hardly been favorites of Bligh. It was Hayward who had been on watch when the Tahitian prisoner held for theft had made his escape; he was subsequently turned before the mast and confined in irons for a full month by way of punishment. No other officer, not even Purcell, had been treated so harshly. Bligh referred in the notes to "Mr Hallett's contumacy" and, even more pointedly, commented to his wife that Hallett "has turned out a worthless impudent scoundrel."

There had been no clique around Bligh—or if there had been, Hayward and Hallett had manifestly not been part of it.

But the two young men stood sharply apart from the other young gentlemen in one important respect: they were both young professionals who had gone to sea by choice. Sons of prosperous middle-class families, they had other careers open to them. Christian and Heywood, on the other hand, were the sons of bankrupts under the shadow of debtor's prison, while Edward Young was the illegitimate son of a noble family. A career at sea was the only way out for these men, whether or not this had been the path of choice.

Whatever his reasons, Christian had not got along with his middle-class colleagues and, as the day's testimony would show, neither had other of the defendants. The mutineers' decision to dump these three officers—Bligh, Hayward and Hallett—into one small boat seems to have had no basis except that the three men were individually not liked.

These considerations must have weighed somewhat heavily on the minds, if not the consciences, of the ten defendants as they were ferried in their own small boat from the *Hector* back to the *Duke* on the third day of their trial. The court called Lieutenant Hayward, "late 3rd Lieut. of His Majesty's ship 'Pandora,' and formerly Midshipman belonging to His Majesty's Armed Vessel the 'Bounty.'" Uniquely, Thomas Hayward could bear witness to the events of both sagas for the prosecution.

On the morning of April 28, 1789, Hayward said, he had been on Christian's watch and actually spoke with him only moments before the mutiny. Christian had relieved the previous watch at four in the morning, as was usual; an hour later, "after giving Orders to prepare for Washing Decks," he ordered Hayward to take the lookout "while he went down to lash his Hammock up." Minutes later, while Hayward was watching a shark following in the wake of the ship, he had looked up to see, "to his unutterable Surprize," Fletcher Christian and eight others coming aft, "[a]rmed with Musquets and Bayonets"; of these men, only Thomas Burkett was among the prisoners.

"On my going forward to prevent their Proceedings I asked Fletcher Christian the Cause of such an Act, he told me to hold my Tongue instantly." Ordering Isaac Martin to stand sentry, Christian had gone below to Bligh's cabin.

"At the time that this happened the People on Deck were Mr. John Hallett, myself, Robert Lamb, Butcher, Thomas Ellison (the Prisoner) at the Helm; and John Mills at the Conn." Mills claimed total ignorance of all that had happened—although he later gleefully joined with the mutineers—but Ellison left the helm and took up a bayonet.

"The Ship's Decks now began to be thronged with Men," Hayward told the listening court, among whom were the prisoners John Millward and William Muspratt, both under arms.

"Peter Heywood one of the Prisoners, George Stewart and James Morrison one of the Prisoners, [were] unarmed on the Booms."

"Murder!" came Bligh's voice from his cabin, and shortly afterward he was led with hands bound on deck, where he was quickly, menacingly, surrounded by most of the men. Some of the other officers, such as Purcell and Fryer, now also came up as Christian gave the order to prepare the cutter.

"We remonstrated against it," Hayward recalled, "she being too small and very leaky to contain us, and he gave us the Launch." As soon as the launch was readied, Christian "order'd Mr. John Samuel, the Clerk, Mr. John Hallett, Midshipman, and myself into her." After asking permission to collect some clothes, Hayward and Hallett were allowed down to their berths one last time. With sentinels placed around the hatchway and another below standing guard over the arms chest, the two midshipmen had made their way with some difficulty. Passing through Bligh's small dining area, they had arrived at their own berths, where they had found "Peter Heywood the Prisoner in his Birth": apparently he too had returned below.

Hayward told the court, "I told him to go into the Boat, but in my hurry do not remember to have received any Answer."

"Mr. Hayward ask'd me what I intended to do," Peter had written to his mother from Batavia of this same moment. He had already, as he told her, mulled over the fact that if he went onshore he risked death at the hands of natives. "I told him to remain in the Ship."

Hayward bundled a few clothes into a bag and went back on deck. His request to take his instruments and charts—proof to his patron, William Wales, of his diligence as a navigator—was "positively refused" by Christian.

Bligh, brought to the gangway by Christian, was then surrounded by a sizable, rambunctious crowd.

"Damn him, I will be Centry over him," Ellison had sworn, brandishing a bayonet. Apparently swept up by the mounting hysteria and confusion, Ellison was transformed from dutiful helmsman to enthusiastic mutineer within the space of two hours.

Once in the boat, the mutineers told Bligh they would give him a tow toward land, but the situation on board the *Bounty* was swiftly deteriorating. A jeering crowd gathered on the taffrail, or stern rail, the better to watch the small boat's humiliating and precarious progress.

"Go see if you can live upon a Quarter of a lb. of Yams per Day," Millward called after them. Hayward's last sight of his ship was of Ellison loosing the topgallant sails, in obedience to Christian's orders.

"Were all the People that were in the Boat ordered or did they go Voluntarily?" the court asked.

"I know no one ordered in except Mr. John Hallet Mr. John Samuel, and myself," Hayward replied, thus confirming the very particular antipathies that Christian had acted upon. Hayward's tough line of testimony fully and unambiguously exonerated only Coleman and Byrn; even Norman and McIntosh, whom he did not "suppose" to be party to the mutineers, he would not personally vouch for. The other six prisoners, armed or not, Hayward supposed to be guilty.

He had not seen Morrison under arms, but was of the opinion that the boatswain's mate had been in league with the mutineers; this was because while he was assisting to launch the boat, Morrison's countenance was "rejoiced," not "depressed" like those of the loyalists.

"What was Mr. Heywood employed about in his Birth when you went below?" the court now pressed.

"Nothing but sitting with his Arms folded on his own Chest," Hayward replied evenly.

"Did you from his Behavior consider him as a Person attached to his Duty or to the Party of the Mutineers?"

"I should rather suppose after my having told him to go into the Boat and he not joining us, to be on the side of the Mutineers," Hayward replied, with one suspects something of the same haughty tone with which he had greeted Peter on the *Pandora*. ("He like all other Worldlings when raised a little in Life received us very coolly," Peter had reported in his letter to his mother.) But, Hayward allowed, this "must be only understood as an Opinion as he was not in the least employed during the active part of it."

The cross-examination from the prisoners began with Morrison in full growl.

"You say that you observed Joy in my Countenance and that you are rather inclined to give it as your Opinion that I was one of the Mutineers," the boatswain's mate began. "[C]an you declare before God and this Court that such Evidence is not the result of a private Pique?"

"No it is not the result of any private Pique," returned Hayward icily, "it is an Opinion that I formed after quitting the Ship, from the Prisoners not coming with us when he had as good an Opportunity as the rest, there being more Boats than one."

"Are you certain that we might have had the large Cutter to have accompanied you?" Morrison demanded pragmatically.

"Not being present at any Conference between you, I cannot say, but perhaps you might," said Hayward, giving the court a strong hint of something suggestive of personal pique.

Morrison concluded his examination with another pertinent query: Did Hayward recollect calling upon him "to give any Assistance to retake His Majesty's Ship?"

"I have a feint Remembrance of a Circumstance of that Nature," Hayward allowed grudgingly.

"Relate the Circumstance," directed the interested court.

"It is so very feint that I can hardly remember it or the Person it was," Hayward stalled, "but on seeing Charles Churchill upon the Booms I thought that had I had a Friendly Island Club, of which there were many on board, I could, had I not been observed, have gone forward, which was behind Churchill, and knocked him down."

"What answer did I give to you?" demanded Morrison.

"I do not remember."

"Did I say, 'go it I'll back you, there is Tools enough'?"

"I do not remember."

Hayward's testimony concluded with a final question from the court: On what basis had he determined that Coleman had been detained involuntarily?

"From hearing from among the Mutineers their Intention to detain him," Hayward replied. They had also planned to detain Ledward, the acting surgeon, but then changed their minds, "saying that they would have Little Occasion for Doctors."

With this, Hayward withdrew and the prisoners were left to reflect upon the damage he had wrought. At this point, too, it was possible to perceive the wisdom of Aaron Graham's ploy to have Peter reserve his right of cross-examination for his full defense. The picture of what had transpired within the few hours the mutiny took place had been subtly changed by every witness; a point-by-point defense—such as Morrison was, with some courage, mounting—carried the great risk of blundering into yet unrevealed contradictions.

Lieutenant John Hallett was the day's next witness. The Admiralty reimbursed all witnesses for the expense of traveling to Portsmouth for the trial, and the punctilious young man had put in his requisition for precisely 351 miles.

Hallett's testimony was brief. He, like Hayward, had shared Christian's watch and so was on deck when the mutiny broke out. His remembrance of the events began with the appearance of Christian and four others armed on deck, with "Thomas Burkitt, the Prisoner," being one of their number. Prevented from going down the fore hatchway by two bayonets thrust before him, he had heard Bligh "sing out 'Murder!'" from his cabin, and minutes later saw his captain led on deck, bound and "naked excepting his Shirt."

The only novel piece of information Hallett offered concerned the lowering of the boats. After the worm-eaten cutter was launched for Bligh, Hayward, Samuel and himself, Cole and Purcell stepped forward to tell Mr. Christian "that they would prefer going in the Boat with the Captain to staying in the Ship." According to Hallett, it was because of these apparently unexpected volunteers that Christian allowed the substitution of the more seaworthy launch, saying "that he did not wish to compel them or any other Person to stay against their Inclinations or to go." With this, the other volunteers streamed forward, in all fifteen men more than Christian had first planned to get rid of; between the nineteen men in the boat and the four men—Coleman, Byrn, McIntosh and Norman—who apparently wished to go, fully half the ship's complement had desired to leave the ship.

Under cross-examination from the court, Hallett recited the names of seventeen men he had seen under arms, including Ellison, Burkett and Morrison; this was the first time Morrison had been so directly placed in the company of the mutineers.

"At what time did you make the Memorandum from which you have named the Prisoners?" was the astute question from the court, and Hallett allowed he had made it "lately."

The court turned its attention to Peter Heywood, whom Hallett had seen on the larboard deck.

"What was he doing at this time?"

"He was standing still, looking attentively towards Captain Bligh," Hallett replied.

"Do you know whether he was or not prevented coming into the Boat?"

"I do not know that he ever offered to go into the Boat."

"Did you hear any Person propose to him to go into the Boat?"

"No."

"Do you know any other particulars respecting him on that Day?"

"When he was standing as I have before related, Captain Bligh said something to him, but what I did not hear upon which he laughed turned round, and walked away."

With this damaging blow, Peter's case became suddenly more precarious. It was one thing to stand bewildered and idle, quite another to stand idle and insolent.

And the general demeanor of the mutineers had grown increasingly, dangerously insolent. Hallett's last view of Morrison had been of him under arms and leaning out over the taffrail to taunt the men in the laboring boat. He called out, said Hallett, "in a jeering Manner, 'If my friends enquire after me, tell them I am somewhere in the South Seas.'"

Hallett added little information about any of the other defendants. But when the court pressed him to return again to his charge that Heywood had laughed at Bligh, the more amplified version was even more disturbing.

"Describe to the court the Situation of Mr. Bligh, Commander of the 'Bounty,' when Mr. Heywood the Prisoner laughed turned round and walked [a]way as you have already related."

"He was standing with his Arms tied behind his Back," Hallett answered, "Christian holding the Cord with one Hand and a Bayonet to his Breast with the other."

His testimony over, Hallett was withdrawn and the last of the *Bounty* men summoned. John Smith, able seaman from Stirling, Scotland, and now in his forties, had been Bligh's servant on the *Bounty;* indeed, he remained with Bligh, departing with him on the *Providence,* but he had been discharged from the Cape on account of ill health, and so was able to attend the court-martial.

Smith had been summoned on deck in the early hours of April 28 by Thomas Hall, the cook, who told Smith that he "was wanted Aft upon the Quarter Deck." Seeing his captain standing in his shirt, Smith went down to his cabin and retrieved his clothes.

"I went and brought up his Cloaths put on his Trowsers and laid his Jacket over his Shoulders," this humbly loyal seaman told the court; the simple act of covering his master's nakedness was one of the very few gestures any man had undertaken on Bligh's behalf during this crisis. Christian then ordered Smith to bring up the rum "and serve every Man under Arms with a Glass." Christian was the first man he had served. Coleman took a dram, perhaps to calm his nerves, but Peter Heywood had refused. Ellison had taken his dram "with a Musquet in his Hand."

"Do you recollect," began Morrison, in his now familiar cross-examination, "that you gave Mr. Cole a Glass into a tin pot and said, 'Morrison, you may as well have a drop, tho' I am ordered to serve none but the Centries'?"

"I do not recall a Word of it," replied loyal John Smith.

Muspratt and Millward followed, briefly invoking actions of their own, but to each Smith denied any recollection.

The drama wrought by the day's witnesses could only have necessitated some readjustment of opinions among the twelve judges. Increasingly it looked as if Bligh's original notations were in fact correct; namely, that only three of the defendants—Coleman, McIntosh, Norman—had been unquestionably loyal. Three of the seven remaining defendants—Burkett, Millward and Ellison—had been consistently described as active mutineers, Millward with some qualifying remarks about his initial reluctance. But it now also transpired that, excluding Michael Byrn, whose role no one took seriously, the remaining prisoners had all been seen by someone at some time under arms.

The day's final witnesses, and indeed the last of the evidences for the prosecution, were Captain Edward Edwards and the officers of the *Pandora*. Only two days before the mutineer trial commenced, Edwards himself had undergone a court-martial for the loss of the *Pandora*, over which the same judges had presided; the court had been assembled, however, not on the *Duke*, but on the *Hector*. Edwards's officers had all sworn to the truthfulness of their captain's version of events, and the court had concluded that the *Pandora*'s loss "was not in any respect owing to Mismanagement or a Want of proper attention to her safety," pronouncing Edwards and his officers "honourably acquitted."

Now called as a witness, Captain Edwards confirmed that Joseph Coleman had attempted to come on board before the *Pandora* even came to anchor and that he helpfully volunteered much information about the whereabouts of the other men. Stewart and Heywood came on board next, Edwards testified, but without his knowledge, presenting themselves to Lieutenant Larkan while he was in his cabin. When they were brought down to the captain's stateroom, Edwards greeted them nonchalantly with "what News?"

"Peter Heywood I think said he supposed I had heard of the Affair of the 'Bounty,'" Edwards recalled. Edwards recalled very little else—strikingly little for an officer who had sailed around the globe specifically to apprehend the men then before him.

"I don't recollect all the Conversation that passed between us," Edwards told the court laconically of his first dealings with Heywood. Apparently this naval professional had taken no notes. "[H]e sometimes interrupted me by asking for Mr. Hayward." Lieutenant Hayward had been summoned and had met Heywood "with a sort of contemptuous look, and began to enter into Conversation with him respecting the 'Bounty.'" ("I asked them how they came to go away with His Majesty's Ship 'Bounty,'" Hayward had told the court in his testimony. George Stewart had responded with the somewhat legalistic retort "that when called upon hereafter he would answer all Particulars.")

This conversation seems to have got out of hand, for Edwards suddenly told Hayward to desist and ordered the two prisoners placed in irons.

Of the prisoners, only Michael Byrn had a question, which prompted Edwards to concede that it was "an Omission" that he had stated in his letter to the Admiralty that Byrn had been "brought on board"; in fact, the fiddler had come on board voluntarily. For once successful in his legal efforts, Byrn was able to establish that he had not only come to the *Pandora* of his own will, but had gone to considerable trouble to do so.

"I believe he did say that he came from a distant Place," Edwards now recalled, dredging his shallow memory, "and that he had travelled in the Night." And with this image of the blind fiddler stumbling through the darkness toward Matavai, Edwards withdrew from the court.

The statements of Lieutenants Larkan and Corner of the *Pandora* were even more perfunctory. The only useful information came from Larkan regarding those prisoners who had been on Morrison's schooner. The schooner, Larkan recalled, had attempted to avoid capture and, sailing "into the offing," was chased by the ship's boats; but who had been on the schooner at that particular time, he could not say. All of the prisoners, once cornered, surrendered without resistance.

At this, the conclusion of the prosecution's evidence, Peter Heywood stepped forward to present the court with another written request.

"After the long Examination which has taken place upon this Trial," he—or, more likely, Aaron Graham—had penned, "it will not I hope be deemed unreasonable, if I request to be allowed the Whole of tomorrow, to prepare my Defence."

The request was granted. Another drear day was drawing to its close. It was Friday. The judges and onlookers alike stirred, stretched their legs, rustled papers and exchanged comments before heading out into the harbor and on to their weekend plans, and the prisoners returned to the *Hector* to prepare and rehearse the words that would damn or save them.

DEFENSE

Meanwhile, events in the outside world had swept on. The newspapers from September 12, the first day of the court-martial, had carried ever more horrifying news from France, where a frenzied massacre of aristocrats and suspected royalist sympathizers was being waged. From the account of a recently escaped English visitor, the *Times* ran columns chronicling the daily atrocities committed by the Parisians against their countrymen: a seventy-year-old man formerly employed in some unremarkable government post had been forced by a murderous mob to sing the "*Ça ira*" before being shoved by pikes into a bonfire; a marauding gang of children on the lookout for "young Aristocrats" had set upon two children, cutting off their heads with penknives. At this unrelenting barrage of soul-numbing news, the English establishment stood aghast; on the Isle of Man, Nessy was moved to compose a poem, "Twilight, On reading an Account of the dreadful Disturbances in France." France was England's oldest and most tenacious enemy, and the Channel separating the savagery of the Parisian streets from the enlightened, well-ordered world of the likes of Sir Joseph Banks was perilously slender. Already the impact had been felt on English soil: the *Times* reported that terrified French refugees had landed all along the Sussex coast and were clogging the Kent and Sussex roads; collections had been taken on their behalf "amongst the porters and common working men at the water side, who each subscribed according to his ability." Of more concern were the murmurings of approval from certain homeland radicals. Every naval man knew that whatever the outcome of events in France, England was unlikely to remain uninvolved.

In Portsmouth the dreary weather continued. After blowing squally for most of Friday, the weather had calmed by day's end, but Saturday was once again hazy with "fresh gales" and showers of rain.

The court-martial transacted only one brief piece of business on this hazy, blowy weekend: Joseph Coleman was summoned to give his defense. Now forty-one, the *Bounty*'s armorer had already been gray-haired at the time of the mutiny. Fair-skinned and, although only five foot six, "Strong made," in Bligh's words, Coleman was from the Dorking-Guildford area of Surrey. Coleman had sailed as an able seaman on Cook's third voyage. Dogged and bone loyal, he had indulged in one discernible act of frivolity—he had himself tattooed, with a heart; the date beneath, "5-7-77," suggests this was a souvenir from his first Pacific voyage, when he—and William Bligh—had been at Tongatapu en route to Tahiti. Coleman's loyalty to Bligh had been proven at every turn; it was he who boldly had dived overboard from the *Bounty* as she left Tahiti for the last time, under Christian's command.

Befitting his undisputed innocence, Coleman's defense was a perfunctory business, the whole proceeding lasting well under an hour. Only one witness, William Cole the boatswain, was called, and he testified that he had heard Christian give the order for Coleman to be detained. On being asked by the court if Coleman had "expostulated" with Christian, the witness demurred; Coleman, he said, "was then surrounded by Armed Men and I saw him crying afterwards."

Apart from this brief transaction, the weekend progressed like any other. On board the *Hector*, John Carter, a seaman, was punished with a dozen lashes "for mutinous expressions," the second punishment administered by Captain Montagu this September. Otherwise, the day's chief activity was taking on fresh beef. Across the harbor, on the *Duke*, casks of water were being stowed. The weather moderated on Sunday while remaining hazy, and divine service was, as usual, performed. As these two days had been expressly allowed for the prisoners' preparation, presumably Stephen Barney and Aaron Graham had been allowed on board to meet their clients for the defense. Since the trial began, Peter had had no further correspondence with his family. But one of Nessy's poems of this time, addressed simply to "Anxiety," could be said to speak for the worried, suspenseful relatives of all the defendants:

Doubting, dreading, fretful guest,
Quit, oh! quit this mortal Breast . . .

Monday, September 17, broke with fair, mild weather. In the *Duke*'s great cabin the much anticipated defense of Peter Heywood began with his statement to the court that "owing to the long and severe Confinement he had suffered," he feared he would not be able to deliver his defense "with that force of Expression which it required, and therefore desired one of his Friends" to be permitted to read it in his stead. The request was granted, and the chosen friend as it turned out was Mr. Const, Peter's second lawyer.

Prepared evidences in general tended to be favorably regarded by courts-martial. As one legal authority had stated, evidences committed in writing were "the most sedate and deliberate acts of the mind" and less corruptible than if "retained in memory only." The prepared statements of all of the other defendants, as it would turn out, were to be read aloud by the Judge Advocate.

"Your attention has already been sufficiently exercised in the painful Narrative of this Trial," Const began, speaking in Peter's voice; "it is therefore my Duty to trespass on it as little as possible," saying which, he launched into a lofty preamble: "The Crime of Mutiny for which I am now arraigned is so seriously pregnant with every danger and Mischief that it makes the Person so accused in the Eyes not only of military Men but Men of every description and of every Nation, appear at once the object of unpardonable guilt and exemplary vengeance.

"In such a Character it is my misfortune to appear before this Tribunal. . . ." The rounded phrases swelled and rolled off Const's tongue; such rhetoric could never have been trusted to a mere Judge Advocate. As it was, one must wonder how this oratorical exercise was squared with the slight, thin-faced young man who stood before the worldly captains, resolute, perhaps, but surely too with signs of nervousness.

Peter addressed at the outset one possible source of embarrassment. Sometime before he had gained the services of Aaron Graham, he had rashly sent to the Earl of Chatham a narrative "containing an account of all that passed on the Fatal morning." The Earl of Chatham was John Pitt, brother of the prime minister, who in 1788 had replaced the illustrious Lord Howe as First Lord of the Admiralty. It is not clear whether this document had circulated among the court. In any event, Peter and his lawyers now took pains to distance him from "a few particulars" of this earlier narrative, which, arising from "the Confusion the ship was in during the Mutiny" and "the errors of an imperfect recollection" might, he now conceded, have been mistaken.

Peter's defense followed three unevenly weighted lines of argument, pursued with varying degrees of conviction and vehemence. First and foremost was his lamentable "extreme youth and inexperience" at the time of the mutiny, which had been the cause of his failing to join his captain in the overloaded boat. On that "Fatal morning," Peter had been awoken from sleep with the news of the mutiny and followed Cole and Purcell up on deck where he had seen Bligh bound, with Christian beside him.

"My faculties were benumbed," Peter said. He did not come to his senses until called upon to help get out the launch by assisting at the tackle fall. In this state of stupor, he took many things as they were handed to him and put them into the launch; it was, he said, at this time that his "hand touched the Cutlass," as Purcell had stated—this last point was in fact contradicted by all other testimony, which made clear that no weapons of any kind were allowed into the boat up until the moment she left the *Bounty*.

Too inexperienced to understand that his own behavior at this time of crisis could be subject to judgment, Peter stood by as a stunned and passive observer. As he candidly stated, the "Boat and Ship . . . presented themselves to me without its once occurring that I was at liberty to choose, much less that the choice I should make would be afterwards deemed Criminal; and I bitterly deplore that my extreme youth and inexperience concurred in torturing me with Apprehensions and prevented me from preferring the former; for, as things have turned out, it would have saved me from the disgrace of appearing before you, as I do this day."

For guidance, Peter looked to the example of his messmates, the more experienced Hallett and Hayward, who appeared "very much agitated" by Christian's order that they join Bligh in the boat, even to the point of shedding tears. This vivid recollection ostensibly served to demonstrate how the terror of Peter's messmates influenced his own decision to remain with the *Bounty*—but it also slyly disparaged the two men who had handed him such damaging testimony. Not mentioned were the actions of the numerous other loyalists that could have guided his inexperience: Purcell facing down Christian; Ledward, the acting surgeon, who had immediately declared he would join his captain; Peckover and Cole; Linkletter, Norton and the others who had given their lives; the fourteen-year-old boy Tinkler. Peter had watched all of these men doggedly gather their gear and make for the launch.

Peter's representation of his dilemma passed into his second, more pragmatic line of argument—that the boat had been so overladen that it appeared, as he had written, "a kind of an act of suicide" to join her.

"I need only refer to the Captain's own narrative," Peter stated, going on to evoke Bligh's claim that the boat had been kept afloat only by his order to fling spare clothing and equipment overboard; apparently, Bligh's narrative had been among those books brought to pass the time by his friends and relatives. Had he, Peter, been in the boat, "she must either have gone down with us or to prevent it we must have light'ned her of the Provisions and other necessary articles and thereby have perished for Want—dreadful alternative!" By staying with the *Bounty*, therefore, Peter had helped save the men in the boat.

This was risky logic to have declaimed by a civilian lawyer before twelve professional sea officers. Between them they had weathered almost every casualty—excepting outright mutiny—that could befall a man at sea. The plea that it was reasonable to avoid an act of duty when dangerous was not one normally honored within the naval code. As for Peter's plea of "extreme youth and inexperience," Peter had been five weeks shy of seventeen on the day of the mutiny. The average age at which the captains sitting in judgment themselves had first gone to sea was twelve; Captain Knight, in company with his father, had seen action off France at the age of ten.

Finally, tangled amid these other arguments was Peter's most sensible—if contradictory—claim; namely, that he had been held below against his will and thus prevented from joining the boat when he had wished to. In his testimony Thomas Hayward had stated that he had advised Peter not to remain with the ship. Of this exchange, Peter now professed a "feint recollection of a Conversation with somebody"; he had thought, however, this had taken place with George Stewart, not with Thomas Hayward, "but be that as it may," Peter was certain that the exchange had taken place "on Deck and not below, for on hearing it suggested that I should be deem'd Guilty if I staid in the Ship, I went down directly." His intent on going down, he now told the court, had been specifically to gather his possessions in order to join the boat. Passing William Cole on his way down, Peter told him his plans "in a low tone of voice." Once below, however, he was prevented from returning on deck by the order of Charles Churchill, one of the armed mutineers.

Significantly, this single claim, which should have rendered all the other excuses beside the point, was not one Peter chose to press with a great deal of energy. More vehement were the personal attacks he directed at Hayward and Hallett: Hallett had been only a callow youth (youthful if not inexperienced!) whose perceptions were not sound; the events he had described were nearly four years past; people's memories could not be trusted. With regard to the midshipman's highly damaging contention that Peter had "laughed turned round, and walked away" when addressed by Bligh—this was unthinkable; Peter's state of mind "rendered such a want of decency impossible." And how had Hallett been able "to particularize the Muscles of a mans Countenance" at any distance?

Having touched glancingly at the claim that he had been detained by force, Peter moved on to the events of the *Pandora*, recalling how on Edwards's orders he had been "chained and punished with incredible severity." The word "punished" was pointed—having already suffered much, he was intimating, he had in effect paid his debt for errors committed.

"My Character and my Life are at your disposal," Peter now told the court, wrapping up his defense. "[A]s the former is as sacred to me as the latter is precious, the consolation or settled misery of a dear Mother and two sisters who mingle their tears together and are all but frantic for my situation—pause for your Verdict!" Given the web of Heywood family interests that touched so many of the judges, this was perhaps not an empty plea.

After solemnly professing that Peter's heart would "rely with confidence on its own innocence" until the day his Spirit faced "that unerring Judge, before whom all Hearts are open, and from whom no Secrets are hid," Const completed the reading of Peter's formal defense. Thus far, Peter had been served by the penmanship of Aaron Graham and the reading of Francis Const, but for this next stage he would be trusting to his own wits. Each defendant was allowed to call witnesses to "establish the facts," and Peter planned to call Fryer, Cole, Purcell and Peckover from the *Bounty*, as well as Captain Edwards and Lieutenant Larkan of the *Pandora*. It was for this moment that Pasley had been justifiably concerned that Peter be properly prepared and coached.

To each of the witnesses, once again summoned into the great cabin before the grave assembly, Peter directed the same essential line of questioning: Had they not seen him assist in the preparation of the larger launch? And had his swift assistance not helped ensure that Bligh was safely in the launch before Christian had time to change his mind about having given his captain the safer boat? What was the height of the gunwale above the water? What was the state of mind of Mr. Hayward— "was he cool and collected or did he seem to be agitated and alarmed?" The tenor of these questions was to suggest that all the young gentlemen had been terrified at the prospect of getting into the boat—and that the only reason Hayward and Hallett were not on trial instead of Peter was that, in his words, they were so "fortunate as to quit the Ship."

Another question was more speculative: "If you had remained in the Ship in hopes of retaking her," Peter demanded of Peckover, "should you from your knowledge of my Conduct from the first Moment you knew me, to the Moment in which you are now to answer the question, have entrusted me with your design and do you believe I would have given you all the assistance in my power?" To this question, Peckover and his shipmates replied gravely in the affirmative: Yes, had they remained on the *Bounty* and not been survivors of a six-week ordeal in the open sea, they would have looked to Peter for assistance. All parties were also in agreement, in Fryer's reverent words, that Peter was "[b]eloved by every body, to the best of my Recollection."

Peter had one key, all-important witness: William Cole, who was now boatswain of the *Irresistible,* moored at Sheerness, and who had traveled down to Portsmouth in company with Captain Pasley. He was the one living person to whom Peter claimed to have confided his intention to quit the ship upon hearing George Stewart's sobering advice. In his own evidence for the prosecution, Cole's statement had tended to support Peter's claim: "I saw Mr. Peter Heywood one of the Prisoners who was standing there lending a hand to get the Fore Stay fall along," Cole had stated, "and when the Boat was hooked on, he spoke something to me, but what it was I do not know, for Christian was threatening me at the time, and Mr. Heywood then went below and I do not remember seeing him afterwards, whilst we were in the Ship." Questioned by the court the previous week, Cole had further recalled that although he had earlier stated that only Coleman, Norman and McIntosh had been detained, he also believed Heywood had been too—he had thought "all along he was intending to come away." Under closer questioning still, Cole had also recalled that he had heard "Churchill call out, 'keep them below'—who he meant I do not know."

Now, pressed by Heywood himself, Cole's memory was further jogged.

"As you have said that when I left the Deck to go below, I said something to you but you cannot now recollect what," Peter prodded, "I would ask you whether it was not that I would go and put some things into a Bag and join you in the Boat?"

"I know it was something about a bag," Cole allowed uncertainly, "but what I could not tell, I supposed he was going to get some things to come into the Boat." Afterward, Peter reminded him, orders had been given to one of the sentinels "not to let them come up again. . . . Do you think he meant me as one of them, whoever they were?"

"Yes, I do," Cole replied. Of the other witnesses summoned, Purcell too stated he had heard Churchill's command to "keep them below."

But Peter had given significantly different versions of these events on at least two different occasions: it is probable that these variant details were among the "few particulars" resulting from "the errors of an imperfect recollection" that, as he had told the court, he had mistakenly submitted to Lord Chatham. Both in his letter to his mother from Batavia and in an early draft of his defense, Peter stated that his pivotal decision to quit the *Bounty* had taken place *after* Bligh was already in the boat.

"I was not undeceived in my erroneous Intention till too late which was, after the Captain was in the Launch," Peter wrote his mother before going on to describe how he had changed his mind.

Similarly, in a more detailed draft of his defense, Peter had written, "[M]y intentions therefore to remain in the Ship were not improper, & I was confirmed in this Opinion by Mr. Bligh's telling several of the Men (when he was in the launch) who were endeavouring to get into the Boat, 'for Gods Sake my Lads don't any more of you come into the Boat, I'll do you Justice if I ever get Home.'"

It is not difficult to see why Aaron Graham edited this last vivid scene out of his lawyerly version of Peter's defense. The image of Bligh in the perilous boat evoking justice could hardly have helped Peter's cause. Yet more damning was the clear evidence the scene gave that Peter had been watching at the rail when his captain was forced into the launch. Since Bligh had been the very last person to enter the launch, Peter's subsequent realization that he should leave the *Bounty* had come at the last possible minute—literally, mere minutes before the launch was cast off. How, then, had he been able to confide his resolution to Cole (". . . on hearing it suggested that I should be deem'd Guilty if I staid with the Ship, I went down directly, and in passing Mr. Cole told him in a low tone of voice that I would fetch a few necessaries in a Bag and follow him into the Boat . . .")? How had Cole and Purcell overheard Churchill's command to "keep them below" if this applied to Heywood and Stewart? Both men had been in the launch for some time, from where, as all testimony had indicated, it had been impossible to hear much of anything (". . . there was so much Noise and Confusion in the Boat that I could not hear one man from the other," Fryer had testified).

"Who were the People that forced Mr. Bligh into the Boat?" the court had asked William Cole, when he had been examined as a witness for the prosecution.

"I cannot tell," Cole had replied, matter-of-factly. "I was in the Boat, I could not see."

Cole and, to a lesser extent, Purcell seem to have entered Peter's account rather late in the day. Pasley had found these men to be "favorable," but had never suggested they had offered anything as welcome as an alibi. One must suspect that the revised details appeared along with Aaron Graham. Was this what had so heartened Pasley and Peter following their respective meetings with this very able adviser?

"I was not undeceived in my erroneous Intention till too late." This straightforward and, one is tempted to say, even innocent summation was Peter's most intimate confession.

The last witnesses Peter summoned were from the *Pandora*. Edwards's treatment of the prisoners, as Peter knew through Pasley, was generally deplored. Accordingly, he had earlier aimed a satisfying barb at this most despised of captains, which had undoubtedly been appreciated by the court: "But tho' it cannot fail deeply to interest the humanity of this Court and kindle in the breast of every Member of it compassion for my sufferings," Peter had declaimed, after evoking the "fear and trembling" that had gripped every prisoner as the *Pandora* went down, "yet as it is not relative to the point, and as I cannot for a moment believe that it proceeded from any improper motive on the part of Captain Edwards whose Character in the Navy stands high in estimation both as an Officer and a Man of humanity . . . I shall therefore waive it and say no more upon the Subject."

Now summoned forth, Edwards, surely discomfitted by his introduction, nonetheless confirmed, in his phlegmatic and noncommittal way, that Peter had voluntarily come on board and had been helpful in relating what had happened to the *Bounty* after the mutiny.

"I had recourse to his Journals," Edwards stated, "and he was ready to Answer any Questions that I asked him."

Similarly, Lieutenant Larkan reported that "Peter Heywood came on board about 2 Hours after the Ship was at Anchor, in a Canoe, and gave himself up to me on the Quarter Deck as one belonging to the 'Bounty.'"

"Mention the Words he made use of?" asked the court, suddenly interested.

"He said, 'I suppose you know My Story,'" Larkan replied.

"Did any Person on board the 'Pandora' to your knowledge inform the Prisoner that any of the 'Bounty's' Crew had arrived in England or did he know that Lieutenant Hayward was on board before you took the Prisoner, down to Captain Edwards?" In other words, had the prisoner known the game was up?

"Not to my Knowledge," was Larkan's reply.

"[K]nowing from one of the Natives who had been off in a Canoe that our former Messmate Mr. Hayward, now promoted to the rank of Lieut. was aboard, we ask'd for him," Peter had written to his mother of his first movements on the *Pandora*. Neither Larkan nor Edwards was privy to the fact that there could be few secrets on Tahiti.

Thus concluded Peter's defense. Mr. Const reappeared one last time to read a summation of the evidence, presented again in Peter's voice. He had been asleep when the mutiny occurred; he had continued on board longer than he should, it was true, "but it has also been proved I was detained by force"; he had surrendered as soon as he was able.

This concluding statement added one new, audacious and vastly fraudulent claim: that Peter had by the absence of Captain Bligh "been deprived of an Opportunity of laying before the Court much, that would have been at least grateful to my feelings, tho' I hope not necessary to my defence." If present, Bligh would "have exculpated me from the least disrespect."

In stark contrast to Peter's extravagant defense, Michael Byrn took exactly four sentences to state his innocence. Born in Ireland, and now thirty-three, the *Bounty*'s fiddler was a slight man, slender built and standing five foot six, with pale short hair and pale skin. The adjective most used to describe him, by Bligh and mutineers alike, was "troublesome." Later events would suggest a fondness for drink. Bligh himself seems to have been unsure of where Byrn had stood, sometimes giving him the benefit of the doubt by referring to him as one of four "deserving of Mercy being detained against their inclinations"; on the other hand, unlike Coleman, Norman and McIntosh, Byrn had been confined in irons for the entire voyage from the Dutch Indies along with those deemed mutineers.

Byrn had gone to sea as an able seaman at nineteen and had served on five naval ships before the *Bounty*. One of the judges of the court-martial was a former shipmate from his first voyage: in 1778, John Ingle-field had been second lieutenant of the *Robust* (under Lord Hood's brother). In a hazardous profession that left many scarred and maimed, Byrn had managed to come through fairly well, if his near blindness is excepted, bearing only one distinguishing mark—a scar on his neck from an old abscess. The fiddler appears to have been one of the few *Bounty* men who was not tattooed.

Read aloud by the Judge Advocate, Byrn's defense was unexpectedly eloquent. Understated but with affecting details, it has a polish and tone that is detectable in some of the other defenses, and one is led to suspect a guiding hand—given the legal tone, Stephen Barney, William Mus-pratt's lawyer, would be one obvious candidate: "It has pleased the Almighty, amongst the Events of his unsearchable Providence, nearly to deprive me of Sight, which often puts it out of my Power to carry the In-tentions of my Mind into Execution," the Judge Advocate read. The spec-tacle of the slight man making his way uncertainly to the witness stand served as a poignant accompaniment to these words.

"I make no Doubt but it appears to this Honorable Court that on the 28th. of April 1789 my Intention was, to quit His Majesty's Ship the 'Bounty' with the Officers, and Men who went away, and that the sorrow I expressed at being detained was real and unfeigned.

"I do not know whether I may be able to ascertain the exact Words that were spoken on the Occasion," he continued, "but some said, 'We must not part with our Fidler,' and Charles Churchill threatned to send me to the Shades, If I attempted to quit the Cutter, into which I had gone, for the Purpose of attending Lieut. Bligh." As the mutiny had gath-ered its curious momentum, amid the taking up of cutlasses, Christian's

threats and Bligh's defiant shouting, and the bullying of the armed mutineers, Byrn sat in the abandoned cutter crying out in confusion and fear.
An entirely different boat, the larger launch, was being cranked out and
he did not appear to know it.

"As to Byrn I do not know what he was crying," William Cole had
stated for the prosecution contemptuously. "I suppose for no other reason he was blind. . . ."

Byrn called upon a solitary witness for his examination. John Fryer,
who had been in Byrn's watch throughout the voyage, was asked to report upon his character, "making Allowance for my want of sight."

"I have nothing to alledge against him," Fryer told the court; "he behaved himself in every respect as a very good Man."

As Fryer was led out, the court shifted in excited anticipation. James
Morrison, the boatswain's mate, was to be next. Sallow-skinned with
long black hair, Morrison had already made a powerful impression upon
the court. He had, as one watching officer recorded, "stood his own
counsel, questioned all the evidences, and in a manner so arranged and
pertinent that the spectators waited with impatience for his turn to call
on them, and listened with attention and delight during the discussion."

In Tahiti, Morrison had been the *taio*, or "particular friend," of Poeno,
the local chief of Ha'apape, and so a man of some importance. It was
Morrison who had planned and supervised the construction of the *Resolution*. This little craft was much admired by naval men; the energy, resolution and skill required for such a feat admirably set Britons like
Morrison apart from the dreamy "Indians" of Tahiti. In later years, Morrison's reputation would be greatly aided by the sentimental belief that a
man who could build his own boat could not be all bad.

On Tahiti, among other embellishments, Morrison had been tattooed
with the Order of the Garter, which now, under the circumstances, suggested either a sardonic sense of humor, or some private and unfathomable twist of patriotism; like Fletcher Christian, George Stewart and
Isaac Martin, Morrison also wore a star tattooed under his left breast.

In the great cabin of the *Duke*, Morrison had already revealed a lawyerly gift for driving a hard logical line of argument in his cross-examination of the prosecution's witnesses. Now he presented the Judge Advocate with his own written defense—undoubtedly disappointing the waiting spectators, who would have preferred to hear the boatswain's mate deliver this himself. Morrison had scattered his statement with emphatic underlined words and phrases, perhaps drawn for his own satisfaction, perhaps to ensure that Greetham delivered his words with the desirable force of expression: "Conscious of my own Innocence of evry *Article* of the Charge exhibited against me, and *fully* satisfied of my Zeal for His Majesty's service," Morrison began, with expected defiance and lack of apology, "I offer the following Narration, in Vindication of *my* Conduct on the 28th, day of April, 1789.

"I was the Boatswain's Mate of His Majesty's Ship 'Bounty.'" On the night before the mutiny, Morrison had come on deck for his watch at eight and remained until midnight, taking the conn, or direction of the steering of the ship.

"There was little wind *all* the Watch, and we were *then* Near the Island of Tofoa."

Relieved at midnight by John Norton, he had turned below and slept until daylight, when Cole woke him to tell him the ship was taken.

"I hope, Mr. Morrison, you have no intention to join Christian's party?" Cole asked.

"I answered him, '*No, Sir,* you may *depend* upon it, that I will *not;* for it is *far* from *my* intentions.'"

In its essential outline, Morrison's account accorded with those already told. After speaking with Cole, he had hastened forward to the head, from where he had cautiously looked out to see the deck ringed with armed men. Bligh was standing between the guns guarded by Christian, who held a bayonet in one hand and had his other on Bligh's shoulder.

Seeing for himself how things stood, Morrison went aft and again bumped into Cole, who asked him to help clear the cutter. After Purcell succeeded in obtaining the bigger launch, Morrison had turned his attention to clearing her. A hasty exchange with Fryer about attempting to retake the ship was interrupted by Quintal, who ordered Fryer back to his cabin. In the meantime, the launch had become so crowded with equipment and possessions "that those who *were* in her began to cry out that she would *sink* alongside if *any more* came into her." From the deck, where he stood guarded, Bligh called out, "you can't *all* go in the Boat, *my lads don't* overload her, some of you *must* stay in the Ship."

When, despite his pleas, Christian ordered Fryer into the boat, Morrison began "to reflect on my own Situation." Like Heywood, he foresaw sure death if he joined the boat. Moreover, as he now told the court, he had witnessed "Mr. Fryer and Most of the Officers go into the boat without the least appearance of an effort to *rescue* the Ship." He had been "heartily *rejoiced*" by Thomas Hayward's hint "that he intended to knock Chal. Churchill down," but when this intention fizzled out, he "gave over all hopes." Morrison's last act on behalf of his captain had been to hand into the boat some twenty-five pieces of pork and several gourds of water. Begging Christian for a musket for the men, he had been curtly refused, but had managed to obtain cutlasses, "two of which I handed in *my self* and Churchill bought the other two and said, '*There*, Captain Bligh! you *don't* stand in Need of *fire arms* as you are Going among your *friends*,'" this last being a mocking reference to Bligh's recent fraught dealings with the Friendly Islanders.

As the boat cast off, Morrison had heard Bligh "desire to speak to Mr. Christian but *he* gave Orders that *no person* should answer."

This ended Morrison's narration of events. The more important part of his defense—and that greatly looked forward to by the court spectators—still remained, the rebuttal of the specific charges made against him by Hayward and Hallett.

The first, and least serious, of these charges was Hayward's claim that Morrison had looked "rejoiced," not "depressed," when he helped prepare the boat for Bligh. It was Morrison's expression, Hayward told the court, that induced him to regard him as a mutineer.

"This Honorable Court knows that *all* men do not bear misfortunes with the *same* fortitude or equanimity of mind," Morrison now countered, "and that the face is *too often* a bad index to the Heart." Interestingly, he did not attempt to deny that he had worn a suspect expression on that day. Rather, as he told the court, he had deliberately dissembled "to deceive those, whose *Act* I abhorred, that I might be at liberty to *seize* the *first* Opportunity that *might* appear favourable, to the retaking of the Ship." Bligh himself, Morrison pointed out, had allowed in his letter that he had erroneously thought "from the Carpenters *sullen* and *ferocious* aspect" that Purcell was a mutineer.

More damaging were the charges made by Hallett that Morrison had appeared at the taffrail under arms.

"Amidst such *Crowd, Tumult,* and *Confusion* might not the Arms in the hands of another wedged by my side *easily* be thought to be in *my possession?*" Morrison now asked passionately of the court. And why, if he had been a mutineer, would he have chosen to wield arms only after Bligh and his men "were placed in a *helpless situation*" and no use of arms was necessary? If after deliberation the members of the Honorable Court found "*any doubts* remain in *their* minds" respecting his innocence, Morrison reminded them that "it has always been Accounted the *Glory* of *Justice* in a *doubtful* Case to throw *Mercy* into the Ballance."

Morrison turned to William Cole, the *Bounty* boatswain and his own immediate superior, to attempt to redress Hallett's second damaging claim, that as the lumbered boat veered away, Morrison had called "in a jeering Manner, 'If my friends enquire after me, tell them I am somewhere in the South Seas.'"

"Do you recollect," Morrison now asked Cole, "hearing me make use of any sneering expressions—particularly over the Stern?"

"I heard him say that if anybody asked for him, to let them know that he was to the Southward of the Line or something to that Purport," replied Cole, no doubt unexpectedly; clearly he was not going to be as cooperative in picking up hints from Morrison as he had been with Peter Heywood.

"Do you recollect that it was by the Clumsiness and Awkwardness of John Norton, that two or three Pieces of the Pork went overboard and that you damned his Clumsy Eyes, and shoved him away from receiving any more of it?" asked Morrison, furiously changing the subject.

"No, I do not remember it," Cole replied, conceding, "I know three or four Pieces went overboard." And when Morrison asked that his "Character at large" be told to the court, Cole had only compliments: "He was a Man of very good Character in the Ship; he was Boatswain's Mate and steered the Captain he was attentive to his duty, and I never knew any harm of him in my life."

Morrison's last witness was William Purcell, who bluntly and briefly denied all that Hallett and Cole had said: he had never seen Morrison under arms, and he had never heard him use "jeering speeches." Questioned by the court, Purcell elaborated. Yes, he had heard *someone* speak jeeringly from the stern, but he could not say who it had been. Like Cole and Fryer, Purcell gave Morrison a very good character, "diligent, and attentive."

It would not appear that Morrison had effectively negated any of the most damaging charges against him; on the contrary, Cole had confirmed Hallett's memory of his jeering speech. But the fact that a lowly boatswain's mate had stood his ground with such consistent, unapologetic fearlessness made a favorable impression on the court.

"This ship appears to have abounded with men above the common herd of uninformed illiterates," wrote the officer reporting on the trial, while singling out "the boatswain's mate" for special commendation. Morrison's clear, emphatic diction, his willingness to attack the most damaging charges head-on and his refusal to make maudlin appeals for mercy were impressive. The boatswain's mate had addressed the superior officers who held his fate man to man—and this was admired.

Morrison's highly ambiguous defense was followed by that of Charles Norman, carpenter's mate, the third of the men generally held to be innocent. Just turned thirty-five, Norman had been baptized in the Holy Trinity Church at Gosport, across Portsmouth Harbour. From the boat that daily ferried him and his fellow prisoners between the *Hector* and the *Duke*, he was able to see his home; on calm, still nights he could hear the church's bells. A Gosport baptism would suggest that his was a naval or seafaring family.

At five foot nine, tall and slender, Norman had light brown hair and fair skin pitted with the scars of smallpox. He had also, as Bligh had described, a "Remarkable Motion with his head and eyes," suggestive of some kind of nervous tic.

Like Hayward and Hallett, Norman had shared Christian's fateful watch. Sometime between five and six in the morning, Norman had been charged by Mr. Christian to "Coil up the Ropes on the quarter Deck."

"When I had done I saw a large Shark alongside and call'd out, 'There's a Shark on the larboad quarter.'"

"Don't make a noise," Hayward said, while Hallett called out for a shark hook. Christian then reappeared and ordered Norman to "go aft and unship the Gangboard ready for Drawing water for washing Decks." While Norman went aft, and Hayward and Hallett watched the shark, the mutiny took place. Norman saw Christian vanish down the fore hatchway and minutes later Churchill and four others armed and "loading as they Came Aft.

". . . [I]n about two Minutes after Christian Came aft with a Drawn Cutlass in his hand and follow'd them down the Hatchway. I was standing by the Larboard Gangway and I heard Captain Bligh Call out, 'What's the matter, What's the matter, Murder!'"

From below, Churchill called out "in terrible threats" for a line to bind Bligh, and John Mills, gunner's mate, complied. Shortly after, Bligh was led up by Christian and Churchill; the captain's "hands were tied and he was in his Shirt without any Breeches or Trowsers." In these humiliating conditions, Bligh was placed between the guns, where Christian assumed guard.

"Churchill then Came to me With a Drawn Cutlass and Pistol and in a Commanding Voice ordered me to Clear the Yams out of the Small Cutter. I ask'd him for What, to which he replied 'Do as I order you.'"

When this notorious, unseaworthy cutter was cleared, she was swung out and launched into the water with Norman still inside her. It was then he, more than anyone else, who had first appreciated just how useless the boat was.

"She was not long Out before I call'd out that she would sink if she was not hoisted in as I could not keep her free with bailing, her bottom being Eaten so much by the Worms." Back on the ship, he assisted Purcell in preparing the bigger launch. He wanted to go with his captain, he told the court, but Christian gave orders that he, along with Coleman and McIntosh, was to remain on the ship.

"[O]n hearing this I was affraid to go over the side for fear of being Shot at, and I can solemnly swear before God and this Honorable Court that I was kept against my Own Consent and I told Mr. Hallet to remember me to my Wife and family."

While the always unaccommodating Hallett could not, under examination, recall the last claim, Norman's account was otherwise borne out not only by Purcell but by William Bligh. Back in March 1790, two weeks after Bligh's return, Norman's brother had written to Bligh and received a welcome response: His "unfortunate Brother" had been kept on the *Bounty* against his will, and Bligh had "recommended him to Mercy— his friends may therefore be easy in their Minds on his account," Bligh concluded in this now all-timely letter, which was presented to the court, "as it is most likely he will return by the first ship that comes from Otaheite. He was in very good health."

The court had no questions for Norman, a fact that in his case probably boded well, and he withdrew to make way for Thomas Ellison, able seaman.

Although he had stated his age as nineteen on the ship muster, Ellison had been between sixteen and seventeen when the mutiny occurred, and as his defense would show, he, like Heywood, would make a plea for his "youth and inexperience." Stocky and stout at five foot three and "strong" made, as Bligh had noted, the youth was dark-haired and fair-skinned.

Ellison had come to the *Bounty* through the recommendation of Duncan Campbell, Bligh's wealthy uncle-in-law, and had sailed with Bligh— and therefore with Christian—all those years ago in the West Indies, on the *Lynx* and the *Britannia*, both Campbell's ships; or as Ellison put it, "both is ship." With his dropping of *h*s, his *w*s for *v*s ("He being wex'd"), Ellison wrote as he spoke, and in doing so betrayed not only his cockney origins, but the fact that he had prepared his defense without mentoring or guidance. Who he was and how he had come to Campbell's notice is not known. The *Bounty* muster lists him as being from "Deptford"; this dockyard community might have been his name or simply the port where he was mustered. That Campbell—and Bligh—looked out for the lad is evident from the affectionate comments Bligh had made in letters to his uncle-in-law on the *Bounty*'s outward journey: "Tom Ellison is improving [and] will make a very good seaman"; "Tom Ellison is a very good Boy and will do very well"; and more indulgently, "Tom Ellison [is] very well but is not a particle taller than when he left home but is fat as he can well be." That the ship's arrival in Tahiti represented a landmark in the boy's life was evident from the single tattoo he bore on his right arm: his own name and "October 25th 1788," the date on which the *Bounty* had sighted the island.

Short and unprepossessing, with the look and accent of "the common herd of uninformed illiterates," as the officer commenting on the trial had put it, Ellison faced his judges. But for all his peculiarities of spelling and diction, Ellison's account was to be one of the most graphic and gripping.

At four o'clock in the morning of April 28, 1789, Ellison had gone to take his turn at the wheel with John Mills at the conn. An hour later, Ellison saw Charles Churchill go aft and speak to Christian "in Close Conversation about ten Minutes," although what they had spoken of he could not hear. A half hour later still, at 5:30 A.M., Ellison saw Christian "and Party" go aft under arms, and return five minutes later with Bligh captive.

"[T]his Proceeding greatly amaz'd and Terifyde me," Ellison told the court, going on to conjure one of the most riveting images of the whole trial proceedings:

"[M]y terror was more Increas'd, at the site of Mr. Christain, he looked like a Madman is long hair was luse, his shirt Collair open." It is extraordinary that no one else in his testimony commented on Christian's appearance, or state of mind. Only Bligh had done so: "As for Christian," he had written in his log, not long after the astonishing turn of events, "he seemed to be plotting instant destruction on himself and every one, for of all diabolical looking Men he exceeded every possible description."

Standing with bayonet in hand, Christian, distraught, his shirt undone, his long hair flowing, was quickly surrounded by armed men.

"Captn. Bligh Wanted to talk with him," Ellison told the court. "I heard Mr. Christian say two or three times, 'Mammoo, sir,' which the meaning of the word is," he elaborated for those ignorant of the Otaheite tongue, "sillence, sir."

Bligh then looked around, Ellison claimed, and seeing the ship was standing off the distant land, "he Disirid me to clap the helm down," or bear up to the wind. Ellison promptly obeyed this order. Ellison's aim was to show the court that he had been obedient to his captain. However, no one else reported this exchange or even suggested that Bligh had been in any position to give any orders whatsoever—although, this being said, such an action would have been entirely characteristic.

Ellison lashed the helm "a lee," and while the cutter was being precariously launched, he had made his way to Lawrence Lebogue, the sailmaker from Nova Scotia, who was now sailing with Bligh on the *Providence,* back in the South Seas. Ellison and Lebogue had been shipmates in the West Indies days, and Ellison turned to him, under pretext of going to the head, or lavatory. "I oney pretended to go to the head For the purpose to speke to him and ask his advice," Ellison told the court, earnestly, "he being an old seaman and had Been many years in His Majtys. Servace. He being wex'd, I believe, answerd me in a Sharp surly manner, told me to go to hell and not bother him; this Reception from my old ship mate quite Disheartened me from making an application to any One else."

Meanwhile, the tension and confusion was mounting around Christian. Hayward and Hallett, ordered into the boat, "weep't Bitterly and Mr. Hayward begged to know what he had done to be sent out of the Ship." All the while Bligh was attempting to speak to Christian, who "with many threats" told him to be silent. Pleas were being made for the launch instead of the leaky cutter. As the second boat was being readied, Christian had continued to look "very severe and by Continual threats Keep every one in fear of him."

Somewhere in this mayhem, young Ellison got hold of a musket or bayonet and in a heady rush of excitement and adrenaline waved it around, shouting over Bligh, "Damn him, I will be Centry over him." Apparently, Ellison's unexpected zeal startled even Christian, and a subsequent report would relate that on seeing the boy brandishing the weapon Christian snapped at him, "You little monkey, what business have you with that?"

"Captn. Bligh, seeing [a] Great many still wanting to come begged for gods sake that no more come In," Ellison now told the court, describing the boat heavy with people and equipment. Bligh, having followed his officers into the boat, called back to the ship, "[M]y lads I will do you all Justice for I know whos and who." Omitted was the fact that Ellison had jumped to answer Christian's command to tend to the sails. The sight of Ellison loosening the main topgallant was the last image many of the loyalists recalled of the *Bounty.*

"This honourable Gentlemen is the reale Truth of all I know about this unhappy affair and I hop your honours will take my Inexpearence'd Youth into Consideration," Ellison now begged the court, wrapping up his defense. "I never did or ment any harm to any one much more to my Commander, to whose care I Was recommended by Mr. Camble." It was also on account of Mr. "Camble," it now transpired, that Bligh "took great pains with me and spoke too Mr. Samule, his Clark, to teach me Writing and Arithmetick." So, indirectly, Ellison owed his ability to prepare his defense to William Bligh.

". . . and I believe Would have taught me further had not this happend," he added miserably. The enormity of what Ellison had thrown away seems to have finally caught up with him. "I hope, honorable Gentlemen yo'll be so Kind as to take my Case into Consideration as I was No more than between Sixteen and Seventeen Years of age when this was done," Ellison concluded, with what was almost an abject confession. "Honourable Gentlemen I leave my self at the Clemency and Mercy of this Honourable Court."

Ellison called only one witness, John Fryer, who was asked if he had seen him under arms on the quarterdeck or the larboard gangway, or jeering from the taffrail.

"[H]e possibly might have been there," Fryer told the court, "but from my Attention to other Things, I had not an Opportunity of seeing him." And with this unhelpful testimonial, Ellison's defense was ended.

After Ellison's desperate bid, the appearance of Thomas McIntosh, formerly carpenter's mate of the *Bounty,* brought a welcome change in tone, McIntosh being the last of the men that most witnesses—including Bligh—had exonerated.

McIntosh, now aged thirty, was from North Shields, a "poor miserable place" strung along the river Tyne, in which it was said there was "scarcely a single house roofed with tiles, and none slated." Nonetheless, it was here McIntosh's mother kept a public house. At some point, perhaps immediately before the *Bounty* voyage, McIntosh had changed his name from "Tosh" to "McIntosh," suggesting that although he had grown up in Northumberland, he felt his allegiance to lie north of the Scottish border.

According to Bligh, the mutineers had prevaricated over whether to retain Purcell or McIntosh for his valuable carpentry skill, and had decided in favor of the latter, knowing Purcell to be, in Bligh's words, "a troublesome fellow." At five foot six, McIntosh was of middle height, slender, with fair, pockmarked skin and light brown hair. He was also the only one of the four men detained against their will who was "tatowed," Coleman's preexisting memento excepted.

McIntosh's testimony was short and uneventful. On the morning of the mutiny, he had been awoken by Cole with the news that "the people had taken the Ship." As he was getting dressed, he was called by Purcell to help prepare first the cutter and then the launch, and he was thus wholly occupied in getting the various parts out of the storeroom. He had also brought up tools and other articles that he "thought might be of Service in the Boat." He heard Christian call to Churchill to prevent him, Norman and Coleman from getting in the boat; Churchill's orders to "detain them," which Peter Heywood had claimed for himself, would seem to have applied to these loyalists.

"I stood by the Gangway alongside of Norman Untill the Captain was Ordered into the Boat, When we both told him that Christian would not suffer us to go with him," McIntosh told the court, "upon which he told us he would do us Justice."

Like Norman, McIntosh was fortunate to be able to produce a letter from Bligh, in this case to his mother, giving reassurance that her son had "remained on board contrary to his inclination" and that she would be unlikely to hear anything more until the return of the *Pandora,* "which will be 18 Months or two Years."

Purcell and Fryer, called upon as witnesses, confirmed both McIntosh's general claim and his character. "I have nothing to say against him," said Fryer. "He always did his duty with Cheerfulness." As had Norman, McIntosh steered clear of calling any of the *Pandora* officers as witnesses. One of the questions never asked was why both men, if innocent, had fled from the *Pandora* on her arrival at Tahiti.

Outside, the fair, fine day had become overcast. The afternoon was wearing on, and still there remained three men to tell their stories. A decision seems to have been made that the court would not adjourn this day until every man had been heard.

William Muspratt, the cook's assistant, now thirty-one, was a striking figure, of medium height and slender, but with dark skin and "a very Strong Black Beard." As well as being noticeably scarred under his chin (hence the beard?), he was also tattooed. Muspratt, with Churchill and his fellow prisoner Millward, had been one of the three men who had so ill advisedly deserted in Tahiti, only to be captured, flogged and imprisoned for their pains. This much, then, could be stated with some assurance: Muspratt would have preferred to have remained on Tahiti.

He had been born in Bray, a parish of Maidenhead on the Thames, where it was busy with the inland barge trade, and was one of his parents' seven surviving children. The year before the *Bounty* sailed, Muspratt's father committed suicide by hanging himself from an apple tree; the subsequent inquest had ruled the cause of death "lunacy."

Muspratt was the only man other than Peter Heywood to enjoy personal legal counsel, and his need for a good lawyer was acute. Two witnesses, Hayward and Cole, had testified to having seen him armed with a musket. And, although the desertion on Tahiti was not formally part of the prosecution's case, the fact that he had on at least one occasion attempted to avoid returning to his native country would suggest a motive for taking the ship.

Aaron Graham's cleverness notwithstanding, it was Muspratt, through Stephen Barney's tactics and language, who was to give the most coherent legal defense. This began with a bold move, a petition to the court to call upon two fellow prisoners, Byrn and Norman, as witnesses; as he noted, it was "every day's practice in the Criminal Courts of Justice on the Land" when trying a number of prisoners for the same charges to acquit those whom "the Evidence does not materially Affect . . . that the other Prisoners may have an Opportunity to call them if advised to do so." In other words, if the innocence of Byrn and Norman was sufficiently proven to justify their acquittal, then, under civil law, he could call on them as witnesses.

At this unexpected turn, the court withdrew to consult, returning only to announce that they were "of the Opinion that they cannot depart from the usual Practice of Courts Martial and give Sentence on any particular Prisoner, until the whole of the Defences of the Prisoners, are gone through." The other might well be a daily practice in courts on land—but on board the *Duke,* this court was at sea.

Apparently undeterred, William Muspratt handed the court his prepared defense to be read by the Judge Advocate. Whereas the defense Aaron Graham had prepared for Heywood had attempted to shroud its legalistic maneuvering behind a smoke screen of sentiment and confusion—as if young Heywood himself were speaking his own words—Muspratt's defense took the legal nature of the proceedings at face value. No attempt was made to obscure the fact that this was his lawyer speaking.

After observing his satisfaction to be "tried under the most Benign Laws, and by a Court attentive equally to the Life and Liberty of the Subject, as to the Honor of the Crown," Muspratt declared, with "God to Witness," that he was innocent of the charges laid against him.

"I was Assistant to the Cook of the 'Bounty,'" he began, matter-of-factly describing how between five and six in the morning of April 28, he had been splitting wood by the starboard fore scuttle.

"Michael Byrn came up just after and asked me what I was about, making such a Noise when the People were just turned into their Hammocks." Hayward then ran by, calling for a hook for the shark that had been spotted. Somebody said that Christian had gone below for a musket to shoot the shark, and shortly after, William McCoy came "up the fore Hatchway with a Musquet in his hand and gave two or three hard thumps with its But-end upon the Deck saying 'bear a hand.'" Other men came on deck and ran aft, and Muspratt learned that Bligh was a prisoner.

Ordered by Churchill to help clear the cutter, with the threat that it would "be the worse for" him if he did not, Muspratt assisted Norman at this task. Having finished, he was sitting on the booms behind the fore hatchway when Millward approached and told him that Fryer was going to attempt to retake the ship.

"I then said I would stand by Mr. Fryer as far as I could." It was for this sole reason that he had taken up a musket.

His account of his own actions given, Muspratt turned to the witnesses who had been so damaging to him, directing a blistering attack on the credibility of Purcell and—above all—Mr. Hayward.

"I should call Mr. Purcell in Aid of my Defense, but I must decline it on observing the very unaccountable manner in which he had given his Evidence to the Honble. Court." On the one hand, Purcell had stated that he could recall nothing in particular about Muspratt on that day; on the other hand, he had later stated that Muspratt was "walking about the Ship handing liquor to the Ships Company."

As for Hayward: "Mr. Haywards Evidence, I trust, must stand so impeached before this Honble. Court as not to receive the least Attention in this Case where the Lives of so many Men are affected by it." As Muspratt reminded the court, Hayward had sworn both that Morrison was a mutineer because he assisted with the boats, and that McIntosh was not a mutineer, although he too had assisted with the boats; he had imputed complicity to Morrison "from the Appearance of his Countenance"; and most damning, Hayward had shown a suspect inability to recall the "most material and striking Circumstances of Morrison's offering to join him to retake the Ship." These and other observations, which he could not "with Decency make," as Muspratt forcefully told the court, "must most materially affect Mr. Hayward's Credit." Nothing he had said about anyone should, therefore, be believed.

"The great Misfortune attending this unhappy Business," Muspratt now ventured, in an audacious summing up, "is that no one ever Attempted to rescue the Ship, it might have been done—Thompson was the only Centinel upon the Arm Chest." This last expression had the vehemence of authentic conviction. But stunned and passive, waiting for someone else to make the first, all-important move, each potential loyalist had dithered as the minutes raced by—and then it was too late.

Thomas Burkett, able seaman, was called next, and one can imagine the faces of the watching judges darkening as he was summoned. There was almost no point in his expending energy to tell his story. He was one of the men specifically named by Bligh who had entered his cabin and forcibly seized him. Every witness who had been on deck recalled seeing Burkett escort Bligh from his cabin at musket point. He was not only a mutineer in the general sense of being of Christian's "party," but had been one of the handful of aggressively active agents.

And yet, as if to belie the fact that his cause was lost, or perhaps as a symptom of his desperation, Burkett was to deliver one of the longest, most detailed and most vivid defenses. Thomas Burkett was now thirty years old. Tall—five foot nine—and slender, with his face "much pitted" from smallpox, he was "very much tatowed." He was also undoubtedly scarred from the wound he had received in the bloody skirmish between mutineers and islanders on Tubuai. There are Burketts found on the Isle of Man, and Burketts in Cumbria, but Burkett of the *Bounty* was from a "liberty," or parish, of Bath in Somersetshire. No further evidence of his family or origins can be found. He had been in naval service for at least two years before joining the *Bounty*, having been a seaman in 1785 on the *Hector*, the same ship on which he was now prisoner.

As if to deflect attention from his actions at the critical moments of the actual mutiny, Burkett drew a detailed picture of what had happened in the preceding two hours. At four in the morning, he had gone on deck "to keep my Watch with Mr. Christian." There was the business with the shark, which had so absorbed Hayward and Hallett.

Hallett then approached Burkett and, although some eleven years the sailor's junior, had told him, "Burkett, it is my catering week and you must draw those three Fowls for me which are hanging to the Main Stay"; such was the prerogative of young gentlemen. Muttering that he did not know how to draw a fowl, Burkett nonetheless retreated to the windlass and set about the work. As he was busy with the birds, he heard Christian say to Coleman, "[G]ive me a Musquet to shoot a Shark with." Behind him, he heard Hayward asking, "What are you about, are you going to Exercise already?," referring to the exercise of arms.

Suddenly there was a lot of activity on deck.

"Hayward is gone to tell the Captain," Churchill said. This in itself, if true, was significant: it was the first suggestion that the midshipmen had caught wind that something was amiss. Turning, Burkett saw Hayward and Hallett disappear aft, and Churchill and others, muskets and bayonets in hand, run down the aft hatchway. McCoy came fore and struck the coamings with the butt end of his musket, while John Williams did the same on the fo'c'sle.

"[T]hen came up Mr. Christian with a Musquet and fix'd bayonet and a Cartouch box in his left hand and a pistol and Cutlass in his right with Fury in his looks, he said, 'Here Burkett lay hold of this,' holding out the Musquet; I ask'd him what I must do with it in a refusing Manner, when he presented his pistol at me, saying, 'Damn your blood lay hold of it and go aft.'"

Going aft on the starboard side, Christian ran into Hayward, and "shaking the Cutlass at Mr. Hayward said, 'Damn your blood, Hayward, Mamoo,'" which the court by now knew was Tahitian for "shut up."

Christian continued down the aft hatchway, and Burkett heard the sound of a door being broken and Mr. Christian say, "Bligh you are my Prisoner." There was the noise of broken glass, and Fryer and Nelson were ordered to stay below, while Hayward and Hallett were standing between the two guns on the quarterdeck, "[s]eemingly much Confused." Churchill called out for seizing, or cord, to bind the captain, and when no one responded called again, "[Y]ou Infernal buggers, hand down a seizing or I'll Come up and play hell with you all."

Shortly after, Bligh was led up, in his nightshirt, with his hands bound behind him. "I was then at the Gangway," Burkett told the court, "and seeing the Captain without Breeches and with his shirt tail tyed up with the seizing that secured his hands I laid down the Musquet by the dripstone."

"What are you going to do?" Christian demanded.

"Let down the Captains shirt," Burkett replied, and did so, "hauling it out of the lashing." Where did this detail come from? Did Burkett really have the audacity, let alone imagination, to invent such an extraordinary scene? And if his account was true—what did this act imply?

"Take up your Arms," Christian ordered him.

"I took no Notice but went to the Companion and said to Jn. Sumner, 'Hand me up the Captain's Cloaths.' In the meantime Jn. Smith, the Captain's Servant, Came aft and I said to him, 'Jack go fetch the Captain's Cloaths it is a Shame to see him stand naked.'"

"Why don't you take up your Arms Burkett," Christian repeated and, drawing his pocket pistol, added, "I would have you take care."

Hayward and Hallett were ordered into the boat, "at which they seem'd verry much surprized."

"What harm did ever I do you, Mr. Christian?" Hayward implored.

"I hope you will not insist upon it, Mr. Christian," Hallett beseeched, with tears in his eyes. But Mr. Christian did insist, telling them curtly to "[g]o into the Boat." On his orders, rum was now served to those under arms, while Norman, from the leaky cutter, called up that the boat was sinking.

"Consider what you are about Mr. Christian," Bligh begged as the larger launch was being prepared. "[F]or God's sake drop it and there shall be no more come of It."

"'Tis too late Captain Bligh," Christian replied.

"No, Mr. Christian, it is not too late yet, I'll forfeit my Honour if ever I speak of it, I'll give you my bond that there shall never be any more come of It."

"You know Captain Bligh," said Christian, "you have treated me like a dog all the voyage. I have been In Hell this fortnight past and I am determin'd to suffer it no longer."

Bligh was joined by Cole and Purcell who also begged Christian to "drop it."

"You know Mr. Cole how I have been Used," replied Christian.

"I know it verry well Mr. Christian, we all know it, but drop it, for God's sake."

"Consider, Mr. Christian What a dangerous Step you have taken," put in Hayward, who was supposed to be getting in the boat.

"Can there be no other Method taken?" asked Bligh; the question was pragmatic more than a plea.

"No," interjected Churchill, who was standing by, "this is the best and only Method."

During this extraordinary exchange, Burkett sought to stay out of Christian's line of sight, retreating by the water cask, behind the wheel. Michael Byrn was "groping about for something in the Fore Rigging" and upon being given a piece of rope, he had groped his way down into the leaky and forsaken cutter.

"I have seen you shifting about, but I have my Eye on you," Churchill said, approaching Burkett in "a surly Manner."

Fryer was let on deck and spoke with Millward and Morrison, who were by the launch, but Burkett could not hear what was said. Suddenly Matthew Quintal ran up carrying a pistol and grabbed Fryer by the collar to take him back down below. Millward then approached Burkett and asked whether he "had a hand in the Affair."

"[N]o more than I was forced to have," Burkett replied, at which Millward told him that Fryer intended to retake the ship.

"I then took up my Arms with a good heart," Burkett now told his judges, "to be ready to Assist in recovering the Ship if any Attempt was Made." The launch was got out, and still there was no such attempt. Christian was talking to all those under arms, but, as Burkett declared, he "did not come to me." Cole was busy trying to remove the compass from the binnacle when he was stopped by Quintal, who asked what need he had of a compass "when land was in Sight."

"Take it," Burkett said, stepping in. Cole removed the compass.

"Damn my Eyes," exclaimed Quintal, "we may as well give him the Ship." The boat was being filled, and the officers were now all on deck. "I look'd for some attempt to be made but, to my utter surprize and astonishment saw None."

Christian gave orders for Coleman, Norman and McIntosh to be detained, but for the others to get into the boat.

"You had better let me stay, Mr. Christian," Fryer said, "for you'll not

Know what to do with the Ship." To this unwise rebuke Christian replied, "We can do verry well without you, Mr. Fryer."

After Fryer was led into the launch, Bligh was untied and led to the gangway.

"Never fear my lads I'll do you Justice if ever I reach England," he called back to those detained on his ship.

Afraid to call to his captain, Burkett instead called to the officers, asking, quaintly, if there was anything he could get them. Peckover replied that he would like some clothes and his pocket book—to this exchange Peckover had indeed already attested. Shortly after, the boat was cast off and Christian called to Burkett with the order to trim the sails.

"I could do no more but give them my hearty blessing and my prayers to God for their welfare," Burkett now claimed, "and bid them farewell."

The narration they had just heard, Burkett now informed the court, had been written shortly after he had left the *Bounty*, when he had "got clear of Christian and his Party—foreseeing, that either, sooner or later, myself, as well as every other person on board, would be obliged to render an account of our Conduct." The vivid specificity of the incidents recalled, especially the conversations which accorded well with other accounts, might well have substantiated this claim—but how, on the other hand, had the narrative survived the wreck of the *Pandora?*

But Thomas Burkett was far from finished. Before summoning his witnesses, the seaman summed up for the court all points in his favor. He obtained the compass for the boat, indicative of "Compassion for the distress of my fellow Creatures" ("I knew that Quintal objected to let the Compass go," Cole had testified in his evidence for the prosecution, "but I do not remember that Burkitt said anything, but he was standing up there. I do not remember what passed; the Confusion was so great that it was impossible that I could take notice of every thing particularly"). There was also Burkett's acquisition of Mr. Peckover's possessions. Even the fact that Christian had chosen him, Burkett now argued, was "greatly in favour of my general good, and peaceable character." He had committed no outrages, but "was simply armed with a Musquet, which I have endeavoured to prove how I came into possession of."

Lieutenant Hayward, it was true, had stated that he had seen Burkett come up the fore hatchway with others under arms, and although "far from desiring to invalidate the testimony of any Witness," it was necessary to point out that this had been a time of great confusion and "the personal fear that might influence the mind on such an occasion, might magnify objects." On the other hand, Hayward had verified that Burkett had voluntarily come down from the mountains in Tahiti, "which" stated Burkett, "certainly argues a consciousness on my part, if not of perfect innocence"—here Burkett was wise enough not to ignore the fact that he had fled to the mountains to avoid capture—"yet innocence in such a degree—as not totaly to exclude every hope of acquittal and forgiveness."

Finally, he begged the court to reflect on the state of mind he had suffered since being on the *Pandora*, "the Hopes and Fears, Doubt, and Anxiety" with which he had been afflicted. Forgiveness, he reminded the court, was "the noblest attribute of the Divinity."

Herewith, Burkett submitted a testimonial of character, from an earlier captain he had served, and summoned his numerous witnesses. Fryer, Cole, Peckover and Hallett variously allowed that they could not "positively swear" that Burkett had not been armed "in Consequence of the fear of immediate Death with which [he] was threatened by Christian." Peckover reiterated that when he was in the boat, Burkett had tossed possessions down to him from the ship. Hallett confirmed, of all things, that yes, indeed, he had asked Burkett to "pick a fowl" before the mutiny. All gave the seaman a good "character" previous to the mutiny.

With all ammunition spent—defense, point-by-point summation, character references, vaguely favorable evidences and a direct, unqualified plea for mercy—Burkett at last surrendered the prisoner's bar. Whether his considerable ingenuity had successfully obscured the single damning image of his emerging from his captain's own cabin under arms, he would have to wait to discover.

There now remained one last defendant. John Millward, another of the *Bounty*'s able seamen and sailmaker, dark-skinned, dark-haired, short and "Strong made," was now twenty-five years old. On his return to Tahiti, Millward had lived with Morrison and his *taio,* the chief. He had been born in Stoke Damerel, the still undeveloped outskirts of Plymouth Dock, site of the most recently developed of the Royal Dockyards of the kingdom. His father was also a "mariner," recently serving on His Majesty's ship *Ocean,* when he had married a young widow in a private ceremony in the Dock Chapel. With only one brother and one sister, John Millward had come from a small family, and although his parents were illiterate, he had learned to read and write. Stoke Damerel had numerous free schools, a number run by dissenters such as Baptists and Methodists, and it may be that the mariner's son had benefited from these charitable institutions. Millward was not a local name, and in other parts of England Millwards were active Methodists.

With Churchill and Muspratt, John Millward had deserted from the *Bounty* on the dark night of January 5, 1789, when heavy rain had obscured his midnight sentry watch. Cole had already testified that Millward had made reference to this "foolish" affair when the mutiny broke: "he said he had a hand in the foolish Piece of Busines before, and that he was afraid they would make him have a Hand in that also." John Fryer had very clearly seen him under arms, although, as he told the court, he had felt Millward "seemed friendly" ("Millward, your Piece is cocked, you had better uncock it as you may shoot some Person").

In addition to the attempt to desert, Millward bore other clear evidence of having taken to the ways of Tahiti. He was, Bligh had written, "[v]ery much Tatowed in Different parts," and bore under the pit of his stomach an elaborate "Taoomy," or tattooed breastplate.

He had been awoken, Millward now told the court through the usual agency of a written deposition, in his berth on the larboard side of the foremast by Cole and Purcell, who told him the ship was taken, adding "they hoped that none of us were Concerned in the Mutiny." Going up to the fo'c'sle, he ran into Charles Churchill, who told him he could either go in the boat or stay with the ship; "to which I answered, 'No Charles, you brought me into one predicament already and I'll take Care you don't bring me into another,'" meaning the desertion.

"As you like it," Churchill said, and Millward continued on deck, where, abaft the windlass, Cole told him to lend a hand with the cutter. As the cutter and then the launch were being prepared, he spoke with Fryer and Morrison, pledging to help them retake the ship. Shortly after, he told the same first to Burkett and then to Muspratt, both of whom promised to assist.

While working with the boat, Alexander Smith approached him carrying a cutlass and said, "Take hold of this, Millward."

"I asked him what I was to do with it, to which he reply'd, 'Never you mind, lay hold of it.'" Millward complied, but as soon as Smith's back was turned, he went "aft and stuck it in the lashing of the Dripstone." But later, as the launch was swung out, he was ordered to take arms again, and this time when he refused, Christian had intervened: "I was affraid to deny and accordingly Obey'd his orders."

Going below once again, he met Fryer and confirmed that the pistols in his hands were those Fryer had been accustomed to keep, supposedly loaded, in his cabin. On asking Fryer if he knew them to be loaded now, Fryer replied that "they only Contained loose powder."

"Then, Sir, said I, 'I won't trust to them.'" A quarter of an hour later, the officers were ordered on deck and into the boat. Fryer, Hayward and Hallett all pleaded to remain, to no avail. As the reluctant officers went over the side, Bligh implored them not to overload the boat, and then turned to address Christian.

"Consider my Wife and family," he had implored; to which Christian had replied, "It is too late, now Captain Bligh you should have thought of them before this time."

Millward recounted, "[W]hen the Boat was Ordered to be Cast off I pull'd my Jacket off and threw it in to George Simpson, who was my Messmate, and with my prayers for their protection." Since he was closely watched, this was all that he could do.

Having cited so many witnesses to his good intentions—Cole, Fryer, Burkett, Muspratt—Millward now called upon only Cole, asking the boatswain whether he recollected how Millward had told him of Fryer's intention to retake the ship. To this forlorn hope, Cole now replied, "I don't remember anything of it at all."

Thus, at last, was the defense of the *Bounty* mutineers concluded. It was late in a long, emotionally exhausting day, and court was adjourned until nine the following morning. Accordingly, on Tuesday, September 18, the ten prisoners were carried one last time back to the *Duke* amid intermittent showers. Admitted to the court, they were asked if they "had anything more to offer to the Court in their Defences." Only Peter Heywood responded, handing over no less than three attestations that his birth had indeed occurred on June 5, 1772, "between the hours of six and seven o'Clock in the Evening," thereby confirming his claim at least of "youth" at the time of the mutiny. None of the other prisoners, it seems, offered a further word. The preceding night had apparently afforded no sober second thoughts—or perhaps no further hope.

The court was cleared, and the twelve post-captains remained to deliberate. Guilt or innocence had to be determined in the case of each and every one of the men before they would pronounce a judgment. The deliberations appear to have taken several hours, for it was not until half past one in the afternoon that the *Duke* hauled down the court-martial signal. By then the prisoners had been reconvened in the great cabin to receive their sentences. Humbly arrayed before their judges, the ten men heard Lord Hood pronounce their fates.

The Court, Lord Hood declared, had found "the Charges had been proved" against Peter Heywood, James Morrison, Thomas Ellison, Thomas Burkett, John Millward and William Muspratt, "and did adjudge them and each of them to suffer Death by being hanged by the Neck, on board such of His Majesty's Ship or Ships of War, at such Time or Times and at such Place or Places" as should be directed.

But, "in Consideration of various Circumstances," the Court did also "humbly and most earnestly recommend the said Peter Heywood and James Morrison to His Majesty's Royal Mercy."

The charges against Norman, Coleman, McIntosh and Byrn were found not proved, and the court "did adjudge them and each of them to be acquitted." And with this, the condemned prisoners were conveyed one last time to the *Hector*.

SENTENCE

The news of Peter's sentencing reached the Isle of Man six days later, on September 24. For a full week contrary weather had held the regular packets at Whitehaven and Liverpool, preventing all communication between the mainland and the island. The news was broken to the Heywood household on the Monday evening "by the son of one of their particular Friends," who ran into the house and abruptly announced "that the Trial was over & all the prisoners condemned—but Peter recommended to Mercy." The boy had heard the news from another man, who had just arrived from Liverpool by fishing boat, and who was at once summoned by the startled and frightened family. On arriving, the man reported that he read the news in a Liverpool newspaper—unfortunately, he had not thought to bring the paper with him.

Three more agonizing days passed before the anguished household received any further information, and this, when it at last came, amounted to a grim confirmation of their earlier intelligence. A letter arrived from James Heywood, the twenty-six-year-old brother of Nessy and Peter, sent from Liverpool along with a copy of the damning article; this account of the *Bounty* verdict had in fact been syndicated in newspapers across the country.

James, like Peter and their younger brother, Henry, had also commenced a naval career of sorts, although he does not appear to have pursued it with any particular energy. He was in Liverpool with Henry, who was just returned from the West Indies, and shortly due to sail again. James wrote Nessy that as she would undoubtedly wish to come to Portsmouth, he would await her arrival in Liverpool, so that they might travel down together.

"Our Friends will not let me go from hence," Nessy wrote back despairingly. Unwilling to pin their faith on a single news item, friends and family were awaiting official word from the expected mail packet.

"We are in an Agony of Suspense—I can scarcely support my own misery, much less keep up poor Mama's dejected spirits," Nessy confided. All at home were in agreement "that there was not the smallest Danger," Nessy reported, briefly rallying. Nonetheless, if there was the least apprehension for Peter's life, she told her brother in a rush of terror, he should "go, for Heaven's sake, to Portsmouth, without waiting for me."

At midnight of the same day, the long awaited packet arrived across now calm seas with a backlog of mainland mail. Amid this flurry of correspondence were letters confirming the newspaper report; the trial was indeed over, the verdict was guilty, and Peter had been recommended to His Majesty's mercy. And yet, bewilderingly, in the very same breath, the letter writers closest to the events all offered unfeigned, unqualified congratulations.

"I have the Happiness of telling you that the Court Martial is this Moment over, & that I think your Son's Life is more safe now, than it was before his Trial," wrote Mrs. Bertie to Peter's mother on the very day the verdict was reached. "[A]s there was not sufficient proof of his Innocence, the Court cou'd not avoid condemning him: but he is so *strongly recommended* to Mercy, that I am desired to assure you, by those who are Judges, that his Life is *safe*." Such judges would include obviously her own husband, Captain Albemarle Bertie. Mrs. Bertie was on her way, as she wrote, to see her father, the well-connected James Modyford Heywood.

The good news was even more unqualified in the letter from Aaron Graham, written "about half an hour" after the conclusion of the trial. Graham, discreet as always, had not presumed to write directly to Peter's family, but had entrusted his letter to Dr. Patrick Scott, a Douglas physician and loyal friend of the Heywoods.

"Before I tell you what is the sentence I must inform you that his *Life* is *safe*,—notwithstanding it is at present at the Mercy of the King," Graham began. "That any unnecessary Fears may not be productive of Misery to the Family I must add that the King's Attorney Gen[era]l, who with Judge Ashurst attended the Trial, desired me to make myself perfectly easy, for that my Friend was as safe as if he had not been condemned." Graham was writing to Scott, he said, so that the news would not be "improperly communicated to Mrs. or the Miss Heywoods whose Distresses first engaged me in the Business."

The unfortunate sentence, for what it was worth, had been the result of "a Combination of Circumstances, Ill-Nature, & mistaken Friendship," but "everybody who attended the Trial is perfectly satisfied in his own Mind, that he was *hardly guilty in Appearance in Intention he was perfectly Innocent.*"

Yet more remarkable was Graham's matter-of-fact discussion of the appropriate course of action once Peter was free. He intended to write to Commander Pasley, he told Scott, and to "take his Advice about what is to be done when Mr. Heywood is released . . . my Intention is afterwards to take him to my House in Town, where I think he had better stay till one of the Family calls for him; for he will require a great Deal of Tender Management after all his Sufferings."

This extraordinary discrepancy between the reactions of those who took the news at face value and those close to the events would continue right to the very bitter end of what Graham called "the Business." And no one, it would appear, took the verdict at more solemn face value than Peter himself. Two days after the conclusion of the trial, Peter wrote Dr. Scott a long letter characterized alternately by naked fear and professed resignation.

"The Morning lowers—& all my Hope of *worldly* Joy is fled far from me!" Peter wrote in this letter from the *Hector.* "On Tuesday Morning the 18th Inst. the dreadful Sentence of *Death* was pronounced upon me!" His letter would come as no shock, Peter ventured, as Aaron Graham had already conveyed his melancholy news. It would appear either that Graham had not shared his own sanguine expectations with the unhappy prisoner, or that Peter was not able to bring himself to believe them.

"I always like to be prepared for the *Worst*," Peter would later tell Nessy, "for if the Worst does happen, 'tis then Nothing more than was expected."

And expecting the worse, he had retreated to that spiritual sanctity he had sought during his more melancholy moments on Tahiti. The task at hand, he now told Dr. Scott, and would soon be telling one and all, was to prepare his soul.

"I bow my devoted Head, with that Fortitude, Chearfulness, & Resignation, which is the Duty of every Member of the Church of our blessed *Saviour* & Redeemer Christ Jesus! To him alone I now look up for Succour; in full Hope, that perhaps a few days more will open to the View of astonished & fearful Soul, his Kingdom of eternal & incomprehensible Bliss." But, despite his sternest efforts, his fear and anger briefly, abruptly, surfaced.

"I have not been found guilty of the slightest Act of the detestable Crime of Mutiny," Peter protested, breaking in on his own higher thoughts. "But—am doomed to die!—for not being active in my Endeavours to suppress it—Cou'd the Evidences who appeared on the Court Martial be tried, *they* would also suffer for the same & only Crime of which I have been guilty—But I am to be the Victim!" The memory of Hayward and Hallett's tears of fear as they had been forced into the boat were bitterly vivid.

"But, so far from repining at my Fate—I receive it with a Dreadful kind of Joy, Composure, & Serenity of Mind!" Peter continued, collecting himself, "—well assured that it has pleased God to point me out, as a subject, thro' which, some greatly useful, tho' at present unsearchable, Intention of the Divine Attributes, may be carried into Execution, for the future Benefit of my Country."

Carried away, he was working toward a great and improbable crescendo: "Then—why shou'd I repine at being made a Sacrifice for the Good of perhaps Thousands of my Fellow Creatures! forbid it Heaven! Why shou'd I be sorry to leave a World in which I have met with nothing but Misfortunes . . . ?"

It would appear that while for Peter the turn of events was devastating and unexpected, for Graham "the Business" was very much under control. Graham may have been relying on a two-pronged approach from the beginning. In the best of all worlds the strangely muted alibi that had been nudged from Cole would have done the trick, but failing this, a pardon could be counted on.

On September 22, the minutes of the court-martial were sent to the Admiralty in London. These, with the written verdict, were to accompany the court's recommendation and to be sent together to the King, currently enjoying the last of his annual outing to Weymouth. Aaron Graham left for London the same day.

At this time too Peter screwed up his courage to write directly to Nessy with his doleful news; every person involved in "the Business" steered away from addressing poor Mrs. Heywood, who had all but collapsed with grief. To Dr. Scott, the trusted family friend, he had allowed himself to vent his fear and anger, along with expressions of resignation. But to his sister, Peter made a valiant, gallant effort to appear tranquil and at peace: "[C]onscious of having done my Duty to God & Man, I feel not one Moment's anxiety on my own Account," he assured her. But, as he imagined the effect of the news on his family, he briefly cracked, "Oh! my Sister—my Heart yearns, when I picture to myself the Affliction— indescribable! which this melancholy News must have caused in the Mind of my much honored Mother! But—let it be your *peculiar Endeavour* to watch o'er her Grief & mitigate her pain . . . we had only Hope then," he recalled of the optimistic days immediately before the trial, "& have we not the same now? Certainly endeavour then my Love to cherish that Hope."

Despite Peter's heartfelt plea that she attend to their mother, it became impossible for Nessy to remain in Douglas. The erratic schedule of the mail packets was driving the household wild, and family and friends were now in agreement that Nessy should go to the mainland, so that at least one member of the family would be in a position to monitor events and be within call of Peter. Amid the flood of delayed mail was a letter from Aaron Graham repeating an offer to play host to Peter's sister if she wished to come to London. This invitation Nessy now spontaneously accepted.

Consequently, only days later, on October 1, while the family was at breakfast, word was brought to the Heywood household that a fishing boat was set to sail from Douglas for Liverpool in half an hour. A glance out the window of the house showed that the weather was bad and the wind contrary; evidently the small boat was hoping to beat a coming storm. Fearful of being isolated once again, Nessy grabbed a few things and raced to the harbor.

The subsequent voyage in tempestuous winter seas was to take forty-nine hours of hard sailing in the face of the driving wind. For two nights, Nessy did not sleep. Wrapped in her plaid shawl, she huddled on the vessel's bare planks and tried only to stave off the piercing, wet cold and the "villainous smells" of the fishing boat.

"[L]et me but be bless'd with chearing influence of *Hope*," she wrote to her mother when she finally arrived in Liverpool, "and I have *spirit* to undertake any thing!" Soaked to the skin by the waves that had broken over her when her boat reached the mouth of the Mersey, Nessy stopped only long enough to meet up with her brother James and dine with family friends; young Henry had already sailed on his next voyage. The same evening, she and James departed by mail coach to London. The following day, as the coach changed horses at Coventry, she dashed off a quick note to her mother, noting that although she had not slept for three days she could "scarcely feel a sensation of Fatigue."

Nessy and James arrived in London at six in the morning of October 5. At the coaching inn, she changed her clothes and took breakfast, and then dispatched her brother with her visiting card to Aaron Graham's house. Within an hour, James returned in Graham's coach accompanied by Graham himself, who warmly greeted Nessy. Shortly afterward, the coach deposited the exhausted siblings at Graham's fine home on Great Russell Street.

Mrs. Graham and one of her two daughters were currently in the country. It is not clear at what point during Nessy's stay Graham's wife returned. The former Sarah Dawes, Mrs. Graham had pretensions of nobility, being a first cousin of Sir Henry Tempest, a roguish and dissolute baronet with whom both Grahams were very close. But of this lady of the house, Nessy had nothing to report in her frequent letters to the Isle of Man. Of Mr. Graham and his younger daughter, Maria, on the other hand, she could not say enough: "[H]e has a most prepossessing Countenance with Eyes in which are strongly pictured the sympathetic Worth & Goodness of his Heart," she gushed to her mother. Maria was "a beautiful Girl about my own Size," of fifteen or sixteen. Most impressive of all, Mr. Graham was full of reports of his conversations with Peter.

"I look upon him to be the most amiable young Man that can possibly exist"; so Mr. Graham had told her, Nessy reported proudly to her mother after a long and highly satisfactory discussion about Peter's situation.

"But Sir may I really be sure it *will* be settled to our Satisfaction?" Nessy had implored Graham.

"You may indeed Ma'am depend upon it" had been the magistrate's prompt and gratifying response. "[W]as not this charming?" Nessy concluded to her mother. Her own eyes were heavy with fatigue and it was now after teatime.

Two days later, James set out for Portsmouth. Once again, Nessy had been absolutely forbidden to see Peter: "Mr. Graham does not wish it," Nessy allowed. But the day after her arrival, she wrote her beloved brother directly, telling him that she was in London and anxiously inquiring after how he was faring.

"[T]ell me for God's sake how you are—if your Health shou'd suffer by the dreadful Evils you have borne with such exemplary Fortitude—but I will not—dare not give Way to the Idea of losing you!" poor Nessy almost wailed. Peter's surprised response came the next day, praising her "little *Bravery* of Spirit" in making the journey and reassuring her of his health—and imploring her "For Gods Sake" to let nothing prompt her to come to see him. To have Nessy's exalted sentiments unleashed in the dark gun room before the other prisoners and awkward guards was a possibility not even to be imagined.

It was the evening of October 7, a Sunday, when one of the guards on the *Hector* informed Peter that a brother of his was waiting in the wardroom, and asked if he "would wish to see him?" Amazed, Peter found himself some minutes later before James. An officer gave the two brothers the privacy of his own cabin for what was Peter's first sight of any member of his immediate family since he had taken leave of his father in the summer of 1787. The two embraced with great emotion, and James was incautious enough to let fall "some *womanish Tears*," in Peter's words, which he suppressed on receiving a "civil Check" from his younger brother. For an hour, the brothers were allowed to meet alone: "the Goodness of the Officers to him is beyond Expression," James reported to Nessy. Spending the night in Portsmouth, he returned to the *Hector* the following day to enjoy a full eight hours with Peter: "when with me he is suffered to be *without Irons*."

These visits considerably lightened Peter's mood, although, as he gently remonstrated with Nessy, he was surprised when James appeared because she "did not mention" in her letter that he was also in London; in her highly strung emotional state, Nessy had edited brother James entirely out of the picture.

"I am sure he will do all he can to supply my place," Nessy wrote to Peter, a little sniffily. The change in Peter's spirits was already evident from his letters. For her part, while James enjoyed the privileges she would have given her heart for, Nessy reconciled herself to sticking close to the Grahams, scarcely leaving their house except on two occasions to take a turn around the Bloomsbury Park neighborhood. Her "chief Recreation & Happiness," she told her sister Mary, was "in talking of Peter" with Mr. Graham, or if he was called away on his frequent "particular business," with young Maria, who was a student of the pianoforte. Nessy had taken a great shine to Maria and was soon contentedly composing poetry for her:

M ild as the vernal Breeze which softly blows
A nd sheds new sweetness on the damask Rose
R estless softness plays in ev'ry Smile
I nsinuation void of Art and Guile
A nd youthful Loveliness our Hearts beguile . . .

In their letters to each other, both Peter and Nessy rarely failed to mention their indebtedness to Mr. Graham's goodness: "Oh! my lov'd Peter—what a Friend he is!" Nessy exclaimed, again and again. And else-

where, "he loves you as his own Son." She was also impatient for Peter
to meet her new friend Maria.

"[T]ake Care of your Heart my dear Peter when you see her," Nessy admonished her brother coyly; and one must wonder what passed through
the young man's mind as, shackled in irons, he read these words by the
vague, low light of the gun shafts. Peter's description of his domestic life
on Tahiti does not appear to have been highly detailed, and he may have
omitted the fact that he and a Tahitian woman had lived as man and wife
for nearly a year in his charming mountain cottage. Maria Graham, "fair
& rather pale than otherwise," with her "most interesting Countenance"
and "soft *speaking* hazle Eyes & . . . most bewitching gentleness of Manner," with her petticoats and pianoforte—suffice to say, Peter was never
to make mention of Maria Graham.

Coleman, Norman, McIntosh and Byrn had all been released immediately following the verdict. Coleman and Byrn eventually washed up as
pensioners of Greenwich Hospital, while McIntosh appears to have entered the merchant service; what happened to Norman at this time remains unknown. Peter Heywood and the other five men found guilty
now existed in a racking state of limbo, returned to their confinement on
the guardship. At the agency of the able Stephen Barney, Muspratt had
filed a petition at the very announcement of the verdict to protest the fact
that he had been "debarred calling Witnesses whose Evidence I have
Reason to believe, would have tended to have proved my Innocence,"
and to lament that "usage of a Court Martial, should be so different from
the Practice of all Criminal courts of Justice on Shore." Now he too, like
Morrison and Heywood, spent each day in anxious anticipation that
news of a pardon might arrive. From a comment of Nessy's that delay
could be expected "on account of the Interest making for some of the
prisoners," it appears that Peter was not alone in clinging to hope.

As October passed, the days of unbroken clouded, drizzly weather
promised a foul autumn. Lord McCartney sailed for China in the *Lion,*
and Inglefield and Sir Andrew Douglas took their ships to be paid off or
decommissioned. Sir Roger Curtis and Sir Andrew Hamond brought

their ships, the 80-gun *Brunswick* and the *Bedford,* from Spithead into the harbor, and John Duckworth and Colpoys took the *Orion* and *Hannibal* around the coast to join the fleet at Plymouth. Captain Bertie does not appear to have been going anywhere. Lord Hood still held the *Duke* just inside the harbor and was occupied once again with the mundane tasks of ship life. On October 10, after the firing of the evening gun, he struck his flag and traveled to London, "His Lordship being wanted at the Admiralty," as his sailing master logged.

These movements were followed closely on the *Hector.* "Lord Hood set off from Hence yesterday for Town, so I hope a few Days will bring this Business to *some kind* of Issue," Peter wrote to Nessy.

On the *Hector,* daily life had of course continued heedless of the prisoners. Captain Montagu's cabin had been freshly painted, seamen were dispatched to and received from the hospital, casks of supplies were emptied and filled. On Friday, October 5, the same day Nessy arrived in town, seven men were punished for going onshore without leave. The following day, on the *Brunswick,* Captain Curtis, the witty, humane confidant of Lord Howe, ordered 84 lashes for various offenses, bringing the total of lashes given in the three and a half weeks since the commencement of the court-martial to 278. On the *Bounty,* William Bligh had punished his crew with 229 lashes in the course of a voyage of seventeen months to the South Pacific.

Meanwhile, Peter was occupying himself with an ambitious and worthy project—employing his "leisure hours," as he put it, in compiling a Tahitian vocabulary. He was, as he had told his mother, "perfectly conversant" in the language, and now under James's amused gaze he absorbed himself completely in this task: "so happy & intent upon it that I have no Opportunity of saying a Word to him," as James told Nessy. He also received visitors. Delafons, Graham and John Spranger (fourth lieutenant of the *Edgar,* a fellow Manxman and a family friend) were regular guests, while the *Hector'*s first lieutenant of marines had also become a friend. The Berties, Uncle James Holwell and old friends like Dr. Scott and a Mr. Southcote were regular correspondents. From Commander Pasley there was an uncharacteristic silence.

"What cou'd I write?" the bluff seaman asked Nessy in a letter explaining his relative lack of correspondence. He was ever, he assured her, "unweariedly employed" in Peter's service. He reiterated that Peter's "flattering situation" was entirely due to "Mr. Graham's Abilities," and one is left with the impression that Graham may have directed him to keep a low profile while matters ran their course.

One relative newcomer who was to play an important role in the events ahead was William Howell, officially the chaplain of the *Bedford* but appointed to minister to the condemned men at the conclusion of the trial. At twenty-eight the Reverend Mr. Howell was the contemporary of most of the six men he was attending. In addition to serving as naval chaplain, Howell was also the minister of St. John's Chapel, Portsea, recently erected on Portsmouth Common—and was apparently "the only minister of St. John's whose relations with his people were unfortunately somewhat marred and interfered with," according to a chapel memorial. This sour relationship with his flock arose principally from the fact that Howell preferred to reside at Purbrook, a quiet village some distance north of Portsea, instead of in the minister's house that had been built at considerable expense close by his chapel. This resentment and his frequent absences notwithstanding, Howell had no qualms about going his own way, and was serenely to hold this desirable living for thirty-two years.

In his capacity as chaplain to the condemned mutineers, Howell found himself spending a great deal of time in their company. He is first referred to indirectly by Peter in a letter to his mother after the trial, informing her that a "Minister of the Gospel" had advised him "not to say *too* much to my dear Relations." Peter's own instinctive religious sensibilities had no doubt been heightened by Howell's ministrations: it may be that in Howell can be found the source of Peter's bizarre notion that his "sacrifice" might in some mysterious way be "for the Good of perhaps Thousands" of his fellow creatures.

Howell was friendly with one of Cook's men, and he was intensely interested in the mutineers' tales of the South Pacific. Thrown into their company, and "daily shut up with them for many Hours every day," the young minister formed sentimental friendships with at least some of the men. In addition to taking a keen interest in Peter's vocabulary, Howell gave encouragement to another important and ambitious literary under-taking—James Morrison's narrative of the events on the *Bounty* and his description of Tahiti. The substantial effect of these two productions would be seen in the years ahead.

Meanwhile, Nessy was also occupied. On October 11, she sent a bold letter directly to Lord Chatham appealing to his lordship's "known Hu-manity & Excellence of Heart" on her brother's behalf. The letter in-cluded a document prepared by Peter that addressed point by point the most incriminating charges emerging from his trial, or, as Nessy termed it, "a few Observations made by my unfortunate & most tenderly beloved Brother."

Pulling out all stops, Nessy laid her heart at his lordship's feet: "When I assure you my Lord that he is dearer & more precious to me than any Object on Earth—nay—infinitely more valuable than even life itself—that, deprived of him, the Word Misery wou'd but ill express my compli-cated Wretchedness—& that on his Fate my own & shall I not add, that of a tender, fond, & alas! widowed Mother depends . . ."

It is unlikely that either Nessy's petition or Peter's "observations" had been drafted without Graham's approval. Although Graham gave no sign of having lost his early complacency, he may have reckoned that some feminine special pleading could not hurt. Whatever the reasons, four days after her plea had been sent, Nessy wrote to her mother with momen-tous news from her Aunt Holwell.

"[S]he has *Assurance*," Nessy wrote ecstatically, "of the royal Mercy be-ing *already extended* & that she has written you a Letter congratulating you on the joyful Intelligence. Now my dearest Mama tho' I cannot doubt its Truth, yet it must be very private, for nobody else has yet heard of it not even Mr. Graham"; Nessy had, of course, passed the news on to Graham, who only made the *"particular request"* that Mrs. Heywood would keep the news to herself: "the Mention of it at *this* Time can do *no* Good, & may do *much* Harm—therefore for Heavens sake be *secret*."

The reassurance was reliable enough to induce Nessy to shed all the anxious cares she had carried since word of the mutiny had reached the Heywood home. On October 15, she dashed off a long poem, "On receiving certain Intelligence that my most amiable and beloved Brother Peter Heywood wou'd soon be restor'd to Freedom."

Ah! Blissful Hour—Oh! Moment of Delight!—
Replete with happiness, with Rapture Bright! . . .

"I have a Letter from Peter to day & have as usual written to him but I dare not mention one Word of what makes me *almost* happy," Nessy told her mother; "is it not a cruel Prohibition?"

As the days passed, the striking disparity between the inner circle and poor Peter was made ever more distinct. On the one hand, Mrs. Heywood wrote to Graham giving her most heartfelt thanks for all his help for a matter now concluded; on the other hand, between his tranquil vocabulary writing and long visits with his brother, Peter despaired of himself as one "banished from this World as a Wretch unworthy to live in it." Graham declared that the "Business tho' not publickly known, is most certainly finished," while the Reverend Mr. Howell continued to administer to Peter and his condemned companions, reminding them of the vanity of earthly existence and of the true and eternal freedom from care that was theirs to come.

Within days, Nessy was writing again to Peter and prattling with happy indiscretion, dropping wild hints about "*sanguine* Hope" and the safety of Peter's "*Honor*," and telling him to give his mind "to every sensation of Delight which the near prospect of Love and Liberty can convey!" Out of delicacy to his "unhappy Companions," he had to keep what she was about to say a sacred secret, which was: "You have no Idea how happy we now are. . . . Oh! gracious—'tis almost too much to support, for I am half bewitched already—I don't know what I have written. . . ."

It was left to John Delafons to hand-deliver this bewildering letter, which Graham had instructed Nessy to leave unsealed. Probably it was from the lips of Delafons himself that all was made clear and for the first time in a long while Peter allowed himself to look forward to life after prison: "I now hope I may for years to come remain & prove myself my dearest Nessy's most truly faithful & fondly affectionate Brother," he signed his subsequent letter.

In the gun room, none of his private good news was communicated to the other prisoners. Still Peter passed much of his days and nights in irons, and he continued to take his meals with his condemned companions. The daily ministrations of the Reverend Mr. Howell undoubtedly kept some part of his imagination on the great hereafter. In such circumstances it was perhaps impossible to believe wholly and absolutely that liberty was just around the corner. On October 21, Pasley sent Nessy "a Letter from Capt Inglefield containing a new & positive Confirmation." Shortly afterward Graham received a letter from John Fryer—by now a voice from the past—inquiring after Peter's release.

"[A]ll that worthy Family are impatient for the happy Conclusion which we have now the utmost *Right* to expect with *Certainty*," Nessy told Peter, after relating the tenor of a letter from Captain Bertie praising Peter. In the face of such conflicting emotion—Nessy's bright certainty and the entrenched terror of his companions—Peter was using all his private reserves to maintain his own equilibrium. On the day he received one of Nessy's most exultant letters, Peter composed a poem in praise of death:

Grim Death itself, in all its Horrors clad,
Is Man's supremest Privilege! . . .

On the night of October 26, Aaron Graham went down to Portsmouth for the last time on this "business," and so was at his client's side when on the following afternoon Peter, along with James Morrison, was summoned before Captain Montagu on the quarterdeck. Here, under mild skies, in the presence of the *Hector*'s entire company, Montagu read to both men His Majesty the King's gracious and unconditional pardon, but also pointed out "the evil of their past conduct; and in language, that drew tears from all who heard him, recommended to them to make atonement by their future good behaviour." According to reports of the event, both prisoners were greatly and visibly affected by these words.

This emotion apart, there is no record of Morrison's reaction to his good fortune; subsequent events would suggest he had revenge on his mind.

Peter's reaction, however, was polished, appropriate and much praised. As the newspapers reported, "Mr. Heywood . . . seemed to have anticipated his inability to speak." With the help of Graham he had prepared a brief statement for this moment, which he now read in his own voice. He hoped he had received the original sentence as became a man and would have met his fate as became a Christian; but "I receive with Gratitude my Sovereign's Mercy, for which my future Life shall be faithfully devoted to his Service."

With few possessions to collect, there was little to delay Peter's departure. From his former shipmates, companions of the terrible, shared intimacy of fear and confinement, he took his final leave. Probably, the men wished one another well. Given Peter's religious feeling, he undoubtedly left his friends with his blessing. After thanking the ship's officers for the kind attention he had received, Peter was led by Graham down to one of the *Hector*'s boats and ferried to the mainland. Here they took a coach and departed for London. The original plan had been to spend the night on the road, but impatience got the better of both, and they pressed on to London.

At half past ten in the morning on the twenty-ninth, Nessy wrote perhaps the shortest epistle of her prolific career: "I have seen him— clasped him to my Bosom—& my Felicity is beyond Expression!" she raved to her mother. "I can write no more but to tell you that the three happiest Beings at this Moment on Earth are your most dutiful & affectionate Children." In happy triumph, the letter was signed by James, by Nessy—and by Peter.

In Portsmouth, the weather continued cloudy but by the afternoon of October 28, it had turned pleasant and mild. Under these briefly benign skies, John Millward, Thomas Burkett and Thomas Ellison were led for the last time down the *Hector*'s gangway and into a gently pitching boat. On this occasion, the *Duke* was not their destination. Following delivery of the verdict, the captains had drawn lots to determine the ship on which the executions would take place. It had fallen to Captain Curtis and the *Brunswick,* half an hour's boat journey away in the harbor.

The gun room of the *Brunswick* had been carefully prepared for the prisoners' reception, with the gun ports closed and screens hung around a marked-off area. Within a corner of this screened enclosure, in turn, was the small "cell" to which the three men were to be consigned.

"Not a ray of light was permitted to obtrude," an officer of the *Brunswick* recorded. "All was silent, solemn, and gloomy." This grim atmosphere had been created out of a kind of perverse delicacy on the prisoners' behalf, intended as a sympathetic, reverential backdrop that would not mock their affliction. Throughout the ship a mood of genuine sadness pervaded.

The prisoners themselves were brought on board under guard and, according to the anonymous officer, "tripped up and down the ladders with the most wonderful alacrity" as they made their way down to the gun room. Their expressions "were perfectly calm, serene, and chearful," although, as the officer confessed, it shocked him to see men so full of life and health and vigor only hours away from death.

As he stood out of sight beyond the screened-off cell, the officer's attention had been drawn early in the evening by the sound of someone reading a sermon, and he had assumed one of the chaplains had been let in to perform this service. On looking around the screen, however, he saw that it was John Millward—the would-be deserter, the reluctant mutineer—who was ministering to his companions. The prisoners continued speaking among themselves, in conversation "chearful, resigned, and manly," until ten o'clock, when they turned to the bedrolls prepared for them and attempted to sleep.

During the night, a shocking incident occurred: The provost-martial, serving as both "gaoler and hangman," had come into the gun room and, within earshot of the prisoners, given his opinion that "[t]he young one's a hardened dog!" Then, as the stunned officers and other guards watched, he pulled a nightcap out of his pocket, exclaiming, "Here is one; I have all three of their caps in my pocket"—these, nightcaps of mutineers of the *Bounty*, would make profitable souvenirs.

At nine in the morning of Monday, October 29, the gun was fired and the yellow flag raised to assemble for the executions. By ten, the *Brunswick* was ringed by boats from all the ships of the fleet, manned and armed. Leaving the gun room, the prisoners thanked Captain Curtis and the officers for the humane treatment they had received during their confinement. On deck, the ship's company stood at attention in solemn columns, "the yard ropes stretched along in each man's hand." Just before eleven, the prisoners were led behind four clergymen through the ranks of men up to the fo'c'sle, where they stood facing the assembled company. The fine weather of their last evening had departed, and it was now clouded over with occasional rain.

Across the harbor, men, women and children thronged the shore and filled the shallow wherries in the water, straining for a view; although, as newspapers would report, the "number of spectators . . . was certainly great, yet many respectable inhabitants purposely left the town till the melancholy scene closed."

Accounts of the last words of these now forlorn mutineers differed wildly. According to the *Brunswick* officer, Millward had stood upon the cathead and "addressed the ship's company, confessed the errors they had been guilty of, acknowledged the *justice* of their sentence" and warned onlookers to avoid their ways. The speech "was nervous, strong, and eloquent, and delivered in an open and deliberate manner." But, according to the popular press, the men had embraced one another repeatedly, "saying, 'God bless you, God receive you in mercy;' but persisted to the last moment of their existence, that they were totally innocent of the crime for which they were to suffer." For this last half hour of their lives, the three men received their final offices—not from the Reverend Mr. Howell or any of the other naval chaplains, but from James Morrison, boatswain's mate, who had remained to minister to his shipmates.

Bags had been placed over the heads of each man, and now nooses were placed around their necks. At 11:26, according to Curtis's log, the gun was fired for execution, and the crews assigned to each prisoner's rope pulled hard away. "Thomas Burkitt was Run up to the Starboard Fore Yard Arm, Milward and Ellison to the Larboard, and There Hung Agreeable to their Sentence," Curtis logged.

For two hours the bodies of the executed men hung from the yards. The rain became heavy, then moderated. At half past one, the bodies were cut down and ferried across the water to Haslar Hospital, that imposing refuge for the naval sick and hurt. The Navy Board was billed seven shillings and sixpence for the cost of each interment. Young Ellison, it was noted in the hospital records, was a "Captain's servant"—another mark of the special privilege he had thrown away.

The following Sunday, the Reverend Mr. Howell, in one of his infrequent appearances in his own chapel, preached a sermon on Hebrews 13:7: "Remember your leaders, those who spoke to you the word of God; consider the outcome of their life, and imitate their faith."

In the very wide coverage of these men's deaths, several newspapers chose to comment on the fact that "the sufferings of the unhappy mutineers of the Bounty were greater than it could be imagined human nature is capable of bearing." Their shipwreck and terrible confinement under Captain Edwards was cited, but it was also curiously reported that "[b]efore the mutiny took place, from the extreme length of the voyage, forty men were put on the allowance of twelve, and even that scanty pittance consisted of food condemned." Where this extraordinary—and false—report originated cannot be known, but it is worth noting that it appears after Morrison's acquittal. As a pardoned mutineer still in Portsmouth, it is likely that he would have been sought out by reporters.

Another point of special interest was flagged by the officer of the *Brunswick,* who noted that "[g]reat murmurs are also carefully breathed, and are assiduously promulged, on the pardon of the midshipman and boatswain's mate: and, according to the vulgar notion, money bought their lives; and that the others fell sacrifices to their poverty." It was perhaps no coincidence that a number of newspapers toward the end of September reported that Mr. Heywood was "an accomplished young gentleman, genteely connected, with a fortune of 30,000l. fallen to him since he has been in confinement," a rumor that appears to be without any basis. These were dangerous sentiments to have bandied around, with the news of the massacres in France still coming in from across the Channel. The *Brunswick* officer raised the point only to shoot it down; his entire report, and most especially his desire to accurately depict the penitents' heartening last words, was motivated, he said, by a desire to correct such vulgar notions.

This view was also shared by Captain Hamond, again the acting port commander in Hood's absence, who noted in his official report to the Admiralty that "the criminals behaved with great penitence, and decency."

Parties from every ship in harbor and at Spithead had attended the execution, and as he noted, from the reports he had received, "the Example seems to have made a great Impression upon the Minds of all the Ships companies present."

The execution over, Morrison returned to naval service. Muspratt was still awaiting the outcome of his petition. By early December he knew himself reprieved, and on February 11, 1793, he learned that he had also received His Majesty's pardon. Deeply shaken by the executions, it was reported, he had "not since spoke a word to any person; nor can he by any means be prevailed on to do so."

After traveling to the Isle of Man to be with his family, Peter too returned to naval service. Offers for midshipman positions came from a number of sympathetic captains, including Lord Hood himself, but Peter's immediate decision was to opt for the *Bellerophon* under his uncle Pasley. This brief service was followed by a more prestigious position on the *Queen Charlotte*—the flagship of Lord Howe, brother-in-law to James Modyford Heywood, Vice Admiral of England and commander of the Channel fleet.

On these ships, Peter discovered, perhaps to his surprise, that he had become a figure of some glamour.

"Amongst the number of our new midshipmen is Mr. Haywood, a very fine young man—who was one of the mutineers in the *Bounty*," a fellow middie wrote excitedly to his father. "[H]e speaks in great raptures of the poeple and climate at Otaheite and would be very much pleased to go back again to his wife and children whom he left there; it is a curious circumstance," the young writer mused, "that his associates were hanged upon the same day by which they had promised to return if cleared by their country."

The Admiralty, Whitehall *(Courtesy of National Maritime Museum, London)*

The sinking of the *Pandora*,
engraving by Lieutenant Colonel Batty, based on a sketch by Peter Heywood
(Courtesy of Dixson Galleries, State Library of New South Wales)

Camp on a sandbar after the wreck of the *Pandora*, from a sketch by Peter Heywood

Nessy Heywood
*(Courtesy of Manx
National Heritage Library)*

Rear Admiral Sir Thomas Pasley,
by Lemuel Francis Abbott *(Courtesy of
National Maritime Museum, London)*

The fleet at Portsmouth, c. 1790 *(Courtesy of National Maritime Museum, London)*

Samuel Hood, First Viscount Hood,
by Lemuel Francis Abbott
(Courtesy of National Portrait Gallery, London)

Captain Sir George Montagu,
by Lemuel Francis Abbott
(Courtesy of National Maritime Museum, London)

Sir Andrew Snape Hamond, by T. Lawrence
(Courtesy of National Maritime Museum, London)

Admiral Sir John Colpoys, by D. Pellegrini
(Courtesy of National Maritime Museum, London)

Vice Admiral Sir John Thomas Duckworth,
by William Beechey
(Courtesy of National Maritime Museum, London)

Vice Admiral John Bazely, by Thomas Langdon
(Courtesy of National Maritime Museum, London)

Sir Roger Curtis
(Courtesy of National Maritime Museum, London)

Sir Richard Goodwin Keats
(Courtesy of National Maritime Museum, London)

Rear Admiral John Knight, by J. Smart
(Courtesy of National Maritime Museum, London)

Sir Andrew Snape Douglas
(Courtesy of National Maritime Museum, London)

Captain John Nicholson Inglefield,
by George Engleheart
(Courtesy of National Maritime Museum, London)

Captain Albemarle Bertie
(Courtesy of National Maritime Museum, London)

Semaphore at Portsmouth, by Edward William Cooke *(Courtesy of National Maritime Museum, London)*

Stephen Barney, oil painting based on surviving miniature
(Courtesy of Lysses House Hotel, Fareham, Hants, UK)

Crown and Sceptre Inn, Greenwich *(Courtesy of Madge Darby and Pitcairn Island Study Group)*

Lambeth, Surrey, 1781, engraving by Wilson Lowry
(Courtesy of Lambeth Palace Library, London, UK/Bridgeman Art Library)

Captain William Bligh, 1791, by John Russell
(Courtesy of Captain Cook Memorial Museum, Whitby, UK)

Elizabeth Bligh, 1802, by John Russell
(Courtesy of Captain Cook Memorial Museum, Whitby, UK)

Government House, Sydney, 1808–9, by George William Evans
(Courtesy of Mitchell Library, State Library of New South Wales)

Sir Joseph Banks, c. 1808, by Thomas Phillips
(Courtesy of Dixson Galleries, State Library of New South Wales)

John Adams, 1829,
from *Voyages aux Îles du Grand Océan,* by J. A. Moerenhout
(Courtesy of New York Public Library)

John Adams's residence on Pitcairn, from *The Eventful History of the Mutiny and
Piratical Seizure of H.M.S. Bounty,* by Sir John Barrow, 1831

Fletcher Christian's son Thursday October Christian, c. 1814, by John Shillibeer
(Courtesy of Dixson Library, State Library of New South Wales)

Descendants of the mutineers Matthew Quintal and John Adams, 1862
(Courtesy of Mitchell Library, State Library of New South Wales)

Captain Peter Heywood, 1822,
by John Simpson *(Courtesy of
National Maritime Museum, London)*

Captain William Bligh, c. 1799, by John Smart *(Courtesy of National Portrait Gallery, London)*

JUDGMENT

Duty.

The backbone of honor.

When in 1794, under heavy fire in the campaign of the Glorious First of June, Admiral George Bowyer lost a leg and was carried to the cockpit for treatment, he had insisted that traditional protocol be observed and that those wounded before him be assisted first. Here, however, he was thwarted, for a sailor who had also lost his own leg swore vehemently that he "would not be dressed before the Admiral." Duty ennobled both the fallen admiral and the common seaman.

In private life duty was the demarcation between honor and discredit, gentleman and scoundrel. In public life the stakes were even higher, and nowhere more so than in the British navy, where each campaign was scrutinized, each failure of duty actionable. Admiralty files are filled with records of courts-martial brought against one officer or another for some alleged dereliction of duty—and filled too with courts-martial that officers who felt their honor impugned petitioned to have called upon themselves to clear their names. Pamphlets issued by two of the *Bounty* court-martial judges—"The reply of Sir Roger Curtis, to the person who stiles himself A neglected naval officer"; "A Refutation of the Incorrect Statements, and Unjust Insinuations . . . as far as the same refers to the conduct of Admiral Sir George Montagu, G.C.B."—were among many similar publications produced by numerous officers to counteract charges that they had failed in some point of their duty. Such publications had even followed Cook's voyages.

Duty was part of the cement that bound the British navy, the code of conduct that enabled the captain of a 90-gun man-of-war to stride his quarterdeck secure in the certainty that the officers and eight hundred men under his direction would perform when and as he required. Duty was what helped to form a loyal company out of a ship's mixed complement of volunteers and impressed men, who, dragooned for the King's service against their will, made up the majority of working seamen.

Duty was invoked at the outset of the most celebrated of all British naval battles. Leading the north column of ships of the line at the onset of the battle of Trafalgar, Admiral Lord Nelson ordered a final rally of encouragement to be signaled to his fleet. Raised aloft flag by flag, his last message had been straightforwardly simple:

ENGLAND—EXPECTS—EVERY—MAN—WILL—DO—HIS—DUTY.

Hours later, the admiral lay mortally wounded.

"Thank God, I have done my duty" were Nelson's last words.

William Bligh had done his duty.

The *Providence,* accompanied by her tender, the *Assistant,* had set sail from Spithead on August 3, 1791, with combined complements of 127 souls all told. Soon, Bligh's log was recording the familiar bustle of cleaning, drying and airing of his ship, the lighting of fires, the ministrations of vinegar. Thrown badly, Bligh was back in the saddle; although battered, he remained unbowed. His orders were given with the same unqualified, uncompromising certitude with which he had commanded the *Bounty.*

"[M]y officers will become habituated to that attention which very few indeed are acquainted is necessary in these Voyages," Bligh reported confidently to Banks. A good officer was made, not born. Others felt this imperious command very differently. According to the *Providence*'s first lieutenant Francis Godolphin Bond, who was also Bligh's half nephew, Bligh's orders were given hastily and in a manner so "devoid of feeling and tact" that he was soon smarting with resentment at his uncle. Bond was particularly incensed by Bligh's insistence on supervising every aspect of his officers' work.

But for all this show of undaunted leadership—demonstrating that despite a full-blown mutiny there was no chink in the armor of his command—Bligh was a very ill man. Four weeks out from Spithead, the *Providence* and *Assistant* rode at anchor under Tenerife, assailed by a strange parching heat that seemed exhaled from the mountainous land. A cricket had somehow found its way to the *Providence,* and on the nights of dreadful, windless calm its high, clear voice could be heard across the water on the *Assistant.*

"[A]t Night light airs off the High land, heated as if they had passed through fire," Bligh wrote in his log. "Myself most materially felt the effect; I was seized with a violent Fever." The raging fever and "most dreadful Head Ach" mounted alarmingly, driving him at times literally out of his mind; on occasion his illogical commands led his anxious men to fear for his sanity. Recognizing this, Bligh took the drastic precaution of relieving himself from command; the enormity of such a step could have been fully appreciated only by himself. Lieutenant Nathaniel Portlock, in command of the *Assistant,* was summoned to take over the *Providence,* while Lieutenant Bond was in turn dispatched to the tender. For the next weeks, Bligh lay in his cabin, dangerously ill; the precautions he had taken by this change of command, as he logged, had been done "while I had power to think" to ensure that the service of the ships "might go on with a greater certainty of success in case of my death."

As the two vessels continued south toward the Cape of Good Hope, Bligh's log kept a record of his health: "continued very ill"; "very ill"; "I still continue very ill." Off Santiago, in the Cape Verde Islands, he dictated a letter to his wife:

"My dear Betsy, I beg you will not be alarmed at not seeing my own writing." The handwriting was that of Surgeon Edward Harwood, who had advised him against attempting even a letter. Bligh was afflicted again with a dreadful headache so severe that the least noise "distracted" his brain, and orders were given to keep a profound silence on the ship; in his log Bligh noted how "wonderfully & kindly" this silence was preserved. His condition was "of a nervous kind," Bligh told his wife, referring to the blinding headaches that deprived him "of reason," the chills and shaking fever that prostrated him; in reality he was almost certainly suffering from a vicious bout of recurring malaria, caught two years ago in pestilential Batavia. Significantly, the two other *Bounty* men who sailed with the *Providence*, Lawrence Lebogue and Bligh's servant, John Smith, also suffered from "Batavia" fever on the voyage.

"God bless you my Dear Love & my little angels," Bligh had scrawled in his own hand as a footnote to the surgeon's letter. His voyage was but five weeks out; his safe return home, if all went well, was nearly two years away.

Three weeks later, Bligh was sufficiently well to read the morning service for his company. However, Portlock, who had been a master's mate on Captain Cook's last voyage, remained de facto in command until mid-November, when the *Providence* and *Assistant* arrived at Table Bay. Here, Bligh was sufficiently recovered to write to the Admiralty: his voyage to date had been without incident, his two vessels were performing to his best expectation and his crew were in good health. But, as for Bligh himself, "I am yet very unwell," he wrote in this brief report. With his familiar, indomitable optimism, he believed that the change of climate would soon "perfectly restore" him to his health. However, the sojourn at the Cape was to last some six weeks, two weeks longer than planned, and it was nearly Christmas before his expedition set forth again. Left behind at the Cape was John Smith, whose illness was too severe for him to continue.

Retracing his own steps, Bligh headed his ships for Van Diemen's Land, where the *Bounty* had stopped for wood and water in August 1788. Arriving in early February 1792, under dark, low skies, Bligh had found many relics of his former visit. The saw-pit where wood had been billeted, and where William Purcell had caused Bligh his first serious confrontation with his officers, had filled only partly with debris over the years. Crops he had sowed for the betterment of this sparsely inhabited outpost remained, although of the numerous apple trees he had planted only one was thriving. More striking was the discovery of a piece of baize fabric dropped by one of the *Bounty*'s men, its red color "perfectly fresh" despite lying at the mercy of the elements.

Wary of his precarious health, Bligh took care to avoid the heavy, soak-ing dews that fell during fine nights. He did, however, make a short, tax-ing excursion to a rocky hill that was covered with small trees and overlooked the beach. He named it Nelson's Hill, after the *Bounty*'s loyal gardener, now buried in Coupang.

The *Providence* and *Assistant* left Adventure Bay in late February for Tahiti, where they arrived six weeks later, on April, 9, 1792. Under bois-terous weather, the ships rounded Dolphin Bank and worked into Ma-tavai Bay, to anchor less than a mile from Point Venus, the site of the *Bounty*'s old nursery. Canoes soon appeared, and in one a native man was seen by Bligh's quick eyes to be wearing a European shirt. This seemingly trivial detail proved to be a harbinger of great and tragic changes wrought in this paradise of the world. Few European ships—the *Pandora*, Vancouver's *Discovery* and *Chatham*—along with the crew of a shipwrecked whaler, had touched at Tahiti since the departure of the *Bounty*, but already European contact had left more than venereal dis-ease, which was rampant as before, and Bligh observed a new fondness among the islanders for liquor. A small arsenal of firearms, gleaned from various ships, was a proud and closely guarded treasure. While Bligh's company remained in Tahiti, they were witness to the flares of re-gional strife that had always undermined island life, but these were deadlier now than ever before, thanks to the European guns, and as a re-sult of such strife, Matavai was a deserted village. The handsome Tahi-tians were dressed in sailors' ragged cast-offs and it was difficult to find, as Bligh noted with sadness, the gleaming white bark cloth that they had worn "with much elegance." Their very language had changed.

"Our country Men must have taken great pains to have taught them such vile blackguard expressions as are in the mouth of every Otahei-tan," Bligh wrote in his log. He had difficulty getting his friends "to speak their own language without mixing a jargon of English." Among Bligh's crew, it was not just the old hands but also those who had never before been to Tahiti who expressed disappointment. "Nothing was as delectable as described," wrote the disillusioned Lieutenant Bond. Even the women did not pass universal muster. "Nothing like European

beauty had been seen among the women," he noted. Their famous se-
ductive arts struck the men as being calculated for gain, rather than arising from any real affection.

Despite these disappointments, Bligh was heartened by the welcome
he received from old friends. Iddeeah soon appeared, and Tynah, who
was away, was quickly summoned; both now went by the name Pomare,
a reference to the disease that had recently killed their daughter. "Nothing could exceed the joy of these People at seeing me," Bligh wrote, and
although he was still unwell his own spirits briefly soared.

"We all thank God that you are safe," Bligh was greeted; "we were told
you were put into a little Boat & set a drift without any thing to eat or
drink, and that you must perish."

Bligh soon had the new nursery under way, and the collection of
breadfruit began again. The *Providence* and *Assistant* remained just over
three months at this task, during which time Bligh resumed his earlier
commentary on the customs and manners of the island. But whereas his
log of the *Bounty* radiated curiosity and tireless discovery—and indeed,
Bligh's own happiness—the log of the *Providence* lacks the consistent
zest of Bligh's earlier record. He was tired and still unwell and the sheer
novelty of the place had worn off.

Some of Bligh's old energy was manifested in his reports of intelligence he received of Christian and the mutineers. Two months after his
own departure, Bligh learned, the *Bounty* returned to Tahiti under Christian's command, where it was greeted with astonishment by the islanders. It was at this time that Christian gave his story about how Bligh had
met with Captain Cook in Whytootackee, where Cook planned to settle.
The generous Tahitians, surprised but cooperative, had given Christian
all he had asked for—hogs, chickens, plants and women—but not, as it
turned out, without some misgivings. Months later, the *Bounty* was back
again, and this time Christian appears not to have come ashore. With
the majority of his men discontent and sensing a suspicious coolness on
the part of the Tahitian chiefs, he had remained long enough only to
drop off "16 of his Associates," Bligh recorded in his log; he had originally written, and then crossed out, "16 of his Villains." Similarly, his
statement of "satisfaction and pleasure in hearing that all these Muti-

neers were taken by Captain Edwards" was a revision of his earlier noted pleasure "to hear of these Wretches all being taken." Bligh was also to hear his own story; as he noted with some amazement, one woman had so perfectly learned it "that she told me the names of all the men who came into my cabin at the time of the mutiny."

George Stewart, Thomas McIntosh and Richard Skinner had left daughters behind, Bligh learned, while Thomas Burkett and John Millward had left sons. No child of Peter Heywood was mentioned. Some of the mutineers' children were now said to be dead, but eventually two were brought for Bligh to see. One of these was George Stewart's daughter, a pretty child about a year old. Her mother had been poor Peggy, "the Woman that Stewart always kept on board the *Bounty*," who had pined and died after Stewart was taken on the *Pandora*. Later, McIntosh's wife, Mary, brought her daughter for Bligh to meet, a baby of about ten months old, "a fine little girl," as Bligh noted.

A few other material relics of the mutineers' lives survived. There was a big drum that Christian had brought from Tubuai. On the dreadful occasion of a human sacrifice, Bligh noted that the king's *maro*, or ritual feather belt, was adorned with human hair "of a pretty auburn colour"; this, he learned, had once belonged to Richard Skinner, formerly the *Bounty*'s barber. Most significantly, Bligh had been able to contemplate the neat houses and cottage gardens laid and tended by Peter Heywood—"the villain who assisted in taking the *Bounty* from me"—and his closes friend George Stewart.

"[T]he house was on the foot of a Hill, the top of which gave him a fine lookout," Bligh wrote; the lookout was that from which Peter had first seen the *Pandora*. "He had regulated the garden and the avenue to his house with some taste."

According to Mary McIntosh, her own husband, Coleman, Hilbrant, Norman, Byrn and Ellison "scarce ever spoke of me without crying. Stewart and Heywood were perfectly satisfied with their situation, and so were the rest of them."

"They deserved to be killed"; so thought Mary, but she "hoped those who cried for me would not be hurt." At the time of Bligh's writing, in May 1792, Hilbrant had long since gone down in chains with the *Pan-*

dora. The *Gorgon* was on her way to England with the captured mutineers, and young Ellison was shortly to be hanged.

Toward the end of June, as the breadfruit were successfully accumulated, Bligh was revisited with another attack of his malady.

"I have now no longer the power of bearing much fatigue," he wrote in his log. "Many necessary duties however cause me to suffer a great deal & I am frequently overcome." Once again, Lieutenant Portlock was obliged to step in. "Besides a constant Head ach, I have frequently in the day a sinking at the pit of my stomach, then a dreadfull heat flies up into my Face, which all but a report seems to fly out at the top of my head, as if shot through me—a lowness & flurry of my spirits takes place." This entire passage Bligh later deleted from his text; such complaints were not consistent with naval duty.

The *Providence* and *Assistant* departed Tahiti on July 19. In addition to 2,126 successfully transplanted and potted breadfruit, his ship also carried 508 "other" plants, one Tahitian passenger, one stowaway, and thirteen crew members from a shipwrecked British whaler, the *Matilda*. Perhaps the tension of preparing for departure had increased Bligh's "nervous" affliction because, as he wrote in his log, his crippling headache was such that he could not "bear the sight of the sun." Tynah and Iddeeah took leave of Bligh, and as Lieutenant Bond reported, their "real friendship with our commander" and sorrow at parting from him were deeply affecting. The loyal Tahitians promised Bligh that they would build him a house at Point Venus, so that he might return and live with them—later visitors would confirm that the islanders kept their word. But reeling under the blue Pacific skies, William Bligh had no thought of return and took final leave of the island he once described, of all places in the world, as harboring happiness "in the highest perfection."

Bligh directed his ships toward and through the Fijis, taking the opportunity to fix more accurately discoveries he had made from the *Bounty* launch. Working in careful tandem with the admirable Lieutenant Portlock, Bligh noted and marked dozens of these small islands. Having completed the survey, the ships continued northwest, and by early September were at the entrance to the Endeavour Strait. Trusting the next perilous steps to no one, Bligh clambered up the masthead from where he conned his ship himself; he did not yet know of the *Pandora*'s fate in these waters. Several days later, an unpleasant encounter with hostile islanders resulted in a number of the ships' party being wounded by arrows. Despite such distractions, Bligh took real interest in his task. Had he a month to spare, he logged, he would have completed the survey of this archipelago himself. As it was, he had to be satisfied with having "opened a way" for someone else, and "with a contrary monsoon advancing" there could be no time for delay.

The navigation of the strait took nineteen days of careful, painstaking vigilance. Midshipman Matthew Flinders, destined to make the first circumnavigation of Australia, later wrote of this passage that "perhaps no space of $3\frac{1}{2}°$ in length presents more dangers." Yet, as he noted—as had the Admiralty—"if a passage moderately free from danger were found ships might save five or six weeks of their usual route." Although the West Indies merchants wanted their breadfruit, and Banks was all for a botanical endeavor of this kind, the Admiralty's real interest—perhaps only real interest—in the breadfruit voyages was the opportunity they afforded for navigation of this unknown and dangerous passage, so strategically placed to the eastern trade routes and the New South Wales colony.

Through the strait and into the Indian Ocean, Bligh's ships made for Coupang, which they reached on October 2. Ironically, Bligh was more gravely ill on this occasion than when he had arrived three years before in the *Bounty*'s launch. He immediately wrote to Betsy.

> My ever Dear Love and my Dear Children,
> I am happily arrived here—I anchored this day & found a Country ship bound to Batavia, by which I have this opportunity to tell you I am well, except a low nervous disease which I have had more or less since I left Tenariffe—I have gone through the most extreme dangers, but after all a gracious God has restored me to this place of safety.

He planned to stay no more than a week—this intention was much on his mind, for it was twice repeated in the letter—and he had only praise for Lieutenant Portlock and his men: "Portlock has been of great service to me & behaved very well, indeed every person has come up to my expectations. This is the last Voyage I will ever make if it pleases God to restore me safe to you," Bligh suddenly exclaimed, and as once before in the Dutch Indies, his yearning for home is achingly palpable:

> I hope I shall live to see you & my Dear little girls.—Success I hope will crown my endeavors & that we shall at last be truly happy. . . . Next June, my Dear Dear Betsy I hope you will have me home to protect you myself—I love you dearer than ever a Woman was loved—You are, nor have not been a moment out of mind, Every joy and blessing attend you My Life, & bless my Dear Harriet my dear Mary, my Dear Betsy, My Dear Fanny, My Dear Jenny & my Dear little Ann. I send you all many Kisses on this paper & ever pray God to bless you—I will not say farewell to you now my Dear Betsy because I am homeward bound. I lose no time every happyness attend you My Dearest Life and ever remember me your best of Friends & most affectionate Husband.
>
> Wm. Bligh.

At Coupang, Bligh and his company had learned of the fate of Captain Edwards and the wreck of the *Pandora;* that they had now brilliantly succeeded where others had miserably failed could only have underscored the deep satisfaction at attaining this landmark on the homeward run. They had survived all the usual vagaries of weather and storm at sea, armed attacks by hostile islanders and the most tortuous and difficult reef-scattered strait in the world.

The *Providence* and the *Assistant* arrived at St. Vincent, in the West Indies, on January 23, 1793. A mere week later, the ships departed for Port Royal, Jamaica; Captain Bligh was very anxious to return to England, as the St. Vincent botanist observed. Although hundreds of breadfruit had died en route, Bligh was able to deposit 544 plants at St. Vincent and 620 in various districts of Jamaica. A token gift of 50 plants, including 12 breadfruit, had been presented to the governor of St. Helena, during a brief call there. The remainder of plants, along with a tub of Otaheite soil, were destined for Banks and for Kew. For his pains, Captain Bligh received public dinners and encomia, memorials and tributes from various island assemblies and councils, as well as a hundred guineas' worth of silver plate. Most remarkably, the Jamaican House of Assembly awarded as token of its thanks a gift of five hundred guineas to Lieutenant Portlock and one thousand guineas to William Bligh.

"[Y]ou have made a good man happy," Banks wrote to a member of the assembly on learning of Bligh's gift, "and a poor man comparatively rich."

Bligh had intended to leave Jamaica at the beginning of April, but a mail packet bearing grim news changed his plans. The King of France had been executed and the French ambassador expelled from England—the British government had no intention of maintaining relations with regicides. British ships had been attacked and now the countries were at war. Wary of an attack on Port Royal, the authorities detained Bligh until mid-June, and it was not until early August that the *Providence* and *Assistant* entered the Thames. Under the drear skies of late summer, the ships made their way upriver past the bodies of executed men hanging in chains from gibbets, a barbaric spectacle that horrified their Tahitian passenger. On August 7, 1793—two years and four days since their departure—they reached Deptford, and Bligh was home.

A local newspaper gave an eyewitness report of the dispersion of Bligh's men, commenting on the "cordial unanimity" of the officers and the "decency of conduct and the healthy and respectable appearance of the seamen, after so long and perilous a voyage." This last in particular bespoke that "good order and discipline" had been observed.

"The high estimation in which Captain Bligh was deservedly held by the whole crew, was conspicuous to all present," the paper noted. "He was cheered on quitting the ship to attend the Commissioner, and at the dock-gates the men drew up and repeated the parting acclamation."

All had not been fair sailing on this hard, long, demanding voyage, as the papers of Bligh's half nephew made abundantly clear. In a letter to his brother sent from St. Helena, which he implored be kept in the utmost secrecy, Lieutenant Bond had railed against Bligh, calling him a "Major Domo" whose elevated opinion of himself had been insupportable. "I don't mean to depreciate his extensive knowledge as a seaman and nautical astronomer, but condemn that want of modesty, in self-estimation,"

Bond had confidentially told his brother. Bligh's imperious manner, he claimed, had made it impossible to take instruction from him.

"[N]otwithstanding his passion is partly to be attributed to a nervous fever, with which he had been attacked most of the voyage, the chief part of his conduct must have arisen from the fury of an ungovernable temper," was Bond's damning summation. Especially galling had been Bligh's discouragement of Bond's ambition to keep an extensive journal of the voyage, having declared that "[n]o person can do the duty of a 1st Lieut. who does more than write the day's work of his publick Journal" or log. He had refused wholly to delegate any authority to his lieutenants; he, Bligh, had given the warrant officers their instructions directly, rather than trusting to the medium of his officers.

Bond's report must be trusted, but it should be read along with the reminiscences of another lieutenant from this same voyage—reminiscences in fact addressed to Bond himself in later years. George Tobin was third lieutenant on the *Providence*, and his recollections, made twenty-four years after the voyage, reflect a mature appreciation of Bligh's management, as opposed to the shredded vanity of a callow officer still nursing fresh wounds.

"I am sure, my dear Friend that in the *Providence* there was no settled System of Tyranny exercised by him likely to produce dissatisfaction," Tobin observed of their former captain. "It was in those violent Tornados of temper when he lost himself, yet, when all, in his opinion, *went right*, when could a man be more placid and interesting. For myself I feel that I am indebted to him. It was the first ship in which I ever sailed as an Officer—I joined full of apprehension,—I soon thought he was not dissatisfied with me—it gave me encouragement and on the whole we journeyed smoothly on. Once or twice indeed I felt the *Unbridled* licence *of* his *power* of *speech*, yet never without soon receiving something like an emollient plaister to heal the wound."

Bond's position on the *Providence* was analogous to that held by Fletcher Christian on the *Bounty*. Both young men served as the officers immediately under Bligh, and both were the particular objects of his attention. The words Bligh had written of his mentoring relationship to Christian (and Heywood) could also have applied to Bond: "with much unwearied Zeal I instructed them, for I considered them very worth of every good I could render to them."

It can be fairly said of Bligh that his great asset as a seaman was not only his unimpeachable professional skills, but his unshakable, complacent, immodest confidence in them. This confidence—the wellspring of his professional optimism, and indeed his courage—was what had enabled him successfully to command the *Bounty* launch on the most historic open-boat voyage yet made. This confidence in turn sprang from a relentless perfectionism, an unwavering and exacting adherence to the strictest letter of the laws of his duty. The gift of perfectionism and all that flowed from it was what Bligh sought to instill in his protégés. However, it may be that the very specialness of his relationship with these chosen young men was the weight that crushed them.

"Sir, your abuse is so bad that I cannot do my Duty with any Pleasure," Fletcher Christian was reported to have complained to Bligh shortly before the mutiny. The master's mate, as perhaps Lieutenant Bond, had not yet learned that duty was not intended to be pleasurable.

No other whiff of dissatisfaction with Bligh's command of the *Providence* voyage was brought to light. This was especially striking in view of the fact that busy inquiries were later made of the *Providence* men by parties who placed a high premium on finding discredit. If Bond's report is given credence, "unhappy" incidents—or, to use Tobin's words, "passing squalls"—surely occurred, but a firewall of loyalty seems to have been erected around Bligh. Perhaps at voyage's end, his men harbored more instructive memories than the miscellaneous slights they may have received: Captain Bligh, shaken with fever, reading the morning service, for example; or, ashen with the headache that made him feel the top of his skull had been blown off by gunshot, conning his ship from the masthead under the Pacific sun he could no longer endure; or, for nineteen days, expertly navigating the treacherous waters of the Endeavour Strait. Perhaps, too, on those days of foul and stormy weather, as the *Providence* pitched and lurched on her two-year voyage to the end of the earth and back, her officers and men looked out upon the roiling seas and imagined what it would have been like to have made the same journey on starvation rations and in a very small boat.

For his part, Bligh was unstinting in his praise of his men. In letters to the Admiralty, as well as privately to Betsy, he indicated throughout the voyage that his company had "come up to expectations." Now, on his return, he attempted to do his duty to them. Shortly after the ships had been paid off, Bligh presented the Admiralty with a list of officers who were "qualified and highly deserving of Promotion." This included, first and foremost, Lieutenant Nathaniel Portlock, whose "vigilance upon every occasion" Bligh commended as deserving his "warmest recommendation." Others in his honor roll included the master, the first officer of the marines, Surgeon Harwood (to whom Bligh felt "highly indebted") and his young gentlemen. The warrant officers were "all of them good Men" and other of the lower officers "from their good conduct during the Voyage" he also recommended. Those serving on the *Assistant* were particularly deserving for bearing with so much cheerfulness "the fatigues of the Voyage increased by the smallness of the Vessel." Such a list, one must imagine, had all gone well, would have concluded the voyage of the *Bounty*.

Since 1789, Bligh and his wife had lived in Lambeth, a pleasant, airy neighborhood on the south bank of the Thames backed by woods and meadows where foxgloves and columbine grew wild, and some twenty minutes' walk from Westminster Bridge. The front rooms faced a large green park, on which in later years Bethlem—or "Bedlam"—Hospital would be built. This modest but elegant brick house was to be the Blighs' home for nearly thirty years, and it was here that William Bligh now returned to his loving wife and daughters.

"My Little Flock are anxious to see me," Bligh had written to Banks, by way of apologizing for not coming to call on him immediately upon his return. Away from the glare of the Pacific sun that had racked his head and inflamed his eyes, he looked forward to rest in the bosom of his family.

Bligh had left England something of a national hero, and indeed the Admiralty's decision to mount a second, more costly expedition for the breadfruit they appear to have cared so little about was in some part a statement of support and confidence in him. But the *Providence* and Bligh returned to a very different political landscape from the one they had left. England was now determinedly at war with her oldest enemy, and rumblings of revolutionary leanings similar to those roiling France were worrisomely present in England. Toward the end of October, the *Times* ran a "very extraordinary report" that as Earl Fitzwilliam was passing through Sheffield in his post chaise, a mob had confiscated the leading pair of his four horses, "observing that two horses were enough for any man." Such incidents, increasingly common in manufacturing towns, bespoke a simmering popular rage that could swiftly turn more murderous.

Once again, then, Bligh was reminded that he was no longer in the age of Captain Cook, when dangerous voyages to exotic places received universal acclamation. Tahiti and the South Pacific were by now old news, in any case, and the successful importation of 1,164 breadfruit trees and other useful plants to the West Indies was not high on the Admiralty's list of events to celebrate.

Less explicable and more disconcerting was the evidence, subtle at first, that the political landscape had also changed within the Admiralty.

Bligh was to receive several clues that he was no longer held with the regard befitting a heroic survivor of the *Bounty,* one of which came in the form of a niggling piece of bureaucratic paperwork. On receiving his pay, Bligh was shocked to discover that he had been given reduced wages for his service as captain of the *Providence.*

"I am informed at the Navy Office, that being Captain & Purser, I am not entitled to any more; the profit of the Pursery being given to the Captain to make up for the two shillings a day taken from his pay," Bligh protested to the Admiralty Board. He had not, as he pointed out, been informed at the outset that he was to undertake the arduous expedition on reduced pay. Moreover, while professional pursers were accustomed to turning their profit by clever buying and selling and stinting of supplies, in the case of the *Providence* voyage, Bligh had made no profit whatsoever.

"Of those profits I shall not receive sufficient to clear my expenses," he wrote indignantly, "which have been occasioned in contribution to the comfort of every individual who was under my command and what were necessary for the outfit of such a voyage." If he had stinted his men, he would have come out ahead; but he had not, and so would now be out of pocket.

As distressing, and humiliating to Bligh personally, was the failure of any of his men to be advanced by promotion. As the father of one of the lieutenants was to observe, "I believe it is the first instance of any such voyage, even when unsuccessful, not being followed by promotion."

The highly personal nature of the Admiralty's new coolness was brought home to Bligh in a very English way. For weeks following his return, Bligh trekked to Westminster Bridge and across the Thames to the Admiralty Office at Whitehall. Here, in the imposing high-ceilinged reception corridor, which so many great men had crossed, Bligh had patiently awaited, or "attended," an audience with Lord Chatham.

But while Bligh continued to attend "from time to time," he never gained admittance. Other captains came, paid their respects and went as Captain Bligh was left to cool his heels very publicly outside. It appears that Joseph Banks attempted to calm Bligh's mounting anxiety regarding his lordship's "unaccountable conduct"; Banks had written a long letter to Lord Chatham praising Bligh's accomplishments and comparing them to those of Cook, shortly after the expedition's return. Nonetheless, in late September, there occurred an incident that rendered all polite pretexts beside the point. While Bligh continued his humiliating vigil, Lieutenant Portlock—his lieutenant, his junior officer—was called inside.

"Astonished at this I determined to have it accounted for," Bligh wrote, distraught, to Banks. Accordingly, he was informed by the Admiralty secretary that his lordship had deferred seeing Bligh "untill he had leisure to have half an hours conversation." But such smooth reassurances could not be trusted. As Bligh told Banks, "His Lordship not seeing me is certainly a slight."

That the problem, whatever its cause, lay squarely in Admiralty circles was demonstrated by a more gratifying circumstance: a visit from Prince William Henry, the Duke of Clarence, who invited Bligh to dine with him at Richmond. "[H]ere is an officer that has acquitted himself in the highest manner, and the First Lord of the Admiralty would not see him!"

Bligh reported that the Duke exclaimed. Whatever mischief had transpired had apparently not seeped outside Admiralty circles—yet.

Ironically, Bligh's men—or at least Francis Bond—may have been
more apprised of the causes of this unaccountable conduct than was
their captain. In November 1792, Lieutenant Bond's brother left a letter
for him in Jamaica, to await his arrival with the *Providence*. In addition to
news of events in France ("Poor Royalists and other innocent people to
the amount of not less than 10,000 were coolly and deliberately Massacred in Paris"), Thomas Bond's letter contained a report on the mutineers' court-martial. Six men had been condemned to die, he wrote, and
three had been executed on board the *Brunswick*. Heywood and Morrison had been pardoned.

"Heywood's friends, have bribed through thick and thin to save him,
and from publick report, have not been backward in *defaming our Uncles
character*," wrote Thomas Bond, adding that "Government in my Judgment, should have waited until Captn. Blighs arrival in England, before
those Mutineers were brought to trial."

Between the time of confinement of the mutineers on the *Hector* and
the return of the *Providence* in August 1793, a sea change had been
wrought in Bligh's reputation. This development was made unequivo-
cally clear by none other than Pasley, now commodore in the Channel
Fleet under Lord Howe.

"Your Capt. will meet a very hard reception," Pasley wrote to former
Providence midshipman Matthew Flinders with grim satisfaction. "[H]e
has Damn'd himself."

But this last was untrue. Bligh's reception was the result of considerable, at times concerted, outside effort. While the Heywood family connections and interest-making had done damage within Admiralty and
naval circles, the most public and audacious attack on Bligh was to come
from, of all quarters, Fletcher Christian's family.

All had not gone well for the Christians over the years since the *Bounty*
had sailed. Mrs. Christian still lived in semi-exile on the Isle of Man. Her
eldest son, John Christian, the attorney whose bankruptcy had resulted

in the very public Cockermouth auction, on the death of his first wife married the widow of a sugar merchant, residing in Pall Mall, London, who was twenty-three years his senior. Then, he died in 1791, at the age of only thirty-nine, "of a gradual decay."

On the return of his disastrous voyage in the *Middlesex,* the third son, Charles, settled in medical practice in Hull, where he was known throughout the town for the "successful Extirpation of Two Womens' Breasts" on account of cancerous afflictions. By 1795, however, his lodgings in the house of a "black-eyed Widow" would cause a local wit to write some facetious "Doggrel Rhyme," and he would move to Leicester. Poor Charles's memoir is a tangled, at times almost incomprehensible, litany of improbable misfortunes and calumnies, goading him onward to ever more confused and high-flown protestations of honor. The youngest Christian son, Humphrey, had died on the coast of Africa in his early twenties—"shortly after reading the account of the mutiny," as a family document pointedly records, although given the death rates at African stations, it is most likely that ill health, not the shock of his brother's deed, killed him.

The only member of Fletcher's immediate family who was flourishing was his elder brother, Edward, the Cambridge-educated lawyer who had been responsible for deftly finessing his mother's finances after she had been declared bankrupt.

A Christian family historian—herself a Christian—noted that "somehow or another there was a strain of eccentricity" among Fletcher's brothers. On the one hand, Edward's career at Cambridge had been full of prizes and full of promise. In 1793, he was a "First Downing Professor of the Laws of England" at Cambridge and was busy preparing what would become a highly successful edition of *Blackstone's Commentaries,* an invaluable legal compendium.

On the other hand, as early as Edward's student days, anecdotes had begun to circulate about his oddities. When some newly planted trees were destroyed in the gardens of his college, for instance, according to a classmate Edward "was requested to draw up a hand bill, offering one hundred pounds reward for the discovery of the offenders." The subsequent bills were so absurd that friends at first believed them to have been made by "some enemy of Christian's in order to render him ridiculous." While offering the reward, Edward had also described the destruction of trees "as being a *capital offence,* punishable with death under the black act; he strongly recommended the perpetrators to come forward & acknowledge their guilt, but he did not offer impunity to them for doing so."

Edward Christian was brought into the *Bounty* fray, as he claimed, in November 1792, when he received an unexpected and shocking letter:

> Sir,
>
> I am sorry to say I have been informed you were inclined to judge too harshly of your truly unfortunate brother; and to think of him in such a manner as I am conscious, from the knowledge I had of his most worthy disposition and character, (both public and private,) he merits not in the slightest degree: therefore I think it my duty to undeceive you, and to re-kindle the flame of brotherly love (or *pity* now) towards him, which, I fear, the false reports of slander and vile suspicion may have nearly extinguished.
>
> Excuse my freedom, Sir:—If it would not be disagreeable to you, I will do myself the pleasure of waiting upon you; and endeavour to prove that your brother was not that vile wretch, void of all gratitude, which the world had the unkindness to think him; but, on the contrary, a most worthy character; ruined only by having the misfortune, (if it can be so called) of being a young man of strict honour, and adorned with every virtue; and beloved by all (except one, whose ill report is his greatest praise) who had the pleasure of his acquaintance.
>
> I am, Sir, with esteem . . .

The letter, dated November 5, was run in the *Cumberland Paquet* two weeks later, and quickly picked up by London papers. In the newspaper the author was identified only as "an officer late of the Bounty"; but in the papers Edward eventually passed along to Joseph Banks, it was evident that it had been written from Aaron Graham's home on Great Russell Street, by "P. Heywood."

Whether the letter was the bolt from the blue that Edward claimed, it was by any reckoning an extraordinarily ill-advised and provocative act on Peter's part; had he expressed any such sentiment in the courtroom, it is doubtful that all the family interest in the world could have saved him—among other things, it tended to give credence to Hallett's contention that he had laughed at his captain's predicament. It was also a blatant contradiction of his defense statement that from Bligh's "attention to and very kind treatment of me personally, I should have been a Monster of depravity to have betray'd him." It may be that Peter never intended for the letter to be aired in a public forum, let alone with his name attached, and had presumed that a professor of law could have been counted on to receive his bold gesture with careful tact—if so, he had not been apprised of the character of Edward Christian. On the other hand, it is possible that the letter had been a calculated move, already ventured to the Christian family. Nessy's earlier confidential correspondence with John Christian Curwen indicates that there were ready lines of communication between these two related families, with their shared Cumbria-Manx backgrounds. It is, moreover, difficult to believe that Peter would have drafted such a letter in Aaron Graham's home without his approval—and Graham always looked to the big picture.

But, whether the letter came to Edward as a great surprise or as a piece in a carefully constructed design, it did the trick. Fletcher's brother now had a respectable pretext to enter the debate—and to conduct his own public "investigation" of what had happened on the *Bounty*. Consequently, by the time Bligh returned to England, Edward had engaged in his *Bounty* researches for close to a year. Evidently, he passed on some of his findings to Joseph Banks, who gave no sign that he had been especially shaken by them, and shortly after the *Providence*'s return Banks in turn passed the papers he had received from Edward on to Bligh.

By way of preface, the *Cumberland Pacquet* suggested that the contents of Peter's anonymous letter would enable the public "to correct the erroneous opinions, which, from a certain false narrative they have long entertained, and to distinguish between the audacious and hardened depravity of the heart which no suffering can soften, and the desperation of an ingenious mind torn and agonized by unprovoked and incessant abuse and disgrace." The "false narrative" referred to Bligh's published account; the "ingenious mind torn and agonized by unprovoked and incessant abuse and disgrace" referred to Fletcher Christian.

> Though there may be certain actions, which even the torture and extremity of provocation cannot justify, yet a sudden act of phrenzy, so circumstanced, is far removed in reason and mercy from the foul deliberate contempt of every religious and virtuous sentiment and obligation, excited by selfish and base gratifications.—For the honour of this county we are happy to assure our readers that one of its natives, FLETCHER CHRISTIAN, is not the detestable and horrid monster of wickedness, which with extreme and perhaps unexampled injustice and barbarity to him and his relations he has long been represented, but a character of whom every feeling heart must now sincerely grieve and lament.

A gentleman who had attended the court-martial as an advocate, the newspaper announced, would shortly "communicate," or publish, astonishing new information arising from the court-martial. As it would turn out, this advocate was to be not Aaron Graham but the more inscrutable Stephen Barney.

But no such revelations had in fact arisen in the court-martial, certainly nothing to raise the eyebrows of twelve seasoned naval captains. Four points could have invited further questioning by the curious: Peckover, the gunner, had reported that David Nelson had said "we know who is to blame"; jeers about living on "three fourths of a Pound of Yams a day" had been aimed at Bligh as he was put in the launch; Christian had been "in hell" for two weeks before the mutiny—according to Fryer, on account of the frequent quarrels with Bligh; and finally, the night before the mutiny Bligh had charged his officers with stealing coconuts. Yet, in a profession in which a captain enjoyed almost total and arbitrary power over all who served under him, the knowledge that Bligh had severely chastised his men over stolen coconuts was not the kind of event to rivet attention. Nor was it likely that any of the presiding captains had served on ships in which there had not been grousing over rations. Whatever concerns had arisen during the period of the court-martial would not seem to have been raised within the actual courtroom.

Following his receipt of this revelatory letter, Edward Christian summoned and interviewed "three other officers" and two of the sailors who had been acquitted at the court-martial, "being all the persons belonging to the *Bounty* who could be found in the neighborhood of London," as the newspapers reported.

Thus began Edward's diligent, in some ways admirable but ultimately mischievous, informal commission of inquiry, the results of which he went on to publish. A panel of eleven legal associates and friends was convened to witness his interviews with the various *Bounty* men. This panel never met as a body, but various combinations of members met sometimes with one witness, sometimes with several; some participants may have attended only once out of curiosity, others may have taken a lively ongoing interest in the cause—the ground rules of participation were not spelled out. Some of the interviews were conducted in Edward's Gray's Inn chambers, but a number were also conducted at a Greenwich public house, the Crown and Sceptre. Built of weathered timber, with back windows that looked out on the Thames, the Crown and Sceptre was not the most respectable venue available, but it was conveniently close to Greenwich Hospital, where three of the *Bounty* men had been admitted.

The pub also provided the kind of familiar, unthreatening atmosphere in which ordinary seamen like Coleman and Byrn would feel most at ease. As it was, some of the comments made by these humble men to Edward Christian and the "several respectable gentlemen" who were his colleagues reeked of class-conscious, cap-in-hand deference, not to mention a little gentlemanly editing:

"Oh ! he was a gentleman, and a brave man," McIntosh was reported to have said "with honest simplicity" of Fletcher Christian. "[E]very officer and sailor on board the ship, would have gone through fire and water to have served him."

"His Majesty might have his equal, but he had not a superior officer in the service."

"He was adorned with every virtue, and beloved by all."

"As much as I have lost and suffered by him, if he could be restored to his country I should be the first to go without wages in search of him."

Edward Christian's committee membership was both eccentric and impressive. At the top of the list was Samuel Romilly, one of the most distinguished legal reformers of his day and a friend of Edward's from their days as law students. An enthusiastic and engaged supporter of the revolution in France, Romilly had been entertained by Lafayette during a visit to France in the late 1780s when they had "talked together of 'American' ideas of patriotism and liberty."

Four theologians were involved. The Reverend Dr. John Fisher had been recently appointed rector of Nether Stowey, where he was shortly to become friends with two young poets resident in the area, William Wordsworth and Samuel Taylor Coleridge. Now a canon of Windsor, Dr. Fisher enjoyed close contact with the King; he was also a close friend of the Laws, another of the Christian family's gifted and well-connected first cousins. The Reverend Mr. William Cookson was also, since 1792, a canon of Windsor. Cookson was in every sense a very weighty man, being close to the King, and also having allowed himself to balloon to almost three hundred pounds. His sister was William Wordsworth's mother. The Reverend Dr. John Frewen had previously been William Wordsworth's tutor at St. John's College, Cambridge, where Edward Christian had also gone. The Reverend Mr. Antrobus, chaplain to the Bishop of London, was from Cockermouth, with family still in the area.

Of John Farhill nothing is known except his address, as stated by Edward. Similarly, little more is known of John Atkinson than that his was a Cumberland name, and he held a position at the College of Arms, the institution that advised on matters of heraldry.

William Gilpin, originally of Cumberland and now of the Strand, was a landscape gardener and watercolor artist, but as a biographer observed, the "inferior quality of his work as a painter was, however, very evident at the first exhibition." William's father was Sawrey Gilpin, a Royal Academy artist of some distinction who specialized in animal paintings, a fact that had undoubtedly helped launch his son's unexceptional career. William was a neighbor of Joseph Christian, the linen draper whom John Fryer had gone to see shortly after his return to England; both men had country residences in Surrey, and town quarters in the Strand.

John France, who was originally from Yorkshire, was a lawyer with chambers in the Inner Temple and a commissioner in bankruptcy. John Wordsworth was a captain in the East India Company (until 1787 under the directorship of Edward's relative Sir Henry Fletcher) and William Wordsworth's father's cousin.

Finally, James Losh, resident for most of his time in Penrith, Cumberland, was, like Romilly, a legal activist and reformer with strong sympathies for the revolutionary cause in France. Also a Cambridge man, Losh was to become a close friend of Wordsworth through radical friends in Bristol. He was also on social terms with John Christian Curwen and with the Speddings—the family of Peter Heywood's mother—and very close to other branches of the Christian family.

Even a very casual glance at this list of participants revealed clear, if curious, fault lines. The Cumberland connection was strong, as less expectedly were the associations with William Wordsworth, at this time a promising if unestablished poet. The Wordsworths and Christians knew one another well. It will be recalled that Fletcher and William had been schoolmates at Cockermouth, and that William was later, very briefly, a pupil at Hawkshead School, where Edward had been headmaster. Edward and William shared a wide circle of college friends and associates. And Edward Christian successfully represented William and his siblings in a legal suit to obtain their father's inheritance, held up for years by the unscrupulous Lord Lonsdale. "We have got a very clever man on our side but as he is young he will not have much authority. His name is Christian," William's sister Dorothy had written in June 1791, regarding the Lonsdale suit. "[H]e is a friend of my Uncle, knows my brother William very well and I am very well acquainted with him, and a charming man he is."

But there were also other more subtle associations. The great majority of Edward's panel were fervent abolitionists. In some cases, as with Romilly and Losh—and William Wordsworth—this arose from strong revolutionary sympathies. St. John's College, where so many of the men had connections, was an important disseminator of the abolitionist movement. William Wilberforce, the great leader of the antislavery movement, had gone here. Wilberforce was in fact an old friend of Edward's from these university days and had written to him a sympathetic letter when news of the mutiny reached England. Edward was also quick to report to his old friend the result of his "inquiry." "Captain Bligh is a detestable villian," he wrote at the end of 1792, "against whom on his return every door must be shut." Wilberforce's closest friend was Prime Minister William Pitt—the brother of Lord Chatham, whom Bligh would wait so long in vain to see.

Edward Christian gave no account of his method of choosing his colleagues. It may be that other men had been asked to participate and declined; it may be the men who were eventually gathered had caught wind of the campaign and volunteered for inclusion. The radical-abolitionist aspect of the eventual "committee" may have been a simple accident of the entirely reasonable association so many of them had with St. John's. But whatever the mechanism by which it had fallen in place, this abolitionist sympathy would prove significant to the outcome.

While Joseph Banks may have been beguiled by the botanical aspects of the *Bounty* voyage, the real goal of the breadfruit expedition had been succinctly expressed by one West Indian planter. Breadfruit would be "of infinite importance to the West Indian Islands, in affording a wholesome and pleasant food to our negroes, which would have the great advantage of being raised with infinitely less labour than the plaintain." By "our negroes," the author meant the thousands of African slaves who worked the vast West Indian plantations, and on whose labor the sugar industry depended. The principal object of the *Bounty*'s voyage, then, was to enable plantation owners to feed their human chattel as cheaply and as efficiently as possible.

William Bligh, purveyor of slave provisions, was unlikely to have aroused much natural sympathy among the men Edward had congregated. In addition, Bligh had worked for his wife's uncle ferrying rum and sugar from the islands. This association with Duncan Campbell in itself was not likely to have impressed Edward's associates.

In short, while Bligh's ship had been renamed *Bounty* for her humane contribution to West Indian Negroes, in certain eyes the breadfruit voyages were nothing to celebrate. And when Edward Christian began his inquiries, William Bligh was back in Tahiti, engaged once again in this same unsavory mission.

Into this atmosphere of radical sympathizers and ardent abolitionists was now flung the saga of the *Bounty*—a story of a young gentleman who, "agonized by unprovoked and incessant abuse and disgrace," stood up for his natural rights and overthrew the oppressive tyrant who was his captain. Bucking the despised authority, he sailed away to freedom in the South Pacific.

That at least some of Edward's committee did in fact make the association between Christian's acts and their own radical interests is evident from James Losh's private diary. In conversation with friends one evening, talk had "turned principally upon the invasion of the liberty. . . . We all agreed that were there any place to go emigration wou'd be a prudent thing for literary men and the friends of freedom," he had recorded with gloomy melodrama. "I explained the real state of a Christian's mutiny." His companions, one of whom was Wordsworth's friend and fellow poet Robert Southey, had been "much struck" by this almost encoded reference to the *Bounty* mutiny.

Sipping their ale in the Crown and Sceptre, Edward's colleagues had undoubtedly listened spellbound to the extraordinary story unfolding, witness by witness. As the dirty winter water lapped at the riverfront outside the window, they heard of hard life at sea, of Tahiti and its black beaches, of the promiscuous customs of the Tahitian women, of the erupting volcano filling the night skies over Tofua—all the rush of images that infused the story with romance and even glamour.

The details that Edward extracted from the *Bounty* men would remain some of the most memorable in all the tellings of this story. Bligh had called his officers "scoundrels, damned rascals, hounds, hell-hounds, beasts, and infamous wretches." When the *Bounty* reached the Endeavour Strait, Bligh had declared, "he would kill one half of the people, make the officers jump overboard, and would make them eat grass like cows."

The general tenor of Edward's published revelations obviously focused on his brother and made vivid the mental anguish that had driven the engaging young man to mutiny.

"What is the meaning of all this?" Bligh had asked indignantly, on being led on deck at bayonet point.

"Can you ask, Captain Bligh, when you know you have treated us officers, and all these poor fellows, like Turks?" Christian replied. Despite all previous testimony that Christian had claimed to have been in hell for "weeks past," or "this fortnight past"—in other words since leaving Tahiti—new evidence now emerged that Bligh had abused Christian on the island and had done so, worst of all, in front of the natives.

"There is no country in the world, where the notions of aristocracy and family pride are carried higher than at Otaheite"—except England, Edward Christian might have added. The Downing Professor of Law was now an Otaheite authority. "[A]nd it is a remarkable circumstance, that the Chiefs are naturally distinguished by taller persons, and more open and intelligent countenances, than the people of inferior condition," Professor Christian continued; hence, it was implied, their affection for Fletcher Christian.

"[T]hey adored the very ground he trod upon," as one of the Bountys had declared. Remarkably, for all the energy invested in these proceedings, nothing emerged to suggest that the direct cause of Christian's breakdown was anything more than the famous theft of coconuts.

"Damn your blood, you have stolen my cocoa nuts," Bligh had said, accosting Christian when the loss was perceived.

"I was dry, I thought it of no consequence, I took one only," Christian plaintively replied, according to one of Edward's new witnesses.

"You lie, you scoundrel, you have stolen one half" and "thief" were Bligh's responses.

("What scurrilous Abuse!" Charles Christian wrote in his own, never published memoir. "What provoking Insult to one of the chief Officers on Board for having taken a Cocoa Nut from a Heap to quench his Thirst when on Watch—base mean-spirited Wretch!!")

"[F]lesh and blood cannot bear this treatment," someone had heard Christian say; the master's mate had been driven to tears, the only time he had been known to cry. After the coconut incident, Christian first planned to set out from the *Bounty* on a raft—in itself a wonderful image—and had that afternoon set about shredding all his personal papers and giving away all his Otaheite souvenirs. But the fireworks over Tofua brought too many men on deck for him to effect this in secret, and so the idea was laid aside. There then occurred the conversation that, all Edward's witnesses agreed, had triggered the mutiny. George Stewart, the husband of poor Peggy, the special friend and messmate of Peter Heywood, knowing of Christian's plans for the raft, had said to him, "When you go, Christian, we are ripe for any thing."

Passing back and forth from one representation to another, from event to event, the document Edward Christian eventually produced was a mass of vivid, confused, riveting statements and details, which had few counterparts in the court-martial testimony. When it was published in 1794, it also contained a number of embarrassments for the Heywoods. That George Stewart and Peter had been close friends had never been concealed; it was Stewart, Peter claimed at his trial, who had told him that he should leave the ship with Bligh. It was Stewart with whom he built his little cottage on Tahiti. How now to account for Stewart's fatal words "we are ripe for any thing"? And how to account for the fact (which "ought not to be concealed," as Edward allowed) that during the mutiny itself Stewart "was dancing and clapping his hands in the Otaheite manner," and saying "It was the happiest day of his life"? Stewart was eventually appointed Christian's second-in-command, although a number of the seamen, it had seemed, had favored Mr. Heywood for this position because of Stewart's renowned "severity."

Edward's published report listed the name of each individual participant of his informal committee along with his address —"38 Mortimer Street," "Lincoln's Inn"—presumably so that each could be further questioned by interested readers. That Edward was confident he had reported the proceedings his colleagues had witnessed cannot be in doubt. What must be doubted, however, was his committee's capacity to understand salient aspects of the story unfolded for them.

"Hence the resolution was taken to put the Capt in a boat, a small distance from Otahitee," William Gilpin reported to a visiting cousin in May 1794, excitedly passing on what had transpired at the Crown and Sceptre; he himself had been present at "several" of Edward's interviews. "Every proper precaution was taken with respect to the safety and convenience of those that went—Notwithstanding, the Capt. made a very contrary report when he came home, declaring their intention to drown him. It is true that afterward he was not suffered to land on Otahitee which was accounted for by Capt. B. on a former occasion having made himself odious to the inhabitants."

That anyone on Edward's panel could have sat through even a single interview and come away with the idea that "every proper precaution was taken with respect to the safety and convenience" of those in the *Bounty* launch must raise serious questions about the entire proceedings. Every man, loyalist and mutineer alike, had testified that to join the launch had seemed, in Peter's words, "a kind of act of suicide." Nor obviously had Bligh touched on Tahiti; nor had he been rebuffed there by the islanders; nor had he made himself odious to them. . . .

William Gilpin's cousin was able to peruse a copy of Edward's pamphlet at the time of his visit, noting that "it was ready for press." Matters were, then, pretty far along at the time of this exchange. In the event, Edward's published version of the inconvenient fact of the boat journey was that the launch had been dangerously laden only because "almost all Captain Bligh's property in boxes and trunks was put on board." Others who had gone voluntarily into the launch "were sure of getting to shore, where they expected to live, until an European ship arrived"—besides, they had the carpenter with them, and he could build a bigger boat. And although the sufferings in the boat were distressful, "they were not the occasion of the death of Mr. Nelson at Timor, or of those who died at Batavia." In any event, Fletcher Christian had been heard to declare that "he would readily sacrifice his own life, if the persons in the launch were all safe in the ship again."

Fletcher Christian's tortured state of mind following the mutiny was another of the indelible images to arise from this new testimony. He was "always sorrowful and dejected after the mutiny; and . . . had become such an altered man in his looks and appearance, as to render it probable that he would not long survive this dreadful catastrophe." After the mutiny, he assumed command of the ship reluctantly, and only after the men "declared that he should be their Captain." Although he kept discipline on the ship, "he was generally below, leaning his head upon his hand." When asked for orders, "he seldom raised his head to answer more than Yes, or No." How could it be otherwise if he deserved the good character "which all unite in giving him"? In fact, severe as had been the sufferings of Captain Bligh and his boat companions, they were "perhaps but a small portion of the torments occasioned by this dreadful event." Before returning to Tahiti for the last time, he had addressed his men in an emotional speech, seeking one favor: "that you will grant me the ship . . . and leave me to run before the wind."

Reformers, men of the cloth, lawyers . . . with the single exception of Captain Wordsworth, the members of Edward's committee were a lubberly crowd and appear to have had not an inkling of life at sea. With their eyes on such issues as social reform and the treatment of slaves, they would have undoubtedly been horrified by much that was matter-of-factly related by the agreeable and pliant seamen—the cramped conditions, bad rationed food and strong language.

"I have heard the Captain damn the people, like many other captains," Lawrence Lebogue would later go on record as saying, "but he was never angry with a man the next minute, and I never heard of their disliking him."

"I will by no means affirm, that I never heard Captain Bligh express himself in warm or hasty language, when the conduct of his officers or people has displeased him," John Hallett would also declare, again on record. "[B]ut every seafaring gentleman must be convinced that situations frequently occur in a ship when the most mild officer will be driven, by the circumstances of the moment, to utter expressions which the strict standard of politeness will not warrant." But he had never, he avowed, "heard Captain Bligh make use of such illiberal epithets and menaces" as Edward had attributed to him.

"I'm damned if I don't sink you, you skulking son of a bitch; I mean to tow you until I work some buckets of tar out of the hawser"—thus another seasoned commander cheerfully reported his captain's words on another, unrelated voyage. Commander James Gardner's memoir of naval service on many ships, under many captains and lieutenants, encompasses exactly the same period of time as the *Bounty* voyage and its aftermath and so gives an excellent, straightforward touchstone for the kind of language commonly used at sea. With affectionate gusto Gardner recalled his various salty encounters: "The admiral, who had an eye like a hawk, would damn him up in heaps"; "No; damn my brains if you shall go," from an "extremely passionate" commander; "you are a damned lubber . . . a blockhead"—this from Sir Roger Curtis, the *Brunswick* captain who had orchestrated the execution of the three mutineers; "I'll hang the fellow"; "Where's that little son of a bitch?"; "Go on the poop and be damned to you"; "such a rage that he swore he would flog the clerk and those who were under him." One captain who "was a very good man at times, but often harsh and severe in his remarks," had informed Gardner, who, as he confessed, had "never forgotten it," that he would never be fit for anything but the boatswain's storeroom.

There was, then, much about life at sea that did not translate well into the civilian world—principally, that naval language was more often than not spiced with profanity, and that officers and men commonly did not like their captains. Ironically, the single incident that would undoubtedly have struck a nerve with naval professionals confronted with the same testimony heard at the Crown and Sceptre was probably the last thing Edward was capable of imagining.

"Damn your blood, you have stolen my cocoa nuts," Bligh had accused Christian.

"I was dry, I thought it of no consequence, I took one only," Christian had plaintively replied, according to Edward.

Bligh's own response to this episode, drafted in the third person after Edward's publication, but never published, was unequivocal and unrepentant: "A heap of Cocoa Nutts were between the guns under the charge of the Officer of the Watch, with orders for no one to touch them untill the Ship was clear of the land, when they would be issued equally and considered highly refreshing, without which caution some would have & waste one half, & others would have none. In one Night (the first) the Officers permitted the whole within a score to be taken away. As this was evidently done through some design Captain Bligh ordered all the Cocoa Nutts to be replaced—The Officers of the Watch declared they were taken away by stelth—Here was a publick theft; a contumacy, & direct disobedience of orders."

Bligh did not require so thorough an explanation. Under the inexorable rules that governed the hierarchy of command and conduct on board a ship in His Majesty's naval service, the removal of a single coconut from the ship's store, if forbidden by order of the superior officer, was a criminal act. And to Bligh's charge that he—the officer of the watch, the acting lieutenant, the second-in-command—had contravened his commanding officer's infrangible injunction, Christian had, in essence, replied, with pain and bewilderment in his voice—"but I was thirsty!"

Bligh appears to have read some version of Edward's report in October 1793, not long after his return with the *Providence,* when Joseph Banks passed along a packet of papers he had received from Edward. This seems to have included a number of letters, notes on Bligh's narrative, perhaps some preliminary report of Edward's interviews—and a narrative by James Morrison. It also apparently contained a number of "news" items containing wildly erroneous reports, such as that the *Providence* had mutinied and taken the ship to Batavia, where Bligh had been delivered up a prisoner.

Such reports, Bligh told Banks, like the "low abuse contained in the Notes upon my Narrative are beneath my Notice." From what he had already heard, the master, boatswain, carpenter and gunner had "made plain their own cowardice and baseness, and nothing would give me more pleasure," he told Banks, "than to have the court martial published." Bligh had had his own informants at the trial: John Hallett Sr. had reported to him that Fryer had been "checked by the Court for contradicting himself," and an officer of the *Duke* had reported to Bligh's brother-in-law that Lord Hood had in conversation "expressed the greatest antipathy" to the prevarications of some of the witnesses. Of the eventuality that the court-martial proceedings would be published, Bligh seemed complacently skeptical, noting that had "Mr. Christian found he was in the right in justifying his Brothers Character I suppose the World would have heard of it before this time in a fair & open Manner." Events would shortly prove Bligh wrong.

Edward Christian's was not the only new account of the *Bounty* story. James Morrison, he of the long black hair and imaginative tattoos, had also been hard at work on his own narrative. He had begun it on the *Hector,* at the same time that Peter had been employed in writing up his Otaheitean vocabulary; indeed, there is evidence that the two works had originally been intended for a single ambitious publication. Morrison's "Journal" was a much expanded version of a shorter "Memorandum" that he had completed in October 1792, a 69-page ad hominem attack on Bligh composed while he was under threat of execution. The "Journal," on the other hand, had a broader focus, and nearly half of this 382-page opus was concerned with Tahitian culture and customs, geography and natural history. Amply illustrating the uncommon abilities that had so impressed the court, the work is an extraordinary and valuable document of Tahitian life as it had been before the coming of the Europeans, and would never be again. The rest was devoted to the events of the *Bounty*, and it was on this part that outside attention was first riveted.

The chief advocate of Morrison's work appears to have been the Reverend William Howell, who had attended the mutineers on the *Hector*. By late November 1792, following the mutineers' trial and execution, Howell was in correspondence with an associate of Joseph Banks. His aim was to get the Morrison manuscript into Banks's hand with the hope, ill concealed, that this would turn Banks against his protégé.

"It is very natural for Sir Joseph Banks not to think so unfavorably of Bligh as you or I may," Howell wrote, in his almost childishly awkward script, "—there was a time when no one could have an higher opinion of an officer than I had of him—so many circumstances however have arizen up against him attended with such striking marks of veracity that I have been compelled to change that idea of him into one of a very contrary nature."

Howell's correspondent was Molesworth Phillips, a man who had a number of connections with Bligh. Phillips had been the first lieutenant of marines on Cook's third voyage and had been present at Cook's death when his ill-commanded marines had fallen back in the panic of that crisis. Bligh's own opinion of him can be gauged from some marginal notes he scrawled beside his name in a published account of that voyage: "This person . . . never was of any real service the whole Voyage, or did any thing but eat and sleep." It was at the feet of Lieutenant Phillips and his panicked marines that Bligh lay blame for Cook's death.

Morrison was getting along well with his "publication," Howell reported to Phillips, and it would be "ready for the press in about six or seven weeks." The narrative was to be a "very particular & diffuse account of the proceedings of Christian & party *after* the mutiny—with a very accurate discription of Taheite." Nothing would be mentioned that might "tend to any disturbance or reflect on any character."

Morrison's manuscript was at this time on the Isle of Wight, for reasons unknown; but some two and a half weeks later, Phillips himself was able to forward the entire, unedited work to Banks. Although there was another account that had been amply revised by "a clergyman," Phillips allowed, he thought that Banks would prefer seeing the original "genuine unsophisticated story . . . in the mans own writing." This was Phillips's calculated method of ensuring that Banks read Morrison's unedited, unbowdlerized criticism of Bligh.

Although Edward Christian had also been in correspondence with Morrison, surprisingly few of Morrison's representations appeared in Edward's report. Reflecting the different preoccupations of their respective social classes, Edward's report was about character and damaged honor—and Morrison's was about food.

Morrison's criticisms of Bligh are strikingly specific: two cheeses had been found missing, and these were alleged to have been taken before the voyage by Bligh for his private use; after crossing the equator, Bligh had pumpkins served at short weight in lieu of bread; beef and pork seemed "light" and officers and men watched in helpless dismay as all the best pieces had been taken to the "cabbin" (as was in practice the prerogative of every commander); a sheep found dead on deck was served to the men; porridge allowance was so scant that brawls broke out in the galley, in one of which the cook suffered a broken rib. . . . More striking, most of these incidents were stated to have taken place on the outward voyage—Morrison was evidently unaware that letters sent home from the Cape by several *Bounty* men and officers tended to contradict his claims.

Some of the allegations were questioned even by Bligh's critics. Was it really credible, as Morrison claimed, that Lieutenant Bligh had ordered the ship's cooper to remove two cheeses from the *Bounty* while at Deptford, and then ordered seaman John Williams, another of his own crew, to ferry these up the Thames, and lug them ashore to his house in Wapping. As for serving the dead sheep, as Bligh pointed out, it was "a general rule on board of Ship, not to suffer any thing that died to be used by the Seamen, because they would always find means to kill any animal if they knew this Rule was not observed." The cook had broken his rib after falling in the bad weather around the Horn, and so on.

Sitting at home in his cozy study in the autumn of 1793, William Bligh plowed through the considerable papers that Banks had provided. Based upon all he knew, it was difficult to take these productions with the seriousness that later events would show they deserved.

"Morrison's accounts are made up of vile falsehoods which no body will dare to publish or sustain, that I will venture to say," Bligh sputtered to Banks. "[My] Dear Sir, my unexpected return has been the effectual means of putting a stop to the malicious insinuations which I have been informed these People were frequently inserting in the Publick Prints." Bligh was calming Banks's fears. Of far greater concern to him was the fact that he had not yet received a new commission. After completing the *Providence* voyage with such success and against such odds, he had presumed he would be entitled "to the command of a Ship of some consequence"—so he had intended to tell Lord Chatham, had he been admitted.

Complacent in his knowledge that he had been scrupulous and unstinting in the performance of his duty, William Bligh did not trouble himself unduly with the complaints of disgruntled petty officers and pardoned mutineers. As he noted, charges had not been made until lawyers got involved. In any case, the rules of his profession were as fixed and sure as if engraved in granite, and he had obeyed the rules. One imagines Bligh reading the *London Chronicle* or the *Times,* while Betsy fussed around him in his parlor, shaking his head over Professor Christian's ill-advised defense of his criminal brother. The implication that a mutiny had occurred because Fletcher Christian's sensibilities had been wounded over the charge of stolen coconuts would have been laughable, had so much death and suffering not resulted. Christian had, after all, been nearly twenty-five at the time of the mutiny. Bligh was grimly entertained by Morrison's account of Christian's preparations for departure on his raft.

" 'That Christian . . . intended to go onshore 10 leagues from the land on a fair Plank with two staves for Paddles with a roasted Pig' is too ridiculous," Bligh scribbled as part of his running commentary on the proceedings.

It took Bligh some time to appreciate how powerful, tenacious and far-reaching were the interests of the various parties who now had stakes in the *Bounty* saga. By the summer of 1794, publication of Edward's report was rumored to be near. That this was now being discussed in London outside naval circles is made clear by a diary entry of Joseph Farington, a member of the Royal Academy, a friend of Hallett's father and an inveterate gossip. After breakfasting one morning with a mutual friend of his and Bligh's, he confided that Captain Bligh was "fully prepared to answer any reflexions on his conduct which may be published by the friends of Christian," adding, in words that have a Bligh-like ring, that indeed Bligh "wishes it may come to that issue." The attacks on Bligh's character "are partly to be imputed to Heywood and his connexions, as at present that young man though pardoned cannot have any promotion."

While Edward's battle was being waged for the honor of his family's name, the Heywoods had more practical concerns. Peter had not after all been acquitted of the crime of mutiny; he had been found guilty and subsequently pardoned, an entirely different matter. And while he had so far enjoyed the eager patronage of so many of his relatives' naval connections, this was not the same thing as advancing to lieutenancy and a proper career.

"Doubts I find, subsist in respect to the fitness, if not legality of advancing Heywood under his particular circumstances," Lord Howe himself wrote during this same July to his friend Roger Curtis, the captain of the *Brunswick*.

In fact, Sir Roger was already at work on his friend's behalf and it was he who took the trouble to consult "an eminent lawyer" on this point. This authority noted that a court-martial was empowered to offer three types of judgment: discretionary, capital and the inability to serve again in the navy. The court, having in this case prescribed death, was not empowered to serve any other judgment—and to this sentence of death, His Majesty had extended his royal pardon.

"I should myself clearly conceive," the eminent lawyer had concluded, summarizing his argument, "that an offence attended with judgment of death, having been pardoned by his Majesty, the supposed offender is in this case, in the same situation as if no such judgment had ever been passed"—or indeed, as if no mutiny had ever happened.

The fact that Peter had been legally adjudged a mutineer was not the only complication in his bid for promotion. In addition to passing an examination, all candidates for lieutenant had to be at least nineteen years of age and have served a minimum of six years at sea, three of these as a midshipman. By the end of 1794, Peter had racked up less than two years' service since his pardon. Previous to the *Bounty*, he had served precisely eleven months, one week and five days at sea. This total fell wide of the necessary mark.

But here, too, a way was found to ensure that Peter stayed on track to achieve his promotion around this impasse. In early January 1795, navy examiners certified that Peter Heywood had served on the *Bounty* from the day of his embarkation, August 27, 1787, until the day his court-martial ended, September 18, 1792; from October 23, 1790—the day following Bligh's court-martial on the loss of the ship—young Peter was on record as having been promoted to midshipman. Thus Peter's *Bounty* experience, under this reckoning, rounded out a satisfying five years, three weeks and one day—a period that covered the loss of his ship, his life on Tahiti and his imprisonment on the *Pandora* and the *Hector*. By contrast, the *Bounty* service of James Morrison, who had received the identical pardon as Peter, was officially noted as having commenced on the day he joined the ship, and ended on April 28, 1789, the day of the mutiny; the notations "Run" and "Mutineer" appear next to Morrison's name. Peter's application for promotion was accompanied by attestations to his "Sobriety and Diligence" from Captains Pasley, Sir Andrew Snape Douglas and Cloberry Christian, the last Fletcher's relative. With this final, inconvenient hurdle overcome, Peter Heywood returned to what would be a respectable naval career. By contrast, nineteen months would pass between the return of the *Providence* in August 1793 and Captain Bligh's subsequent commission.

That Peter had been successfully promoted in the face of stiff odds warned Bligh that his enemies wielded very considerable power. In any case, he had by this time been made to take seriously the charges leveled against him. Despite Bligh's early skepticism, Edward had indeed published his report. This appeared toward the end of 1794, as an "Appendix" attached to a partial transcription of the court-martial proceedings, as prepared by Stephen Barney; the whole was entitled *Minutes of the Proceedings of the Court-Martial held at Portsmouth, August [sic] 12, 1792, on Ten Persons Charged with Mutiny on Board His Majesty's ship the Bounty: With an Appendix Containing a Full Account of the Real Causes and Circumstances of that Unhappy Transaction, the most material of which have hitherto been withheld from the Public.*

Barney's transcription included only the arguments for the prosecution, omitting all the arguments for the defense. Edward would later declare that he desired to publish the whole, but had not been able to obtain the Admiralty's permission. Whether this was true or not, the incomplete version ensured that the public did not see representations made by certain of the defendants that, although winning sympathetic support in the emotionally charged courtroom, might not have held up to more dispassionate scrutiny.

The sea of intrigue in which Bligh found himself entangled remains unfathomable. Heywoods and Christians and disgruntled petty officers, he knew, were gunning for him. But what was meant by Nessy's casual comment after the court-martial that sentencing might be delayed "on account of the Interest making for some of the prisoners"? Which prisoners, other than Peter? Was there something more than merely an anxious brother's goodwill behind Muspratt's ability to retain legal counsel? William Muspratt's family came from Bray and nearby Cookham; was it only coincidence that Cookham was the seat of Sir George Young, uncle of mutineer Edward Young, one of Fletcher Christian's inner circle? In this regard, what is to be made of a very curious provision in the will of

Sir George Young; how did it come to pass that one of the executors was Aaron Graham?

Joseph Banks remained Bligh's loyal protector. That Morrison's "Journal" was never, after all, brought forth in any published form was almost certainly due to Banks's discreet interference. But the appearance of Edward's "Appendix" forced Bligh into the open.

"The appendix endeavours to palliate the behaviour of Christian, and the Mutineers, and to criminate Captain Bligh," a review in the *British Critic* observed, "to which he will, without doubt, think it necessary to make reply."

This, with characteristic energy and irritation, Bligh did. His swift response was made to the world the following month, and consisted of a series of documents and affidavits, or as he entitled them a "List of Proofs," preceded by a statement noting, among other things, that although Edward Christian had cited the names of all participants in his inquiry, no single statement was ever attributed to a specific individual. "The mixing together the names of men, whose assertions merit very different degrees of credit, and blending their evidence into one mass" ensured, Bligh wrote, "the impossibility of tracing the author of any particular assertion." This was, however, not only good storytelling technique on Edward's part, but a clever lawyerly ploy to protect against libel. Bligh's uneven miscellany of proofs included such items as his standing orders at Tahiti regarding the regulation of trade, the deserters' letter of apology and contrition, the examination of all survivors of the mutiny by Dutch authorities in Batavia, and various notarized statements by some of the men Edward had already interviewed.

Less colorful than Edward's document, Bligh's response nonetheless had its own striking images. Christian had been drinking at least until midnight on the night before the mutiny, although he had to be up at four to take the morning watch; also revealed was the fact that throughout the voyage Christian had been indulged with the use of Bligh's private liquor cabinet. To the Dutch authorities, the boat survivors had testified (with Bligh absent) that they had "heard at the time several expressions and huzzas in the ship, which makes them believe that the mutineers are returned to Otaheite."

"Huzza for Otaheite!" Bligh had stated in his *Narrative* that this cheerful cry had been heard "frequently" from the ship as it sailed away. In his "Appendix," Edward had vehemently denied that these words had ever been uttered, just as he denied that Fletcher had a "favorite woman" ("if that was the case," a former shipmate from West Indies days dryly noted in a letter to Bligh that was included with the other attestations, "he must have been much altered since he was with you in the *Britannia;* he was then one of the most foolish young men I ever knew in regard to the sex"). For Edward to concede these small points would be to play to Bligh's claim that the mutiny had occurred because his men wanted to return to a life of sensual leisure; the picture Edward strove to depict was of his brother's tortured soul.

Of the supporting affidavits that Bligh attached, some carried more credibility than others: "I never knew Christian and Captain Bligh have any words particular"; "I never knew any thing that Christian intended to make a raft, or ever heard of it until the Mutineers arrived in the Pandora"; "I never knew any thing of Christian intending to make a raft, to quit the ship"; "I never heard, or told Mr. Edward Christian, about his brother's expression that 'he had been in hell for weeks past with you.'" Here, the stern and indignant presence of William Bligh leaning heavily over the shoulders of Joseph Coleman and John Smith, his faithful servant, was all too evident.

On the other hand, the novel facts and idiosyncratic language of the statements of Hallett and Lebogue bore the ring of unscripted truth—in particular, the latter's claim that Edward Christian had summoned him to ask "whether Captain Bligh did flog his people, and why he kept them at short allowance," and about his behavior on the *Providence.*

"Captain Bligh was not a person fond of flogging," Lebogue had answered, adding that "some of them deserved hanging, who had only a dozen." Hallett took strong exception to a "discovery" Edward had reported, that he and Hayward had been asleep at their watch when the mutiny broke out. It required some temerity to float this theory in the face of all the testimony given at the trial that both young gentlemen were excitedly tracking a shark at the time. On a more personal note, Hallett felt compelled to address, of all things, Edward's claim that Fletcher was a "fine scholar." This could not be, Hallett reported haughtily, "as he did not appear to have received any portion of classical education, and was ignorant of all but his native language."

Bligh's rebuttal was received with respectful acceptance in most public circles. The *British Critic* acknowledged that Bligh had replied to the "Appendix," as its reviewer suggested, "in the properest manner," through documents and testimonies. The follow-up concluded with some advice: "We cannot help thinking, that the friends of Christian will act the wisest part, in throwing as much as possible into oblivion, the transaction in which that young man acted so conspicuous, and so criminal a part."

Edward made one final public and very indignant rebuttal of Bligh's response, invoking the respectability of his committee, and lashing out against the *Bounty* men who had stood by their captain. Joseph Coleman, he now ventured, had the "appearance of a decent and honest man, but he is old and dull." Moreover, Edward allowed, his bluster running ahead of his reason and inadvertently shedding new, unflattering light on his committee's interviewing methods, "I never saw him but in the company of other persons belonging to the Bounty, who took the lead in conversation; but to their information he certainly in every instance assented by his silence." Edward Christian also took particular exception to Hallett's dismissal of his brother's education; Fletcher had been educated at St. Bees, in Cumberland, he felt compelled to retort, "where the young men of the best families in that country receive their education."

Bligh retired from the field with his considerable pride intact and the belief that he had successfully silenced the villainous wretches, and it was true that news of the *Bounty* would be muted and very sporadic for the next twenty years. But the damage done to him in naval circles would prove irreparable. While Bligh had defended himself in crisp, logical naval fashion, he failed to comprehend that he was doing battle with a force more formidable and unassailable than any enemy he would meet at sea—the power of a good story. In a great seafaring nation, now beset

by revolution and the travails of war, this fantastic tale of escape to paradise at the far end of the world had the allure of something epic. And at
the very dawn of the Romantic age, now in the process of being invented
by men like William Wordsworth and his friend Coleridge, Edward
Christian had elicited the perfect Romantic hero—the tortured master's
mate, his long hair loose, his shirt collar open, he with his gentlemanly
pedigree and almost mythic name: Fletcher Christian.

Whatever else might be implied from William Wordsworth's striking
association with so many key parties, this much is secure: the story of
the *Bounty* was to enjoy a healthy run through the annals of Romantic
poetry. Wordsworth himself borrowed from it in his verse tragedy *The
Borderers*, published in 1795, which describes how the crew of a ship
conspired to leave their despised captain without food or water on a remote island:

Marmaduke   *A man by men cast off,*
                    Left without burial! nay, not dead nor dying,
                    But standing, walking, stretching forth his arms,
                    In all things like ourselves, but in the agony
                    With which he called for mercy; and—even so—
                    He was forsaken?
Oswald   *There is a power in sounds:*
                    The cries he uttered might have stopped the boat
                    That bore us through the water—
                    . . . Some scoffed at him with hellish mockery,
                    And laughed so loud it seemed that the smooth sea
                    Did from some distant region echo us.

Less overt was the trace of the *Bounty* saga in another, majestic work
of this time. At some point between December 1795 and January 1796,
Wordsworth's bosom friend Samuel Taylor Coleridge made a simple entry in his notebook of ideas for future essays and poems: "Adventures of
CHRISTIAN the Mutineer." No great poem Coleridge ever wrote was
woven from less than a hundred strands of inspiration; nonetheless, em-
bedded amid much else (including images from Cook's voyages), one
can discern in the story of the haunted Ancient Mariner, doomed to wan-

der the ocean for having committed a single crime, the shadow of
Fletcher Christian:

> *Alone, alone all all alone,*
> *Alone on the wide wide Sea;*
> *And Christ would take no pity on*
> *My soul in agony.*

("I am in hell, I am in hell . . .")

It was Lieutenant Bligh's ill luck to have his own great adventure coin-
cide exactly with the dawn of this new era, which saw devotion to a code
of duty and established authority as less honorable than the celebration
of individual passions and liberty. Coleridge's Ancient Mariner was a
crude forerunner of the full-blown Romantic hero to be glamorized by
Byron; but Fletcher Christian was the forerunner of them all. And in the
clumsy, erratic testimonies of his "Appendix," Edward Christian had unleashed the most irresistible elements of the story now known as "the
Mutiny on the *Bounty*."

LATITUDE 25° S,
LONGITUDE 130° W

The revolutionary movement that led to the decapitation of the French King evolved by 1804 to crown a French emperor; and for England, the war with France that began in early 1793 was to continue, with little respite, for twenty-two years. On land, Napoleon's armies had consumed whole countries, but Britain still retained command of the sea and in October 1805 won a historic victory at the battle of Trafalgar. Under the command of Lord Nelson, the British defeated the combined French and Spanish fleets—but lost Nelson, who had died on his ship thanking God he had done his duty. The navy was now perpetually engaged in a strategy of blockade and skirmish with few further major battles. On the bright side of things, there were no more officers on half pay. Amid this grave turmoil the affair of the *Bounty,* a small transport vessel in the Pacific, was no longer a matter of consequence. In any case, the navy had undergone important reforms and change, and events of the 1780s belonged to a bygone age.

The Pacific had been "opened." The penal colony at Port Jackson was succeeding, there was missionary activity in the islands, and a steady if still sparse traffic of mostly American whalers and sealers patrolled these seas. And it was an American sealer, the *Topaz,* that in February 1808, cruising at latitude 25° 04' south, longitude 130° 06' west, spied land where no land was indicated on the charts.

Over the next hours, as the *Topaz,* under the command of Captain Mayhew Folger, drew closer, the island was seen to be about two miles long and a mile wide, green and forested, with precipitous, dangerous cliffs that admitted no anchorage—"iron bound," as it would later be described. From its latitude, Captain Folger guessed this must be Pitcairn's Island, discovered forty years ago by the British sloop *Swallow,* Captain Philip Carteret, but wrongly laid down on all sea charts as lying nearly 180 miles farther west. Folger had come to a place, then, that was literally off the map.

Sailing through the night, the ship was off Pitcairn by the early hours of the morning. At daylight, Folger joined a boat party to go ashore in search of seals, wood and water. Approaching the plunging cliffs, Folger and his men were startled to see smoke drifting lazily from the trees in the fresh dawn light.

"I was very much Surprised," Folger wrote in his log. The island had been represented by Carteret as being "destitute of Inhabitants." Folger had thought he was at least eight hundred miles from the nearest inhabited land.

Suddenly, skimming toward them through heavy surf, came a double canoe, expertly paddled by three young men. And to their utter amazement, Folger's party heard themselves hailed in English by the three dark-skinned men, asking for the captain of the ship.

Turning to his crew, Mayhew asked them who they thought the men could be.

"Curse them, they must be Spaniards," his mate had replied, judging from the young men's tawny good looks. The canoe and the boat now bobbed beside each other and it was seen that the three friendly strangers had brought a hog, fruit and coconuts as presents for their visitors, Tahitian fashion.

"Where are you from?" one of the young men asked. Folger, believing the men would know little about America, answered, "England."

"Don't you know my father?" asked another islander, who appeared to be in his late teens. "He is an Englishman." Folger did not know his father, and the youth tried again. "Did you ever know Captain Bligh?" he asked, adding that "his father had sailed with him." And thus it dawned on Folger that he had solved the mystery of what had become of Fletcher Christian and the *Bounty*.

Ferried by the adroit canoeists through the violent surf that guarded the island, Folger arrived onshore. He was met by the island's small colony of thirty-five inhabitants of mostly women, youths and children—the widows and offspring of the *Bounty* mutineers. Ranging from one week to some eighteen years of age, the *Bounty* children were a handsome people, the young men standing over six feet, men and women alike strong-limbed and athletic—they not infrequently swam around the island for pleasure and exercise, they said. Dark-haired, with perfect white teeth and tawny skin, they stood nearly naked, the men dressed only in loincloths and straw hats, the young women with long skirts and shawls of bark cloth draped over their shoulders. They had plenty of old clothes from the *Bounty*, as it turned out, but preferred not to wear them. The oldest of the young men, a youth of eighteen, with a recognizably English face under his dark tan and long, plaited hair, was Fletcher Christian's son, Thursday October Christian. His father had named him for the day and month of the child's birth, much as another mutineer had tattooed himself, nearly twenty years before, with the date of his arrival and rebirth on Tahiti.

Reluctantly, tentatively, and much against the misgivings of his suspicious wife, the island patriarch came out to meet with Folger. Alexander Smith, former able seaman, had been about twenty-three when the *Bounty* sailed. Short and stocky, at five foot five, and badly scarred by smallpox, he had been, as Bligh reported, "very much tatowed on his Body, Legs, Arms & feet" while at Tahiti. Smith was in his midforties but looked much older, his brown hair mixed with white and hanging in long strands from his bald pate. He was the sole surviving mutineer.

Smith's principal concern at this first meeting with the outside world, and the source of his wife's anxiety, was that a King's ship might carry him away to serve justice in England. Folger had caught wind of this fear, and revised his own introduction, disclosing to his three young guides that he was not after all from England but from America.

"Where is America?" they had asked, and then settled among themselves that it was "some Irish place." Now, reassured by Folger personally on this count, Alexander Smith relaxed and became more expansive.

"Old England forever!" the mutineer had exclaimed, on learning of the great naval victories won by Lords Howe and Nelson.

For his part, Folger does not seem to have been particularly inquisitive about the events on the *Bounty.* Smith had kept "a regular Journal, which had become very voluminous," from which he invited Folger to copy any extracts he chose—an offer Folger declined in light of the fact that he was staying "only five hours." The information Folger did pick up was somewhat murky, in part because he left no account of how it was obtained: Had Smith volunteered information, or had Folger asked leading questions, based upon what he knew of this by now famous story?

The mutiny, said Smith, looking back to those few fraught hours almost two decades ago, "originated with Lieutenant Christian, who at the time was Officer of the Watch," and its cause was the "overbearing and tyrannical Conduct of the Captain." Alexander Smith had been fast asleep in his hammock when it broke out and on learning of the events had come on deck bewildered and disoriented. "Arms were put into his hands."

("I saw Chas. Churchill, Isaac Martin, Alexr. Smith, Jn. Sumner, Matthew Quintell, come armed with Musquets and bayonets, loading as they Came Aft," Charles Norman had testified.)

After leaving sixteen men and cutting the ship's cable in the night at Tahiti, Christian steered the *Bounty* for a group of islands said to have been discovered by the Spanish. When no such islands were found, the company had struck out for Pitcairn's, which they had at last hit upon despite its wrong position on the charts. Running the *Bounty* aground on the island's rocky, treacherous shore, they had then broken up the ship that had carried them on so many adventures.

The little band of mutineers had forged a successful settlement, with each Englishman building his own thatched house and tending his own garden, together with his wife. Good, rich soil and an abundance of fruit, coconut, fish and wild birds made it possible to build new lives from scratch. The breadfruit tree was found in abundance.

The colony had prospered, although two of the mutineers died in the first two years, one of "sickness," one by jumping off the towering rocks in a fit of insanity. Four or five years later, six of the seven remaining mutineers, including Fletcher Christian, were killed in the night by their "Otaheite servants," who had risen against them. Only Alexander Smith had been left alive, although badly wounded. The widows of the mutineers then in turn killed their Tahitian kinsmen in revenge, and so Smith had been left with all the women, and their various offspring.

This much came from Smith alone. As Captain Folger noted, it was peculiar, but all the children spoke only English and all the Tahitian widows only Tahitian. It was, then, obviously not possible to interview the women who had been eyewitnesses, if not participants, in the events Smith so dispassionately described.

Before they parted, Smith gave Folger two generous and significant gifts: the *Bounty*'s Kendall chronometer and her azimuth compass, along with provisions and a length of mulberry bark cloth. Folger for his part presented Smith with a silk handkerchief, with which the mutineer seemed much pleased. Folger then departed, making his way back to the *Topaz* through the high, dangerous surf that protected the island from landfall, and continued on his sealing voyage.

Before leaving Pitcairn's, Folger asked Alexander Smith if he objected to having an account of his discovery published "in the papers," and Smith said no—"he did not care for all the Navy of England cou'd never find him." But in fact the story of the *Bounty* mutineers, which had evoked so much attention back in the old days, now received surprisingly little comment. Folger and his first mate made a report to a British lieutenant, Fitzmaurice, in Valparaíso, who in turn reported the discovery to his admiral, Sir William Sidney Smith, who passed the information on to the Admiralty.

In this roundabout manner, the news reached England, eventually prompting mention in the London press. In early 1810, the *Quarterly Review* printed the whole of Fitzmaurice's report, although not as an item of interest in itself, but only as a brief aside within a longer, unrelated article. "If this interesting relation rested solely on the faith that is due to Americans, with whom, we say it with regret, truth is not always considered as a moral obligation, we should hesitate in giving it this publicity," the *Review* reported frostily to its Tory readers. The editors, however, had checked their facts, and independently ascertained that Alexander Smith did indeed appear on the *Bounty* muster, and it also appeared that "the *Bounty* was actually supplied with a time-piece made by Kendall."

In his report Lieutenant Fitzmaurice duly recorded Folger's observation that the mutineers' offspring all spoke English and had been educated "in a religious and moral way." His report also made mention of a curious fact: the second mate of the *Topaz* asserted to him that "Christian the ringleader became insane shortly after their arrival on the island, and threw himself off the rocks into the sea." Alexander Smith had of course told Folger that Christian had been killed in the uprising of the Otaheite "servants." This discrepancy was reported without comment.

More unexpected than the lukewarm reception of Folger's news in the popular press was the apparent total lack of interest on the part of the Admiralty. Perhaps the war with France was too great a distraction, or the Pacific was simply too far away, or the fact that Americans had broken the story may have rendered it unappealing; perhaps the *Bounty* was a story that nobody in the Admiralty particularly wished to see revived.

Whatever the reasons, the silence from the Admiralty was so profound that when six years later, in 1814, two British naval ships also chanced upon Pitcairn, they were completely ignorant of the events relating to the *Topaz*. Captain Sir Thomas Staines of the *Briton* accompanied by the *Tagus* under Captain Philip Pipon, coming from the Marquesas Islands, "fell in with an island where none is laid down in the Admiralty, or other charts"; evidently, the Admiralty had not seen fit to revise its sea maps.

As the two ships approached the picturesque island, with its forested heights and severe crags, they, like Folger, were surprised to see evidence of habitation in the form of striking huts and houses "more neatly constructed than those on the Marquesas islands" and tidy plantations. When the ships were about two miles from shore, according to Pipon, "some natives were observed bringing down their canoes on their shoulders, dashing through the heavy surf" toward the ships. Like Folger and his crew, Captains Staines and Pipon were astonished when one of the natives hailed them in English with the cry "Won't you heave us a rope, now?"

The tall, young man of some twenty-four years who first climbed on board was Thursday October Christian; his companion, also a fine young man of about eighteen, was George Young, son of Edward Young who had been, with Christian, one of the only two officers among the nine Pitcairn mutineers. Evidently, at this second visit from their fathers' world, the young men were bolder and willingly accepted an invitation to join the astonished company for a meal. The company's astonishment was increased when one of the loincloth-clad visitors suddenly rose from the table "and placing his hands together in a posture of devotion, distinctly repeated, and in a pleasing tone and manner, 'For what we are going to receive, the Lord make us truly thankful.'"

With these words—or rather the report of these words that would eventually be read with avid and approving interest in England—the Pitcairn Islanders at last strode onto the stage of history. With the assistance of their young guides, Captains Staines and Pipon made their way toward the ironbound shore, where a murderous surf pounded the cliff face. Scrambling ashore with "difficulty and a good wetting," they were led from the rocky beach up a steep, zigzagging trail that passed beneath trees of coconut and breadfruit to the island's settlement. Here, on a small plateau stood a square of neat houses laid out around a lawn on which chickens ran, and which bore the appearance, in the eyes of the wistful Englishmen, of a village green. Surveying these relics of the mutineers' domestic history, the two captains were much impressed by the neat arrangement of the "village" and its surpassing cleanliness, all betraying the "labour & ingenuity of European hands." Alexander Smith's house stood at one end of the square, facing that of Thursday October Christian, the two symbolizing the poles of authority around which the community revolved. This trim village also enjoyed a grand lookout over the Pacific, a point from which any chance ship might be observed.

At the settlement the captains were met by the daughter of Alexander Smith, "arrayed in Nature's simple garb, and wholly unadorned," but, as Pipon later told his shipmates, "she was Beauty's self and, needed not the aid of ornament." This cautious beauty had been sent out as a spy to find out what might have brought the English ships. On being reassured that the men came alone and did not intend to apprehend her father, she led them to the patriarch himself. Thus Smith at last appeared, leading his wife, a very old, blind Tahitian woman, and introduced himself to the English captains as "John Adams." This reversion to what was in fact his true, christened name was one of the many layers of truth that would be peeled away from Smith/Adams's story over the coming years, as ship after ship came, went and made report to the outside world. Adams took the alias of Smith on joining the *Bounty*, enticed, one suspects, by the fact that her destination was as far from England as it was possible to travel; he may have been a deserter from another ship, or perhaps his reasons for wishing to escape detection were more personal.

Captain Sir Thomas Staines, in his forties and with one arm lost in battle, and his colleague Captain Philip Pipon found much to admire as they strolled around the settlement. There was the island's own rich bounty, the coconuts, wild birds and fruit, as well as the produce garnered by the residents' industry in their carefully tended fields. The captains admired the unconcealed joy the "poor people manifested, on seeing those whom they were pleased to consider their countrymen." In Fletcher Christian's son they had been happy "to trace in his benevolent countenance, all the features of an honest English face. . . . He is of course of brown cast, not however, with that mixture of red, so disgusting in the wild Indians," Pipon recorded. Other Englishmen, as Pipon hardly needed reminding, had not found the Tahitian tincture so offputting. Thursday October was now married "to a Woman much older than himself"; in fact, he had married Edward Young's widow, a woman of his own mother's generation.

Above all else, the Englishmen admired Pitcairn's young women— their "bashfulness that would do honour to the most virtuous nation," their tall, robust forms, their regular, ivory teeth and most of all "the upper part" of their bodies, so frequently displayed whenever they laid aside the shawls that formed their only upper dress.

"[I]t is not possible to behold finer forms," Pipon observed delightedly. Venerable John Adams, the island patriarch, had complemented the young women's native modesty by instilling in them "a proper sense of religion and morality." According to Adams, since Christian's death, "there had not been a single instance of any young woman proving unchaste; nor any attempt at seduction on the part of the men." To the English captains wandering beneath the luxuriant trees among the bare-breasted virgins, it seemed they had entered a kind of paradise—a rich Eden with its own Adam, innocent of civilized wiles. Pitcairn had many of the attractions of Tahiti, enhanced by a recognizably English decency, the *Book of Common Prayer* and blushing modesty. Here, in short, a decent man might feel no shame in gawking at the island's naked girls.

The Englishmen's admiration increased when on entering the houses they found feather beds on proper bedsteads, tables, chests all with neat cloth coverings. There were shutters at night, but no locks upon the doors, as the notion of theft did not exist among the pious colonists. In lieu of candles, a certain oily nut was burned for light. John Adams was not bashful about letting his visitors view his library, which "consisted of the books that belonged to Admiral Bligh." Bligh had written his name on the title page of every volume, beneath which Fletcher Christian had inscribed his own signature.

Adams was assured by the captains that the authorities in England were "perfectly ignorant of his existence," and indeed it was he who informed them of the visit of the *Topaz*. Relaxing in his library, the old mutineer dropped his guard somewhat and chatted about the colony's early history. His voluminous journal turned out to be a kind of landsman's log more than a personal diary, containing only brief notations of each day's principal events. From this, Staines and Pipon learned that one other ship had approached Pitcairn before the *Topaz*, in 1795. Adams elaborated on this event and in doing so contradicted his journal: three ships had arrived, he said, one in December 1795, one shortly after, and later still a third, which had come close enough to the island to see them and their houses. In later reports, he would say that one of these ships had actually sent a boat ashore, for the islanders had afterward seen evidence of its landing.

The *Bounty* had arrived at Pitcairn on January 15, 1790, with the nine mutineers, eleven Otaheite women, one child, and six "black men," by which was meant Otaheite men; the insistence on the men only being "black" while the women were "Otaheitian" is in itself striking. Despite the error of the island's position on all the *Bounty*'s charts, Christian himself was certain they had found Pitcairn's. The mutineers drove the ship into a creek against the spray-beaten cliffs, unloaded all they could carry, and then set her on fire. Adams's account of this point of no return, the climactic and symbolic firing of the *Bounty,* would change over the years with different tellings. For now, to the English captains, he claimed that it was Fletcher Christian who had been responsible.

Christian himself was never the same after the mutiny. He became, Adams said, sullen and morose and "having, by many acts of cruelty and inhumanity, brought on himself the hatred and detestation of his companions, he was shot by a black man whilst digging in his field, and almost instantly expired." This had taken place less than a year after they were on the island. The black man was himself later assassinated, so justice had been served. Christian's behavior had so alienated his people from him that divisive parties had formed, with feelings running very high and each seeking occasion to put the other to death. One act in particular had incurred the hatred of the black men: when Fletcher Christian's wife died, he had then seized upon one of their wives, which had "exasperated them to a degree of madness."

As for old John Adams, the English captains were in agreement that on him the "welfare of the colony entirely depends." It was he who had taught the Pitcairn Islanders the Lord's Prayer and the Creed. Other, somewhat contradictory information was given by the young men who had first romped through the treacherous surf to greet the ships. Their religion had been learned by Fletcher Christian's order, they had reported, and "he likewise caused a prayer to be said every day at noon."

"And what is the prayer?" the young men were asked.

"It is 'I will arise and go to my Father, and say unto him, Father, I have sinned against Heaven, and before thee, and am no more worthy of being called thy son.'"

Before Staines and Pipon left the island they asked Adams if he would wish to see his native land again, and to their surprise he said he would. Alone with the captains in his house when this bold ploy was discussed, Adams turned to summon his family for a consultation. Suddenly, it seemed the entire community was gathered outside his door.

"Oh, do not, Sir, take from me my father: do not take away my best—my dearest friend," Adams's daughter had implored the captains, before breaking down entirely. The whole company was soon in tears. Adams's daughter in particular was lovely in her tears, "for each seemed to add an additional charm." With much feeling, Staines and Pipon assured their hosts that they had no intention to take the old man from his flock. And should he ever return to England, perhaps "his unremitting attention to the government and morals of this little colony" might win him his sovereign's pardon.

With regrets and brimming hearts, the captains bade farewell to the picturesque colony, and to the former able seaman of His Majesty's service. Both Staines and Pipon wrote accounts of their remarkable discovery, as did their lieutenant of marines, John Shillibeer, who had remained on the ship. Following their return to England, a lengthy story appeared in the *Naval Chronicle*. Consisting of Captain Staines's report filed from Valparaíso and largely paraphrasing Pipon's more personal account, the editors of the *Chronicle* made discreet editorial cuts in the interest of good taste. Pipon's observation that Christian's death "[t]hus terminated the miserable existence of this deluded young man, whose connexions in Westmoreland were extremely respectable" was subtly revised to read simply that Christian was a man who "was neither deficient in talent, energy, nor connexions, and who might have risen in the service, and become an ornament to his profession."

A similar toning down was effected by the exclusion of a striking and key paragraph in which Pipon had described Christian's actions on the death of his wife: "Christian's wife had paid the debt of nature, & as we have every reason to suppose sensuality & a passion for the females of Otaheite chiefly instigated him to the rash step he had taken, so it is readily to be believed he would not live long on the island without a female companion." The attachments of the mutineers to the women of Otaheite was of course the cause Bligh had ascribed to the mutiny.

The editors of the *Chronicle* also took the opportunity to impress an important point upon their readers: Adams, that venerable and sage old patriarch, would one day also pay the debt of nature, and it was "exceedingly desirable, that the British nation should provide for such an event, by sending out, not an ignorant and idle missionary, but some zealous and intelligent instructor." For on Pitcairn's Island "there are better materials to work upon than missionaries have yet been so fortunate as to meet with"—namely, men and women of English blood.

This time, the discovery—or rediscovery—of Pitcairn and the fate of the *Bounty* mutineers incited wide interest. As with the story of the mutiny itself, back in 1790, this new chapter in the *Bounty* saga was quickly exploited in the theater. *Pitcairn's Island, "A new Melo Dramatic Ballet of Action,"* opened in Drury Lane in April 1816; this distinguished theater had been managed for several seasons by the multitalented Aaron Graham.

Snuggled expectantly in the grand auditorium, the London audience watched as the curtain rose to reveal the picturesque colony of maids and youths against the painted Pacific scenery. Entering from offstage and sporting a remarkable, long beard, Fletcher Christian suddenly appeared behind the footlights. The script describes his entrance: "he extends his arms in giving them a general Benediction." Two ships appear:

"With what Terror do I recognize the Ensigns of my Country," Christian exclaims. As the English crew approach, dressed as captains and jolly tars, Christian departs into hiding, admonishing his people to show the visitors "the graves of the departed and let them think that my family lie buried there with my companions." There is playful interaction between the sailors and the handsome children of the mutineers, and a midshipman chats up a native daughter. Later Christian reappears, disguised and pretending to be John Adams, to preside over various sporting games between his people and the sailors. Finally, the visitors return to their boats as tearful women cling to them, waving flowers and with hearty cries of "when we meet again!"

The single most interesting detail of this "spectacle" is of course that its writer understood that the hero of this story, whether in fact dead or alive, must be Fletcher Christian. John Adams, venerable patriarch and survivor though he may have been, did not possess the drawing power of the arch-mutineer. This very public fantasy that Fletcher Christian was alive and ruling an island kingdom did not appear to raise eyebrows in any circles.

Following this new account, British ships became not infrequent visitors to the remote island colony. Sir William Sidney Smith, who had been in command of the South American station at the time Captain Folger made his report, now learning of plans to "send some succour to the semi british colony" and feeling it his duty as an Englishman to contribute to the moral and intellectual improvement of his countrymen, begged the Admiralty to forward the islanders a gift. His gift was "the *academic edition*," as he emphasized, of *Robinson Crusoe*, with its elaborate and instructive notes, which would doubtless be of value to these ingenious islanders—one can imagine the face of Alexander Smith, now John Adams, as he cautiously handled the unexpected volume.

One more ship, the American whaler *Sultan*, under Captain C. Reynolds, in 1817, was to discover the island for herself, without prior knowledge of its history. The *Sultan* was also the first ship that Adams himself was induced to board. Apparently "elated" to feel the unsteady motion of a deck again beneath his feet, the old mutineer had pulled at the rigging and sung songs, to the appreciation of the Yankee crew. The *Sultan* carried away much of importance. Adams presented Captain Reynolds with "an old spy glass, and two blank books which belonged to the *Bounty*," doubtless the spoils of Captain Bligh's possessions. As it turned out, one of the notebooks was not entirely blank, for it contained Adams's touching efforts at writing his own biography: "I was Born at Stanford Hill in the parrish of St. John Hackney, Middellsex of poor But honast parrents My farther Was Drouned in the Theames thearfore he left Me and 3 More poore Orfing."

One of these other poor orphans was Adams's brother Jonathan who, while his brother had been reinventing himself as a Pacific island patriarch, was himself more prosaically employed as a fireman of the London Assurance Company. In time, through the medium of visiting ships and the friendly assistance of the occasional fully literate visitor, the two brothers were able to enjoy an intermittent correspondence:

> Pitcairn's Island, March 3, 1819
>
> Dear Brother,
>
> . . . it gives me much pleasure to hear that you are in health . . . hope with the blessings of Providence you will continue so, and likewise that your worldly circumstances will be improved: but we must leave all to the all-wise disposer of events. As to my coming to England, that is not much to be expected. . . .

As the years passed, a visit to the Pitcairn Island community became a kind of obligatory port of call for Pacific-going ships anywhere in the vicinity, which dropped off clothes, farm implements, fishing hooks, bedding and improving texts donated by missionary groups or other well-wishers. For as long as Adams was alive, a meeting with the "patriarch"—as he was invariably called, despite being only in his fifties—became an equally obligatory component of the pilgrimage. Always the early history of the community, if not the events of the mutiny, was discussed, and as the years passed each ship departed bearing with it some new, often contradictory fact or detail: the massacre of the white men had not happened in a single night, but over several years, with McCoy and Quintal escaping to the woods, while Adams and Edward Young lived in the village with the women. Christian's wife had not died, but was in fact still alive, although there is no evidence that a single visitor solicited her reminiscences. It was Edward Young who had taught Adams to read and write; Young, who was half West Indian and half English, appears to have been the only mutineer to have maintained good relations with the Tahitian "blacks": Young had died of asthma in 1800, and had not been killed. As for Christian, he variously committed suicide, went insane, was killed by the blacks who shot him in the back while he was tilling his yam field. In this last account, his final words, on falling in his field, had been "Oh dear." On the other hand, Captain Folger himself was reported to have stated in some private correspondence that Adams had reassured him that Christian "became sick and died a *natural death*."

<hr>

The visit of one ship in particular produced especially important narratives. In 1825, the *Blossom* under Captain Frederick Beechey enjoyed a lengthy sojourn off the island—sixteen days, as opposed to the usual half-day tour. The *Blossom* was by most accounts the sixteenth ship to visit Pitcairn (counting the *Tagus* and the *Briton* as a single visit). By this time Adams was confident that he would never be carried away, that indeed it increasingly seemed that in the eyes of the English authorities justice had been served, and the books closed on the *Bounty*. Adams was now one of only six remaining of the original party that had walked off the *Bounty*—although again it does not appear that Beechey interviewed any of the five surviving women. This visit had been looked forward to with much anticipation and fanciful speculation by the *Blossom*'s crew; as the first lieutenant allowed, there were some who looked forward to finding in Adams "Fletcher Christian the Master's Mate." Evidently, the "Melo Dramatic Ballet" had picked up on a wishful, popular theory.

According to Beechey, Adams had achieved "considerable corpulency." Beechey's sure eye caught a number of telling details. The patriarch had retained his sailor's rolling gait and wore a low-crowned hat, which he instinctively doffed and held in his hand, "smoothing down his bald forehead whenever he was addressed by the officers." The old mutineer had never surrendered his British loyalties—it was he and he alone who had instilled in the young colonists the belief that they were servants of King George—and this in turn gave Captain Beechey of His Majesty's Navy an advantage over his American counterparts when it came to an interview. Beechey was also wise enough to avail himself of a previously underexamined source of information—the diary of Edward Young, now dead these twenty-five years.

Although a number of the *Blossom*'s officers were to go ashore to explore the island, Beechey's principal interview with Adams took place in the privacy of his own cabin, with only his clerk in attendance to take notes. Beechey ensured that on this occasion at least Adams's story would be professionally recorded and unfolded at leisure, without the distraction of the twelve eager young men who had accompanied him excitedly to the ship and were now entertaining the officers below. Yet, despite these precautions, it was the opinion of one officer, Lieutenant Edward Belcher, that Beechey "did not get as accurate an account" as he and other of the officers were to come by later, when Adams returned to the ship as a "Guest in the Gun Room." Additionally, Beechey's published report of this historic interview, as will be seen, displayed some tactful editing. It also incorporated some "additional facts" derived, as he claimed, from other inhabitants, but in some cases betraying his own prior understanding of the story.

According to Adams, the falling-out between Bligh and Christian had begun at the Cape, where Christian came "under some obligations to him of a pecuniary nature, of which Bligh frequently reminded him when any difference arose." Bligh's relations with his officers had suffered throughout the voyage—this much had been clear from Bligh's own log, although Master John Fryer and Acting Lieutenant Fletcher Christian were the only two men singled out by name, in Adams's recollection, as objects of Bligh's criticism. But, Adams told Beechey, "whatever might have been the feelings of the officers, there was no real discontent among the crew; much less was there any idea of offering violence to their commander."

Sometime before the by now infamous coconut incident, Christian, smarting under Bligh's nagging, had "in a moment of excitation told his commander that sooner or later a day of reckoning would arrive." So at least John Adams in hindsight recalled those events of thirty-six years ago. Following the blowup over the coconuts, Christian declined Bligh's invitation to dinner. It was now the night of April 28, 1789, "one of those beautiful nights which characterize the tropical regions, when the mildness of the air and the stillness of nature dispose the mind to reflection": Were these the words of seaman Adams, or of the reflective Captain Beechey? In any event, it was on this still, limpid night that Christian planned his escape from Bligh's constant tongue-lashings. "New connexions" had been formed at Otaheite (Beechey had earlier apologized to his readers for spelling Tahiti in the "old" way), making him receptive to "ideas which the situation of the ship and the serenity of the moment particularly favoured"; again, one catches the echo of Beechey's editorializing.

This had been the moment when Christian had conceived his mad plan to float away on a raft—a plan "strange as it must appear," Beechey could not help adding, "for a young officer to adopt, who was fairly advanced in an honorable profession." In this case, Beechey's bluff aside reveals that the instinctive reaction of a career officer to the events described was incomprehension. Nothing Adams had related—of Bligh's conduct or anything else—apparently explained Christian's conduct to Beechey. Why, the master's mate was well advanced in his career! What business had he with rafts and such?! This voyage would soon blow over—so it would seem, if one may editorialize on Beechey, that he had reasoned.

Now came the fateful intervention of Christian's Iago, the voice in his ear at this moment of mortal weakness in the predawn hours.

"Take the ship." By all accounts—from Adams, from the men Edward Christian interviewed, on every occasion this event was described—this speaker was George Stewart. Stewart, as was by this time well-known, was passionately attached to his "Peggy," the woman he had left behind on Otaheite; his objective, at least, for wishing to return required little speculation. In Beechey's published narrative, Stewart is identified as "a young officer, who afterwards perished in the Pandora." In his working manuscript, however, Beechey named him as "Stewart." The reason for this slight revision—as much else about the Blossom's visit—would shortly be revealed.

Stirred by Stewart's words, Christian now relieved the officer on duty, Peckover, and assumed charge of the morning watch. Turning to Quintal, "the only one of the seamen, who Adams said, had formed any serious [female] attachment at Otaheite," Christian sounded him out about taking the ship. Unexpectedly, Quintal, demurred, saying "he thought it a dangerous attempt, and declined taking a part." Annoyed with the rebuff, Christian dramatically opened his jacket to reveal "a hand lead slung to his neck, adding that would soon carry him out of reach"; this detail was reported by Beechey's officers. It was, then, do or die. "What, are you afraid?" Christian taunted Quintal, urging him to consider that "success would restore them all to the happy island, and the connexions they had left behind." But still Quintal refused, telling Christian that he had better sound out someone else. That someone else was Isaac Martin, who slapping his thigh, declared, "By God, he was for it; it was the very thing."

With this small momentum, Christian went to every man of his watch, working them over to him; then the "news soon spread like wildfire through the crew." To judge by his earlier tactics with Quintal, Christian's argument to the crew would seem to have been that they could all return to "the happy island." As a footnote to his narrative, almost an afterthought, Adams allowed to Beechey that in his opinion the reason "the majority of the Crew yielded so easily to the persuasions of Christian was, that the Captain stinted them in their allowance, and that during the greater part of the time the Ship was lying at Otaheite no Ships Provisions of any kind was served out and the Men were obliged to their own recourses to get a meal, except that when Hogs were received on board, after the Meat was cut from the bones, they were served out to the Crew. If a Man was detected bringing a yam or any thing else in the Ship for his own use it was taken from him and he was punished."

Adams's complaint echoed that of James Morrison, who had also been unmoved by Bligh's directive that all food that came on board was to be considered common stock, and that trade was to be strictly regulated by a designated officer (Peckover) to ensure an orderly market. The hog meat that had been cut from the bones was for the salt pork that, as Bligh had noted with enormous satisfaction, filled his puncheons in readiness for the long voyage home. Bligh was very proud of the fact that, like Cook, he and his men had lived off the land during this sojourn, both eating incalculably better food than at any time in the voyage—if not in their lives—and safeguarding the precious ship stock for the months ahead.

To the men excitedly gathered on deck on the fine, calm night of April 28, however, pumped with the adrenaline of new and outrageous opportunity, the subtleties of Lieutenant Bligh's ship "economy" were undoubtedly not discussed. Ahead lay travail and hardship and the certainty of being nagged and harangued through the Endeavour Strait—as the *Providence* voyage would show, navigation of the strait was hard work. Behind lay female "connexions" and the happy island of plenty.

Adams, lying peacefully asleep in his hammock, was at this point awokened. At first he declined to participate, as he said, but seeing "Christian handing the arms out of the Arm Chest and many of my friends employed thought I might as well make one of them." Adams had been flogged with twelve lashes in Tahiti for allowing the rudder gudgeon to be stolen, a fact that may or may not have been of significance. Many men who had taken up arms innocently in the belief that they were to resist an attack by natives "now laid them down again." Lieutenant Belcher, drawing on his gun-room interview, made an important observation: the actions of these briefly armed loyalists showed "the influence Christian possessed as they would not resist him." Christian's watch had included the gunner's mate John Mills, Thomas Burkett and Thomas Ellison, as well as loyalists Charles Norman, Thomas Hayward and John Hallett.

Armed and full of fury, Christian went down with his party to Bligh's cabin, "the door of which was always open." Bligh was seized and rudely treated.

"I heard the Master at Arms strike him with the flat of the Cutlass," Adams reported; but as the canny Lieutenant Belcher observed, it was more likely that this strike had been seen by Adams, not heard.

"And you too Smith against me," Bligh said, standing bound by the binnacle and addressing Adams by his *Bounty* alias. "I went with the rest," Adams replied to his captain.

Some ten leagues from Tofua, the overcrowded launch in tow behind the ship had been cast off, "and immediately 'Huzza for Otaheite!' echoed throughout the Bounty."

The officers of the *Blossom* later made strenuous explorations of Pitcairn, traveling farther off the beaten track than ship companies before them. The strength and agility of the island's youths as they ran and leaped along the undulating mountain trails were much admired: of George Young and Edward Quintal, the grown sons of the mutineers, it was claimed that each had on his own "carried, at one time, without inconvenience, a kedge anchor, two sledge hammers, and an armourer's anvil, amounting to upwards of six hundred weight." Lieutenant Belcher, "who was admitted to be the most active among the officers on board," above all in his own estimation, was soon engaged in a kind of undeclared and ill-advised competition of strength with these youths. En route to Pitcairn, Belcher had entertained himself by testing his "swimming jacket" in high surf off various other islands and landfalls. Now, against the advice of his officer friends, Belcher plunged after one of the islanders down a "perilous descent," and as Captain Beechey seemed pleased to report, "Mr. Belcher was obliged to profess his inability to proceed," and to take the hand his native companion innocently offered in assistance.

According to Adams, once the *Bounty* departed Tahiti for the third and final time, following the failed settlement and bloodshed in Tubuai, there was no definite destination. The Marquesas Islands were first discussed, but Christian, availing himself of the volumes of voyages of discovery in Bligh's library, read Captain Carteret's description of Pitcairn. The island was very remote, uninhabited and devoid of anchorage, ensuring that a passing ship would be less inclined to loiter; and so it was there he had steered the *Bounty*'s course.

On arrival, Christian and a reconnaissance party went ashore and returned greatly satisfied. They had found wood, water, fruit trees and rich soil. They had also discovered a mountainous and difficult land with narrow, easily defensible passes and a number of caves; the island was the perfect outlaw's redoubt. (Christian had returned to the ship with "a joyful expression such as we had not seen on him for a long time past," Adams told a later visitor.) The ship was slowly unloaded and then burned. While the settlement was being built, the mutineers lived under the *Bounty*'s sails; and when these were no longer required for shelter, the cloth had been cut up to fashion clothes. Thus had this small ship served her company to the very end. Her guns and anchors were observed by later visitors to be lying in the shallow water of Bounty Bay.

The massacre of the mutineers and the blacks had taken place in several waves of violence, and principally arose from the fact that the Englishmen had come to regard their Otaheitean friends as slaves. Fletcher Christian was killed in the first wave as he tilled his yam field. McCoy

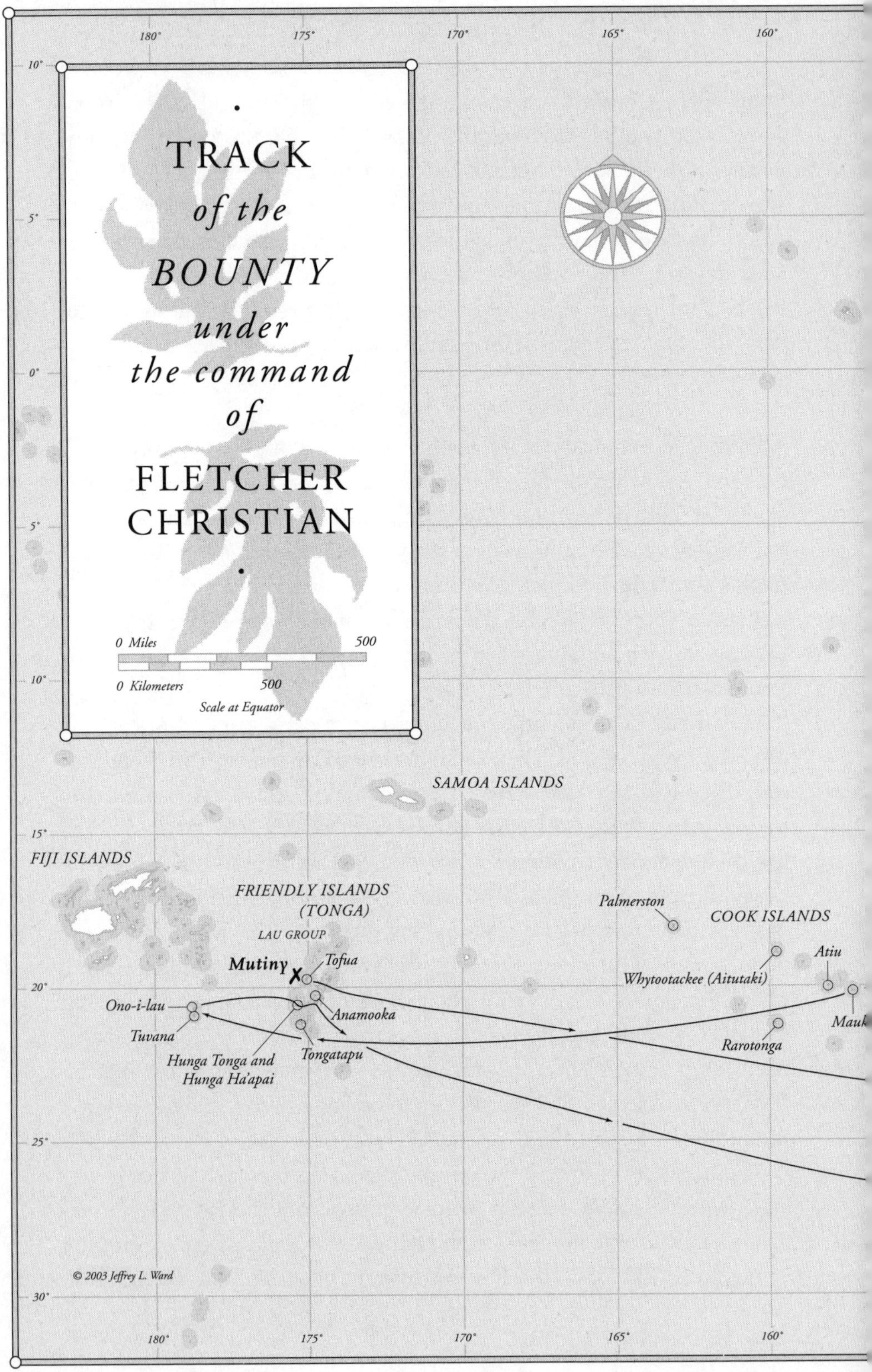

TRACK
of the
BOUNTY
under
the command
of
FLETCHER
CHRISTIAN

0 Miles 500

0 Kilometers 500
Scale at Equator

SAMOA ISLANDS

FIJI ISLANDS

FRIENDLY ISLANDS
(TONGA)
LAU GROUP

Mutiny X *Tofua*

Palmerston

COOK ISLANDS

Atiu

Whytootackee (Aitutaki)

Ono-i-lau *Anamooka*

Tuvana

Mauk

Hunga Tonga and
Hunga Ha'apai

Tongatapu

Rarotonga

© 2003 Jeffrey L. Ward

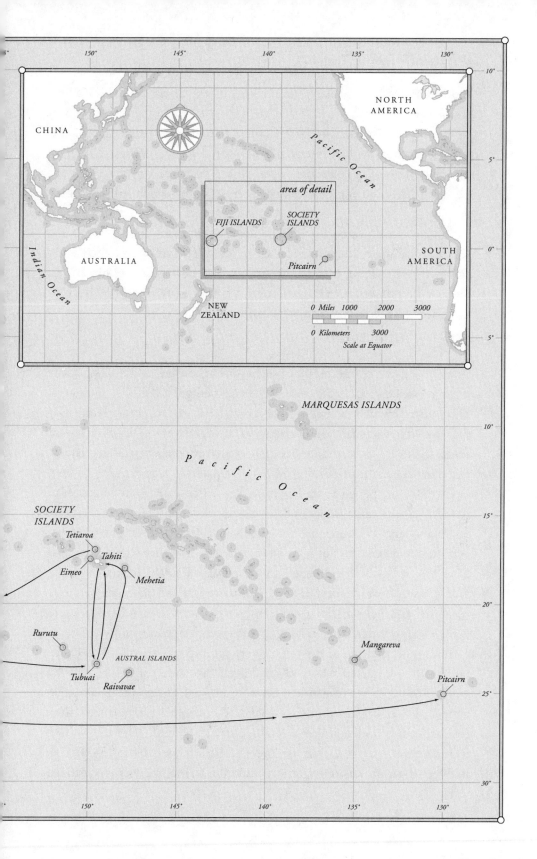

CHINA

NORTH
AMERICA

Pacific Ocean

area of detail

FIJI ISLANDS

SOCIETY
ISLANDS

SOUTH
AMERICA

Indian Ocean

AUSTRALIA

Pitcairn

NEW
ZEALAND

0 Miles 1000 2000 3000

0 Kilometers 3000

Scale at Equator

MARQUESAS ISLANDS

Pacific Ocean

SOCIETY
ISLANDS

Tetiaroa

Tahiti

Eimeo

Mehetia

Rurutu

Mangareva

AUSTRAL ISLANDS

Tubuai

Raivavae

Pitcairn

and Mills heard his groans, but decided it was Christian's wife calling him to dinner.

"Thus fell a man, who, from being the reputed ringleader of the mutiny, has obtained an unenviable celebrity," wrote Beechey, adding by way of another of his editorials, "and whose crime may perhaps be considered as in some degree palliated, by the tyranny which led to its commission."

Captain Beechey and the *Blossom* departed Pitcairn on December 20, 1825, continuing on their own voyage of discovery throughout the Pacific and Bering Strait, as part of the Admiralty's new polar ventures. The *Blossom* did not return to England until 1828. The full import of this voyage would be made manifest two years later.

One of the items of interest that Beechey brought away on the *Blossom* was the diary of Edward Young, one of the most enigmatic of the mutineers. The journal, which Young started toward the end of 1793, some two months after the death of Christian in the first wave of massacres—in some accounts—was said by Beechey to give evidence of Young's education and "serious turn of mind." His journal, which was never to be seen or cited again, opened a window on a dark, largely undisclosed aspect of island life—the unhappiness of the island's women. Only one of the female pioneers—Teehuteatuaonoa, nicknamed Jenny—ever gave her own version of the early days of settlement, and that only after she had escaped from Pitcairn—she had hitched a passage with Captain Reynolds on the *Sultan,* some years before, in 1817. From Young's and Teehuteatuaonoa's accounts, and the occasional incautious remark of John Adams, a more complete and complicated history of this exemplary community emerged.

With the exception of the female companions of Christian and Quintal, and Jenny herself who had once been the "wife" of Adams, all the women brought to Pitcairn had been kidnapped. When the *Bounty* had arrived at Matavai Bay on its final visit, the usual friendly visitors came on board, including eighteen women, one with a child. After the women went below for supper, Christian ordered the anchor cable cut. Although told that the ship was only going around the island, the women realized the truth when they passed through and beyond the reef; one courageous woman had dived overboard. After this, Christian had been careful not to bring the ship too close to other landfalls, knowing, as Jenny said, that several of the women would have tried to swim to shore. Off the island of Eimeo, five or six leagues from Tahiti, six of the women "who were rather ancient" and presumably deemed physically unattractive were sent ashore.

After scouting several islands, Christian set out for Pitcairn, a search during which two full months would pass without seeing land. During this time, "all on board were much discouraged: they therefore thought of returning to Otaheite." But at last, on the evening of January 15, 1790, the island was seen rising like a great rock from the ocean. For three days a fierce wind held them at bay, preventing any landing; that the island was so effectively defended by the elements may have been seen as a favorable omen.

With the aid of a raft, the men methodically unloaded the *Bounty,* and when everything had been removed they debated what to do with the ship. "Christian wished to save her for awhile," Jenny said, but while they were debating, Matthew Quintal had gone on board and set a fire in the bow; later, two others followed and fired other parts of the ship. But during the night "all were in tears at seeing her in flames. Some regretted exceedingly that they had not confined Capt. Bligh and returned to their native country, instead of acting as they had done."

Prisoners now of the island, the women set to work. It would be their skills of homemaking, their knowledge of preparing the familiar fruits and fish and fowl, and their traditions of making bark cloth and clothes that would carry the settlement. Passed around from one "husband" to the other, as men died and the balance of power shifted, they rebelled.

"[S]ince the massacre, it has been the desire of the greater part of them to get some conveyance, to enable them to leave the island," Edward Young recorded in his diary. Shortly before, he had come upon Jenny handling the skull of Jack Williams and learned to his amazement and horror that the women had refused to bury the slaughtered men.

"I thought that if the girls did not agree to give up the heads of the five white men in a peaceable manner, they ought to be taken by force, and buried," wrote Young indignantly; he was after all a gentleman. One of these unburied skulls belonged to Fletcher Christian, whose head, according to Jenny, had been "disfigured" with an axe after he was killed.

The women's desperation finally prompted the men to build them a small boat, according to Young, who also reported that Jenny in her zeal had ripped boards out of her own house for building material. On August 13, 1794, the little vessel was completed, and two days later launched. But the women's hopes of a return to their native land were bitterly dashed when the vessel foundered, "according to expectation," as Young wrote, with masculine amusement. Miserably, the women returned to their captors. The "wives" of McCoy and Quintal—who, as Beechey had to comment, "appear to have been of very quarrelsome dispositions"—were frequently beaten.

A grave was duly dug for the murdered men's bones. Three months later "a conspiracy of the women to kill the white men in their sleep was discovered." No punishment was inflicted, but as Young recorded, "We did not forget their conduct; and it was agreed among us, that the first female who misbehaved should be put to death." And so the years passed. A multitude of offspring were born to the women, who had been passed promiscuously around the male survivors. Jenny herself had formerly been the "wife" of John Adams, who as Alexander Smith had tattooed her with his initials while they were on Tahiti. When he left her, she was turned over to Isaac Martin. With the arrival of the *Sultan* in 1817, Jenny at last made good her escape, returning in a roundabout fashion after a voyage of some years, to her native Tahiti thirty-one years after she had departed. As the newsman who first recorded her story reported, she had been "apparently a good looking woman in her time." Her hands were hard from manual labor.

Mauatua (Christian's wife, known by him affectionately as Mainmast, perhaps for her height), Vahineatua, Teio (and her little daughter, Teatuahitea), Faahotu, Teraura, Obuarei, Tevarua, Toofaiti, Mareva, Tinafornea, and Jenny or Teehuteatuaonoa . . . the names of the women who made the Pitcairn experiment succeed had rarely been evoked. Also evocative were the familiar names with which Jenny referred to the *Bounty* men— Billy Brown, Jack Williams, Neddy Young, Matt Quintal—the names of

English lads one might run into on any waterfront. Christian on the other hand, as Adams reported reverentially, was always addressed as "Mr. Christian." As Lieutenant Belcher had been shrewd enough to perceive, the authority Christian possessed had held in check even those against his desperate scheme. Sleepless and the worse for drink, he seems to have succeeded with his mutiny in great part because he was the most popular man on board.

How much of his authority he retained to the end is difficult to tell. He clearly lost his grasp at Tubuai, and also the confidence of the sixteen men who at the last chose to leave him and take their chances on Tahiti. Events related by Jenny suggest that he was having difficulty holding his small band intact during the months in which they roamed the sea, seeking their new home. Adams, as often, contradicts himself: Christian "was always cheerful," he told Beechey, and was "naturally of a happy, ingenuous disposition." Yet, when discussing the island's geography Adams pointed out a cave, "the intended retreat of Christian, in the event of a landing being effected by any ship sent in pursuit of him, and where he resolved to sell his life as dearly as he could." In this cave, Adams told other ships, Christian was wont to retreat and brood. And what of Adams's earlier statements to Captains Staines and Pipon that Christian had "by many acts of cruelty and inhumanity, brought on himself the hatred and detestation of his companions"?

Despite the heartfelt pronouncements of almost every visitor that "for good morals, politeness of behavior," as well as their "strict adherence to the truth, and the principles of religion," the Pitcairners had, thanks to John Adams, "not their equals to be found on earth," it is very unclear how much of anything Adams himself said was to be taken as truth. Most suspicious were his inconsistent stories of Christian's death. Was the story he spontaneously told Captain Folger, the first visitor to catch him unawares, the real truth? If so, then Fletcher Christian was killed in a single massacre that occurred on the island about four years after arrival. Or was the truth that which he related, after a sober second thought, to Folger's second mate—that Christian committed suicide? Why, when Christian's own wife was living, had Adams insisted that she had predeceased her husband? And what of his statement to Captain Pipon that the mutineers had divided into parties, "seeking every opportunity on both sides to put each other to death"? Had Adams and Christian been of the same "party"? Or had they been adversaries? What importance is to be attached to the striking fact that Adams was one of only two men left standing in the wake of the massacres? Was it Adams's party that killed Christian? Could it even be—impossible as it would seem of the venerable patriarch!—that it was Adams who killed Christian?

With the arrival of each ship eager to pay homage to the Christian miracle of Pitcairn, the wily survivor made subtle adjustments to his narration. From the tenor of the questions he was asked, he must have soon caught hold of the shape his story had taken in England. By the 1820s, Adams had introduced a new element: the mutiny had been caused by the "remorseless severity" of Bligh, who had even subjected his mate, Fletcher Christian, "to corporal chastisement."

Adams died in March 1829, on the day after his sixty-sixth birthday—if the date he had told the captain of the *Maryland* on her visit in 1824 was true. His power to shape and embellish the story, however, continued posthumously. Just before the pious old mutineer expired, one reverential tribute—uniquely, and many years after the fact—reported, "[H]e said in a whisper as his countenance lighted up with joy 'Let go the anchor' and fell back upon his pillow and died."

After Adams's death, the next generation continued the tradition of telling the story of the *Bounty* to the steady stream of curious visitors, if with some fuzziness as to details. In relating the famous coconut scene, for example, a Pitcairn narrator described how some "fruit, which had been sent on board for the captain's cabin . . . disappeared; Captain Bligh was exceedingly angry," and had berated Christian by saying, "I suppose you have eaten it yourself, you hungry hound!" ("Can we be surprised at insults of this nature rankling in the mind of a susceptible man, and driving him at last to the desperate deed . . . ?" the visitor interjected.) These new narrators brought new details to light and accorded old ones new scrutiny. It was more openly recognized that Adams's safeguarding of his own daughters' virtue was in great part due to the fact that if they married they would cease to till his own fields. His stepdaughter was reported to retain "most unpleasant recollections of John Adams, who she insists killed her mother by his cruel treatment of her." The patriarch's insistence on religious observances had been rigorous, "even to severity of discipline," whatever that might have entailed. It was also said that when the *Bounty* arrived at Pitcairn and Christian went ashore to scout the island, there had been a plot afoot among those, such as Adams, who had remained on board to leave their ringleader and take the ship back to Tahiti.

The growing legend was, however, able to absorb all its discrepancies as well as all its darker elements. Truly unfavorable reports were largely ignored—such as an account that the pious youths had been caught red-handed brewing spirits very much like whiskey; or that when Thursday October Christian had come on board the *Briton,* he had abruptly left the table when a West Indian member of the company entered, muttering, "I don't like that black fellow, I must go." Fletcher Christian's offspring were generally treated with great tact and only very occasionally received anything less than flattering descriptions—such as the opinion of a visitor in 1830 that "Thursday and Charles Christian, the sons of the mutineer, are ignorant, uneducated persons, unable to maintain superiority."

As long ago as 1791, when the *Pandora* had been roaming the broad Pacific in her hapless search for the *Bounty,* Surgeon George Hamilton had mused on a far-fetched and, under the circumstances, inappropriate fantasy: should Christian "elude the hand of justice, it may be hoped he will employ his talents in humanizing the rude savages, so that, at some future period, a British Ilion may blaze forth in the south, with all the characteristic virtues of the English nation, and complete the great prophecy, by propagating the Christian knowledge amongst the infidels." And so, improbably, it had come to pass. Few in England, apparently, were able to discern that the Pitcairn Islanders' traits were more readily traced to their Polynesian ancestry than to English Christendom. Their selfless and communal identity, the much marveled lack of locks on their doors, their open-handed generosity, their cleanliness—these were Otaheite characteristics that the men of the *Bounty* had admired, and not found in the society that had only recently ceased to gibbet executed criminals along the Thames.

This chapter of the *Bounty* saga was also to serve English poetry. "Christina, the Maid of the South Seas" was written by Mary Russell Mitford in 1811, following the news of the discovery by the *Topaz*—the poem was then one of the few public responses to the event. Relating the love of Christian's daughter Christina for "Henry," an English sailor somehow serving on the American *Topaz*, the poem received editorial assistance from two old *Bounty* hands: Rear Admiral James Burney, who had edited Bligh's log for publication, and Samuel Taylor Coleridge. In an ill-advised preface, the authoress expressed some anguish at both having to recognize "the sufferings of Captain Bligh" on the one hand and "irritating the feelings of a highly respectable family" on the other; one may be sure that this in itself succeeded in irritating the Christian Curwens.

Another poet inspired by this most romantic tale of love and exile was none other than that arch-romantic Lord Byron. By the time he published *The Island* in 1823, Byron was near the end of his wild life and had perfected his self-image as the dark-haired exile, dragging his intriguing taint of unspecified wrongdoing across Europe. Who better to immortalize the charismatic mutineer! And yet, in a role reversal of breathtaking unexpectedness, Byron championed William Bligh.

> *Awake, bold Bligh! the foe is at the gate!*
> *Awake! awake!—Alas it is too late!*
> *Fiercely beside thy cot the mutineer*
> *Stands, and proclaims the reign of rage and fear.*

As for the mutineers—

> *Young hearts, which languish'd for some sunny isle,*
> *Where summer years and summer women smile;*
> *Men without country, who, too long estranged,*
> *Had found no native home, or found it changed,*
> *And, half uncivilised, preferr'd the cave*
> *Of some soft savage to the uncertain wave—*

(Perhaps Byron's uncharacteristic disapproval of so romantic a figure arose from pique, a wounded sense that Fletcher Christian—his long hair loose, his shirt collar open—had out-Byroned Byron.)

A number of the survivors of the *Bounty* did not live to learn of Fletcher Christian's fate. Loyalist Charles Norman died in December 1793, which would explain his absence as a "witness" in the dueling pamphlets of Bligh and Edward Christian. He had been buried in the Gosport church of his baptism, and so had not strayed far from Portsmouth Harbour after his acquittal and release.

After the court-martial John Hallett joined the *Penelope* as third lieutenant, and a little over a year later, while the ship was in the West Indies, the muster indicates that he was "Invalided" for the remainder of the voyage. Hallett died in Bedford in December 1794, "after a long and severe illness," as the *Times* reported. Another obituary indicated he had lost the use of his limbs following the open-boat voyage, and although recovered sufficiently to make another voyage, he "again lost the use of his limbs, and recovered them no more." Hallett was only twenty-two years old at the time of his death. His parish church registry noted he had been a "gentleman."

A later tradition put out by the Heywood family represented that Mr. Hallett had died on board the *Penelope*—and that in "his last moments he expressed his contrition for the unfavorable evidence he had given against his friend Peter Heywood." He had been bewildered by the events of the mutiny and too much under the influence of Lieutenant Bligh—so Hallett had himself confessed to "one of the most distinguished flag-officers in the service, who was then first lieutenant of the *Penelope*." The first lieutenant of the *Penelope* had been Pulteney Malcolm—another of Thomas Pasley's nephews as it turns out, although this striking fact was not publicized. Doubtless, the rumor of Hallett's "death on board," instead of by slow and dreadful paralysis allegedly resulting from his ordeals in the open boat, was intended to deflect invidious attention from those persons who had made him suffer. An elaborate memorial tablet of white marble in the chancel of St. Mary's,

Bedford, reflected both his proud parents' grief and their social pretensions: amid engrailed sable arms and a demi-lion rampant was inscribed
his epithet: "*Juvenis Laboris patiens, Virtute praeditus, nec Tempestate nec
Fama nec Periculo Fracta:* A youth patient in his duties, outstanding in
his valour, broken neither by tempest, nor rumour nor danger." The notion that "Fama"—rumor—could be a threat to a naval officer of only
twenty-two is so curious that one must suspect that it was pointed.

Lawrence Lebogue died in the spring of 1795, on board the *Jason*,
while she was moored in Plymouth Harbour. Lebogue was forty-eight at
the time of his death and had served Bligh loyally in the West Indies, on
both breadfruit voyages, and in his outspoken affidavit on Bligh's behalf
once back in England; for this latter he had incurred the full wrath of Edward Christian who had declared that Lebogue's was "the most wicked
and perjured affidavit that ever was sworn before a magistrate, or published to the world." That the open-boat journey had ruined his health,
as it had ruined so many others', is suggested by his suffering, like Bligh
and John Smith, from fever on the *Providence*. Yet, when a friend of
Bligh's looked the sailmaker up for a glass of grog after his ordeal, remarking wryly that this was "better than being in the boat," Lebogue had
been dismissive.

"Oh damn me, I never think of the boat!" he had replied.

Following his return to England with the last of the *Pandora*'s crew in
September 1792, Thomas Hayward had joined the *Diomede* as second
lieutenant. Incredibly, he was to endure yet another shipwreck, albeit
less dramatic than that of the *Pandora*. Off the coast of Ceylon in August
1795, working against a strong wind, the ship struck a rock and gained
water so quickly that there had only just been time to evacuate. The next
year, Hayward received what was to be his last commission. Appointed
commander of the 18-gun sloop *Swift*, he was en route from Macao to
England with a convoy of merchantmen when overtaken by a violent ty-
phoon in the South China Sea. The sloop was observed making signals
of distress before foundering with all souls lost. Thomas Hayward was
twenty-nine years old. In his short life he had served in ten ships and survived a mutiny, two historic open-boat voyages and two shipwrecks, before succumbing to the sea. He left behind him a series of unremarkable

charts, which indicated ambition if no particular talent. His watchful father had given his son some blank logbooks for the *Bounty* voyage. One
of these was found in the Pitcairn library of old John Adams, still bearing the name of Thomas's father and a fanciful coat of arms with the
motto "*Pro Deo patria et amicis*"—For God, country and friends.

George Simpson, the *Bounty*'s quartermaster's mate, was found dead
in his hammock on the *Princess of Orange* in 1801. No cause of death was
given, and his personal effects were turned over to his father in the Lake
District.

William Muspratt had remained on the *Hector* until early February
1793, and following his successful legal plea had been discharged to the
Royal William, a ship on which it appears, however, he did not serve.
Later the same year, however, he wrote a will identifying himself as "a
Seaman belonging to His Majesty's Ship *Bellerophon*"; if this was correctly stated, Muspratt had joined his former shipmate Peter Heywood
on his uncle Pasley's ship—however, his name is not listed on the ship's
muster; it is possible that, given his history, he took a "purser's name."
Muspratt's will was "proved" in 1798, indicating that the *Bounty* steward
was dead by this time. Shortly after receiving his pardon, Muspratt had
been bold enough to disconcert the Admiralty with a petition for his
back wages; only two prior cases could be found to bear any similarity to
his, and in one, as the Admiralty secretary reported, the recipient had already been hanged. Whether or not his *Bounty* wages were included in
his estate, William Muspratt left everything to his "dearly beloved
Brother Joseph" of Fareham.

Befitting his temperament, James Morrison's career following his
pardon was full of action, smoke and thundering explosions. Reverting
to the profession for which he had qualified before the *Bounty*, Morrison
eventually achieved the rank of master gunner, and in this capacity saw
heated action in the Mediterranean. In 1801, Morrison's service took
him back to Jamaica and the West Indies; here, one may be sure, he
added to the island's knowledge of the breadfruit expeditions. In 1803,
Morrison was in the *Tonnant*, which, while engaged in a blockade off the
Spanish coast during tempestuous weather, found herself unable to re-
supply. Eventually, the captain was reduced to sending his purser ashore

to a safe cove to seek out local provisions. One wonders how the long-haired master gunner endured this pinch—with many a knowing conversation, discussing pounds and ounces and equivalent weights owed, and dire grumblings of short rations? Or had he mellowed somewhat since his *Bounty* days?

Following a stint as a gunnery instructor in Plymouth, Morrison joined the distinguished Rear Admiral Sir Thomas Troubridge, with whom he had served before, apparently to mutual satisfaction, in the *Blenheim*. In 1806, en route to the Cape of Good Hope (now British), at which station he was to take command, Troubridge grounded the *Blenheim* on a sandbar. The damage sustained by the ship was severe, and, broken and gaining water, she had limped to safe harbor in Madras. But Troubridge was a proud man and, despite being warned of the *Blenheim*'s obvious defects, flattered himself that he could overcome yet one more challenge, and determined to continue to the Cape. The *Blenheim* was last seen by another of His Majesty's ships off the coast of Madagascar, lying fatally low in the water in the wake of a severe gale. Morrison had expended considerable energy railing against Bligh on matters that would have appeared in hindsight to have been very slight—especially when reviewed, say, from a broken ship commanded by a captain who had chosen to bet his men's life against his own pride.

At some point after the *Bounty* voyage, Morrison had returned to his native Stornoway and entertained his relatives with stories of his life in Otaheite, central to which seems to have been the considerable status he had enjoyed as the *taio* of a local chief. Long after specific personalities had been forgotten, Morrison's family retained the tradition that a forebear of long ago had been king of a South Pacific island.

HOME IS THE SAILOR

One person who did not comment on the Pitcairn Island miracle, although he was very much alive, was Rear Admiral William Bligh, who was far from England when the news of the *Topaz* broke. And when the report of the *Tagus* and *Briton* reached England in 1815, he was still recovering from his wife's death and approaching the end of his own life. In the course of the intervening years he had both achieved great distinctions and weathered additional squalls; his life's voyage, as an old shipmate would reflect, had been a turbulent one.

Following the return of the *Providence*, Bligh had remained on half pay for over a year and a half. In April 1795, he was ordered to the North Sea fleet under the command of Admiral Adam Duncan, first as captain of the 24-gun armed transport *Calcutta*, and subsequently in the more prestigious role as captain of the 54-gun *Director*. And it was as captain of the *Director* that Bligh endured what is sometimes referred to as his "second mutiny."

The mutiny at the Nore anchorage in the spring of 1797 was one of the landmark events in the British navy, and Bligh's minor role in these tumultuous events is instructive. The Nore mutiny was not so much a mutiny as a labor strike, inspired by a similar strike at Spithead that had ended only days earlier. The Spithead mutiny had addressed such longstanding grievances as the fact that seamen's wages had not been raised since 1653, that their food was deficient and that their sick and wounded were not properly cared for. By refusing to weigh anchor until their complaints had been met, the seamen had paralyzed the Channel fleet. Lord Howe, drawing on the enormous credibility and respect he enjoyed with the seamen, had adroitly negotiated with the mutineers, conceding most of their demands and guaranteeing their pardon.

This success at Spithead immediately led to a larger and more serious mutiny at the Nore, which eventually spread to the North Sea fleet, in which Bligh was stationed. This time, the mutineers' demands descended to what might be termed second-tier grievances—complaints over the distribution of prizes, shore leave, the harsh terms of some of the Articles of War. Most tellingly, the mutineers also demanded that certain unpopular officers be removed from their ships. And to illustrate their seriousness, they peremptorily sent ashore a stream of disfavored commanding officers, lieutenants, midshipmen and masters in varying degrees of popular disgrace: several captains who had served as judges on the *Bounty* mutineers' court-martial bore the brunt of these events. The surgeon of the *Montagu,* under the command of Captain John Knight, was tarred and feathered; John Colpoys's first lieutenant barely escaped being hanged, and Colpoys himself was for twenty-four hours in fear of his own life; several unpopular midshipmen were ducked. William Bligh was not among these "offenders."

It was also in this crisis that Aaron Graham was called upon to exercise officially those abilities he had earlier revealed only discreetly, and in yet another of his many roles he now served the Admiralty as a spy. In boardinghouses and inns throughout the seamier parts of Sheerness, agent Graham conducted interviews with sailors, bawdy women, dockyard workers, innkeepers, even the mothers of sailors, seeking to learn which way the crisis was blowing, who stood where and where the ringleaders were. ("I assume I can spend money freely," Graham had written to his boss, the Duke of Portland.)

The Nore mutiny had been under way for a week before Bligh was relieved of command of the *Director;* during this time the crisis escalated to the point where the Admiralty had begun to plan for the use of force. On surrendering his command, Bligh wrote to inform the Admiralty of the turn of events in a letter conspicuous for its startling lack of rancor.

The trouble arose from the interference of the crew of the *Sandwich*, Bligh reported, adding of his own men that "hitherto never did a ship's company behave better or did ever a ship bear more marks of content and correctness."

The mutiny was eventually quelled by a strategic use of limited force and the threat of much greater. This time the chief mutineers were hanged, flogged or transported. Bligh had been one of a delegation of captains commissioned to go among the seamen and urge them to return to duty—and his inclusion in this group would suggest some faith in his relations with the sailors. Of the few concessions awarded this time around, Lord Howe agreed to the removal of those officers whom the seamen most resented. A list of more than a hundred names was duly submitted; William Bligh's was not among them.

After the quelling of the Nore mutiny, Bligh regained command of the *Director* and joined Admiral Duncan and the North Sea fleet in a blockade off the Dutch coast. In the ensuing Battle of Camperdown, in October 1797, the *Director* played an important and gallant role in Duncan's victory, directing a spirited broadside at close quarters (twenty yards) against the Dutch flagship *Vrijheid*. Despite her bold action, the *Director* escaped with only seven men wounded—for which Bligh's officers came forth to congratulate him. Along with other flag officers and captains, Bligh received the gold medal issued to commemorate this important victory.

Following this engagement, Bligh requested leave of absence from the Admiralty, pleading the need for medical attention.

"I want much to have advice on account of an alarming numbness which has seized my left arm from a rheumatic affliction," he wrote— perhaps a relic of the long, cold, wet days and nights in the open boat. Between campaigns, Bligh was engaged in the more peaceable activity of hydrographic survey. While studiously engaged in surveying Helford Harbour in Cornwall, he had been mistaken for a French spy and taken under arrest to be held at the local vicarage.

"In an act of duty, he had been roughly treated; and he resented it" was the vicar's diplomatic account. But, he added, after Bligh's anger had subsided, he had joined "in commending the loyal zeal of my parishioners." Over the ensuing peace-making dinner of woodcock and "a variety of wines," Bligh delighted the erudite vicar with his conversation, and the two sat talking until two in the morning. "But a moment's conversation with Captain Bligh discovered all the gentleman" was the vicar's summary.

In 1801, Bligh participated in the most important naval engagement of his career, when in command of the 54-gun *Glatton* he joined Lord Nelson at the battle of Copenhagen. Egged on by Napoleon, the Russians, Danes and Swedes had conspired to block English trade in the Baltic. It was in this campaign that Nelson, the second-in-command, had famously ignored what he regarded as his admiral's pusillanimous orders. ("I really do not see the signal," Nelson had reported of the admiral's signal to "discontinue the action," holding the telescope to his blind eye.) His insubordination resulted in a sound victory, and for his role as what Nelson termed his "second," Bligh was summoned on board by his lordship for personal commendation.

Four years later, Bligh was the recipient of another of Sir Joseph Banks's fated tokens of kindness. Banks had been busy behind the scenes on Bligh's behalf on a number of occasions over the years, supporting his application to join the Royal Society (membership in which enabled Bligh to put a coveted "F.R.S." after his name), and seeking a stable land-based commission for the aging captain, whose health had "by the Voyage from the *Bounty* to Timor been utterly ruined." After a number of rebuffs, Banks was at last able to come to Bligh with a solid if unlikely offer: the governorship of New South Wales.

"I apprehend that you are about 55 years old," Banks wrote with the warmth that characterized what was by now an old and comfortable friendship (in fact, Bligh was fifty-one). "[I]f so, you have by the tables an expectation of 15 years' life," he continued, with admirable if disconcerting exactitude, "and in a climate like that, which is the best that I know, a still better expectation." The job would bring in £2,000 a year, of which he could save half, plus a pension, which at compound interest of 5 percent Banks calculated would produce "more than £30,000." These were arguments that spoke convincingly to Bligh.

Eventually, despite misgivings about taking up a position outside the arena of his professional expertise and so far from home, Bligh accepted the offer. It would mean another long voyage to the Pacific, and an exile of sorts. Above all, it meant separation from his wife. Although he was to be accompanied by his daughter Mary and her husband, Mrs. Bligh would not be joining him. As Bligh told Banks, "her undertaking the Voyage would be her Death owing to her extreme horror of the Sea, the Sound of a gun, or Thunder."

The governorship of New South Wales was to be the final debacle in Bligh's eventful career. The story of the state of the penal colony at the time he assumed command and of the organized thuggery of the Rum Corps that characterized its "government" is a subject too vast to do justice here. Suffice it to say that in 1808, Governor Bligh, inexperienced in and perhaps temperamentally unfit for the backroom strategizing and gamesmanship of political leadership, was ousted from office in a well-orchestrated coup. As one local correspondent reported to Banks, "[T]he plans against Bligh have been extensively laid and artfully conducted." Dragged unceremoniously from Government House, Bligh was to pass some two years on a ship offshore before relief came from England, during which time he refused to recognize the usurpers, considering himself to be, quite correctly, the government in exile: William Bligh was not one to desert his post or duty.

Eventually, a long and exhaustive court-martial of the usurpers was held in England, which resulted in their disgrace and ban from all future service. As a central witness, Bligh was involved once again in defending his honor, which he did with expected uncompromising energy and fearlessness. Inadvertently, however, these proceedings of 1811 revealed how corrosive had been the effects of the *Bounty*'s aftermath, nearly twenty years ago.

"How often has it happened, in the course of your service in the navy, that you have found it necessary to bring officers or others to courts martial for mutiny or other similar offences?" Bligh was asked as the second question of his cross-examination by Lieutenant Colonel George Johnston, the defendant.

"I think about twice, I have brought persons to a court martial," Bligh responded, "twice or thrice, I suppose, in the course of forty years of constant and active service."

"How many courts martial have you obtained against individuals for other offences?"

"Really, gentlemen, it is hard for me to answer such a question," Bligh replied impatiently; he could see where this was going. "[T]he world knows perfectly well that in 1787 there was a mutiny on board the ship Bounty: I presume that is what they allude to; I don't know any other mutiny that I have had any thing to do with, except that dreadful mutiny at the Nore, in which, of course, I was not particularly concerned."

"Have you ever been brought to a court martial, and for what?" Johnston continued later.

"I was brought to a court martial for the loss of the Bounty: and my lieutenant, who, I understand, is now turned out of the service, brought me to a trial when I commanded His Majesty's ship the Warrior, a seventy-four."

"And for what?" Johnston continued; he had done his homework.

"I cannot say how the charge was worded; but the amount of it, I recollect, was, that I had sent for him to do his duty when he had a lame foot, that I sent for him and he refused to come, because he had a lame foot, which he had embarked on board the ship with, but made a pretence of it when I sent for him on duty, and said that it was an act of tyranny on my part to send for him, or the word might be, oppression."

The case that Johnston had touched upon, Bligh's second court-martial, had occurred in 1805. The causes were indeed as Bligh outlined; the injured lieutenant, a man named Frazier, had in fact been allowed to take his watch sitting down, but while doing so had begun an argument with the Warrior's steward that had become so heated it had reached Bligh in his cabin. Coming out in one of his passions, Bligh had, as the affronted lieutenant reported, grossly insulted and ill-treated him "by calling me a rascal, scoundrel and shaking his fist in my face." The ensuing court-martial revealed a calculated awareness of the reputation Bligh had gained as a result of the Bounty business. The charges preferred against him from this squall were for behaving toward his officer in a "tyrannical and oppressive and unofficerlike manner." The stream of witnesses summoned by both sides yielded the revelation that Captain Bligh was often hasty in his language, which was variously regarded by different men as offensive and "irritating," or of no consequence. It was also revealed that Captain Bligh habitually used "a great deal of action with his hands, without having any particular meaning in it." The general consensus of the officers was that "they were sorry Lieutenant Frazier should be so ill-advised as to bring his Captain to a Court-martial upon grounds which appeared so frivolous."

For his part Bligh had directed to the court an unapologetic statement: "I candidly and without reserve avow that I am not a tame & indifferent observer of the manner in which Officers placed under my orders conducted themselves in the performance of their several duties," he declared, in a self-assessment that could apply to his entire career. "[A] signal or any communication from a commanding officer has ever been to me an indication for exertion & alacrity to carry into effect the purport thereof, & peradventure I may occasionally have appeared to some of those officers as unnecessarily anxious for its execution."

The charges were "in part proved," and Bligh had been reprimanded, "admonished to be in future more correct in his language," and restored to his command. As one historian has noted, however, "[T]he officers comprising the bench of magistrates must in private have grinned broadly to themselves when they sent him back to his ship after admonishing him to swear a little more mildly in future. . . ." But once this particular box of mischief had been opened, it proved both difficult to close again and extremely easy to manipulate the contents brought to light.

"Did any soldiers ever complain to you of having received gross abuse from the Governor?" one of the Rum Corps officers was now asked at the court-martial held on Governor Bligh's removal from office.

"I heard several complaints from the soldiers, of having received abuse from Gov. Bligh, and often the language was too gross to be repeated," replied the officer priggishly. Putting aside the very real question of how much personal contact Governor Bligh would have had with these troops, one is asked to believe that Rum Corps soldiers policing the world's largest penal colony had been shocked and offended by Governor Bligh's unprecedented bad language. More credible is the probability that this line of attack had been inspired by an opportunistic awareness of Bligh's record for such behavior.

Bligh's case against the usurpers was won to his satisfaction, but this case, too, represented a kind of Pyrrhic victory. As the events of his life receded over time into a fuzzy unclarity, they came to suggest a damning record of tyranny and mismanagement. First the *Bounty,* then the Nore mutiny, then the mutiny in New South Wales—clearly Captain Bligh, Breadfruit Bligh, that Bounty Bastard, had been cursed with some fatal inability to command.

With the conclusion of the Rum Corps court-martial, Bligh returned to a brief period of untroubled domesticity, which was ended sadly by the death of Betsy in the spring of 1812. A striking and fulsome obituary in the *Gentlemen's Magazine* praised her as "a rare example of every virtue and amiable quality" and gave some insight into why her husband had so revered her. Mrs. Bligh had collected "a choice and extensive library" in English, Italian and French literature, and had also owned a world-class collection of rare shells, undoubtedly supplemented from her husband's travels. Her knowledge, "excellent understanding" and unfailing good taste were matched only by her sweetness of temper. Poor Bligh now buried his wife of thirty-one years in the churchyard of St. Mary's, Lambeth. She was not yet sixty.

The same year also saw the loss of another important figure in Bligh's life, although it is doubtful that he had concerned himself much with John Fryer for many years. The *Bounty*'s former master had rebounded from his travails to build a solid and apparently unproblematic career. By the end of his life he had enjoyed the command of three storeships, and the commendation of one of his captains as a "very good navigator, a very sober man, well informed in his profession and of great exertion." Commander of a storeship, to be sure, was fairly far down on the naval chain of command, and Fryer's daughter would state in later years that her father was "the oldest Master but one" on the naval lists at the time of his death, not necessarily cause to boast.

Fryer's bitterness toward Bligh never waned; Bligh had been "as Tyrannical in his temper in the Boat as in the Ship," he had told his daughters, and in the boat Bligh had thought chiefly of his own comfort—a quaint notion, given the circumstances of that ordeal. Fryer had also conveyed to his family his many friendships with numerous other captains—Sir Andrew Snape Hamond, who had served on the court-martial of mutineers, was "amongst those whom he considered his best friends." However, when Fryer came to petition the Admiralty for a pension after ill health forced him to retirement, he does not appear to have enjoyed their "interest"—in any event, his petition had met with no success.

The ordeal of the boat voyage had, according to his daughter Mary Ann, "laid the foundation for a premature old age." A surgeon's report made for Fryer at the time he surrendered command of his last ship described him as suffering from "general debility, spasmodic rigidity of almost the whole body, great anxiety of mind, with much loss of memory, the whole forming a disease of extreme nervous irritability." Again, his daughter's assessment was insightful; the debility from the boat voyage "combined with a naturally anxious mind" had reduced him to a state of almost complete helplessness. This "naturally anxious mind" had probably not been the happiest combination to have paired with Bligh's "tornados" of temper. A series of pathetic letters written (by or for him) at the very end of his life speak eloquently of this earnest, dogged and quietly ambitious officer's anxieties. After years of zealous and faithful service, and many perils and dangers, Fryer found himself "unable to maintain himself and family of five Daughters with the half-Pay to which he is entitled." He died, in his daughter's words, "as helpless as an infant," unable even to put food to his mouth, yet another survivor of the boat voyage afflicted with a mysterious paralysis.

John Fryer was a few months shy of sixty when he was buried in his native Wells-next-the-Sea. Despite the representations of his pension petition, the former master owned a number of tidy, modest cottages at the time of his death and was able to bequeath to each of his daughters £200 as well as silver forks and teaspoons. Judging from the easy, confident style of his daughter Mary Ann's letter writing, he had also left his family a legacy of some education. A son, Harrison, had served as a midshipman under Nelson at the battle of Copenhagen—a remarkable distinction—and so would have been present to witness Nelson's public commendation of Bligh after that battle, on his ship.

Fryer's young brother-in-law, Robert Tinkler, the youngest by far of those condemned to the boat voyage, died some eight years after Fryer. Tinkler had joined the *Bounty* at the age of twelve as an able seaman destined for the quarterdeck, and indeed eventually achieved the rank of commander. He was only forty-six when he died at his home in Norwich and was reputed to have received some twenty-one wounds in the course of his intrepid service. His death too does not appear to have come at sea.

Robert Tinkler was the probable source of an anecdote that, if true, offers significant insight into the relationship of the *Bounty* crew with Bligh and Christian. Many years later, in 1857, George Borrow, a collector of folk and Romany tales, recalled "an individual who was turned adrift with Bligh, and who died about the year '22, a lieutenant in the navy, in a provincial town in which the writer was brought up"; Tinkler died in 1820, in Norwich, which was indeed the same provincial town in which Borrow had spent his youth. Tinkler died a commander, not a lieutenant, but this inconsistent detail may have been a slip of youthful memory. The ringleaders in the mutiny, this survivor of the boat voyage had told Borrow, those "two scoundrels" Fletcher Christian and Edward Young, had enjoyed great influence with the crew "because they were genteelly connected." William Bligh, son of a Plymouth customs officer, was also of solid "gentleman's" background, and certainly his naval career had progressed along the lines typical of a young gentleman; but in the calibrated social order that governed their universe, as the *Bounty*'s canny sailors, "above the common herd of uninformed illiterates," would have appreciated, a nephew of Sir George Young and the heir to the seven-hundred-year-old Christian name enjoyed birthrights—and interest—that outranked that of William Bligh.

Others of the *Bounty*'s crew—William Peckover, John Samuel, Michael Byrn, Joseph Coleman, Thomas McIntosh, John Smith—all eventually vanish from view. Joseph Coleman was in and out of hospitals for a number of years following the court-martial. He served with Bligh on two later ships, the *Director* and the *Calcutta*. On the latter, he wrote his will, which left all effects to his wife, Elizabeth, and which was witnessed by William Bligh. Coleman was last recorded as being discharged from the *Director* to the Yarmouth Hospital Ship in November 1796—and then is heard of no more. Michael Byrn is briefly glimpsed serving with Bligh's nephew, Francis Bond, on the *Prompte*. Bond interviewed Byrn at his uncle's behest during the Edward Christian affair, scrupulously following an exacting list of questions Bligh had prepared. Byrn's answers, scribbled by Bond, are often inadvertently comical: Had Byrn ever recalled Bligh calling Mr. Edward Christian's brother "a Thief"? No, said Byrn, he could only remember Captain Bligh calling the ship's company by this term. Had he ever seen Bligh shake his fist in Fletcher Christian's face? "I cannot see" had been poor Byrn's plaintive response.

Bligh was less than happy with the entirety of Byrn's performance, although a more dispassionate reading should have shown him that Byrn had done him good, not harm. He had been particularly put out that Bond had been unable to get Byrn to state that he remembered Captain Bligh's "kindness to us was such that I made songs on him." Evidently, Bligh had been wont to take his evening stroll around the *Bounty* quarterdeck as his men danced away, warm with the cozy belief that his fiddler's words about their captain were kindly meant. He had not apparently appreciated the lower deck's gift for sardonic dark humor. Almost unremarked was the fiddler's extraordinary statement that George Stewart had not "clapped his hands and said the day of the Mutiny was the happiest day of his life"—this, said Byrn, had been done by Peter Heywood.

Of the other men named, John Smith seems to have stayed with the Blighs at least until 1801, and McIntosh was to join the merchant service. And after this, nothing more has been found about them. Captain Edward Edwards was rumored to have retired to Cornwall to become an innkeeper of an establishment he named, with a monstrous lack of tact, Pandora Inn. He died in 1815, still living on his naval half pay.

Bligh apart, the man who was to achieve the greatest professional distinction of all the men who had sailed with the *Bounty* was Peter Heywood. After serving under Captains Pasley, Cloberry Christian and

Douglas, Heywood had been present with Curtis as an aide-de-camp on the quarterdeck of the *Queen Charlotte,* Lord Howe's flagship, at the defeat of the French off Ushant on June 1, 1794—reverentially spoken of afterward as the battle of the Glorious First of June. All these gentlemen, as Heywood later wrote, became "his most sincere and warm friends."

In 1803, at the age of thirty-one, Heywood was promoted to post-captain—he was two years younger than Lieutenant Bligh had been when he took command of the *Bounty*. Heywood remained in constant service until his early retirement in 1816. In addition to proving a competent and diligent officer, he made a name for himself as a hydrographic surveyor. His beautifully drafted charts—of the Malabar coast, the north coast of Morocco, the River Plate, the north coast of Sumatra and the northwest coast of Australia—often accompanied by evocative landscapes, recall the precocious sketches he had made for his family of the wreck of the *Pandora*.

"[W]ith much unwearied zeal I instructed them," Bligh had written of his tutelage of Heywood and Christian, "for I considered them very worthy of every good I could render to them, and they really promised as professional Men to be an honor to their Country."

Despite the ease with which he had been advanced through the service, and the innumerable tokens of special treatment he enjoyed, Peter's life after the court-martial had not been altogether happy. The year following her brother's release, Nessy Heywood died after catching cold at a ball on a visit to a family friend near Tunbridge Wells. Her grieving mother left a specific account of this sudden, sad illness, noting that Nessy had caught "a violent cold, and not taking proper care of herself, it soon turned to inflammation on her lungs." Later literature could do better than this, however, and when some years afterward the first comprehensive account of the mutiny on the *Bounty* was published, Nessy's death had been deftly attributed to the strain of Peter's trial: "This impassioned and most affectionate of sisters, with an excess of sensibility, which acted too powerfully on her bodily frame, sunk, as is often the case with susceptible minds, on the first attack of consumption." In later versions still, readers would learn that "protracted anxiety" had worn out Nessy's "naturally delicate constitution . . . [s]he had never recovered the effects of the tempestuous voyage to Liverpool," made when she had fled to Peter's aid. From this, it was but a small step to the final version of the legend—that Nessy had died saving her brother.

Fortunately for posterity, Nessy had compiled a book of her poems and correspondence relating to Peter's trial. Several copies of this were made and discreetly passed around. "I am glad you were pleased with my poor Nessy's little Book," Peter wrote to a fellow officer in 1808. "[T]he impression it has made on the mind of those who have read it has been favorable to me. . . ."

Nessy had not been Peter's only loss. Young Henry had died in Madras, on Peter's own ship, in 1802, and his eldest brother, James, had died in late 1804. Things had not gone so well for James, who in 1793 had fled the Isle of Man at night to escape his creditors; it appears that he had inherited the debts his father owed the Duke of Atholl. Three years later, James spent several months in Winchester Gaol, also for debts ("my present truly disagreeable situation," as he had referred to his predicament, with a young gentleman's hauteur). The year 1805 saw the death of Mrs. Bertie, Peter's relation who had tended him so kindly during his confinement. An affair she had been conducting with one of her husband's officers was discovered when her lover's ship was wrecked and her correspondence was found in a desk floating on the water. Discarded by her husband, she was rumored to have died of disgrace. Uncle Pasley had died in 1808, a baronet, having earned this distinction for his bravery in the Battle of the Glorious First of June, in which he had lost a leg.

When, those years ago, young Heywood had been summoned before the assembled company of the *Hector* to receive His Majesty's pardon, he had pledged his "future Life" would be faithfully devoted to his sovereign's service. This pledge he held good. A humble awareness that he had been reprieved—when others had not—combined with his strong religious feeling seemed to have forged of his life a kind of penance. A portrait of Captain Heywood in full-dress uniform, painted in 1822, captured the former mutineer with what his family referred to as his "thoughtful countenance." An expression of wary reserve informs his watchful face. That Captain Heywood did not indulge himself often or deeply is evident from the stark record of his service: as he himself tellingly summarized, at the time of his retirement after twenty-nine years, seven months and one day of naval service, he had been "actively employed *at sea* twenty-seven years, six months, one week and five days."

During one of his brief stints ashore, in 1806, Heywood got engaged, but ten years would pass before the marriage took place and was consummated. That he had been not entirely successful in sublimating his lurking passions is suggested by a curious document he drew up in the presence of fellow officers while at sea on the *Nereus* in 1810. On a squally late summer day, somewhere between the Downs and Spithead en route to Buenos Aires, Peter drafted a brief last will and testament. Addressed to his brother Edwin with the stern injunction that it was "to be opened at death and not before," it expressed Heywood's intention to "make some provision for an Infant under my care & protection and at present at Nurse." Payments for the care of "Mary Gray" were to be to a Mr. Makin, a color and dye merchant in London.

From his eventual marriage in 1816 to Frances Joliffe, the widow of an East Indiaman captain, there would be no children. Beneath the blue cloth and gold braid of his portrait, Heywood still wore the blue-black tattoos so attractive to Otaheite women, and one must wonder how the widow Joliffe was prepared to behold this sight. She was from a Stirlingshire family, and after her husband's death had come from Bombay to London with her infant daughter. She eventually fell under the protection of her great-uncle—Aaron Graham.

The years immediately following Heywood's marriage and retirement saw successive deaths of several figures who had cast long shadows over his life. In 1817, William Bligh, Vice Admiral of the Blue, dropped dead in Bond Street on a visit to his surgeon. He was sixty-three years old and had been living quietly with his daughters on a comfortable estate he had purchased in Kent. The cause of his death was probably stomach cancer.

Just over a year later, Aaron Graham died at the age of sixty-six, the victim of "a long train of nervous disorders," as his obituary read, romantically, if implausibly, attributed to the care he had expended in squaring the accounts of the Drury Lane theater. Among his other accomplishments, Graham had found time to overhaul the hulk prison system. He "left behind him a prudent and respectable widow," his obituary noted with just a whiff of defensiveness, "who has lately succeeded, by the death of a relation, to a great fortune." This relative was her first cousin Sir Henry Tempest, Aaron's good friend—for whom Mrs. Graham had in fact deserted her husband. Living with Sir Henry as his common-law wife, Sarah Graham had borne her cousin several children who were diplomatically given the surname "Tempest Graham."

Closing out the circle of Heywood's *Bounty* past, Sir Joseph Banks died in 1820 at seventy-seven. The slim, alert young man whose restless energy had explored all there was to know or experience, in Otaheite and elsewhere, had become heavy and gouty over the years. His influence and boundless interests had survived unchanged, however, and he had remained the president of the Royal Society up until weeks before his death—a long, unmatched run of forty-two formidable years. True to character, Banks requested in his will to be buried "in the most private manner in the Church, or Church yard of the Parish in which I shall happen to die." He entreated his "dear relatives to spare themselves the affliction of attending the ceremony" and implored them to erect no monument to his memory.

The death of Sir Joseph Banks represented more than the passing of a landmark figure in the *Bounty* saga. With Banks had gone William Bligh's most loyal and influential protector. "My Dear Admiral" was how Banks had come to address his old friend. Bligh's need of Banks would, however, outlive his death. His career was no longer at stake—but his reputation was. Of this, Peter Heywood would show himself to be keenly aware.

Whereas Bligh had never been able to free himself of the stigma of the *Bounty*, the same events appear to have intruded very little on Peter Heywood's life or career. Very occasionally an enigmatic glimmer of something that might have touched on buried memory flickers forth: "[T]he only way to get at Mens' Characters & to find what sort of stuff their Brains are composed of is to come in close contact," Heywood wrote to polar explorer James Clark Ross. Had he learned this on the *Bounty*? And what had passed through his mind when in 1813 he dutifully made note of the secret codes to be used to telegraph a naval crisis:

"242 = A disposition to mutiny; 353 = Have mutinied—I shall quell them; 414 = I shall not be able to quell them . . ."?

Retired after a career of blameless service, with the more haunting ghosts of his youth vanished to the shades, Heywood was at last in a position to relax and live more expansively. Settled comfortably in an elegant home in Highgate, with his wife and stepdaughter, Heywood enjoyed a low-key but stimulating social life. Charles Lamb was a good friend, as was the gifted Francis Beaufort, originator of the Beaufort wind scale and now the Admiralty's hydrographer. Heywood's step-daughter, Diana, reported on evenings at the home of the Duchess of St. Albans, a neighbor whom Heywood had met at Aaron Graham's.

"Peter!" the Duchess was wont to greet him, slapping him heartily on the back. The Duchess was the former Harriet Mellon, the actress whom Aaron Graham had helped pair with banker Thomas Coutts. Old Coutts had died some years before, leaving his widow the wealthiest woman in England. Mrs. Coutts's marriage to the bankrupt Duke of St. Albans, twenty-five years her junior, had been the means of adding a title to her wealth. Another Highgate neighbor, who complained about the noisy stream of "Carriages, Coachmen and other such Cattle" convening on the spectacular house of the Duchess (whom he called "Mrs. Cootes"), was Samuel Taylor Coleridge. Peter's stepdaughter would recall seeing him, to a child a somewhat frightening figure, walking with a dazed ex-pression in his eyes, which were "like boiled gooseberries."

Within his affectionate inner circle of family and friends, Captain Heywood was known as the "Capitan." To them he told his stories of the old naval school, admirals of old, "Capital fighting fellows," if some-times "rough and prejudiced," as he now recalled with nostalgic affec-tion. One of his stories told how a crusty captain had dressed his lieutenant down.

"I thought I was acting for the best," the lieutenant had protested.

"'Thought, sir!' returned the other furiously, 'and pray what business had you to think? I'll have no one think on board my ship but myself.'" Yes, they were capital fellows all.

Heywood's health was not sound and a chronic shortness of breath gave evidence of a bad heart—the effects, his family believed, of his own boat ordeal following the loss of the *Pandora*. In 1829, he removed his family to a quieter residence on the edge of Regent's Park, an area still under development, covered with flowering gorse on which partridges flew and hares and pheasant ran. It was a place "for quiet people," unattracted to the frivolities of fashionable London. His experience in life had taught him, the Capitan told his family, "that it was not desirable to know more people than were necessary, except to do them good." Optimistically, he took a lease on this place on the outer fringes of London's last wilderness for twenty-one years.

It was at this time of quiet winding down that there strode into Heywood's life a figure who threatened to overturn all that he had so carefully constructed. Edward Belcher was last seen five years earlier as a brash lieutenant on the *Blossom,* when she had made her extended visit to Pitcairn Island in 1825. Even then, as a lieutenant of twenty-six, his name buried amid many others in his captain's published report, Belcher snags one's attention. A distant, vaguely discernible warning bell sounds at each mention of his name. One hears it when Beechey relates how his lieutenant had ignored all warnings about attempting to compete with the Pitcairn youths' feats of strength and agility; one hears it too in Belcher's own description of his solo swims in heavy surf, which with casual arrogance he noted to be "more formidable in appearance than reality." And above all, one hears it in his almost lazy surety of opinion that although his captain had personally interviewed old John Adams, he "I am inclined to think did not get as accurate an account as we did below." Belcher's journal is devoid of the usual sentimental asides that characterize such works of aspiring officer-authors, nor did he wax eloquent on the morals of the Pitcairn community; he was far more interested in what had previously happened, on the island and on the *Bounty.*

When Edward Belcher, now a captain himself, entered Peter Heywood's life, he was well on his way to becoming both one of the most brilliant and one of the most despised officers in His Majesty's naval service. His surveying skills were formidable, and he was to produce magnificent charts of large parts of the globe—Africa, the Americas, the China Seas, the East Indies. The secret commissions and diplomatic duties with which he was from time to time entrusted very much suited his reckless self-assurance. He was also soon renowned for his ability, as one historian has succinctly put it, to make "life a living hell for his officers on every ship he had . . . commanded." At least two courts-martial were the usual toll of his voyages, although on one he was to instigate as many as eight. Voyages under his command often concluded with a number of his men brought into harbor already under arrest.

"Perhaps no officer of equal ability has ever succeeded in inspiring so much personal dislike" was the assessment of the famously staid *Dictionary of National Biography*. When Belcher was eventually chosen, ill advisedly, to lead four ships in the Admiralty's last-gasp polar enterprise in search of the vanished explorer John Franklin, he found a rush of volunteers for the arduous and hateful task of man-hauling sledging; life on the ice, anywhere, was preferable "to the prospect of life under Belcher." His crew, wrote one officer, were "a body of men especially chosen to serve with one of the most diabolical creatures ever allowed to rule on earth."

It was this man who in the summer of 1830 was invited to the Regent's Park home of Captain Peter Heywood. Belcher shared a number of interests, such as surveying, with the retired captain, and they also had mutual acquaintances. All this notwithstanding, it comes as a surprise to find, three months later, Belcher married to Heywood's beautiful, educated, twenty-six-year-old stepdaughter.

Diana, compliant, protected and adoring of her adoptive father, would have obeyed Heywood on the matter of marriage, as much else. But Peter's wife, the young woman's mother, was beside herself with grief and rage at what was destined to be a fatally unhappy union. Years after the marriage, a friend visiting their home found on the flyleaf of a family Bible "a diatribe against Captain Belcher written by Mrs. Heywood." The outraged mother's worst suspicions were quickly confirmed when on her wedding night Diana contracted a virulent form of venereal disease.

"I confess it requires a considerable stretch of belief to think that any man would be beastly enough to pox his own wife, and that too on their first connexion," one of Edward's own surgeons wrote him. "But you know that you did so, having a perfect knowledge of what would be the consequence from my having warned you of it in strong language."

Her fever and inflammation, "effusion of blood," pain in the groin and bladder, scalding sensation when passing water, offensive discharge—all would be aired before the public when Diana was eventually induced to petition, unsuccessfully, for divorce, and her personal correspondence relating to her marriage was published. She would return to her husband once again, and again suffer the same results.

"As long as life endures," Belcher wrote to his wife, responding to the suggestion of their separation, "by this title, and no other, I address you; you are my wife. . . . Hear the decision of your husband, whose very existence is wrapped up in yours:—No power on earth that can be available, shall be left unmoved until you are restored to me."

Before he died, Heywood was clear-sighted enough to make provisions for Diana to receive an income free and clear of her husband's interference. This amounted, in its way, to his confession of having grievously erred.

"Captain Heywood was fond of the navy, and had a justly high opinion of Captain Belcher's abilities," wrote a close friend of Diana's, after her death and by way of explanation of Heywood's role in this act of astounding bad judgment. "[T]hat officer having visited Pitcairn in the *Blossom*, gave them a ground of common interest." But the visit to Pitcairn had furnished Belcher with something more than common ground. While his captain had nattered on with Adams about the early days of the settlement, Belcher alone, of all the visitors to the island, left evidence of having raised hard, specific questions while he had Adams in the gun room.

"Those who wished to go were now sent into the boat excepting the Carpenters Mate & Armourer whom Mr. Christian detained as they might be of service," Lieutenant Belcher had written in his log of the *Blossom*, taking dictation from Adams about the last moments of the mutiny. One can imagine him sitting, one arm flung lazily over the back of a chair, listening as the garrulous old mutineer spilled his secrets. "No one else was detained. Mr. Heywood was on the Gangway and might have gone if he pleased. All the party being in the boat, the Captain was put into her. . . ."

That Peter had perjured himself at his court-martial undoubtedly formed part of the burden of penance he seemed to have voluntarily assumed in his post-*Bounty* life. On the day of the mutiny, then a tattooed boy of sixteen, he had watched from the gangway as Bligh was led toward the boat. He had, of course, not been "kept below," as he had represented, and as his uncle and Aaron Graham had bribed the boatswain to swear. On balance and in its roundabout way, in his case, justice could be said to have been fairly served; he had been found guilty, but had been pardoned to redeem himself—which he had done with, it would seem, penitence and humility. But others had been hanged—and there was the rub.

With his marriage, the ambitious Captain Belcher gained valuable connections with a still powerful family. Belcher's greatest and most useful patron, as it would turn out, was to be Francis Beaufort, since 1829 the Admiralty hydrographer—and one of Peter's very closest friends; indeed, Beaufort owed his post to Heywood, who had been offered it himself, but who had declined for personal reasons in favor of his good friend.

Years back, in 1816, at the conclusion of Heywood's final voyage after so many years' service, there had occurred an event that had deeply stirred him. As commander of the *Montagu,* Heywood was informed that there were two Tahitian men on board one of the ships in his convoy. Summoning them, the English captain greeted them in his cabin: "Mă nōw, wa, Ehō, māa?"—Welcome, my friends! Their names were "Tĕ,ăy.re'" and "Pyē,ă.hўe," Heywood later reported to the Admiralty, the precision of his spelling and inflection suggesting the relish he may have found in speaking what had briefly been the language of his youth. The Tahitians had been kidnapped and taken to Lima by an English vessel, thence made their way to Cádiz, eventually ending up on the *Calypso,* where Heywood had found them. Heartsick and homesick, they wanted badly to return to their native land. To this cause Heywood gave considerable effort, finding and paying for their passage and personally attending to the necessary paperwork. A merchant ship going to New South Wales would carry them to Port Jackson, whence they could get passage to Tahiti, or nearby Eimeo.

How easy it now was to voyage to Otaheite! For Peter Heywood, freshly retired from his unbroken and penitential service, the departure of the youths stirred up long and carefully suppressed emotion. "And after all that is said and done among us great and wise people of the earth, pray what do we all toil for, late take rest, and eat the bread of carefulness, but to reach, at last, the very state to which they are born," he wrote to a close friend, dropping his habitual guard, "—ease of circumstances, and the option of being idle or busy as we please?" There had been his cottage close by the mountains, the hill with its view over the sea; his neat garden; black beaches under the rattling palms; his wife and children. . . .

"But," he continued, as if shaking off the sudden spell that had briefly claimed him, "if I go on this way you will say I am a *savage,* and so I believe I am, and ever shall be in *some* points; but let that pass."

Toward the end of 1830, the year of his daughter's marriage, Heywood's shaky health took a sudden, alarming turn for the worse. His shortness of breath became painful, and he found even speaking difficult. From his bed, he watched the sun and wind that blew over the fields of gorse beyond his house, commenting to Diana when she drew the curtains that it was a fine wind to beat out of the Channel, where her husband was then bound. He died on February 10, 1831, at fifty-eight, and was buried in the vault of Highgate churchyard; the worldlier part of London claimed him at the last. Three years later, another body would be laid in the same vault—that of Samuel Taylor Coleridge. Thus the poet of the "Ancient Mariner" and the midshipman who had shared the voyage that had partially inspired him were brought together.

Reserved as he had been, Peter had also proven a zealous and watchful guardian of the *Bounty* saga; his complicity with Belcher apart, he left compromising fingerprints all over the later story. In his lifetime, he had cooperated with a historian in preparing an account of his own career for a series of naval biographies, and to this historian he had made available James Morrison's "Journal." In fact, Morrison was placed front and center of this work, as indicated on its title page: "This narrative is from the private journal of the late Mr. James Morrison, Gunner of H.M.S. Blenheim, who had the misfortune to witness all he has related." Joseph

Banks was dead, and there was now no other check to having it published.

This, the "Biography of Peter Heywood, Esq.," published in 1825, quickly got down to its business. Regarding the voyage of the *Bounty*, the author stated on the first page, "it would be folly" to look to her commander's *Narrative* "for any statement having a tendency to implicate his own conduct." Instead, "a private journal, long in our possession, the publication of which was only prevented by the death of its original owner, the late Mr. James Morrison . . . enables us at length to withdraw the veil by which the world has been so long blinded."

There then follows a paraphrase of all Morrison's charges against Bligh. The paraphrase itself, laced with its editorial commentary—"To this grievance another quickly succeeded"; "To this imperious menace they bowed in silence"—tended to confer additional authority. The manuscript of Morrison's "Journal" that is known to have survived—whether or not other copies, or versions once existed or now exist—shows that a second hand made amendments to the text. Some of these are merely stylistic; others are of more import, such as the consistent obliteration of George Stewart's name. The revelation that Stewart had played a central role in the mutiny had, at all costs, to be obscured in view of Heywood's own repeated reference to their close friendship.

In 1831, following Heywood's death, there appeared the first comprehensive account of the several dramas making up the story of the mutiny on the *Bounty*. Sir John Barrow was second secretary of the Admiralty when he published, at first anonymously, *The Eventful History of the Mutiny and Piratical Seizure of H.M.S. Bounty: its Causes and Consequences*. That the Heywood family was complicit in this is evident from Barrow's access to Morrison's manuscript, which was by now in Diana Belcher's hands. Barrow himself knew Heywood well and was also close to Edward Belcher, the latter from their involvement in the Admiralty's ongoing polar expeditions. It was undoubtedly for the sake of the Heywoods that Barrow included in his book the text of a letter Peter had written to Captain Beechey regarding the "confusion" over George Stewart's role. That Fletcher Christian was recommended to take the ship by George Stewart was "entirely at variance with the whole character and conduct of the latter," Heywood had written heatedly. A gentleman's word being quite enough, that ended the matter.

Barrow's classic book was the beginning of the *Bounty* book industry. Following it was an account that further sentimentalized Heywood's role, written by Diana, now Lady Belcher—Edward, the most violent and despised officer in the service, had been knighted. The piety of the Pitcairn Island community formed the greater part of Lady Belcher's book, which pointed out, as had Barrow's, that Peter's Tahitian vocabulary, drawn up to while away the hours of imprisonment on the *Hector,* had "proved of great value to the missionaries" who were first sent to Otaheite.

Published in 1870, over eighty years after the events, Lady Belcher's book, *The Mutineers of the Bounty and their Descendants . . .* , together with Barrow's, cemented the many falsehoods that had insinuated their way into the narrative up to this point: Bligh met the Heywoods at their ancestral home, "the Nunnery" (in fact, sold for debts in the year of Peter's birth), and wrote to "Deemster Heywood" to offer his son a position on the *Bounty;* Hayward and Hallett, the loyalists, were asleep on their watch and so the *passive* cause of the mutiny; Bligh knew that Heywood had been "kept below" from joining him in the boat, and by omitting this fact from his own narrative deliberately jeopardized the boy's life; the reason Heywood, with Stewart, had been kept below was that the mutineers had thought that if they were allowed to leave "there would be no one capable of navigating the ship in the event of any thing happening to Christian." Christian had spent the last hours before the *Bounty*'s final departure from Tahiti in soulful conversation with Peter and George Stewart "at the house of a worthy chief"; as "the day began to dawn," Christian prepared for departure and Peter and Stewart accompanied him to the beach. "You are both innocent," the mutineer told the young men as the sun rose over the sand, "no harm can come to you, for you took no part in the mutiny," and he confided to Peter a secret message for Christian's family that would "extenuate" his crime. In reality, of course, as Edward Christian's inquiry had determined, Christian had never come ashore during the *Bounty*'s last, fleeting visit, but had secretly cut the ship's cable and left in the night. One detail alone allegedly conveyed by Christian might well have been true. On the night before the mutiny, he had gone to bed "about half-past three in the morning, feeling very unwell," and when Stewart woke him half an hour later for his watch, "his brain seemed on fire." This was consistent with the report that he had been drinking.

―――――――

It was also from Heywood, by way of John Barrow's book, that there arose one of the most tenacious and intriguing of the *Bounty* legends. "About the years 1808 and 1809," Barrow wrote,

> a very general opinion was prevalent in the neighborhood of the lakes of Cumberland and Westmoreland, that Christian was in that part of the country, and made frequent private visit to an aunt who was living there. Being the near relative of Mr. Christian Curwen, long member of Parliament for Carlisle, and himself a native, he was well known in the neighborhood. This, however, might be passed over as mere gossip, had not another circumstance happened just about the same time, for the truth of which the Editor does not hesitate to avouch.
>
> In Fore Street, Plymouth Dock, Captain Heywood found himself one day walking behind a man, whose shape had so much the appearance of Christian's, that he involuntarily quickened his pace. Both were walking very fast, and the rapid steps behind him having roused the stranger's attention, he suddenly turned his face, looked at Heywood, and immediately ran off. But the face was as much like Christian's as the back, and Heywood, exceedingly excited, ran also. Both ran as fast as they were able, but the stranger had the advantage, and, after making several short turns, disappeared.

Heywood, said Barrow, thought about making further inquiry, "but on recollection of the pain and trouble such a discovery must occasion him, he considered it more prudent to let the matter drop; but the circumstances was frequently called to his memory for the remainder of his life." Barrow was himself from the Lake District, so his knowledge of this local "gossip" may have been firsthand.

The rumor that Fletcher Christian had not died on Pitcairn was not new, although Heywood's story gave it compelling credibility. As Barrow and others had pointed out, John Adams had never given a consistent report of the manner in which Christian had died: what was he hiding? That ships found Pitcairn before the *Topaz* was evident from Adams's own journal, which had recorded both sightings and an actual landing of several strange vessels. Whalers' logs indicate how close they came to this island, so strategically situated between the great whaling fields of the Pacific, and American ships in particular might have been sympathetic to a British mutineer. A passage back to England by way of China, where the sealers plied their trade, the East Indies or even America was not out of the question. There was also the mysterious fact that the ducats and Spanish dollars that the Admiralty had given Bligh were never found; surely, the mutineers had not let them vanish with the ship? And while nails, notebooks, furniture and clothes from the *Bounty* surfaced on Pitcairn over the years, of this hard currency there has never been a glimpse.

As early as 1796, an account of the mutineer's later adventures purportedly written by Fletcher Christian had been circulating around London. In this pamphlet, "Christian" had described his travels and eventual shipwreck off the coast of South America while rescuing "Don Henrique, Major General of the Kingdom of Chili," an act of courage that resulted, as one review stated, in Christian's "present lucrative establishment under the Spanish Government in South America."

"[I]s it possible that Wretch can be at Cadiz?" Bligh wrote to Banks in steaming outrage, "and that he has intercourse with his Brother, that sixpenny Professor, who has more Law about him than honor—My Dear Sir, I can only say that I heartily dispise the praise of any of the family of Christian and I hope & trust yet that the Mutineer will meet with his deserts."

The Christians, as it turned out, were as alarmed as Bligh about this representation; the last thing they desired was a colorful rumor floating about that would keep this family shame alive. None other than William Wordsworth loyally took up his pen in their cause to repudiate the pamphlet. In a letter to *The Weekly Entertainer*—the only letter he ever deigned to write to a newspaper under his own name—Wordsworth informed the editors "that I have the best authority for saying that this publication is spurious." Far from putting the rumor to rest, however, Wordsworth's letter only fueled further speculation. While its most sensible interpretation was that through his own wide literary connections Wordsworth knew the wag responsible for this hoax, conspiracy theorists saw it differently: what had he meant by "the best authority"? That the Christian family had told him the truth—namely, that Fletcher was in England?

One of the more intriguing questions that Edward Christian had put to the *Bounty* survivors was revealed by Lawrence Lebogue: "Mr. Christian asked me if I thought Captain Bligh could hurt his brother, if he ever came home." Lebogue's astonishingly misinformed answer—"I said Captain Bligh had such a forgiving temper, that I did not think he would"—is of less importance than the evidence that the Christians had at least contemplated Fletcher's homecoming.

That the rumors of Christian's return just happened to be in circulation precisely around the time of the *Topaz*'s discovery—"about the years 1808 and 1809," according to Barrow—was surely no coincidence. Although the Admiralty had not seen fit to act upon or broadcast the news it had received from the American sealer, Peter Heywood had been informed of it at the time. The discovery, he would recall, "naturally interested me much when I first heard of it in 1809, at the Admiralty." The story had also seen light of day in the press and probably incited much excited gossip. At least one other spurious publication appeared around this time, *Statements of the Loss of His Majesty's New Ship The Bounty . . . As Communicated by Lieutenant Christian, the Ring-leader to a Relation in England*. Very likely, the report that Fletcher Christian's island had been discovered with one of the mutineers still alive had metamorphosed in the course of its transmission from London to the Lake District into something more suggestive.

For poor Heywood, securely a post-captain with the *Bounty*, as he thought, far behind him, the news from the *Topaz* must have aroused a host of troubled, guilty thoughts. What else had John Adams told the visitors? Deep in thought, hastening along Plymouth Dock where the busy traffic brought ships from all over the world, Peter may very well have conjured his friend of old, Fletcher Christian.

Less easy to rationalize, however, although also written in this critical period of 1809, was another series of letters that came from a far less susceptible source. Away up in the Lakes, Robert Southey, future poet laureate, kept a lively correspondence with his many friends and associates. Southey was many things—a prolific wordsmith, an outpourer of often wholly unreadable masses of verse, biographer of Nelson, brother-in-law of Coleridge, friend of Wordsworth, and originator of the tale of Goldilocks and the Three Bears. His lifelong friend and most faithful correspondent was Grosvenor Charles Bedford, a resident of Brixton, and to him, in October 1809, Southey casually dropped an electrifying piece of information. In a recent review of "South Sea Missions" published in the *Quarterly Review,* Southey had made reference to "the notorious Capt. Bligh." Bedford had queried his friend on this remark and Southey made reply: "I called Captain Bligh *notorious* as the only way in which I could imply that he was a thorough rascal," Southey explained, adding a weak pun about missionaries and Christians.

"I know a great deal of that affair of the *Bounty* from James Losh," he continued. Losh had been on Edward Christian's committee of inquiry; he was the radical who had been in France, and it was he who had made the veiled reference in his diary to the *Bounty:* "I explained the real state of a Christian's mutiny." One of the men present and "much struck" at this conversation of 1798 had been Robert Southey.

"I know too," said Southey, "or have every reason to believe that Fletcher C. was within these few years in England and at his fathers house—an interesting circumstance in such a history, and one which I hardly ought to mention—so do not you let it get abroad. For tho the Admiralty would be very sorry to hang him, some rascal or other would gladly enough apprehend him for the price of blood, and hung of course he would be, but if every man had his due Bligh would have had the halter instead of the poor fellows who we brought from Taheite. Is not that a sad story of Stewart and the Taheitian Girl? . . ."

Bedford does not appear to have cared much about the revelation that the Admiralty would be sorry to hang Christian—one reason, perhaps, for their remarkable lack of action on learning the *Topaz*'s news—but was eager for details of his appearance in England, with which Southey, a week later, obliged:

"I will tell you all I know concerning poor F.C.," he wrote to his friend.

> F. is a native of this country. One of our country gentlemen (a very remarkable and strong headed man) who was his schoolfellow and knows his person as well as you know mine told me, that about five or six years ago, as he was walking near his own house with his daughter, he saw two Gentlemen riding towards him, and recognized one of them time enough to say to his daughter—look at this man—it is F.C.—and also to consider that it would be better not to speak to him—which he was on the point of doing. There was a dog with the horsemen, and presently afterwards some boys came along who had picked up a collar, bearing the name of F.C.'s father. My friend had no doubt before of his identity, and this was a confirmation of the fact. What is become of him since God knows. . . .

Fletcher Christian: aged twenty-three at the time the *Bounty* sailed, tall, dark-skinned and with long brown hair. Strong made, and now covered with exotic tattoos; a gentleman, genteelly connected.

"[I]t was very easy to make one's self beloved and respected on board a ship," Fletcher was said to have told his family, after his return from India on the *Eurydice*. "[O]ne had only to be always ready to obey one's superior officers, and to be kind to the common men, unless there was occasion for severity, and if you are severe when there is a just occasion, they will not like you the worse for it."

"Fletcher when a Boy was slow to be moved," his brother Charles had observed, in anguished incomprehension, on learning of the mutiny. He remembered his younger brother "full of professional Ambition and of Hope." Baring his arm at their final meeting, Fletcher had delightedly amazed the other with his brawniness.

"This," said the future mutineer, "has been acquired by hard labour." He said "I delight to set the Men an Example. I not only can do every part of a common Sailor's Duty, but am upon a par with a principal part of the Officers." This was to be the last time Charles saw his brother; they had parted in stormy weather, Charles back to the *Middlesex*, Fletcher to the *Bounty*.

What caused the mutiny on the *Bounty*? The seductions of Tahiti, Bligh's harsh tongue—perhaps. But more compellingly, a night of drinking and a proud man's pride, a low moment on one gray dawn, a momentary and fatal slip in a gentleman's code of discipline—and then the rush of consequences to be lived out for a lifetime. As Edward Christian wrote at the conclusion of his *Appendix*, had his brother "perhaps been absent from the Bounty a single day, or one ill-fated hour," the story might have turned out very differently. How tempting, then, to imagine him safe returned to his native land, wandering the woods and byways of the wild north country. Later tradition would have him working as a smuggler, just over the Scottish border, but known "by the authority of his family," as one Scottish newspaper reported, to have died in 1804. By this account, Fletcher Christian lived to the middle age of forty.

Charles Christian died in 1822, aged sixty. He had spent some of the intervening years working as a surgeon on a slave ship that had traveled to the Guinea coast and West Indies. He returned to live with his mother on the Isle of Man, a damaged, if not broken man, as the tenor of his writing suggests. His and Fletcher's mother predeceased him by nearly four years. Their personal effects were sold at auction a month after Charles's death.

The following year, 1823, also saw the death of the last member of this perplexing family. Edward Christian had married, but had no children, and settled in Hoddesdon, outside London, from where he ran his variegated careers as professor of common law at Downing College, Cambridge, and chief justice of Ely. He died, as his sly cousin Lord Ellenborough remarked, "in the full vigour of his incapacity." Among possessions handed down to his wife's relatives was "a strange native hat" from Pitcairn Island. Like his brother Charles, but very strangely for a lawyer, Edward did not leave a will.

Greenwich Hospital records indicate that a William Cole died in March 1833 at the age of seventy-one. Following the court-martial, the former boatswain of the *Bounty* had enjoyed what must have been a relatively comfortable ten-year stint on a single ship, *Irresistible*, with two of his sons doing duty as his "servants." He was admitted to his pension in 1805; if he was indeed the William Cole who died at Greenwich, then he had a good long run at his retirement.

William Purcell went out to the West Indies after the court-martial; eventually, he would serve in fourteen more ships before retirement. Sometime after 1800, he married Hannah Maria Mayo, a widow. Purcell died in 1834, after having "shown symptoms of derangement," in Haslar Hospital, across the water from Portsmouth. His death was thought to warrant a notice in the *Gentlemen's Magazine*, in which he was referred to as "the last surviving officer of the Bounty, and one of those turned adrift in an open boat on the Pacific ocean." Touchingly, his wife's gravestone also commemorated this event, referring to Mrs. Purcell as the relict of one who had been "an adherent of Captain Bligh's."

Purcell was indeed the last of the officers to die, but the last survivors who had sailed on the *Bounty* were still alive on Pitcairn. Mauatua— Maimiti, Mainmast, "Isabella"—the widow of Fletcher Christian, was to die in 1841, at a very advanced age. White-haired but still mentally alert, she had "frequently said she remembered Captain Cook arriving at Tahiti," as the Pitcairn Island register recorded. She had, then, seen it all, from the long-ago age of discovery when the white men descended on her island, through the death—or departure—of her famous husband. She was attended by Teraura, the widow of both Edward Young and, spanning two generations, Fletcher's son, Thursday October Christian. Teraura died in 1850.

Bligh himself did not live long enough to see the end of his own story. He had known himself to be "notorious," and read countless cruel summations of his character that appeared unchecked in every variety of literature. Doubtless he knew he was said to have pushed "the discipline of the service to which he belonged, . . . to its extreme verge . . . goaded into a mutiny a crew of noble-minded fellows, the greater part of whom it has been since discovered, pined away their existence on a desolate island." In the final telling, he "was an unfeeling tyrant, and induced the mutiny by his harshness and cruelty." Over the years, Bligh's "cruelty" would be made brutally physical; a comparison was even made

between the necessary atrocities committed by the French revolution-
aries and the deeds of the mutineers; "we will merely draw a parallel by
observing . . . the *excessive* folly and tyranny of her government." Lieutenant Bligh, who had hoped to complete the *Bounty* voyage without a single flogging, would be transformed into "Captain Bligh of the *Bounty*," a
sadistic bully who bloodied his men with the lash.

To none of these many specious charges did Bligh pay public attention; instead, he had doggedly carried on, from commission to commission. On hearing of his old commander's death, George Tobin, now
post-captain but a former lieutenant of the *Providence,* wrote to Bligh's
nephew, Francis Godolphin Bond, offering both his condolences and a
humane assessment of the man they had both served: "He has had a
long and turbulent journey of it," wrote Tobin, "—no one more so, and
since the unfortunate Mutiny in the *Bounty,* has been rather in the
shade. Yet perhaps was he not altogether understood. . . . He had suffered much and ever in difficulty by labour and perseverance extricated
himself."

Bligh was buried beside his wife in the same tomb in St. Mary's
churchyard, Lambeth. Over the years, the churchyard fell out of use
and became overgrown, and eventually was used as a rubbish dump. At
length, some 170 years after Bligh's death, a renovation was begun and
the covered graves and tombs at last dug out. In clearing the ground, exca-
vators moved a large oblong block—and found themselves looking at the
entrance to a vault. Four steps led down into an arched brick chamber,
where stood a number of lead coffins, embellished with garlands and
swags. The two standing side by side, less than two feet apart, contained
the remains of William and Betsy Bligh, while tiny coffins at the back held
the remains of twin sons, who had lived but a single day. The wooden cof-
fin lids had collapsed, revealing the adult skeletons; that of Bligh still held
tufts of mortal hair. Stunned, the intruders quickly conferred; pho-
tographs of Captain Bligh of the *Bounty* would fetch a very good price . . .

"No," recalled one, "we couldn't possibly do it." Replacing the lids,
they exited the vault, and sealed it. (Duty; they had done their duty. . . .)

Cleared and scrubbed, the inscription on the handsome monument
could be read again. Beneath a miniature graven shield, crested with a

knight's hand holding a battle axe, read a succinct summation of Bligh's life:

Sacred
to the memory of
William Bligh, Esquire, F.R.S.
Vice Admiral of the Blue,
The celebrated Navigator
who first transplanted the Bread Fruit Tree
From Otaheite to the West Indies,
bravely fought the battles of his country;
and died beloved respected and lamented
on the 7th day of December 1817
aged 64.

Surmounting the whole, in letters that had once been gold, was a simple phrase:

"In coelo quies"—There is peace in heaven.

A NOTE ON SOURCES

ABBREVIATIONS

Adm.   Admiralty papers, Public Record Office, Kew, Richmond, Surrey, UK
ATL   Alexander Turnbull Library, Wellington, New Zealand
BL   British Library, London
DTC   Dawson Turner Copies, Natural History Museum, Botany Library, London
ML   Mitchell Library, State Library of New South Wales, Sydney, Australia
MNHL   Manx National Heritage Library, Manx Museum, Douglas, Isle of Man
NLA   National Library of Australia, Canberra, Australia
NMM   National Maritime Museum, Greenwich, UK
OIOC   Oriental and India Office Collections, British Library, London
PROB   Probate Records, Public Record Office, Kew, Richmond, Surrey, UK
SLNSW   State Library of New South Wales, Sydney, Australia
VOC   Verenigde Oost-indische Compagnie (United East India Company) manu-
       script holdings, The Hague and Jakarta

PRELUDE

All of the correspondence quoted is held by the Mitchell Library (hereafter ML), State Library of New South Wales, Sydney, Australia (hereafter SLNSW). That with Duncan Campbell is found at "William Bligh, Letters 1782–1805," Safe 1/40 (letters of December 10, 1787; December 22, 1787; January 9, 1788; February 17, 1788; May 20, 1788). Bligh's correspondence with Banks is found in SLNSW: the Sir Joseph Banks Electronic Archive (February 17, 1788, Series 46.21). Bligh's letter to his wife from Coupang is found in ML, "Bligh, William—Family correspondence," ZML Safe 1/45, pp. 17–24.

Bligh's correspondence from the Dutch East Indies to Campbell, Banks, and Elizabeth Bligh is published in facsimile in Paul Brunton, ed., *Awake Bold Bligh!* (Sydney, 1989).

PANDORA

The descriptions of Peter Heywood's last day on Tahiti and his capture are found in a letter to his mother, written in Batavia on November 20, 1791, and preserved in an album of correspondence relating to his court-martial that was kept by his sister Hester (Nessy) Heywood. There are five known copies of this album; the one cited throughout this book is "Correspondence of Miss Nessy Heywood," E5. H5078, the Newberry Library, Chicago. This is also the source for Peter Heywood's poetry. Peter's Isle of Man tattoo is referred to by William Bligh in his descriptive list of the mutineers, of which there are several versions;

the earliest being that given in his notebook, held by the National Library of Australia, Canberra (NLA MS 5393) and published in facsimile, John Bach, ed., *The Bligh Notebook* (Sydney, 1987). Other details about the mutineers—their ages and places of origin—are taken from the *Bounty* Muster Book, Admiralty papers, Public Record Office (hereafter Adm.) 36/10744.

Early news of the mutiny is found in numerous contemporary newspapers: *English Chronicle or Universal Evening Post* (March 13–16, 1790), the *General Evening Post* (March 16–18, 1790), the *London Chronicle* (March 16, 1790) and the *World* (March 16, 1790), to cite only a few. The possibility of the *Bounty*'s being apprehended by the Spanish is reported in *British Mercury*, no. 20, May 15, 1790 (p. 212). The report that news of the *Bounty* mutiny had inspired Botany Bay convicts to attempt escape is found in the *London Chronicle*, April 21–24, 1792.

The transcription of the court-martial of the mutineers of the *Narcissus* is found in Adm. 12/24, and is in itself fascinating: in 1782, as newly appointed captain to the 20-gun *Narcissus*, Edwards was patrolling the eastern coast of North America when word came through the quartermaster that a mutiny was planned for that night. Swiftly, all officers had armed themselves, come on deck, and together forced the apprehension of the would-be mutineers. In the ensuing court-martial it was revealed that some forty-six men had signed up for the mutiny with the intention of securing the captain in irons and making for "Philadelphia or the first rebel fort." Once within sight of land, the plan had been to put the captain and officers into the longboat with a compass, sail the ship to port, sell her, and divide the spoils. The code word signifying that the mutiny had commenced was to have been "wine."

Edwards's papers are found in Adm. 1/1763, which includes his correspondence with the Admiralty before *Pandora* left England, his long official report, and his official correspondence following his return home. Other pertinent papers are found in Admiralty Library Manuscript MSS 180, "The Papers of Edward Edwards," held at the Royal Naval Museum and Admiralty Library in Portsmouth (and read on microfilm provided by ML: reel FM4 2098 [AJCP reel M 2515]), which includes the log of the *Pandora* (and of the open-boat journey and voyage to Batavia); Edwards's extracts from the journals of Peter Heywood and George Stewart; a memorandum written by Edwards at Tahiti; a statement written by Edwards on the loss of the *Pandora;* as well as the original sailing orders he received from the Admiralty and an account of his career. These papers were lost until 1966, having spent many years in a brown-paper parcel in a forgotten corner of the Admiralty Library (H. E. Maude, "The Edwards Papers," *Journal of Pacific History* 1 [1966], pp. 184–85).

Surgeon George Hamilton published his account of the *Pandora* voyage in *A Voyage Round the World, in His Majesty's Frigate Pandora* (London, 1793). Hamilton's account and Edwards's report have been published together as Edwards and Hamilton, *Voyage of H.M.S. "Pandora" Despatched to Arrest the Mutineers of the "Bounty" in the South Seas, 1790–91, Being the Narratives of Captain Edward Edwards, R.N., the Commander, and George Hamilton, the Surgeon* (London, 1915).

Biographical material about Edwards is found in "The Pandora Again!," *United Service Magazine*, no. 172 (March 1843), pp. 411–20.

The history of seaman John Brown and the *Mercury*, the ship that left him on Tahiti, is found in Lieutenant George Mortimer, *Observations and Remarks Made During a Voyage to the Islands of Teneriffe, Amsterdam, Maria's Islands Near Van Diemen's Land, Otaheite, Sandwich Islands, Owhyhee, the Fox Islands on the North West Coast of America, Tinian, and from thence to Canton, in the Brig Mercury, Commanded by John Henry Cox, Esq.* (London, 1791).

James Morrison wrote two accounts of the mutiny and its aftermath, both held by the

Mitchell Library: an extensive "journal" (about which more later), "Journal on HMS Bounty and at Tahiti, 1792," ZML Safe 1/42; and the much briefer "Memorandum and particulars respecting the Bounty and her crew," Safe 1/33.

For the Articles of War, see N. A. M. Rodger, *Articles of War: The Statutes which Governed Our Fighting Navies, 1661, 1749, and 1886* (Homewell, Hampshire, 1982).

The wreck of the *Pandora* is currently being excavated by the Queensland Museum, Australia; it can be followed online at www.mtq.qld.gov.au.

The story of the Botany Bay convicts is well told in Frederick A. Pottle's *Boswell and the Girl from Botany Bay* (London, 1938).

Edwards's transactions with the Dutch authorities in the East Indies are documented in manuscript holdings of the Verenigde Oost-indische Compagnie (hereafter VOC), or United East India Company. These include ARA VOC 3917, pp. 1841 and 1843; VOC 827 (Resolutions of the Governor General and Council, November 8 and 18, 1791); VOC 3940, pp. 8 verso, 9, 32, 32 verso, and 52 (all in the Algemeen Rijksarchief, The Hague); and the Minuut Resolutie Nov.–Dec. 1791 (in the Arsip Nasional Republik, Jakarta). A glimpse of Edwards's transactions at the Cape is found in Council of Policy, vol. C 202 Resolutions, Edwards, p. 185, in the Cape Town Archives Repository, Cape Town.

The fate of the *Resolution* is told by D. Renouard, "Voyage of the Pandora's Tender," 1791, ML, *D377. An edited version of this account was published as "The Last of the Pandoras," *United Service Magazine*, no. 166 (September 1842), pp. 1–13. The schooner's itinerary is reconstructed in H. E. Maude, "The Voyage of the *Pandora*'s Tender," *Mariner's Mirror* 50 (1964), pp. 217–35. Morrison gives an elaborate description of the schooner's construction in his "journal."

The *Pandora*'s complicated expenses are documented in Adm. 106/2217, Adm. 2/268, and Adm. 2/269.

Adm. 51/383 contains the *Gorgon*'s log; other relevant files are Adm. 36/11120, the *Gorgon*'s muster, and Adm. 1/1001, Captain's Letters, which includes the carpenter's report on the state of the ship on her return to Spithead.

Mary Ann Parker, the wife of the *Gorgon*'s captain, wrote an account of her voyage to Botany Bay and back, by way of the Cape, of which she gives a vivid description. Mary Ann Parker, *A Voyage round the World, in the Gorgon Man of War: Captain John Parker, Performed and written by his widow* (London, 1795). Captain Parker died shortly after he and his wife returned to England and Mrs. Parker learned that one of her children had died in their absence. The preface to her book states that it has "been most unjustly and injuriously reported, that the Authoress is worth a considerable sum of money," and goes on to explain that while Captain Parker had indeed been entitled to a share of prize money "accruing from success in the West-Indies," his debts were larger than that sum.

Even in the random accounts cited in this chapter, one finds casual references to the presence of women on board. In the transcript of the *Narcissus* court-martial, for example, one of the men on trial offers a Mrs. Collins as his alibi, stating nonchalantly that "I lye near Mrs. Collins and her two children." Similarly, in the account of the *Mercury* one learns that while on Tahiti, "Otoo happening to see a pair of [scissors] with a long chain suspended to them, given by our second mate to his wife, had a great desire to possess them, and demanded them of her; but she positively refused to give them up" (p. 32). An interesting examination of the role of usually unremarked women in the British navy is Suzanne J. Stark, *Female Tars: Women Aboard Ship in the Age of Sail* (Annapolis, 1996).

Lieutenant Clark's journal is published as *The Journal and Letters of Lt. Ralph Clark, 1787–1792* (Sydney, 1981). The description of the Botany Bay convicts is given in Watkin Tench,

A Complete Account of the Settlement at Port Jackson, in New South Wales, including an accurate description of the situation of the colony, of the natives; and of its natural productions: taken on the spot, by Captain Watkin Tench (London, 1793). Another journal covering the *Gorgon's* homeward voyage is James Scott (Sargeant of Marines), *Remarks on a Passage to Botany Bay, 1787–1792,* Dixson Library, SLNSW, MS Q43.

The anonymous poem is found in Bligh's papers in the Mitchell Library: "A Copy of Verses on the Loss of his Majesty's Ships Bounty And Pandora, the former by Mutany, the Latter by Accident upon the Coast of New holland near Endeavour Straits. A Sad Catastrophe to the Latter On the 29th of August 1791," ML, Safe 1/44.

Hamond's orders are found in the Captain's Letters for 1792, Adm. 1/1001. Montagu's log of the *Hector* is found in Adm. 51/448. Burkett's service is confirmed in Adm. 36/10544 (*Hector* muster book) and Adm. 35/758 (paybook).

The account of Peter Heywood's prayer book is given in the Reverend Thomas Boyles Murray, *Pitcairn: The Island, the People and the Pastor, to which is added a short notice of the original settlement and present condition of Norfolk Island,* 11th ed. (London, 1858), pp. 72–73.

Details of the *Chatham's* visit are found in Edward Bell's log of the *Chatham,* held by the Alexander Turnbull Library, Wellington, New Zealand (hereafter ATL): "Chatham, H.M.S., Journal of a voyage with Vancouver, 1792–4," qMS-2071–2072. The story of Peggy and George Stewart was to be the inspiration of many poems, including Byron's *The Island or Christian and His Comrades* ("There sat the gentle savage of the wild/In growth a woman, though in years a child . . .").

BOUNTY

Patrick O'Brian's biography of Banks is first-rate, as one would expect: *Joseph Banks: A Life* (Chicago, 1997). A good biographical summary is also given in J. C. Beaglehole, ed., *The Endeavour Journal of Joseph Banks, 1768–1771* (Sydney, 1962). Beaglehole also wrote the definitive biography of James Cook, which, in its account of the *Endeavour* voyage, has a great deal to say about Banks. Banks as the "lion of London" is from Beaglehole's *The Life of Captain James Cook* (Stanford, Calif., 1974), p. 273.

Banks's Tahitian adventures were first published in John Hawkesworth, *An Account of the Voyages Undertaken by the Order of His Present Majesty for making Discoveries in the Southern Hemisphere, And Successively Performed by Commodore Byron, Commodore Wallis, Captain Carteret and Captain Cook, in the* Dolphin, *the* Swallow, *and the* Endeavour, *drawn up from the journals which were kept by the several commanders, and from the papers of Joseph Banks, Esq.,* 3 vols. (London, 1773); vol. 2, pp. 79–249, covers the *Endeavour's* Tahitian sojourn. Cook objected to this popular rendition of his voyage and subsequently insisted on publishing his own account of his later expeditions.

The facetious verses come from *An Epistle from Mr. Banks Voyager, Monster-Hunter, and Amoroso, To Oberea, Queen of Otaheite* (London, c. 1773). Banks's own account of his interlude in Oberea's canoe is given in his journal entry of May 28, 1769 ("I repaird to my old Freind Oborea who readily gave me a bed in her canoe much to my satisfaction. I acquainted my fellow travelers with my good fortune and wishing them as good took my leave. Oborea insisted that my cloths should be put in her custody . . .").

The State Library of New South Wales holds one of the most important collections of Banks correspondence in the world; the Sir Joseph Banks Electronic Archive is available online at www.sl.nsw.gov.au/banks. Quoted here are Bligh's letters to Banks of August 6, 1787 (46.02), November 5, 1787 (46.08), December 5, 1787 (46.13), December 6, 1787 (46.14),

December 8, 1787 (46.15), January 9, 1788 (46.20), February 17, 1788 (46.21), and June 28, 1788 (46.25). The Natural History Museum, Botany Library, London, holds the Dawson Turner Copies (hereafter DTC), an extensive collection of transcriptions made of Banks's correspondence.

A selection of Banks's correspondence has been published by the Banks Archive Project: Neil Chambers, ed., *The Letters of Sir Joseph Banks: A Selection, 1768–1820* (London, 2000). Warren Royal Dawson, ed., *The Banks Letters: A Calendar of the Manuscript Correspondence of Sir Joseph Banks Preserved in the British Museum, the British Museum (Natural History) and Other Collections in Great Britain* (London, 1958), offers a synopsis of more than seven thousand letters. There can be few other bibliographic catalogues that are in themselves as engrossing as this mammoth publication. As the opening sentence of the preface states, "There is scarcely an aspect of British public life in the reign of George III that is not represented at first hand in the Correspondence of Sir Joseph Banks."

There were several mermaid sightings, of which that of William Munro, on June 9, 1809, is the most confidently stated: ". . . in the course of my walking on the Shore of Sandside Bay, being a fine warm day in Summer, my attention was arrested by the appearance of a figure, resembling an unclothed human female, sitting upon a rock extending into the Sea; and apparently in the action of combing its hair, which flowed around its shoulders" (DTC 17.322–324).

For Banks supplying Coleridge with Indian hemp, see Earl Leslie Griggs, ed., *Collected Letters of Samuel Taylor Coleridge*, vol. 2 (Oxford, 1956), pp. 918 ff.

Valentine Morris's letter to Banks, April 17, 1772, is in British Library, Additional Manuscripts, London (hereafter BL Add. MS), 33977.18.

The political background of the breadfruit expedition and the West India Committee's lobby is described in "The Romance of the Bread-fruit," *The West India Committee Circular*, no. 590 (May 12, 1921), pp. 197–99; and David MacKay, "Banks, Bligh and Breadfruit," *The New Zealand Journal of History* 8 (1974), pp. 61–77.

Matthew Wallen's letter to Banks of May 6, 1785, is in BL Add. MS 33978.11–12. Banks notes his own lack of good breadfruit specimens in a letter to Johann Georg Adam Forster, May 20, 1782, DTC 2.132–133.

For Banks's approval of a distinct breadfruit expedition, see his letter to Lord Liverpool, March 30, 1787, DTC 5.143–146. For Lord Sydney's letter to Banks of August 15, 1787, see DTC 5.208–209.

There are two standard and very good biographies of William Bligh: George Mackaness, *The Life of Vice-Admiral William Bligh R. N., F. R. S.*, rev. ed. (Sydney, 1951); and Gavin Kennedy, *Bligh* (London, 1978), later revised and published as *Captain Bligh: The Man and His Mutinies* (London, 1989). Mackaness is the more detailed and exhaustive, Kennedy the more insightful. Bligh's ships of service are listed on the flyleaves of a family Bible held by the Mitchell Library: "Bligh Family, Genealogy of, and Memoranda, 1754–1885," ML A2049. Cook's remarks on the duties of young officers serving him are found in Cook, *A Voyage to the Pacific Ocean. Undertaken, By The Command of His Majesty, For Making Discoveries in the Northern Hemisphere*, vol. 1 (London, 1784), p. 5. The events surrounding Cook's death are described in Gavin Kennedy, *The Death of Captain Cook* (London, 1978). Bligh's remarks made in the margins of a copy of Cook's *Voyage* are described in Lieutenant Commander Rupert T. Gould, "Bligh's Notes on Cook's Last Voyage," *Mariner's Mirror* 14 (1928), pp. 371–85. For Bligh's remarks on "improving" himself, see his letter to John Bond, April 7, 1783, published in George Mackaness, ed., *Fresh Light on Bligh* (Sydney, 1953), pp. 16 ff.

Bligh's physical description is given in the Reverend Thomas Boyles Murray, *Pitcairn:*

The Island, the People and the Pastor: to which is added a short notice of the original settlement and present condition of Norfolk Island, 8th ed. (London, 1857), pp. 60–61. Depictions of Bligh are discussed in Geoffrey Callender, "The Portraiture of Bligh," *Mariner's Mirror* 22 (1936), pp. 172–78.

The A to Z of the *Bounty*'s acquisition, dimensions, and refitting, including diagrams of the ship and a description and plan of the ship's launch, is C. Knight, "H.M. Armed Vessel *Bounty*," *Mariner's Mirror* 22 (1936), pp. 183–99; also see John McKay, *The Armed Transport Bounty* (London, c. 1989). The original blueprints of the *Bounty* are in the National Maritime Museum, Greenwich (ID 3190). Bligh's own description of his ship and her refitting is given in his second published narrative: William Bligh, *A Voyage to the South Sea, Undertaken by Command of His Majesty, for the Purpose of Conveying the Bread-Fruit Tree to the West Indies in His Majesty's Ship the* Bounty *commanded by Lieutenant William Bligh. Including an Account of the Mutiny on Board the Said Ship, and the Subsequent Voyage of Part of the Crew, in the Ship's Boat, from Tofoa, one of the Friendly Islands, to Timor, a Dutch Settlement in the East Indies* (London, 1792). This account also includes the history of European discovery of the breadfruit, Bligh's sailing orders, and his quotation regarding "the object of all previous voyages." Gavin Kennedy was the first to underscore the implications of the *Bounty*'s small size and cramped quarters, a subject elaborated upon more directly in Greg Dening, *Mr. Bligh's Bad Language* (Cambridge, 1992).

The saga of Banks's refitting of the *Resolution* is given in Beaglehole, *The Life of Captain James Cook*, pp. 293ff. Banks's reaction to the undoing of his careful adaptations is found in "Memoirs of the early life of John Elliott," BL Add. MS 42714, folios 10–11. ("He *swore* & *stamp'd* upon the *warfe*, like a Mad Man.")

For Banks's stern injunctions to "the Master & Crew," see DTC 5.210–216 (to an unknown correspondent). The possibility of an astronomer on board the *Bounty* is referred to in Banks to Lord Howe, September 9, 1787, SLNSW: the Sir Joseph Banks Electronic Archive, 45.09.

The *Bounty*'s muster provides the name, age, place of origin and date of entry on the ship's books of each member of the crew, and is found in the Admiralty records, Adm. 36/10744. The ship's establishment is reprinted in D. Bonner Smith, "Some Remarks About the Mutiny on the *Bounty*," *Mariner's Mirror* 22 (1936), pp. 200–237.

John Fryer's birth, death, and marriage records are preserved in the parish records of Wells-next-the Sea, Norfolk; I am indebted to Mike Welland of Wells for sharing his careful biographical work on John Fryer and his family. Much information is also found in the "Statement of service of John Fryer, recorded by one of his children" (National Library of Australia, MS 6592) and in Fryer's Memorial to the Admiralty (Adm. 1/4585). Robert Tinkler's birth certificate is also in the parish records (Baptisms for 1775).

Information about Thomas Denman Ledward's background is from "Memoir in MSS of the Life of Dr. Thomas Denman in the Handwriting of His Sister Sophia," Archives and Manuscripts, 5620, Wellcome Trust, London; I am indebted to Lord Denman for the Denman family tree. The excerpts from Ledward's correspondence are taken from Arthur Denman, ed., "Captain Bligh and the Mutiny of the Bounty," *Notes and Queries* 9th ser., 12 (December 26, 1903), pp. 501–2.

Hayward's recommendation is found in the letter of William Wales to Sir Joseph Banks, August 8, 1787, written from Christ's Hospital (Webster Collection), University of California, Los Angeles, Special Collections, Collection 100, Box 171, and is quoted with their kind permission. Details of Wales's teaching career were kindly provided by Christ's Hospital, London. Charles Lamb's description of Wales can be found in his *Recollections of Christ's*

Hospital (London, 1835). Francis Hayward, Midshipman Hayward's father, was the brother-in-law of a Charles Green, who was almost certainly the astronomer Charles Green, who sailed on the *Endeavour* with Banks—and who was in turn the brother-in-law of William Wales (see Francis Hayward to Sir R. M. Keith, April 6, 1787, BL Add. MS, 35538 f.106).

Hayward's biography can be pieced together from the register of St. John's, Hackney, and his lieutenant's passing certificate, Adm. 107/13. Adm. 36/8189 contains the muster of the *Halifax*, and Adm. 36/11054 that of the *Porcupine*.

William Cole's service record is in Adm. 29/1. Biographical material about James Morrison is taken from James Shaw Grant, *Morrison of the Bounty* (Stornoway, Scotland, 1997). The author is a kinsman of the *Bounty*'s boatswain's mate; the quotation from the report of Morrison's examiner is taken from p. 36.

William Peckover's career prior to joining the *Bounty* can be traced in Adm. 32/258 (pay book of the *Endeavour*), and Adm. 36/7672 and Adm. 36/8013, the muster books of the *Resolution* and *Discovery*, respectively. William Purcell's career can be traced in Adm. 2915, "Carpenters 1817–1833."

Joseph Coleman's service on the *Discovery*, with Cook, is also recorded in Adm. 36/8013. The terms of David Nelson's service are given in Banks's letter of March 30, 1787, to Lord Liverpool, DTC 5.143–146. The description of Nelson by a former shipmate is found in SLNSW: the Sir Joseph Banks Electronic Archive, "Letter received by Banks from Charles Clerke, 23, 29 November 1776," 11.03. William Brown's midshipman service is confirmed by Adm. 36/8712.

Evidence of past service with Bligh is found for Lawrence Lebogue in William Bligh, *Answer to Certain Assertions contained in the Appendix Entitled "Minutes of the Proceedings on the Court Martial held at Portsmouth August [sic] 12th 1792 on Ten Persons Charged with Mutiny on Board his Majesty's Ship the Bounty"* (London, 1794), p. 25. This rare pamphlet has been reprinted in facsimile by the Australiana Society (Melbourne, 1952). Past service for John Norton is confirmed by Bligh's *Bounty* Log, entry of May 3, 1789, and for Tom Ellison in his own testimony at his court-martial—see Owen Rutter, ed., *The Court-Martial of the "Bounty" Mutineers* (Edinburgh, 1931), p. 176.

Stephen Barney and Edward Christian, *Minutes of the Proceedings of the Court-Martial held at Portsmouth, August [sic] 12, 1792, on Ten Persons Charged with Mutiny on Board His Majesty's Ship the Bounty: With an Appendix, Containing a Full Account of the Real Causes and Circumstances of that Unhappy Transaction, the most material of which have hitherto been withheld from the Public* (London, 1794; this is also included in the Australiana Society facsimile, above). Fletcher Christian's past service both on the *Eurydice* and with Bligh in the West Indies is described in Edward Christian, "Appendix" to Barney's *Minutes*, above, pp. 76 ff. Christian's service in the *Eurydice* is confirmed by the ship's muster, Adm. 36/10359. Christian's "bright, pleasing countenance" is described in Lady Diana Belcher, *The Mutineers of the Bounty and their Descendants in Pitcairn and Norfolk Islands* (London, 1870), p. 164n.

Other material about the Christian family is found in the Christian family papers now held by the Manx National Heritage Library, Douglas, Isle of Man (hereafter MNHL; MS 09381); Mrs. William Hicks Beach, *The Yesterdays Behind the Door* (Liverpool, 1956); William Fletcher, "Fletcher Christian and the Mutineers of the 'Bounty,'" *Transactions of the Cumberland Association for the Advancement of Literature and Science*, part 2 (1876–1877), pp. 77–106; and above all in Glynn Christian's *Fragile Paradise*, rev. ed. (Sydney and New York, 1999). Incredibly, Glynn Christian, a sixth-generation direct descendant of Fletcher, was the first *Bounty* scholar to attempt to write a comprehensive biography of his famous forebear. His sleuth work unearthed a cache of hitherto unknown Christian family papers; it is these papers that are now on the Isle of Man. I am also indebted to Ewan Christian for use of family papers in his possession.

Additional information about Fletcher's father is found in *Gentleman's Magazine* 38, pt. 1 (March 1768), p. 143. The quotation from the will of Charles Christian Sr. is from *Fragile Paradise*, p. 14.

Isaac Wilkinson, another classmate of Fletcher's who became a poet, left a tribute to his boyhood friend, stating that "I can with truth say a more amiable youth I have never met with: he was mild, generous, and sincere":

> His heart was open, generous, and humane,
> His was a heart that felt for others' pain;
> Yet quick of spirit as the electric beam
> When from the clouds its darting lightnings gleam.

The quotation is from Isaac Wilkinson's *Poetical Works* (1824). The poem was written in response to Byron's damning portrait of the mutineer in his poem *The Island*.

The arresting description of the north country is from Daniel Defoe, *A Tour Through the Whole Island of Great Britain*, rev. ed., vol. 2 (London, 1962), p. 270.

A contemporary description of Cockermouth is given in William Hutchinson, *The History of the County of Cumberland* (Carlisle, 1794).

Wordsworth's lines are from *The Prelude*, Book First, lines 288ff.

Evidence of the Christian family finances is found in "The Solicitors Papers of the Christian family of Unerigg [Ewanrigg]," in the Cumbria Record Office, Carlisle (D/Ben Box 254–256).

Information about Fletcher's brother John Christian can be found in the *Cumberland Pacquet*, October 19, 1779, and *Gentleman's Magazine*, June 1791, pp. 588–89.

For an outline of the life of Fletcher's brother Edward Christian, see his entry in the *Dictionary of National Biography* (London, 1917). Edward Christian's letter to his cousin is found in the Cumbria Record Office and Local Studies Library, Whitehaven (D/Cu/3/9). Permission to quote was kindly given by Mrs. Susan Thornely.

Biographical material about Fletcher's brother Charles Christian is found in the Christian family papers, MNHL MS 09381. All quotations from the collection are made with the kind permission of the Manx National Heritage. The letter from Sir George Savile, Bart., is found in the Wentworth Woodhouse Muniments at Sheffield Archives (Rockingham Papers at Sheffield Archives—WWM R1/1982); I am grateful to the Head of Leisure Services, Sheffield City Council, for permission to use the papers.

Details of Douglas life are from Joseph Farrington, *The Farington Diary*, vol. 1 (London, 1923)—see his entry for October 4, 1796, p. 671. Description of Douglas at this time comes from A. W. Moore, *Nessy Heywood* (Douglas, Isle of Man, 1913). Other details are found in modern guides such as John Kitto, *Historic Homes of the Isle of Man* (Braddan, Isle of Man, 1990).

Heywood family history is found in Heywood family papers in the MNHL MS 09519 and in the Cumbria Record Office and Local Studies Library, Whitehaven. A valuable family pedigree ("The Heywoods of Heywood, in the County of Lancaster") was kindly provided by the Devon Record Office. Moore's *Nessy Heywood* also gives the family history. The Heywood family finances are made very plain by correspondence to and from Peter John Heywood (the *Bounty* midshipman's father) in the hitherto unregarded Duke of Atholl papers, MNHL MS AP 122 (4th) and x/5.

Peter's naval service is recorded in Adm. 6/94. His service on the *Powerful* is confirmed by Adm. 36/10590. Information about Peter's education is given in Lady Belcher, *The Mutineers of the Bounty . . .*; and Derek Robson, *Some Aspects of Education in Cheshire in the Eighteenth Century* (Manchester, 1966).

Betham's letter to Bligh, dated Douglas, September 21, 1787, is found in "William Bligh, Correspondence," ML, Safe 1/45.

Sir George Young's biography is found in the *Dictionary of National Biography;* the *Naval Chronicle* 31 (1814), pp. 177–83; Sir George Young, 3rd Bart., *Young of Formosa* (Reading, Berks., 1927); and the erratic John A. Kempe, ed., *Autobiography of Anna Eliza Bray* (London, 1884).

Information about Edward Young is given in Rosalind Amelia Young, *Mutiny of the Bounty and the story of Pitcairn Island, 1790–1894* (Oakland, Calif., 1894). The death of Captain Robert Young is reported in Oriental and India Office Collections (hereafter OIOC), L/MAR/B/46E and N/6/1/33.

Bligh describes his meeting with Stewart in *A Voyage to the South Sea . . .*, p. 161. Details of old Stromness were kindly provided by Bryce Wilson of the Orkney Museum. Genealogical history is found in Barbara Juarez Wilson, *From Mission to Majesty* (Baltimore, 1983). Lady Belcher quotes correspondence of Stewart's sister in *The Mutineers of the Bounty*, pp. 18 ff. Other correspondence is found in A. Francis Steuart, "Orkney News from the Letter-Bag of Mr. Charles Steuart," *Old-lore Miscellany of Orkney, Shetland, Caithness and Sutherland* 6 (1913), pp. 41–49 and 101–9.

The biography of John Hallett, midshipman, is established by three wills: his own (Probate Records, Public Record Office, Kew—hereafter, PROB 11/1254), that of his father, John Hallett Sr. (PROB 11/1535), and that of his aunt (PROB 11/1425), all of which cross-reference common names and addresses. His birth and baptismal certificate, as well as his naval service record, is found in Adm. 107/14. Hallett Sr.'s profession is established by numerous references in Joseph Farington's priceless gossipy multivolume diary. The service of the other Hallett brothers with the East India Company is confirmed by OIOC, J/1/14 and O/1/2.

The Hallett residence is named in two of the wills. Descriptions of Manchester Buildings is found in Walter Thornbury and Edward Walford, *Old and New London: A Narrative of Its History, Its People, and Its Places,* vol. 3 (London, 1875), p. 381.

The letter from Hallett Sr. to Banks is in BL Add. MS 33978.143. Details of Hallett's service on the *Alarm*'s commission are in Adm. 36/9639.

David Nelson's letter to Banks, dated December 18, 1787, is in BL Add. MS 33978.163.

The list of "Articles for the Voyage" is found in SLNSW: the Sir Joseph Banks Electronic Archive (45.02).

The classic account of life at sea during this age of sail is N. A. M. Rodger, *The Wooden World* (Annapolis, 1986). See also the encyclopedic and beautifully illustrated reference book by Brian Lavery, *Nelson's Navy* (Annapolis, 2000); descriptions of the duties of the warrant officers are paraphrased from p. 100. The quotation describing the boatswain's mate is found on p. 135.

Bligh's letters to Banks of September 7, 1787, and September 14, 1787, are in SLNSW: the Sir Joseph Banks Electronic Archive (45.10 and 45.11, respectively). Selkirk's closeness to the Bethams is revealed by his letter to Dr. Cullen of October 4, 1785, regarding the schooling of one of Betham's nephews, then living with Selkirk and his wife (Glasgow University Library Special Collections, GB 247 MS Cullen 87). Selkirk had another North American connection—it was he whom John Paul Jones, the famous rebel and founder of the American navy, had returned to Scotland in 1778 to kidnap.

Bligh's correspondence with Duncan Campbell, including his angry letter of December 10, 1787, is found in "William Bligh Letters, 1782–1805," ML, Safe 1/40. Duncan Campbell's correspondence with other parties (about the war on September 29; his "poor fellow" of November 7) is found in "D. Campbell, Business Letter Books" 5, December 1784–June 1788, ML, A3229.

Banks's admonition to Nelson is in DTC 5.217–225.

The discovery of Charles Christian's memoir was one of Glynn Christian's great coups, and is related in *Fragile Paradise*. A reference to trouble on the *Middlesex* led Glynn Christian to examine the ship's log, where he found details of the mutiny. Charles Christian's autobiography is now in MNHL (MS 09381). The log of the *Middlesex* is in OIOC L/MAR/B/450F.

To these sources can be added additional India Office files containing the affidavits, or "Memorials," of the aggrieved mutineers, which provide the details of what transpired on the day of the mutiny (E/1/81 [part 3], folios 153ff.). Other pertinent material is found in Madras Dispatches, E/4/873 f. 700–701; and in E/1/226 f. 122, f. 146–147, f. 171, f. 513, f. 537; Court Books B/105 f. 593, f. 595, f. 613; in B/106, f. 835; and in B/107 f. 204, f. 404, and f. 459. Service records of Aitken and Rogers are found in L/MAR/C/654 f. 15 and L/MAR/C/654 f. 8, respectively.

Additionally, a hitherto unregarded and very obscure pamphlet published by Charles Christian many years after the fact confirms that the captain of the *Middlesex* was found guilty and that the mutineers consequently received compensation for damages: Charles Christian, *An Abridged Statement of Facts, Supported by Respectable and Undeniable Evidence: with Strictures on the Injurious Influence of Calumny, and a Display of the Excellence and Invincibility of Truth* (Douglas, Isle of Man, 1818). Readers will find themselves awash in the most purple of high-strung prose. Charles Christian's impassioned description of his intervention on Grece's part is found on p. 22.

The rise of civil suits against merchant captains who had taken punitive action while at sea became a matter of concern, as is evident by a memorial drawn up on January 9, 1788, by "Sundry Commanders in the Service of the Honourable the United East India Company" (E/1/82, f. 14). In this document, it is complained that "your Memorialists having at present no legal authority to quell Mutiny and punish Delinquents on board the Ships under their command are exposed to great difficulties and dangers." The petition, which was drawn up in the Jerusalem Coffee House, was signed by forty-seven memorialists, including Captains John Rogers and John Wordsworth, a relative of the poet. As a footnote to the *Middlesex* saga, it is pleasing to observe that Seaman John William Grece went on to make "a fortune" as an underwriter at Lloyd's.

VOYAGE OUT

Information regarding the *Bounty*'s voyage to Tahiti, the twenty-three-week sojourn in Tahiti, and commencement of the return voyage, as reported by William Bligh, is taken from Bligh's log: his first draft, or personal log, is preserved in ML, "Log of the Proceedings of HMS *Bounty*," December 4, 1787–October 22, 1788 (Safe 1/46), and April 5, 1789–March 13, 1790 (Safe 1/47); his official copy submitted to the Admiralty is now in the Public Record Office (Adm. 55/151). Unless otherwise indicated in the text, all quotations are taken from the official log. This has in turn been published in a limited edition: Owen Rutter, ed., *The Log of the Bounty* (London, 1937).

Bligh names Fletcher Christian as the officer delegated to visit the governor in Tenerife in his *Voyage to the South Sea* . . . (London, 1792), p. 15.

Bligh's letters to Campbell are found in the Mitchell Library, "William Bligh Letters, 1782–1805," ML, Safe 1/40 (see letters for January 9, February 17, and June 28, 1788).

Bligh's correspondence with Banks is found in SLNSW: the Sir Joseph Banks Electronic Archive; quoted here are letters of January 9, 1788 (42.20), June 20, 1788 (46.24), and June 28, 1788 (46.25).

For Captain Cook's management, see J. C. Beaglehole, *The Life of Captain James Cook* (Stanford, Calif., 1974); Cook's punishment of men with dirty hands is referred to on p. 320.

Matthew Quintal is named as the first man flogged in Bligh's *Voyage to the South Sea . . . ,* pp. 26 ff.

Details of the attempted passage around the Horn not found in the log (such as the breaching of the whales) are taken from Peter Heywood's letter published in the *Cumberland Pacquet,* November 26, 1788.

The report that Bligh's decision to make for the Cape was returned with three cheers is recorded by James Morrison, "Journal on HMS Bounty and at Tahiti, 1792," ML, ZML Safe 1/42, p. 14. This is the source for Morrison's and other remarks on the outward voyage.

That the quarrel between Bligh and Christian began at the Cape is found in John Adams, "Narrative, 1825," ML, MS A1804. Bligh confirms his loan of money to Christian in "Attestation Mr. Wm. Bligh Plaintiff," ML, Safe 1/43, p. 21.

The description of festivities at the Cape is found in the *Diary of L. Macquarie,* entries for June 13 and 18, 1788 (ML, Lachlan Macquarie Papers, 1787–1824; A768/2). Macquarie—like William Bligh—would later be appointed governor of New South Wales.

The excerpts from Thomas Denman Ledward's letters are found in Arthur Denman, ed., "Captain Bligh and the Mutiny of the Bounty," *Notes and Queries* 9th ser., 12 (December 26, 1903), pp. 501–2.

The proposed newspaper article is found in SLNSW: the Sir Joseph Banks Electronic Archive, Series 46.26. The authorship of this article is a vexed issue. The article was sent to Joseph Banks with a note indicating that "[t]he above is transcribed from a Letter from the Master at Arms of the Bounty armed Ship to the Revd. J. Hampson Tunbridge Wells." A note in another hand at the top of the manuscript, however, states that the article was sent from "the Armorer to Mr. Hamson." Charles Churchill was the master-at-arms; Joseph Coleman, the armorer.

Despite resistance to the belief that the future mutineer was the author of this elegant memoir, evidence strongly supports the authorship of Churchill. First, the note to Banks ascribing the article to the master-at-arms was sent shortly after receipt of the article ("It came by the French Packet to Havre & here by last Friday's Post"), and apparently by Hampson himself or someone close enough to Hampson to have access to the text.

By contrast, the note ascribing the article to Coleman contains no reliable details and could have been added at any later date; it also misspells Hampson's name. More to the point, later evidence indicates that Coleman was illiterate.

A credible basis for a relationship between Hampson and Churchill can be established: Poll and rate books indicate that John Hampson, cleric, was a nonconformist minister occupying a school in Tunbridge, Kent, from 1791 on. In January 1795, his obituary appears in *Gentleman's Magazine,* p. 85: "1795 January 6 died in his 63d year, the Rev. Mr. Hampson, of Southborough in Kent, master of the free school in Southborough, pastor of a congregation of Protestant Dissenters at Tunbridge Wells, and father of the Rev. Hampson of Sunderland."

The Alumni Oxoniensis and Cantabrigensis states that John Hampson of Sunderland was in turn the son of "John Hampson of Manchester, Lancashire." The *Bounty* muster indicates Manchester as being the place of origin of Charles Churchill; it is possible, then, that Hampson was known to the master-at-arms before he moved to the dissenting school in Kent. Later circumstances suggest that Churchill was indeed literate—perhaps Hampson had been his teacher? The article does not, in any case, appear to have been published.

Details about Bligh's collision with William Purcell are found in Adm. 1/5328.

Fletcher Christian's physical prowess is described in A. G. K. L'Estrange, *Lady Belcher and Friends* (London, 1891); Christian's ease with the lower deck is described in Edward Christian's "Appendix" to Stephen Barney's *Minutes of the Proceedings . . .* (London, 1794), p. 28.

Regarding falsification of a ship's books, Article XXXI reads: "Every Officer or other Person in the Fleet, who shall knowingly make or sign a false Muster or Muster-book, or who shall command, counsel, or procure the making or signing thereof, or who shall aid or abet any other Person in the making or signing thereof, shall, upon Proof of any such Offence being made before a Court-martial, be cashiered, and rendered incapable of further Employment in his Majesty's Naval Service." Bligh's command that Fryer sign or explain his reasons for refusing is found in "Attestation Mr. Wm. Bligh Plaintiff," ML, Safe 1/43, p. 48.

TAHITI

As there was no fixed orthodoxy at this time, Bligh's spelling of all Tahitian personal names is used. A succinct and accessible account of the bewildering name changes of the Tahitian chiefs is found in Sven Wahlroos's "encyclopedia" of the *Bounty, Mutiny and Romance in the South Seas: A Companion to the* Bounty *Adventure* (Topsfield, Mass., 1989); see entries under each name.

Bligh's rules of conduct while at Tahiti are given in his *An Answer to Certain Assertions . . .* (London, 1794), p. 4.

Cook's description of his disrupted trade market is given in J. C. Beaglehole, ed., *The Journals of Captain James Cook on His Voyages of Discovery,* vol. 2 (Cambridge, 1961), p. 369.

The record of men treated for "venereals" is found in the *Bounty's* muster, Adm. 36/10744.

Morrison's account of Bligh's interference in the ship's trade is given in James Morrison, "Journal on HMS Bounty and at Tahiti, 1792," ML, Safe 1/42, pp. 25ff. Morrison's report of Christian's denial of knowledge of the desertion is at p. 371, Bligh's rebuke of his shore officers at p. 39.

The apprehension of Cook's deserter is discussed by J. C. Beaglehole, *The Life of Captain James Cook* (Stanford, Calif., 1974), pp. 565ff. The tale of near mutiny on the *Endeavour* is related in a letter from James Maria Matra to Joseph Banks, May 7, 1790, BL Add. MS 33979.29–30. Matra (born Magra) was from New York but later served as British consul in Tangier, and had his own problematic and colorful history on the *Endeavour*. The captain's clerk, having gone to bed drunk one night, some "Malicious person or persons in the Ship took the advantage of his being drunk and cut off all the cloaths off from his back, not being satisfied with this they some time after went into his Cabbin and cut off part of both his Ears." The "Malicious person" was thought to have been Mr. Midshipman Matra, who was known to have cut off the victim's clothes before in "drunken frolicks" and had been heard to say "that if it was not for the Law he would Murder him" (Beaglehole, *The Journals of Captain James Cook on His Voyages of Discovery,* vol. 1, pp. 234ff.). Although later officially acquitted of the charges, Matra never wholly shook off all suspicion.

The assertion that others intended to desert the *Bounty* at Tahiti is found in the "Affidavit of Joseph Coleman," Dixson Library, SLNSW MS Q163, p. 29.

Bligh's contention that Christian and Heywood's names were on Churchill's list is found in his letter to Francis Bond, July 26, 1794; see George Mackaness, ed., *Fresh Light on Bligh: Being Some Unpublished Correspondence of Captain William Bligh, R.N., and Lieutenant Francis Godolphin Bond, R.N., with Lieutenant Bond's Manuscript Notes Made on the Voyage of HMS Providence, 1791–1795* (Sydney, 1953), pp. 56–57. The original correspondence is in the NMM (BND/1).

Bligh's index to the missing portion of his personal log, is in ML, Safe 1/46a.

Article XVI applies to desertion, Article XXVII to sleeping on watch; see N. A. M. Rodger, *Articles of War: The Statutes which Governed our Fighting Navies, 1661, 1749, and 1886* (Homewell, Hampshire, 1982), pp. 25 and 27, respectively. Courts-martial held, for example, on deserters during the same period as the trial of the *Bounty* mutineers in the latter part of 1792 give evidence of harsh sentencing; see, for example, Adm. 1/5330.

Banks's letter to David Nelson, written some time in 1787, is found in DTC 5.217–225.

It is gratifying to note that the Tahitians received at least one great benefit from their otherwise destructive commerce with Europeans: namely, the introduction of the indispensable cat, which, as Bligh noted, kept both ship and island remarkably free of rats. The first cats arrived with Captain Wallis, the "discoverer" of Tahiti, on the *Dolphin* in 1767. Wallis noted in his log, "I gave them a Cat big with Kittens of which they were very fond—and Surprized to see her attack the Rats so eagerly" ("Log of Captain Samuel Wallis on the Dolphin During His Voyage Round the World, 1766–1768" [ML, Safe 1/98]). The Tahitians' affection for cats is made evident by a number of incidents recorded by Bligh: On November 25, 1788, Banks's old friend Oberea visited the *Bounty* by canoe: "I now got her below with her Attendants and a favorite Cat that she had bred from one that was given her by Captn. Cook," Bligh recorded.

The value of cats was also acknowledged by His Majesty's Navy, as is evident from a court-martial held off New York on December 16, 1776, on two officers of the armed schooner *St. Lawrence*. Court-martial records indicate that a Mr. Thomas Page Christian, Acting Surgeon, "put a dog into the Steerage to drive out a cat belonging to Lieut. John Graves, Commander of the said Schooner." When the dog wantonly killed the cat, the lieutenant "went to the Surgeon, and some high words passed between them. Soon after they went off in a boat ordered by the Lieutenant, and within half an hour returned, the Lieutenant being wounded in the left arm." The court found that Lieutenant Graves, the owner of the cat, had "acted unbecoming an officer" and was to be dismissed from command of the *St. Lawrence;* but that Mr. Thomas Christian was to be "mulcted one twelve month's pay" and "to be dismissed from His Majesty's Naval Service, and rendered incapable of serving in it in any capacity" (Adm. 1/5307); *sic semper tyrannis!*

MUTINY

Lebogue's statement about events after passing Whytootackee is found in William Bligh, *An Answer to Certain Assertions . . .* (London, 1794), p. 25.

Bligh's denial of frequent quarrels is found in "Attestation Mr. Wm. Bligh Plaintiff," ML, Safe 1/43, p. 28.

Quotations from Morrison's account of events preceding the mutiny are found in James Morrison, "Journal on HMS Bounty and at Tahiti, 1792," ML, ZML Safe 1/42, pp. 42 ff.

John Fryer's recollection of events before the mutiny is found in his unpublished narrative in the Mitchell Library: John Fryer, "Narrative, letter to his wife and documents. 4 April 1789–16 July 1804," ML, Safe 1/38, p. 1ff. His quote of David Nelson appears on p. 19; Hayward's acceptance of Bligh's invitation to dine is on p. 16.

For the sojourn of Cook and Bligh at Tonga in 1777, see J. C. Beaglehole, *The Life of Captain James Cook* (Stanford, Calif., 1974), pp. 531ff. The flogging of the chief is described in J. C. Beaglehole, ed., *The Journals of Captain James Cook on His Voyages of Discovery*, vol. 3 (Cambridge, 1967), entry for May 8, 1777, p. 101. John Rickman describes the flogging and cutting of thieves: "During our stay here, more capital thefts were committed, and more Indians punished than in all the friendly islands besides; one was punished with 72 lashes, for only stealing a knife, another with 36, for endeavouring to carry off two or three drinking glasses; three were punished with 36 lashes each, for heaving stones at the wooders; but what was still more cruel, a man for attempting to carry of an axe, was ordered to have his arm cut to the bone, which he bore without complaining" (John Rickman, *Journal of Captain Cook's Last Voyage to the Pacific Ocean, on Discovery* [London, 1781], p. 121). The destruction of the canoes and houses is described in Cook's *Journals*, vol. 3, October 8–10, 1777, pp. 229ff. The account of the man punished by cutting off his ears is given by Rickman: ". . . [i]n this bleeding condition he was sent on shore" (p. 174).

For the sinister drama leading to Cook's death, see Gavin Kennedy, *The Death of Captain Cook* (London, 1978).

Readers of Herman Wouk's *The Caine Mutiny* will recognize this coconut scene as the inspiration for the brilliant strawberry episode on the *Caine*. Edward Christian's "Appendix" to Stephen Barney's *Minutes of the Proceedings . . .* (London, 1794), pp. 63ff., records the further details of the confrontation over the coconuts. It should be observed that the word "break," as Christian used with Purcell, meant to disrate him.

The words of Edward Lamb, Christian's former shipmate, are found in Bligh's *An Answer to Certain Assertions . . .* , pp. 30–31.

Cook's *heivas* and other displays of his "hasty temper" are discussed by Beaglehole, *Life of James Cook*, pp. 710ff., who in turn quotes James Trevenen, then a midshipman on the third voyage: "*Heiva* the name of the dances of the Southern Islanders, which bore so great a resemblance to the violent motions and stampings on the Deck of Capt Cooke in the paroxysms of passion, into which he often threw himself upon the slightest occasion that they were universally known by the same name, & it was a common saying amongst both officers & people: 'The old boy has been tipping a *heiva* to such or such a one.'"

The lowly status of inferior officers is described in Edward Thompson, *Sailor's Letters*, vol. 1 (London, 1767), pp. 141ff.

Bligh's description of Christian's excessive perspiration suggests that Christian suffered from a condition known as hyperhidrosis, which is discussed by Glynn Christian, *Fragile Paradise*, rev. ed. (Milsons Point, NSW, and Auckland, 1999), pp. 306ff.

Bligh's pleas to Christian are recorded in Edward Christian, "Appendix," p. 69. Other details of the day of mutiny are from Bligh's log and his *Voyage to the South Sea . . .* (London, 1792).

Christian's surprise at the number of men voluntarily entering the launch is described in James Morrison's "Journal on HMS Bounty and at Tahiti, 1792," ML, ZML Safe 1/42, p. 61.

RETURN

Bligh's feat was praised in *English Chronicle or Universal Post*, March 16–18, 1790. His forthcoming book was advertised in a number of papers—see, for example, *Diary or Woodfall's Register*, May 29, 1790.

Descriptions of the voyage of the *Bounty*'s launch are taken from Bligh's *A Narrative of the Mutiny, on Board His Majesty's Ship* Bounty; *and the Subsequent Voyage of Part of the Crew, in the Ship's Boat, From Tofoa, one of the Friendly Islands, to Timor, a Dutch Settlement in the East Indies* (London, 1790); and from Bligh's logs. A book of signals that Thomas Hayward carried with him was used by Bligh as a notebook, from which in turn he kept his running log. A memorandum by Bligh at the back of the notebook explains his methodology: "This account was kept in my bosom as a common memorandum of our time & transposed into my fair Journal every day when the weather would admit with every material circumstance which passed." The notebook is held by the National Library of Australia (William Bligh, "Notebook and List of Mutineers," 1789, NLA MS 5393) and is published in facsimile: John Bach, ed., *The Bligh Notebook* (Sydney, 1987). The "fair Journal" is Bligh's personal log, held by the Mitchell Library (William Bligh, "Log of the Proceedings of HMS *Bounty*," April 5, 1789–March 13, 1790, ML, Safe 1/47). Bligh's official copy submitted to the Admiralty is in the Public Record Office, Adm. 55/151. Except where noted, quotations are from the official log.

The accuracy of Bligh's log is indicated by some latter-day investigations at Tofua. In 1985, efforts were made by Marie-Thérèse and Bengt Danielsson, distinguished historians of the South Pacific, to locate the cave in which Bligh and his men had camped while on Tofua. The Danielssons found the cave on the island's northwest corner, as described by Bligh, and also found that the cave's dimensions (one hundred yards wide) and situation on the beach exactly accorded with Bligh's account. More remarkably, the position Bligh had determined by sextant was tested by the captain of the ship that had brought the Danielssons to Tofua, and who with "infinitely more sophisticated navigational equipment at his disposal, arrived at exactly the same figure" (Marie-Thérèse and Bengt Danielsson, "Bligh's Cave: 196 Years On," *Pacific Islands Monthly*, June 1985, pp. 25–26).

It is instructive to contrast these findings with those of a similar investigation conducted on Tubuai, where the mutineers had attempted to construct a fort. According to James Morrison, "the Fort was laid out in a quadrangular form, measuring 100 yards on each square," but when Glynn Christian visited in 1980, he found the remains to measure "48 yards square" (Glynn Christian, *Fragile Paradise*, rev. ed. [Sydney and New York, 1999], pp. 211ff.). Morrison's inaccuracy may be a result of both the distance in time from which he was describing the events and his overly grandiose recollection of the mutineers' achievements.

The rationing of food that Bligh's men swore to honor is best appreciated from artifacts of the voyage, the actual tiny cup, coconut scale, and bullet weight that were used to measure each meal (now in NMM). The bullet, which remained in the Bligh family for generations, was identified by Bligh with the following label: "This bullet, ⅟₂₅ of a lb. was the allowance of Bread which supported 18 men for 48 days, served to each person three times a-day" (the Reverend Thomas Boyles Murray, *Pitcairn: The Island, the People, and the Pastor; With a short account of the mutiny of the Bounty* [London, 1853]. Bligh still wore the bullet weight, "strung on a blue ribbon round his neck," at the end of his life (Alfred Gatty, "Barker and Burford's Panoramas," *Notes and Queries*, 4th s., 7, [May 20, 1871], p. 432).

Bligh's role in the European exploration of the Fiji Islands is described in G. C. Henderson, *The Discoverers of the Fiji Islands: Tasman, Cook, Bligh, Wilson, Bellingshausen* (London, 1933). For a succinct overview of this work as it pertains to Bligh, see Owen Rutter, "The Vindication of William Bligh," *The Quarterly Review* 261 (October 1933), pp. 279–91.

Bligh's letter from Coupang to his wife is in the Mitchell Library, ZML Safe 1/45, pp. 17–24 (published in facsimile in Paul Brunton, ed., *Awake Bold Bligh!* [Sydney, 1989]).

The mutinous incident at Surabaya and the formal inquiry held on his men is described by Bligh in his personal log (his official log of events between his departure from Coupang and his arrival in England is missing; it may be that the Admiralty did not require an account of this portion of the voyage). Bligh's account is substantiated by VOC records, which contain a lengthy dispatch regarding Bligh's arrival from the governor of North-East Java, Jan de Greve, to the governor general and council, dated September 25, 1789. Following Bligh's insistence on the arrest and interrogation of the troublemakers, Governor de Greve, "according to the enclosed documents, had reported that these three persons had nothing against their commander and therefore had asked him immediately to excuse them and had been forgiven by him, while on the contrary the other two rebels Fryer and Purcell according to the request of Bligh had been put on spice vessels" (VOC 3862). Bligh's remarks about Fryer's "vicious" disposition, that his men wished to stay in Batavia town, and that the Dutch captain of the *Vlijt* was afraid are also from her personal log.

The unfavorable impression left by Bligh's interaction with his officers in the Dutch Indies is recorded by Amasa Delano, *Narrative of Voyages and Travels, in the Northern and Southern Hemispheres: Comprising Three Voyages Round the World; Together with a Voyage of Survey and Discovery in the Pacific and Oriental Islands* (Boston, 1817), pp. 145 ff.

Bligh's remarks about the sale of the *Bounty* launch are found in his *Voyage to the South Sea . . .* (London, 1792), p. 257.

John Fryer, "Narrative, letter to his wife and documents. 4 April 1789–16 July 1804," is in ML, Safe 1/38.

For Ledward's letter, see Arthur Denman, ed., "Captain Bligh and the Mutiny of the Bounty," *Notes and Queries* 9th ser., 12 (December 26, 1903), pp. 501–2.

Bligh's voyage in the *Bounty* launch is generally reckoned, among historically known and documented voyages of survival at sea, to be challenged only by Sir Ernest Shackleton's great boat voyage in the *James Caird*, made in April–May 1916, from Elephant Island to South Georgia in the South Atlantic.

Bligh's presentation to the King is reported in the *General Evening Post*, March 16–18, 1790.

Advertisements for the more titillating account of the mutiny are found in a number of papers—for example, the notice under the caption "MUTINY—OTAHEITIAN FEMALES" in *Diary or Woodfall's Register*, June 4, 1790. Similarly, the Royalty Theatre Drury Lane production of *The Pirates* is advertised in a number of London papers; see *Gazetteer and New Daily Advertiser*, May 15, 1790, and *Diary or Woodfall's Register*, May 11, 1790.

Fanny Burney's characteristically vivid account of meeting with Windham is found in *Diary and Letters of Madame D'Arblay, edited by her niece*, vol. 3 (London, 1843), pp. 113 ff.

For letters of commiseration to Banks on the failure of the breadfruit expedition, see Joshua Steele to Banks, May 24, 1790, BL Add. MS 33979.34; Johann Friedrich Blumenbach (the cranial enthusiast) to Banks, June 9, 1790, BL Add. MS 8097.261–262; Olof Swartz to Banks, March 31, 1790, BL Add. MS 8097.344–345. The expression of hope that the mutineers would be hanged is made by Hinton East in a letter of October 6, 1790, Kew (BC 2.19); quoted with permission of the trustees of the Royal Botanic Gardens, Kew, England.

James Mario Matra's letter to Banks of May 7, 1790, is found at BL Add. MS 33979.29–30.

For the public description of Fletcher Christian, see *English Chronicle or Universal Evening Post*, March 16–18, 1790.

Charles Christian's memoir, which includes Bligh's conversation with Captain Taubman, is found in MNHL MS 09381, pp. 27 ff.

The biography of Captain Sir Hugh Cloberry Christian is given in *The Naval Chronicle* 21 (1809), pp. 177–89. For the biography of John Christian Curwen, see Edward Hughes, *North Country Life in the Eighteenth Century*, vol. 2 (Oxford, 1965); and Henry Lonsdale, *The Worthies of Cumberland* (London, 1867).

Bligh's theory that Fletcher Christian deliberately mishandled the ship is given in Edward Christian's "Appendix" to Stephen Barney's *Minutes of the Proceedings . . .* (London, 1794), p. 71.

The majority of correspondence to or from the Heywood family is from "Correspondence of Miss Nessy Heywood," E5. H5078, the Newberry Library, Chicago. Some letters are printed in Edward Tagart, *A Memoir of the Late Captain Peter Heywood, R.N., with Extracts From his Diaries and Correspondence* (London, 1832).

Bligh's letters to Elizabeth Bligh, Duncan Campbell, and Joseph Banks are in Brunton, *Awake Bold Bligh!*

The *Times*'s comments remarking on the lack of resistance to the mutineers are from March 26, 1790.

The transcripts of the courts-martial held for both the loss of the *Bounty* and William Purcell are in Adm. 1/5328 (part 2). Purcell's mutinous behavior is described in Bligh's *Narrative . . .* , p. 55. The suggestion that Purcell was recommended by Banks is made in Edward Christian, *A Short Reply to Capt. William Bligh's Answer* (London, 1795), p. 10.

Bligh's comments to Banks about the courts-martial are given in his letter of October 24, 1790, SLNSW: the Sir Joseph Banks Electronic Archive, 46.03.

Purcell and Fryer played modest but significant roles in another naval drama at the Cape, en route from Batavia to Europe. Toward the end of February 1790, the *Guardian*, a British ship that had been crippled by an encounter with an iceberg, limped into Table Bay under the skillful and courageous command of Lieutenant Edward Riou—another of Cook's men. Finding the remainder of the *Bounty*'s company on hand, Riou had gratefully taken the opportunity to recruit skilled British seamen to help him make necessary repairs and had officially taken on Purcell, Fryer, and Robert Tinkler. Purcell, who was in no blazing hurry to get back to England, being still technically a "prisoner at large," was as a professional carpenter an especially welcome addition to Riou's shattered crew. As for John Fryer, this stint at the Cape was probably the high point of his long and dogged ordeal and, spreading his cramped wings, he had risen to the occasion, proving a reliable and invaluable mover of stores. When, in early June, Riou at last prepared to send the detained men home, he had entrusted Fryer with letters for his family and the Admiralty. "Mr. Fryer will give you this," he had written to his family, "he is [a] good honest plain modest man." Riou's correspondence is found in M. D. Nash, ed., *The Last Voyage of the Guardian: Lieutenant Riou, Commander, 1789–1791* (Cape Town, 1990).

Francis Masson discusses John Fryer and the seeds in a letter to Banks of May 27, 1790, SLNSW: the Sir Joseph Banks Electronic Archive, 13.45. Masson used a number of the other Bountys as seed couriers.

John Fryer's visit to Joseph Christian is referred to in the pamphlet by Edward Christian, *A Short Reply . . .* , p. 4 (reprinted in facsimile by the Australiana Society, Melbourne, 1952). For Jane Austen's patronage, see Deirdre Le Faye, ed., *Jane Austen's Letters*, 3d ed. (Oxford, 1997), p. 211 and note on p. 506. That John Christian resided with Joseph Christian following his elopement is evident from Andrew Oliver, ed., *The Journal of Samuel Curwen, Loyalist*, vol. 2 (Salem, Mass., 1972), pp. 879 ff.

The merchandise "proposed to be Shipped for Capt. William Bligh" from Joseph Christian is found in Adm. 1/1507; the fact that this invoice survives amid official Admiralty papers, and not Bligh's personal correspondence, is in itself intriguing. Bligh's list of personal losses to the Admiralty is also found at Adm. 1/1507.

Correspondence of Bligh and Banks regarding the second breadfruit voyage is found in SLNSW: the Sir Joseph Banks Electronic Archive; for Bligh's memo, see "Capt. Bligh, Hints for an outfit, March 1791," 49.05; Banks's orders to his new gardeners are found in his memo of June 25, 1791, "Instructions for Mr. James Wiles," 49.09; Bligh's letter to Banks concerning Peckover, dated July 17, 1791, is in 50.05.

For Fanny Burney's remark about her brother and Bligh's narrative, see *Diary and Letters . . .* , part 3, pp. 101ff. James Burney's role in the preparation of Bligh's published accounts is discussed in Rolf du Rietz, "Three Letters from James Burney to Sir Joseph Banks," *Ethnos*, no. 1–4 (1962), pp. 115–25.

PORTSMOUTH

Descriptions of Portsmouth at this time can be found in *A New Portsmouth Guide; Being a Description of the Ancient and Present State of the Place* (Portsmouth, 1790); and G. J. Marcus, *A Naval History of England*, vol. 1 (Boston, 1962), pp. 394ff.

Advance press concerning the capture of the mutineers is found, for example, in *Scots Magazine* 54 (April 1792), pp. 196f.; the *General Evening Post*, April 10–12, 1792, describes Heywood's tattoos.

The description of Nessy Heywood is found in Lady Diana Belcher, *The Mutineers of the Bounty and their Descendants in Pitcairn and Norfolk Islands* (London, 1870), p. 142. Nessy's biographer was A. W. Moore; his *Nessy Heywood* (Douglas, Isle of Man, 1913) also gives descriptions of Douglas at this time. Both of these works also quote from the Heywood family correspondence, as does Edward Tagart, *A Memoir of the Late Captain Peter Heywood, R.N. with Extract from his Diaries and Correspondence* (London, 1832). The petition served on Mrs. Heywood and her daughters for debts, with reference to their "contumacious" behavior, is found in MNHL (MS M4 Lib. Wills, 9L 725 1791 [1], Braddon and Douglas—Episcopal, 13/8/02). Nessy's claim that her father died of gout is found in Nessy Heywood to Dr. Thorkelin, October 9, 1790, Edinburgh University Library, Edinburgh, Scotland, La. III. 379/446ff. 818–19. All quoted correspondence between Nessy and other members of the Heywood family is from "Correspondence of Miss Nessy Heywood," E5. H5078, the Newberry Library, Chicago.

The *Dictionary of National Biography* (London, 1917) has entries for a number of the naval officers referred to in this chapter.

Information about Thomas Pasley is found in *The European Magazine, and London Review*, September 1805, pp. 162ff.; Louisa M. Sabine Pasley, *Memoir of Admiral Sir Thomas Sabine Pasley* (London, 1900); and Rodney M. S. Pasley, ed., *Private Sea Journals 1778–1782, Kept by Admiral Sir Thomas Pasley, Bart. when in command of H. M. Ships* Glasgow *(20),* Sybil *(28) and* Jupiter *(50)* (London, 1931).

Captain Edwards's letter to C. Christian of July 17, 1792, is in the Papers of Edward Edwards, Admiralty Library MSS 180, held at the Royal Naval Museum and Admiralty Library, Portsmouth. The only known contenders for this "C. Christian" are Fletcher's brother Charles Christian, whose own papers make no mention of the Heywoods, and Captain Hugh Cloberry Christian, known as Captain Christian—and whom John Curwen informed Nessy he would be meeting, and whom he recommended to her as the person most likely to be of assistance to Peter.

Montagu's career is given in James Ralfe, *Naval Biography of Great Britain*, vol. 2 (Boston, 1828), p. 6; and John Marshall, *Royal Naval Biography*, vol. 1 (London, 1823–1835), p. 39.

For the career of Colpoys, see *Naval Chronicle* 11 (1804), p. 265. Hamond's biography is found in Marshall, *Royal Naval Biography*, vol. 2, pp. 54–60; and Records of the Trinity House (Adm. 81449).

Lord Hood's correspondence with the Admiralty regarding the allocation of ships, and other matters relating to the court-martial, is found in Captains Letters, Adm. 1/1002.

A number of memorials describe Duckworth's life and career: G. G. Cunningham, *Lives of Eminent and Illustrious Englishmen* (Glasgow, 1836), pp. 198–202; *The Annual Biography and Obituary* (London, 1818), pp. 136ff.; *British Naval Biography: Comprising the lives of the most distinguished admirals, from Howard to Codrington; with an outline of the naval history of England, from the earliest period to the present time* (London, 1839), pp. 597ff.; his physical description is given in *Gentleman's Magazine*, September 1817, p. 275, and October 1817, pp. 372ff. His fondness for his own pigs is described in Mrs. Cornwell Barron-Wilson, *Memoirs of Miss Mellon, Afterwards Duchess of St. Albans* (London, 1886).

The scant career notes of Captain Bazely can be found in David Syrett and R. L. DiNardo, eds., *The Commissioned Sea Officers of the Royal Navy 1660–1815*, rev. ed., vol. 1 (Brookfield, Vt., 1994), p. 52; and *Gentleman's Magazine*, April 1809, p. 389. Details of his finest hour on the *Alert* are found in William Laird Clowes and Clements Robert Markham, *The Royal Navy: A History from the Earliest Times to the Present*, vol. 4 (London, 1899), pp. 8ff.

Curtis's biography is given in *The Annual Biography and Obituary* (London, 1817), pp. 380–91; *Naval and Martial Biography* (1806), pp. 120–24. The anecdote about his coach ride is told in "Old Sailor," *The Log Book; or Nautical Miscellany* (London, 1830), p. 461.

Keats's biography is from his obituary in the *Times* (London), April 8, 1834; and Marshall, *Royal Naval Biography*, vol. 1, pp. 342–47.

For biographies of Captain John Knight, see Marshall, *Royal Naval Biography*, vol. 1, pp. 154–65; and *Naval Chronicle* 11 (1804), p. 425.

An obituary in the *Maidstone Journal*, February 24, 1807, contains biographical information about Colonel Holwell. In his will much can be learned about this military man from the cherished objects he passes on: a Falkland Island stone seal "with my crest set in gold," "my pistols and fiddle," a "model of the monument erected over the Black Hole Calcutta 'in petrified water,'" "my faithful horse Dicky" (PROB 11/1457, 201).

The outline of Aaron Graham's biography is given most straightforwardly in *Dictionary of Canadian Biography*, vol. 5, *1801–1820*, (Toronto, 1991), pp. 361–62, where he is referred to as "incomparably the greatest civil servant in the history of Newfoundland"; and in *The Annual Biography and Obituary* (1820), pp. 402–22. His family details are confirmed by the records at Holy Trinity Church, Gosport. Adm. 36/7517 confirms Graham's naval service with Pasley. Other aspects of his multifaceted career must be pieced together from other sources. His early love of theatrics is attested to in Sir R. Vesey Hamilton and John Knox Laughton, eds., *Recollections of James Anthony Gardner, Commander R.N.* (London, 1906), Publications of the Navy Records Society, vol. 31; Gardner served with Graham in Newfoundland. Graham's correspondence with Sheridan is found in Cecil Price, ed., *The Letters of Richard Brinsley Sheridan*, vol. 2 (Oxford, 1966), passim. Graham's service during the Nore mutiny is documented in James Dugan, *The Great Mutiny* (New York, 1965), passim; his relationship with Coutts and Harriet Mellon is found in Ernest Hartley Coleridge, *The Life of Thomas Coutts, Banker* (London, 1920), passim.

There is a tantalizing suggestion that Aaron Graham was related to Dr. James Graham, a Scottish quack doctor who had achieved enormous notoriety for his Temple of Health, a

London "spa" in which nubile beauties were displayed clad in healthful mud and not much else before a leering public; Emma Hart, the future Lady Hamilton beloved by Nelson, made her London debut here. The relation to James Graham is suggested by A. G. K. L'Estrange, *Lady Belcher and Friends* (London, 1891), p. 13.

The various legal considerations before and after the court-martial are discussed in D. Bonner Smith, "Some Remarks About the Mutiny of the *Bounty*," *Mariner's Mirror* 22 (1936), pp. 200–237, which also discusses the mustering of the witnesses.

Events at Portsmouth for September 8 are described in *Gentleman's Magazine*, September 1792, p. 860.

The life of the Right Honorable Samuel Lord Viscount Hood, Baron of Catherington and a Baronet, is amply covered in a number of memorials and biographies: see, for example, *The Annual Biography and Obituary* (1817), pp. 371–79; *British Naval Biography* . . . , pp. 414–18.

The letter from Lord Hood to Lord Bridport is found in BL, Bridport Papers, Add. MS, 35194 f. 166.

Contemporary news accounts of the French massacres are found, for example, in *Gentleman's Magazine*, September 1792, pp. 854 ff.; and the *Times*, September 12, 1792.

Morrison's and Muspratt's letters of character are published in Owen Rutter, ed., *The Court-Martial of the "Bounty" Mutineers* (Edinburgh, 1931).

PROB 11/1301 establishes Cam's Hall, Fareham, as the place of employment of Muspratt's brother Joseph. Information on the Delmé family is found in Christine Bartlett et al., *Titchfield: A History* (Titchfield, Hampshire, 1982). Information about Stephen Barney was kindly provided by the Portsmouth City Council, Museums and Records Service, taken from the Hampshire Directories of 1784 and 1792, Fareham sections; St. Peter & St. Paul, Fareham records; and Corporation records 1782–1788 (CF 18/2); and by the Isle of Wight Record Office (JER/BAR/3/12/45–48, 212). Barney's house in Fareham is now the Lysses House hotel.

Captain Douglas's career and tragic life are described in the *Naval Chronicle* 25 (1811), pp. 353–82; and J. W. Norie, comp. and arr., *The Naval Gazetteer, Biographer and Chronologist* (London, 1842), pp. 101 ff.

For Inglefield's colorful biography, see Marshall, *Royal Naval Biography*, vol. 2, pp. 62–70. An account of his travails at sea is given in John Nicholson Inglefield, *Capt. Inglefield's Narrative, concerning the loss of His Majesty's ship, the Centaur, of seventy-four guns: and the miraculous preservation of the Pinnace* (London, 1783). Byron's borrowings can be seen in *Don Juan*, Canto II; verse LXI is quoted. Inglefield's travails on the domestic front are chronicled in *New annals of gallantry: containing, a complete collection of all the genuine letters which have passed between Captain Inglefield, and Mrs. Inglefield; signed with their respective names, relative to a charge brought by the former against the latter, for partiality to her black servant. To which are added, the black's affidavits, pro and con, and Mrs. Inglefield's also, upon this extraordinary business. Likewise, the letters of Mr. Mills, man-midwife, of Greenwich, relative to his conduct since the suspicion of this strange connection* (London, 1785). Adm. 1/1988 contains correspondence relating to the *Centaur* and Inglefield's letter on behalf of the pirates.

Captain Bertie's meager record is given in Marshall, *Royal Naval Biography*, vol. 1, p. 195; and in an obituary in *Gentleman's Magazine*, May 1824, pp. 459 ff. His meeting with Jane Austen is recorded in her letters; see Deirdre Le Faye, ed., *Jane Austen's Letters*, 3d ed. (Oxford, 1997), p. 117.

James Modyford Heywood's biography is found in *Gentleman's Magazine*, April 1798, p. 356; important details are also found in A. Aspinall, ed., *The Later Correspondence of George III*, vol. 1 (Cambridge, 1962), pp. 15–16. Evidence of Heywood's relationship and close friendship with Richard, Earl Howe is found in his will, PROB 11/1305, of which Lord Howe was named as executor. The royal visit of 1789 is described by Fanny Burney in *Diary and Letters of Madame D'Arblay, edited by her niece*, vol. 2 (London, 1843), p. 56; and in the local press, see for instance *Exeter Flying Post*, August 27, 1789. Details of the colorful life of Sophia Heywood Musters are given in a short description of the Musters family found in the Norfolk Record Office (HMN 5/235/4–8). This famous beauty was painted by Reynolds, Romney, and Stubbs; a portrait of Mr. Musters and his wife on horseback was later returned to Stubbs by the jealous husband with the request that Sophia, whom he believed to have been unfaithful to him, be painted out. Stubbs complied and, until restored, this painting showed a stable lad leading a horse with a vacant side saddle (*John and Sophia Musters Riding at Colwick Hall*, dated 1777, by George Stubbs; in a private collection).

That James Modyford Heywood read Peter's letter from the Cape to Lord Howe is evident from Peter John Heywood's letter to his son Peter of December 15, 1788, MNHL MS (AP 122 [4th]—33[a]); this letter also contains Mr. Heywood's version of the events between himself and the Duke of Atholl. Howe's letter to Captain Curtis of September 8, 1792, is in HO 119 Howe; Richard, Earl Howe to Sir Roger Curtis, Huntington Library, San Marino, Calif.

COURT-MARTIAL

Day-to-day events are taken from the contemporary press and logs of the *Hector* and *Duke*: Adm. 51/448 and Adm. 52/3097 contain the captain's and master's logs of the *Hector*; Adm. 51/265 and Adm. 52/2985, the same of the *Duke*.

The transcription of the court-martial of the mutineers is found at Adm. 1/5330. These records were published by Owen Rutter, ed., *The Court-Martial of the "Bounty" Mutineers* (Edinburgh, 1931); this was reprinted by the Notable Trials Library—with an introduction by Alan Dershowitz (Birmingham, Ala., 1989).

Stephen Barney, Muspratt's lawyer, also published a partial, less accurate transcript, *Minutes of the Proceedings . . .* (London, 1794).

Several books outlined court-martial protocol, including a work by one of Peter Heywood's advisers: John Delafons, *A Treatise on Naval Courts Martial* (London, 1805). This manual uses incidents from both Bligh's court-martial of 1790 and that of the *Bounty* mutineers as instructive examples.

Hood's opinion that the defendants should be tried together is found in Adm. 1/1002.

Distinguished members of the audience attending the trial are cited by *The Star* • *Daily Evening Advertiser*, September 19, 1792.

Biographical information on John Fryer's family was kindly supplied by Mike Welland, from parish records in Wells-next-the-Sea.

John Hallett's travel expenses are found in Adm. 106/2217.

For John Smith's continued service with Bligh, see Edward Christian, *A Short Reply to Capt. William Bligh's Answer* (London, 1795), p. 6 (reprinted in facsimile by the Australiana Society, Melbourne, 1952).

The record of the court-martial on Captain Edwards and the officers of the *Pandora* is found at Adm. 1/5330.

DEFENSE

The atrocities of the French Revolution are reported in the *Times*, September 12, 1792; the influx of refugees reported in articles of September 14 and 15.

The age of Joseph Coleman is a vexed question. Adm. 36/8013, the muster of the *Discov-*

ery, records his age as twenty-five in March 1776; Adm. 36/10744, the muster of the *Bounty*, as thirty-six in August 1787; Adm. 35/298, the muster of the *Calcutta*, as forty-eight in 1795; and Adm. 6/271, a hospital record, as forty-eight in January 1793. I have chosen to follow the age stated in the muster of the *Bounty*, which is at least consistent with that of the *Discovery*.

The superiority of written testimony is stated in John McArthur, *Principles and Practice of Naval and Military Courts Martial: with an appendix illustrative of the subject*, 4th ed., vol. 2 (1813), pp. 161–62.

Early versions of Peter Heywood's defense, entitled "The Defence of Peter Heywood at a Court Martial held on him & others on board H. M. Ship the Duke at Portsmouth September 12th, 13th, 14th, 15th, 16th, 17th & 18th 1792," are found in "Correspondence of Miss Nessy Heywood," E5. H5078, the Newberry Library, Chicago; and MNHL MS 09519/2/1. A slightly more polished version was published in Edward Tagart, *A Memoir of the Late Captain Peter Heywood, R.N., with Extracts From His Diaries and Correspondence* (London, 1832).

Byrn's service record is outlined in Adm. 73/2, his admission form for entrance to Greenwich Hospital. The muster of the *Robust*, Adm. 36/8495, confirms his service with Lieutenant Inglefield. That he was held in irons throughout the voyage of the *Gorgon* is stated by James Scott (Sargeant of Marines), *Remarks on a Passage to Botany Bay, 1787–1792* (Sydney, 1963), from the original manuscript held by Dixson Library, SLNSW, MS Q43; see entry for April 5, 1792.

For Morrison's stint as a *taio* of a chief, see James Morrison, "Journal on HMS Bounty and at Tahiti, 1792," ML, ZML Safe 1/42, pp. 140 ff.

The article describing the uncommon caliber of men on the *Bounty*, written by an unidentified officer of the *Brunswick*, appeared in *Gentleman's Magazine*, December 1792, pp. 1097–98.

The baptismal record of Charles Norman, son of Charles and Mary Norman, is found in the archives of Holy Trinity Church, Gosport. Bligh's letter to Norman's brother is found with other documents of the court-martial, in Adm. 1/5330 and in Owen Rutter, ed., *The Court-Martial of the "Bounty" Mutineers* (Edinburgh, 1931).

Bligh's indulgent remarks about Ellison were made in his letters to Duncan Campbell, cited in "Voyage Out." Christian's calling Ellison a monkey is in Edward Christian's "Appendix" to Stephen Barney's *Minutes of the Proceedings . . .* (London, 1794), p. 74, note.

The description of North Shields is taken from William Whellan & Co., *History, Topography, and Directory of Northumberland* (London, 1855), pp. 467 ff. That McIntosh's mother ran a public house is stated by Edward Christian, "Appendix," p. 62. Bligh's letter to Mrs. Tosh is found in the court-martial documents, as cited above.

William Muspratt's baptismal certificate is found in the Bray parish records, in the Berkshire Records Office. London Guildhall Records, MS 21543, p. 27, indicate that John Muspratt, William's father, was admitted to the Bray almshouse on June 8, 1781. Evidence of John Muspratt's suicide is found in the coroner's account book, in the Berkshire Records Office, noting the day of death as December 6, 1786; and an article in the *Reading Mercury*, December 11, 1786.

William's brother Joseph married a Rebecca Fryer less than a year after the court-martial in nearby Fareham; "Fryer" is not a Fareham name; there is, however, a Rebecca Fryer in the family of the *Bounty*'s master—a relative who accompanied John Fryer to Portsmouth, there to meet William Muspratt's brother? This would be too delicious. . . .

Burkett's earlier service on the *Hector* is confirmed by Adm. 36/10544 and Adm. 35/758.

John Millward's biography is drawn from parish records of Stoke Damerel, Plymouth, which records both his own christening on June 15, 1767, and the marriage of his parents,

Henry Millward, a mariner "lately discharged from H.M.S. *Ocean,*" and Mary Simmons, widow, on March 18, 1762, in the Dock Chapel. John Millward's trade as a sailmaker is recorded in Adm. 102/271. Descriptions of Stoke Damerel of the time are found in Daniel and Samuel Lysons, *Magna Britannia: Being a Concise Topographical Account of the Several Counties of Great Britain,* vol. 6 (London, 1822)—Samuel Lysons, incidentally, was a friend of William Bligh.

SENTENCE

The account of the Heywood family's reaction to Peter's sentence and all correspondence between Nessy and other members of the Heywood family, including that of Aaron Graham, are taken from the "Correspondence of Miss Nessy Heywood," E5. H5078, the Newberry Library, Chicago.

Information about James Heywood's naval career is found in Adm. 36/11467 and Adm. 36/12747, which show him as a twenty-nine-year-old master's mate on the *Caesar,* Captain Nugent, in 1795.

Peter's letter to Dr. Patrick Scott is held by the National Maritime Museum, Greenwich (A GC/H/26/2).

Reports of the conclusion of the court-martial appear in a great many papers; see, for example, the *Times,* September 18, 1792; the *Hereford Journal,* September 26, 1792; the *Reading Mercury,* September 24, 1792; and the *Observer,* September 23, 1792.

Aaron Graham's marriage to Sarah Dawes is confirmed by Guildhall Library Doc. MS 10091/135; and Sir Henry Tempest's will, Ref. PROB 11/1613, 386 ff., the latter also giving proof of her relationship to Sir Henry.

The admission of Coleman and Byrn to Greenwich Hospital is confirmed by Adm. 73/2, Adm. 73/5, Adm. 73/38, Adm. 6/271, and Adm. 2/1136. The later activities of McIntosh are mentioned in Edward Christian's "Appendix" to Stephen Barney, *Minutes of the Proceedings . . .* (London, 1794), p. 62.

Muspratt's petition is discussed, with quotations from the Admiralty's legal briefs, by Bonner Smith, "Some Remarks About the Mutiny of the Bounty," *Mariner's Mirror,* 22 (1936), pp. 200–237. The muster of the *Hector* shows that Muspratt was discharged, in theory to the *Royal William,* on February 10, 1793, the day before his reprieve—although the ship's papers show no record of Muspratt.

Information about the post-court-martial movements of the various ships is found in ship's logs and the local press; see, for example, the *Times,* September 26 and 28, 1792.

Records of punishment are found in the logs of the ships: for the *Hector,* Adm. 51/448; the *Brunswick,* Adm. 51/112; the *Bounty,* Adm. 55/151.

William Howell's biography comes from Gavin Kennedy, *Bligh* (London, 1978), pp. 199ff.; *Gentleman's Magazine,* January 1822, p. 92; the *Bury and Norwich Post,* January 16, 1822; Suffolk Record Office, Bury St. Edmund's Branch, FL 574/3/15; "Recollections of St. Johns' Portsea, from 1872–1880" (kindly provided by the Museums and Records Service, Portsmouth City Council); and Adm. 36/11296.

The account of Howell's hours spent with the mutineers is reported in the journal of the Reverend Thomas Haweis, under his entry for September 16, 1796, ML, MSS 633. For a detailed examination of Howell's interaction with the mutineers and later missionaries, see Rolf E. Du Rietz, *Peter Heywood's Tahitian Vocabulary and the Narratives by James Morrison: Some Notes on Their Origin and History* (Uppsala, 1986).

Reports of the pardon appear in many newspapers; see, for instance, the *Times,* October

30, 1792, and the *Evening Mail*, October 29, 1792. The fullest report is found in the *Oracle*, October 30, 1792, which describes Graham's escort of Peter off the ship in the *Hector's* boat. Peter Heywood's inheritance is reported, for example, in the *Observer*, September 23, 1792.

Events of the last days of the condemned mutineers are described in the logs of the *Hector* and the *Brunswick;* and the fulsome report by an anonymous officer of the *Brunswick* in *Gentleman's Magazine*, December 1792, pp. 1097f., which contains the account of Morrison's ministration to his former shipmates. The account of the boats ringing the *Brunswick* is found in the *Hampshire Chronicle*, November 5, 1792, as is the report of the condemned men's exit from their "cell" and thanks to their captors. The report of the men's farewells to one another and insistence on their innocence is found in the *Reading Mercury*, November 5, 1792, and the *Diary or Woodfall's Register*, October 31, 1792, for example, the latter recording the absence of respectable people. The official report of the execution is found in Captain Curtis's log of the *Brunswick*.

Haslar Hospital records are found in Adm. 102/271.

The whereabouts of the manuscript of Howell's sermon are now unknown; it is known only by its title: William Howell, "Original Autograph ms Sermon preached on the Sunday after the Execution of Three Mutineers on the text: Hebrew 13v. 17. 16pp. 4 to. Portsmouth, 1792."

See the *London Chronicle*, October 30 to November 1, 1792, and the *Times*, October 31, 1792, for accounts of the reported sufferings of the mutineers.

Andrew Snape Hamond's report to the Admiralty is found in Adm. 1/1002.

Morrison's later service is documented in James Shaw Grant's *Morrison of the Bounty* (Stornoway, Scotland, 1997). Muspratt's reaction to the executions is described in the *Caledonian Mercury*, December 10, 1792.

Heywood's later career is documented in John Marshall, "Peter Heywood, Esq.," *Royal Naval Biography*, vol. 2, part 2 (London, 1825), pp. 747–97.

The remarkable letter by the midshipman of the *Queen Charlotte* was written by James Clerk to his father, John Clerk, on December 12, 1793; the letter is quoted here with the kind permission of Sir Robert Clerk, Bart., and is located in the National Archives of Scotland, GD18/4250.

JUDGMENT

For the incident with Admiral Bowyer, see, for example, Joseph Farrington, *The Farington Diary*, vol. 1 (London, 1923), p. 217 (entry for July 18, 1794).

The pamphlets cited are: Sir George Montagu and Edward Pelham Brenton, *A Refutation of the Incorrect Statements, and Unjust Insinuations, contained in Captain Brenton's Naval History of Great Britain, as far as the same refers to the conduct of Admiral Sir George Montagu, G.C.B. In a letter addressed to the author* (London, 1821); and Sir Roger Curtis, *The reply of Sir Roger Curtis, to the person who stiles himself A neglected naval officer* (London, 1784). For a similar series of pamphlets following Cook's second voyage, see Johann Georg Adam Forster, *A Voyage Round the World in His Britannic Majesty's Sloop, Resolution, commanded by Capt. James Cook, during the Years 1772, 3, 4, and 5* (London, 1777); the same author's *Reply to Mr. Wales's Remarks* (London, 1778); and William Wales, *Remarks on Mr. Forster's Account of Captain Cook's last Voyage round the World, in the Years 1772, 1773, 1774, and 1775* (London, 1778).

There are many sources reporting Nelson's famous signal; see, for example, Ernle Bradford, *Nelson: The Essential Hero* (London, 1977), pp. 338ff. This book also contains Nelson's prayer before the action, remarkable, amid much else, for its failure to request personal safety: "May the Great God, whom I worship, grant to my Country, and to the benefit of Europe in general, a great and glorious Victory; and may no misconduct in any one tarnish it; and may humanity after Victory be the predominant feature in the British Fleet. For myself, individually, I commit my life to Him who made me, and may his blessing light upon my endeavours for serving my country faithfully. To Him I resign myself and the just cause which is entrusted to me to defend. Amen. Amen. Amen."

Bligh's letters to Banks relating to the *Providence* voyage are found in SLNSW: the Sir Joseph Banks Electronic Archive, Series 50. Bligh's remarks about the *Providence* officers, and the ill health of the two men formerly with him on the *Bounty*, are found in his letter of August 30, 1791 (50.13); his comment regarding Portlock was made in a letter of July 17, 1791 (50.05). His report of returning to his "little flock" is in a letter of August 4, 1793 (50.29). Bligh's description to Banks of his treatment by Lord Chatham and his reaction to the allegations made by Edward Christian and Morrison are found in his letter of October 30, 1793 (50.32).

Lieutenant Francis Godolphin Bond was the son of Bligh's half sister (from Bligh's mother's first marriage). Bond had been badly burned and disfigured in an explosion on an earlier voyage. The somewhat complicated Bligh-Bond family tree is discussed in George Mackaness, ed., *Fresh Light on Bligh: Being Some Unpublished Correspondence of Captain William Bligh, R.N., and Lieutenant Francis Godolphin Bond, R.N., with Lieutenant Bond's Manuscript Notes Made on the Voyage of HMS Providence, 1791–1795* (Sydney, 1953). Bond's forcibly expressed complaints against Bligh are found in an undated letter to his brother Thomas Bond (pp. 68ff.). The original correspondence is in the National Maritime Museum, Greenwich (BND/1).

For Bond's log, see above and George Mackaness, "Extracts from a Log-Book of HMS Providence Kept by Lt. Francis Godolphin Bond RN," *Royal Australian Historical Society Journal* 46 (1960), pp. 24–66. The log itself is in Adm. 55/96.

Bligh's personal log of the *Providence* is found in ML A564-2; his official log is found in Adm. 55/152–153. The latter has been published in a limited edition: William Bligh, *The Log of H.M.S. Providence* (London, 1976). For several years following his return to England, Bligh had hoped to publish an account of this second voyage, but never did—the Admiralty's coolness may well have deterred him.

Bligh's letters to his wife of September 13, 1791 (on the outward voyage), and October 2, 1792 (from Coupang), are in the Mitchell Library ("Bligh, William—Family correspondence," ZML Safe 1/45, pp. 31ff., 35ff., respectively). Bligh's letters to the Admiralty from the Cape are found in Adm. 1/1507.

For the significance of Bligh's several visits to Van Diemen's Land, see George Mackaness, *Captain William Bligh's Discoveries and Observations in Van Diemen's Land* (Sydney, 1943).

The Reverend William Ellis, *Polynesian Researches*, vol. 1 (London, 1829), p. 63, records that the first missionaries to Tahiti "were conducted to a large, oval-shaped native house which had been but recently finished for Captain Bligh, whom they expected to return."

Matthew Flinders's quote on the Endeavour Strait is found in Matthew Flinders and Robert Brown, *A Voyage to Terra Australis*, vol. 1 (London, 1814), p. xxix. The relationship of Matthew Flinders, *Providence* midshipman and future navigator, with William Bligh is examined in Madge Darby, "Bligh's Disciple: Matthew Flinders's Journals of HMS *Providence* (1791–1793)," *Mariner's Mirror* 86, no. 4 (November 2000), pp. 401–11. A close account of the navigation of the strait by Bligh and Portlock is given in George Mackaness, *The Life of Vice-Admiral William Bligh, R.N., F.R.S.,* rev. ed. (Sydney, 1951), pp. 276 ff.

Alexander Andersen's report of January 23, 1793, to Joseph Banks of Bligh's arrival at St. Vincent's is found in SLNSW: the Sir Joseph Banks Electronic Archive, 56.03. Reports of the Jamaican House of Assembly's generous award to Bligh and Portlock and Banks's response to the awards are preserved in two newspaper cuttings, found at 50.26 and 50.09, respectively. Bligh's correspondence regarding the payment of this award is held by the Somerset Record Office (DD/DN508-511). Bligh's lists of all plants delivered to the several destinations are in Adm. 1/1508.

The reaction of Mydiddee, the Tahitian passenger, to the gibbeted men along the Thames is described by Lieutenant George Tobin in his private log in the Mitchell Library (ZML A562). His official log is in Adm. 55/94–95. Mydiddee died shortly after arrival in England. The Tahitian stowaway remained in Jamaica to help the gardeners; see Madge Darby, *The Story of Mydiddee* (London, 1988).

Bligh's departure from the *Providence* to the warm applause of his men is described in the *Kentish Register,* September 6, 1793.

George Tobin's letter to Francis Bond of December 15, 1817, is from a transcript in ML of the privately owned original, Ab 60/8; the letter is published in George Mackaness, ed., *Some Correspondence of Captain William Bligh, R.N., with John and Francis Godolphin Bond, 1776–1811* (Sydney, 1949).

The report of Fletcher Christian's words to Bligh about his duty is made in John Fryer, "Narrative, letter to his wife and documents. 4 April 1789–16 July 1804," ML, Safe 1/38.

Bligh's recommendations of his men to the Admiralty are found in Adm. 1/1508, pp. 173 ff.; his letters to the Admiralty concerning his pay and expenses are found in Adm. 1/1509. The failure of the *Providence* men to gain promotion is remarked on by James Guthrie (senior) to Lieutenant Bond, January 3, 1794, published in Mackaness, *Fresh Light on Bligh,* p. 72.

For a vivid description of Lambeth at this time, see Aline Grant, *Ann Radcliffe* (Denver, 1951), pp. 77 ff.

The attack on Earl Fitzwilliam is reported by the *Times,* October 29, 1792.

Banks's letter of September 1, 1793, praising Bligh to Lord Chatham is found in SLNSW: the Sir Joseph Banks Electronic Archive, 54.01.

The Heywood family's attacks on Bligh are reported in Francis Godolphin Bond, "Letter from Thomas Bond, November 1792," ML, MSS 6422.

Pasley's remarks to Matthew Flinders, of August 7, 1793, are quoted by the kind permission of the National Maritime Museum (NMM FLI/1).

Information about the later years and death of John Christian is found in *Gentleman's Magazine,* June 1791, pp. 588 ff.; Richard Holworthy, *Monumental Inscriptions in the Church and Churchyard of Bromley, County Kent* (London, 1922), p. 60, number 478; Centre for Kentish Studies, Maidstone, Microfilm of Bromley burials, see sub. June 22, 1791, and January 7, 1800 (Mrs. Sarah Christian); PROB 11/1335, 12.

Information about Charles Christian is taken from his unpublished autobiography, MNHL MS 09381, with the kind permission of the Manx National Heritage.

Information about Edward Christian, including his attempts to apprehend the tree vandal, is from the Christian family pedigree, MNHL MS 09381/8/2, and quoted with the kind permission of the Manx National Heritage; J. Venn, *Alumni Cantabrigienses* (Cambridge, 1922); and material kindly provided by St. John's College, Cambridge. The remark about a strain of eccentricity in the family is made by Mrs. Hicks Beach in *The Yesterdays Behind the*

Door (Liverpool, 1956), p. 68. A copy of the letter addressed to Edward Christian that first appeared in the *Cumberland Packet* can be found in SLNSW: the Sir Joseph Banks Electronic Archive, 46.35.

A number of the men participating in Edward Christian's inquiry, including Edward Christian himself, have entries in the *Dictionary of National Biography* (London, 1917). See also C. S. Wilkinson, *The Wake of the Bounty* (London, 1953), p. 71.

The quotation regarding Samuel Romilly's discussion of "'American' ideas" is found in Simon Schama, *Citizens: A Chronicle of the French Revolution* (New York, 1989), p. 295. A glimpse of Romilly's friendship with Edward Christian is seen in Samuel Romilly, *Memoirs of the Life of Sir Samuel Romilly, written by himself with a selection from his correspondence edited by his sons*, vol. 1 (London, 1840), p. 67.

For the Reverend William Cookson, see A. Aspinall, ed., *The Later Correspondence of George III*, vol. 1 (Cambridge, 1962), pp. 370, 579, and passim. For Cookson's weight, see Farrington, *The Farington Diary*, p. 196 (entry for June 5, 1794).

Information about William Gilpin is found in Barnes and Mortlake History Society publication no. 30, September 1969, p. 4; for evidence of a neighborly connection between Gilpin and Joseph Christian, see John Eustace Anderson, *A Short Account of the Mortlake Company of the Royal Putney, Roehampton and Mortlake Volunteers Corps 1803–6* (Richmond, 1893), provided by the London Borough of Richmond upon Thames Local Studies Library, along with an undated newspaper cutting about the Gilpins from "an old ledger" (22.9.1906). The quotations from Gilpin's visiting cousin regarding Edward Christian's inquiry are from Peter Benson, ed., *My Dearest Betsy: A Self-Portrait by William Gilpin, 1757–1848* (London, 1981), pp. 133 ff.

From a document in the London Metropolitan Archives, John France would seem to have been a commissioner of bankruptcy (London Deeds, ref. O/014/014, date 1804); additional information was kindly supplied by the Temple Inns of Court. Captain John Wordsworth is glimpsed in an account of the loss at sea of William Wordsworth's brother: Alethea Hayter, *The Wreck of the Abergavenny* (London, 2002).

James Losh has an entry in the *Dictionary of National Biography* "Missing Persons" supplement (Oxford, 1993). His remark regarding Christian's mutiny is found in James Losh, "Diary," held by the Jackson Collection, Carlisle Library (entry for April 3, 1798). For his relationship to Wordsworth, see Paul Kaufman, "Wordsworth's 'Candid and Enlightened Friend,'" *Notes and Queries*, n.s., 9, (November 1962) pp. 403–8. Excerpts of Losh's diary have been published: Edward Hughes, ed., *The Diaries and Correspondence of James Losh*, 2 vols. (Durham, 1962–63).

Dorothy Wordsworth's description of Edward Christian is found in her letter to Jane Pollard of June 26, 1791; see Alan G. Hill, ed., *Letters of Dorothy Wordsworth: A Selection* (Oxford, 1981), pp. 9 f. Wordsworth's college days at St. John's are described in Mary Moorman, *William Wordsworth: A Biography*, vol. 1 (Oxford, 1957), which also makes mention of Wordsworth's relation to Frewen and Fisher.

For the remarks about breadfruit as food for West Indian slaves, see Hinton East to Banks, July 19, 1784, Royal Botanic Gardens, Kew (BC 1. 168). The economic and political issues behind the breadfruit venture are discussed in David MacKay, "Banks, Bligh and Breadfruit," *The New Zealand Journal of History* 8 (1974), pp. 61–77.

A favorite fiction inserted at the end of many accounts of Bligh's Tahitian voyages is that the breadfruit was disliked and spurned in Jamaica, and hence Bligh's efforts had been useless. By contrast, see Dulcie Powell, "The Voyage of the Plant Nursery, H.M.S. *Providence,*

1791–1793," *Bulletin of the Institute of Jamaica*, Science Series no. 15 (1973), p. 7, which asserts that the fruit is "absolutely relied upon in rural areas, where breadfruit in its season, is eaten three times a day."

Edward Christian's letter to Wilberforce reporting on his "inquiry" is in the Bodleian Library, Oxford (Bod Ms. Wilberforce d.15/1 Fol.22r–23v.). Wilberforce's friendship with Edward Christian is discussed in John Pollock, *Wilberforce* (New York, 1977), p. 8. The striking abolitionist character of Edward Christian's committee and its remarkably numerous associations with William Wordsworth and his circle were first established and explored by Wilkinson, who was the first scholar of the *Bounty* to look beyond the particulars of its own history to the wider contemporary world of English politics and letters. This in itself was enlightening, but such observations serve only as a backdrop to his main contention—which must for the moment be reserved for the following chapter. Suffice it to say at this point that central to Wilkinson's thesis is the highly convincing premise that Coleridge's "Rime of the Ancient Mariner" was in part inspired by Fletcher Christian's adventures.

Edward Christian's report was made in the form of an appendix to Stephen Barney's publication of the minutes of the court-martial: Stephen Barney, *Minutes of the Proceedings of the Court-Martial held at Portsmouth, August [sic] 12, 1792. On Ten Persons charged with Mutiny on Board His Majesty's Ship the Bounty. With an Appendix, Containing A full Account of the real Causes and Circumstances of that unhappy Transaction, the most material of which have hitherto been withheld from the Public* (London, 1794).

For examples of language commonly employed by naval officers in this great age of sail, see Sir R. Vesey Hamilton and John Knox Laughton, eds., *Recollections of James Anthony Gardner, Commander R.N.* (London, 1906), Publications of the Navy Records Society, vol. 31, pp. 43ff., 61, 66, 69ff., 160, 169ff.

James Morrison's two narratives are held by the Mitchell Library: "Memorandum and particulars respecting the Bounty and her crew," Safe 1/33; and "Journal on HMS Bounty and at Tahiti, 1792," ML, ZML Safe 1/42.

The Reverend Mr. Howell's letter to Molesworth Phillips of November 25, 1792, is found in SLNSW: the Sir Joseph Banks Electronic Archive, 48.01. Phillips's letter to Banks of December 12, 1792, apparently accompanying Morrison's "Journal," is found in BL Add. MS 33979.188–189.

Bligh's public rebuttal of Edward Christian's charges is made in William Bligh, *Answer to Certain Assertions contained in the Appendix to a Pamphlet, entitled "Minutes of the Proceedings on the Court Martial held at Portsmouth August [sic] 12th 1792 on Ten Persons Charged with Mutiny on Board His Majesty's Ship the Bounty"* (London, 1794), also published in facsimile by the Australiana Society. Bligh's unpublished remarks on Edward Christian's charges, on the court-martial testimony, and on Morrison's narrative are found in William Bligh, "Attestation Mr. Wm. Bligh Plaintiff" and "Remarks on Morrison's Journal," both held by the ML (Safe 1/43).

For Joseph Farington's report concerning Bligh's intention to answer all charges against him, and the actions of the Heywood family, see Farrington, *The Farington Diary*, vol. 1, p. 56 (entry for June 23, 1794).

Howe's letter regarding Peter Heywood's difficulties in getting promoted is found in HO 119 Howe; Richard, Earl Howe to Sir Roger Curtis, July 23, 1794, Huntington Library, San Marino, Calif. The lawyer's report is given in John Marshall, "Peter Heywood, Esq.," *Royal Naval Biography*, vol. 2, part 2 (London, 1825), pp. 747–97. Peter Heywood's "Lieutenant's Passing Certificate" and statement of service are found in Adm. 107/19 and Adm. 6/94; for comparison with James Morrison, see Adm. 106/2217.

The will of Sir George Young is found in PROB 11/1515.

The reviews of Edward Christian's "Appendix" and Bligh's response are found respectively in the *British Critic* 4 (November 1794), p. 559, and 4 (December 1794), p. 686. Edward Christian's final word is given in Edward Christian, *A Short Reply to Capt. William Bligh's Answer* (London, 1795), published in facsimile by the Australiana Society (Melbourne, 1952).

The verses from *The Borderers* can be found in *The Poetical Works of William Wordsworth*, vol. 1 (Oxford, 1963), verses 1727 ff.

For Coleridge's notebook entry, see Kathleen Coburn, ed., *The Notebooks of Samuel Taylor Coleridge*, vol. 1 (New York, 1957), #174 G.169.22 or folio 25". For Coleridge's dazzling poetic process, see Jonathon Livingston Lowes, *The Road to Xanadu* (Boston, 1927); or immodestly, this author's own *The Way to Xanadu* (New York, 1994), about traveling to the landmarks of *Kubla Khan*. The line from "The Rime of the Ancient Mariner" can be found in *The Complete Poetical Works of Samuel Taylor Coleridge*, vol. 1 (Oxford, 1975), part 4, verses 232 ff.

LATITUDE 25° S, LONGITUDE 130° W

The discovery of Pitcairn ("Pitcairn's" in earliest accounts) is recorded in Admiral Philip Carteret, "An Account of a Voyage Round the World," in John Hawkesworth's *Voyages*, vol. 1 (London, 1773). The meandering and remarkable voyage of the *Bounty* under Christian's command until arrival at Pitcairn is described in H. E. Maude, "In Search of a Home: From the Mutiny to Pitcairn Island (1789–1790)," *Journal of the Polynesian Society* 67, no. 2 (June 1958), pp. 104–31.

The log of the *Topaz*, Captain Folger (April 5, 1807–February 10, 1808) is found in the Nantucket Historical Association Research Library, MS 220: ship's logs, no. 105. News of the *Topaz*'s discovery was first published in Mayhew Folger, "Mutineers of the Bounty," *Naval Chronicle* 21 (1809), pp. 454–55; it was later reported in a review of *Voyage de Dentrecasteaux . . .*, *Quarterly Review*, February 1810, pp. 21–43; Lieutenant Fitzmaurice's report appears at pp. 23 ff. The *Bounty* Kendall chronometer had a long and colorful history of its own. Months after leaving Pitcairn, with his crew suffering from scurvy, Folger called in at the Spanish colony of Juan Fernández, where the Spanish garrison, in contravention of all sea law, impounded his ship, imprisoned his crew, and confiscated the *Bounty* chronometer. This was then purchased at an unknown date by a Señor Castillo for three doublons. On his death in 1840, his family sold it to Captain Thomas Herbert, HMS *Calliope*, who gave it to what was then the United Service Museum in London. It was then acquired by the National Maritime Museum in Greenwich, where it can be seen today (along with John Adams's pigtail)—still, reportedly, keeping good time. Walter Hayes, *The Captain from Nantucket and the Mutiny on the Bounty* (Ann Arbor, Mich., 1996), contains most material relating to Folger's visit, along with vivid background information. Finally, a letter from Folger's wife describes what her husband had told her of his discovery (Mary Folger to Mary Rappee, 1846, Nantucket Historical Association Research Library, Folger Family Papers, MS 118, folder 32).

Manuscript copies of Pipon's report are found in SLNSW: the Sir Joseph Banks Electronic Archive: "Papers concerning the discovery of Pitcairn Island and the mutineers of HMS Bounty, 1808–1809, 1813–1815" (Series 71.05). Pipon's account was published in a review of *Journal of a Cruize made to the Pacific Ocean, Quarterly Review* 13, no. 26 (July 1815), pp. 352–83. This report was closely paraphrased, along with a copy of Captain Staines's report, in "Nautical Anecdotes and Selections; Mutineers of the Bounty," *Naval Chronicle* 35 (1816), pp. 17–25. An expanded version of Pipon's account was published as "The Descendants of the Bounty's Crew," *United Service Journal* (1834), part 1, pp. 191–99.

Lieutenant John Shillibeer of the Royal Marines on board the *Briton* also left an account: John Shillibeer, *A Narrative of the* Briton's *Voyage to Pitcairn's Island* (Taunton, 1817); it was Shillibeer who reported Thursday October's reaction to the West Indian. An important article based on Shillibeer's report was also published in an unnamed newspaper (possibly the *Sydney Gazette*) in 1817, preserved in ATL, qMS-2259. "Account of Pitcairn's Island Received from Mr. Rodney Shannon, Lieutenant on Board the King's Ship, 1815," Suffolk County Record Office, Bury St. Edmund's (Ref 941/56/92), is also from this voyage. A brief report was also made by Lieutenant H. B. Willis, along with a marvelous sketch of the island and the picturesque inhabitants clad like ancient Greeks; this is found in ATL, qMS-2259. Finally, an amusing anecdote is related in Mordecai M. Noah, *Travels in England, France, Spain and the Barbary States, in the Years 1813–14 and 15* (New York, 1819), pp. 6 ff. Noah was on a ship taken captive by the *Briton*. Captain Staines received his prisoners with "politeness and civility" but no "unmeaning expressions of regret."

The script of *Pitcairn's Island, Melo Dramatic Ballet of Action in Two Acts, Thomas John Dibdin, Theatre Royal, Drury Lane, April 10, 1816* (LA 1918), is in the Huntington Library, San Marino, Calif.

Sir W. Sidney Smith's letter of March 5, 1816, is found in ATL, MS-Papers-3102.

For Adams's history, see Brian W. Scott, "The True Identity of John Adams," *Mariner's Mirror* 68 (1982), pp. 31–39. As an improbable footnote, Adams's genealogy reveals him to be the great-uncle of Mary Moffat, who married the missionary David Livingston. The report of Adams's visit to the *Sultan* and the first published account of his autobiography (and a brief but fascinating biographical sketch of mutineer Matthew Quintal) is recorded in *The New England Galaxy*, January 12, 1821, in a letter to the editor by Samuel Topliff.

Adams's letter to his brother, with information about his brother's employment, was published in the *European Magazine*, September 1819, pp. 210–11.

The visit in 1825 of the *Blossom*, Captain Beechey, is amply documented. The speculation that Fletcher Christian might be found on Pitcairn was made by Lieutenant George Peard, "Journal Kept on HMS Blossom, Captain Beechey in 1825," BL Add. MS 35141. Beechey's manuscript draft of Adams's account, "John Adams, Narrative, 1825," is found in ML, A1804; for Beechey's published account, see F. W. Beechey, *Narrative of a Voyage to the Pacific and Beering's Strait, to co-operate with the Polar Expeditions, performed in His Majesty's Ship Blossom, under the command of Captain F. W. Beechey* (London, 1831). See also James Wolf, "Journal of a voyage on board the HMS Blossom" (WA MS 533), in the Yale Collection of Western Americana, Beinecke Rare Book and Manuscript Library; this log emphasizes Stewart's role in the mutiny. Finally, the inexplicably unexamined account of Lieutenant Belcher, "Private Journal and remarks etc. H.M. Ship Blossom on discovery during the years 1825, 6, 7 Captn. F. W. Beechey Commander, by Edward Belcher, Supy. Lieut. & Assistant Surveyor," is found in ATL, MS-0158. A review of Beechey's book with substantial commentary and quotation is [W. H. Smyth], "Capt. Beechey's Narrative," *United Service Journal* (1831), part 1, pp. 527–31.

Adams's quote about Christian's "joyful expression" on returning to the *Bounty* after scouting Pitcairn is found in J. A. Moerenhout, *Voyages aux Îles du Grand Océan* (Paris, 1837), translated by Arthur R. Borden, as *Travels to the Islands of the Pacific Ocean* (Lanham, Md., 1993).

The remains of the *Bounty* were excavated in the 1950s; see Luis Marden, "I Found the Bones of the *Bounty*," *National Geographic Magazine*, December 1957, pp. 725–89.

Jenny's narratives were published in the *Sydney Gazette*, July 17, 1819, and more expansively as "Pitcairn's Island—The Bounty's Crew," *United Service Journal* (1829), part 1, pp. 589–93. This latter is a handier version of the same originally published in the *Bengal Hurkaru*, October

2, 1826. The Tahitian women who were brought to Pitcairn are listed with sources for information about them in Alan S. C. Ross and A. W. Moverley, *The Pitcairnese Language* (New York, 1964), p. 52. See also Sven Wahlroos, *Mutiny and Romance in the South Seas: A Companion to the Bounty Adventure* (Topsfield, Mass., 1989), for entries under each woman's name.

The very plausible theory that Adams was responsible for Fletcher Christian's death is aired at length by Glynn Christian, who traces the rumor of Adams's role back to an early work of fiction, whose author had spent significant time on Pitcairn and claimed to have heard this from the islanders. See Glynn Christian, *Fragile Paradise*, rev. ed. (Sydney and New York, 1999), pp. 340 ff.

Adams gave his birth date to Captain O. Folger of the *Maryland*, 1821–1824; see the log of the *Maryland*, Kendall Whaling Museum, Sharon, Massachusetts, Log 0673.

Adams's "cruel treatment" of his wife is reported in a letter from Rosalind Young to Captain and Mrs. Gibbon, April 1882, Phillips Library, Peabody Essex Museum, Salem, Massachusetts, MS E33.

For other ships that visited Pitcairn, see the following:

The *Elizabeth*, Captain Henry King, arrived in 1819; see "Extract from the Journal of Captain Henry King of the *Elizabeth*," *Edinburgh Philosophical Journal* 3, no. 6 (October 1820), pp. 380–88.

The *Surry*, Captain Raines, left several accounts of its 1821 visit—one clear-eyed report found Adams disappointingly a little cool on being disturbed by his unexpected visitor; it was also Captain Raines's company who found the island's young men cheerfully swigging their home-distilled spirits ("Journal on the ship, *Surry*, 1820–1821," ML, A131; and also "Various documents and notes re the Ship *Surry*," ML As 125/1–5). Readers of Nathaniel Philbrook's *In the Heart of the Sea* (New York, 2000) will recognize the *Surry* as the ship that rescued survivors of the *Essex* from nearby Henderson Island.

The account of the *Russell*, Captain Frederick Arthur, which stopped at Pitcairn in 1822, is found in an undated news article in the Nantucket Historical Association Research Library, Edouard A. Stackpole Collection, Folder 947, Whaling—Captains "A."

Otto von Kotzebue and Johann Friedrich Eschscholtz, *A New Voyage Round the World, in the years 1823, 24, 25, and 26* (London, 1830), pp. 225 ff., reports that he was told that Bligh had subjected "even his mate, Christian Fletcher, to corporal chastisement" (p. 229). Kotzebue makes reference to two other unrecorded visits to the island, by an English captain in 1803, and the American *Eagle* in 1821. Similarly, the log of the *Cherub*, Adm. 51/2206, gives an account of passing the island in August 1814, before the arrival of the *Topaz*.

Adams's "dying words" are reported in the American Seaman's Friend Society, *The Sailors' Magazine, containing the life of Peter Heywood, Midshipman of the Bounty; Also a sketch of the principal Mutineers of the Bounty* (New York, n.d. [c. 1860s]).

The Journal of the Royal Geographical Society of London 3 (1833), pp. 156–69, reports visits of the *Seringapatam* (1830), the *Comet* (1831), and the *Challenger* (1833). The account of the first gives the unflattering description of the abilities of Fletcher Christian's sons.

The report that Bligh called Christian a "hungry hound" is from Walter Brodie, *Pitcairns Island, and the Islanders, in 1850* (London, 1851), pp. 50 ff.

Frederick Debell Bennett, *Narrative of a Whaling Voyage Round the Globe, from the Year 1833 to 1836* (London, 1840), recounts his voyage as a passenger in the *Tuscan*, by which time one has come to the post-Adams era.

The Reverend Thomas Boyles Murray, *Pitcairn: The Island, the People and the Pastor; With a Short Account of the Mutiny of the Bounty* (London, 1853), went through many editions.

Sir Charles Lucas, ed., *The Pitcairn Island Register Book* (London, 1929), is a transcription of the official island records.

Rosalind Amelia Young, *Mutiny of the* Bounty *and the story of Pitcairn Island, 1790–1894* (Oakland, Calif., 1894), is the story of life on the island; Young was a great-granddaughter of John Adams.

The descendants of the mutineers live on Pitcairn to this day. For an account of these people in modern times, see H. L. Shapiro, *Descendants of the Mutineers of the* Bounty (Honolulu, 1929), and his *The Heritage of the* Bounty: *The Story of Pitcairn Through Six Generations* (New York, 1936); David Silverman, *Pitcairn Island* (Cleveland, 1967); and H. E. Maude, *Of Islands and Men* (Melbourne, 1968). For a darker view of life on the island, see Dea Birkett, *Serpent in Paradise* (New York, 1997).

Evidence of Charles Norman's death, on December 16, 1793, is found in the burial records of Holy Trinity Church, Gosport, kindly provided by the Portsmouth City Council, Museum and Records Office.

John Hallett's will is found in PROB 11/1254, 21; his service on the *Penelope* is confirmed by Adm. 35/1253 and by the ship's muster, Adm. 36/11981. His obituaries appear in the *Times* (London), December 6, 1794, and in *Gentleman's Magazine*, December 1794, p. 1157. His burial is listed in the parish burial registry for 1794, of St. Mary's, Bedford; this record and a description of his "Mural Monument" (Doc. Reference X69/52.) were kindly provided by the Bedfordshire and Luton Archives and Record Office, Bedford.

The tradition of Hallett's "confession" was first raised by Sir John Barrow, *The Eventful History of the Mutiny and Piratical Seizure of HMS* Bounty: *its Causes and Consequences* (London, 1831), p. 202, note; this was then elaborated on by Lady Diana Belcher, *The Mutineers of the Bounty and their Descendants in Pitcairn and Norfolk Islands* (London, 1870), p. 147, where she has upgraded the informant from "first lieutenant" to "captain" of the *Penelope*. The identity of the first lieutenant is found in the muster of the *Penelope,* above; John Marshall, *Royal Naval Biography,* vol. 1, part 2 (London, 1823), pp. 582–83, reveals that Malcolm was the maternal nephew of Sir Thomas Pasley. Pulteney had formerly served as a young gentleman under his uncle Pasley, at the age of twelve. Pasley's opinion of this time of his young nephew, whom he refers to as "an idle little vagabon," is amusingly described in his journal: Rodney M.S. Pasley, ed., *Private Sea Journals*. Another erroneous tradition arose independently that Hallett had joined Bligh on the *Providence*.

The log of the *Jason*, Adm. 51/1164, shows "Lawrence Lebogue Sailmaker, departed this life" on June 3, 1795; Adm. 102/604, "Hospital muster books, Plymouth, 1795," indicates that he was "Received on shore" on June 5 as a "Corpse." Edward Christian's remark regarding Lebogue's testimony is found in his *Short Reply to Capt. William Bligh's Answer* (London, 1795), p. 7. Lebogue's remarks about the boat journey were described by the Reverend James Bligh; see his "Papers, 1790–1792, 1834," ML, vol. Z C695.

Thomas Hayward's service on the *Diomede* is confirmed by Adm. 36/14096, the ship's muster; the travails of the *Diomede* are reported by her captain in Adm. 1/168, pp. 66–71. The loss of the *Swift* under Hayward's command is recorded in Sir William Laird Clowes and Sir Clements Robert Markham, *The Royal Navy: A History from the Earliest Times to the Present* (London, 1897–1903), p. 549, under "British Losses, 1793–1802." Information about Hayward's surveys was kindly provided by A. C. F. David, the United Kingdom Hydrographic Office. The blank logbook given to Hayward by his father was described in Bennett, *Narrative of a Whaling Voyage*, p. 47.

George Simpson's death is recorded in Adm. 35/1323 and Adm. 44/S2, Seaman's Effects.

William Muspratt's will is found in PROB 11/1301. For his transfer to the *Royal William,* see the muster of the *Hector,* Adm. 36/11187. The muster of the *Bellerophon* is Adm. 36/ 11904. The report from the solicitor general and council for the Admiralty to Secretary Stephens regarding Muspratt's back wages is found in Adm. 106/2217.

A remarkable exercise in collective family memory is described in James Shaw Grant, *Morrison of the Bounty* (Stornoway, Scotland, 1997), a biography about his forebear that was inspired by the memory of his aunt Jessie, "an elderly and timid spinster," informing him that Morrison "was a relative of ours" (after seeing the Charles Laughton film, she had reported that "the family resemblance was unmistakable"). Aunt Jessie had received this information from "Maggie the captain's daughter," who was the granddaughter of Lillias Morison, who lived to be a hundred and was a "cousin" of James Morrison. Thus, as Grant points out, there was only one link between his informant, Aunt Jessie, and "a woman who was in her twenties when the mutiny took place."

HOME IS THE SAILOR

For Bligh's life on his return to naval service after the *Providence* voyage, see George Mackaness, *The Life of Vice-Admiral William Bligh, R.N., F.R.S.,* rev. ed. (Sydney, 1951).

The story of the Nore mutiny, and of Aaron Graham's role as Admiralty agent, is colorfully told in James Dugan, *The Great Mutiny* (New York, 1965).

For Bligh's role in the battle of Camperdown, see Rear-Admiral A. H. Taylor, "William Bligh at Camperdown," *Mariner's Mirror* 23, no. 4 (October 1937), pp. 417–33. For the battle of Copenhagen, see Dudley Pope, *The Great Gamble* (London, 2001).

Bligh's arrest on suspicion of being a spy is told in the Reverend R. Polwhele, *Traditions and Recollections; Domestic, Clerical, and Literary* (London, 1826), pp. 376 ff.

An early attempt by Banks to get a shore commission for Bligh is found in his letter to Spencer, George John, 2nd Earl, December 10, 1795 (58.02), in SLNSW: the Sir Joseph Banks Electronic Archive. Bligh's remarks about his wife's inability to go to sea are in a letter to Banks of March 21, 1805 (58.29).

Banks's letter to Bligh broaching the governorship of New South Wales is quoted in Mackaness, *The Life of Vice-Admiral William Bligh,* pp. 352 f.; the letter itself cannot now be located.

The *Warrior* court-martial is found in Adm. 1/5367 and Adm. 1/5368. The case of the *Warrior* court-martial was first discovered and examined by Mackaness, *The Life of Vice-Admiral William Bligh,* pp. 333–51. This excellent and balanced overview quotes at length from the trial transcript. His quote about Bligh's bemused judges "grinning broadly" is on p. 336. For the Rum Corps, see, for example, Herbert Vere Evatt, *Rum Rebellion: A Study of the Overthrow of Governor Bligh by John Macarthur and the New South Wales Corps* (Sydney, 1939).

For the court-martial held on the deposers of Governor Bligh, see George Johnston and J. Bartrum, *Proceedings of a General Court-Martial Held at Chelsea Hospital, Which commenced on Tuesday, May 7, 1811, and continued by Adjournment to Wednesday, 5th of June following, for The trial of Lieut.-Col. Geo. Johnston, Major of the 102d Regiment, late [of] the New South Wales Corps, on A Charge of Mutiny . . . Exhibited Against Him By the Crown, For Deposing On the 26th of January, 1808, William Bligh, Esq. F.R.S.* (London, 1811). The report that plans against Bligh had been well laid was made by Greville, Hon. Charles Francis, to Banks, September 20, 1808, DTC 17.212–13.

The fulsome obituary of Elizabeth Bligh was published in *Gentleman's Magazine,* May 1812, pp. 486–87.

Material relating to John Fryer's later years is found in the National Library of Australia, and is quoted with the library's kind permission; see the "Statement of service of John Fryer, recorded by one of his children," NLA MS 6592. Adm. 1/4585 contains Fryer's petition to the Admiralty, while Adm. 1/4593 contains his daughter's petition to the same. "The Naval Service of John Fryer, Master in His Majesty's Navy 1781–1817," compiled by Owen Rutter in 1932, quotes both letters of commendation and the surgeon's report made on Fryer when he was forced from ill health to retire his command. Rutter's useful fact sheet is found in the Mitchell Library, as a preface to John Fryer's "Narrative, letter to his wife and documents. 4 April 1789–16 July 1804," ML, Safe 1/38; this also includes information about Fryer's son, Harrison. An article in the *Eastern Daily Press* (Norfolk), October 13, 2000, pp. 30–31, describes the exciting discovery of Fryer's tombstone by Mike Welland, Tom Sands, and Allan Leventhall in the graveyard of St. Nicholas Church, Wells. Information about John Fryer's cottage and other property was kindly supplied by Mike Welland. Details of John Fryer's will are found in Owen Rutter, ed., *The Voyage of the Bounty's Launch as Related in William Bligh's Despatch to the Admiralty and the Journal of John Fryer* (London, 1934).

Robert Tinkler's obituary appeared in *Gentleman's Magazine*, September 1820, p. 282. The remarks attributed to Tinkler are found in George Borrow, *The Romany Rye; A sequel to "Lavengro,"* vol. 2 (London, 1857), pp. 331–32.

Joseph Coleman's hospital records are found in Adm. 73/38, which shows him being discharged from Greenwich in May 1795. Coleman's service on the *Calcutta* is confirmed by Adm. 35/298; Adm. 142/3, "Register of Seamen's Wills," shows his will was drawn on the *Calcutta*, while Adm. 48/15 shows it was witnessed by William Bligh. Adm. 35/524 indicates that he was discharged to the Yarmouth Hospital Ship in November 1796, although his name does not appear in the Yarmouth muster.

Bligh's last interaction with Michael Byrn is glimpsed in his correspondence with his half nephew, Francis Bond, preserved in the National Maritime Museum, Greenwich (BND/1), and published in George Mackaness, ed., *Fresh Light on Bligh: Being Some Unpublished Correspondence of Captain William Bligh, R.N., and Lieutenant Francis Godolphin Bond, R.N., with Lieutenant Bond's Manuscript Notes Made on the Voyage of HMS Providence, 1791–1795* (Sydney, 1953). Adm. 102/606 and 102/608 show Byrn in and out of the *Edgar* with a fractured knee, until he is eventually discharged in January 1797 with "Consumption."

Mention is made by Bligh of a John Smith in a letter to his wife of January 27, 1800 (cited with the kind permission of the Kerpels Museum, Santa Barbara).

Captain Edwards's retirement activities are described in Robert Langdon, "Ancient Cornish Inn Is Link with the Bounty," *Pacific Islands Monthly* (April 1961), pp. 75–76.

Several important biographies relate Peter Heywood's later life and career: John Marshall, "Peter Heywood, Esq.," *Royal Naval Biography*, vol. 2, part 2 (London, 1825), pp. 747–97; E. Tagart, *A Memoir of the Late Captain Peter Heywood, R.N., with Extracts from his Diaries and Correspondence* (London, 1832); and A. G. K. L'Estrange, *Lady Belcher and Friends* (London, 1891); the latter describes the relationship of Peter's wife to Aaron Graham, and attributes Peter's fondness for Edward Belcher to their shared interests. Heywood's hydrographic career is discussed in Andrew David, "From Mutineer to Hydrographer: The Surveying Career of Peter Heywood," *International Hydrographic Review* 3, no. 2 (New Series) (August 2002), pp. 6–11; and also by A. C. F. David, "Peter Heywood and Northwest Australia," *The Great Circle: Journal of the Australian Association of Maritime History* 1, no. 1 (April 1979), pp. 4–14, both kindly supplied by the author. From the latter one learns that Heywood carried a chart of these waters drawn by his former shipmate Thomas Hayward.

Nessy Heywood's fate is described first by Nessy's mother, quoted in Tagart (above),

p. 160, and embellished by Sir John Barrow, *The Eventful History of the Mutiny and Piratical Seizure of HMS Bounty; its Causes and Consequences* (London, 1831), pp. 210 ff.; and again by Lady Diana Belcher, *The Mutineers of the Bounty and their Descendants in Pitcairn and Norfolk Islands* (London, 1870), p. 141.

Peter Heywood's letter to Captain Jeff Raigersfield of November 24, 1808, about Nessy's poems, is found in MNHL MS Heywood Papers, 09519; the flight of James Heywood from the Isle of Man is attested to in MNHL MS AP x5(2nd)-18ADM; both are used with the kind permission of the Manx National Heritage. Adm. 106/1353 is the petition of James Heywood written to the Admiralty from prison for an advance of wages; Adm. 36/11467, the muster of the *Caesar,* Captain Nugent, confirms details in the petition.

The fate of Emma Bertie is told in the Musters' family memoir in the Norfolk Record Office: HMN5/235/5.

Peter Heywood's 1810 handwritten "last will and testament" is found in MNHL MS MD 400, and is used with the kind permission of the Manx National Heritage; Adm. 52/4196, the log of the *Nereus,* gives details of the day on which the will was drafted. John Makin's profession is listed in *Kent's Directory, For the Year 1794. Cities of London and Westminster, & Borough of Southwark,* available at www.londonancestor.com/kents/kents-m.htm.

Aaron Graham's obituary is found in *The Annual Biography and Obituary* (1820), pp. 402–22. The story of Aaron Graham, his wife, Sarah, and her first cousin Sir Henry Tempest, although a wild digression, is too diverting to pass over. Sir Henry, having squandered his own meager fortune, set his sights upon Susannah Pritchard Lambert, the only daughter and heiress of Henry Lambert of Hope End, Hereford. Disguising himself as a female gypsy, Sir Henry met with the impressionable girl on her village green and told her that she would meet her future husband if she went at a certain hour to Colwall Church. This she did, where she met Sir Henry, now in his own guise. The subsequent marriage placed all the young woman's property in her husband's hands, and Sir Henry was shortly to turn both his wife and father-in-law out of their homes, while he assumed the Lambert estate. Following the court-martial, Nessy Heywood had been caught up in a whirl of social activity, and one finds her writing giddily of her recent visit to Lady Tempest, "a charming girl about my own age." The dynamics of the dark drama being played out beneath her nose apparently entirely escaped her. Lady Tempest was eventually disowned by her dispossessed father and toward the end of her short life could be found wandering forlornly and destitute up the Holloway Road. Her death was the origin of a local legend of the "ghost of Holloway."

Graham appears to have remained on good terms with his errant wife after she left him for Sir Henry, for he spoke warmly of her in his will, and left her his estate (PROB 11/1612, 167r–169l), as did Sir Henry (PROB 11/1613, 386l–389r). Regrettably, nothing more is known of this intriguing woman. Material relating to the life of Sir Henry was kindly provided by H. R. Tempest, and by the Hereford Record Office (Documents AE33/2; AE33/3; E27/1). I am particularly grateful to John Harnden for digging into Sir Henry's unsavory life. Hope End was sold in 1809 to the Moulton-Barretts, formerly of Jamaica and the parents of Elizabeth Barrett Browning, who evokes the estate in her poem "The Lost Bower." The Moulton-Barretts eventually sold Hope End to antiquary Thomas Heywood.

Banks's final years and excerpts from his will are described in Patrick O'Brian, *Joseph Banks: A Life* (Chicago, 1997), pp. 303 ff. "[T]o leave Joseph Banks on his deathbed, with the usual remarks about his will and his funeral, and extracts from the obituaries, would not only be sad but also misleading," O'Brian writes. "[T]here was such a fund of life there, such a zest and eager intelligent curiosity that no one who has dwelt with him long enough to write even a very small biography can leave him without wishing to show him in his vigour."

Peter Heywood's letter to James Clark Ross, January 25, 1829, is found in the National Library of Scotland, MS 9819, ff. 160–611, and is quoted with their kind permission. Heywood's notation of secret signals is found in "Seven Official orders received and given by Captain P. Heywood. 1810–1815," in ATL, MS 56/068, and is quoted with the library's kind permission.

Coleridge's comments about the Duchess of St. Albans, his neighbor, are found in Earl Leslie Griggs, ed., *Collected Letters of Samuel Taylor Coleridge*, vol. 6, 1826–1834 (Oxford, 1971), p. 468. The comment by Heywood's stepdaughter on Coleridge is in L'Estrange, *Lady Belcher and Friends*, p. 70.

For a summation of Edward Belcher's career, see the *Dictionary of National Biography* (London, 1917); and Alfred Friendly, *Beaufort of the Admiralty: The Life of Sir Francis Beaufort, 1774–1857* (London, 1977), p. 257. The quote regarding life on the ice being preferable to life with Belcher is from Fergus Fleming's *Barrow's Boys* (New York, 1998), p. 391. The sentiment that Belcher was an agent of the devil is found in Christopher Lloyd, *Mr. Barrow of the Admiralty* (London, 1970), p. 200. Edward Belcher was also the first cousin of Captain Frederick Marryat, the author of the celebrated series of sea novels (L'Estrange, *Lady Belcher and Friends*, pp. 100 ff.).

The astonishing divorce case of *Belcher v. Belcher,* a great document of social history of the time, is found in Joseph Phillimore and Sir Robert J. Phillimore, *A Report of the Judgment Delivered on the Sixth Day of June, 1835 by Joseph Phillimore, In the Cause of Belcher, the Wife, against Belcher, the Husband* (London, 1835). This also contains correspondence between husband and wife relating to Peter Heywood. I am enormously indebted to Terry Martin for drawing my attention to this, and for the loan of his working manuscript, "There Rises Something Bitter: The Poisoned Marriage of Edward and Diana Belcher, 1830–1835."

Belcher's log of the *Blossom,* "Private Journal and remarks etc. H.M. Ship Blossom on discovery during the years 1825, 6, 7 Captn. F. W. Beechey Commander, by Edward Belcher, Supy. Lieut. & Assistant Surveyor," MS-0158, is quoted with the kind permission of the Alexander Turnbull Library.

Heywood's intercession for the Tahitians is found in Captains Letters "H," Adm. 1/1953. His letter regarding the Tahitians is quoted in Tagart, *A Memoir of the Late Captain Peter Heywood,* pp. 285 ff.

For Heywood's last months and his death, see Diana Belcher's letters of October 20 and 22, 1830, in Phillimore and Phillimore, *Report of the Judgment.* For a description of the burial and vault of Coleridge, see "Appendix A: The Death and Burial of Coleridge," in Griggs, *Collected Letters,* vol. 6, pp. 991–97. Heywood's vault is described in John Richardson, *Highgate: Its History Since the Fifteenth Century* (Hertfordshire, 1983), p. 109.

Peter's remarks on the role of George Stewart were published in Barrow, *Eventful History of the Mutiny,* p. 85; the rumor of Christian's return is found at pp. 233 ff.

The earliest spurious pamphlet is *Letters From Mr. Fletcher Christian, Containing a Narrative of the Transactions on Board His Majesty's Ship Bounty, Before and After the Mutiny, With His Subsequent Voyages and Travels in South America* (London, 1796). This was reviewed in the *True Briton,* September 13, 1796; the same newspaper then disavowed the letters in a retraction published on September 23, 1796.

Bligh's comments to Banks about Christian in a letter of September 16, 1796, are in SLNSW: the Sir Joseph Banks Electronic Archive, 58.09. Wordsworth's letter appeared in *The Weekly Entertainer,* November 1796, p. 377.

For the later spurious account, see *Statements of the Loss of His Majesty's New Ship The Bounty, W. Bligh, Esq. Commander, By a Conspiracy of the Crew . . . "As communicated by Lieu-*

tenant Christian, the Ringleader, to a Relation in England" (London, c. 1809). Heywood's reaction to the news is recorded in Tagart, *A Memoir of the Late Captain Peter Heywood*, p. 288.

Lebogue's report that Edward Christian inquired after the possibility of his brother's return is found in William Bligh, *An Answer to Certain Assertions . . .* (London, 1794), p. 26.

The remarkable letters regarding Fletcher Christian's return can be found in Kenneth Curry, ed., *New Letters of Robert Southey*, vol. 1, *1792–1810* (New York, 1965), pp. 519 ff. Curry draws attention to the letters in both his preface and in a footnote, noting that this sighting would place the mutineer's return to England much earlier than was usually rumored. Curry also draws attention to C. S. Wilkinson's *The Wake of the Bounty* (London, 1953), which first examined the story of Christian's return and posits the conspiracy theory that Wordsworth and Coleridge were complicit in this return—a theory untenable for the simple reason that Coleridge would not have been capable of holding such a secret. Despite the fact that Curry assiduously drew attention to the letters, they seem to have fallen beneath the radar of *Bounty* researchers.The letters are in the Bodleian Library, Oxford University (Robert Southey to Grosvenor Charles Bedford, October 23, 1809, MS Eng. lett. c. 24, fols. 120–121, and October 30, 1809, MS Eng. lett. c. 24, fol. 122), and are quoted with its kind permission.

Charles Christian's last meeting with his brother is described in his unpublished memoir, MNHL MS 09381. Fletcher's death by 1804 is reported in the *Aberdeen Chronicle*, April 15, 1815.

The *Manx Daily Advertiser* of December 19, 1822, reports the auction of Charles Christian's effects in his house on Fort Street. The burial of Ann Christian is recorded on January 8, 1819; that of Charles on November 17, 1822, both in St. George's Chapel (MNHL MS Braddan Burials 1624–1699 and 1800–1849).

Accounts of Edward Christian's later life and his death are given in the Christian family pedigree, MNHL MS 09381/8/2; he was buried in Broxbourne Church (with a monument by Flaxman)—see Martin Faragher, "Broxbourne and the Bounty," *Herts. Countryside* 33, no. 236 (1978), pp. 28–29. The story of Edward's "native hat" is found in Anne Fremantle, *Loyal Enemy* (London, 1938), p. 13.

The muster of the *Irresistible*, Adm. 36/11349, shows William Cole with his two sons as "servants"; one of the boys died early, however, in 1794. Adm. 29/1 contains his pension record, including all ships on which he served. RG 4/1674, the Greenwich Hospital burials, shows the death of a William Cole at the age of seventy-one—Cole's age was never given on any muster of any ship on which he served, so it is impossible to confirm if the burial is of the boatswain of the *Bounty*.

Purcell's record of service is found in Adm. 29/5, "Carpenters 1817–1833." The reference to his "derangement" is found in "The Last of the 'Pandoras,'" *United Service Magazine*, September 1842, pp. 1–13. Purcell's obituary is in *Gentleman's Magazine*, June 1834, p. 668. Information about his widow, Hannah Purcell, is taken from "Tower Hamlets Cemetery Trail," reprinted in Peter Gardner, "The Bounty Grave—Tower Hamlets," *UK Log*, July 2002, p. 39.

The deaths of the widows of Fletcher Christian and Edward Young, Isabella and Susannah, are recorded in Sir Charles Lucas, ed., *The Pitcairn Island Register Book* (London, 1929).

Quotes about Bligh's tyranny are found in W. C. Wentworth, *A Statistical, Historical, and Political Description of The Colony of New South Wales* (London, 1819), pp. 167 ff.; and "The Mutiny of the Bounty," *The Edinburgh Review* 4, no. 24 (January 1832), pp. 673–85. The comparison of the mutineers' uprising with the French Revolution is found in [W. H. Smyth], "The *Bounty* Again!," *United Service Journal* (1831), part 1, pp. 305–14.

George Tobin's humane assessment of his former captain is found in a letter to Francis Bond, of December 15, 1817, now preserved as a copy of the privately held original in ML, Ab 60/8.

The description of entering Bligh's tomb is given in an interview in the television documentary *Bligh of the Bounty* (Rolf Harris Productions, 1998).

A description of Bligh's vault is found in two short letters in *Notes and Queries*, July 29, 1899, p. 97, and September 23, 1899, p. 253. Bligh's age at death is wrongly stated in the vault; he was in fact sixty-three. St. Mary, Lambeth, is now—suitably—a museum of garden history. Although the fact that Bligh's tomb is actually in the old churchyard is, strangely, omitted, the museum does have numerous displays about Banks and the transplantation of exotic plants from around the world. With reference to the breadfruit expeditions, a display notes that the mutiny on the *Bounty* occurred as a result of Bligh's appropriation of his men's drinking water for his plants.

SELECT BIBLIOGRAPHY

For unpublished materials, see "A Note on Sources," page 411.

An Account of the Mutinous Seizure of the Bounty, with the Succeeding Hardships of the Crew, to which are Added Secret Anecdotes of the Otaheitean Females. London: Robert Turner, 1792.

Aitken, Robert T. *Ethnology of Tubuai.* Honolulu: Bernice P. Bishop Museum, 1930.

Alexander, Caroline. *The Way to Xanadu.* New York: Knopf, 1994.

American Seamen's Friend Society. *The Sailors' Magazine, containing the life of Peter Heywood, Midshipman of the Bounty; Also, a sketch of the principal Mutineers of the Bounty.* New York: American Seamen's Friend Society, n.d. (1860s).

Anderson, John Eustace. *A Short Account of the Mortlake Company of the Royal Putney, Roehampton and Mortlake Volunteer Corps 1803–6.* Richmond, Surrey: Simpson, 1893.

The Annual Biography and Obituary, for the year ———. Annual. 21 vols. London: Longman, Hurst, Rees, Orme, and Brown, 1817–1837.

Anson, George Anson, Lord. *A Voyage Round the World, in the Years MDCCXL, I, II, III, IV.* Edited by Richard Walter and Benjamin Robins. London: John and Paul Knapton, 1748.

Anstey, Roger. *The Atlantic Slave Trade and British Abolition, 1760–1810.* London: Macmillan, 1975.

Askew, John. *A Guide to the Interesting Places In and Around Cockermouth, with an account of its Remarkable Men and Local Traditions.* Cockermouth, Cumbria: Isaac Evening, 1866.

Aspinall, Arthur, ed. *December 1783 to January 1793.* Vol. 1 of *The Later Correspondence of George III.* Cambridge: Cambridge University Press, 1962.

Australiana Society. *Narrative of the mutiny on board H. M. Ship Bounty ... Minutes of the court martial ... Bligh's answer to certain assertions ... Edward Christian's short reply to Captain William Bligh's answer.* 1790, 1792, 1794, 1795. Facsimiles. Melbourne: Georgian House, 1952.

Bach, John, ed. *The Bligh Notebook: Rough Account, Lieutenant Wm. Bligh's Voyage in the Bounty's Launch from the Ship to Tofua and from Thence to Timor, 28 April to 14 June 1789, with a Draft List of the Bounty Mutineers.* Facsimile ed., 2 vols. North Sydney, N.S.W.: Allen & Unwin in association with the National Library of Australia, 1987.

Ball, Ian M. *Pitcairn: Children of the Bounty.* London: Victor Gollancz, 1973.

Banks, Sir Joseph. *An epistle from Mr. Banks, voyager, monster-hunter, and amoroso, to Oberea, Queen of Otaheite. Transfused by A.B.C. Esq. second professor of the Otaheite, and of every other unknown tongue. Enriched with the finest passages of the Queen's letter to Mr. Banks.* London: Jacobus Opano, n.d. (c. 1773).

Barnes and Mortlake History Society. Publication no. 30 (September 1969): 4.

Barney, Stephen, and Edward Christian. *Minutes of the Proceedings of the Court-Martial held at Portsmouth, August* [sic] *12, 1792, on Ten Persons Charged with Mutiny on Board His Majesty's ship the Bounty: With an Appendix Containing a Full Account of the Real Causes and Circumstances of that Unhappy Transaction, the most material of which have hitherto been withheld from the Public.* London: J. Deighton, 1794.

Barron-Wilson, Cornwell, Mrs. *Memoirs of Miss Mellon, Afterwards Duchess of St. Albans.* New ed. 2 vols. London: Remington, 1886.

Barrow, Sir John. *The Eventful History of the Mutiny and Piratical Seizure of H.M.S. Bounty: its Causes and Consequences.* London: J. Murray, 1831.

———. *The Life of Richard Earl Howe, K.G., Admiral of the Fleet, and General of Marines.* London: J. Murray, 1838.

———. "Recent Accounts of the Pitcairn Islanders," *Journal of the Royal Geographical Society of London* 3 (1833): 156–69.

Bartlett, Christine, et al. *Titchfield: A History,* edited by George Watts. Repr. with corrections. Titchfield, Hampshire: Titchfield History Society, 1982.

Barton, G. B., and Alexander Britton. *History of New South Wales from the Records,* edited by Frank Murcot Bladen. 2 vols. Sydney: Charles Potter, 1889–1894.

Basker, James G., ed. *Amazing Grace: An Anthology of Poems About Slavery, 1660–1810.* New Haven: Yale University Press, 2002.

Baynham, Henry. *From the Lower Deck: The Old Navy, 1780–1840.* London: Hutchinson, 1969.

Bazely, John, obituary in "Obituary of Remarkable Persons, with Biographical Anecdotes." *Gentlemen's Magazine* 79, pt. 1 (April 1809): 389.

Beaglehole, J. C. *The Life of Captain James Cook.* Stanford, Calif.: Stanford University Press, 1974.

Beaglehole, J. C., ed. *The Endeavour Journal of Joseph Banks, 1768–1771.* 2 vols. Sydney: Trustees of the Public Library of New South Wales in association with Angus and Robertson, 1962.

———. *The Voyage of the Endeavour, 1768–1771.* Vol. 1 of *The Journals of Captain James Cook on His Voyages of Discovery.* Extra series xxxiv. Cambridge: Hakluyt Society for the University Press, 1955.

———. *The Voyage of the Resolution and Adventure, 1772–1775.* Vol. 2 of *The Journals of Captain James Cook on His Voyages of Discovery.* Extra series xxxv. Cambridge: Hakluyt Society for the University Press, 1961.

———. *The Voyage of the Resolution and Discovery, 1776–1780.* Vol. 3 of *The Journals of Captain James Cook on His Voyages of Discovery.* Extra series xxxvi. Cambridge: Hakluyt Society for the University Press, 1967.

Becke, Louis, and Walter Jeffery. *The Mutineers: A Romance of Pitcairn Island.* London: T. Fisher Unwin, 1898.

Beechey, Frederick William. *Narrative of a Voyage to the Pacific and Beering's Strait, to co-operate with the Polar Expeditions performed in His Majesty's Ship Blossom, under the command of Captain F. W. Beechey, R.N., F.R.S. &c. in the years 1825, 26, 27, 28.* 2 vols. London: Henry Colburn and Richard Bentley, 1831.

Belcher, Lady Diana Jolliffe. *The Mutineers of the Bounty and their Descendants in Pitcairn and Norfolk Islands.* London: J. Murray, 1870.

Bennett, Frederick Debell. *Narrative of a Whaling Voyage Round the Globe, from the Year 1833 to 1836: comprising sketches of Polynesia, California, the Indian Archipelago, etc.; with an ac-*

count of southern whales, the sperm whale fishery, and the natural history of the climates visited. 2 vols. London: Richard Bentley, 1840.

Benson, Peter, ed. *My Dearest Betsy: A Self-Portrait of William Gilpin, 1757–1848, Schoolmaster and Parson, from His Letters and Notebooks.* London: D. Dobson, 1981.

Bertie, Admiral Albemarle, obituary. *Gentlemen's Magazine* 94, pt. 1 (May 1824): 459–60.

"Biographical Memoir of John Knight, Esq. Rear Admiral of the White Squadron." *Naval Chronicle* 11 (January–July 1804): 425–31.

"Biographical Memoir of Sir George Young, Knt., Admiral of the White." *Naval Chronicle* 31 (1814): 177–83.

"Biographical Memoirs of Sir John Colpoys, K.B. Admiral of the Blue Squadron." *Naval Chronicle* 11 (January–July 1804): 266–72.

Birkett, Dea. *Serpent in Paradise.* New York: Anchor Books, 1997.

Bladen, F. M. "The Deposition of Governor Bligh." *Australian Historical Society, Journal and Proceedings* 1 (June 1908): 192–200.

Bladen, F. M., ed. *Bligh and Macquarie, 1809, 1810, 1811.* Vol. 7 of *Historical Records of New South Wales.* Sydney: Government Printer, 1901.

———. *King and Bligh, 1806, 1807, 1808.* Vol. 6 of *Historical Records of New South Wales.* Sydney: Government Printer, 1898.

Blake, Nicholas, and Richard Russell Lawrence. *The Illustrated Companion to Nelson's Navy.* London: Chatham, 1999.

Blane, Sir Gilbert. *Observations on the diseases incident to seamen.* London: J. Cooper, 1785.

Bligh, Elizabeth, obituary in "Additions to former Obituaries." *Gentlemen's Magazine* 82, pt. 1 (May 1812): 486–87.

Bligh, William. *Answer to Certain Assertions Contained in the Appendix Entitled "Minutes of the Proceedings on the Court Martial held at Portsmouth August [sic] 12th 1792 on Ten Persons Charged with Mutiny on Board His Majesty's Ship the Bounty."* London: G. Nicol, 1794.

———. *Bligh's Voyage in the Resource from Coupang to Batavia, Together with the Log of His Subsequent Passage to England in the Dutch Packet Vlydt and His Remarks on Morrison's Journal. All Printed for the First Time from the Manuscripts in the Mitchell Library of New South Wales, with an Introduction and Notes by Owen Rutter, and Engravings on Wood by Peter Barker Hill.* London: Golden Cockerel Press, 1937.

———. *The Log of the Bounty: Being Lieutenant William Bligh's Log of the Proceedings of His Majesty's Armed Vessel Bounty in a Voyage to the South Seas, to Take the Breadfruit from the Society Islands to the West Indies.* 2 vols. Edited by Owen Rutter. London: Golden Cockerel Press, 1937.

———. *The Log of H.M.S. Providence 1791–1793.* Guilford Surrey: Genesis Publications, 1976.

———. *A Narrative of the Mutiny, on Board His Majesty's Ship Bounty; and the Subsequent Voyage of Part of the Crew, in the Ship's Boat, From Tofoa, one of the Friendly Islands, to Timor, a Dutch Settlement in the East Indies.* London: G. Nicol, 1790.

———. *A Narrative of the Mutiny, on Board His Majesty's Ship Bounty; and the Subsequent Voyage of Part of the Crew, in the Ship's Boat, From Tofoa, one of the Friendly Islands, to Timor, a Dutch Settlement in the East Indies.* 1790. Reprint, London: Sign of the Unicorn; New York: M. F. Mansfield, 1901.

———. *A Voyage to the South Sea, Undertaken by Command of His Majesty, for the Purpose of Conveying the Bread-Fruit Tree to the West Indies in His Majesty's Ship the Bounty commanded by Lieutenant William Bligh. Including an Account of the Mutiny on Board the Said Ship and the Subsequent Voyage of Part of the Crew, in the Ship's Boat, from Tofoa, one of the Friendly Islands, to Timor, a Dutch Settlement in the East Indies.* London: G. Nicol, 1792.

———. *A Voyage to the South Sea, Undertaken by Command of His Majesty . . .* 1792. Facsimile. Honolulu: Rare Books, 1967.

Bonhams Knightsbridge. "William Bligh and the *Bounty* Mutineers: The Property of Angela and Stephen Walters." Catalogue for auction, March 20, 1996. London, 1996.

Borrow, George Henry. *The Romany Rye: A Sequel to "Lavengro."* 2 vols. London: J. Murray, 1857.

Bradford, Ernle Dusgate Selby. *Nelson: The Essential Hero.* London: Macmillan, 1977.

British Naval Biography: Comprising the lives of the most distinguished admirals, from Howard to Codrington; with an outline of the naval history of England, from the earliest period to the present time. London: Scott, Webster and Geary, 1839.

Brodie, Walter. *Pitcairns Island, and the Islanders, in 1850. Together with extracts from his private journal, and a few hints upon California; also, the reports of all the commanders of H. M. ships that have touched the above island since 1800.* London: Whittaker & Co., 1851.

Brunton, Paul, ed. *Awake Bold Bligh! William Bligh's Letters Describing the Mutiny on HMS Bounty.* Sydney: Allen & Unwin, State Library of New South Wales, 1989.

Burney, Fanny. *Diary and Letters of Madame d'Arblay, edited by her niece* [Charlotte Barrett]. 7 vols. London: H. Colburn, 1842–1846.

Byron, Lord George Gordon Noel. "Don Juan" in *Lord Byron: The Major Works.* Oxford World's Classics. Edited by Jerome J. McGann. Oxford: Oxford University Press, 2000.

———. *The Island, or Christian and his comrades.* London: John Hunt, 1823.

Callender, Geoffrey. "The Portraiture of Bligh." *Mariner's Mirror* 22 (1936): 172–78.

Chambers, Neil, ed. *The Letters of Sir Joseph Banks: A Selection, 1768–1820.* London: Imperial College Press, 2000.

Chamier, Frederick. *Jack Adams, the mutineer.* London: H. Colburn, 1838.

Christian, Charles. *An Abridged Statement of Facts, Supported by Respectable and Undeniable Evidence: with Strictures on the Injurious Influence of Calumny, and a Display of the Excellence and Invincibility of Truth.* Douglas, Isle of Man: 1818.

Christian, Edward. *Charges delivered to Grand Juries in the Isle of Ely: upon libels, vagrants, criminal law, religion, rebellious assemblies, &c., &c. For the use of magistrates and students of the law.* 2d ed. London: T. Clarke and Sons, 1819.

———. *A Short Reply to Capt. William Bligh's Answer.* London: J. Deighton, 1795.

Christian, Fletcher [pseud.]. *Letters from Mr. Fletcher Christian, Containing a Narrative of the Transactions on Board His Majesty's Ship Bounty, Before and After the Mutiny, With His Subsequent Voyages and Travels in South America.* London: H. D. Symonds, 1796.

———. *The Letters of Fletcher Christian.* 1796. Reprint, Guildford, Surrey: Genesis Publications, 1984.

———. *Statements of the Loss of His Majesty's New Ship The Bounty, W. Bligh, Esq. Commander, By a Conspiracy of the Crew; Including the Wonderful Escape of the Captain and about Twelve Men in an open Pinnace; Also, the Adventures of the Mutineers, As Communicated by Lieutenant Christian, the Ring-leader to a Relation in England.* London: Thomas Tegg, n.d. (c. 1809).

Christian, Glynn. *Fragile Paradise: The Discovery of Fletcher Christian, Bounty Mutineer.* Boston: Little, Brown, 1982.

———. *Fragile Paradise.* Rev. ed. Sydney and New York: Doubleday, 1999.

Christian, John, in "Lists of Deaths, Promotions, &c." *Gentlemen's Magazine* 38, pt. 1 (March 1768): 143.

Christian, John, obituary in "Obituary of Considerable Persons; with Biographical Anecdotes." *Gentlemen's Magazine* 61, pt. 1 (June 1791): 588–89.

Clark, Ralph. *The Journal and Letters of Lt. Ralph Clark, 1787–1792.* Edited by Paul G. Fidlon and R. J. Ryan. Sydney: Australian Documents Library in association with the Library of Australian History, 1981.

Clowes, Sir William Laird, and Sir Clements Robert Markham. *The Royal Navy: A History from the Earliest Times to the Present.* 7 vols. London: S. Low, Marston, 1897–1903.

Coburn, Kathleen, ed. *1794–1804.* Vol. 1 of *The Notebooks of Samuel Taylor Coleridge.* New York: Pantheon, 1957.

Coleman, Everard Home. "Bligh." Letter to *Notes and Queries,* July 8, 1899, 33–34.

Coleridge, Ernest Hartley. *The Life of Thomas Coutts, Banker.* 2 vols. London: John Lane, 1920.

Coleridge, Samuel Taylor. *The Complete Poetical Works of Samuel Taylor Coleridge.* Edited by Ernest Hartley Coleridge. 2 vols. Oxford: Clarendon Press, 1912, 1975.

Cook, James. *Cook's Third Voyage.* 3 vols. London: Lord's Committee of the Admiralty, 1784.

———. *A Voyage to the Pacific Ocean. Undertaken, By The Command of His Majesty, For Making Discoveries in the Northern Hemisphere. To Determine The Position and Extent of the West Side of North America; its Distance from Asia; and the Practicability of a Northern Passage to Europe. Performed under the Direction of Captains Cook, Clerke, and Gore, In His Majesty's Ships the Resolution and Discovery. In the Years 1776, 1777, 1778, 1779, and 1780. In Three Volumes.* Vol. 1. London: W. and A. Strahan for G. Nicol and T. Cadell, 1784.

Craine, David. *Manannan's Isle: A Collection of Manx Historical Essays.* N.p.: Manx Museum and National Trust, 1955.

Creswell, John. *British Admirals of the Eighteenth Century: Tactics in Battle.* Hamden, Conn.: Archon Books, 1972.

Cunningham, Sir Charles. *A Narrative of Occurrences that took place during the Mutiny at the Nore, in the Months of May and June, 1797; with a few Observations upon the Impressment of Seamen, and the Advantages of those who are employed in His Majesty's Navy; also on the necessity and useful operations of the articles of war.* Chatham, Kent: W. Burrill, 1829.

Cunningham, George Godfrey. *Lives of Eminent and Illustrious Englishmen: from Alfred the Great to the latest times, on an original plan.* 8 vols. Glasgow: A. Fullarton, 1836–1837.

Curry, Kenneth, ed. *1792–1810.* Vol. 1 of *New Letters of Robert Southey.* New York: Columbia University Press, 1965.

Curtis, Sir Roger. *The reply of Sir Roger Curtis, to the person who stiles himself A neglected naval officer.* London, 1784.

"Curtis, Sir Roger." In *The Annual Biography and Obituary for the Year.* Vol. 2: 136ff. London: Longman, Hurst, Rees, Orme, and Brown, 1818.

Danielsson, Bengt. *What Happened on the* Bounty? Translated by Alan Tapsell. London: George Allen & Unwin, 1962.

Danielsson, Marie-Thérèse, and Bengt Danielsson. "Bligh's Cave: 196 Years On." *Pacific Islands Monthly,* June 1985, 25–26.

Darby, Madge. "Bligh's Disciple: Matthew Flinders's Journals of HMS *Providence* (1791–1793)." *Mariner's Mirror* 86, no. 4 (November 2000): 401–11.

———. *The Causes of the Bounty Mutiny. A short reply to Mr. Rolf du Rietz's comments. With a few concluding remarks by Rolf du Rietz.* Vol. 2 of *Studia Bountyana.* Uppsala, Sweden: Almqvist & Wiksell, 1966.

———. *The Story of Mydiddee.* London, 1988.

———. *Who Caused the Mutiny on the* Bounty? Sydney: Angus and Robertson, 1965.

David, Andrew C. F. "Bligh's Notes on Cook's Last Voyage." *Mariner's Mirror* 67, no. 1 (February 1981): 102.

———. "Broughton's Schooner and the Bounty Mutineers." Mariner's Mirror 63 (1977): 207–13.

———. "From Mutineer to Hydrographer: The Surveying Career of Peter Heywood." International Hydrographic Review n.s., 3, no. 2 (August 2002): 6–11.

———. "The Glorious First of June: An Account of the Battle by Peter Heywood." Mariner's Mirror 64, no. 4 (November 1978): 361–66.

———. "Peter Heywood and Northwest Australia." The Great Circle: Journal of the Australian Association for Maritime History 1, no. 1 (April 1979): 4–14.

———. The Surveyors of the Bounty: A Preliminary Study of the Hydrographic Surveys of William Bligh, Thomas Hayward and Peter Heywood and the Charts Published from Them. Taunton, Somerset, 1976.

———. "The Surveys of William Bligh." Mariner's Mirror 63, no. 1 (1977): 69–70.

Davis, John. The Post-Captain; or, The wooden walls well manned; comprehending a view of naval society and manners. London: T. Tegg, 1813.

Dawson, Warren Royal, ed. The Banks Letters: A Calendar of the Manuscript Correspondence of Sir Joseph Banks, Preserved in the British Museum, the British Museum (Natural History) and Other Collections in Great Britain. London: Trustees of the British Museum, 1958.

Defoe, Daniel. A Tour Through the Whole Island of Great Britain. Rev. ed. 2 vols. London: Dent/Everyman's Library, 1962.

Delafons, John. A Treatise on Naval Courts Martial. London: P. Steel, 1805.

Delano, Amasa. Narrative of Voyages and Travels, in the Northern and Southern Hemispheres, Comprising Three Voyages Round the World; Together with a Voyage of Survey and Discovery in the Pacific Ocean and Oriental Islands. Boston: House, 1817.

Dening, Greg. Mr. Bligh's Bad Language: Passion, Power, and Theatre on the Bounty. Cambridge: Cambridge University Press, 1992.

Denman, A., ed. "Captain Bligh and the Mutiny of the Bounty," Notes and Queries 9th ser., 12 (December 26, 1903): 501–2.

Dillon, Peter. "Pitcairn's Island—The Bounty's Crew." United Service Journal (1829), part 2: 589–93.

Duckworth, Admiral Sir John, obituary. Gentlemen's Magazine 87, pt. 2 (September 1817): 275. And "Memoir." Gentlemen's Magazine 87, pt. 2 (October 1817): 372–74.

"Duckworth, Sir John." In The Annual Biography and Obituary for the Year. Vol. 1: 380–91. London: Longman, Hurst, Rees, Orme, and Brown, 1817.

Dugan, James. The Great Mutiny. New York: Putnam, 1965.

Duncan, Archibald. "Narrative of the loss of the Bounty through a conspiracy," 21–35; "Narrative of the total loss of His Majesty's Ship the Bounty, including the transactions of the mutineers, after they gained possession of the vessel. Extracted from the letters of Lieutenant Christian," 49–62 in vol. 4; and "Loss of the Pandora Frigate," 271–73 in vol. 5 of The Mariner's Chronicle, or, Authentic and Complete History of Popular Shipwrecks. 6 vols. London: James Cundee, Ivy-Lane, 1810.

DuRietz, Rolf E. The Bias of Bligh. Uppsala, Sweden: Dahlia Books, 2003.

———. The Causes of the Bounty Mutiny: Some Comments on a Book by Madge Darby. Vol. 1 of Studia Bountyana. Uppsala, Sweden: Almqvist & Wiksell, 1965.

———. Fresh Light on John Fryer of the Bounty. Uppsala, Sweden: Dahlia Books, 1981.

———. Peter Heywood's Tahitian Vocabulary and the Narratives by James Morrison: Some Notes on Their Origin and History. Banksia 3. Uppsala, Sweden: Dahlia Books, 1986.

———. "Three Letters from James Burney to Sir Joseph Banks: A Contribution to the History of William Bligh's A Voyage to the South Sea." Ethnos 1–4 (1962): 115–25.

———. "The Voyage of HMS Pandora 1790–1792: Some Remarks upon Geoffrey Rawson's

Book on the Subject." Review of *Pandora's Last Voyage*, by Geoffrey Rawson. *Ethnos* 2–4 (1963): 210–18.

Edwards, Edward, Captain R. N., and George Hamilton. *Voyage of H. M. S. "Pandora" Despatched to Arrest the Mutineers of the "Bounty" in the South Seas, 1790–91; Being the Narratives of Captain Edward Edwards, R. N., the Commander, and George Hamilton, the Surgeon.* Edited by Basil Thomson. London: F. Edwards, 1915.

Egan, Elizabeth, comp. *Guide to the Papers of William Bligh and the Bligh Family in the Mitchell Library, State Library of NSW.* Sydney: Library Council of New South Wales, 1989.

Ellis, William. *Polynesian Researches, during a residence of nearly six years in the South Sea Islands, including descriptions of the natural history and scenery of the Islands, with remarks on the history, mythology, traditions, government, arts, manners, and customs of the inhabitants.* 2 vols. London: Fisher, Son, & Jackson, 1829.

Evatt, Hon. Herbert Vere. *Rum Rebellion: A Study of the Overthrow of Governor Bligh by John Macarthur and the New South Wales Corps. Including the John Murtagh Macrossan Memorial Lectures Delivered at the University of Queensland, June 1937.* 2d ed. Sydney: Angus and Robertson, 1939.

Faragher, Martin. "Broxbourne and the *Bounty*." *Hertfordshire Countryside: A Panorama of County Life* 33, no. 236 (1978): 28–29.

Farington, Joseph. *The Farington Diary.* Edited by James Greig. 8 vols. London: Hutchinson, 1923–1928.

Fiske, Nathan Welby. *Aleck and the Mutineers of the Bounty: A Remarkable Illustration of the Influence of the Bible.* New ed. Boston: Massachusetts Sabbath School Society, 1855.

Fleming, Fergus. *Barrow's Boys.* New York: Atlantic Monthly Press, 1998.

Fletcher, Isaac. *The Diary of Isaac Fletcher of Underwood, Cumberland, 1756–1781.* Edited by Angus J. L. Winchester. Extra series 27. Kendal, Cumbria: Cumberland and Westmorland Antiquarian and Archaeological Society, 1994.

Fletcher, William. "Fletcher Christian and the Mutineers of the 'Bounty.'" *Transactions of the Cumberland Association for the Advancement of Literature and Science*, pt. 2 (1876–1877): 77–106.

Flinders, Matthew, and Robert Brown. *A Voyage to Terra Australis; undertaken for the purpose of completing the discovery of that vast country, and prosecuted in the years 1801, 1802 and 1803, in His Majesty's Ship the Investigator, and subsequently in the Armed Vessel Porpoise and Cumberland Schooner. With an account of the Shipwreck of the Porpoise, Arrival of the Cumberland at Mauritius, and Imprisonment of the Commander during six Years and a half in that Island.* 2 vols. London: W. Bulmer and Co.; G. and W. Nicol, 1814.

Folger, Mayhew. "Mutineers of the Bounty." *Naval Chronicle* 21 (1809): 454–55.

Forster, Johann Georg Adam. *Reply to Mr. Wales's Remarks.* London: B. White, J. Robson, and P. Elmsly, 1778.

———. *A Voyage Round the World, in His Britannic Majesty's Sloop, Resolution, commanded by Capt. James Cook, during the Years 1772, 3, 4, and 5.* 2 vols. London: B. White, J. Robson, P. Elmsley, and G. Robinson, 1777.

Foster, Joseph, ed. *Alumni Oxonienses, the members of the University of Oxford, 1500–1714: their parentage, birthplace, and year of birth, with a record of their degrees. Being the matriculation register of the University, alphabetically arranged, revised and annotated.* Oxford, London: Parker and Co., 1891–1892.

Fremantle, Anne Jackson. *Loyal Enemy.* London: Hutchinson, 1938.

Friendly, Alfred. *Beaufort of the Admiralty: The Life of Sir Francis Beaufort, 1774–1857.* London: Hutchinson, 1977.

Frost, Alan. *Dreams of a Pacific Empire: Sir George Young's Proposal for a Colonization of New South Wales (1784–5); A Parallel Edition of the Texts, Together with an Introduction Discussing Their Historical Background and Foreground.* Sydney: Resolution Press, 1980.

Furneaux, Robin. *William Wilberforce.* London: Hamish Hamilton, 1974.

Gamble, Mary Ann Fryer. *John Fryer of the Bounty: Notes on His Career.* Edited by Owen Rutter. London: Golden Cockerel Press, 1939.

Gardner, Peter. "The *Bounty* Grave—Tower Hamlets." *UK Log* 24 (July 2002): 39.

Gatty, Alfred. "Barker and Burford's Panoramas." Letter to *Notes and Queries*, 4th series, 7 (May 20, 1871): 432.

Gill, Conrad. *The Naval Mutinies of 1797.* Manchester: University Press, 1913.

Goldman, Irving. *Ancient Polynesian Society.* Chicago: University of Chicago Press, 1970.

Gould, Rupert T. "Bligh's Notes on Cook's Last Voyage." *Mariner's Mirror* 14 (1928): 371–85.

"Graham, Aaron." In *The Annual Biography and Obituary for the Year 1820.* Vol. 16: 402–22. London: Longman, Hurst, Rees, Orme, and Brown, 1820.

———. In *Dictionary of Canadian Biography* 5 (1801–1820): 361–62. Toronto: University of Toronto Press, 1991.

Grant, Aline. *Ann Radcliffe: A Biography.* Denver: A. Swallow, 1951.

Grant, James Shaw. *Morrison of the Bounty: A Scotsman, Famous but Unknown.* Stornoway, Isle of Lewis, Scotland: Acair, 1997.

Griggs, Earl Leslie, ed. *Collected Letters of Samuel Taylor Coleridge.* 6 vols. Oxford Scholarly Classics. Oxford: Clarendon Press, 1971, 2000.

Haan, Frederik de. *Oud Batavia gedenkboek uitgegeven door het Bataviasch Genootschap van Kunsten en Wetenschappen naar aanleiding van het driehonderdjarig bestaan der stad in 1919.* 2 vols. Batavia: G. Kolff, 1922–1923.

Hallett, John, obituary in "Obituary of Remarkable Persons, with Biographical Anecdotes." *Gentlemen's Magazine* 64, pt. 2 (December 1794): 1157.

Hamilton, George. *A Voyage Round the World, in His Majesty's Frigate* Pandora, *Performed Under the Direction of Captain Edwards in the years 1790, 1791, and 1792.* Berwick, Northumberland: W. Phorson, 1793.

Hamilton, Sir Richard Vesey, and John Knox Laughton, eds. *Recollections of James Anthony Gardner, Commander R.N. (1775–1814).* Publications of the Navy Records Society, vol. 31. London: Navy Records Society, 1906.

Hampson, John, obituary in "Obituary of Remarkable Persons, with Biographical Anecdotes." *Gentlemen's Magazine* 65, pt. 1 (January 1795): 85.

Hawkesworth, John. *An Account of the Voyages Undertaken by the Order of His Present Majesty for making Discoveries in the Southern Hemisphere, And Successively Performed by Commodore Byron, Captain Wallis, Captain Carteret, and Captain Cook, in the Dolphin, the Swallow, and the Endeavour, drawn up from the journals which were kept by the several commanders, and from the papers of Joseph Banks, Esq.* 3 vols. London: W. Strahan and T. Cadell, 1773.

Hayes, Walter. *The Captain from Nantucket and the Mutiny on the Bounty: A Recollection of Mayhew Folger, Mariner, Who Discovered the Last Mutineer and His Family on Pitcairn's Island, Together with Letters & Documents Never Previously Published.* Ann Arbor, Mich.: William L. Clements Library, 1996.

Hayter, Alethea. *The Wreck of the Abergavenny.* London: Macmillan, 2002.

Henderson, George Cockburn. *The Discoverers of the Fiji Islands: Tasman, Cook, Bligh, Wilson, Bellinghausen.* London: J. Murray, 1933.

"HMS *Pandora*," www.mtq.qld.gov.au. Museum of Tropical Queensland, Queensland Museum, South Brisbane.

Heywood, James Modyford, obituary in "Obituary of Remarkable Persons, with Biographical Anecdotes." *Gentlemen's Magazine* 68, pt. 1 (April 1798): 356.

Hibbert, Christopher. *The French Revolution.* London: Allen Lane, 1980.

———. *George III: A Personal History.* London: Penguin, 1998.

Hickman, William. *A treatise on the law and practice of naval courts-martial.* London: J. Murray, 1851.

Hicks Beach, Mrs. William. *The Yesterdays Behind the Door.* Liverpool: University Press, 1956.

Hill, Alan G., ed. *Letters of Dorothy Wordsworth: A Selection.* Oxford: Oxford University Press, 1981.

Holmes, Richard. *Coleridge: Darker Reflections, 1804–1834.* London: HarperCollins, 1998.

———. *Coleridge: Early Visions.* London: Hodder & Stoughton, 1989.

Holworthy, Richard. *Monumental Inscriptions in the Church and Churchyard of Bromley, County Kent.* London: M. Hughes, 1922.

"Hood, Rt. Hon. Samuel Lord Viscount, Baron of Catherington, Bart." In *The Annual Biography and Obituary for the Year.* Vol. 1: 371–79. London: Longman, Hurst, Rees, Orme, and Brown, 1817.

———. In *British Naval Biography.* 414–18. London: Scott, Webster and Geary, 1839.

"Horrid Massacres in the Capital of France." *Gentlemen's Magazine* 62, pt. 2 (September 1792): 854–56.

Horwood, Richard. *The A to Z of Regency London.* 1813. Reprint with an introduction by Paul Laxton; index compiled by Joseph Wisdom. London: London Topographical Society, 1985.

Hough, Richard Alexander. *Captain Bligh and Mr. Christian: The Men and The Mutiny.* New York: E. P. Dutton, 1973.

Houston, Neal B. "Fletcher Christian and 'The Rime of the Ancient Mariner.'" *Dalhousie Review* 45 (Winter 1965–1966): 431–46.

Howay, F. W. "Some Lengthy Open-Boat Voyages in the Pacific Ocean." *American Neptune,* January 1944, 53–57.

Howell, William, obituary in "Obituary; with Anecdotes of remarkable Persons." *Gentlemen's Magazine* 92, pt. 1 (January 1822): 92.

Hughes, Edward. *North Country Life in the Eighteenth Century.* 2 vols. London: Oxford University Press, 1952–1965.

Hughes, Edward, ed. *The Diaries and Correspondence of James Losh.* 2 vols. Durham, Eng.: Andrews & Co. for the Surtees Society, 1962–1963.

Hunter, Rosemary. "Surviving the Pacific: Captain Bligh's Record of Health and Disease." *Pacific Island Focus* 1, no. 2 (1989): 23–44.

Hutchinson, William. *The History of the County of Cumberland, and Some Places Adjacent, from the Earliest Accounts to the Present Time, Comprehending the Local History of the County; its Antiquities, the Origin, Genealogy, and Present State of the Principal Families, with Biographical notes, its Mines, Minerals, and Plants, with other Curiosities, either of Nature or of Art.* 2 vols. Carlisle, Cumbria: F. Jollie, 1794.

Inglefield, John Nicholson. *Capt. Inglefield's-Narrative, concerning the loss of His Majesty's ship, the Centaur, of seventy-four guns: and the miraculous preservation of the Pinnace, with the captain, master, and ten of the crew, in a traverse of near 300 leagues on the great western ocean, with the names of the people saved.* New ed., corrected. London: J. Murray and A. Donaldson, 1783.

Jarrett, Derek. *England in the Age of Hogarth*. New Haven: Yale University Press, 1974, 1986.

Johnston, George, and J. Bartrum. *Proceedings of a General Court-Martial Held at Chelsea Hospital, Which commenced on Tuesday, May 7, 1811, and continued by Adjournment to Wednesday, 5th of June following, for The trial of Lieut.-Col. Geo. Johnston, Major of the 102d Regiment, late [of] the New South Wales Corps, on A Charge of Mutiny . . . Exhibited Against Him By the Crown For Deposing on the 26th of January, 1808, William Bligh, Esq. F.R.S*. London: Sherwood, Neely and Jones, 1811.

Johnston, Kenneth. *The Hidden Wordsworth: Poet, Lover, Rebel, Spy*. New York: W. W. Norton, 1998.

Jong, C de. *Reizen naar de Kaap de GH, 1791–7*. Haarlem, 1802.

Kaufman, Paul. "Wordsworth's 'Candid and Enlightened Friend.'" *Notes and Queries*, n.s., 9 (November 1962): 403–8.

Kempe, John A., ed. *Autobiography of Anna Eliza Bray*. London: Chapman and Hall, 1884.

Kennedy, Gavin. *Bligh*. London: Duckworth, 1978.

———. "Bligh and the *Defiance* Mutiny." *Mariner's Mirror* 65 (1979): 65–68.

———. *Captain Bligh: The Man and his Mutinies*. London: Duckworth, 1989.

———. *The Death of Captain Cook*. London: Duckworth, 1978.

Kent, William George Carlile. *Interesting naval trial minutes of a court martial . . . for the trial of Lieut. W.G. Carlile Kent, late acting commander of H.M.S. Porpoise . . . on charges exhibited against him by the said William Bligh . . . including the whole of the evidence and documentary proof on the part of the prosecution, and on the defence, with the different addresses from the prosecutor and prisoner, as also the sentence of the court*. Portsmouth, Hampshire: Mottley, Harrison, & Miller, 1811.

Kent's Directory for the Year 1794. Cities of London and Westminster, and Borough of Southwark, www.londonancestor.com/kents/kent=m.htm. London Ancestor, London.

King, Capt. Henry. "Extract from the Journal of Captain Henry King of the *Elizabeth*." *Edinburgh Philosophical Journal* 3, no. 6 (October 1820): 380–88.

Kitson, Peter J., and Debbie Lee, eds. *Slavery, Abolition, and Emancipation: Writings in the British Romantic Period*. 8 vols. London: Pickering & Chatto, 1999.

Kitto, John. *Historic Homes of the Isle of Man*. Braddan, Isle of Man: Executive Publications, 1990.

Knight, C. "H. M. Armed Vessel *Bounty*." *Mariner's Mirror* 22, no. 2 (April 1936): 183–99.

Knight, Roger. "The First Fleet. Its State and Preparation 1786–1787." In *Studies from Terra Australis to Australia*, edited by John Hardy and Alan Frost. Canberra: Australian Academy of Humanities, n.d. (c. 1989).

Kotzebue, Otto von, and Johann Friedrich Eschscholtz. *A New Voyage Round the World in the years 1823, 24, 25, and 26*. 2 vols. London: H. Colburn and R. Bentley, 1830.

Lamb, Charles. *Recollections of Christ's Hospital*. London: E. J. Stirling, 1813, 1835.

Langdon, Robert. "Ancient Cornish Inn Is Link with the Bounty." *Pacific Islands Monthly*, April 1961, 75–76.

———. *Tahiti, Island of Love*. 5th ed. Sydney: Pacific Publications, 1968, 1979.

Laprade, William Thomas. *England and the French Revolution, 1789–1797*. Baltimore: Johns Hopkins Press, 1909.

"The Last of the 'Pandoras.'" *United Service Magazine* no. 166 (1842): 1–13.

Lavery, Brian. *Nelson's Navy: Its Ships, Men and Organization, 1793–1815*. Annapolis, Md.: Naval Institute Press, 2000.

Lee, Ida. *Captain Bligh's Second Voyage to the South Seas*. London: Longmans, 1920.

Leeson, Ida. "The Morrison Myth." *Mariner's Mirror* 25 (1939): 433–38.

Le Faye, Deirdre. *Jane Austen's Letters*. 3d ed., new ed. Oxford: Oxford University Press, 1995, 1997.

L'Estrange, Rev. Alfred Guy Kingan. *Lady Belcher and Friends*. London: Hurst and Blackett, 1891.

Lewis, Michael Arthur. *England's Sea-Officers: The Story of the Naval Profession*. London: George Allen & Unwin, 1939.

Liddel, Robert. *A Detail of the Duties of a Deputy Judge Advocate; with Precedents of Forms of the Various Documents used in Sommoning, Assembling and Holding a Naval Court Martial; with The Proceedings Thereof, To The Passing Of Sentence; also Records of Sentences, with Cases and Opinions On Special Points*. London: G. Wilkie and J. Robinson, 1805.

Lloyd, Christopher. "Cook and Scurvy." *Mariner's Mirror* 65 (1979): 23–28.

———. *Mr. Barrow of the Admiralty: A Life of Sir John Barrow, 1764–1848*. London: Collins, 1970.

London Missionary Society. *Narrative of the Mission at Otaheite, and other islands in the South Seas; commenced by the London Missionary Society, in the year 1797; with a map, and a geographical description of the islands*. London: London Missionary Society, 1818.

Lonsdale, Henry. *The Worthies of Cumberland*. 6 vols. London: George Routledge & Sons, 1867.

Lowes, John Livingston. *The Road to Xanadu: A Study in the Ways of the Imagination*. Boston: Houghton Mifflin, 1927.

Lucas, Sir Charles Prestwood, ed. *The Pitcairn Island Register Book*. London: Society for Promoting Christian Knowledge, 1929.

Lysons, Daniel, and Samuel Lysons. *Devonshire*. Vol. 6 of *Magna Britannia: Being a Concise Topographical Account of the Several Counties of Great Britain*. London: T. Cadell and W. Davies, 1822.

Mackaness, George. *Captain William Bligh's Discoveries and Observations in Van Diemen's Land: Read Before the Royal Society of Tasmania at Its Centenary Meeting, Hobart, Oct. 14, 1943*. Sydney: D. S. Ford, 1943.

———. "Extracts from a Log-Book of HMS *Providence* Kept by Lt. Francis Godolphin Bond RN." *Royal Australian Historical Society Journal* 46 (1960): 24–66.

———. *The Life of Vice-Admiral William Bligh, R. N., F. R. S.* New and rev. ed. 1931 Reprint, Sydney: Angus and Robertson, 1951.

———. *Sir Joseph Banks: His Relations with Australia*. Sydney: Angus and Robertson, 1936.

Mackaness, George, ed. *Fresh Light on Bligh: Being Some Unpublished Correspondence of Captain William Bligh, R.N., and Lieutenant Francis Godolphin Bond, R.N., with Lieutenant Bond's Manuscript Notes Made on the Voyage of H.M.S. Providence, 1791–1795*. Sydney: D. S. Ford, 1953.

———. *Some Correspondence of Captain William Bligh, R.N., with John and Francis Godolphin Bond, 1776–1811*. Sydney: D. S. Ford, 1949.

MacKay, David. "Banks, Bligh and Breadfruit." *The New Zealand Journal of History* 8 (1974): 61–77.

Maltby, Isaac. *A Treatise on Courts Martial and Military Law: containing an explanation of the principles which govern courts martial and courts of inquiry*. Boston: Thomas B. Wait, 1813.

Manwaring, George Ernest. *My Friend the Admiral: The Life, Letters, and Journals of Rear-Admiral James Burney, F.R.S., the Companion of Captain Cook and Friend of Charles Lamb*. London: G. Routledge & Sons, 1931.

Marcus, Geoffrey Jules. *The Age of Nelson: The Royal Navy, 1793–1815*. New York: Viking, 1971.

———. *The Formative Years*. Vol. 1 of *A Naval History of England*. Boston: Little, Brown, 1962.

Marden, Luis. "I Found the Bones of the *Bounty*." *National Geographic Magazine*, December 1957, 725–89.

———."Wreck of H.M.S. *Pandora*." *National Geographic*, October 1985, 422–51.

Mariner, William. *An Account of the Natives of the Tonga Islands in the South Pacific Ocean. With an original grammar and vocabulary of their language. Compiled and arranged from the extensive communications of Mr. William Mariner, several years resident in those islands.* Edited by John Martin. 2 vols. London, 1817.

Marshall, John. "Captain Albemarle Bertie." In *Royal Naval Biography or, Memoirs of the Services of All the Flag-Officers, Superannuated Rear-Admirals, Retired-Captains, Post-Captains, and Commanders, whose names appeared on the Admiralty List of Sea Officers at the commencement of the present year, or who have since been promoted; Illustrated by a Series of Historical and Explanatory Notes, Which will be found to contain an account of all the Naval Actions, and other important Events, from the Commencement of the late Reign, in 1760, to the present period. With Copious Addenda.* Vol. 1: 195. London: Longman, Hurst, Rees, Orme, and Brown, 1823–1835.

———. "Sir Andrew Snape Hamond." In *Royal Naval Biography*. Vol. 2: 54–60. London: Longman, Hurst, Rees, Orme, and Brown, 1823–1835.

———. "Peter Heywood, Esq." In *Royal Naval Biography*. Vol. 2, pt. 2: 747–97. London: Longman, Hurst, Rees, Orme, and Brown, 1823–1835.

———. "John Nicholson Inglefield." In *Royal Naval Biography*. Vol. 2: 62–70. London: Longman, Hurst, Rees, Orme, and Brown, 1823–1835.

———. "Richard Goodwin Keats." In *Royal Naval Biography*. Vol. 1: 342–47. London: Longman, Hurst, Rees, Orme, and Brown, 1823–1835.

———. "Captain John Knight." In *Royal Naval Biography*. Vol. 1: 154–65. London: Longman, Hurst, Rees, Orme, and Brown, 1823–1835.

———. "Pulteney Malcolm." In *Royal Naval Biography*. Vol. 1, pt. 2: 582–83. London: Longman, Hurst, Rees, Orme, and Brown, 1823–1835.

———. "Sir George Montagu." In *Royal Naval Biography*. Vol. 1: 39. London: Longman, Hurst, Rees, Orme, and Brown, 1823–1835.

Maude, H. E. "The Edwards Papers." *Journal of Pacific History* 1 (1966): 184–85.

———. "In Search of a Home: From the Mutiny to Pitcairn Island (1789–1790)." *Journal of the Polynesian Society* 67, no. 2 (June 1958): 104–31.

———. *Of Islands and Men: Studies in Pacific History*. Melbourne: Oxford University Press, 1968.

———. "Tahitian Interlude: The Migration of the Pitcairn Islanders to the Motherland in 1831." *Journal of the Polynesian Society* 68, no. 2 (June 1959): 115–40.

———. "The Voyage of the *Pandora*'s Tender." *Mariner's Mirror* 50 (1964): 217–35.

McArthur, John. *Principles and Practice of Naval and Military Courts Martial: with an appendix illustrative of the subject*. 4th ed. 2 vols. London: A. Strahan, 1813.

McKay, John. *The Armed Transport* Bounty. London: Conway Maritime, n.d. (c. 1989).

McKee, Alexander. *The Truth About the Mutiny on the* Bounty. London: Mayflower Books, 1961.

"Memoir of the Public Services of the late Sir Hugh Cloberry Christian, K.B. Rear Admiral of the White Squadron." *Naval Chronicle* 21 (January–June 1809): 177–89.

"Memoir of the Public Services of the late Captain Sir Andrew Snape Douglas, Knt. Colonel of Marines, who commanded Lord Howe's Flag-Ship, The Queen Charlotte, on the First of June, 1794." *Naval Chronicle* 25 (January–June 1811): 353–82.

Mitford, Mary Russell. *Christina, the Maid of the South Seas; A Poem.* London: A. J. Valpy for F. C. and J. Rivington; J. Hatchard, 1811.

Moerenhout, Jacques Antoine. *Voyages aux Îles du Grand Océan.* Paris: A. Bertrand, 1837. (Translated as *Travels to the Islands of the Pacific Ocean* by Arthur R. Borden. Lanham, Md.: University Press of America, 1993.)

Moffat, Hugh. "George Tobin RN." *Sea Breezes* 39 (1965): 562–66.

Montagu, Sir George, and Edward Pelham Brenton. *A Refutation of the Incorrect Statements, and Unjust Insinuations, contained in Captain Brenton's Naval History of Great Britain, as far as the same refers to the conduct of Admiral Sir George Montagu, G.C.B. In a letter addressed to the author.* London: J. Murray, 1823.

Montgomerie, H. S. "The Morrison Myth." *Mariner's Mirror* 27 (1941): 69–76.

Moore, A. W. *Nessy Heywood.* Douglas, Isle of Man: Brown & Sons, 1913.

Moorman, Mary Trevelyan. *The Early Years, 1770–1803.* Vol. 1 of *William Wordsworth: A Biography.* Oxford: Clarendon Press, 1957–1965.

———. *The Later Years, 1803–1850.* Vol. 2 of *William Wordsworth: A Biography.* Oxford: Clarendon Press, 1957–1965.

Morrison, James. *The Journal of James Morrison, Boatswain's Mate of the Bounty, Describing the Mutiny and Subsequent Misfortunes of the Mutineers, Together with an Account of the Island of Tahiti.* Edited by Owen Rutter. London: Golden Cockerel Press, 1935.

Mortimer, George. *Observations and Remarks Made During a Voyage to the Islands of Teneriffe, Amsterdam, Maria's Islands Near Van Diemen's Land, Otaheite, Sandwich Islands, Owhyhee, the Fox Islands on the North West Coast of America, Tinian, and from thence to Canton, in the Brig Mercury, Commanded by John Henry Cox, Esq.* London: T. Cadell, 1791.

Murray, Thomas Boyles. *Pitcairn: The Island, the People, and the Pastor; With a short account of the mutiny of the Bounty.* 2d ed. London: Society for Promoting Christian Knowledge, 1853.

———. *Pitcairn, The Island, The People, and The Pastor: to which is added a short notice of the original settlement and present condition of Norfolk Island.* 8th ed. London: Committee of General Literature and Education for the Society for Promoting Christian Knowledge, 1857.

———. *Pitcairn: The Island, The People and The Pastor, to which is added a short notice of the original settlement and present condition of Norfolk Island.* 11th ed. London: Committee of General Literature and Education for the Society for Promoting Christian Knowledge, 1858.

"The Mutiny of the *Bounty.*" *Edinburgh Review* 4, no. 24 (January 1832): 673–85.

Nash, M. D., ed. *The Last Voyage of the* Guardian: *Lieutenant Riou, Commander, 1789–1791.* Cape Town: Van Riebeeck Society, 1990.

Nausistratus [Samuel Greatheed]. "Authentic History of the Mutineers of the *Bounty.*" *Sailor's Magazine and Naval Miscellany* 1 (1820): 402–6, 449–56; 2 (1821): 1–8.

"Nautical Anecdotes and Selections; Mutineers of the Bounty." *Naval Chronicle* 35 (January–June 1816): 17–25.

Naval and Martial Biography, Or memoirs of several hundred illustrious British naval and military characters . . . and a brief history of the rise and progress of the British Navy and other important particulars relative to the subject. With portraits of the most distinguished characters. Ormskirk, Lancashire: J. Fowler, 1806.

"Naval Anecdotes, Commercial Hints, Recollections, &c.; Mutineers of the Bounty." *Naval Chronicle* 21 (January–June 1809): 454–55.

New annals of gallantry: containing, a complete collection of all the genuine letters which have passed between Captain Inglefield, and Mrs. Inglefield; signed with their respective names, relative to a charge brought by the former against the latter, for partiality to her black servant. To which are added, the black's affidavits, pro and con, and Mrs. Inglefield's also, upon this extra-ordinary business. Likewise, the letters of Mr. Mills, man-midwife, of Greenwich, relative to his conduct since the suspicion of this strange connection. London: R. Randall, 1785.

A New Portsmouth Guide; Being a Description of the ancient and present State of the Place . . . Its Buildings, Charitable Foundations, Fairs, Markets, Playhouse, and Assembly-Room . . . Interspersed with many Particulars, Useful, Curious and Entertaining. Portsmouth, Hampshire, 1790.

Nicholls, Christine Stephanie, and Godfrey Hugh Lancelot Le May. "James Losh." In *The Dictionary of National Biography: Missing Persons.* Oxford: Oxford University Press, 1994.

Nicol, John. *The Life and Adventures of John Nicol, Mariner.* 1822. Reprint, edited by Tim Flannery. Edinburgh: Canongate, 2000.

Nicolson, Robert B., and Brian F. Davies. *The Pitcairners.* Sydney: Angus and Robertson; San Francisco: Tri-Ocean Books, 1965.

Noah, Mordecai Manuel. *Travels in England, France, Spain, and the Barbary States, in the Years 1813–14 and 15.* New York: Kirk and Mercein, 1819.

Norie, John William, comp. and arr. *The Naval Gazetteer, Biographer and Chronologist, containing a history of the late wars from 1793 to 1801 and from 1803 to 1815, and continued, as to the biographical part to the present time.* London: C. Wilson, 1842.

Oberea, Queen of Otaheite [pseud.]. *An epistle from Oberea, Queen of Otaheite [pseud.] to Joseph Banks, esq. Translated by T.Q.Z., Esq. [pseud.] Professor of the Otaheite Language in Dublin and of all the languages of the undiscovered islands in the South Sea.* London: J. Almon, 1774.

———. *A Second Letter from Oberea, Queen of Otaheite [pseud.] to Joseph Banks, Esq.* London: T. J. Carnegay, 1774.

O'Brian, Patrick. *Joseph Banks: A Life.* Chicago: University of Chicago Press, 1997.

Old Sailor. *The Log Book; or Nautical Miscellany.* London: J. & W. Robins, 1830.

Oliver, Andrew, ed. *The Journal of Samuel Curwen, Loyalist.* 2 vols. Cambridge, Mass.: Harvard University Press, for the Essex Institute, Salem, 1972.

Oliver, Douglas L. *Ancient Tahitian Society.* 3 vols. Honolulu: University Press of Hawaii, 1974.

———. *Return to Tahiti: Bligh's Second Breadfruit Voyage.* Carlton, Victoria: Melbourne University Press, at the Miegunyah Press, 1988.

Page, John T. "Bligh." Letter to *Notes and Queries,* July 29, 1899, 97.

Parker, Mary Ann. *A Voyage Round the World, in the Gorgon Man of War: Captain John Parker, Performed and written by his widow.* London: J. Nichols, 1795.

Pasley, Louisa Maria Sabine. *Memoir of Admiral Sir Thomas Sabine Pasley.* London: E. Arnold, 1900.

Pasley, Rodney Marshall Sabine, ed. *Private Sea Journals, 1778–1782, Kept by Admiral Sir Thomas Pasley, Bart., when in command of H.M. Ships Glasgow (20), Sybil (28), and Jupiter (50).* London: J. M. Dent and Sons, Ltd., 1931.

Peacock, James. "Bligh." Letter to *Notes and Queries,* August 19, 1899, 150.

Philbrick, Nathaniel. *In the Heart of the Sea: The Tragedy of the Whaleship* Essex. New York: Viking, 2000.

Phillimore, Joseph, and Sir Robert Joseph Phillimore. *A Report of the Judgment Delivered on the Sixth Day of June, 1835 by Joseph Phillimore, In the Cause of Belcher, the Wife, against Belcher, the Husband.* London: Saunders and Benning, 1835.

Pipon, Philip. "The Descendants of the Bounty's Crew." *United Service Journal* (1834), part 1: 191–99.

Pollock, John Charles. *Wilberforce.* New York: St. Martin's, 1977, 1978.

Polwhele, Rev. Richard. *Traditions and Recollections; Domestic, Clerical, and Literary; in which are included letters of Charles II, Cromwell, Fairfax, Edgecumbe, Macaulay, Wolcot, Opie, Whitaker, Gibbon, Buller, Courtenay, Moore, Downman, Drewe, Seward, Darwin, Cowper, Hayley, Hardinge, Sir Walter Scott, and other Distinguished Characters.* 2 vols. London: J. Nichols and Son, 1826.

Pope, Dudley. *The Great Gamble: Nelson at Copenhagen.* 1972. Reprint, London: Chatham, 2001.

"Port News; Portsmouth, Sept. 5." *Gentlemen's Magazine* 62, pt. 2 (September 1792): 860.

Pottle, Frederick Albert. *Boswell and the Girl from Botany Bay.* London: Heinemann, 1938.

Powell, Dulcie A. "The Voyage of the Plant Nursery, H. M. S. *Providence,* 1791–1793." *Bulletin of the Institute of Jamaica,* Science Series no. 15 (1973): 7.

Price, Cecil John Layton, ed. *The Letters of Richard Brinsley Sheridan.* 3 vols. Oxford: Clarendon, 1966.

Purcell, Mr. [William], obituary. *Gentlemen's Magazine* 1 n.s., pt. 1 (June 1834): 668.

Raine, T. "Captain Raine's Narrative of a Visit to Pitcairn's Island in the ship Surry, 1821." *The Australian Magazine, or, Compendium of Religious, Literary and Miscellaneous Intelligence* 1 (1821): 80–84; 109–14.

Ralfe, James. "George Montagu." In *The Naval Biography of Great Britain: Consisting of Historical Memoirs of Those Officers of the British Navy who Distinguished Themselves During the Reign of His Majesty George III.* Vol. 2: 6. London: Whitmore & Fenn, 1828.

Rawson, Geoffrey. *Pandora's Last Voyage.* London: Longmans, 1963.

Rees, Siân. *The Floating Brothel: The extraordinary true story of an eighteenth-century ship and its cargo of female convicts.* London: Headline, 2001.

Retraction of review of *Letters from Mr. Fletcher Christian, Containing a Narrative of the Transactions on Board His Majesty's Ship Bounty, Before and After the Mutiny, With His Subsequent Voyages and Travels in South America,* by Fletcher Christian. *True Briton,* September 23, 1796.

Review of *Answer to Certain Assertions Contained in the Appendix Entitled 'Minutes of the Proceedings on the Court Martial held at Portsmouth August 12th 1792 on Ten Persons Charged with Mutiny on Board His Majesty's Ship the* Bounty, by William Bligh. *British Critic* 4 (December 1794): 686.

Review of *Journal of a Cruize made to the Pacific Ocean by Captain David Porter, in the United States Frigate Essex, in the years 1812, 1813, and 1814, containing Descriptions of the Cape de Verd Islands, Coasts of Brazil, Patagonia, Chili and Peru, and of the Gallapagos Islands. Also, a full Account of the Washington Group of Islands; the Manners, Customs, Dress of the Inhabitants, &c., &c.,* by David Porter. *Quarterly Review* (London) 13, no. 26 (July 1815): 352–83.

Review of *Letters from Mr. Fletcher Christian, Containing a Narrative of the Transactions on Board His Majesty's Ship Bounty, Before and After the Mutiny, With His Subsequent Voyages and Travels in South America,* by Fletcher Christian. *True Briton,* September 13, 1796.

Review of *Minutes [taken by Stephen Barney] of the Proceedings of the Court-Martial held at Portsmouth, August [sic] 12, 1792, on Ten Persons charged with Mutiny on Board His Majesty's Ship the* Bounty. *With an Appendix Containing A full Account of the real Causes and Circumstances of that unhappy Transaction, the most material of which have hitherto been withheld from the Public,* by Joseph Coleman and Edward Christian. *British Critic* 4 (November 1794): 559.

Review of *Voyage de Dentrecasteaux, envoyé à la Recherche de la Pérouse, publié par Ordre de Sa Majesté L'Empereur et Roi, sous le Ministère de S.E. le Vice-Amiral Decrès, Comte de l'Empire,* by M. de Rossel. *Quarterly Review* (London) 3, no. 5 (February 1810): 21–43.

R. F. P. "Bligh." Letter to *Notes and Queries,* September 23, 1899, 253.

Richardson, John. *Highgate: Its History Since the Fifteenth Century.* Herts.: Historical Publications, 1983.

Rickman, John. *Journal of Captain Cook's Last Voyage to the Pacific Ocean, on Discovery: Performed in the Years 1776, 1777, 1778, 1779.* London: E. Newberry, 1781.

Robertson, George. *The Discovery of Tahiti: a Journal of the Second Voyage of H.M.S. Dolphin Round the World Under the Command of Captain Wallis, R.N., in the years 1766, 1767, and 1768.* Edited by Hugh Carrington. London: Hakluyt Society, 1948.

Robinson, A. H. W. "Captain William Bligh R.N., hydrographic surveyor," *Empire Survey Review* 11, no. 85 (1952): 301–6.

Robson, Derek. *Some Aspects of Education in Cheshire in the Eighteenth Century.* Manchester: Chetham Society/Manchester University Press, 1966.

Rodger, N. A. M. *Articles of War: The Statutes which Governed our Fighting Navies, 1661, 1749, and 1886.* Homewell, Havant, Hampshire: Kenneth Mason, 1982.

———. *The Wooden World: An Anatomy of the Georgian Navy.* Annapolis, Md.: Naval Institute Press, 1986.

"The Romance of the Bread-fruit." *The West India Committee Circular,* no. 590 (May 12, 1921): 197–99.

Romilly, Samuel, Sir. *Memoirs of the Life of Sir Samuel Romilly, written by himself with a selection from his correspondence edited by his sons.* 2d ed. 3 vols. London: J. Murray, 1840.

Ross, Alan Strode Campbell, and A. W. Moverley. *The Pitcairnese Language.* New York: Oxford University Press, 1964.

Rutter, Owen. "Bligh's Log." *Mariner's Mirror* 22 (1936): 179–82.

———. "The Vindication of William Bligh." Review of *The Discoverers of the Fiji Islands,* by G. C. Henderson. *Quarterly Review* (London) 261, no. 518 (October 1933): 279–91.

Rutter, Owen, ed. *The Court-Martial of the "Bounty" Mutineers.* Edinburgh: W. Hodge & Company, Ltd., 1931.

———. *The Court-Martial of the "Bounty" Mutineers.* 1931. Reprint, with a new introduction by Alan M. Dershowitz. Birmingham, Ala.: Notable Trials Library, 1989.

———. *The Voyage of the* Bounty's *Launch as related in William Bligh's Despatch to the Admiralty and the Journal of John Fryer.* London: Golden Cockerel Press, 1934.

Samwell, David. *A Narrative of the Death of Captain James Cook. To which are added some particulars, concerning his life and character, and observations respecting the introduction of the venereal disease into the Sandwich Islands.* London: G.G.J. and J. Robinson, 1786.

Schama, Simon. *Citizens: A Chronicle of the French Revolution.* New York: Knopf, 1989.

Scott, Brian W. "The True Identity of John Adams." *Mariner's Mirror* 68 (1982): 31–39.

Scott, James. *Remarks on a Passage to Botany Bay, 1787–1792.* Sydney: Trustees of the Public Library of New South Wales in association with Angus and Robertson, 1963.

Shapiro, Harry Lionel. *Descendants of the Mutineers of the* Bounty. Honolulu: Memoirs of the Bernice P. Bishop Museum 11, 1929.

———. *The Heritage of the* Bounty: *The Story of Pitcairn Through Six Generations.* New York: Simon and Schuster, 1936.

Shillibeer, John. *A Narrative of the Briton's Voyage to Pitcairn's Island: Including an Interesting Sketch of the Present State of the Brazils and of Spanish South America.* Taunton, Somerset: J. W. Marriott, 1817.

Silverman, David. *Pitcairn Island.* Cleveland: World, 1967.

Smith, Bernard. "Coleridge's *Ancient Mariner* and Cook's Second Voyage." *Journal of the Warburg and Courtauld Institutes* 19, no. 1–2 (1956): 117–54.

Smith, D. Bonner. "More Light on Bligh and the *Bounty*." *Mariner's Mirror* 23 (1937): 210–28.
———. "Some Remarks About the Mutiny of the *Bounty*." *Mariner's Mirror* 22 (1936): 200–237.
Smith, Howard M. "The Introduction of Veneral Disease into Tahiti: A Re-Examination." *Journal of the Polynesian Society* 10 (1975): 38–45.
[Smyth, W. H.] "The *Bounty* Again!" *United Service Journal* (1831), part 3: 305–14.
———. "Capt. Beechey's Narrative," Review of *Narrative of a Voyage to the Pacific and Beering's Strait, to co-operate with the Polar Expeditions performed in His Majesty's Ship* Blossom, *under the command of Captain F. W. Beechey, R.N., F.R.S. &c. in the years 1825, 26, 27, 28*, by Frederick William Beechey. *United Service Journal* (1831), part 1: 527–31.
———. "The *Pandora* Again!" *United Service Magazine* no. 172. (1843): 411–20.
———. "Review of *A Memoir of the late Captain Peter Heywood, R. N.* by Edward Tagart." *United Service Journal* (1833), part 1: 92–93.
———. "Sketch of the Career of the Late Capt. Peter Heywood R. N." *United Service Journal* (1831), part 1: 468–81.
Staines, Sir Thomas. "Account of the Descendants of Christian and Other Mutineers of the Bounty." *Naval Chronicle* 33 (1815): 217–18.
Stark, Suzanne J. *Female Tars: Women Aboard Ship in the Age of Sail*. Annapolis, Md.: Naval Institute Press, 1996.
Statements of the Loss of His Majesty's New Ship the Bounty, W. Bligh, Esq., Commander, By a Conspiracy of the Crew; including the Wonderful Escape of the Captain and about Twelve Men in an Open Pinnace; also, the Adventures of the Mutineers, As Communicated by Lieutenant Christian the Ringleader, to a Relation in England. London: T. Tegg, 1800.
Stephen, Sir Leslie, and Sir Sidney Lee, eds. *The Dictionary of National Biography, Founded in 1882 by George Smith*. 22 vols. London: Oxford University Press, 1917.
Steuart, A. Francis. "Orkney News from the Letter-Bag of Mr. Charles Steuart." *Old-lore Miscellany of Orkney, Shetland, Caithness and Sutherland* 6 (1913): 41–49; 101–9.
Syrett, David, and R. L. DiNardo, eds. *The Commissioned Sea Officers of the Royal Navy, 1660–1815*. Revised from 1954 Admiralty edition. Aldershot, Hampshire: Scolar Press for the Navy Records Society; Brookfield, Vt.: Ashgate, 1994.
Tagart, Edward. *A Memoir of the Late Captain Peter Heywood, R.N., with Extracts From His Diaries and Correspondence*. London: E. Wilson, 1832.
Taylor, Rear-Admiral A. H., O.B.E. "William Bligh at Camperdown." *Mariner's Mirror* 23, no. 4 (October 1937): 417–33.
Teehuteatuaonoa ["Jenny"]. "Account of the mutineers of the Ship *Bounty*, and their Descendants at Pitcairn's Island." *Sydney Gazette*, July 17, 1819, 817.
———. "Pitcairn's Island—The Bounty's Crew," *United Service Journal* (1829), part 1: 589–93.
Tench, Watkin. *A Complete Account of the Settlement at Port Jackson, in New South Wales, including an accurate description of the situation of the colony; of the natives; and of its natural productions: taken on the spot, by Captain Watkin Tench*. London: G. Nicol, 1793.
Terrill, Anne Elizabeth. *Memorials of a Family in England and Virginia, A.D. 1771–1851*. London: Hazell, Watson, & Viney, 1887.
Thompson, Edward. *Sailor's Letters, Written to His Select Friends in England, During his Voyages and Travels in Europe, Asia, Africa, and America, from the year 1754 to 1759*. 2 ed., corrected. 2 vols. London: T. Becket & P. A. de Hondt; W. Flexney; and C. Moran, 1767.
Thompson, Thomas William. *Wordsworth's Hawkshead*. Edited by Robert Woof. London: Oxford University Press, 1970.
Thornbury, Walter, and Edward Walford. *Old and New London: A Narrative of Its History, Its People, and Its Places*. 6 vols. London: Cassell, Petter, & Galpin, 1873–1878.

Tinkler, Robert, obituary in "Obituary; with Anecdotes of remarkable Persons." *Gentlemen's Magazine* 90, part 2 (September 1820): 282.

Topliff, Samuel. "Pitcairn's Island." *New-England Galaxy* (Boston), January 12, 1821.

"T. W." "John Adams of Pitcairn Island." Letter to *Gentlemen's Magazine: and Historical Chronicle* 88, part. 2 (July 1818): 38–39.

Venn, John, and John Archibald Venn. *Alumni Cantabrigienses: a Biographical List of All Known Students, Graduates and Holders of Office at the University of Cambridge, from the Earliest Times to 1900.* Cambridge: Cambridge University Press, 1922.

Wahlroos, Sven. *Mutiny and Romance in the South Seas: A Companion to the* Bounty *Adventure.* Topsfield, Mass.: Salem House, 1989.

Wales, William. *Remarks on Mr. Forster's Account of Captain Cook's last Voyage round the World, in the Years 1772, 1773, 1774, and 1775.* London: J. Nourse, 1778.

Walker, Charles Frederick. *Young Gentlemen: The Story of Midshipmen from the XVIIth Century to the present day.* London: Longmans, Green, 1938.

Watkin, R. C. "Mutiny on the Bounty." *Proceedings—Isle of Man Natural History and Antiquarian Society* 7 (1970): 374–400.

Welford, Richard. *L–Y.* Vol. 3 of *Men of Mark 'twixt Tyne and Tweed.* London: Walter Scott, 1895.

Wentworth, William Charles. *A Statistical, Historical, and Political Description of The Colony of New South Wales, and Its Dependent Settlements in Van Diemen's Land: With a particular enumeration of the advantages which these colonies offer for emigration, and their superiority in many respects over those possessed by the United States of America.* London: G. and W. B. Whittaker, 1819.

West India Merchants. *West India Committee Minutes* 3 (1787): 54.

White, John. *Journal of a Voyage to New South Wales.* 1790. Edited by Alec H. Chisholm, F.R.A.H.S. Introduction by Rex Rientis. Sydney: Angus and Robertson in association with the Royal Australian Historical Society, 1962.

Wilkinson, Cuthbert Selby. *The Wake of the* Bounty. London: Cassell, 1953.

Wilkinson, Isaac. *Poetical Works.* Cockermouth, Cumbria: Edward Banks, 1824.

William Whellan & Co. *History, Topography, and Directory of Northumberland, comprising a general survey of the county, and a history of the town and county of Newcastle-upon-Tyne, with separate historical, statistical, and descriptive sketches of the boroughs of Gateshead and Berwick-upon-Tweed, and all the towns . . . wards, and manors. To which is subjoined a list of the seats of the nobility and gentry.* London: Whittaker and Co., 1855.

Wilson, Barbara Juarez. *From Mission to Majesty: A Genealogy and History of Early California and Royal European Ancestors.* Baltimore: Gateway Press, 1983.

Wilson, William, and James Wilson. *A Missionary Voyage to the Southern Pacific Ocean, performed in the Years 1796, 1797, 1798, in the Ship* Duff, *Commanded by Captain James Wilson. Comp. from Journals of the Officers and the Missionaries; and Illustrated with Maps, Charts, and Views, Drawn by Mr. William Wilson, and engraved by the most eminent Artists. With a preliminary discourse on the geography and history of the South Sea islands; and an appendix, including details never before published, of the natural and civil state of Otaheite; by a committee appointed for the purpose by the directors of the Missionary society.* London: S. Gosnell for T. Chapman, 1799.

"W. L." "Letter to Mr. Urban," *Gentlemen's Magazine* (December 1792): 1097–98.

Wood, Arthur Skevington. *Thomas Haweis, 1734–1820.* London: Church Historical Society [by] S.P.C.K., 1957.

Wordsworth, William. Letter to *Weekly Entertainer*, November 1796, 377.

————. *The Poetical Works of William Wordsworth*. 5 vols. 1940–1949. Reprinted from corrected sheets of the first edition. Vols. 2 and 3, second edition; vols. 3, 4, and 5 edited by E. de Selincourt and Helen Darbishire. Oxford: Clarendon Press, 1963–1966.

————. *The Prelude, or, Growth of a Poet's Mind: An Autobiographical Poem*. London: E. Moxon, 1850.

X. Y. Z. [pseud.]. "Letter to the Editor." *United Service Journal* (1829), part 2: 366–67.

Young, Sir George, 3rd Bart. *Young of Formosa*. Reading, Berks., 1927.

Young, Rosalind Amelia. *Mutiny of the Bounty and the story of Pitcairn Island, 1790–1894*. 3d ed. Oakland, Calif.: Pacific Press, 1894.

MAGAZINES AND NEWSPAPERS

Aberdeen Chronicle, April 15, 1815.

British Mercury, no. 20 (May 15, 1790): 212.

Bury and Norwich Post; or, Suffolk, Essex, Cambridge, Ely, and Norfolk Telegraph. (Bury St. Edmunds, Suffolk), January 16, 1822.

Caledonian Mercury (Edinburgh), December 10, 1792.

Cumberland Pacquet and Ware's Whitehaven Advertiser, October 19, 1779.

Diary, or, Woodfall's Register (London), May 11 and 29, 1790; June 4, 1790; October 31, 1792.

Eastern Daily Press (Norfolk), October 13, 2000: 30–31.

English Chronicle or Universal Evening Post (London), March 13–18, 1790.

European Magazine, and London Review, September 1805: 162 ff; September 1819: 210–11.

Evening Mail (London), October 29, 1792.

Gazetteer and New Daily Advertiser (London), May 15, 1790.

General Evening Post, March 16–18, 1790; April 10–12, 1792.

Hampshire Chronicle (Southampton), November 5, 1792.

Hereford Journal, September 26, 1792.

Kentish Register, September 6, 1793.

London Chronicle, March 16, 1790; April 21–24, 1792; October 30–November 1, 1792.

Maidstone Journal and Kentish Advertiser, February 24, 1807.

Manx Advertiser and Weekly Intelligence, December 19, 1822.

Observer (London), September 23, 1792.

Oracle (London), October 30, 1792.

Reading Mercury and Oxford Gazette, December 11, 1786; September 24, 1792; November 5, 1792.

Scots Magazine 54 (April 1792): 196ff.

Star (and Daily Evening Advertiser) (London), September 19, 1792.

Times (London), March 26, 1790; September 12, 14, 15, 18, 26 and 28, 1792; October 29–31, 1792; December 6, 1794; April 8, 1834.

Trewman's Exeter Flying-Post, or Plymouth and Cornish Advertiser, August 27, 1789.

World, March 16, 1790.

ACKNOWLEDGMENTS

Even a cursory glance at the source material will reveal my debt to a great number of archives and individuals. Those deserving of special mention include: the Mitchell Library, State Library of New South Wales, Sydney, whose collection of *Bounty*-related material is unrivaled. I am grateful to Martin Beckett for his friendly assistance over several years, and to Jennifer Broomhead for helping me navigate the various collections and references. This is the second project for which I am indebted to the Mitchell Library.

The Public Record Office, Kew, holds, amid much else, Admiralty files going back centuries. The retention of prosaic items such as ships' musters, logs, lieutenants' certificates, hospital records, invoices, and seamen's wills, as well as the extraordinary bounty of actual records of naval courts-martial, makes possible the detailed reconstruction of events long past. I am grateful not only to be able to use this material, but for the opportunity to have delved into it.

The Manx National Heritage Library holds extraordinary material for *Bounty* scholars, such as the Christian and Heywood family papers and the underused Atholl papers. I am extremely grateful to the Manx National Heritage for the use of this valuable material, and to Roger Sims and Wendy Thirkettle for their assistance.

The Newberry Library, Chicago, holds one of the collections of Nessy Heywood's correspondence, so central to this story. I am grateful for the use of this correspondence, and to Elizabeth Freebairn for her assistance.

I am grateful to the National Maritime Museum, Greenwich, for use of both its manuscript and picture holdings. To Kiri Ross-Jones I am grateful for answering my relentless stream of queries, and to David Taylor for his help with pictures.

The Alexander Turnbull Library, Wellington, has important Pacific and *Bounty* holdings. I am grateful for the use of this material, and particularly indebted to Tim Lovell-Smith for his unfailingly friendly assistance; he too is a colleague from a former project.

The Natural History Museum, London, holds one of the great repositories of Sir Joseph Banks's correspondence. The material used was by courtesy of the Trustees of the Natural History Museum, for which I am deeply grateful. I would particularly like to thank Neil Chambers for his friendly and invaluable assistance, and Malcolm Beasley for his help in managing the reproduction of much Banks material.

I am indebted to the British Library for use of its matchless holdings, and in particular for the use of material in the Oriental and India Office Collections.

My thanks are also due to the Bodleian Library, University of Oxford, and to Clare Brown and Greg Colley for much assistance.

The National Library of Australia holds much material valuable to the story of the *Bounty*, and I am grateful for its use. To Kay Nicholls and Graeme Powell I am grateful for their assistance with manuscript holdings, and to Wendy Morrow for her help with pictures.

The Huntington Library has extraordinary collections pertaining to eighteenth-century England. I am especially grateful to Gayle Barkley for her guidance and steady help over the past years.

I am grateful to the Algemeen Rijksarchief, Den Haag, for information about the Dutch East Indies Company (VOC) holdings; I am particularly grateful to Victor van den Bergh for his assistance. Yosephine Hutagalung of the VOC archives in Jakarta was of great assistance to me.

I am grateful to the Trustees of the Royal Botanic Gardens, Kew, for use of the Banks Collection, and to Kate Pickard for her patient help.

The Cumbria Record Office and Local Studies Library, Whitehaven, and the Cumbria Record Office, Carlisle, hold material important to the Christian and Curwen families, and also to the Heywoods. I am grateful for the use of this material, and also to David Bowcock, Catherine Clark, S. A. Gilder and Peter Eyre for fielding numerous requests.

To the Trustees of the National Library of Scotland I am grateful for furnishing me with a variety of material, and to Sally Harrower for her assistance.

I am grateful to the Nantucket Historical Association for the use of its marvelous collection of whaling records, and to Elizabeth Oldham for her assistance.

I also owe a debt of gratitude to a great number of individuals. To Aude and Airlie Holden-Hindley for their characteristic generosity and hospitality, I am more grateful than I can say. Long months of research were sustained by the comfort of their home away from home, in both London and Cumbria.

I am grateful to Maurice Bligh for both information and support.

To Glynn Christian I am grateful for his helpful guidance at the outset of my research, and for his book *Fragile Paradise;* we undoubtedly differ in our conclusions, but I do so with much respect.

I am indebted to Madge Darby for her thorough, detailed and patient responses to my numerous inquiries and for her tactful suggestions on the text. I look forward to her own book on the *Providence* voyage.

To Laura Bemis Rollison I am indebted for being my right hand over several years, and in particular for managing the tangled mass of bibliographic correspondence. It would have been difficult to undertake this project without her indefatigable backup.

I am grateful to Pieter Van Der Merwe for his careful reading of my text, and for saving me from many a lubberly slip; any errors retained are my own.

A number of people helped me comb archives and files; to Sara Lodge I am indebted for her careful investigations at the very earliest stage of this venture. To Bob O'Hara and Imelda Lauris I am grateful for much work in the Public Record Office. I am similarly grateful to Carole Carinne and Roger Nixon for help on the Isle of Man.

I am indebted to Gillian Rickards for much assistance in Kent. To Stephen Walters I am grateful for the use of key pictures, and for his early enthusiasm.

To Anne Kulig, Gary McCool, Susan Noel and indeed Lamson Library, Plymouth State College, in general, I am deeply grateful. Similarly, once again, I am indebted to Mary Delashmit of the Holderness Free Library, for her knowledgeable and efficient acquisition of a wealth of interlibrary loan material.

David Ransom of the Pitcairn Island Study Group, Andrea Martin at the Lincolnshire County Council, and Sophie Forgan at the Captain Cook Memorial Museum were of great assistance in assembling pictures.

Other people and archives that provided key assistance are:

Lyn Scadding and Kevin Ward, Bedfordshire and Luton Archives and Record Services; Jeremy Taylor and Lisa Spurrier, Berkshire Record Office; Rachel McGregor, Birmingham Record Office; Bill Faucon, Boston Public Library; Liz Wigmore, Bury St. Edmunds Records Office; Lesley Akeroyd, County Record Office, Cambridge; Stephen White, Jackson Collection, Carlisle Library; J. Gill, Durham Record Office; Theresa Thom, Gray's Inn; Michael Bosson, Sandon Hall, Harrowby Manuscripts Trust; Alan Akeroyd, County Record Office, Huntingdon, Cambridge; Clare Rider, Inner Temple; Catherine Howard, Institute of Commonwealth Studies; John Hodgson and Peter Nockles, John Rylands University Library of Manchester; Anna Watson and Bruce Jackson, Lancashire Record Office; Guy Holborn, Lincoln's Inn; Jane Battye, London Borough of Richmond upon Thames; Rhys Griffith and Bridget Howlett, London Metropolitan Archives; Cathy Williamson, Mariners' Museum; Robert Fotheringham, National Archives of Scotland; Christine Abbot, Newcastle City Council; Eric Hollerton, North Tyneside Council; Mrs. Sue Wood, Northumberland County Council; Bryce Wilson, Orkney Museum; Diana Gregg and Sarah Speller, Portsmouth City Council, Museums and Records Office; Alan Harkin, Reading Borough Council, Reading Central Library; Mark Pomeroy, Royal Academy of Arts; Clara Anderson, the Royal Society Archives; Alastair Brookham and Jonathan Harrison, St. John's College, Cambridge; Phil Hocking and Andrea Pring, Somerset Record Office; Michael Page, Surry County Council; E. A. Rees, Tyne and Wear Archives; Tony Lawless, University College, London; Janet Bloom, William Clements Library, University of Michigan; Dr. Lesley Hall, Wellcome Trust; Stephen Parks and Ayesha Ramachandran, Beinecke Rare Book and Manuscript Library, Yale University; Elizabeth Pridmore, York Minster Archives.

The following institutions provided useful material and services:

American Philosophical Society; Arizona State University; Atlanta University Center, Robert W. Woodruff Library; Australian National Maritime Museum; Bath and North East Somerset Record Office; Bibliothèque Publique et Universitaire de Genève; Birmingham Record Office; Bishop Museum; Brandeis University Library; Centre for Kentish Studies; Churchill Archives Centre, Cambridge University; Columbia University, Butler Library; Cornell University, Olin Library; Courtauld Institue of Art; Dartmouth College, Berry/Baker Library; Department of Navy Library; Derbyshire County Council; Devon Record Office; Dorset Record Office; Fishmongers' Company; Flintshire County Council; Florida State University; Getty Museum; Glasgow City Archives; Hampshire Record Office; Harvard University, Widener Library; Herefordshire and Luton Archives and Record Services; Hertfordshire Archives and Local Studies Service; Highgate Literary and Scientific Institute; Hydrographic Office of Taunton, Somerset; Isle of Wight Record Office; the Kerpels Museum, Santa Barbara; the Linnean Society; McGill University, McLennan Library; Manchester Archives and Local Studies; Mystic Seaport Museum, G. Blunt White Library; National Archives of Scotland; National Library of Wales; New York Public Library; Norfolk Record Office; Ohio State University Library; Public Record Office of Northern Ireland; Reading Local Studies Library; Rice University, Woodson Research Center, Fondren Library; the Royal Archives; Firepower, Royal Artillery Museum; Royal Naval Academy, Portsmouth; Society of Antiquaries; Staffordshire Record Office; Surrey History Centre; Sutro Library, San Francisco; Union Theological Seminary, New York; University of Arizona; the University of British Columbia Library; University of California, Charles E. Young Research Library; University of Hawaii at Hilo, Edwin

Mookini Library; University of Massachusetts; University of Michigan; University of New Hampshire, Dimond Library; University of Nottingham, Hallward Library; U.S. Military Academy; Warwickshire County Record Office; West Yorkshire Archive Service; Wiltshire & Swindon Record Office; Yale University Library.

Other individuals who provided information and expertise, and in some cases permissions, are: John Bach, James Basker, Vivien Burgess, Evangeline Clare, Sir Robert Clerk, A. C. F. David, Lord Denman, Rolf E. DuRietz, Valerie Facey, Dan Finamore, John Harnden, Rolf Harris, Mrs. M. Holland, Gill McKenna, Terry Martin, John Maggs, Peter Nockles, Amanda Norris, Kay Priestly, Eric Probert, Sarah Scully, Daniella Shippey, Henry Tempest, Mrs. Susan Thornely, Leonie Twentyman, Hugo Vickers, Sven Wahlross, Mike Welland, Stephen White, Frances Wilkins, Lindon Williams, Carol Woodcock and Sir George Young.

I am grateful to Laurence and Judy Webster, Captain Gerry Christian and Dorothy Wickenden for providing good omens for the voyage ahead.

On the domestic front, I am indebted to Linda Baker and John and Belinda Knight for their unwavering support. To George Butler and Smokey, Joanna Alexander and Ron Haskins, and my mother, Elizabeth Kirby, I am grateful for listening to *The Bounty* over the years. I am, as always, indebted to my friend Laura Slatkin.

Finally, I acknowledge an enormous debt of gratitude to Clare Ferraro, to my editors, Wendy Wolf at Viking Penguin and Arabella Pike at HarperCollins UK, and to the many long-suffering people responsible for production; to Bruce Giffords, who oversaw the copyediting, and to Trent Duffy; to Carla Bolte for design; to Cliff Corcoran; and to Cathie Arrington for zealous picture hunting. I am indebted to Randy Hartwell for his bibliographic work.

And I am grateful too, again, to Anthony Sheil, now my friend and agent of many years.

INDEX